The Global Cigarette

The Global Cigarette

Origins and Evolution of British American Tobacco 1880–1945

Howard Cox

OXFORD
UNIVERSITY PRESS

Great Clarendon Street, Oxford OX2 6DP

Oxford University Press is a department of the University of Oxford.
It furthers the University's objective of excellence in research, scholarship,
and education by publishing worldwide in

Oxford New York

Athens Auckland Bangkok Bogotá Buenos Aires Calcutta
Cape Town Chennai Dar es Salaam Delhi Florence Hong Kong Istanbul
Karachi Kuala Lumpur Madrid Melbourne Mexico City Mumbai
Nairobi Paris São Paulo Singapore Taipei Tokyo Toronto Warsaw

with associated companies in Berlin Ibadan

Oxford is a registered trade mark of Oxford University Press
in the UK and in certain other countries

Published in the United States
by Oxford University Press Inc., New York

First published 2000

British Library Cataloguing in Publication Data
Data available

Library of Congress Cataloging-in-Publication Data

Cox, Howard, 1954–
The global cigarette: origins and evolution of British American Tobacco, 1880–1945/
Howard Cox.
p. cm.
Includes bibliographical references and index.
1. British American Tobacco—History. 2. Tobacco industry. I. Title.
HD9141.9.B7 C69 2000
338.8'87797—dc21 99–086915

ISBN 0–19–829221–X

3 5 7 9 10 8 6 4 2

Typeset in Bembo by
Cambrian Typesetters, Frimley, Surrey

Printed in Great Britain
on acid-free paper by
Biddles Ltd.,
Guildford and King's Lynn

This book is dedicated to my parents and to R. Glyn Davies, who, like my father, sadly passed away before it could be completed.

Foreword

In 1934, when I was working as a solicitor in the City of London, I was approached by the British–American Tobacco Company to fill the vacant position of Company solicitor in Shanghai. Already tempted by the opportunity of working in China, Sir Hugo Cunliffe-Owen's suggestion at the subsequent interview that I should be better placed as 'a small frog in a big pond' helped to persuade me to chance my arm with BAT.

Circumstances led my time in China to be rather brief, but not my association with BAT. Six months after my arrival in Shanghai I was transferred back to the company's London headquarters as deputy head of its legal department. Although disappointed not to remain longer in China, the unexpected promotion was welcome, of course, especially as it gave me the chance to work closely with Sir Hugo as secretary of his Chairman's Committee which met daily and at which all important decisions were made.

As vice-chairman of BAT after the war I travelled extensively around the company's many subsidiaries, gaining insights and experience that proved to be of immense benefit during my period as chairman from 1953 to 1966. In a career with BAT spanning nearly 40 years, therefore, I accumulated a considerable store of knowledge relating to the company and its history.

In the light of this I was most interested to read the accounts of BAT's development that Howard Cox had written during his earlier research and was impressed by the depth and accuracy of the papers he had published. Accordingly, I did my best to encourage the company to support the work he was undertaking for the present book and have been most gratified by the help he has received from BAT's Director of Public Affairs, Michael Prideaux, and his staff.

Over the past few years I have engaged in a number of discussions with Howard at BAT's headquarters in London as the draft of this book has taken shape. The depth and thoroughness of his research means that now, as the company approaches its centenary, we finally have an accurate account of this fascinating and in many respects unique company from its foundation up until the Second World War.

Sir Duncan Oppenheim

Preface

On Tuesday 8 September 1998, after having traded for more than two decades as a diversified conglomerate, British American Tobacco plc once again became listed on the London Stock Exchange as a dedicated tobacco firm. A little over four months later the company surprised city analysts in London by announcing that it had reached an agreement to merge with the rival tobacco firm Rothmans International. The arrangement, under which shareholders in Rothmans hold a minority interest in the company, places British American within touching distance of Philip Morris as the world's leading manufacture of tobacco goods and takes the company another significant step towards regaining pole position in the global cigarette industry.

As most of the people reading this book will be perfectly aware, the resumption of leadership within the global industry merely restores British American Tobacco's birthright as the world's pre-eminent international tobacco manufacturing concern. Historically, the company owes this position to the competitive forces that were unleashed in Britain, and even more dramatically in America, during the closing years of the nineteenth century as a direct result of the mechanization of cigarette manufacturing. James Bonsack's machine initiated a revolution in this most fashion-conscious industry and served to draw a product, which hitherto had been of little consequence for tobacco users in these two countries, into the pivotal role of a remarkable transformation in consumer preferences. During the subsequent course of the twentieth century, tobacco markets throughout the globe have fallen increasingly under the sway of this image-laden product in a rise to prominence paralleled by that of the marketing industry itself.

The principal objective of this book has been to chart the international expansion of cigarette production from its origins, based on the export of American hand-rolled brands in the 1880s, through to the truly internationalized industry structure that was in place by the time of the Second World War. Because BAT Co. was specifically created in 1902 to operate as the international arm of the American Tobacco and Imperial Tobacco Companies, the story of the global cigarette is, in large measure, a history of this one company. What follows, therefore, is not a conventional corporate history, but rather an attempt to use a detailed appreciation of BAT's evolution as a means of analysing a broader process at work: the internationalization of a manufacturing industry in the period before multinational enterprises had gained their current pre-eminent position in the global economy.

To do this has required the gathering of a diverse collection of information from sources based mainly in Britain, but also located in the United States and China. The initial phase of the research was undertaken as an aspect of my doctoral thesis at Birkbeck College, University of London, under the expert guidance of my supervisor Ron Smith and with the assistance of Paul Auerbach. It was during this period that I found myself entering the realm of business history and, in doing so, I was given great encouragement by the support and advice of many academics engaged in this field, and in particular by Geoffrey Jones. In addition, both Sherman Cochran and Mira Wilkins provided invaluable support as I sought to develop my original thesis into the present work.

A major turning point along this path occurred in 1995 when I was awarded a grant by the Nuffield Foundation to engage in research at the Shanghai Academy of Social Sciences. The materials that I was able to access here, thanks to the assistance of Professor Huang Han Ming and his team, as well as Tim Wright, and Kai Yiu Chan, represented a quantum leap forward in my understanding of the company's organization. This research helped to bring my work to the attention of Sir Duncan Oppenheim and, through him, to Eleanor Elliott, both of whom have provided me with consistent support since that time. I am especially indebted to Sir Duncan for agreeing to provide the book with his endorsement through the contribution of a foreword.

At the end of 1995, Sir Duncan approached the then-retiring chairman of BAT Industries, Sir Patrick Sheehy, in order to solicit the company's support for the project. I had already received help from individuals within the company, most notably the late R. Glyn Davies and Trevor Bates, and to this was now added the critical backing of Michael Prideaux, head of the company's Public Affairs department. Michael's willingness to support this work by allowing access to the company's archives, coupled with his disinclination to interfere in any way with the resulting output, represents an extraordinary act of faith coming from within an industry that has been obliged to become instinctively suspicious and defensive.

Since 1996 I have received help and advice from many people within the organization. Suzanne Fisher deserves a great vote of thanks for providing many forms of practical assistance, in particular with the photographs, and for putting me in touch with retired BAT staff whose recollections were of great help. In this respect, I should like to acknowledge the discussions and correspondence I engaged in with J. H. Maslen, E. J. Symons, P. Tindley, and the late D. S. F. Hobson, and the earlier assistance given by T. Wilson and the late B. Hearnshaw. Much important information was gleaned from the archive material accessed through Valerie Rice and her team at the company's library in Southampton. This is a private company archive which has been organized only for internal use, but I have endeavoured to use the reference system employed by the company in order to acknowledge the use of these sources in the text. Murray Anderson and Tony Holliman of the company's secretarial department both provided me with extremely valuable source material, and Tony Holliman took time to read through draft chapters as I worked on the manuscript. Thanks are also due to Jane Smith, Paul Richmond, Wendy Black, Kate Haseldine, Caroline Martin, Michael Groves, Kathy Neeves, John Lewis, and Ken Street. At the company's Indian associate, ITC, I received help from A. Basu, S. Ghoshal, R. Prakash, and A. Syam. In the autumn of 1996 the company kindly supported me in a visit to the archive held at the Special Collections Department of the William R. Perkins Library at Duke University, where I obtained much help and advice from William R. Erwin and his colleagues and had some helpful and enjoyable discussions with Gordon and Evelyn Boyce.

At Oxford University Press, David Musson oversaw the long process of bringing this project to fruition with a judicious mixture of encouragement and patience. A great many fellow business historians have provided me with advice during the past decade or so, particularly my colleagues in the Centre for International Business History at Reading University. I received invaluable help with Chinese language sources from Li Yaqing at South Bank University. I am also deeply indebted to this institution for providing me with a period of study leave to work on the book and I am grateful to my many colleagues and friends in the Business School, particularly to Grazia Ietto-Gillies, who have supported my efforts to do writing and research.

Finally, and most of all, my wife Jill has provided a combination of practical and emotional support to me throughout the duration of this project, and much more, without which it would simply have been an impossible task.

Howard Cox

South Bank University, London
October 1999

Conventions

1. I have used the term BAT Co. to refer to the parent company and BAT to refer to the organization as a whole.
2. Chinese proper nouns have been transliterated using the Wade–Giles system that was utilized in documents of the time.
3. Place names have been retained in their contemporary form, but where the present name differs this has been given in parentheses following the first appearance.

Contents

Part Two: Pioneers of an International Mass Market

Part Three: Commerce and Colonialism in Asia

Part Four: International Business in an Unstable World

Conclusion

List of Figures and Maps

FIGURES

MAPS

List of Plates

List of Tables

Introduction

I

The Growth of an International Cigarette Industry

Introduction

THREE product features serve to characterize the modern international cigarette. First, it is manufactured from types of tobacco leaf whose species and method of curing both originated in the United States. Second, it is packaged and sold as a branded product using marketing methods whose earliest exponents were American firms. Third, it is a standardized product made using methods of mass production which originally became known as the American system of manufacture, and on a machine whose inventor was an American entrepreneur. In short, the modern international cigarette is an American invention.

During the course of the twentieth century this method of consuming tobacco rolled up in paper—practically unknown before the mid-nineteenth century—has come to prevail throughout the globe as the most common form of smoking.[1] The purpose of the present book is to explore the process through which this global industry was established during the first half of the twentieth century, and in particular to analyse the role played by the firm which became the world's leading international cigarette manufacturer; the British–American Tobacco Company, Ltd. (BAT Co.).

[1] Cigarettes using paper as a wrapper, as opposed to other vegetable matter, seem to have originated in Spain, perhaps as early as the seventeenth century. However, the manufacturing of such a product developed in France during the mid-nineteenth century and spread from there into other parts of Europe. These early French cigarettes featured American tobacco leaf; only later was Turkish and Balkan tobacco utilized in the product. J. Goodman, *Tobacco in History: the Cultures of Dependence* (1993), pp. 94–7. Since the late 1980s, at least 80 per cent of all tobacco grown in the world has been used to manufacture cigarettes, ibid., p. 97.

Phases of Competition

The evolution of the international cigarette manufacturing industry before the Second World War occurred in four broad phases. From around 1880 to 1902 the industry witnessed an initial competitive period which was marked by a shift from hand-rolled to machine-made products, and from export-led growth to one based increasingly on foreign direct investment. Even before the process of production had been successfully mechanized, American firms such as Kimball, Kinney, Goodwin, and Allen & Ginter had developed an export market in Europe for their colourfully-packaged hand-rolled cigarettes. During the early 1880s, these companies pioneered the growth of branded cigarettes in Britain and stimulated similar forms of production among local firms, such as Players and Wills, and manufacturers elsewhere—notably firms operating in Cairo using oriental leaf.

As these hand-rolled cigarettes were expensive to produce, they were sold as luxury or novelty products. In order to expand the market for cigarettes the American firms who had promoted cigarettes sought a rolling machine that could replace the huge numbers of women engaged in their factories and, thereby, significantly reduce unit production costs.[2] The economic benefits that mechanized production could provide stimulated a number of engineers to experiment during the early 1880s with a variety of manufacturing devices, and the design that proved most successful was patented by an American, James A. Bonsack, in 1881. However, because the reputation of the leading American firm, Allen & Ginter, had been built on the hand-rolled product this company was initially reluctant to adopt the Bonsack machine, and the first manufacturers to do so were the French tobacco monopoly and the British firm of W. D. & H. O. Wills. Indeed, the first American company to fully adopt the Bonsack machine in 1885 was the firm of W. Duke, Sons, & Co., led by James B. Duke, which had begun to manufacture cigarettes only four years earlier.

The effect of mechanization during the second half of the 1880s was to increase rapidly the productive capacity of individual cigarette manufacturers, enabling a much smaller number of firms to satisfy consumers' demand for the product compared with other branches of tobacco manufacturing. The resulting rapid concentration of output in the American cigarette manufacturing

[2] In 1876, the labour costs of one brand of cigarettes in America were 96.4 cents per thousand, of which 86.2 cents was required for the operation of rolling the cigarette itself. A hand-roller could roll no more than 3,000 cigarettes in a ten-hour day. By the mid-1880s, the best machine could manufacture 200 cigarettes per minute. R. B. Tennant, *The American Cigarette Industry: A Study in Economic Analysis and Public Policy* (1950), p. 17.

industry prompted Duke to spearhead a series of negotiations that culminated in the creation in 1890 of the American Tobacco Company (ATC) as an amalgamation of the five leading tobacco firms that specialized in cigarette manufacturing. As the problem of excess capacity had built up through the 1880s cigarette manufacturers were given a strong incentive to develop sales in foreign markets, and during these years many of the leading American and British tobacco firms sent representatives around the world seeking orders for their products. In the 1890s annual exports of American-made cigarettes, now dominated by the products of ATC, increased from 300 million to over one billion,[3] with the Asian markets of Japan and China proving the most receptive. However, competition from local tobacco firms in many of these foreign markets, together with the tendency for tariffs on imported tobacco goods to rise, meant that from 1894 ATC were encouraged to transfer production of their goods directly into foreign markets by means of partnership or outright acquisition. Thus, by the turn of the century, strategies of international expansion by the world's leading cigarette manufacturer had begun to feature foreign direct investment as well as the traditional export route. In contrast, British firms who ventured abroad did so on the basis of exports. And although Wills, as Britain's leading firm, did experiment with the system of licensing a local manufacturer in South Africa, they did not manage any factories of their own abroad before 1900. Nevertheless, as the volume of cigarette exports from Britain grew, Wills and ATC found their brands in direct competition across a range of foreign markets during the latter part of the 1890s.

The shift towards foreign direct investments by ATC created the circumstances for the second phase of the evolution of the international cigarette industry which began in 1902 and lasted effectively until the end of the First World War. In 1901, frustrated by the import tariffs levied on its cigarette exports to Britain, Duke's ATC made a bid to acquire shares in some of the leading British cigarette manufacturers as it had already done in Canada, Australia, Japan, and Germany. In this case, however, only one of the smaller British manufacturers, Ogden's of Liverpool, was prepared to accept Duke's offer of merger. Meanwhile, a number of the most important British tobacco companies, including Wills and Players, combined together to fight Duke's advances

[3] See Tables 2.2 and 2.3. Official trade statistics for the UK do not enumerate cigarette exports separately before 1906 (see Appendix 3). Wills, the leading British cigarette exporter, began its trade in the product during 1885, but this only began to gather pace during the second half of the 1890s. In 1895 the company's export sales exceeded 100 million sticks for the first time, and by 1900 they had reached a level of around 500 million, or just under one half of total US cigarette exports. In 1906, the UK exported around 2 billion sticks (5 million lb.). Figures for Wills' exports (given by weight rather than number) are provided in B. W. E. Alford, *W. D. & H. O. Wills and the Development of the UK Tobacco Industry, 1796–1965* (1973), p. 460.

by consolidating their enterprises under the banner of the Imperial Tobacco Company. After a period of commercial warfare lasting twelve months, ATC and Imperial agreed to a truce under which each party confined its own activities to their respective national markets, and all their foreign investments and export trade was transferred to a British-registered joint venture called the British–American Tobacco Co. (BAT Co.). ATC's greater contribution of international assets to the new company allowed the American firm to claim two-thirds of BAT Co.'s initial equity stake, although the degree of control exercised by its American directors was tempered by the decision to locate the company's main headquarters in London rather than New York.

With no international competitors of comparable size BAT Co. was able to develop its activities abroad opposed only by domestic competitors in the countries where it invested. In those markets where tobacco manufacturing was still largely in a pre-industrialized condition, such as China and India, BAT Co.'s branches and subsidiaries pioneered the development of modern cigarette manufacturing. For a decade at the beginning of the twentieth century, therefore, BAT Co. was the only British or American tobacco firm with an international market for its products, as well as being the leading manufacturer in the tobacco industries of various countries, most notably Australia, Canada, South Africa, India, and China.

Although BAT's monopoly position in the international cigarette industry lasted effectively until the end of the First World War, it had in fact begun to be undermined when, in 1911, the Supreme Court in America ordered the dissolution of ATC into a number of competing elements. The impact of the dissolution of ATC on BAT was twofold. First, the court ordered ATC to dispose of its institutional shareholding in BAT Co., and thereby established the Imperial Tobacco Company as the leading minority shareholder in the international organization, allowing the two companies to establish closer links which were to be of great significance during the First World War.[4] This shift in the balance of ownership within BAT Co. towards Britain, where most of ATC's liberated shares were traded, was reinforced by Duke's decision in 1912 to resume active management of BAT's affairs and spend more of his time at the company's London headquarters. Even though this initiative was disrupted in 1914, when the outbreak of the First World War persuaded Duke to forsake his residence in Britain and return to New York, by the war's end BAT Co. had emerged decisively as a British-controlled firm.

[4] The territorial agreement between Imperial and BAT Co. was cancelled in 1972, shortly before entry of the UK into the EEC. Imperial's one-third shareholding in BAT Co. declined only gradually until the early 1970s; thereafter a process of disinvestment saw the two companies completely independent by 1982.

The second impact of the Supreme Court's successful challenge to ATC's monopoly of the American tobacco industry was that it created a group of independent firms who were now free to engage in foreign expansion and thus to compete with BAT for a share of the international cigarette market. Four main successor manufacturers were formed from the assets of ATC—Liggett & Myers, R. J. Reynolds, Lorillard, and a reformed ATC—but this potential source of rivalry was delayed by the frantic struggle that developed between them for shares of the US market and, during this hiatus, BAT Co. strengthened its international position still further by making significant investments in the large South American markets of Argentina and Brazil.

By the time of the cessation of hostilities in Europe, therefore, competitive conditions had been restored in the international cigarette industry. Of the four main successor firms to ATC, only Liggett & Myers made a serious attempt to take up the cudgels against BAT Co. in foreign markets, when it established operations in China during the early 1920s. A more concerted attack on BAT Co. during this period came from an organization which was created as a new concern in 1912, called the Tobacco Products Corporation (TPC), which was constructed on the base of the tobacco retailing operations that Duke's monopoly had created in America.[5] This company initially purchased a number of independent tobacco manufacturers in the United States with a view to competing for a share of the American domestic cigarette market. In the process, however, it also acquired operations outside of the US and these were formed into a group called the Tobacco Products Export Corporation (TPEC) in 1919 and for a period of time this organization competed actively with BAT in China and elsewhere.

BAT Co. also continued to expand its range of international operations during the 1920s, and intensified competition still further in 1927 when Duke's successor as chairman, the Englishman Hugo Cunliffe-Owen, decided to enter the cigarette market in America through the purchase of the small independent firm of Brown & Williamson. This in turn stimulated the reformed ATC to resume operations in Britain where Imperial's leadership of the market was already coming under increased competitive pressure from a number of quarters. The British firms which challenged Imperial in the UK such as Carreras, Godfrey Phillips, Ardath, and Gallaher also, to a varying degree, developed an export trade in competition with BAT Co. during the 1920s, and even began to make some direct investments abroad. Thus the period 1918–29 can be seen as a phase of renewed competition within the international cigarette industry, although the wide geographical spread of

[5] These retailing operations were called the United Cigar Stores.

BAT Co.'s foreign operations meant that overall its position as the dominant international firm was never more than briefly threatened.

The onset of the world trade depression in 1929 initiated the fourth phase of competition in the international cigarette industry, during which formal cartels and informal agreements largely replaced competitive rivalry between manufacturers. By the end of the 1920s, BAT Co. had already assumed control over the Chinese operations of both Liggett & Myers and TPEC, and in 1929 the company also acquired the remaining foreign assets of TPEC. As trading conditions deteriorated during the early 1930s BAT Co. engaged in co-operative arrangements with its main British rivals, Carreras and Gallaher, and at the same time formed cartel agreements with domestic firms in various markets, as tobacco manufacturers in general sought to maintain profitability by avoiding price competition and excessive marketing expenditure, and by pooling their operations to control output. Thus when the growing political forces of nationalism exploded into the military conflict that engulfed much of Asia and Europe, the international cigarette industry had effectively collapsed into a collection of national markets, and BAT Co., as the only remaining multinational organization, operated its large group of foreign subsidiaries as a collection of independently managed enterprises under the strategic control of a small group of directors based in London.

Historical Source Materials

In setting out the early history of the international cigarette industry, and in particular the development of BAT Co., the account which follows has drawn upon a range of primary and secondary sources of material. In terms of quantitative sources, three data series have helped to provide the study with its statistical skeleton. The first of these are figures on the tobacco export trade collected by the statistical bureaux of the United Kingdom and the United States. In America, the export volume of cigarettes by number can be traced through government records dating back to the beginning of the 1890s and this provides a clear picture of the geographical development of the industry during its earliest phase. In Britain, cigarette exports were not enumerated separately by the government in its trade statistics before 1906, but from this year on a detailed breakdown by destination is available based on the weight of tobacco contained in the product.[6] Naturally, the destination to which

[6] For comparative purposes these British cigarette exports have been converted from weight to number using a standard conversion factor of 1000 cigarettes to 2.20462 lb. of tobacco.

these cigarettes were consigned does not necessarily represent their ultimate location of consumption, and a certain amount of transshipment will have occurred. Nevertheless, these export statistics provide a good picture of the aggregate growth in the cigarette trade for the two main exporting countries, and the consignment destinations certainly provide a broadly accurate picture of the geographical shape which this trade took. Table 1.1 compares British and American aggregate cigarette exports for the period 1906–40 and also shows the proportion of these cigarettes that were shipped to China.[7] A breakdown of the British figures by principal destinations in Asia and Africa for the period 1906–48 is given in Appendix 3. Geographical breakdowns of American exports are given in Tables 2.2 and 5.2 for the period 1890–1911. Until the financial crash of 1929, the bulk of American cigarette exports were directed to China (see Table 1.1). During the 1930s, however, around one half of all cigarettes exported from the United States went to the Philippines, a market from which BAT Co. had been formally excluded by the agreement of 1902.[8]

The two remaining statistical series are based on BAT Co. sources, and these comprise sales data and financial results. The sales data represent the monthly sales statistics cabled to BAT Co. headquarters by its operating subsidiaries abroad, and are available complete from October 1920. A summary of BAT Co.'s total sales and the proportion made within China is provided in Table 1.2 and a full breakdown by market is shown in Appendix 4. These figures can be taken as an accurate guide to the international development of BAT Co.'s cigarette empire, and provide a picture of the company's sales performance as it would have been received by the BAT Co. board of directors in London. They show that the vast majority of the company's sales were made through its foreign subsidiaries and sales branches, with only a relatively small proportion coming from direct sales by BAT Co. itself, mainly through sales to ships' stores.

The financial performance of the company, as detailed in its annual report and accounts, is rather more problematic as a record of performance. In the era before consolidated accounts, the performance as a whole of the group of companies which comprised BAT Co. is difficult to judge, and that of individual subsidiaries is of course completely obscured. The declared profits of BAT Co. were based largely on dividends paid by these subsidiaries, set against losses elsewhere, with the overall performance being something of an

7 Figures for shipments to China include cigarettes sent to Hong Kong. Some small proportion of these cigarettes are likely have been shipped on to other parts of South East Asia.

8 The other two main destinations for American cigarette exports after 1930 were Panama (including the Canal Zone) and France.

TABLE 1.1. UK and US cigarette exports by volume: total and per cent to China, 1906–40

Year	UK		US	
	Total (bn. sticks)	To China (%)	Total (bn. sticks)	To China (%)
1906	2.2	34	1.7	53
1907	2.9	38	2.0	49
1908	3.5	49	1.5	36
1909	4.2	53	1.6	39
1910	5.0	62	1.6	38
1911	5.4	60	1.2	31
1912	6.4	61	1.6	34
1913	8.6	65	1.9	33
1914	8.4	62	2.6	43
1915	8.3	57	2.1	34
1916	9.2	47	2.6	59
1917	6.0	14	6.5	73
1918	4.8	9	9.1	62
1919	5.7	4	16.2	38
1920	7.4	12	15.8	54
1921	4.3	23	8.5	75
1922	5.4	11	11.5	75
1923	6.6	13	12.5	75
1924	6.7	15	10.5	72
1925	7.6	9	8.2	66
1926	9.0	9	9.5	72
1927	10.0	7	7.1	61
1928	12.1	12	11.7	74
1929	14.9	14	8.5	57
1930	14.1	21	4.9	27
1931	8.9	27	3.0	4
1932	7.1	12	2.4	3
1933	7.5	5	2.5	3
1934	8.9	3	3.3	3
1935	10.0	3	3.9	3
1936	11.0	2	4.6	2
1937	12.5	3	5.7	2
1938	12.0	2	6.4	1
1939	11.4	2	6.8	1
1940	10.1	3	6.6	2

Notes: UK exports have been converted from weight to number using a standard conversion factor of 1000 cigarettes = 2.20462 lb. of tobacco.
US exports to 1918 are for year ending June; thereafter the figures are for calendar years.
Exports to China include shipments to Hong Kong.
Sources: UK: Annual Statement of the Trade of the UK; US: Foreign Commerce and Navigation of the US.

TABLE 1.2. BAT Co. world-wide cigarette sales and sales in China, 1921–41

Year	Total sales (bn. sticks)	China sales (bn. sticks)	China sales (%)
1921	38.0	18.7	49
1922	40.0	21.0	52
1923	48.9	26.4	54
1924	59.2	32.3	55
1925	61.0	29.8	49
1926	67.2	29.5	44
1927	72.4	28.6	40
1928	77.0	26.4	34
1929	98.0	41.6	42
1930	99.1	44.0	44
1931	90.2	42.2	47
1932	89.9	40.1	45
1933	95.5	39.7	42
1934	98.0	35.5	36
1935	108.8	37.8	35
1936	122.1	43.7	36
1937	145.0	55.4	38
1938	140.9	45.9	33
1939	142.0	43.9	31
1940	143.4	44.4	31
1941	151.3	44.9	30

Note: Sales to China include Hong Kong.
Source: BAT Co. Monthly Sales Returns.

averaging-out exercise.[9] Nevertheless, the accounts show quite well the relative prosperity of the company up until the depression, demonstrated by its ability to issue fresh shares on the basis of accumulated profits, and the more straitened circumstances in which the company found itself after 1929, illustrated by the decision to halve its final dividend after 1931 (see Appendix 1).[10] Moreover, the balance sheet gives some indication of the changing proportion of the company's assets held in subsidiaries and also shows, for example, how the extremely conservative financial approach of Sir Hugo Cunliffe-Owen led to goodwill being practically written out of the company's

9 For a more detailed discussion see H. Cox and R. Smith, 'An Assessment of BAT Co.'s Profitability between the Wars', paper presented to the Accounting, Business, and Financial History First Annual Conference held at Cardiff Business School, 26–27 September 1990.

10 The first reduction in the final dividend paid to ordinary shareholders was in respect of the financial year ending September 1931 but was actually paid, and recorded in the accounts, during the following financial year.

accounts from 1921, after having accounted for one-quarter of BAT Co.'s total assets in 1903 (see Appendix 2).

In addition to these quantitative data, the company also made available to the author a wide variety of other source material from its own records.[11] Particularly useful in relation to tracing the company's evolution before the Second World War have been two in-house series, the *BAT Bulletin* which was published between 1915 and 1931 and provides a wealth of detailed information covering the evolution of the company up until this point, and *BAT News*, edited by R. Glyn Davies, which was published biannually from 1982 until 1990 and featured many items of a historical nature. A third source of information concerning the company's general evolution has been provided by its legal department's series of corporate histories which give a detailed explanation of the process of subsidiary formation by BAT Co. in each of its markets. As a whole, these sources provide the present corporate history of BAT Co. with a qualitative counterpart to the sales and financial records outlined above.

Of the various other records held in storage by the company, private documents of both a formal and informal nature were utilized. Among the most useful of the formal papers were a letterpress book of the London depot of ATC containing correspondence from the period immediately prior to ATC's purchase of Ogden's in 1901, various papers retained by the secretarial and legal departments of BAT Co., and the minutes of the Chairman's Daily Committee for the period 1932–9 which allowed many insights into the company's strategic decision-making under Cunliffe-Owen. The study also benefited from a number of discussions with Sir Duncan Oppenheim who was secretary to this latter committee from 1935 and rose to become chairman of the company between 1953 and 1966. Insights into Cunliffe-Owen's personality and business philosophy were also gained as a result of these interviews, as well as through Sir Hugo's correspondence with Lord Beaverbrook held in the library of the House of Lords in London.

Among the informal papers in the BAT Co. collection were a variety of brief histories written by retired staff that dealt with the operations of the company in those parts of the world in which they served. These papers, together with interview transcripts undertaken in respect of earlier projected histories of the company and my own interviews and correspondence with retired BAT Co. staff, formed a large body of factual accounts of the company's develop-

[11] British–American Tobacco has no formal archive of its historical papers, but retains a large number of documents in storage off-site which were accessed mainly through the company's library at Southampton. The most useful of these documents for the present study are described in the rest of this section.

ment. Obviously the reliability of these recollections is a matter for conjecture, but an effort has been made in what follows to reconcile wherever possible individual accounts both with one another, and with more definitive primary and secondary sources of information. Among these latter materials are a collection of subsidiary histories, published by the overseas company in question.

Research into the period predating the formation of BAT Co. drew on materials dealing with a variety of companies that acted in the role of precursors. Papers of W. D. & H. O. Wills held by the Public Record Office in Bristol provided some evidence of its early international activities and the attitude of the Wills board to Duke's strategy of entry by acquisition. More important for the present study, however, was the published history of Wills by B. W. E. Alford which provided a wealth of important information and has been cited copiously in the text. A second important source of material for the early part of the study was contained in the Special Collections Department at Duke University, North Carolina. This collection contains the private and business papers of James B. Duke, together with those of a number of other individuals who were directly involved in the development of the international cigarette industry during the late nineteenth and early twentieth centuries, notably R. H. Gregory, E. J. Parrish, J. A. Thomas, and R. H. Wright. The library also holds the papers of various companies who engaged in the international cigarette trade as competitors of ATC before becoming absorbed into BAT Co. after 1902, including the firms of David Dunlop, Cameron and Cameron, and T. C. Williams.

Of the collected papers of individual businessmen held at Duke University, those of Edward J. Parrish have been of great importance in gaining an understanding of ATC's early operations in Japan, China, and South-East Asia, whilst those of James A. Thomas provided details both of BAT's operations in China between 1905 and 1915, and of the shift in power within BAT Co. which occurred between the dissolution of ATC in 1912 and the end of the First World War. Further appreciation of Thomas' career and personality has been gained through conversations and correspondence with his daughter, Eleanor Elliott, who provided introductions to a variety of other people connected with the tobacco industry in China and America, including Noel Pugach.[12]

[12] Dr Pugach has written a number of papers on Thomas, dealing mainly with his career after he left BAT in 1919 to work for the Chinese–American Bank of Commerce. See N. Pugach, 'Keeping an Idea Alive: the Establishment of a Sino-American Bank, 1910–1920', *Business History Review*, 26 (1982), 266–93; idem., 'Second Career: James A. Thomas and the Chinese–American Bank of Commerce', *Pacific Historical Review*, 56 (1987), 195–229; idem., *Same Bed Different Dreams: a History of the Chinese–American Bank of Commerce, 1919–1937*, Centre for Asian Studies, University of Hong Kong, 1997.

The importance of the Chinese market to the development of the international cigarette industry, and to BAT Co. in particular, has made access to materials dealing with China of special significance for this study. The initial point of departure in this respect was the work of Sherman Cochran, whose detailed account of BAT's development in China was absolutely invaluable as an overview of events there.[13] Research into the operations of BAT and its rivals in the Chinese tobacco industry was subsequently deepened through two sources of archive material. First, by reference to the collection of papers which BAT's China subsidiary was forced to abandon at the time of its withdrawal from the market there, which are now held at the Centre for Chinese Business History at the Shanghai Academy of Social Sciences. These provided a wealth of information based on internal and external correspondence, along with statistical materials, enabling a detailed picture of the company's operations there to be drawn.[14] Second, the papers of the British Foreign Office contained in the Public Record Office in London which provided information and insights into a range of BAT operations abroad, in particular relating to the company's affairs in China. From these papers it was possible to identify the diplomatic and consular support afforded to BAT as it attempted to develop the potential of the Chinese market for British products.

The present study has attempted to contrast BAT's operations in China with those in another large, pre-industrialized colonial market, India. Important source material for this part of the book was obtained from the India Office Library and Records section of the British Library, particularly in relation to the decision by BAT to expand local manufacturing capacity there around 1909.[15] BAT Co.'s own collected papers are also relatively rich in respect of the company's operations in India, including a very detailed typescript by Reginald Baker who worked for the company's ITC subsidiary there between 1911 and 1945, and who assumed the position of chairman of ITC in 1935. In addition, ITC's own commissioned history by Champaka Basu, published on the occasion of the company's 75th anniversary in 1988, provided much helpful detail.[16]

Various government reports provided authoritative accounts of the development of the tobacco industry in individual countries. The Government of

13 S. Cochran, *Big Business in China: Sino-Foreign Rivalry in the Cigarette Industry, 1890–1930* (1980).

14 H. Cox, 'Learning to do Business in China: The Evolution of BAT's Cigarette Distribution Network, 1902–41', *Business History*, 39 (1997), 30–64.

15 H. Cox, 'International Business, the State and Industrialisation in India: Early Growth in the Indian Cigarette Industry, 1900–19', *Indian Economic and Social History Review*, 27 (1990), 289–312.

16 C. Basu, *Challenge and Change: The ITC Story, 1910–1985* (1988).

India put out a report on the marketing of tobacco in India and Burma during 1939, and BAT Co.'s own leaf development company also published an account of its activities in support of tobacco growing there two years later.[17] Important anti-monopoly reports on the tobacco industry were published by the US Bureau of Corporations in 1909 and by the UK Monopolies Commission in 1961.[18] The former provided much detail on the growth of James Duke's ATC, whilst the latter outlined developments in the British cigarette industry, particularly in the inter-war years. Other existing histories of these two countries' tobacco industries also provided extremely valuable information, but were relatively silent on international developments.[19] Finally, throughout the entire study, the commentary provided by the tobacco trade press, particularly the London-based monthly *Tobacco* journal, has been an indispensable guide to the industry's international development,[20] although it is interesting to note that this journal's coverage of foreign affairs dwindled after 1929 except in relation to the growth of tobacco leaf within the British Empire.

Research Objectives of the Study

The sources outlined above have facilitated the construction of a detailed account of the international cigarette industry as it developed between 1880 and 1945; a process which, after 1902, was dominated by BAT Co. An important function of the present study, therefore, is to provide a work of reference through which this particular case of international industrial and corporate expansion may be appraised and integrated into broader-based studies dealing

[17] Government of India, *Report on the Marketing of Tobacco in India and Burma* (1939); ILTD Co., 'Indian Tobacco Leaves: Story of Co-operation in India', BAT Co., London, n.d. (*c.*1941).

[18] US Bureau of Corporations, *Report of the Commissioner of Corporations on the Tobacco Industry* (1909); UK Monopolies Commission, *Report on the Supply of Cigarettes and Tobacco and of Cigarette and Tobacco Machinery*, HMSO (1961).

[19] The most useful of these existing histories are M. Corina, *Trust in Tobacco: the Anglo-American Struggle for Power* (1975); R. Cox, *Competition in the American Tobacco Industry 1911–1932: A Study of the Effects of the Partition of the American Tobacco Company by the United States Supreme Court* (1933); R. Kluger, *Ashes to Ashes: America's Hundred-Year Cigarette War, the Public Health, and the Unabashed Triumph of Philip Morris* (1996); R. B. Tennant, *The American Cigarette Industry* (1950). Corina's study considers both Britain and America, whilst Kluger's outlines the international growth of Philip Morris in the post-Second World War period.

[20] The tobacco trade press, together with the *BAT Bulletin*, was particularly useful in my earlier published account of BAT's initial international development, see H. Cox, 'Growth and Ownership in the International Tobacco Industry: BAT 1902–27', *Business History*, 31 (1989), 44–67.

with the question of international business before the Second World War. In addition, however, the study attempts to provide evidence in relation to a number of issues that, in the absence of a corporate history of BAT, have been either imperfectly understood or, in some cases, misinterpreted.

Five issues in particular warrant careful attention. First, the study attempts to set out the background and surrounding circumstances that encouraged ATC to invade the British market in 1901, paying special attention to the international context in which this invasion occurred. Second, it explores the nature of BAT's relationship with the two companies that set it up and assesses the widely held claim that BAT was effectively American controlled until the 1920s. Third, it considers why the American tobacco firms that succeeded ATC after its dissolution in 1911 made little impression in cigarette markets between the wars. Fourth, the study explores the way in which BAT Co. managed its collection of international subsidiaries which, by the inter-war years, controlled production and distribution operations in almost fifty countries. Fifth, it assesses how the varying political environments in which the company operated affected its conduct, with particular reference to the contrasting forms of colonialism that confronted the company in the important markets of China and India. These questions provide an implicit agenda which informs the historical narrative of the case study. Overall, the purpose of the book has been to understand the microeconomic aspects of the international cigarette industry, in relation to firm behaviour, whilst taking into account the main macroeconomic and political contexts within which these firms have operated.

The basic structure of the book is chronological, with Part One addressing the early competitive phase of the industry (*c.*1880–1902), Part Two dealing with the period of BAT Co.'s effective control of the international industry (1902–*c.*1918), and Part Four assessing the two phases of the inter-war years being, respectively, the re-emergence of international competition (*c.*1918–29) and cartelization (1929–*c.*1945). Part Three adopts a different point of departure by concentrating on developments within two of BAT's important national markets, China and India, covering the period as a whole (although developments before 1900 in these countries are previewed in Part One). This change of focus enables the operations of BAT Co. to be considered from the perspective of the host countries, rather than purely from the viewpoint of the headquarters, and affords some insights into the developmental consequences of the industry's international operations in pre-industrialized economies. It also allows for a comparison of BAT's operation in two colonial markets operating under quite different political conditions.

Part One

Origins

2

A Product with Global Potential

Introduction

In October 1901 the London-based trade journal *Tobacco* presented its readers with written confirmation of a long-anticipated development. An item under the heading 'Purchase of Ogden's Limited' began with the following statement: 'Considerable sensation was caused in the tobacco trade throughout the country when it became known, about the middle of September, that negotiations were practically completed for the purchase by the American Tobacco Company of the extensive business, plant, goodwill, &c., of Ogden's Limited, the well-known tobacco and cigarette manufacturing company of Liverpool.'[1]

The president of the American Tobacco Company (ATC), James Buchanan Duke, had arrived in England barely three weeks prior to the publication of this news item and had immediately set about capturing for his company an increased share of the protected British market for manufactured tobacco products.[2] He was determined, in particular, to make an impact on the rapidly expanding market for machine-made cigarettes, and a war chest of £6 million had been set aside for the purpose of capturing a share of this lucrative market.

It came as little surprise to British tobacco manufacturers, therefore, when within a few days of gaining control of the Ogden company Duke had circulated the distribution trade with two offers designed to push the sales of his new firm's goods. Under the new terms, all orders for the packet tobacco 'Coolie Cut Plug' were to be granted a rebate of 3d. per lb. provided that, for

1 *Tobacco (London)*, 21 (250) (1901), 451.

2 J. K. Winkler, *Tobacco Tycoon: The Story of James Buchanan Duke* (1942), pp. 138–9.

every 5 lb. ordered, an additional 2 lb. of 'St Julien' tobacco was also ordered. With regard to cigarettes, the circular promised that any dealer who ordered 1,000 of Ogden's 'Guinea Gold' brand would be handed an additional 200 'Tab' cigarettes free of charge, on condition only that the prices of these brands were maintained at a specified level. These circulars effectively represented a declaration of war by the American invader against the élite group of tobacco manufacturers who dominated the trade in Britain; a declaration to which the latter were not slow to respond.

The response chosen by the principal British firms was a defensive amalgamation. Two days before Ogden's issued its circulars to the trade, representatives of five leading British tobacco manufacturers held a meeting in Birmingham and agreed to band together to fight the American invasion. The leading role in these negotiations was played by the Bristol firm of W. D. & H. O. Wills, led by its charismatic chairman William H. Wills.[3] As early as 1895, the Wills board had discussed the possibility of an amalgamation with other prominent firms in the industry, primarily as a way of combating any possible attempt by Duke's firm to corner the market in American leaf tobacco. Although it proved unnecessary to pursue the matter at the time, the possibility of such a combination continued to exercise the Wills directors and three years later the Board passed a resolution approving in principle the amalgamation of their company with three major rivals from other parts of England—Hignett Bros. of Liverpool, Lambert & Butler of London, and John Player & Sons of Nottingham—along with the possibility of extending the arrangement to cover some Scottish manufacturers.[4] Thus when the American threat finally materialized in September 1901 these four firms, together with the Glasgow-based manufacturer Stephen Mitchell & Son, were in a position to react with speed.

Having reached agreement among themselves, the group extended the opportunity of participation in the consolidated venture to a number of other leading firms in the industry. On 3 October it was formally announced that a group of thirteen firms were joining together under the banner of the Imperial Tobacco Company (of Great Britain and Ireland) Ltd., and that an organizing committee drawn from amongst the members of the firms would formulate a common strategy to combat Duke's Ogden initiative. A circular was issued to the trade by this committee on 14 October informing dealers of

[3] Compared with other members of the Wills family, William Henry Wills was an outgoing, relatively flamboyant character. Politically a radical member of the Liberal Party, he was awarded a peerage in 1893 and took the title Lord Winterstoke. Wills' historian describes him as 'a man of Affairs', see B. W. E. Alford, *W. D. & H. O. Wills and the Development of the UK Tobacco Industry, 1786–1965* (1973), p. 279.

[4] Alford, *W. D. & H. O. Wills*, pp. 251–4.

the new circumstances, and this was followed two weeks later by the announcement that dealers in Imperial's goods would receive a bonus, although no specific details were made available immediately.[5]

While the British firms deliberated, Duke, his finance director W. R. Harris, and ATC's legal counsel, W. W. Fuller, along with Ogden's solicitor James Hood, travelled to London in order to register a new company bearing the name of the British Tobacco Company.[6] This entity, capitalized at just £100, was designed to act as a holding company into which ATC's British interests could later be subsumed. Although it was never utilized for this purpose, the registration of the British Tobacco Company carried a clear warning to the British manufacturers of Duke's intentions; at the same time it foreshadowed the turn of events that lay ahead.

Having completed his opening gambit, Duke paid a visit to ATC's depot at High Holborn in London, withdrew £100 in cash together with a stock of fine cigars, valued at over £40, and settled down for a protracted period of commercial warfare. The resolution of this 'tobacco war' in Britain, when it came almost exactly one year later, would serve to shape the future of the international tobacco industry throughout the remainder of the twentieth century.

Origins of the American Cigarette Industry

Duke's invasion of the British tobacco market in 1901 was not the first occasion on which American cigarette manufacturers had sought to influence the consumption patterns of Britain's smoking public. During the early 1880s, imported cigarettes from America carved out a small but significant market among the more affluent smokers in Britain's large cities. Four firms in particular had succeeded in winning customers for their hand-rolled paper cigarettes. Three of these firms, Kinney Bros., Goodwin & Co., and Kimball & Co., were based around New York, where the smoking of imported Turkish-leaf cigarettes had become fashionable in the 1850s, shortly before the outbreak of the American Civil War; the fourth, Allen & Ginter, was a southern-based firm, located in Richmond, Virginia. This latter firm had been particularly successful in Britain, building up sufficient trade by 1883 to be considered the market leader in ready-made cigarettes.[7]

The move towards cigarette production in the United States, had first been

5 *Tobacco (London)*, 21 (251) (1901), 490.

6 Reported in *Cigar and Tobacco World*, 13 (1901), 503.

7 *Tobacco (London)*, 4 (38) (1884), 18.

stimulated by changes in the process of curing leaf tobacco. Traditionally, farmers had processed their tobacco crop either by means of air-curing, in which the green tobacco leaves would be hung out in large curing barns and simply left to dry, or through the method of fire-curing, in which the tobacco would be hung over log fires and dried through contact with the ensuing smoke. This latter method had been employed by farmers in the Piedmont region of Virginia and North Carolina to treat the relatively poor strain of Bright tobacco grown in the sandy soil of that region. In 1839, a slave-worker supervising the curing of a crop of tobacco had placed hot charcoal on the log fire and, in doing so, unwittingly altered the form of tobacco produced. As a result of his action, the transformation of the leaf had occurred, not through contact with the smoke from the wood, but rather through its exposure to the heat thrown out by the coals, and the effect had been to produce a tobacco which was bright yellow in colour and exceptionally mild.[8] Initially, this new form of tobacco was found to be suitable as a wrapper for plug (chewing) tobacco, and tobacco farmers were therefore encouraged to further develop this curing process through the use of flue-pipes which channelled heat from a furnace into a curing barn. This new method, which became known as flue-curing, allowed for much greater control of the curing process, and enabled the final colour of the leaf to be fixed both more rapidly and with much greater precision.[9]

The possibility of using flue-cured Bright tobacco as a filler for cigarettes first emerged towards the end of the American Civil War. Union soldiers from the North, already familiar with cigarettes as a form of tobacco smoking and who now found themselves stationed in the Piedmont region, adopted the new strain of tobacco for use in their own cigarettes. On returning home at the end of the war, many of them sought to obtain the product through their local tobacco dealers, and hence bags of granulated, flue-cured Bright tobacco began to be shipped north to satisfy the demand of these Civil War veterans. By the early 1870s, therefore, two distinct types of cigarette were in use in America; the traditional high quality cigarettes, hand-rolled in factories using imported Turkish tobacco and purchased almost exclusively by well-to-do city-dwellers, and the crude form of cigarette, rolled up by the smoker himself using pouches of granulated Bright tobacco, and prevalent in both urban and rural communities of the northern United States. The creation of the modern

[8] N. M. Tilley, *The Bright Tobacco Industry, 1860–1929* (1948); J. Goodman, *Tobacco in History: the Cultures of Dependence* (1993), pp. 98–9.

[9] According to Corina, the system of flue-curing was developed around 1860. See M. Corina, *Trust in Tobacco: the Anglo-American Struggle for Power* (1975), p. 48. For a summary of the different types of tobacco and the process of cigarette production from farm to factory, see D. Tucker, *Tobacco: An International Perspective* (1982), chs. 1 and 2.

American cigarette industry required an integration of these two elements in order to produce a factory-made and packaged, hand-rolled cigarette that contained the cheaper flue-cured Bright tobacco.[10]

The firm which first succeeded in achieving this combination was one set up by Francis S. Kinney in New York. After some experimentation, Kinney produced a cigarette which blended together Turkish Latakia and flue-cured Virginia Bright leaf, along with some exotic flavourings, and named the resulting product 'Sweet Caporal'. The brand quickly caught on and, having captured a large share of the market in New York, Kinney developed a distribution network of jobbers (wholesalers) who successfully marketed 'Sweet Caporal' in other major American cities.[11] Naturally, rival companies soon began to follow Kinney's lead. William S. Kimball of Rochester, in upstate New York, developed a variety of cigarette brands including 'Vanity Fair' and 'Old Gold', and Goodwin & Co. of New York City developed a product similar to Kimball's which they branded 'Old Judge'. Later, Goodwin also created a brand specifically for the English export market which carried the name 'Chancellor'.[12]

One figure who emerged as a leading actor during this initial phase of the industry was based not in New York, but in the tobacco-growing region of the south. Major Lewis Ginter was a northerner who before the war had settled in Richmond and enlisted in the Confederate army. He had returned to New York at the end of the conflict where he witnessed the boom in cigarettes containing Virginia Bright leaf, and this prompted him to join forces with an established tobacco manufacturer John F. Allen and to begin the production of cigarettes. Under Ginter's leadership, the new firm of Allen & Ginter set up manufacturing facilities in Richmond in 1875, and began to produce and heavily advertise cigarette brands using flue-cured Virginia leaf with names such as 'Richmond Straight Cut' and 'Richmond Gem'. Displaying a gift for innovation, Ginter focused on the packaging of his products and developed attractive labels and new, stronger forms of packaging which were less prone to crushing. Allen & Ginter's brands, for example, became the first to incorporate printed cards which both served to stiffen the paper packet and, at the same time, allowed the firm to advertise its product. These little

[10] Note that the price advantage of roll-your-own cigarettes made from the domestically grown Bright tobacco was enhanced between 1864 and 1867 by the imposition of a Federal tax on all ready-rolled cigarettes. R. Sobel, *They Satisfy: the Cigarette in American Life* (1978), pp. 17–18.

[11] The demand for low-priced Bright tobacco cigarettes seems to have been boosted by the onset of economic depression in 1873. See R. Kluger, *Ashes to Ashes: America's Hundred-Year Cigarette War, the Public Health, and the Unabashed Triumph of Philip Morris* (1996), p. 18.

[12] *Tobacco (London)*, 4 (38) (1884), 18.

cards developed into numerous series, featuring a variety of subject matters, encouraging consumers to continue buying the same brand. By 1880, as the American cigarette craze hit Britain, sales of the product in the United States had reached 500 million and Allen & Ginter had emerged as the nation's leading cigarette manufacturer.[13]

These hand-rolled cigarettes had initially been developed using a blend of domestic Bright and imported Turkish leaf, but one of Ginter's main innovations had been to replace the expensive imported leaf with a strain of tobacco grown in Kentucky, called White Burley, which readily lent itself to the absorption of flavourings and sweeteners such as glycerine, rum, liquorice, sugar, and tonka bean.[14] By incorporating flavoured Burley together with the Virginia Bright tobacco, Ginter and others created the American-blend cigarette, comprising entirely of domestically produced leaf. Flavourings of the kind used in American-blend cigarettes, however, were frowned upon by the authorities in Britain, and in 1883 a number of consignments of American cigarettes were impounded by the Board of Customs on the grounds that they were adulterated with added sugar.[15] Although the claims of adulteration were eventually shown to be unfounded, the result of these constraints was that the British consumer developed a taste for American cigarettes which were produced from pure Virginia tobacco—as the flue-cured Bright leaf came increasingly to be termed—rather than the American-blend of cigarettes featuring flavoured Burley leaf which found favour with smokers in the United States.

The Dukes of Durham

The rise in American cigarette consumption involved sales of both factory-made and roll-your-own forms of the product. One firm which had been very successful in selling the latter type was W. T. Blackwell of Durham, North Carolina, most notably under the 'Bull Durham' brand name. Blackwell's president, Julian Carr, claimed in 1883 that his firm had spent over $250,000 during the year on various forms of advertising, including the organization of four gangs of painters who travelled around the country—following the railroad network—in order to publicize the firm's products.[16] Carr was an enthusiastic supporter of the power of advertising, in much the

[13] Kluger, *Ashes to Ashes*, p. 18.

[14] Sobel, *They Satisfy*, pp. 24–5.

[15] *Tobacco (London)*, 4 (38) (1884), 16.

[16] The painting gangs, who were partly employed on contract and partly hired on a daily basis, travelled the length and breadth of America, as far west as Seattle and down beyond the border with Mexico. *Tobacco (London)*, 3 (36) (1883), 156.

same way as Lewis Ginter, and by the mid 1870s the Blackwell concern was reputed to control the largest smoking-tobacco factory in the world.[17] The success of the Blackwell enterprise made progress very difficult for its local rivals in Durham, such as the firm of W. Duke, Sons & Co. This latter enterprise had been founded by Washington Duke on his farm outside Durham at the end of the Civil War, and had made some progress with its brand of smoking tobacco 'Pro Bono Publico'. In 1874, Washington Duke moved the business into Durham town, where he built a small factory, and four years later he formally organized the firm into a partnership with his three sons, Brodie, James Buchanan, and Benjamin, together with an experienced wholesale tobacconist, George Watts.[18]

After the formation of W. Duke, Sons & Co. as a partnership, the management of the company fell increasingly into the hands of Washington Duke's youngest son James 'Buck' Duke. Indeed, in 1880 Washington Duke felt sufficiently redundant to sell his own share of the business to Richard H. Wright, another local tobacco manufacturer, and withdraw into retirement. In an effort to extend the market for Duke's products, Wright began to travel on the firm's behalf. To begin with he was posted to Chicago to develop the firm's business there and in the west of the country, but in 1882 he embarked on a world tour in an ambitious effort to promote the Duke company's brands abroad. The tour extended for two years, and saw Wright travel widely through Europe, South Africa, India, and elsewhere in Asia, and finally to Australia and New Zealand, before returning in 1884.[19]

Back in Durham, meanwhile, James Duke had concluded that the only way his firm could succeed against the Bull Durham concern was to engage in the manufacture of the increasingly popular hand-made cigarettes.[20] With no local expertise in the hand-rolling of cigarettes available to him in Durham, Duke had begun by hiring a well-known Russian-born Jewish cigarette-maker, J. M. Siegel, to help train a workforce of local people and to act as the factory superintendent.[21] Towards the end of 1880, he had also become aware of a dispute between the hand-rollers of the New York firm Goodwin & Co. and their management who were attempting to introduce machinery and cut wages. Late that year, Duke approached the leader of the workers' union, Moses Gladstein, and offered to maintain the current wages of the workforce on condition that they relocated to North Carolina. Gladstein and

17 R. F. Durden, *The Dukes of Durham, 1865–1929* (1975), p. 18.

18 Durden, *Dukes of Durham*, p. 18.

19 Durden, *Dukes of Durham*, p. 19.

20 American Tobacco Company, ' "Sold American!"—The First Fifty Years' (1954), p. 19.

21 B. W. C. Roberts and R. F. Knapp, 'Paving the Way for the Tobacco Trust: From Hand Rolling to Mechanized Cigarette Production by W. Duke, Sons and Company', *The North Carolina Historical Review*, 69, (1992), 257–81.

125 of his fellow workers accepted Duke's proposal, and by the autumn of 1881 these workers had begun producing cigarettes at his factory in Durham.[22]

Along with his first brand of cigarettes, called simply 'Duke's of Durham', Duke launched a variety of inducements to jobbers and customers alike. To begin with Duke's firm made little impression on the fledgling cigarette market; however, between 1883 and 1884 the position of W. Duke, Sons & Co. in the American tobacco industry was transformed by two of Duke's most inspired decisions. The first of these moves demonstrated Duke's tactical business brain at its very sharpest as he outwitted and outmanoeuvred his rivals in the face of a golden opportunity. Early in 1883, the jobbers who dealt in tobacco goods had been reluctant to take on extra stocks of cigarettes due to the pressure that was being applied to Congress for a reduction in the duty on the product, which stood at $1.75 per 1,000. In March a new rate of $0.50 was duly agreed, drastically reducing the retail price of the product, but the change was not scheduled to take force until 1 May. Duke, however, acted quickly. Immediately the new level of duty was announced, Duke's cigarette brands were made available to dealers at a 50 per cent discount, on the important proviso that three-quarters of the order would not be called for delivery until after the new rate of duty had gone into effect. The jobbers, who had run down their inventories in anticipation of the rate cut were thus offered cut-price cigarettes in return for bulk orders, and Duke's products became the first to arrive on the streets at the substantially reduced price of 5 cents for ten. In the final nine months of 1883, Duke's firm sold 30 million cigarettes and had emerged as a force to be reckoned with.[23]

Duke's clever scheme had brought his products into the public eye at precisely the moment when cigarettes were about to enjoy a consumer boom. Having stimulated the demand for his brands, he now sought to revolutionize the method by which they were produced. Duke's second critical decision, therefore, related to the adoption of a cigarette-making machine.

Mechanization and the Bonsack Machine

The potential savings that could be effected in the cost of production by the successful mechanization of cigarette manufacturing were such that, almost as soon as they set up their factory in 1875, Allen & Ginter had felt it appropriate

[22] Sobel, *They Satisfy*, pp. 31–2.

[23] R. B. Tennant, *The American Cigarette Industry: A Study in Economic Analysis and Public Policy* (1950), p. 22; P. G. Porter, 'Origins of the American Tobacco Company', *Business History Review*, 43 (1969), 59–76.

to offer the extravagant prize of $75,000 to the first person who was able to produce a cigarette-rolling machine that the company was prepared to adopt for its products.[24] One such machine, developed piecemeal by a Virginia-based mechanic James A. Bonsack, was granted its first patent in March 1881, and was quickly offered to Allen & Ginter for their consideration. When they tried it out in their Richmond factory later that year, however, they were not sufficiently impressed to take it up, partly due to its limitations in operation, but partly, too, because the firm had by this time begun to entertain fears that consumers would not take to machine-made cigarettes after all.[25] It was an error of judgement which, within a few years, was to cost Allen & Ginter their position as leaders of the American manufactured cigarette business.

Undaunted by Allen & Ginter's negative response, Bonsack found some financial backing and set up the Bonsack Machine Co. under the presidency of his brother-in-law D. B. Strouse, a lawyer,[26] before taking his invention off to Europe and exhibiting it in Paris early in 1883. The mechanism quickly attracted the interest of W. D. & H. O. Wills' agent there, and in May 1883 Bonsack scored his first major success when Wills agreed to take out a contract for the exclusive use of his machine in Britain and in other British territories for a period of five years.[27]

No doubt encouraged by the news of Wills' adoption of the machine in Britain, but equally mindful of the problems that would be engendered among his workforce in the event of introducing machine production, James Duke decided in April 1884 to invite Bonsack to set up one of his machines in the factory at Durham. Aided by the support of a mechanic supplied by Bonsack, William T. O'Brien, the machine began to show sufficient promise for Duke to enter into detailed negotiations with Strouse. Duke's objective was to ensure that, if his firm fully adopted the Bonsack, his rival manufacturers would not be in a position to jump on the bandwagon and compete against him on equal terms. Just as Wills had been granted exclusivity in their use of the machine in Britain, in exchange for the risk that they were taking, so Duke wanted some measure of protection if, having adopted the machine, it eventually proved to be a success. Unwilling or unable to grant Duke exclusive rights to the machine in America, Strouse eventually came to an agreement in April 1885 with Duke that, whatever rate per 1,000 cigarettes was charged to other firms for use of the machine, Duke's firm would be charged

[24] Tennant, *American Cigarette Industry*, p. 17; Roberts and Knapp, 'Paving the Way', p. 266 (who give the date as 1876).

[25] Kluger, *Ashes to Ashes*, p. 20.

[26] The Bonsack Machine Co. was established at Salem, Virginia, 27 March 1882. Roberts and Knapp, 'Paving the Way', p. 271.

[27] Alford, *W. D. & H. O. Wills*, pp. 144–50. It does not seem to have been specified precisely which countries the term 'other British territories' embraced.

at a rate that was 25 per cent lower. With the 65 per cent reduction in unit cost allowed by mechanization, coupled with a guaranteed advantage in the marginal cost of production over any rival firm who used the machine, Duke was now poised to move into a position of leadership in the American cigarette industry.[28]

Naturally, the decision to adopt the Bonsack machine created unrest among Duke's workforce. Within three months of the installation of the first machine at the factory, members of Duke's workforce who had been brought from Goodwin's factory in New York set up a local chapter of the Cigarmakers Progressive Union, the first such union branch to be created in the south-eastern United States.[29] In an effort to press for an improvement in the working conditions of their members in Durham, Duke was persuaded to attend a meeting with the New York committee of the union at which he agreed to put in hand certain changes. However, the negotiations backfired on the union. On his return, Duke instituted a maximum daily production quota of 1,000 cigarettes for those employees who were members of the union, effectively halving their wages, whilst allowing non-union members to continue to work a full 11½ hour day. As a result many of the ex-Goodwin hand-rollers began to leave Durham and return to find work in New York. Their departure, coupled with soaring demand, created acute problems for Duke in the short term and despite the fact that the number of machines employed at his factory rose from four to fifteen during the course of 1886 many new hand-rollers were still required. In the autumn of that year W. Duke, Sons & Co. were said to be 'offering inducements for five hundred girls and boys to learn the business'.[30]

Finding consumers for the cigarettes that his increasingly mechanized factories were producing, however, never seemed to present a problem to Duke. He had soon grasped the importance of sales promotion, in much the same way as Ginter and Carr had done before him, and he was particularly well-served by one of his main salesmen, Edward Small, whom he had employed soon after his firm had moved into the cigarette trade. Small, a naturally gifted salesman, had first made a big impression in Atlanta, when he persuaded a well-known French actress, Madame Rhea, to endorse Duke's 'Pin Head' brand as part of her own promotional material. Subsequently,

[28] The agreed rate of royalty to be paid by Duke's firm per 1000 cigarettes was \$0.24 compared with the standard rate charged to other users of \$0.33. As well as the agreement to maintain this differential rate, Strouse also agreed to reduce the rate further, to \$0.20 per 1000, as soon as Duke had transferred all his production on to the Bonsack. Durden, *Dukes of Durham*, p. 32.

[29] Roberts and Knapp, 'Paving the Way', p. 273.

[30] *Tobacco (London)*, 9 (105) (1899), 258.

Small followed up this coup by employing an attractive widow as a saleswoman in St Louis. In both cases, the effect was to create a minor sensation and to generate vast amounts of free publicity. Later schemes employed by Small included the creation of a Duke-sponsored ice-hockey team named after a popular brand of cigarettes, 'Cross Cut'.[31] When, in 1884, Duke took the decision to set up a headquarters in New York city, one of the reasons that prompted this move was a desire to secure better advertising facilities.[32] The move also served to place his organization at the focal point of American business life, leaving him closer to his main markets and well placed to develop his international sales, and the company soon built a factory there on the Lower East Side.[33]

The sales generated by Duke's international envoy, his partner Richard H. Wright, were also beginning to emerge as a factor of some importance to the firm. A visitor to the Durham factory in 1886, who casually enquired as to the destination of the vast quantities of cigarettes and smoking tobacco stored there, was handed bills of lading by the general manager showing that goods were being shipped to Hamburg, Honolulu, Singapore, Madras, Antwerp, Rotterdam, Montreal, Auckland, and Sourabay in the Dutch East Indies (Indonesia). The firm claimed by this time to have established a large trade in China and Asia, and India and Arabia.[34] Impressive as this must have sounded to an observer at the time, it represented merely the first trickle of a trade in cigarettes and tobacco which was set to rise sharply after 1890.

To some extent, the potential growth in foreign markets was undermined by Wright's resignation from the Duke partnership shortly after returning from his world tour. Wright's decision created a series of legal problems for James Duke and his other partners and led to the formation of W. Duke, Sons & Co. as a joint stock company in 1885. Wright himself invested heavily in a rival cigarette manufacturing company, the Lone Jack Co. of Lynchburg, and was quickly installed as its managing director. Having recognized the potential profits to be made through mechanization of cigarette production, Wright then used his position as a cigarette manufacturer to cultivate his contacts with the Bonsack Machine Co., in which he ultimately became a substantial shareholder. Thereafter Wright, particularly through his activities in

[31] Durden, *Dukes of Durham*, pp. 20–2. The endless variety of promotional schemes developed by Duke's company has been well documented. See P. G. Porter, 'Advertising in the Early Cigarette Industry: W. Duke, Sons & Company of Durham', *The North Carolina Historical Review*, 48 (1971), 31–43.

[32] Porter, 'Advertising in the Cigarette Industry', p. 33.

[33] A. D. Chandler, *Strategy and Structure: Chapters in the History of the Industrial Enterprise* (1962), p. 27.

[34] *Tobacco (London)*, 6 (67) (1886), 156.

the international cigarette market, became a thorn in the side of James Duke and his ambitions.[35]

Formation of the American Tobacco Company

Once the Bonsack machine was operating efficiently, it was capable of producing an output of around 200 cigarettes per minute. To satisfy the entire national demand for cigarettes in America in 1885, therefore, would require only thirty such machines working 10 hours per day.[36] Provided that consumers could be persuaded to switch from hand-rolled to machine-made cigarettes—and of the large manufacturers only Allen & Ginter seemed to hold out much belief that this would not be the case[37]—it was clear that the growth of mechanization would lead to a process of industrial concentration in the cigarette manufacturing business. The principal manufacturers had already lined up behind different machines, with Goodwin & Co. developing the Emery machine themselves and Kinney & Co. and W. S. Kimball & Co. taking out ownership of the Allison machine. During the 1880s, however, the Bonsack machine emerged decisively as the industry leader and Duke's favourable rate gave him a crucial advantage over his main rivals as they too began to adopt Bonsack's invention. During the latter part of the 1880s Duke tried hard to persuade Strouse to restrict the use of his firm's machine to the major manufacturers in order to prevent a profusion of small firms gaining a share of the market by reducing prices and thereby causing a fall in profits.[38] Clearly the development of industrial concentration among firms involved in manufacturing machine-made cigarettes was viewed by Duke as the only way

[35] Wright's dispute with Duke in 1885 and his subsequent career are covered in Durden, *Dukes of Durham*, pp. 28–36 and *passim*. In fact, Wright negotiated with the Bonsack company a better rate for the Lone Jack Co. than that granted to Duke, due to his willingness to allow the Bonsack engineers to experiment with the machines at his plant. Indeed, the Lone Jack Co. seems to have played the role of Bonsack's research and training facility during the late 1880s. The firm, however, was much too small-scale to compete effectively with the main cigarette manufacturers.

[36] Tennant, *American Cigarette Industry*, p. 20.

[37] Having established their position as the leading producer and exporter of cigarettes on the strength of the hand-rolled article, Allen & Ginter were the most reluctant to make the switch to mechanized production. An account of their Richmond factory in 1889 indicated that 1,300 girls were still employed in the hand-rolling of cigarettes. *Tobacco (London)*, 9 (106) (1899), 285. Even after the company began to produce their better brands on Bonsack machines, they were still apparently sent out as being 'hand-made'. See letter from D. B. Strouse to J. B. Duke dated 28 June 1890 in the papers of J. B. Duke, Special Collections Library, Perkins Library, Duke University, hereinafter J. B. Duke papers.

[38] This is a continuing theme of Duke's correspondence with Strouse between 1887 and 1889. See Durden, *Dukes of Durham*, pp. 37–45, citing J. B. Duke papers.

forward for the industry, and he took it into his own hands to advance this process via horizontal integration.

As a prelude to a formal merger between the main cigarette manufacturers, Duke and his leading competitors engaged in a form of quasi-integration during the late 1880s by forming a leaf-purchasing cartel. As Chandler has pointed out, the profitability of high volume production in industries like cigarette manufacturing was reliant upon more active management of the chain of production activities as a whole.[39] The need to guarantee the necessary supplies of tobacco leaf, therefore, led the main cigarette manufacturing firms to engage in backward vertical integration through the construction and operation of large warehouses and curing facilities. Since the Dukes, as tobacco farmers, had begun by producing their own leaf, the company already possessed the necessary expertise to develop these facilities for handling the leaf. However, as their raw material requirements began to rise rapidly, so the company began to purchase leaf by means of its own salaried leaf buyers rather than through the existing system of middlemen.[40] These developments were complemented by the creation of wholesale distribution facilities in the major American cities through which, with Duke's firm leading the way, the retailers and local jobbers could be reached without the need for large scale commission merchants and even some of the larger jobbers.[41]

By 1889, the five leading American cigarette manufacturers were producing a level of output in excess of 2 billion sticks per year—a combined market share of between 90 and 95 per cent[42]—with Duke's firm alone accounting for 834 million (see Table 2.1). Under Duke's initiative, discussions had been taking place during the previous two years regarding the possibility of an amalgamation between the five firms, but progress had been slow. However, some moves towards industrial concentration had begun to emerge. Between 1888 and 1889, the Bonsack Machine Co. had bought out the patents of both the Emery and Allison machines, thus giving them control of the machinery of cigarette production, and in 1899 the five cigarette manufacturing firms had agreed to pool their leaf-buying activities.[43] Full amalgamation now only depended upon the time required to reach an

[39] See A. D. Chandler, *The Visible Hand: The Managerial Revolution in American Business* (1977), esp. pp. 382–98.

[40] Porter, 'Origins of the American Tobacco Co.', p. 66; G. Porter and H. C. Livesay, *Merchants and Manufacturers: Studies in the Changing Structure of Nineteenth Century Marketing*, Johns Hopkins Press, Baltimore (1971), pp. 203–4.

[41] Porter and Livesay, *Merchants and Manufacturers*, p. 205.

[42] Durden, *Dukes of Durham*, p. 58.

[43] Porter, 'Origins of the American Tobacco Co.', pp. 72–3; Tennant, *American Cigarette Industry*, p. 25.

TABLE 2.1. Cigarette sales of the five principal US producers (million sticks), 1889

Company	Cigarettes
W. Duke, Sons & Co.	834
Allen & Ginter	517
Kinney Tobacco Co.	432
William S. Kimball & Co.	237
Goodwin & Co.	168

Source: R. B. Tennant, *American Cigarette Industry*, Table 2. Yale University Press, © Yale University Press.

acceptable agreement. The final negotiations centred around the question of a division of ownership, with Duke eventually agreeing to an equal holding in the new corporation to that allocated to Ginter's firm, on condition that Duke himself was appointed as the new company's president. Thus ATC was incorporated in January 1890 in New Jersey with an authorized capital of $25 million. This total share capital was allocated between the constituent firms as follows: W. Duke, Sons & Co. and Allen & Ginter each took 30 per cent, the Kinney Tobacco Co. was allocated 20 per cent, and William S. Kimball & Co. and Goodwin & Co. each received 10 per cent. The company's headquarters were located in prestigious offices in New York at 111 Fifth Avenue.[44]

Expanding Foreign Sales

Announcing the creation of this new American tobacco trust in February 1890, the London trade journal *Tobacco* pointed out that, 'The "Trust" proposes to extend the sale of its cigarettes in foreign markets. Doubtless they will favour England in due course.'[45] Certainly, the development of an export trade was one of the key factors that had motivated Duke's desire for a merger and after its formation this trade was stepped up through the appointment of sales representatives in key markets. As Table 2.2 indicates, in the ten years following its formation, the United States' cigarette exports grew practically fourfold in volume terms. Comparison with Table 2.3 indicates that this trade was dominated by ATC which, during the 1890s as a whole, accounted for around 96 per cent of the country's export trade in cigarettes. As a result of

[44] Porter, 'Origins of the American Tobacco Co.', pp. 73–4; Tennant, *American Cigarette Industry*, p. 26.

[45] *Tobacco (London)*, 10 (110) (1890), 29.

TABLE 2.2. US exports of cigarettes (million sticks), 1890/1–1899/1900 (year ending June)

	1890/1	1891/2	1892/3	1893/4	1894/5	1895/6	1896/7	1897/8	1898/9	1899/1900
Europe	**111.5**	**130.9**	**147.4**	**134.6**	**164.1**	**193.0**	**232.9**	**216.8**	**230.7**	**202.6**
Germany	*17.6*	*19.8*	*24.7*	*15.3*	*13.3*	*12.8*	*20.1*	*16.0*	*10.8*	*13.2*
United Kingdom	*69.0*	*83.1*	*97.1*	*89.0*	*114.1*	*134.5*	*158.2*	*131.4*	*148.3*	*109.9*
North America	**15.0**	**15.2**	**18.3**	**23.6**	**35.8**	**40.0**	**47.5**	**36.5**	**32.1**	**15.9**
British W. Indies	*10.3*	*11.8*	*14.3*	*18.1*	*30.4*	*33.9*	*38.9*	*30.1*	*24.9*	*8.7*
South America	**3.2**	**2.6**	**1.8**	**2.0**	**3.2**	**2.8**	**0.7**	**0.3**	**1.1**	**3.6**
Asia	**59.9**	**62.4**	**151.3**	**161.3**	**150.5**	**283.9**	**448.2**	**554.8**	**677.3**	**599.7**
Japan	*45.0*	*39.4*	*102.9*	*76.6*	*50.0*	*130.5*	*216.0*	*263.4*	*297.1*	*78.3*
Chinese Empire	*9.1*	*13.9*	*21.2*	*52.3*	*62.9*	*117.7*	*161.2*	*218.6*	*222.8*	*357.9*
Hong Kong	*3.1*	*4.7*	*7.4*	*7.9*	*2.4*	*3.2*	*10.7*	*8.5*	*11.8*	*17.1*
British E. Indies	*2.8*	*4.4*	*19.9*	*24.5*	*35.1*	*32.5*	*60.2*	*64.3*	*144.2*	*143.0*
Oceania	**106.6**	**66.5**	**60.6**	**53.1**	**65.7**	**72.5**	**105.2**	**142.8**	**143.8**	**155.7**
British Australasia	*103.1*	*62.8*	*57.2*	*50.2*	*61.7*	*67.8*	*98.7*	*128.4*	*114.9*	*120.7*
Africa	**22.8**	**28.8**	**31.4**	**33.9**	**45.3**	**41.6**	**87.0**	**54.7**	**84.7**	**186.3**
British Africa	*22.8*	*28.8*	*31.4*	*33.9*	*45.3*	*40.0*	*86.7*	*54.3*	*84.5*	*186.1*
Total	**319.0**	**306.5**	**410.9**	**408.6**	**464.6**	**633.8**	**921.3**	**1005.9**	**1169.5**	**1164.4**

Notes: British East Indies relates to sales in British India and the Straits Settlements (Malaysia and Singapore); British Africa relates principally to South Africa; British Australasia relates to Australia and New Zealand.

Figures in italics are components of regional subtotals. Totals may not sum due to rounding.

Source: Foreign Commerce and Navigation of the US, 1900.

TABLE 2.3. Total output and foreign exports of cigarettes by ATC, 1891–1901

Year	Total output (million sticks)	Exports (million sticks)	Export share (per cent)
1891	2,788.8	309.3	11.1
1892	2,883.5	324.6	11.3
1893	3,122.2	427.9	13.7
1894	3,131.7	394.1	12.6
1895	3,565.9	514.9	14.4
1896	3,987.8	780.0	19.6
1897	3,753.4	816.5	21.8
1898	3,872.0	1,215.6	31.4
1899	3,547.4	983.3	27.7
1900	3,380.1	1,132.6	33.5
1901	3,354.7	1,232.8	36.7

Source: US Bureau of Corporations, *Report on the Tobacco Industry*, Table 41.

this rapid growth, the importance of export sales in ATC's cigarette business rose progressively during its first ten years in operation, increasing from just over 10 per cent of the company's total sales in 1890 to around one-third at the turn of the century.

In developing this export trade, ATC initially utilized local agents to promote and arrange for the distribution of their goods. In China, for example, the company developed links with an agency in Shanghai called Mustard & Co. in 1890, and in India with the firm of George Atherton & Co. around the same time. However, ATC's management quickly became convinced of the uselessness of conducting its business in the old-fashioned way of placing its goods on a commission basis in the hands of a local commission agent or manufacturer's agent.[46] In order to raise the profile of the company's products, therefore, Duke began to post his own salaried sales representatives abroad, primarily within the British colonies, and used these members of staff to push the company's imported goods to local dealers. As a result, one such ATC representative, Alfred I. Hart based in South Africa, was able to claim in 1893 that, 'in the United Kingdom and all the British possessions our goods are the recognised favourites'.[47]

The success of this export-based approach, however, required the provision of a supply of low-priced cigarettes and, in certain markets, high tariffs made such a strategy problematic. Thus, according to the company's management, 'It soon

[46] The American Tobacco Co., 'A few facts relating to the development of its export business', BAT Co. internal paper, n.d. (*c.*1907), BAT Co. Southampton Archive, Box 87, p. 5.

[47] *Tobacco (London)*, 13 (152) (1893), 90.

became evident that in order to secure anything like a large share of the Tobacco business in such countries as Canada, New Zealand, Australia and others where the "import" duties were high, it would be necessary to establish factories on the ground.'[48] In Australia, ATC faced not only the problem of high tariffs, but also strong competitive pressure both from the products of local firms, notably the Dixson Tobacco Company, and from another American tobacco manufacturing group, the Camerons. The Cameron family of Petersburg and Richmond in Virginia had made substantial investments in the Australian market well before ATC made its first impact there, building tobacco manufacturing factories in Melbourne, Sydney, Adelaide, and Brisbane, and developing a large export trade in their smoking tobacco.[49] In the 1890s, one of the Cameron group of companies, the firm of Cameron & Cameron of Richmond, acquired a number of Bonsack machines and began to develop its own cigarette export trade with Australia in competition with Duke's company.[50] Spurred by this threat to ATC's export market, Duke made the decision to set up subsidiary companies within the main states of the Australian colony.[51] Hence in 1894, ATC made their first foreign direct investment by organizing and investing in the American Tobacco Co. of Victoria Ltd., the American Tobacco Co. of New South Wales Ltd., and the American Tobacco Co. of South Australia Ltd. In each case, the subsidiary companies were formed in conjunction with local interests, notably Hugh Dixson and the Cameron brothers in the case of New South Wales and South Australia, and the Cameron group and Jacobs Hart & Co. in the case of Victoria. The subsidiaries were licensed to produce ATC's brands and were granted sole agency for the sale of cigarettes imported from America. As the parent company, ATC took a 57.5 per cent share of the issued stock of each subsidiary.[52] The following year, the company formed the American Tobacco Co. of New Zealand which included a tobacco manufacturing business called Austin Welsh & Co. that had been acquired earlier. In the case of the New Zealand subsidiary, ATC took a share of 80 per cent. Altogether, ATC invested $172,000 in the capital stock of these companies.[53]

48 American Tobacco Co., 'A few facts', p. 2.

49 *Tobacco (London)*, 16 (188) (1896), 286.

50 Cf. W. R. Erwin, The papers of the British–American Tobacco Co., Ltd., unpublished mimeo, Part V; Foreign Letterpress Books of Cameron & Cameron, 1895–1901, both in the Special Collections Department, Perkins Library, Duke University.

51 Before Federation in 1901, tariff controls severely restricted interstate trade within the Australian colony, hence separate arrangements needed to be made for operating in each of the states. R. Walker, *Under Fire: A History of Tobacco Smoking in Australia* (1984), p. 45.

52 Copy of Agreements relating to the American Tobacco Company, Inc. and Australia. BAT Co. Southampton Archive, Box 51.

53 US Bureau of Corporations, *Report of the Commissioner of Corporations on the Tobacco Industry* (Part I) (1909), Table 34.

In September 1895, the year after these investments had been commenced in Australia, ATC undertook a similar programme of investment in the Canadian cigarette industry when it created the American Tobacco Co. of Canada Ltd. This company was capitalized at $1 million and was used to acquire the interests of the two main cigarette manufacturing businesses in Canada, B. Goldstein & Co. and D. Ritchie & Co., both located in Montreal.[54] Of the total issue of stock by the new Canadian subsidiary, 89.5 per cent was assigned to ATC.[55]

The twin problems of tariff restrictions and local competitors continued to provide problems for ATC's export trade in the two main European markets that Duke coveted, Germany and Great Britain, and in each case the export trade expanded much more slowly—scarcely at all in the case of Germany—than the company would have wished during the 1890s. Nevertheless, there was a brighter side to the foreign trade picture during these years, which was to be found in the tenfold growth in cigarette exports to markets in the Far East.

Progress in the Far East

The export market which brought ATC its greatest success in Asia before 1900 was that of Japan. As early as 1881 Mr Dusel, the manager of Kimball & Co., had signed a contract appointing Mr Matsuhei Iwaya of Tokyo as sole agent for the company's 'Old Gold' cigarettes in the Orient,[56] and it is probable that Richard Wright's tour on behalf of W. Duke, Sons & Co. between 1882 and 1884 would have taken him to Japan also. By the 1890s Japan had blossomed into ATC's leading export market with the company's 'Pin Head' and 'Old Gold' brands proving particularly popular among Japanese consumers. With the Japanese authorities constrained by treaty to levy a nominal import tariff of 5 per cent on the trade, the American-manufactured cigarettes were sufficiently cheap to compete with the locally produced pipe tobacco and mouthpiece cigarettes made from domestically grown leaf.

[54] According to an unpublished typescript in the BAT Co. archive, the B. Goldstein concern had been set up in 1885 as the American Cigarette Company and had been licensed to manufacture and sell in Canada the 'Sweet Caporal' brand of the Kinney Tobacco Co. By 1895 it was therefore effectively operating on behalf of ATC. D. Ritchie & Co. had also been set up in 1885, according to this account, and had imported its first Bonsack machines in 1888. S. Mercier, 'A Brief History of Tobacco in Canada', BAT Co. Southampton Archive, Box 42.

[55] US Bureau of Corporations, *Report on the Tobacco Industry* (Part I), pp. 69–71.

[56] Translation of newspaper article enclosed with letter from E. J. Parrish to BAT Co. London dated 17 March 1904, Parrish Letterpress Book, Papers of E. J. Parrish, Special Collections Department, Perkins Library, Duke University, hereinafter Parrish Papers.

The booming trade attracted other Western cigarette manufacturers to Japan. W. D. & H. O. Wills built up its trade with Japan during the 1890s to the point where it constituted the company's largest overseas market, accounting for one-fifth of its exports by 1898.[57] The American firm of Cameron & Cameron also made a concerted effort to gain a share of the market in Japan by appointing ATC's erstwhile representative in South Africa, Alfred I. Hart, to market their cigarettes there in 1897. Cameron's strategy had been to promote their 'Purity' brand to Japanese consumers as a high-quality product, but the approach was fundamentally flawed because of the need to compete with ATC's low-priced cigarette brands. On his arrival at Yokohama Hart reported to Cameron's home office that 'the bulk of the trade in Cigarettes is of the cheap grades, of "Pin Head" and "Old Gold" and that there is less than twelve millions of the fine grade sold'.[58] Faced with such a well-established rival, Hart became increasingly frustrated with Cameron's management in Richmond as they cajoled him to develop a market for their high-grade cigarettes, complaining with some justification that ATC's existing good contacts with local firms and their ability to bargain for lower shipping rates on the strength of their bulk cargoes from America made his task well-nigh impossible.[59]

ATC's successful expansion of their cigarette exports to Japan was undermined after 1898, however, as the Meiji regime gained treaty concessions which enabled it to abolish the system of extraterritoriality and gain some control over the level of import tariffs that could be levied.[60] Soon after these treaty revisions were announced the Japanese government gave notice that the duty on tobacco imports would rise, and from 1 January 1899 rates of 35 per cent on leaf tobacco and 40 per cent on manufactured tobacco were imposed.[61] The Meiji government was well aware of the potential that tobacco presented for the purposes of revenue generation and in 1898 it had created a state monopoly for the purchase of all domestically grown leaf upon which it had then imposed an excise tax at the rate of 100 per cent *ad valorem*. For a time this benefited importers of foreign leaf tobacco, and led one Japanese tobacco manufacturer, the Murai Brothers Tobacco Company of Kyoto, to substitute imported American leaf for domestically grown tobacco in its

[57] Alford, *W. D. & H. O. Wills*, p. 218.

[58] Letter Cameron & Cameron (C&C) to Alfred I. Hart, Yokohama, dated 7 January 1898, Hart Letterpress Book, Papers of the British–American Tobacco Co., Ltd., Special Collections Department, Perkins Library, Duke University, hereinafter BAT Papers.

[59] Letter C&C to Alfred I. Hart dated 20 April 1898, BAT Papers.

[60] P. Francks, *Japanese Economic Development: Theory and Practice* (1992), p. 43. Full tariff autonomy was not gained by Japan until 1911.

[61] *Tobacco (London)*, 19 (217) (1899), 18.

products.[62] However, this avenue was closed in August 1899 when the state monopoly was extended to cover imported tobacco leaf as well.[63] At the same time the import tariff on tobacco goods was raised from 40 per cent to 100 per cent.[64]

This latter decision effectively torpedoed the trade in imported manufactured cigarettes and left the Western firms to consider their response. Although these companies had been aware for some time that import duties would be raised on tobacco products following the revision of the treaties, the steep increase to 100 per cent had not been anticipated. W. D. & H. O. Wills had sent a leading director, Harry Wills, to Japan in 1898 to investigate the situation, and he had returned to report that the proposed tariff levels would not be unduly disruptive for the firm's sales. Once the news of the 100 per cent tariff reached the Wills board in Bristol, however, it became apparent that the impact would be devastating. To combat the problem, Harry Wills arranged a deal with the Osaka Tobacco Company by which the Japanese firm would be invoiced Wills' products at cost price, in order to minimize the duty payable, and in return would remit half of the profits earned on their sales to Wills through the London-based finance house E. Hunt & Co., which had an arrangement with the Osaka Company. This was viewed by Wills as a purely temporary measure, to prevent a complete collapse of export sales in the Far East, and the company now turned its attention to advancing its growing trade in north China centred on Shanghai.[65]

Wills' lack of direct representation in Japan seems to have prevented any serious consideration by the firm of engaging in the local manufacture of their products as a way of overcoming the higher tariff. However, with a revision of the Commercial Law in 1899 allowing for foreign direct investment in Japan,[66] both ATC and the Cameron firm gave serious attention to the possibility of manufacturing their goods locally. Early in 1899 Alfred Hart approached N. Kimura & Co. of Tokyo, a Japanese tobacco manufacturer with whom he had generated some successful business, to suggest that the

[62] Letter E. J. Parrish to BAT Co., London, dated 17 March 1904, Parrish Papers. According to this report, Murai Brothers was able to persuade the Mitsubishi Bank to advance ¥4 million to support its purchase of American leaf tobacco.

[63] *Tobacco (London)*, 21 (242) (1901), 57. Two dealers were appointed by the government to deal in imported leaf tobacco, Yezoye and Kansai & Co. The latter was subsequently displaced by the Mitsui Bussan Kaisha. See letter from E. J. Parrish to W. R. Harris, New York, dated 31 December 1901, Parrish Papers.

[64] *Tobacco (London)*, 19 (227) (1899), 444.

[65] Alford, *W. D. & H. O. Wills*, pp. 218–19.

[66] R. P. T. Davenport-Hines and G. Jones, 'British Business in Japan since 1868', in R. P. T. Davenport-Hines and G. Jones (eds.), *British Business in Asia since 1860*, Cambridge University Press, Cambridge (1989), p. 225.

Tokyo-based firm should manufacture Cameron's 'Richmond Belle' cigarettes under licence.[67] However, Kimura was not minded to accept Hart's proposal and the American firm turned its attention to the market in British India instead.

In contrast to Cameron's licensing approach, ATC's management adopted a strategy of direct investment in the Japanese market in order to overcome the tariff barrier. At the time of the tariff hike, ATC was represented in Japan by Captain J. W. Lee who had developed the company's trade in cigarettes principally through the Tokyo-based firm Yezoye & Co. During 1899, Lee was joined by Dusel who had been sent from New York with clear instructions to acquire a local manufacturing firm able to produce the company's cigarettes within Japan.[68] The firm targeted was the Kyoto-based Murai Brothers Tobacco Company, the largest cigarette manufacturer in Japan and one which had already begun to produce cigarettes from American leaf tobacco.[69] Towards the end of 1899, Dusel reached an agreement with the owner of the Murai Brothers firm, Kichibei Murai, to form a jointly owned company capitalized at a value of US$5 million (¥10 million) in which ATC took a 50 per cent shareholding, paying $2 million in cash and transferring to Murai its existing Japanese assets. Shortly afterwards, ATC purchased $500,000 of Murai's share of the stock, to give Duke's company a controlling 60 per cent interest.[70]

With this arrangement in place, Duke posted an experienced tobacco executive, Edward J. Parrish, to Japan as Murai's first vice-president under chairman Kichibei Murai. Parrish effectively took control of the development of the Murai Brothers' cigarette business and stepped up American forms of marketing designed to promote the company's 'Old Gold' and 'Pin Head' cigarettes, as well as locally produced brands such as 'Hero' and 'Peacock'. A huge new factory was constructed in Tokyo, and this city became Parrish's headquarters for the Murai company.[71] From here, Parrish developed Murai into

[67] Letter C&C to Alfred I. Hart dated 17 March 1899, BAT Papers.

[68] Letter C&C to Alfred I. Hart dated 10 June 1899, BAT Papers.

[69] *Tobacco (London)*, 20 (231) (1900), 85. According to this report, Murai Brothers operated three factories and had an annual output of 2.5 billion cigarettes. Interestingly, the intelligence on conditions in the tobacco market in Japan seem to have been gleaned by the London-based newspaper from reports in the German tobacco trade journal *Deutsche Tabak Zeitung*.

[70] US Bureau of Corporations, *Report on the Tobacco Industry* (Part I), pp. 83–4, 183; S. Cochran, *Big Business in China: Sino-Foreign Rivalry in the Cigarette Industry, 1890–1930* (1980), p. 40. The Murai Brothers was the first joint venture investment by a foreign firm under the revised treaties. See letter from E. J. Parrish to W. R. Harris, New York, dated 31 December 1901, Parrish Papers.

[71] R. F. Durden, 'Tar Heel Tobacconist in Tokyo, 1899–1904', *The North Carolina Historical Review*, 53 (1976), 347–63.

ATC's main Asian-based operation, supplying markets in China, the Straits, and India as well as the domestic market in Japan, but at the same time maintaining a detailed dialogue with ATC's William R. Harris in New York.

Despite the early progress made, Parrish faced pressure from the Japanese government as the Murai Brothers' American business methods came under criticism from nationalist elements in Japan. The main danger posed to the company concerned the possible extension of the Meiji government's tobacco monopoly from leaf trading to manufacturing itself. A symptom of the political pressure on the industry was witnessed when, in August 1900, the duty on tobacco leaf was increased to 130 per cent and further advances were intimated to Kichibei Murai by his political contacts in Tokyo. Parrish considered that the time had come to consolidate the American-leaf cigarette business in Japan through amalgamation. The Murai Brothers had already expanded its activities into printing through its ownership of the Oriental Printing Company and Parrish now suggested to Harris that horizontal integration was in order:

> The advanced duty on leaf tobacco to our minds will help stop the agitation among politicians of the monopoly of manufacturing. We think that it shows that the officials have at last abandoned any such intentions. This being so, it seems a good time to buy up Kimura & Co. and if possible get hold of all the machines we can now in Japan, even to the taking over of all the leaf tobacco and factories of the Osaka Tobacco Co. and Tonoi . . . and then by a wise and gradual advance of prices corresponding somewhat with and at the time of the advances of duty made by the Government, we would be on the road to great success.[72]

The scheme clearly found favour in New York. The Kimura business was purchased later in 1900, and the following year ATC's main dealer in Tokyo, Yezoye & Co., was also acquired.

The financial benefits accruing to Murai Brothers from its growing dominance of the market for American-leaf cigarettes in Japan, however, was dissipated by a continuing demand for the more traditional Japanese-style mouthpiece cigarettes. Murai developed their own version of these cigarettes and set up a special factory in Tokyo to produce the company's 'Chu Yu' brand. The company also began to manufacture a brand of the cigarette using American, rather than domestic leaf, to which it gave the name 'Time'. Despite the fact that the low prices of these cigarettes cut into the American-leaf cigarette trade in Japan and involved the company in actual losses on the sales of mouthpiece cigarettes that they made, Parrish was unwilling to collude with or purchase the main local manufacturers of these products, Iwaya & Co. and Chiba & Co. As he explained to Harris in New York:

[72] Letter E. J. Parrish to W. R. Harris, New York, dated 25 August 1900, Parrish Papers.

> If Iwaya and ourselves were able to agree and raise prices, it would simply build up Chiba, Minano and others, who would take advantage of the opportunity to increase the sale of their goods. The fact is: *we cannot afford to agree to any terms or agreement with Iwaya* . . . We do not think it wise to make any effort to buy Iwaya or Chiba. In fact think it would operate against us to buy either one. The Chief of the Monopoly has said rather confidentially that it would be unwise to do so. Suppose he says this from a diplomatic or political standpoint. Our opinion is that it would raise quite a howl, and as the Japanese people are rather peculiar and so sentimental that there might be great danger. If we should buy either Iwaya or Chiba and raise prices we would certainly fear the result.[73]

In fact, rather than attempting to solve the problem of competition from mouthpiece cigarettes by joining forces with Iwaya, Parrish attempted to undermine the rival firm by terminating its licence to manufacture ATC's popular 'Old Gold' brand of non-mouthpiece cigarettes.[74]

The profitable expansion of Murai's trade in Japan was also constrained by political factors. The main strategy adopted by Parrish in an effort to improve the company's political position was to place a strong emphasis on Murai's export trade.[75] In 1901, for example, when Parrish began to experience difficulties in obtaining leaf from the government monopoly at a reasonable price, he pointed out to the officials in charge of the monopoly that higher prices for leaf tobacco would damage Murai's exports to India, China, and the Straits where now, as a result of the conflict between British and American firms spilling over from ATC's purchase of Ogden's, Murai's sales were being squeezed by rival British manufacturers such as Wills. The government officials seemed very anxious to facilitate exports, Parrish confided to Harris.[76] The Japanese government had instituted a system of drawback on the duty paid against cigarettes destined for export and Parrish pointed out that:

> The drawback, added to Invoice makes these [new cheap] brands pay us good profits . . . and we think they should be able to run out of China, Straits and India, the Shanghai Cigarette Co.'s goods and all other wild cat or cheap brands.

73 Letter E. J. Parrish to W. R. Harris, New York, dated 31 October 1901, Parrish Papers (emphasis in original).

74 Shortly after raising this issue of collaborating with Iwaya, Parrish wrote to Harris, 'We think Iwaya has seen his biggest day. Old Gold selling well. The loss of Old Gold to Iwaya about broke his back bone.' Iwaya had been marketing this brand in Japan for twenty years. Letter E. J. Parrish to W. R. Harris, New York, dated 31 December 1901, Parrish Papers.

75 Parrish even tried to market Murai Brothers cigarettes to a company in Germany, but was informed that the domestic consumers held a decided preference for cigarettes made from Turkish tobacco. Letter E. J. Parrish to Messrs Achenbach & Co., Hamburg, dated 4 October 1901, Parrish Papers.

76 Letter E. J. Parrish to W. R. Harris, New York, dated 31 December 1901, Parrish Papers.

In fact, at this point in time over one-third of the output of Murai's factories in Japan was being exported, mainly to Mustard & Co., ATC's agents in Shanghai.[77]

A further difficulty that faced Parrish in Japan at this time related to the question of machinery, where rights to the Bonsack cigarette-making machine were held by Duke's ex-partner Richard H. Wright. After splitting from W. Duke, Sons & Co. acrimoniously in 1885 and trying his hand at the management of the rival Lone Jack Co., Wright sold up his shares in this latter concern and purchased a major shareholding in the Bonsack Machine Co. Whilst in charge of the Lone Jack Co., Wright had ingratiated himself with D. B. Strouse, the president of the Bonsack concern, by virtue of his willingness to allow Strouse's company to experiment on the machines which had been leased to him.

After Wright had joined the Bonsack company, Strouse gave him the task of using his previous experience as Duke's overseas salesman to develop a market for the company's cigarette-making machines abroad, giving Wright control of the Bonsack patent for China, Japan, the Philippines, India, and Africa (notably South Africa and Egypt).[78] Duke was furious when he discovered that Strouse had done this, declaring to the president of the Bonsack company, 'The world is now our market for our product and we do not propose sitting idly down and allowing you or anyone else to cut off any of the channels of our trade by establishing factories where there have been none and tying up your machinery with them, and afterwards you could say to us, "You must manufacture your goods in the United States; this country and that country is taken." '[79] Wright, however, intended to make the most of his opportunity.

The patent for the Bonsack machine in Japan had been registered by Wright with the Japanese Patent Bureau following his sale to the Kimura company of fifteen machines for their factory in Tokyo.[80] When Murai acquired the Kimura company in 1900, Parrish refused to purchase these machines and Kimura brought an action against Wright in an effort to force

[77] Letter E. J. Parrish to W. R. Harris, New York, dated 31 October 1901, Parrish Papers. Note that the reference to the Shanghai Cigarette Co. probably refers to the American Cigarette Co. of Shanghai.

[78] See biography of Wright in S. A. Ashe (ed.), *Biographical History of North Carolina*, Vol. V (1906), p. 497.

[79] Cited by Durden, *Dukes of Durham*, p. 41.

[80] Wright offered to grant ATC exclusive rights for use of the Bonsack machine in Japan early in 1899, proposing to sell up to thirty machines for $1,500 each. However, it is clear that the management in New York turned this offer down. See letter from R. H. Wright to ATC, New York, dated 12 May 1899, papers of R. H. Wright, Special Collections Department, Perkins Library, Duke University, hereinafter Wright Papers, and letter from E. J. Parrish to W. R. Harris, New York, dated 24 December 1901, Parrish Papers.

the cancellation of the Bonsack patent. By this means, Parrish attempted to put pressure on Wright to transfer the Japanese rights for the Bonsack machine to Murai Brothers. As the date for the hearing of Kimura's case became subject to a series of delays and postponements Wright and Parrish engaged in protracted negotiations in respect of the question of machinery. Given the high cost of procuring leaf tobacco in Japan, the low wastage rates achieved by the Bonsack machines made them far more economical than the output produced by the Winston and Phillippe models that were being used by the Murai Brothers' factories. Faced with the possibility that Wright would win the case against him and grant exclusive use of the Bonsack machine for Japan to the Iwaya company or to the Imperial Tobacco Company, who were stepping up activities in China at the time, Parrish eventually settled an agreement with Wright in February 1902 which gave Murai non-exclusive rights to use the full range of Bonsack equipment in Japan but which prevented Wright from making exclusive arrangements with other firms in Japan.[81] For his part, Wright then turned his attention back to the competitive situation which was developing in the cigarette industry in Shanghai.

Although China represented a potentially enormous market for cheap machine-made cigarettes, at the end of the nineteenth century cigarette sales there were mainly confined to the areas designated as treaty ports. Beyond these regions the up-country trade was handled by the Chinese themselves and even as late as 1890 the main commodity import reaching the Chinese interior was Indian opium.[82] ATC had begun to develop a trade in its 'Pin Head' cigarettes in Shanghai around 1890 through Mr Laurits Andersen, a partner of the managing agency Mustard & Co., and had subsequently appointed C. E. Fiske to act as the company's representative there.[83] The trade in cigarettes had developed gradually during the early 1890s but had begun to pick up appreciably during the latter part of the decade. No doubt

[81] Letters from E. J. Parrish to W. R. Harris dated 6 November 1901, 7 November 1901, 24 December 1901, 20 February 1902, and 17 June 1902; letters from R. H. Wright to E. J. Parrish dated 14 December 1901, 16 December 1901, and 21 December 1901, Parrish Papers.

[82] P. J. Cain and A. G. Hopkins, *British Imperialism: Innovation and Expansion, 1688–1914*, Longman, London (1993), p. 426.

[83] A special edition of the monthly magazine of BAT Co. (China) contains a history of the early years of the company's operations in China and specifies that 'Pin Head' cigarettes were first imported into Shanghai by Mustard & Co. around 1890 and that these were the first cigarettes seen on the Shanghai market. *Ying Mei Yien Kung Ssu Yueh Pao* [*British–American Tobacco Co. Monthly Journal*], September 1923, p. 10. This source makes no reference to C. E. Fiske but he was certainly acting as ATC's representative in Shanghai, in collaboration with Mustard & Co. as distributors, by 1900. See letter from E. J. Parrish to C. E. Fiske, Shanghai, dated 6 February 1900, Parrish Papers.

this had been helped by the railway investment boom which had followed the signing of the Treaty of Shimonoseki in 1895 which ended the Sino-Japanese war. The development of a railway system within China under foreign control significantly increased the possibility of exploiting the Chinese interior market. The Treaty of Shimonoseki also granted foreign powers the right to set up their own factories within the treaty ports, which had previously provided them merely with trading facilities.[84] Thus after 1895 a variety of manufacturing enterprises were launched in Shanghai, boosting the local economy there and no doubt stimulating cigarette sales as well.

The first serious attempt to satisfy the demand for machine-made cigarettes in Shanghai by means of local manufacture had been commenced in 1891, soon after the arrival of ATC's imports but before such forms of enterprise had been sanctioned by formal treaty. Perhaps for this reason the first cigarette factory in Shanghai was built outside the limits of the treaty port in Pootung (Pudong). The initiative had been taken by a long-standing Shanghai resident, Mr E. Jenner Hogg, who had registered the name of his business as the American Cigarette Company (ACC).[85]

Around the middle of 1898, Richard Wright held discussions with the directors of ACC in Shanghai and the parties agreed a contract for the supply of ten Bonsack machines for a total of $25,000, arranged through the offices of the American Trading Company.[86] Shortly afterwards the ACC directors lodged another order through the American Trading Company for a further five machines, allowing them to secure the option for a ten-year monopoly over the use of the Bonsack machine in China which had been specified by Wright in the original contract.[87]

Wright himself took up a substantial shareholding in the expanded concern and the Bonsack Machine Co. sent a representative, Mr Collins, to assist with the setting up and operation of the machines. Within a short space of time, however, Wright became extremely disenchanted with the management of ACC in Shanghai. The cigarettes produced on the machines were

[84] Strictly speaking, the concession to allow manufacturing in the treaty ports was granted by the Chinese to Japan in a subsidiary treaty to the Treaty of Shimonoseki signed on 21 July 1896. The privilege granted to Japan was automatically extended to the other powers by virtue of the 'most favoured nation' clause of the treaty conditions. F. L. Hawks Pott, *A Short History of Shanghai* (1928, reprinted), p. 128.

[85] According to a report in BAT Co.'s in-house journal, Mustard & Co. had made an early attempt to manufacture cigarettes in Shanghai even before the factory was set up by Jenner Hogg. *BAT Bulletin*, 17 (1926), 30–1.

[86] Letters from R. H. Wright to the American Trading Company, Shanghai, dated 1 October 1898 and 1 November 1898, Wright Papers.

[87] Letter R. H. Wright to American Trading Company, Shanghai, dated 5 December 1898, Wright Papers.

imperfect due to a lack of local expertise in the handling of cigarette tobacco leaf under the humid conditions of Shanghai. Moreover, the employee who was given responsibility for purchasing the company's leaf requirements, a Mr Emiss, was very inexperienced. Wright chided his fellow shareholders in Shanghai, 'The American Tobacco Co. pay their head leaf man $10,000 gold per year and several others $5,000. They certainly are not clever businessmen to pay such salary if men can do it successfully with Mr Emiss' limited knowledge and experience.'[88]

Eventually, Wright's frustration with the situation in Shanghai led him to reconsider his position with regard to the Bonsack patent for China. In May 1899, shortly after he had agreed to sell ACC the machines for use in China, Wright corresponded with the management of Duke's concern in New York. From his letter it is clear that the idea of gaining control of the Bonsack patent in China by means of direct acquisition of ACC had been under discussion amongst ATC's directors, but Wright counselled them that, 'If you don't want to buy out the [American] Cig[arette] Co. then I have another suggestion to make when I see you.'[89] Quite what this suggestion amounted to was never articulated, and the following month Wright set off for England in order to discuss developments with the Wills company. Scarcely had he returned to America before Duke and his colleagues themselves set off across the Atlantic Ocean for the same destination, and sparked off the 'tobacco war' of September 1901.

[88] Letters from Wright to American Trading Company, Shanghai, dated 5 December 1898 and 2 January 1899, Wright Papers.

[89] Letter Wright to R. D. Patterson, American Tobacco Co., dated May 1899, Wright Papers.

3

Formation of an Anglo-American Alliance

Introduction

Of the group of British companies that banded together in 1901 to form the Imperial Tobacco Co., it was the London-based firm of Lambert & Butler who appear to have displayed the earliest interest in the market for cigarettes. According to the writings of the tobaccophile Sir Compton Mackenzie, entries for cigarettes appear in that firm's stockbooks even before the generally accepted date for the introduction of cigarette manufacturing in Britain by Robert Gloag in 1856.[1] Certainly London was the focal point for the development of cigarette smoking in Britain, paralleling the position that New York would later play in the American history of the product, and although this form of tobacco consumption made little initial impact on the market, it is no surprise to find that when the Bristol-based firm of W. D. & H. O. Wills manufactured its first cigarettes, in 1871, it did so at its factory in London.[2] It was in London, too, that the American John Morgan Richards established his agency in 1876 to promote the products of the US cigarette manufacturer Allen & Ginter, who had started up production in Richmond, Virginia, only the previous year.[3]

The influx on to the British market of these American hand-rolled cigarettes,

[1] C. Mackenzie, *Sublime Tobacco*, Chatto & Windus, London (1957), p. 275. The circumstances surrounding Gloag's claim that he constructed the first cigarette factory in Britain have been called into question, see B. W. E. Alford, *W. D. & H. O. Wills and the Development of the UK Tobacco Industry, 1786–1965* (1973), p. 123.

[2] Alford, *W. D. & H. O. Wills*, p. 123. The brand name chosen for the first cigarette Wills made was 'Bristol'.

[3] Richards' agency dealt in the products of various American cigarette manufacturers including, in later years, W. Duke, Sons & Co. Mackenzie, *Sublime Tobacco*, p. 277.

with their accompanying 'sumptuous' advertising, generated a spurt in demand during the early 1880s which was credited with quadrupling sales of the product within a matter of months.[4] The boom in these American Bright-leaf cigarettes was relatively short-lived, however, and during the military occupation of Egypt by British troops in 1882 many of the officers discovered a taste for a type of cigarette incorporating Turkish Latakia leaf.[5] Enterprising Egyptian and Greek tobacco manufacturers, such as Melachrino and Vafiades, set up cigarette factories in Cairo and exported these hand-rolled Turkish-style cigarettes to the newly converted smokers back in England, making particular progress among the clientele of London's gentlemen's clubs. The popularity of these Egyptian-made products, which was further enhanced by the development of a tourist trade to Egypt during the late nineteenth century, is indicated by a report of the US Consul-General at Cairo in 1894 which stated that eighty-three factories were operating in that city for the purpose of producing cigarettes, giving employment to 1,300 workers.[6]

As the tobacco industry moved towards the final decade of the nineteenth century, therefore, cigarette smoking in Britain was still strongly wedded to expensive imported products such as these and, as a result, was considered by many in the trade to be nothing more than a temporary fashion.[7] Indeed, the relative insignificance of cigarettes to the tobacco-consuming population of Britain is well captured by an article that appeared in the London trade journal *Tobacco* in July 1889, entitled 'The Future of Cigarettes', which concluded, 'To us the smoking of cigarettes savours of the effeminate, and is not suited to the English nation. If this is a correct assumption, it follows that the practice is but a passing fancy, which may hardly last out the present generation.'[8] The statement could hardly have been less prophetic, for at the very moment that these words were committed to print the market for machine-made cigarettes in Britain stood poised on the verge of a period of spectacular growth.

[4] *Tobacco (London)*, 9 (103) (1889), 198.

[5] Mackenzie, *Sublime Tobacco*, p. 281.

[6] The report indicates that Egypt exported 140 million cigarettes during 1883, with the principal customers being England and Germany. *Tobacco (London)*, 14 (164) (1894), 227. The report also explains that most of these firms were owned by Greeks, although Kluger states that the Melachrino firm, which gained a reputation for high-class cigarettes in Britain, Germany, and the United States, was owned by an Egyptian national, Miltiades Melachrino. This firm certainly established a branch in New York around the turn of the century which remained independent of ATC and enjoyed some success when Turkish cigarettes experienced a boom in sales there in the early 1900s. R. Kluger, *Ashes to Ashes: America's Hundred-Year Cigarette War, the Public Health, and the Unabashed Triumph of Philip Morris* (1996), p. 73.

[7] Although by 1883 some of the more established British tobacco manufacturers, such as Players and Wills, were beginning to market hand-rolled cigarettes, it constituted a very small fraction of their total sales (less than 1 per cent in the case of Wills). Alford, *W. D. & H. O. Wills*, p. 460.

[8] *Tobacco (London)*, 9 (103) (1889), 198.

The Growth of Wills' Cigarette Business

Evidence of the potential demand for cigarettes, provided by the boom in sales of imported American cigarettes in the early 1880s, had given British tobacco manufacturers an incentive to explore the possibility of developing a machine-made version of the product. An early example of a British firm actively engaged in mechanized cigarette production can be found in the November 1883 edition of *Tobacco* relating to a company based in south-east London. This firm had begun to utilize a machine built by P. Everitt able to produce up to 7,000 cigarettes an hour, reducing the cost per 1,000 cigarettes by anything between a factor of six and a factor of ten. However, the mechanism was less than entirely automatic and required a team of five girls in order to operate it successfully. Certainly, the members of the Wills firm who visited London to inspect Everitt's machine in operation were less than enthusiastic about its proficiency.[9] Only a few days previously the Wills company had witnessed a demonstration of James Bonsack's machine in operation at their own factory in Bristol, and on comparing the two machines the Wills directors quickly came down in favour of the American's invention. Thus on 9 May 1883, Wills signed an agreement with D. B. Strouse, president of the Bonsack Machine Co., which granted them sole rights to the machine in Britain and other British territories for a period of five years with provision for subsequent years. The price paid by Wills for this privilege was £4,000.[10]

Control of the Bonsack patent gave Wills a head start in the embryonic market for machine-made cigarettes in Britain, and Table 3.1 illustrates the progress made by the firm in this segment during the remaining years of the nineteenth century. Sales of cigarettes for the half-year 1883 were 8,724 lb., rising to 21,276 lb. during the first full year of mechanized production. During the next four years growth in the cigarette side of the business, whilst steady, remained relatively slow, and even by 1888 cigarettes accounted for less than 2 per cent of Wills' tobacco sales by weight. The decade of the 1890s, however, witnessed a radical transformation in the fortunes of this part of Wills' business as, courtesy of a new marketing policy, cigarettes were suddenly thrust into the position of the company's leading product.

The new marketing strategy was based on an idea which Harry Wills, one of the younger generation of directors, had formulated at the onset of the

[9] *Tobacco (London)*, 3 (35) (1883), 144; Alford, *W. D. & H. O. Wills*, p. 147. The report in *Tobacco* simply refers to this company as the Cigarette Manufacturing Co., but Alford's discussion indicates that the firm was called Bettleheim. The Everitt machine had been granted a patent in 1882 and seems to have been the first in the field within Britain.

[10] Alford, *W. D. & H. O. Wills*, pp. 144–50.

TABLE 3.1. Sales of Wills' tobacco products in the UK, 1883–1900

Year	Total tobacco sales (lb.)	Cigarette sales (lb.)	Cigarette sales as % of total	Wills' share of UK cigarette market (%)
1883	3,529,507	8,724	0.3	n.a.
1884	3,818,805	21,276	0.6	n.a.
1885	4,008,959	28,952	0.7	n.a.
1886	4,065,671	41,228	1.0	n.a.
1887	4,080,343	58,898	1.4	n.a.
1888	4,229,699	74,298	1.8	60.9
1889	4,492,023	137,709	3.0	58.4
1890	4,699,789	204,126	4.3	59.2
1891	4,944,974	307,632	6.2	53.9
1892	5,472,291	493,030	9.0	55.0
1893	5,472,907	751,407	13.7	54.2
1894	6,190,106	1,192,632	19.3	54.7
1895	6,676,462	1,709,277	25.6	55.4
1896	7,334,508	2,342,311	31.9	54.5
1897	7,988,349	3,146,702	39.4	54.8
1898	8,666,910	4,139,649	47.8	55.8
1899	9,238,674	4,933,352	53.4	54.4
1900	10,079,569	5,793,757	57.5	54.6

Source: Derived from Alford, *W. D. & H. O. Wills*, Table 29 and Appendix Table 1.

machine-made era but which had not been implemented due to the resistance of the older members of the firm, notably the chairman Sir William H. Wills. Harry Wills had argued that the key to exploiting the potential for high-volume output presented by the Bonsack machine lay in the marketing of a low-priced product. However, the senior directors pointed out that such a policy might easily damage the company's reputation, and thus its sales, in the market for smoking tobacco where the vast majority of its revenues were still generated. Five years therefore elapsed before cigarette sales were sufficiently strong for the firm to feel persuaded to launch a product of the type which would test the validity of Harry Wills' idea. In August 1888, two new machine-made brands were introduced by Wills—'Wills Woodbine' and 'Cinderella'—which were designed to retail at the low price of five for 1d. The immediate success of these products, illustrated clearly in Table 3.2, quickly led the firm to adopt a number of bold marketing strategies in an attempt to capitalize on the penny cigarette's popularity. Increased discounts to retailers were arranged, new packaging was developed with an increase in supporting advertising, and a new promotional device, the insertion of cigarette cards in the packets, was introduced and was rapidly popularized in

TABLE 3.2. Wills' cigarette sales by number and type (million sticks), 1888–1891

Year	Ordinary cigarettes	Penny cigarettes	Total
1888	21.6	4.8	26.4
1889	23.6	27.8	51.4
1890	24.5	48.9	73.4
1891	41.5	84.5	126.0

Note: Penny cigarette sales for 1888 are for final five months only.
Source: Alford, 'Penny Cigarettes', Table 3.1.

Britain through the medium of Wills' low-priced cigarettes. During 1889, the first full year in production, the penny cigarettes outstripped the sales of all Wills' other cigarette brands combined, ushering Britain into the era of the cheap, mass-produced smoke.[11] By 1905, cigarettes accounted for around 25 per cent of all tobacco sales in Britain by weight.[12]

The development of a machine-made cigarette, as well as transforming the tobacco market within Britain, was also instrumental in the growth of an international market for British manufactured tobacco goods during the 1890s. An export trade in manufactured tobacco had first been encouraged by the migration of many British tobacco consumers to the settler colonies of the British Empire, and had been facilitated by the development of improved techniques of packaging utilizing air-tight tins. The arrangements for exporting tobacco goods out of Britain had also been assisted by the passage of the Manufactured Tobacco Act of 1863, which allowed the firms who manufactured products for foreign markets to do so in bonded factories. Production of tobacco goods in bond enabled manufacturers to avoid the time-consuming process of claiming import duty refunds on their tobacco exports under the prevailing drawback arrangements and, more significantly, reduced the level of circulating capital required simply to finance their holdings of these duty-paid tobacco stocks.

In 1883, Wills opened its first bonded tobacco factory in Bristol, and the following year this concern was placed under the supervision of Harry Wills. The company had begun to develop an export trade in its tobacco products during the 1870s and, whilst this had mainly involved the use of traditional specialized import–export agencies, in Australia the company had established its first exclusive dealership with a tobacco manufacturing firm, Heyde, Todman & Co. of Sydney. Shortly before the foundation of the bonded factory, arrangements for exporting the company's products into Europe were stepped up through the

[11] B. W. E. Alford, 'Penny Cigarettes, Oligopoly, and Entrepreneurship in the UK Tobacco Industry in the Late Nineteenth Century', in B. Supple (ed.), *Essays in British Business History* (1977), pp. 49–68.

[12] Calculated from figures provided in Alford, *W. D. & H. O. Wills*, Appendix Table X.

establishment of a continental branch based in Hamburg. In the early 1880s various travelling salesmen were employed by the firm to explore potential markets for Wills' products, and by 1886 a network of agents had been established across western Europe, Scandinavia, Egypt, South Africa, and Australia.[13]

To begin with the company's foreign trade was based almost exclusively on packet tobaccos but the popularity of cigarettes in Britain was soon reflected in the pattern of Wills' foreign tobacco sales. In 1886, the Wills board discovered that one of its customers in South Africa, Holt & Holt of Kimberly, were making up a portion of its imports of 'Three Castles' tobacco into cigarettes, which it was selling under the same brand name. Other South African firms were also imitating Wills' cigarettes, and were doing so using tobacco not even purchased from Wills. In an effort to protect the company's trademark Wills instructed a solicitor in Kimberley to prevent the practice, but the firm which bore the brunt of this intervention was the Holt & Holt company itself, which protested to Wills directors that, unlike other firms in South Africa, it was at least using Wills' own tobacco to manufacture these cigarettes.[14] Unable to effectively protect its trade marks at arm's length in this way, Wills instead began to develop an export trade in cigarettes to South Africa, utilizing a newly developed type of air-tight tin, and appointed Holt & Holt as its sole agents for South Africa in 1887, having developing two new brands specifically for export: 'Diamond Queen' and 'Pirate'.[15] The granting of a sole agency gave Holt & Holt an incentive to obtain legal protection for any infringement of the Wills trade mark and enabled the two firms to develop close links. By 1894, as the trade in cigarettes grew, the Bristol firm had been persuaded to grant a subsidiary of Holt & Holt, the Acme Cigarette Co., the right to manufacture Wills cigarettes directly in South Africa on a royalty basis using Bonsack machines.[16] During the 1890s cigarettes became

[13] Alford, *W. D. & H. O. Wills*, pp. 131–3, 163–5.

[14] See letters from Holt & Holt, Kimberley, to W. D. & H. O. Wills dated 31 May 1886 and 12 July 1886, and letter from Wills to Holt & Holt dated 20 August 1886. See also letter from Edward P. Wills to George A. Wills dated 24 August 1886. W. D. & H. O. Wills Archive, Bristol Public Record Office (hereinafter Wills Archive), File No. 38169/HAF/19(F).

[15] According to Alford, the agency granted to Holt & Holt in South Africa was defined in global terms as constituting, 'any point 20° south lat. except such territory above the Limpopo River, being Portuguese, and the Islands of Madagascar and Mauritius'. Alford, *W. D. & H. O. Wills*, p. 165. The Nottingham firm of John Player & Son also entered into a sole agency agreement for distributing its products in South Africa with the Cape Town-based merchant house of Ernest Ebert & Co. in 1888. This arrangement was set up and supervised by the London-based tobacco merchant Adolph Frankau & Co. Letter from A. Frankau & Co. to John Player & Co., dated 6 February 1888, enclosing agreement of same date, John Player & Sons Archive, Nottingham Record Office, (hereinafter Player Archive), File No. DD PL 4/11/1–2.

[16] The issue as to the ownership of the rights to the Bonsack patent in different parts of South Africa, as between Wills and the Bonsack company itself (and its agreement with Richard Wright) was a vexed one. After some dispute, in 1897 Bonsack's president, D. B. Strouse, agreed to allocate exclusive rights to Wills for the use of the machine in the Transvaal for a period up to the end of 1903. Alford, *W. D. & H. O. Wills*, pp. 229–30.

an increasingly important segment of Wills export sales, allowing the firm to consolidate its position as Britain's leading exporter of manufactured tobacco products (see Table 3.3).[17]

Branded Cigarettes and the Tobacco Industry in Britain

In the closing years of the nineteenth century, therefore, Wills' dominance of the cigarette market secured its position as Britain's largest tobacco manufacturer. As long as the Bonsack machine remained the pre-eminent technology, and continued to stay under Wills' exclusive control within Britain, this

TABLE 3.3. UK versus Wills' exports of manufactured tobacco goods ('000 lb.), 1883–1900

Year	UK exports of manufactured tobacco	Wills' exports of manufactured tobacco	Wills' cigarette exports as a % of Wills' tobacco exports	Wills' share of UK tobacco exports (%)
1883	443.0	44.6	neg.	10.1
1884	537.0	127.5	neg.	23.7
1885	570.0	156.3	1.4	27.4
1886	623.0	219.8	2.1	35.3
1887	689.0	259.4	1.1	37.6
1888	868.0	292.6	2.4	33.7
1889	964.0	297.6	1.4	30.9
1890	1169.0	377.4	5.7	32.3
1891	1287.0	457.4	7.0	35.5
1892	1498.0	538.5	10.8	35.9
1893	1684.0	617.2	14.2	36.7
1894	1727.0	793.0	19.2	45.9
1895	2544.0	1080.3	23.9	42.5
1896	2960.0	1479.5	31.9	50.0
1897	3644.0	1735.7	37.6	47.6
1898	4272.0	1987.0	42.6	46.5
1899	4752.0	2077.6	40.8	43.7
1900	5525.0	2613.5	45.6	47.3

Source: Derived from Alford, *W. D. & H. O. Wills*, Tables 26, 27, 29, and Appendix Table IV.

[17] Wills' first main domestic challenger in the export market for cigarettes seems to have been the London-based firm of Lambert & Butler, which set up its own bonded factory in 1891. *Tobacco (London)*, 11 (135) (1891), 360.

position of leadership was virtually assured. However, other firms were keen to emulate Wills' success, and as alternative machines to the Bonsack became available, so rival manufacturers began to produce cigarettes to compete directly with their phenomenally popular 'Woodbine', 'Cinderella', and 'Gold Flake' brands. During the 1890s Wills' technological lead began to recede, and after 1895 a number of Britain's largest tobacco firms began to make heavy investments in cigarette-making machinery to enable them to obtain a share of this rapidly growing market.[18] A variety of rival cigarette manufacturing machines to the Bonsack were marketed during the 1890s, originating mainly from the United States. The American Luddington Machine Co. developed a cigarette machine which could manufacture different sizes of cigarettes, allowing much more economical production of a range of brands, and this had been adopted by the Belfast-based firm of Gallaher & Co. at their London branch by 1895.[19] Another American machine, the Briggs, was imported from North Carolina by the firm of J. S. Molins and sold to various manufacturers.[20] Also at this time, a machine called the Munson was put on the market, claiming a manufacturing capacity of 18,000 cigarettes an hour, and was taken up by the Salmon & Gluckstein chain of retail tobacconists to manufacture their own cheap brands.[21]

The most frequently used rival machine to the Bonsack, however, was that developed in America by Bernhard Baron and registered in Britain as the Elliot. Following the formation of the American Tobacco Co. in the United States, Baron had used the ability of his machine to compete with the Bonsack to set up the National Cigarette and Tobacco Co., and during the 1890s Baron's firm constituted ATC's only major rival in the cigarette business in America. The machine was marketed in Britain, and was adopted by the important Nottingham-based tobacco firm of John Player & Sons to manufacture its cigarettes in 1893.[22] In an effort to capitalize on the success of his machine with Players, Baron incorporated a company in England during 1896,[23] the Baron Cigarette Machine Co., and by the end of 1899 Players were operating eighteen of their machines and the Glasgow firm of Stephen Mitchell & Son were operating sixteen. As these alternative machines became available, a relatively small group of firms emerged behind Wills as the leaders in the industry, and the vast fringe of smaller firms was increasingly

[18] *Tobacco (London)*, 16 (181) (1896), 2.

[19] *Tobacco (London)*, 15 (176) (1895), 281. This report notes that the running costs of the machine involved the attention of an engineer 'almost daily' and a girl for feeding tobacco.

[20] R. Hill, *The Making of Molins* (1978), p. 3.

[21] *Tobacco (London)*, 15 (171) (1895), 89.

[22] On Player's negotiations for the patent rights to use the Elliot cigarette-making machine between 1890 and 1892 see Player Archive, File Nos. DD PL 4/2/1–182.

[23] *Tobacco (London)*, 16 (189) (1896), 366.

squeezed. By 1900, the tobacco industry in Britain was moving rapidly towards the oligopolistic structure which was to become the characteristic feature of manufacturing industry more generally during the twentieth century.[24]

As the dominant firm in the cigarette industry, Wills was content to maintain its position as market leader without attempting to strengthen its hold towards that of a monopoly. Thus, in contrast to Duke's American Tobacco Co., the Wills firm was much less inclined to engage in a policy of corporate growth based upon horizontal and vertical integration by means of merger and acquisition. Horizontal integration was viewed mainly as a defensive measure, to be entered into with the agreement of other firms in order to combat an external threat.[25] Thus, as noted in Chapter 2, the possibility of amalgamation with other manufacturers was first raised in the context of a possible need to secure supplies of raw leaf. However, as it became clear that ATC was not in a position to control the market for leaf tobacco, the plan was shelved. Even when it was faced with a particularly aggressive rival cigarette manufacturer in the Liverpool-based Ogden company, Wills was reluctant to pursue a policy of acquisition until it became clear that the Liverpool firm was on the point of selling out to the Americans. Eventually, when a meeting did take place between the directors of Wills and Ogden's with a view to merging their interests against the American threat, differences in personality and strategy quickly led Wills to decide against an alliance.[26]

Interestingly, the strategic issue which divided the two companies concerned the possibility of forward vertical integration into the retailing of tobacco. The advent of heavily advertised brands of cigarettes and smoking tobaccos in Britain had the effect of concentrating demand within the industry into a much narrower range of products. The high volume of turnover generated by these products supported the development of a small group of multiple retailers, along the lines of the American chain stores, which operated in both the wholesale and retail sectors of the market simultaneously. By taking advantage of bulk discounts, retailing chains specializing in tobacco goods became much more prevalent during the 1890s. Thus the concentration in manufacturing output within the industry at this time was mirrored at

[24] Alford points out that by the late 1890s tobacco manufacture had effectively segmented into two industries; one concerned competition between small manufacturers supplying loose tobaccos and the less popular brands of packet tobaccos whilst the other concerned competition between a relatively small group of firms who produced the most popular brands of packet tobaccos and, increasingly, cigarettes. The creation of Imperial in 1901 enormously strengthened this shift towards oligopoly. Alford, *W. D. & H. O. Wills*, pp. 224–5.

[25] Wills did, in fact, acquire the firm of Sales, Pollard & Co., a general tobacco manufacturer which had fallen into decline, for £18,000 in 1893, and a small cigar manufacturer for £1,000 the following year. However, these were minor exceptions to the normal policy of purely organic growth. Alford, *W. D. & H. O. Wills*, p. 210.

[26] Alford, *W. D. & H. O. Wills*, pp. 254–5.

the distribution stage in the growth of firms such as Salmon & Gluckstein, Arthur Baker, and Singleton & Cole, all of whom quickly gained notoriety within the tobacco retail trade for cutting prices on the leading brands of cigarettes and tobacco goods.

The attitude of the leading tobacco manufacturers towards these bulk retailers was ambivalent. On the one hand, they were an important factor in creating the massive growth in the sales of branded cigarettes that took place during these years, and which therefore served to consolidate the position in the industry of the leading manufacturers. On the other hand, as a manifestation of countervailing power, they limited the manufacturers' room for manoeuvre in regard to the distribution process as a whole, weakening their direct links with the trade and undermining the traditional role played by the firms' travelling salesmen in supporting the retailers who operated outside of the urban areas. Indeed, this loss of influence over the distribution of products threatened serious repercussions if the leading retailers chose to play the large manufacturers off against one another, or when they began to retail their own manufactured products, as Salmon & Gluckstein did after 1895.

Not surprisingly, therefore, the large manufacturers made some efforts to co-ordinate their response to these cut-price retailers. Wills held discussions with Lambert & Butler, Taddy & Co., Cope Bros., Hignett Bros., and John Player & Sons, rapidly becoming known as the 'big six', whilst four other companies, Wm. Clarke & Son, Ogden's, J. & F. Bell, and Gallaher, banded together to form the National Association of Tobacco Manufacturers. Some attempts were made to impose standard retail prices, through the threat of non-supply, but these met with very limited success, particularly within the huge markets of London and Birmingham. Increasingly, the popularity of cut-price cigarettes allowed non-specialist retailers to use them as a means of attracting extra customers, and attempts to maintain retail prices became futile. Ultimately, the introduction of branded tobacco products, especially the machine-made cigarette, seriously undermined the specialist tobacco goods retailer.[27]

In their meeting with Wills, Ogden's management had argued that, as part of an amalgamation, the manufacturers should buy out certain discount retail chains and create a system of tied retailers, matching a practice that was commonplace in the brewing industry. This policy of forward vertical integration would, they argued, give the manufacturers the whip-hand, enabling them to exert much greater control over the prices at which cigarettes were sold. However, this argument did not find favour with the management of Wills,

[27] For a discussion of the attempts made by the specialist tobacco retailers to resist this trend, see M. Hilton, 'Retailing History as Economic and Cultural History: Strategies of Survival by Specialist Tobacconists in the Mass Market', *Business History*, 40 (1998), 115–37.

who pulled out of further negotiations.[28] Wills displayed the same reluctance towards backward vertical integration in the case of a scheme floated by the American Luddington and Baron machinery interests which would have given Wills a share in a pooling operation called the United Cigarette Machine Co. Ltd. In this case, however, Wills' involvement may have also compromised its continued exclusive control of the Bonsack machine.[29]

The process of industrial concentration in Britain's tobacco industry therefore arose principally as a result of the larger manufacturers' success in persuading consumers to adopt the new, heavily advertised, branded goods in preference to the traditional products of small manufacturers, and in particular due to the willingness of smokers to purchase machine-made cigarettes.[30] This process was greatly assisted by changes in the distribution and retailing of tobacco goods. Indeed, the activities of these discounting wholesale/retailers, as they sought to capitalize on the market demand of low-income urban consumers, may have acted as a greater catalyst for change in the industry than the policies adopted by the manufacturers themselves.[31]

Management Strategy of the American Tobacco Company

Many of the changes which were brought about by the growth in popularity of cigarettes in Britain occurred somewhat earlier in America. Unlike in Britain, where Wills held exclusive control over Bonsack's machine and was thus able to delay the introduction of low-priced cigarettes for five years without losing its first-mover advantage, in America James Duke needed to exploit quickly the cost advantage that the agreement with the Bonsack company had granted his firm. In the years that preceded the formation of ATC in 1890, therefore, Duke had pressed home his advantage by cutting the prices of his cigarettes to dealers and by using every form of sales promotion imaginable in order to raise his firm's sales volume at the expense of his main rivals.[32] Once in place, the five-firm partnership that created ATC acted to

[28] Alford, *W. D. & H. O. Wills*, p. 255.

[29] On its formation in 1899, the United Cigarette Machine Co. became the sole agents in Britain for the Briggs and Elliot machines, as well as two other rival American cigarette makers, the Venner and the Peerless. Alford, *W. D. & H. O. Wills*, p. 231.

[30] These products also widened the market for manufactured tobacco goods, encouraging boys as young as seven and eight to take up smoking, much to the distaste of the trade press which urged controls on such practices. *Tobacco (London)*, 14 (164) (1894), 279.

[31] Wilson, for example, points out that the development of branded goods in Britain was supported by a revolution in retailing methods. J. Wilson, *British Business History, 1720–1994* (1995), pp. 96–7.

[32] R. Sobel, *They Satisfy: The Cigarette in American Life* (1978), pp. 43–5; Kluger, *Ashes to Ashes*, pp. 25–6.

rationalize the productive capacity of the group. Less profitable brands were abandoned and small, less efficient, factories closed down.[33]

The new corporation brought to the tobacco industry an unprecedented degree of vertical integration, extending backwards into leaf procurement and handling, and forward into bulk distribution through regional warehouses. Of perhaps even greater importance at this stage was the increasing control of the organization exercised by the head office in New York. From here the overall strategy of the group was planned and all advertising and sales campaigns were co-ordinated. Under the guidance of W. R. Harris, elaborate systems of management and cost accounting were introduced to control the movement of stock and monitor the group's overall financial position. In creating this organizational framework, Duke's American Tobacco Co. became one of the earliest and best examples of a modern, hierarchically managed American business organization.[34]

Organizing the flow of materials through the manufacturing and distribution process involved a much greater investment in management personnel than had been the case in earlier forms of business enterprise. Forward and backward integration was achieved by means of internalizing key market functions concerning the throughput of resources. Thus the company did not become involved in growing leaf, but in processing, storing, and handling the huge quantities required in the production process. Fears that ATC would corner the market in Bright leaf were unfounded because such an action was not needed in order to achieve the principal objective of securing supplies to the company's factories.

Similarly, in terms of distribution, Duke's firm invested in a nation-wide system of warehouses, supervised from the New York headquarters, which could manage the high volume of output generated by ATC's factories. As Table 3.4 demonstrates, the output of cigarettes and small cigars rose rapidly in America during the first half of the 1890s as ATC stepped up its activities. The key to supporting growth in output was the organization of a network of depots spanning the entire United States market, managed by a small staff under the guidance and supervision of the New York headquarters. The method of organizing these depots is illustrated by a letter from Duke to the staff of the San Francisco depot. Each of the three members of staff, Messrs Bruton, Godsey, and Mason, were allocated specific responsibilities by Duke, in order to avoid misdirected effort. Bruton, the senior staff member, was to

[33] P. G. Porter, 'Origins of the American Tobacco Company', *Business History Review*, 43 (1969), 74.

[34] A. D. Chandler, *The Visible Hand: The Managerial Revolution in American Business* (1977), pp. 382–98; C. J. Schmitz, *The Growth of Big Business in the United States and Western Europe, 1850–1939* (1993), pp. 38–9.

TABLE 3.4. Cigarette and small cigar output in the USA (ATC v. Independents) (million sticks), 1891–1901

Year	Total output of the United States	Output of ATC	Output of independent tobacco companies	Market share	
				ATC	Independents
1891	3,137.3	2,788.8	348.5	88.9	11.1
1892	3,282.0	2,883.5	398.5	87.9	12.1
1893	3,660.8	3,122.2	538.6	85.3	14.7
1894	3,620.7	3,131.7	489.0	86.5	13.5
1895	4,237.8	3,699.8	538.0	87.3	12.7
1896	4,967.4	4,142.4	825.1	83.4	16.6
1897	4,927.3	3,939.7	987.6	80.0	20.0
1898	4,842.6	4,094.5	748.1	84.6	15.4
1899	4,367.3	3,887.9	479.4	89.0	11.0
1900	4,255.8	3,750.2	505.6	88.1	11.9
1901	4,505.8	3,923.0	582.8	87.1	12.9

Source: US Bureau of Corporations, *Report on the Tobacco Industry* (Part 1), Table 36.

manage the consignment agreements with jobbers 'pending specific instructions from [the New York] Office' and to visit the jobbing trade as frequently as possible in order to keep them informed of all new schemes pertaining to brands, writing to 'the New York Office frequently with reference to all matters of interest'. Mason's role was to take responsibility for the introduction of new brands, for advertising generally, and for relations with the retail trade, thereby acting as a monitor for the New York headquarters of the state of trade and of the activities of competitor firms. Finally, Godsey was to act as depot manager and was responsible for the 'correct accounting for [goods shipped] to the Auditor'. He was advised to consult regularly with Messrs. Bruton and Mason 'with reference to probable requirements in the way of stock of new brands so as to anticipate as far as possible, the demand that may be created by special work, advertising, etc'.[35]

Despite the importance of distribution, however, the company did not attempt to subsume the downstream element of the distribution of tobacco products. Duke's attitude towards distribution can be discerned from the following comments, made in reply to Mr E. T. Bedford of the Corn Products Refining Co. of New York:

[35] Letter J. B. Duke to Messrs Bruton, Godsey, and Mason, San Francisco Territory, dated 18 March 1897, Business Papers of J. B. Duke, Special Collections Dept, Perkins Library, Duke University, hereinafter J. B. Duke Papers.

> I know that we have problems of distribution somewhat similar in their nature, distributing, as we do, packaged goods of advertised brands. Frankly, though, there is no condition in our distribution that would induce us at present to consider any attempt to do our own distribution. It is, of course, true that we have to create a consumers' demand for our product by advertising, sampling and by giving quality and uniformity to our product. We do not find, though, that there is any difficulty, when we secure this consumers' demand, in having a distribution of our products through jobbers into the hands of retailers for satisfying this consumers' demand.[36]

Duke's relations with jobbers after 1890 was based on a system of indirect control, offering distributors a rebate in return for their agreement to maintain prices and deal exclusively with the products of ATC.[37] Although this system was temporarily withdrawn in 1892, in the face of a barrage of legal actions, a similar form of consignment was re-introduced under which ATC retained title to the goods until they were sold to retailers, and a commission was then paid to the jobbers. Under this system, contracts were issued to jobbers which obliged them to act in the company's interest and ATC was able to vary commissions in cases where it deemed the actions of jobbers contravened this clause. These contracts also allowed jobbers freedom to decide whether or not to deal exclusively in ATC products , but non-exclusivity carried a severe penalty in terms of the commission paid.[38] In 1897, this form of relationship with the jobbers came under legislative attack for being unduly restrictive and was changed.[39] Under the revised system, goods were sold outright to the jobbers and they were allowed to sell them on at a price of their own choosing, although if they maintained the recommended price ATC would pay them a premium. The competitive pressure to discount the price of the goods to retailers, however, meant that many jobbers were worse off under this system than under the earlier arrangements, since the margins were slim.[40] Thus, in distribution, Duke's company created a system of depots that spanned the

[36] Letter J. B. Duke to E. T. Bedford dated 25 April 1911, J. B. Duke Papers.

[37] G. Porter and H. C. Livesay, *Merchants and Manufacturers: Studies in the Changing Structure of Nineteenth Century Marketing* (1971), p. 209.

[38] Duke wrote to C. N. Churchill, president of the Wholesale Grocers Association of Memphis, Tennessee, '. . . if you choose to become agent for our cigarettes exclusively we will pay you a commission of 11 per cent upon sales made by you. Clause 7 provides that if you do not desire to become such an exclusive agent, but desire to act for us in common with any, or all other manufacturers of cigarettes we will pay you a commission of 2½ per cent of the amount of your sales of our cigarettes.' Letter J. B. Duke to C. N. Churchill, dated 13 March 1896, J. B. Duke Papers. The 11 per cent offered here for exclusivity may have been exceptional, since the normal differential in commission seems to have been 7½ per cent. See *Tobacco (London)*, 15 (180) (1895), 439.

[39] US Bureau of Corporations, *Report of the Commissioner of Corporations on the Tobacco Industry* (Part 1) (1909), p. 309.

[40] See letter from J. B. Duke to the jobbing firm Karnes, Hagerman, & Kranthoff of Kansas City, Montana, dated 19 May 1899, J. B. Duke Papers.

United States, and attempted to use its strength as the predominant source of supply to cajole jobbers into acting in the firm's best interests. Only in the huge market of New York did the company eventually develop a subsidiary company of jobbers, the Metropolitan Tobacco Co., to take direct control of the firm's distribution arrangements.[41]

Horizontal Integration and the 'Plug War' in America

Effective resistance to the expansion of ATC's cigarette business during the early 1890s was very limited. A spate of fires, which destroyed two ATC factories in New York and another in Richmond, Virginia, within the space of a few months late in 1892 and early in 1893, raises the possibility that some forms of direct opposition may have surfaced at this time, and spare Bonsack machines were kept available as a precaution for such eventualities.[42] In terms of legitimate competition, only the National Cigarette & Tobacco Co. of New York, using the cigarette machines engineered by one of its founders and managing director, Bernhard Baron, represented a serious threat.[43] One other important rival cigarette manufacturer based in New Orleans, Hernsheim Bros. & Co., was bought out by ATC in 1892.[44] Baron's firm launched the 'Admiral' brand after it set up in opposition to Duke in 1893 but its impact on ATC's national brands was very limited. Duke was later reported to have said that it cost ATC $1,500,000 to fight the 'Admiral' cigarette, but that 'Sweet Caporal' got such advertising through the fight that the money all came back, and more, too.[45] During 1895, the Consolidated Cigarette Co. of New York, H. Ellis & Co. of Baltimore, and Thomas H. Hall of New York, all manufacturers of cigarettes and small cigars, sold out to Duke's expanding concern as he stepped up a programme of acquisitions across the American tobacco industry.[46]

Unlike in Britain, where the surging sales of cigarettes in the 1890s automatically lifted the Wills company into the position of industry leader, control of the cigarette segment of the industry in America would not, by itself,

41 The Metropolitan Tobacco Co. was incorporated in New York on 21 January 1899, being a combination of the leading New York and Brooklyn jobbing houses under the leadership of Bendheim Brothers, and later absorbed a large number of smaller concerns. US Bureau of Corporations, *Report on the Tobacco Industry* (Part 1), pp. 309–11.

42 The fires involved the factories that had belonged to Duke & Son and Kinney in New York, and to Allen & Ginter in Richmond. *Tobacco (London)*, 13 (151) (1883), 35; 13 (154) (1883), p. 163.

43 *Tobacco (London)*, 13 (151) (1893), 35.

44 US Bureau of Corporations, *Report on the Tobacco Industry* (Part 1), p. 69.

45 *Tobacco (London)*, 19 (221) (1899), 202.

46 US Bureau of Corporations, *Report on the Tobacco Industry* (Part 1), pp. 180–1.

have given ATC leadership in tobacco manufacturing in the United States. Rather, James Duke's assumption of that role was dependent upon a process of horizontal integration across the different branches of tobacco manufacturing, requiring a succession of hostile acquisitions. The key event which marked the accession of ATC to the position of unchallenged leadership among the tobacco manufacturers of the United States came as a result of the so-called 'plug war' of 1895–9, when the company set out to wrest control of the market for plug (chewing) tobacco.

A programme of acquisitions had been initiated almost as soon as ATC had been formed. In 1891, the company increased its authorized capital by $10 million, to $35 million, and used these additional funds, along with its cash reserves, to initiate a programme of acquisitions. During that year ATC purchased two manufacturers of smoking tobacco and snuff in Baltimore, G. W. Gail & Ax, and Marburg Bros., for $242,218 in cash and $2.9 million in ATC stock, quickly rationalizing their production capacity.[47] It also acquired a major manufacturer of cheroots, P. Whitlock of Richmond, for $300,000 cash, and its first plug tobacco firm, the National Tobacco Works of Louisville, Kentucky, for $600,000 cash and $1.2 million in stock. This latter acquisition brought with it a plug brand by the name of 'Battle Ax', a weapon which would later be put to good use.

These purchases gave ATC a presence in each of the main tobacco markets, other than large cigars, but which, as Table 3.5 indicates, still left it as a minor player in all but cigarettes. As these new concerns were being integrated into the ATC organization, the programme of acquisitions subsided for a while. Between 1894 and 1895, Duke turned his attention more towards foreign markets, making the investments in Canada and Australia outlined in Chapter 2. These acquisitions provided a new element in the strategy employed by Duke because they functioned in a relatively independent way, as ATC's operating subsidiaries abroad, rather than simply falling under the direct managerial control of New York in the way that the export business had done.[48] Duke appreciated that the limits of organizational scope would be reached as the company expanded, and that further growth would involve managing a group of interrelated businesses, rather than a single integrated concern. It was in such a way that the absorption of most of the plug tobacco producers of the United States was handled, via the creation of a sister company to ATC, the Continental Tobacco Co.

The fight to gain the lion's share of America's plug tobacco capacity ran through two distinct phases. The first phase began in late 1894 when the

47 Kluger, *Ashes to Ashes*, pp. 32–3.

48 US Bureau of Corporations, *Report on the Tobacco Industry* (Part 1), p. 165.

TABLE 3.5. US ouput of tobacco goods excluding large cigars (ATC v. Independents), 1891

Product	Total US output	Output		Market share	
		ATC	Independents	ATC	Independents
Cigarettes and little cigars (million sticks)	3,137.3	2,788.8	348.5	88.9	11.1
Manufactured tobacco and snuff (million pounds)	270.5	19.2	251.3	7.1	92.9
Plug tobacco (million pounds)	166.2	4.4	161.7	2.7	97.3
Smoking tobacco (million pounds)	76.7	13.8	62.9	18.0	82.0

Source: US Bureau of Corporations, *Report on the Tobacco Industry* (Part 1), pp. 29–34.

company began to cut the price of its 'Battle Ax' brand as part of a price war.[49] Using the profits from its cigarette business to cross-subsidize its plug sales, ATC at one point was selling 'Battle Ax' to jobbers at 13 cents per lb. which, allowing for revenue tax, was certainly below the unit cost of production.[50] To cope with the additional orders, ATC managed to purchase one independent plug producer in 1895, the J. G. Butler Co. of St Louis, and erected another plant of its own. The large plug producers responded to Duke's invasion of their market by producing their own cigarette brands, practically doubling the output of independent cigarette producers between 1894 and 1896 (cf. Table 3.4). Notwithstanding this upsurge of competition, ATC was able to absorb large losses on its plug sales between 1895 and 1898 (see Table 3.6).

By 1897, ATC had captured one-fifth of the total output of chewing tobacco in America, and during the following year Duke's firm became the country's leading producer of plug tobacco when two of the major plug producers in St Louis, the Brown Brothers Tobacco Co. and the Drummond Tobacco Co., sold out to ATC for a total consideration of $4.66 million. Finally, on 10 December 1898, having launched a further assault on his rivals by discounting the leading 'Horseshoe' brand that had been acquired

[49] M. R. Burns, 'Outside Intervention in Monopolistic Price Warfare: The Case of the "Plug War" and the Union Tobacco Company', *Business History Review*, 56 (1982), 33–53. Note that the author suggests that ATC may not have initiated this price war, see pp. 39–40.

[50] For evidence that ATC did follow a policy of pricing below average total cost, see M. R. Burns, 'New Evidence on Predatory Price Cutting', *Managerial and Decision Economics*, 10 (1989), 327–30.

TABLE 3.6. ATC losses on plug and profits on cigarettes, 1894–8

Year	Plug sales ('000 lb.)	Plug losses ($'000)	Cigarette profits ($'000)
1894	9,000	−110	3,529
1895	20,000	913	3,530
1896	31,000	1,378	3,290
1897	38,000	890	2,886
1898	33,000	942	2,690

Note: Negative figure for plug losses in 1894 indicates profit.
Source: R. B. Tennant, *American Cigarette Industry*, Table 4. Yale University Press. © Yale University Press.

from the Drummond concern, Duke completed the first phase of the plug war by setting up the Continental Tobacco Co. Into this enormous holding company he transferred the plug businesses of ATC, Drummond, and Brown Bros., together with six more of the remaining plug firms who had finally capitulated to the remorseless competitive pressure and thrown in their lot with Duke.[51] On its incorporation, the Continental Tobacco Co. issued a total of $62,290,700 in stock, with ATC as the main minority shareholder.[52]

The formation of the Continental Tobacco Co. gave the Duke interests 46 per cent of the market in chewing tobacco and brought to a conclusion the first phase of the plug war.[53] The second phase of the war centred around the last independent producer of plug tobacco of any significance in America, the Liggett & Myers Tobacco Co. of St Louis, which still held a market share roughly equal to one-third that of Continental's, and fiercely resisted Duke's attempt to steam-roll all opposition.[54] As Duke set about completing his conquest of the plug tobacco market through the acquisition of Liggett & Myers, however, certain financial interests in the United States began to appreciate the potential for huge profits which stood to be gained from monopoly control of the tobacco industry. In concluding his take-over of America's chewing tobacco market, therefore, Duke found himself in a battle of strategy, not with tobacco people, but with pure financial capitalists.

[51] The six companies in question were P. Lorillard (which sold out only 60 per cent of its capital), P. J. Sorg, Daniel Scotten, John Finzer, J. Wright, and P. H. Mayo. At the time, these six firms between them accounted for just under 17 per cent of America's national output of both plug and smoking tobacco. Burns, 'Outside Intervention', Table 1.

[52] US Bureau of Corporations, *Report on the Tobacco Industry* (Part 1), pp. 2–3.

[53] Burns, 'Outside Intervention', p. 43.

[54] It was Liggett & Myers who had taken the lead in launching a counter-attack on the cigarette market following Duke's first plug offensive. *Tobacco (London)*, 15 (178) (1895), 357.

Involvement with financial interests outside the tobacco industry had already begun when several of ATC's founding directors, including Lewis Ginter, had become concerned over Duke's monopolization strategy. In an effort to oust Duke from control these directors had sought the support of Colonel Oliver H. Payne, a financier who had become a millionaire through his involvement with Standard Oil and who now constituted one of the shrewdest operators on Wall Street. When Payne and Duke confronted one another, however, there was an immediate meeting of minds and Payne, far from forcing Duke out, teamed up with him. It proved to be a decisive moment. By the spring of 1897 Ginter, Kinney, Kimball, and Emery, the owners of the four other founding companies of ATC, had all resigned their directorships with the company and during 1898 Duke, with the financial support of Payne, was able to complete his campaign against the plug producers and set up the gigantic Continental holding company.

Payne's collaboration with Duke brought to an end any internal opposition to his strategy, but left numerous other rivals seeking an opportunity to make good at his expense. In October 1898, as Duke embarked on the final stages of his campaign against the plug manufacturers, ATC's main rival in the cigarette business, Bernhard Baron, agreed to sell his company to a group of financiers led by the sophisticated businessman Thomas Fortune Ryan. A few months earlier, Ryan and his collaborators had set up a holding company which they called the Union Tobacco Co., and following its purchase of Baron's National Cigarette & Tobacco Co. they incorporated this company at a nominal value of $10 million. In the five months that followed, Union used opposition within the tobacco industry to Duke's monopolizing tactics to consolidate its position.[55]

In December the group purchased Duke's old Durham adversary, W. T. Blackwell's Bull Durham Tobacco Co. for $4 million, gaining an important stake in the smoking tobacco market. With Baron's and Blackwell's concerns in hand, the Union directors now approached the management of Liggett & Myers and succeeded in persuading the directors of the St Louis company to sell them an option to purchase Liggett & Myers at a price of $11 million. With Liggett & Myers on board the Union Tobacco Co. would control a good segment of the plug market, thus enabling it to compete with Duke across the three main markets in which he operated. However, Ryan's agenda was not to compete with Duke, but rather to make money out of him,

[55] Ryan and a number of his collaborators in the Union initiative, such as P. A. B. Widener, Anthony N. Brady, and William C. Whitney, had made fortunes by replacing horse-drawn street railways with new electric-powered trolleys and subways. A. D. Chandler, *Scale and Scope: The Dynamics of Industrial Capitalism* (1990), p.80.

and thus immediately the Liggett & Myers option was in place negotiations between the directors of Union and ATC began.[56]

These negotiations were soon brought to a conclusion. In April 1899 Duke agreed to exchange $12.5 million of ATC's total capital stock of $35 million in return for the assets of the Union Tobacco Co., including the option to buy Liggett & Myers. Shortly afterwards, a syndicate embracing Duke, Payne, Ryan, and other Union directors arranged the purchase of Liggett & Myers, together with a sum of $5 million in cash, in exchange for $35 million in the stock of the Continental Tobacco Co.[57] A large segment of the American tobacco industry was now under the control of Duke's trust, but with the exception of Duke himself it was no longer principally under the direction of men whose background lay in tobacco.[58]

The financial sophistication of these new directors was perfectly illustrated by their formation in 1901 of the Consolidated Tobacco Co. as a holding company for both ATC and Continental, which was launched with an initial capital of $30 million. The expansion of Duke's tobacco concerns during the 1890s had been funded predominantly through the issue of stock and had therefore led to a situation in which the shares of the ATC and Continental companies were distributed over a large number of shareholders. In the two years following the formation of the Continental company, however, no dividends had ever been paid against the ordinary shares, and even the shares of ATC had paid at only 6 per cent. The principal directors of the ATC and Continental companies were aware, however, that the monopolistic position of the group, together with the likelihood of lower duties on tobacco following the end of the Spanish–American war, made very high future earnings highly probable.

On the formation of the Consolidated company, therefore, the directors issued 4 per cent company bonds which were offered in exchange for the ordinary shares of both the Continental Tobacco Co., at equal par value, and ATC at the rate of 2:1 (i.e., a return of 8 per cent).[59] Based on the recent record of earnings on these shares, the offer did not appear ungenerous and it carried with it the bonus of security of return; it was therefore generally accepted. Based on future profit levels, however, the return offered was miserly. The effect of this shrewd financial manoeuvre was twofold. First, the

[56] Burns, 'Outside Intervention'; Kluger, *Ashes to Ashes*, p. 34.

[57] US Bureau of Corporations, *Report on the Tobacco Industry* (Part 1), p. 4.

[58] Ten years after the 'Plug War' had ended, when giving evidence to the US Circuit Court in 1908, Duke accepted that he had paid a high price for the Union Tobacco Co., but argued that it had been necessary in order to get 'ourselves [in with] a lot of rich financial people to help finance our properties'. Testimony of J. B. Duke, in *United States v. American Tobacco Company*, US Circuit Court, 1907–11, pp. 3276–514, extracted in J. B. Duke Papers, p. 3357. See also R. D. Durden, *The Dukes of Durham, 1865–1929* (1975), pp. 67–70.

[59] R. B. Tennant, *The American Cigarette Industry* (1950), p. 28.

issue of bonds brought about a substantial increase in the capital resources of the group allowing further expansion of the company, most especially into new markets overseas. Secondly, it acted to concentrate the future surplus profits of the group predominantly into the hands of just six men.[60]

Delegating Managerial Responsibility within American Tobacco

The programme of acquisitions that had brought Duke control of the plug industry was continued in the period leading up to the foundation of the Consolidated holding company. These acquisitions involved not only tobacco manufacturing concerns, but machinery producers, box, tin-foil, and sacking manufacturers, a firm producing liquorice, and a cigar distributor. Even a company called the Health Tobacco Co., producing nicotine-free cigars, was purchased for $75,000 in 1899 but it did not prove an enduring success and was soon closed down.[61] As the number of acquisitions grew, Duke increasingly came to realize that a fully integrated management structure was neither feasible nor desirable. If a business over which ATC gained control was well-run Duke was inclined to allow the existing management to continue, under the financial supervision of the head office in New York, rather than try to impose his direct control. As the trust grew, therefore, the delegation of managerial responsibility became Duke's principal concern. This was particularly the case with those tobacco products which, unlike cigarettes, gained relatively little from scale economies and the rationalization of production facilities. Thus when, in 1899, the Continental Tobacco Co. gained control of the non-cigarette-producing R. J. Reynolds Tobacco Company of Winston-Salem, North Carolina, through the purchase of shares from independent shareholders, Duke acceded control to the antagonistic Richard J. Reynolds, subject only to the posting of some ATC accountants in the offices at Winston to keep track of the parent company's financial interests.[62]

As his later evidence to the Circuit Court indicates, Duke found that the strategy of managerial delegation worked in his interest. Asked about his

[60] The Consolidated Tobacco Co. issued $157.4 million bonds in exchange for $54.3 million American common stock (at 2:1) and $48.8 million Continental common stock (at par). Over half of the shares in the Consolidated Tobacco Co. were held by the following six people: James B. Duke, A. N. Brady, O. H. Payne, Thomas F. Ryan, P. A. B. Widener, and William C. Whitney. US Bureau of Corporations, *Report on the Tobacco Industry* (Part 1), pp. 7–9.

[61] Another company, called the Health Cigar Company, did market a low nicotine cigar in America in the late 1930s. Sobel, *They Satisfy*, p. 124.

[62] Sobel, *They Satisfy*, pp. 72–5.

policy of purchasing majority interests [as opposed to full control] in other tobacco companies, Duke gave the following replies:

> . . . they were acquired with the idea that we would build up a lot of other organizations. Our crowd had about all they could handle and we concluded that the best way would be if we went into things in that way was to let them continue an interest in it and they would manage it.
>
> Q. You mean the previous owners would continue the management of it and continue an interest in it?
> A. Yes, sir; we wanted them to push and drive hard against us. If they could take our trade let them have it; we didn't care, or at least I didn't. The manager of a department, he cared; it made him work hard to keep them from getting his trade.
>
> Q. You had already had an experience with the separate organizations with the previous owners interested in the case of R. J. Reynolds Tobacco Co.?
> A. Yes; I think that is one of the mistakes the American Tobacco Co. made in the beginning that we didn't keep a separate organization for all the principal businesses we bought.
>
> Q. Why did you think that?
> A. Because we would have got better service and better management; we would have had competition and would have built and extended the business.
>
> Q. You mean competition between those various branches of the ATC?
> A. Yes, sir.[63]

The first occasion that this policy of non-integration of a majority-owned concern was applied to a firm manufacturing cigarettes arose in June 1900 when ATC acquired a 51 per cent share in the stock of the John Bollman Co. in San Francisco, California. This company manufactured Russian cigarettes, a type of product which featured a mouthpiece. These cigarettes were particularly popular in Eastern Europe and parts of Asia, including Japan and North China, but their manufacture involved a quite different production process to that employed by the Bonsack machine. The Bollman company was profitably run under the management of a German émigré, a Mr Gutschow, and Duke delegated to Gutschow a good deal of managerial autonomy.

The policy of managerial delegation became especially important to the development of the company's overseas business. Given the difficulties involved in transoceanic transport and communications, the appointment of reliable and competent managers abroad was critical to the strategy of foreign

[63] Testimony of J. B. Duke, pp. 3392–3, J. B. Duke Papers. Of course, it needs to be borne in mind that in his testimony Duke was attempting to demonstrate to the authorities that there had been no attempt by ATC to create a monopoly organization and, as such, the importance of this policy of managerial delegation would have been emphasized. Nevertheless it is clear that as the scope of the company's activities grew, particularly abroad, direct supervision of management gave way to more indirect, financial controls based on performance.

direct investment that was proving increasingly necessary to compete effectively abroad. Thus when Duke made his first European acquisition by purchasing two-thirds of the capital stock of the Dresden-based tobacco firm of Georg A. Jasmatzi in February 1901[64]—reputedly the third largest tobacco manufacturer in Germany[65]—he asked Gutschow to take charge of the American firm's interests there.[66]

Foreign Expansion and the 'Tobacco War' in Britain

As Table 2.3 illustrated, the export trade in cigarettes had been a major area of growth for ATC during the 1890s, rising from around 10 per cent of the company's cigarette output in 1890 to over one-third by the turn of the century. This growth was uneven, however, and was subject to the constraints imposed by competition from local manufacturers and by governments using protective tariffs on manufactured tobacco goods through which they were able to provide a cost advantage to domestic producers. Duke had already circumvented these problems in Australia, Canada, and Japan, during the 1890s, by setting up foreign subsidiaries of ATC to operate directly within those markets with encouraging results. By 1901, the Canadian factories were producing 100 million cigarettes per year, and the Australian factories around double that number. Thus, taken together, these two markets added a further 30 per cent to the volume of ATC's export trade. Even greater success had been achieved in Japan, however, where the level of output was stated at this time to have reached 8 million cigarettes daily.[67] Naturally, these sales were generating a healthy profit for Duke's concern, and now, using the capital resources raised by the flotation of the Consolidated company, the same strategy was about to be applied to the protected markets of Europe.[68]

Duke's acquisition of the Jasmatzi concern in Germany was thus a prelude

[64] F. Blaich, *Der Trustkampf, 1901–15* (1975), p. 46. A factor which helped to determine the timing of ATC's acquisition of Jasmatzi was a concern regarding changes in the income tax laws affecting foreign businesses operating in Germany which threatened to levy taxes on the companies' world-wide profits. Letter S. J. Gillchrest to T. D. Asten dated 28 December 1900, Letterpress Book of the London depot of ATC, BAT Co. Southampton Archive, Box 49.

[65] According to *Tobacco*, the Jasmatzi company had an annual production of 200 million cigarettes. The report also indicates that ATC bought out a smaller business in Germany at this time, Kyriazi Bros. of Berlin, which controlled the most popular brand of Egyptian cigarettes sold in Europe at that time. *Tobacco (London)*, 22 (253) (1902), 16.

[66] Testimony of J. B. Duke, pp. 3387–8, J. B. Duke Papers.

[67] These figures are drawn from Duke's own testimony. See US Bureau of Corporations, *Report on the Tobacco Industry* (Part 1), p. 165.

[68] The profits reported from the joint venture with the Murai Bros. firm in Japan in 1900 were ¥772,641 rising to ¥1,408,623 in 1901. S. Cochran, *Big Business in China: Sino-Foreign Rivalry in the Cigarette Industry, 1890–1930* (1980), p. 41.

to the main objective of his European campaign, which was to expand his business interests in Britain. The depot which ATC had set up in London helped to boost the company's export sales in Britain dramatically during the mid-1890s.[69] However, the continuation of this export-based approach to the British market was severely hampered by the structure of import duties levied on tobacco brought into the UK. Throughout most of the 1890s the duty on manufactured tobacco products, including cigarettes, had stood at 4s. 0d. per lb. as against 3s. 2d. per lb. on unmanufactured tobacco leaf; a differential of 10d. or 20 per cent. Given that the value of tobacco, including the duty, accounted for approximately 90 per cent of the material and labour costs of producing 1000 'Wild Woodbine' cigarettes, this differential duty rate acted strongly in favour of domestic cigarette manufacturers as they began to generate increased scale economies in production to match those of ATC.[70] Reductions in the rate of duty on cigarettes and unmanufactured tobacco by 7d. and 6d. per lb. respectively in the spring budget of 1898 allowed ATC a little respite and helped the company's sales in Britain to briefly revive. Two years later however, following the outbreak of war in South Africa, these duty reductions were largely reversed and the original tax differential between manufactured and unmanufactured tobacco of 10d. was restored. As a result of the increased duties, ATC's sales in Britain began to fall sharply[71] and the company's London depot, which had merely been breaking even, began to accumulate losses.[72] Shortly after the imposition of the higher duties in 1900, the manager of ATC's London depot wrote to Duke arguing that, 'Any change in our business [in Britain] will require us to either open a factory or buy one.'[73] Thus it was that Duke set out for England in September 1901 to purchase an interest in the British tobacco industry.[74]

Wills had received an intimation from Bernhard Baron in the spring of 1901 that ATC was negotiating for the purchase of a substantial shareholding

69 Figures for US cigarette exports to Britain are given in Table 2.2. Comparing the total exports of cigarettes from the United States with those of ATC given in Table 2.3 shows that Duke's company completely dominated this segment of the American tobacco industry.

70 Detailed figures for the production costs of 'Wild Woodbine' cigarettes as at 1896 and 1900 are provided in Alford, *W. D. & H. O. Wills*, Table 31.

71 Between 1899 and 1900, sales of ATC's cigarettes in Britain fell from 115 million to 80 million. Letter S. J. Gillchrest (ATC's assistant depot manager in London) to T. D. Asten dated 8 January 1901, Letterpress Book of the London depot of ATC, BAT Co. Southampton Archive, Box 49.

72 US Bureau of Corporations, *Report on the Tobacco Industry*, p. 166.

73 Letter, T. D. Asten to J. B. Duke dated 23 May 1900, Letterpress Book of the London depot of ATC, BAT Co. Southampton Archive, Box 49.

74 The Bureau of Corporations report suggests that Duke was accompanied by C. C. Dula, who had joined Duke's concerns with the acquisition of Liggett & Myers. US Bureau of Corporations, *Report on the Tobacco Industry*, p. 166. However, this is not supported by contemporary reports in the trade press and it seems more likely that Duke and Harris were accompanied by W. W. Fuller, ATC's legal counsel. Certainly it was these latter three who registered the British Tobacco Co. in London on 25 September 1901. See *Tobacco (London)*, 21 (250) (1901), 451–4, and *Cigar and Tobacco World*, 13 (1901), 503.

in Ogden's,[75] and it is clear that a meeting between the directors of Ogden's and the Secretary of ATC, Mr R. L. Patterson, had been set up in Liverpool as early as August 1900.[76] On his arrival in England, however, Duke's first move was to discuss the possibility of a take-over with the directors of the Nottingham-based business, John Player & Sons. His strategy was clearly to acquire control of as many of Britain's leading tobacco firms as possible, placing them under the banner of the British Tobacco Co., and then engage in direct competition with the remaining firms from a position of strength. The directors of Players were clearly aghast at these tactics and quickly fell in behind Wills' efforts at resistance.[77] Apart from the Ogden acquisition, Duke was unable to persuade any of Britain's other big tobacco businesses to come over to his side.[78] Meanwhile, the creation of the Imperial amalgamation within a few weeks of Duke's arrival in Britain had thwarted any chance that the American may have had of gaining market leadership, or anything close to it, through a strategy of acquisition. Thus within a matter of weeks the battle for control of the British tobacco market had effectively been lost by Duke. The war itself continued, however, and Duke now set himself the objective of winning the peace instead.

The purchase of Ogden's had given Duke a useful platform from which to make an impact on the tobacco market in Britain. The Liverpool firm had developed as an unusually aggressive competitor within the British market for manufactured cigarettes, devoting 25 per cent of its net profits to advertising compared with Wills' expenditure of between 1 and 2 per cent.[79] Between 1895 and 1899, at a time when sales of Wills' cigarettes were rising extremely rapidly, the value of Ogden's sales rose from 12.5 per cent of Wills' to nearly 18 per cent. In fact by 1900 Ogden had emerged as Wills' leading rival and in

[75] Letter B. Baron to J. Inskip dated 16 April 1901, Wills Archive, File No. 38169/M/1(g).

[76] Letter T. D. Asten to W. B. Ogden dated 17 August 1900, Letterpress Book of the ATC's London Depot, BAT Co. Southampton Archive, Box 49.

[77] Alford, *W. D. & H. O. Wills*, p. 258. It is reputed that Duke's opening gambit at his meeting with the directors of Players—'Hello, Boys, I'm Duke from New York come to buy your business'—effectively killed the negotiations stone dead.

[78] Duke had sought an interview with Wills directors through a letter to their board written by R. H. Walters of Ogden's dated 21 September 1901. Minutes of a Wills board meeting three days earlier indicate that some members of the family, notably Harry Wills, were minded to sell out to Duke. However, the prevailing view was that the company should resist the American challenge through amalgamation with other leading British firms. By the following week, the Wills board had agreed not to enter into any negotiations with Duke for the sale of their business. Minutes of a Special Board Meeting, 18 September 1901, and an Extraordinary Board Meeting, 25 September 1901, Wills Archive, File No. 38169/M/1(c/d). According to *Tobacco*, by the end of 1901 it had become apparent that none of the firms Duke had shown an interest in purchasing (other than Ogden) were willing to sell. *Tobacco (London)*, 22 (253) (1902), 2.

[79] Wills' advertising expenditure during the late 1890s averaged out at about £5000 per annum. Alford nevertheless argues that this relatively small advertising budget did not weaken the firm's competitive position because the quality of their goods was so superior to those of Ogden's. See Alford, *W. D. & H.O. Wills*, p. 234.

that year had launched its own brand of cigarettes selling at five for one penny—'Tabs'. The company had also made progress in its foreign trade, operating a bonded factory in Liverpool and investing in a factory in Sydney, New South Wales, which had gained a foothold for the firm's products in that market.[80] However, it was also Ogden's market segment that was most directly threatened by ATC's imported cigarettes, since brand loyalty among its customers was likely to be based on the transient effects of promotions and low prices.[81] This vulnerability, together with the generous price proposed for the company's stock, no doubt helped to persuade Ogden's directors to accede to Duke's offer.

Duke's early efforts to expand Ogden's sales in Britain by offering dealers free cigarettes and rebates with their regular orders, made little impact because they did not allow any supporting price reductions to the actual consumers and led simply to a rise in unsold stocks. Thus the offers of free cigarettes were withdrawn in favour of a strategy based on cutting the prices of Ogden's leading brands and supporting the lower prices with expensive promotional schemes. In contrast, Imperial bided its time in its marketing strategy, publicizing only the promise of a loyalty bonus to dealers in the near future.[82] Nevertheless, it acted quickly to protect its supplies from American acquisition, bringing its main packaging firm, Mardon, Son & Hall into the Imperial group on 1 January 1902. Moreover, as sales of Ogden's 'Tabs' and 'Guinea Gold' cigarettes began to rise following the new policy, Imperial moved to support its distribution network in two ways early in 1902. First, it bought control of the 140 discount shops operated by the Salmon & Gluckstein chain for a sum of £400,000. Then, following a suggestion put forward by Harry Wills, it promised to pay an annual bonus amounting to £50,000 to retailers who signed an agreement promising that they would display only Imperial's brands and would not stock or sell any brands of Ogden's or ATC.[83]

The exclusive nature of Imperial's bonus scheme created some problems within the trade, who felt that the company was using the American threat in an attempt to gain monopoly control. Duke quickly made capital out of this discontent, responding with his own bonus scheme in which he offered to share out among Ogden's dealers the whole of the Liverpool firm's profits plus £200,000 each year for four years, based on the proportion of their sales

[80] *Tobacco (London)*, 22 (253) (1902), 26.

[81] When outlining a proposed new promotion of ATC's 'Cameo' brand of cigarettes in England during 1900, the manager of ATC's London depot explained to Duke in a letter that, 'If the scheme were adopted and turned out trumps Ogden's business could be bought cheap, as it would be from them we should take a good part of the increase.' Letter T. D. Asten to J. B. Duke dated 23 May 1900, Letterpress Book of ATC's London depot, BAT Co. Southampton Archive, Box 49.

[82] *Tobacco (London)*, 21 (251) (1901), 490–2.

[83] Alford, *W. D. & H. O. Wills*, p. 264.

of Ogden's goods. Although the offer carried no restrictions to prevent dealers from selling other companies' brands it was treated with some scepticism within the trade and was not very widely taken up. Nevertheless, it pressured Imperial into retracting the exclusive nature of their bonus scheme—much to Harry Wills' annoyance. Moreover, the level of scepticism relating to the Ogden bonus scheme declined markedly when, at the end of June 1902, the company duly paid the registered dealers their first quarter's bonus of £50,000.[84] Thus by the middle of 1902 the war in Britain was raging more strongly than ever.

The conflict in Britain influenced market conditions in a variety of countries where the firms that founded Imperial were in competition with ATC. This normally involved the Wills branch of the company, whose foreign trade was the most advanced. In the case of Jamaica, however, an export business had been developed by Lambert & Butler on the strength of its 'Trumpeter' and 'Needle Point' brands. As the tobacco war intensified Lambert & Butler's Jamaican representative became engaged in a process of protracted commercial warfare against ATC's 'Harp' brand for the custom of smokers in the capital, Kingston. Commenting on the struggle, the trade press noted that, 'Both [representatives] advertise largely and push their wares by all sorts of ingenious bonuses, prizes and similar attractions. Latterly the battle has raged between the bill posters of the rival agents. Day after day—or, rather, night after night—they cover up each others bills wherever found in the city.'[85]

In Australia, where the advent of Federation in 1901 stimulated inter-state trade and investment, Wills organized local manufacturing for its products. This took the form of a partnership with the company's distributor in Sydney, Heyde, Todman & Co., who in April 1901 contracted to manufacture Wills' brands and distribute them throughout Australia. The strategy was complicated by the fact that Heyde, Todman & Co. also acted as agents for ATC and were bound by an agreement with that firm not to manufacture cigarettes in New South Wales. For this reason, the manufacturing business was organized under the name of W. D. & H. O. Wills (Australia) Ltd.[86] Developments of this kind led Duke to observe that, 'England is our chief competitor . . . in all the foreign markets.'[87]

Duke's comment was especially appropriate to the circumstances that were developing in south and east Asian markets where competitive pressures

[84] *Tobacco (London)*, 22 (260) (1902), 377–8. The item pointed out that, as the number of dealers who signed up to Ogden's scheme was small, so the bonus paid was quite large, amounting to 17 per cent of the invoiced sales.

[85] *Tobacco (London)*, 22 (260) (1902), 402.

[86] R. Walker, *Under Fire: a History of Tobacco Smoking in Australia* (1984), p. 45; Alford, *W. D. & H. O. Wills*, pp. 218–19; *Tobacco (London)*, 21 (245) (1901), 213 and 21 (248) (1901), 364.

[87] *Tobacco (London)*, 22 (261) (1902), 436.

intensified after 1900. In India, both ATC and Wills had developed their export business in conjunction with the same managing agency in Calcutta, George Atherton & Co., and during the 1890s this firm had utilized the native tobacco firm of Bukhsh Ellahie & Co. to distribute Wills' 'Flag' and ATC's 'Pin Head' cigarettes. However, shortly before the conflict began in Britain ATC withdrew their business from Atherton and set up their own depot in Calcutta under the management of E. A. Woodward and three assistants. Meanwhile, the Bukhsh Ellahie firm began to push Wills' products more strongly—notably the dedicated export brand of cigarettes 'Scissors'.[88]

Around this time Duke also posted representatives to Singapore (J. A. Thomas) and Hong Kong (J. B. Warfield) to push ATC's business in these two outposts of the British Empire. Together with the company's representative in Shanghai (C. E. Fiske) ATC was now prepared to make a substantial advance in the region. These representatives were also utilized by the manager of ATC's business in Japan, E. J. Parrish, to develop the export sales of Murai Brothers' brands. Between May and June 1901, Parrish wrote to Thomas, Woodward, and Warfield explaining that he was preparing to transfer to them the Murai Brothers' trade in Singapore, Penang, Calcutta, and Hong Kong from the existing agencies.[89] Subsequently, as the war with Wills' cigarettes in the region intensified, Parrish developed low-priced export brands at the company's Kyoto factory which were designed to be 'cheap enough and good enough to knock out Wills' and American Cigarette Co.'s goods'.[90] Parrish also kept these ATC representatives informed of rival brands of cigarettes that were being exported into their markets by other manufacturers in Japan, using intelligence from drawback returns.[91]

In China, the Murai Brothers had developed a sufficient trade in their cigarettes by the beginning of 1901 to warrant the appointment of their own comprador in Shanghai, Yang Ting Tsai.[92] In New York, however, ATC's

88 See *Thakar's Indian Directory*, editions for 1901 and 1902.

89 See letters from E. J. Parrish to J. B. Warfield (Hong Kong) dated 24 May 1901; to J. A. Thomas (Singapore) dated 20 June 1901; to E. A. Woodward (Calcutta) dated 19 June 1901, Parrish Papers. These letters indicate that Murai had previously been dealing with Messrs Kim Hin & Co. in Singapore, Messrs S. A. Aljunid in Penang, Mr Savermo Diacono in Bangkok, and various firms in Kobe and Osaka who had exported the goods themselves. Murai had also developed a trade in Calcutta with Messrs Haji Karam Ellahie and Mohamed Shafi, as well as a trade with Bukhsh Ellahie which was underwritten by Atherton & Co. In China, Murai had been dealing with Mustard & Co. but wrote to C. E. Fiske in May 1901 to acknowledge 'the transfer of our China business over to your Company [the American Tobacco Co.]' who had set up a depot of their own in Shanghai. See letters from E. J. Parrish to C. E. Fiske and The American Tobacco Co. Depot both dated 17 May 1901, Parrish Papers.

90 These brands were 'Top', 'Camelia', 'Pointer', and 'Ideal' selling at ¥1.40, ¥1.50, ¥1.60, and ¥1.75 per 1000 respectively. Letters from E. J. Parrish to J. A. Thomas and to E. A. Woodward both dated 11 September 1901, Parrish Papers. The citation is taken from the letter to Woodward.

91 See letter from E. J. Parrish to E. A. Woodward dated 17 September 1901, Parrish Papers.

92 See contract between Murai Brothers Company, Shanghai branch, and Yang Ting Tsai, dated 5 April 1901, Parrish Papers.

management became concerned by the possibility that the factory operated in Shanghai by the American Cigarette Company (ACC)—and, more significantly, the exclusive contract for the use of the Bonsack machine in China which this company had purchased from R. H. Wright in 1899—might fall under the control of the British. Thus early in 1902, ATC dispatched their export manager Harold Roberts to the Far East to investigate the situation, presumably with a view to buying out the rival concern. Roberts met up with ATC's Shanghai representative C. E. Fiske in April and together they travelled to Japan to discuss with Parrish the possibility of ATC's Japanese subsidiary acquiring control of ACC. Parrish declared that he thought it would be a mistake for Murai Brothers to purchase a factory in Shanghai because it would reduce the company's export trade and thus jeopardize their attempt to cultivate favoured relations with the Meiji government. Given that it was possible to transport goods from Japan to China in five or six days, and since the government gave generous drawback terms on exported goods, Parrish felt the move would be counter-productive. In a letter to W. R. Harris in New York, Parrish suggested that 'the [Japanese] government would rather *subsidise* than *lose* Exports', and that in his opinion ATC should simply buy out the factory in Shanghai under another name and leave it to stand idle.[93]

Unable to persuade Parrish to support them, Roberts and Fiske returned to China. There they were joined by J. A. Thomas and together the three took up negotiations with E. Jenner Hogg, chairman of ACC, regarding the purchase of the Shanghai plant and the Bonsack contract. On 6 May Murai's Kyoto factory suffered a serious fire in which three buildings were completely gutted and seventy-five cigarette machines destroyed.[94] A little over a week later, on 14 May, Roberts and Hogg drew up a contract setting out the terms by which ATC would purchase the plant, assets, and outstanding commitments of ACC, and which placed a value on the Shanghai factory of 102,500 Taels. The terms of the agreement included the transfer to ATC of the contract with R. H. Wright relating to the exclusive control of Bonsack machines for China which had been signed on 2 August 1899.[95]

Shortly after this contract had been drawn up Hogg travelled to Tokyo and

93 Letter from E. J. Parrish to W. R. Harris dated 1 May 1902 (emphasis in original), Parrish Papers.

94 Telegram from Murai to Powhattan (ATC) New York dated 7 May 1902, Parrish Papers; *Tobacco (London)*, 22 (260) (1902), 422. The telegram suggested that work would recommence in Kyoto in about four weeks and that production would be stepped up in Tokyo in the meantime. The report in the trade press pointed out that the insurance of the factory had been switched from a Japanese firm to a foreign insurer offering a lower price within the previous month.

95 Agreement between E. Jenner Hogg and H. Roberts dated 14 May 1902, Document Nos. 13-C-176 to 178, BAT Archive, Centre for Chinese Business History, Shanghai Academy of Social Sciences, hereinafter BAT Archive (SASS).

THE LATEST NOVELTY
IN
PRESSED CIGARETTES
IS

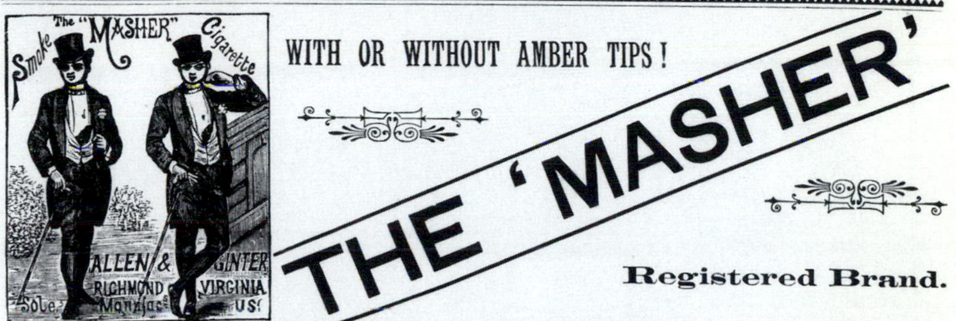

These Cigarettes are made from the Fragrant Virginia Gold Leaf, combined with the Aromatic Dubec Turkish Tobacco.

'Yes, we're Mashers, you bet,
'With the Light Cigarette,
'And the quite unapproachable stick.'
(*As sung by the* MISSES WATSON, *in the Burlesque of Blue Beard at the Gaiety.*)

PACKETS OF 10 PRICE SIXPENCE.

Allen & Ginter, *Manufacturers,* Richmond, Va. U.S.A.

ALSO MANUFACTURERS OF THE WELL-KNOWN BRANDS OF

RICHMOND GEM, OUR LITTLE BEAUTIES (PRESSED OR ROUND), **OPERA PUFF, THE PET, AND PERFECTION CIGARETTES.**

OUR Cigarettes have a reputation that has made them a STANDARD ARTICLE in all parts of the world.

They have received the HIGHEST AWARDS of Merit at the great exhibitions in Philadelphia, Paris, Sydney, and Melbourne.

In addition to their immense sale in this country, we export them to ALL PARTS OF THE WORLD; there is scarcely a country in which they are not sold.

While the sale of the adulterated brands of many of the American manufacturers has been prohibited in Great Britian, OUR ABSOLUTELY PURE GOODS have attained the largest popular sale ever known in Cigarettes in that country, with a steadily increasing demand.

Our Cigarettes are made with different degrees of strength, to suit all tastes.

We USE THE TASTELESS French Rice Paper **(papier de riz,)** made in France expressly for us; it has no smell and its purity is such that in burning, scarcely an atom of ash remains.

London Depot: 55, Holborn Viaduct. H. K. TERRY & Co., *Sole Consignees.*

PLATE 1. Advertisement for imported American cigarettes in British tobacco trade press, 1883.

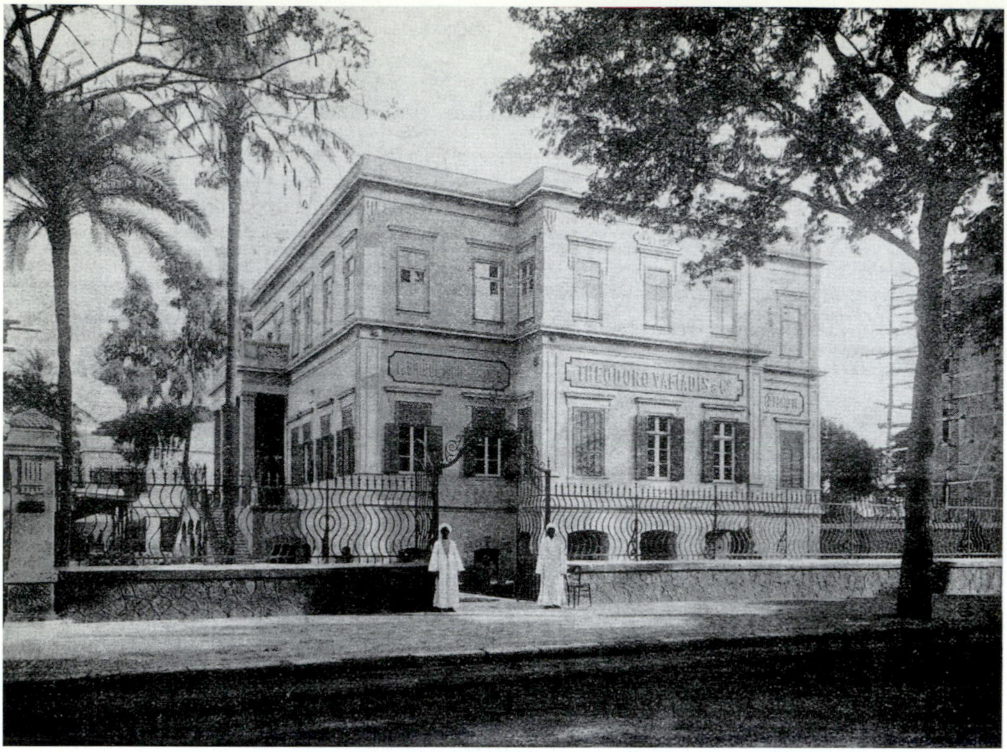
THEODORO VAFIADIS & Cº

PLATE 2. Headquarters of Greek cigarette manufacturer Theodoro Vafiades in Cairo, 1903.

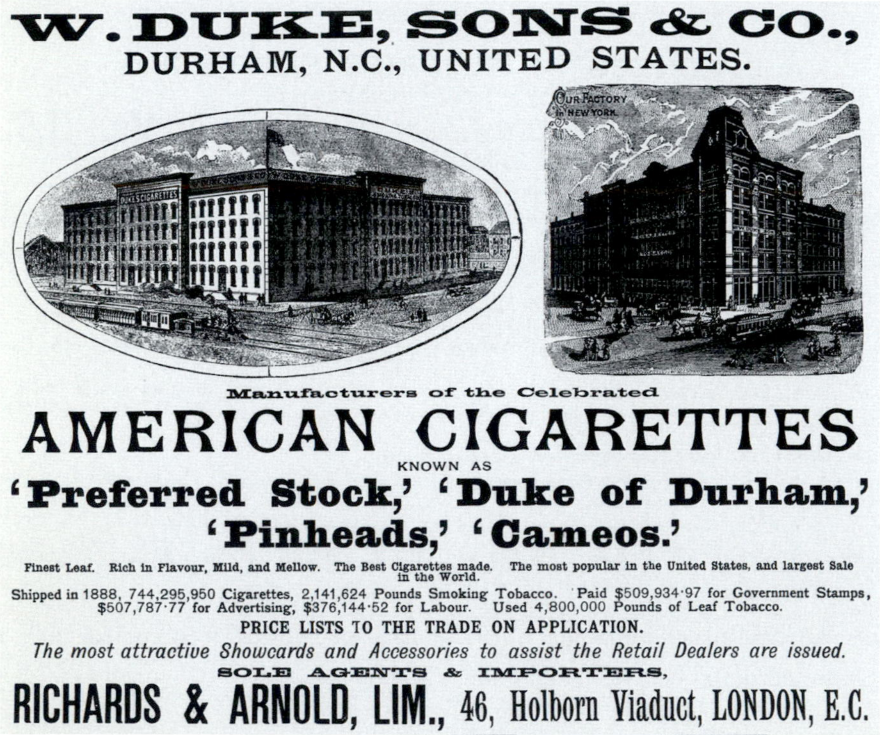
W. DUKE, SONS & CO.,
DURHAM, N.C., UNITED STATES.
OUR FACTORY IN NEW YORK.
DUKE'S CIGARETTES
Manufacturers of the Celebrated
AMERICAN CIGARETTES
KNOWN AS
'Preferred Stock,' 'Duke of Durham,'
'Pinheads,' 'Cameos.'
Finest Leaf. Rich in Flavour, Mild, and Mellow. The Best Cigarettes made. The most popular in the United States, and largest Sale in the World.
Shipped in 1888, 744,295,950 Cigarettes, 2,141,624 Pounds Smoking Tobacco. Paid $509,934·97 for Government Stamps, $507,787·77 for Advertising, $376,144·52 for Labour. Used 4,800,000 Pounds of Leaf Tobacco.
PRICE LISTS TO THE TRADE ON APPLICATION.
The most attractive Showcards and Accessories to assist the Retail Dealers are issued.
SOLE AGENTS & IMPORTERS,
RICHARDS & ARNOLD, LIM., 46, Holborn Viaduct, LONDON, E.C.

PLATE 3. W. Duke, Sons & Co. promoting its cigarette brands in Britain, 1889.

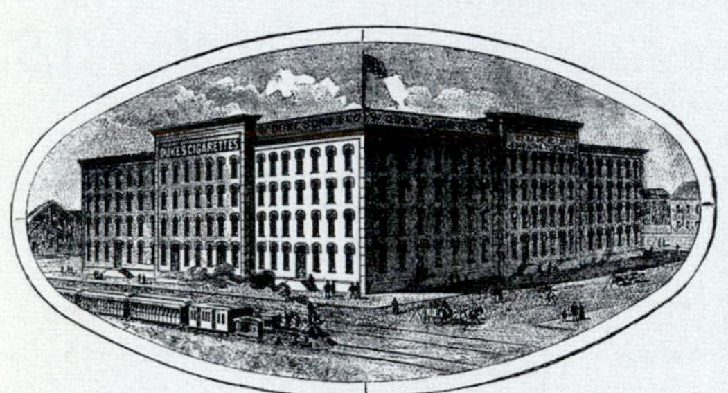

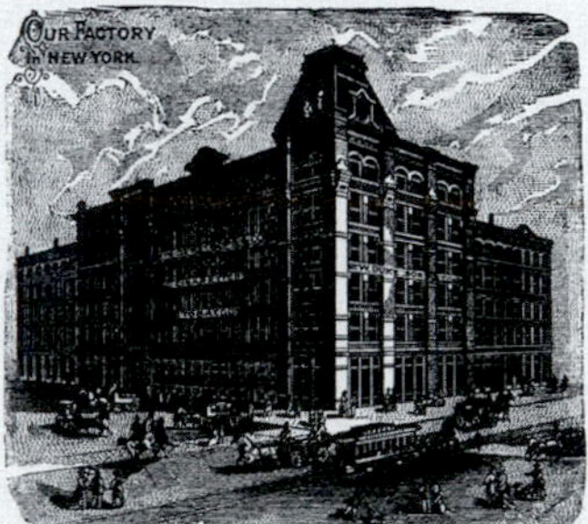

PLATE 4. Female workers processing tobacco leaf in a Cairo factory, 1899.

PLATE 5. The future King Edward VII featured in a trade advertisement for Melachrino cigarettes, 1895. Melachrino's business was sold to the Tobacco Products Corporation in 1912 and acquired by BAT Co. in 1930.

PLATE 6. Example of an Ogden's window display during the 'Tobacco War' in Britain, 1901.

Form No. 3

CABLE MESSAGE.
THE WESTERN UNION TELEGRAPH COMPANY.
INCORPORATED
THOS. T. ECKERT, President and General Manager.

TWO AMERICAN CABLES FROM NEW YORK TO GREAT BRITAIN.
CONNECTS ALSO WITH FIVE ANGLO-AMERICAN AND ONE DIRECT U. S. ATLANTIC CABLES.
DIRECT CABLE COMMUNICATION WITH GERMANY AND FRANCE.
CABLE CONNECTION WITH CUBA, WEST INDIES, MEXICO AND CENTRAL AND SOUTH AMERICA.
MESSAGES SENT TO, AND RECEIVED FROM, ALL PARTS OF THE WORLD.

OFFICES IN AMERICA:
All Offices (22,000) of the Western Union Telegraph Company and its Connections.

OFFICES IN GREAT BRITAIN:
LONDON: 21 Royal Exchange, E. C. 40 Mark Lane, E. C. Effingham House, Arundel Street, W. C. 109 Fenchurch Street, E. C. 2 Northumberland Avenue, W. C. Hay's Wharf, Tooley Street.
LIVERPOOL: 8 Rumford St. and Cotton Exchange. BRISTOL: Backhall Chambers, Baldwin Street. BRADFORD: 10 Forster Square. DUNDEE: 1 Panmure Street. EDINBURGH: 50 Frederick Street.
GLASGOW: 4 Waterloo Street. 29 Gordon Street. LEITH: Exchange Buildings. MANCHESTER: 7 Royal Exchange, Bank Street. NEWCASTLE-ON-TYNE: 1 Side.

NUMBER 5 Bg SENT BY Rh RECD BY P No. OF WORDS 21 FROM Londontown 27

RECEIVED at 1:07 PM Sept 27 1902

W. B. Duke, Durham, NC.

Have just completed great deal with British manufacturers covering world securing great Benefit to our companies

Duke.

PLATE 7. Duke's telegram messages to Col. Oliver H. Payne and his father following the agreement with Imperial to set up BAT Co. in September 1902.

W B Duke N.C.
Durham
Just Completed great deal with British Manufacturers Covering the World securing great benefit to our Companies

CARLTON HOTEL.
PALL MALL.
LONDON

Col Payne
Papers signed ~~insuring~~ great deal for our Companies
Duke

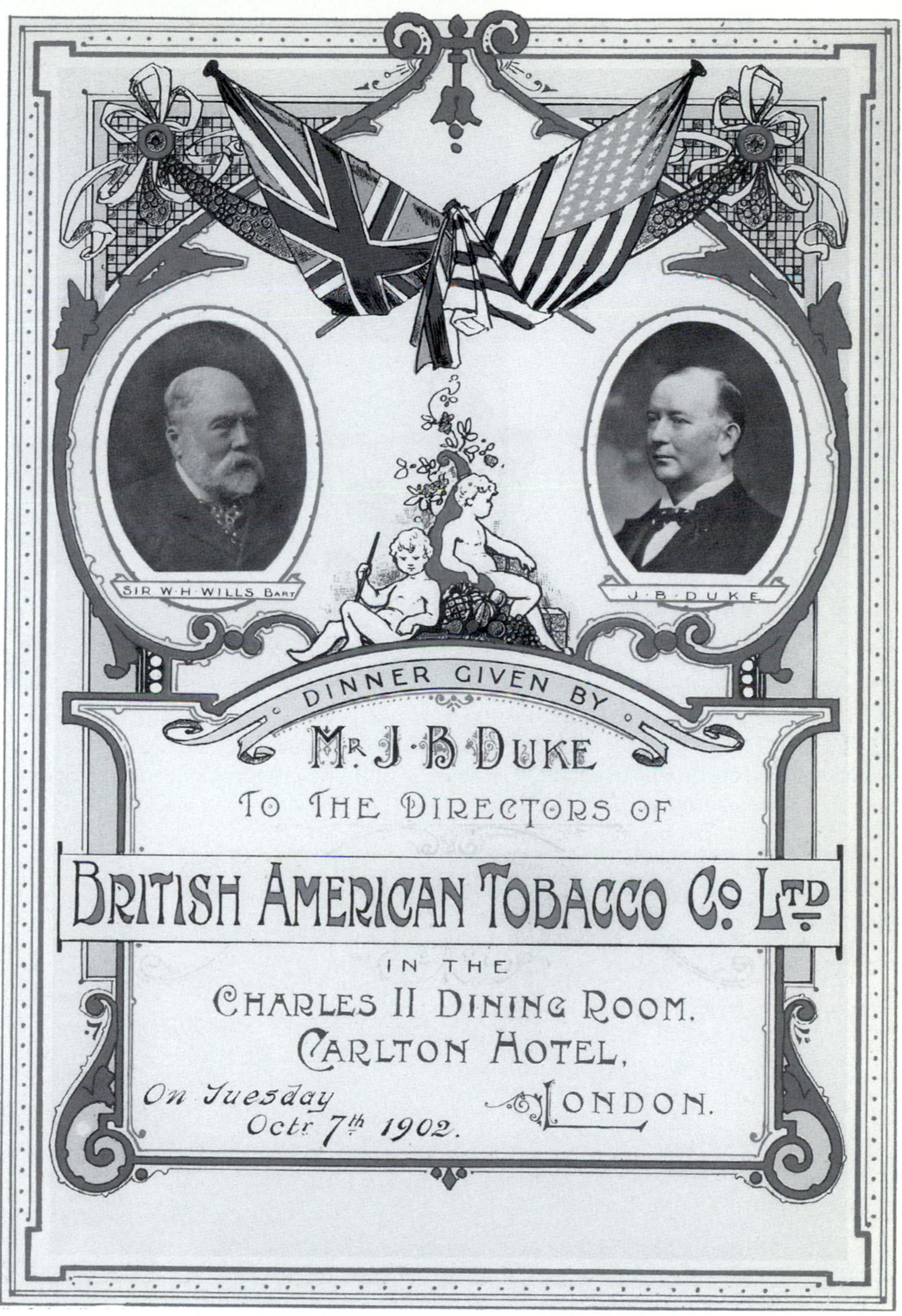

PLATE 8. Cover of menu for celebration dinner hosted by Duke in London to mark the formation of BAT Co.

PLATE 9. The cartoon by 'Spy' which W. H. Wills sent to Duke as a reciprocal token of friendship following the establishment of the British-American joint venture in 1902.

PLATE 10. Harry H. Wills, instigator of Wills' highly successful 'Wild Woodbine' cigarette brand and vice-chairman of BAT Co. under Duke until his sudden resignation in 1904.

PLATE 11. Girls making boxes for 'Springbok' cigarettes in South Africa, *c.*1900.

PLATE 12. Hugo Cunliffe-Owen (standing, centre) photographed during negotiations with Australian cigarette manufacturers in Sydney, 1903. William R. Harris, who assumed the chairmanship of BAT Co. from Duke between 1905 and 1911, is also present (seated, extreme right).

PLATE 13. Affixing tax stamps to BAT Co.'s 'Flag' brand of cigarettes in South Africa, *c.*1910.

PLATE 14. Bonny McGinn dressed to promote ATC's 'Sweet Caporal' cigarettes, *c.*1900.

PLATE 15. Cartoon in the American tobacco trade press of Uncle Sam embarking on the dissolution of ATC, 1907.

explained the situation regarding the sale of the factory to Parrish in a meeting at which he intimated that the deal had been satisfactorily concluded.[96] However, on 9 July Wills' agent in Shanghai, Rex & Co., wrote to J. S. Fearon, of the American merchant house Fearon, Daniel & Co., addressing him as the acting chairman of ACC. In this letter Rex explained that he had been instructed by W. D. & H. O. Wills to offer the shareholders of ACC an improved bid of 110,000 Taels for their factory in Shanghai, with all the other terms of the agreement of 14 May between Hogg and Roberts maintained. Fearon wrote back to Rex & Co. the following day, accepting Wills' offer on behalf of the directors of ACC, and at the same time gave notice of an Extraordinary General Meeting of ACC shareholders scheduled for 25 July to consider the proposal from Wills.[97] This meeting duly passed the resolutions put forward and thus confirmed the sale of the ACC's Shanghai factory to Wills and not to ATC as originally agreed. In Tokyo, Parrish was clearly stunned by the development and wrote in reply to letters from Fiske outlining the news:

> We are decidedly of the opinion that if you intend starting a factory in Shanghai, you should not let the [additional] 7,500 Tls. prevent the consummation of the deal with the American Cigarette Co., especially as we understand that Company has the *exclusive right* to the Bonsack machine for *China*.[98]

On 3 September Parrish wrote to Harris in New York expressing his concern that Wills was now on the point of extending its activities from Shanghai to Japan through an arrangement with the Osaka Tobacco Company who had distributed Wills' products in Japan prior to the tariff rise in 1899.[99] Thus the events in Shanghai had added another, unexpected, twist to the competitive struggle between Imperial and ATC; and one which worked to the decided benefit of the British combination.

By the time ACC had fallen under Wills' control, at the end of July 1902, the conflict between Duke and the Imperial group was reaching a critical stage. In Britain, the payment of the first quarterly bonus to the Ogden dealers had considerably raised the stakes in the battle for dealers' loyalty and threatened to create even greater dislocation within the distribution sector for Imperial. At the same time, Imperial's strength had been reinforced by the addition of another three significant tobacco manufacturers to the original group of thirteen, and the Ogden's promotions were beginning to cost the

96 Letter E. J. Parrish to C. E. Fiske, dated 1 August 1902, Parrish Papers.

97 Letter Rex & Co. to J. S. Fearon, dated 9 July 1902; letter J. S. Fearon to Rex & Co., dated 10 July 1902; Notice of Extraordinary General Meeting of the shareholders of the American Cigarette Co. dated 11 July 1902, BAT Archive (SASS), Document Nos. 13-C-174–180.

98 Letter E. J. Parrish to C. E. Fiske, dated 1 August 1902 (emphasis in original), Parrish Papers.

99 Letter E. J. Parrish to W. R. Harris, dated 3 September 1902, Parrish Papers.

American invader substantial sums of money.[100] In America, moreover, Duke and his allies had also set up in 1901 the American Cigar Co., embarking on a costly attempt to expand the interests of the trust into this final area of the domestic tobacco industry.[101] Meanwhile the Imperial group was busily finding other methods to exert financial pressure on Duke. Bristol City Council accepted a plan put forward by Wills to build huge warehouses at Bristol docks in an effort to draw the shipments of leaf tobacco away from their traditional location in Liverpool.[102] In May 1902, three members of the Imperial company travelled to New York and began to explore the potential for setting up production facilities to compete with Duke in his home market. By August, reports were circulating in the trade press that Imperial was on the verge of forming an alliance with the Universal Tobacco Co. in order to commence manufacture of a full range of their tobacco products within the United States.[103] For this threat to remain credible, however, these rumours would soon need to be backed up with hard cash.

Increasingly, therefore, both parties began to see the benefit of bringing the conflict to a mutually satisfactory conclusion. No doubt the three representatives of Imperial who had travelled to America engaged in informal soundings among Duke's confidants. More actively, Harry Wills arranged for his assistant, Hugo Cunliffe-Owen, to visit the proprietor of the Paris-based cigarette paper manufacturer, Braunstein Frères, and persuade him to visit Duke in New York, apparently to raise the question of an amalgamation between Imperial and ATC.[104] However, negotiations really began to make significant progress in July 1902 when Thomas F. Ryan, Duke's co-director of the Consolidated Tobacco Co., arrived in England and met with the directors of Imperial. Adopting a more conciliatory approach, Ryan appears to have been instrumental in smoothing the way for a final series of meetings to take place between Duke and the directors of Imperial. Thus in the late summer of 1902, Duke returned to England and negotiated an end to the conflict.

The final settlement, agreed on 27 September 1902, essentially divided into two components. The first concerned the domestic markets of Britain and America. Imperial achieved its principal objective when Duke agreed to withdraw from the British tobacco market by selling to Imperial ATC's interest in the Ogden concern. However, he drove a hard bargain, setting a price

[100] The Ogden bonus scheme was ultimately reputed to have resulted in a loss of £376,000 for the American concern. M. Corina, *Trust in Tobacco: the Anglo-American Struggle for Power* (1975), p. 67.

[101] By 1903 the American Cigar Co. had acquired control of about one-sixth of the cigar production in America, but had been forced to accept heavy losses in the process. US Bureau of Corporations, *Report on the Tobacco Industry*, pp. 6–7.

[102] *Tobacco (London)*, 22 (260) (1902), 378.

[103] *Tobacco (London)*, 22 (258) (1902), 287; 22 (259) (1902), 351; 22 (260) (1902), 389; 22 (261) (1902), 425–6.

[104] Alford, *W. D. & H. O. Wills*, p. 268.

of £3 million which amounted to practically three times the cost of acquisition. Thereafter, it was agreed that the parties would trade exclusively in their own domestic markets. This partitioning of markets was strengthened through a transfer of trade marks, such that Imperial held the rights to ATC's brands in Britain and vice versa. In return for the sale of Ogden's, ATC gained a minority shareholding in Imperial and three seats on its board of directors.

The second component of the agreement related to the trade beyond Britain and America, and here the approach adopted took the form of a joint venture. A subsidiary company was set up, with Duke as chairman, which was granted the rights to the trade marks of all the brands currently owned by ATC and Imperial for markets outside of Britain and America. To this subsidiary was to be transferred all the export capacity of the two parent companies, together with all the foreign assets owned by them. The company was called the British–American Tobacco Company (BAT Co.), and its £6 million authorized share capital was divided in the ratio of 2:1 in favour of the American parent, reflecting ATC's extensive foreign investments in Canada, Australia, Germany, and Japan which were now transferred to BAT Co.'s control.

Thus had the tobacco world been divided. On concluding the agreement, Duke rushed from the negotiating table and quickly scribbled in an excited hand two telegram messages on the Carlton Hotel's headed paper. On the front sheet, he wrote to his financial ally Colonel Payne: 'Papers signed insuring [*sic*] great deal for our Companies', on the back was a message to his father, Washington Duke, reading: 'I have just completed great deal with British manufacturers covering the world securing great benefit to our Companies.' To celebrate the new world order, a few days later Duke hosted a grand dinner at the same hotel. The speech he made at this gathering is not recorded, but his sentiments were clearly expressed when the normally reticent Duke spoke to the press about the new venture: 'Is it not a grand thing in every way that England and America should join hands in a vast enterprise rather than be in competition? Come along with me and together we will conquer the rest of the world.'[105]

[105] *Tobacco (London)*, 22 (262) (1902), 475.

Part Two

Pioneers of an International Mass Market

4

Birth of a Multinational Enterprise

Introduction

In the three years that followed the formation of BAT Co. in 1902 James Duke and his fellow directors set about the task of consolidating the company's various assets and integrating them into a coherent corporate structure. An export business, based on factories in both Britain and America, was placed directly under the aegis of BAT Co., whilst a number of foreign-based affiliates were used to manage the company's main investments abroad. In addition, two tobacco leaf-purchasing subsidiaries were incorporated in the United States to provide the organization with its primary raw material. These developments saw BAT Co. emerge as one of the earliest examples of a modern-style multinational corporation although, of course, the company itself continued to be a joint venture, fully owned by ATC and Imperial.

The fact that ATC owned two-thirds of BAT Co.'s shares allowed Duke to exert his control over the organization. His strongest influence can be seen in the company's early developments in Japan and China, but it was also evident in Canada, Australia, and Germany. In each of these markets the managerial composition of BAT Co.'s operating subsidiary was decisively influenced, if not actually determined, by Duke. Only in South Africa was Wills' existing market strength such as to give the British management in London more influence over developments there, although in India too, after 1905, operations passed into the hands of a management team with a much greater affinity towards the Imperial elements within BAT Co.

The decision to locate the company's headquarters—and two-thirds of its directors—in London meant that this became the focal point for the organization's administrative offices. Under Duke's leadership, however, the managers appointed by him to oversee BAT Co.'s foreign subsidiaries were given a good measure of autonomy in the day-to-day management of their businesses. This was particularly true of the firms that operated in the markets of the British Dominions where BAT Co.'s subsidiaries quickly established themselves as quasi-autonomous corporations. Moreover, the British and American-based export operations were themselves effectively in competition with one another for their foreign sales, and a separate committee of US-based directors was formed in New York to manage the American factories' trade.

Despite his efforts to facilitate a degree of managerial autonomy within the BAT group of companies, Duke's desire to exercise his ultimate authority over decision-making soon provoked a clash with the Imperial elements in the British-based management which precipitated the resignation from BAT Co.'s board of Harry H. Wills and William G. Player in 1904. Duke's own decision to stand down within a year of these resignations, together with the death of William Ogden in 1906, left the fledgling multinational with a management team of relatively limited experience. However, Duke's growing expertise in the area of managerial delegation seems to have provided the company with wise governance under the chairmanship of the more conciliatory William R. Harris in New York, whilst at the same time the grooming of Hugo Cunliffe-Owen as his eventual successor was a conscious decision made at a very early stage of BAT Co.'s life. Of particular importance in this latter respect was Duke's insistence, during his initially brief period of tenure as BAT Co.'s chairman, that Cunliffe-Owen should take management decisions at the highest level in both the American and Chinese parts of the operation.

There is no clear evidence to indicate whether Duke's decision to stand down as BAT Co. chairman in 1905 was conceived as a temporary measure, in the face of difficult personal circumstances and under the weight of competing business demands, or whether it represented a deliberate step away from his tobacco industry roots in search of a more diversified business career. In the event he was soon obliged to direct his energies back towards tobacco matters when the US anti-trust authorities stepped up their campaign against ATC's virtual monopoly of the US tobacco market. During the four and a half years between the initiation of legal proceedings on 19 July 1907 and the final ruling of the Supreme Court on 16 November 1911, a significant portion of Duke's time was devoted to defending his American companies against the charge of unlawful conspiracy. It was only after the case against them had been lost, and his American tobacco trust had been dissolved, that the management of BAT Co. once again became one of Duke's central concerns.

BAT Co.'s Initial Production Capacity

The agreement of 27 September 1902 between ATC and Imperial, which brought BAT Co. into existence, created at a stroke one of the world's first manufacturing-based multinational corporations. Largely due to the activities of its American parent, BAT Co. began its commercial life with manufacturing subsidiaries located in five countries outside of Britain and America. ATC owned manufacturing plants in Canada, Australia, Germany, and Japan, and these were formally transferred to BAT Co., along with the foreign investments of the Wills company in Shanghai and Sydney, both of which had been acquired during the previous two years.[1] In addition, a factory operated by Ogden's in Sydney, which had fallen under the control of ATC in 1901, was transferred to the new Anglo-American joint venture.[2]

These foreign investments were purchased by BAT Co. in exchange for £2.82 million of its authorized ordinary share capital of £4.5 million, with the shares being allocated two-thirds to ATC and one-third to Imperial in line with the terms agreed. The shares were issued in June 1903, and together with £900,021 of ordinary shares that had been sold to the parent companies for cash in October 1902, they represented the extent of the issued ordinary share capital of the company during its first ten years in business. Subsequent to these transactions, just under £1.25 million was paid by BAT Co. in exchange for the export-related assets transferred to the new company in Britain from the Imperial group and Ogden, and in America from ATC. At this point the full authorized preference share capital of BAT Co., amounting to £1.5 million, was issued to the parent companies.

Altogether, five bonded tobacco manufacturing factories in Britain were specifically transferred to BAT Co. by the agreement of 27 September. One was a factory at Cornwallis Street in Liverpool which had been built by Ogden as that company developed its export trade,[3] while the remaining four were transferred from companies within the Imperial group. These comprised Lambert & Butler's bonded factory in Bucknall Street, near Long Acre in London, two factories of the Richmond Cavendish Company located in Liverpool[4] and, finally, the most valuable property transferred to BAT Co.,

[1] W. D. & H. O. Wills (Australia) had been registered in July 1901, whilst the American Cigarette Co. of Shanghai had been purchased only two months before the formation of BAT Co. On the Australian subsidiary, see B. W. E. Alford, *W. D. & H. O. Wills and the Development of the UK Tobacco Industry 1789–1965* (1973), pp. 219–20. See also *Tobacco (London)*, 21 (245) (1901), 213 and idem., 21 (248) (1901), 364.

[2] *Tobacco (London)*, 22 (253) (1902), 25–6. This report on the absorption of Ogden's business in Australia by ATC indicated that the local managers of the Ogden company in Sydney had made magnificent progress and were 'not at all pleased with the turn events have taken'.

[3] *Tobacco (London)*, 19 (221) (1899), 200.

[4] BAT Co.'s own records indicate that they inherited a total of five factory sites in Liverpool. Two of these were the Cornwallis Street factory of Ogden and the Roberts Street factory of Richmond Cavendish. The others mentioned are Greenock Street, Paisley Street, and Old Hall Street (which was sold almost at once). BAT Co. Corporate Index, BAT Co. Southampton Archive, Box 114.

the export factory built by W. D. & H. O. Wills at Ashton Gate in Bristol, which Wills had constructed as part of its export drive under Harry Wills' initiative. This latter plant was a modern factory which had only begun production in May 1901,[5] and it seems to have been the main location for BAT Co.'s export trade from Britain during the early years.[6] In the United States, meanwhile, two of ATC's export factories, one in Rochester, New York, formerly belonging to W. S. Kimball & Co., and Duke's own factory in Durham, North Carolina, were given over to the production of BAT Co.'s export goods.[7] However, James Duke soon ensured that these American plants were supplemented by fresh acquisitions.

Shortly after his return to the United States, following the completion of the deal with Imperial, Duke sent a telegram to the BAT Co. board of directors in London intimating that he had come to an arrangement to purchase the Petersburg-based tobacco manufacturer T. C. Williams. The Williams organization had developed a substantial trade in plug tobacco with Australia and Duke was concerned that any delay in finalizing the deal would result in the company being sold to rival Australian manufacturers.[8] The proposed deal was ratified by the directors in London and the T. C. Williams Company was duly bought out by BAT Co., who then sold the domestic part of the business to the Continental Tobacco Company, Duke's American plug tobacco manufacturing subsidiary. Soon after this deal had been completed, Duke entered into an agreement with another tobacco manufacturing company located in Petersburg, David Dunlop. Like Williams, Dunlop had also developed a significant trade in plug tobacco with Australia before the turn of the century, and in 1903 this business was formally transferred to a newly regis-

5 According to Alford, work on the Ashton Gate factory had begun in 1897 on land purchased for the sum of £15,000. On completion, the buildings alone (independent of fittings, machinery, and plant) were estimated to have cost £67,000. This compares with Ogden's investment of between £40,000 and £50,000 for the factory in Liverpool. See Alford, *W. D. & H. O. Wills*, p. 234. See also *Tobacco (London)*, 20 (233) (1900), 203.

6 According to an account of BAT Co.'s operations in Liverpool, production at the Richmond Cavendish facilities and at Ogden's Cornwallis Street factory commenced only in 1907 and 1910 respectively. This same source indicates that the Ashton Gate factory was where BAT Co. had started in 1902. J. Jones, 'Cigarettes—Liverpool 5: the Story of the Liverpool Branch of British–American Tobacco Company Ltd', pp. 7–8.

7 US Bureau of Corporations, *Report of the Commissioner of Corporations on the Tobacco Industry* (Part I), US Department of Commerce and Labor, Government Printing Office, Washington (1909), p. 304; Cartophilic Society of Great Britain, *Tobacco War and BAT Co. Booklets* (Reference Booklets Nos. 18 and 21, originally issued 1951 and 1952) (1978), (Booklet 18) p. 6.

8 Telegram from J. B. Duke to BAT Co. London, dated 31 March 1903. Business papers of J. B. Duke (Box 5, No. 282), Special Collections Dept, Perkins Library, Duke University, hereinafter J. B. Duke Papers.

tered company, David Dunlop Inc., in which BAT Co. held 66.7 per cent of the capital stock.[9] Further production capacity was acquired in Petersburg, and in nearby Richmond,[10] when BAT Co. purchased the business of the Cameron group of companies in 1904, another tobacco manufacturing concern which had been active in the Australian market.[11]

During these early years, the export trade remained the most important aspect of the company's business. Even in some of those markets where BAT Co. had invested in local production facilities, for example in China and Australia, export sales continued to be of significance for some time. The first task which confronted the management of the new company, therefore, was the consolidation of its productive capacity in Britain and America. For the first ten years of its life, BAT Co. operated in this respect as two independent companies. Orders received for Imperial brands were processed by the company's factories in England, whilst those pertaining to the brands of ATC were dealt with in the United States. Tables 4.1–4.4 provide a breakdown by brand of the main locations for BAT Co.'s cigarette exports from its American plants during the company's first ten years in operation in order to illustrate the extensive nature of this trade.

To support its tobacco manufacturing activities, BAT Co. also made investments in leaf buying and handling facilities. Soon after the company's formation Duke seconded the manager of ATC's leaf-purchasing department, Peter Arrington, to BAT Co. in order to set up the Export Leaf Tobacco Co. in Danville, Virginia, to handle the group's purchase of raw leaf.[12] An interest in another American leaf-dealing firm, W. S. Mathews & Sons of Louisville, Kentucky, was acquired by BAT Co. in May 1903. This firm was engaged in the buying and preparation of dark leaf tobacco for sale principally in Mexico and the West Indies. Two further companies were incorporated into the Mathews operation, the Black Horse Tobacco Co.

[9] US Bureau of Corporations, *Report on the Tobacco Industry* (Part I), pp. 196 and 304. See also W. R. Erwin (ed.), The Papers of the British–American Tobacco Co., Ltd. Petersburg, Virginia. Unpublished mimeo. Special Collections Department, Perkins Library, Duke University, n.d., Part II, hereinafter referred to as BAT Co. Papers.

[10] The Richmond factory, operated by Cameron & Cameron, does not appear to have been incorporated into the BAT Co. organization and was probably transferred to the Liggett & Myers branch of the ATC. Erwin notes that the books of Cameron & Cameron were sent to the New York office of BAT Co. at the time of the acquisition in 1904, presumably as a prelude to the transfer, whilst Mullen illustrates that Cameron & Cameron's brands were marketed by Liggett & Myers at the Richmond factory. Erwin, 'The Camerons', BAT Co. Papers, Part V, p. 2; C. Mullen, *Cigarette Pack Art* (1979).

[11] On the origins of the Dunlop and Cameron firms, see J. C. Robert, *The Tobacco Kingdom: Plantation, Market, and Factory in Virginia and North Carolina, 1800–1860* (1938).

[12] *BAT Bulletin*, 3 (75) (1916), 354.

TABLE 4.1. BAT Co. US factories' cigarette shipments to Asia by brand, 1903–11

Brand	Burma	Ceylon	North China	South China	Korea	India	Java	Siam	Straits S'ments
Acorn		x	x	x		x	x	x	x
Akbah Shah		x				x			
Atlas			x						
Battle Ax			x					x	
Bramtoco				x		x		x	
Cameo	x		x						
Colonial						x			
Columbia			x			x			
Cross Cut			x					x	
Cycle	x		x	x	x	x	x	x	x
Cyclone			x					x	
Duke of Durham			x			x			
Eagle Bird				x				x	x
Egyptian Dieties #3				x					
Electric Light			x			x			
Especiales		x		x		x			x
Fragrant Vanity Fair			x						
Ghoorka						x			
Gold Fish			x						
Golden Light						x		x	
Gunga						x			
Gypsy Queen						x			
Harp			x						
Heart			x						
Imperiales			x	x					
La Marquise			x						

Lis Combatants				x					
Maritana			x						
Mogul			x	x					
Motor			x	x		x			
Old Gold						x			
Old Judge			x			x			
Old Rip			x	x					
Pall Mall			x						
Peacock			x						
Pedro			x			x			
Pin Head			x			x			
Railway	x		x			x			
Richmond Gem Mild	x								
Richmond Gem Medium	x	x	x	x		x			x
Richmond Straight Cut #1			x	x		x			
Sita						x			
Sweet Caporal	x		x	x		x			
Tiger			x			x			
Turkish Trophies	x		x	x				x	
Victoria						x			
Watch						x			
Wideawake						x			
Wild Duck						x			
Total cigarette brands	7	4	31	15	1	28	2	9	5

Source: BAT Co. Archive.

TABLE 4.2. BAT Co. US factories' cigarette shipments to main European markets by brand, 1903–11

Brand	Belgium	Denmark	Finland	France	Germany	Holland	Norway	Sweden	Switzerland
Bee Hive									x
Cameo	x	x				x	x	x	
Caporal Halves					x				x
Casino									x
Chancellor				x					x
Cross Cut V.M.P.						x			
Cyclone					x	x			x
Duke of Durham		x			x	x	x	x	
Especiales	x	x				x	x	x	x
Excelsior		x						x	
Excelsior #2		x							
Helmar									x
Kedive									x
King Bee	x								
Kinney Bros. Straight Cut		x							x
Lis Combatants				x		x			
Motor		x					x	x	
Murad									x
Old Gold		x	x						x
Old Judge			x		x				x
Old Judge Medium									x
Old Rip						x			
Old Virginny									x
Pall Mall									x
Pall Mall Kings									x
Picayune					x				

Ramses				x					
Richmond Gem Mild	x			x	x	x		x	x
Richmond Gem Medium	x	x	x	x		x			x
Richmond Straight Cut #1		x		x	x			x	x
St James		x			x				
St James Half and Half					x				
Sport		x			x				x
Sweet Caporal	x	x		x	x	x			x
Turkish Trophies									x
Virginia Beauties					x				
Total cigarette brands	6	13	3	7	12	10	4	7	22

Note: Small shipments also made to Austria–Hungary, Gibraltar, Greece, Portugal, Rumania, Russia, Spain, Turkey. Other shipments also made to Channel Islands and unspecified Mediterranean ports.

Source: BAT Co. Archive.

TABLE 4.3. BAT Co. US factories' cigarette shipments to Africa, Australasia, and North America by brand, 1903–11

Brand	Canada	Newfoundland	Australia	New Zealand	East Africa	South Africa	West Africa	Egypt
Abdullah	x	x						
Acorn	x	x	x	x				
Admiral			x					
Atlas				x				
Bairam	x							
Bramtoco					x			
Cairo	x							
Cameo		x	x	x	x	x		
Carlton Club	x		x					
Casino	x							
Cycle		x		x	x			
Duke of Durham					x			
Egyptian Dieties	x	x	x					
Egyptian Dieties #1	x		x					
Egyptian Dieties #3	x		x					
Egyptian Dieties After Dinnner	x		x					
Egyptian Dieties Ladies Gold	x							
Egyptian Dieties Ladies M.P.	x							
Egyptian Ibis			x					
Egyptian Ibis #3	x							
Egyptian Luxury	x							
Egyptian Straights	x		x					
Electric Light					x			
Especiales				x	x			
Fatima	x							
Fragrant Vanity Fair	x	x	x	x				
Full Dress					x			
Hassan	x							
Helmar	x		x					
Horse Guard	x							
Imperiales	x							

Japanese	x							
Kedive	x	x						
King Bee							x	
Kinney Bros. Straight Cut								x
La Marquise	x		x					
Ladies #4	x							
Lord Salisbury	x		x					
Mecca		x						
Mogul	x	x	x	x				
Mon Plaisir	x							
Murad	x	x	x	x				
Nadine	x	x						
Old Gold	x	x			x	x		
Old Judge			x	x		x		
Old Judge Medium			x	x				
Old Mill							x	
Pall Mall	x	x	x					
Pall Mall Kings	x	x	x					
Pedro		x						
Picadilly	x							
Piedmont	x							
Pin Head			x		x	x		
Princess Lillian	x							
Ramleh	x							
Richmond Gem Mild					x			
Richmond Gem Medium	x	x	x	x	x		x	
Richmond Straight Cut #1	x	x	x	x				x
Sweet Caporal	x	x	x	x	x			x
Turkish Trophies	x	x	x	x				
Turkey Red			x					
Two Seas			x					
Virginia Brights					x			
Total cigarette brands	40	19	27	14	13	4	3	3

Source: BAT Co. Archive.

TABLE 4.4. BAT Co. US factories' cigarette shipments to main markets in Latin America and the Caribbean by brand, 1903–11

Brand	Chile	Costa Rica	Guatemala	Honduras	British Honduras	Mexico	Nicaragua	Panama	Bermuda	West Indies	Jamaica
Acorn					x	x		x			x
American Beauty								x			
Bramtoco			x								
Cameo			x		x	x			x	x	
Colonial										x	
Corona		x									
Coupon		x	x	x			x	x			
Cycle	x		x					x	x	x	
Cyclone										x	
Duke of Durham						x					
Egyptian Dieties						x		x	x	x	
Egyptian Dieties #1						x				x	x
Egyptian Dieties #3						x				x	
Electric Light	x										
Especiales			x	x	x	x	x			x	x
Fatima					x	x		x		x	
Full Dress			x							x	
Golden Light										x	
Harp	x								x	x	x
Hassan				x				x	x	x	x
Helmar			x	x				x	x	x	
Home Run		x		x	x		x	x		x	
King Bee		x	x	x	x	x	x	x		x	
Kinney Bros. Straight Cut										x	
Ladies #4						x					
Latest English				x							
Minaret						x					

Mogul		x	x	x		x	x	x	x	x	x
Motor	x									x	
Murad		x	x	x		x		x	x	x	x
Old Gold								x		x	
Pall Mall						x		x	x	x	x
Picayune				x	x			x			
Piedmont								x			
Pin Head	x	x	x		x		x			x	
Railway	x										
Ramleh								x			
Richmond Gem Medium						x		x			
Richmond Straight Cut #1				x		x				x	x
Sultana						x					
Sweet Caporal				x		x	x	x	x	x	
Talisman		x									
Tolstoy #1						x					
Tolstoy #2						x					
Turkish Trophies		x	x	x	x	x	x	x	x	x	x
Turkey Red			x				x				
Virginia Brights			x								
Virginia Extras				x			x	x			
Volga						x					
Total cigarette brands	6	9	14	14	9	22	10	21	11	26	10

Note: Small shipments also made to Argentina, Bahama Islands, Brazil, Colombia, Cuba, Danish West Indies, Dutch Guiana, Haiti, Peru, Venezuela.

Source: BAT Co. Archive.

which operated a factory in Monterey, Mexico, and the West Indian Tobacco Co. which was active in Trinidad.[13]

Creating a Management Team

BAT Co. effectively began its operational life on 6 October 1902, when the first board of directors was appointed. It had been agreed at the outset that the joint venture should have its headquarters in London, rather than in New York, most probably to minimize the threat from the American anti-trust authorities,[14] and for a few weeks Duke personally supervised arrangements from the company's first registered office at 53 Holborn Viaduct. These offices had previously housed ATC's London depot, but the increased size of the new organization meant that they would no longer be adequate and the company sought out more spacious and prestigious accommodation. A suitable site was quickly located at Cecil Chambers, 86 Strand, and these premises became the company's new registered headquarters on 22 October 1902. Shortly after this change, Duke handed over temporary control of BAT Co.'s operations in London to his deputy William R. Harris and returned to New York.[15]

The composition of BAT Co.'s founding directors, shown in Table 4.5, was designed to reflect the 2:1 distribution of power within the organization as a whole. Eighteen directors were appointed, twelve of whom were members either of ATC or Ogden, and the remaining six of whom were connected with Imperial. In New York, a committee of directors was formed to manage the company's affairs in America which comprised of Duke, John B. Cobb, Percival S. Hill, Caleb C. Dula, and Harold Roberts. Two remaining ATC officers featured among the founding directors; Harris, who joined the New York committee following his return from London, and William W.

[13] BAT Co. Corporate Index, BAT Co. Southampton Archive, Box 114. As well as dealing in dark leaf tobacco, the West Indian Tobacco Co. also manufactured cigarettes using imported American leaf. This company had originally been set up in 1896 by John Phillips, and was reincorporated on 21 September 1904 as a three-way joint venture between BAT Co., Phillips, and W. S. Mathews & Sons. West Indian Tobacco Co., Ltd., 'West Indian Tobacco Company Limited, 1904–1964', BAT Co. Southampton Archive, Box 86, p. 2.

[14] Corina makes the point that the decision to register BAT Co.'s headquarters in London provided a point of satisfaction for the Wills family, to be set against the concession of two-thirds of the share capital being allocated to ATC. M. Corina, *Trust in Tobacco: the Anglo-American Struggle for Power* (1975), p. 103. Duke no doubt felt able to control the operation despite spending the majority of his time in New York. As a British-registered company, moreover, operating in the markets of the British Empire was likely be much more straightforward.

[15] *Tobacco (London)*, 22 (264) (1902), 583.

Fuller, ATC's legal counsel. In London, meanwhile, two vice-chairmen were appointed from the British-based directors to take charge of the UK operation. These were Harry Wills, whose branch of Imperial had provided the company's main factory in Bristol, and William B. Ogden, the senior director of the Ogden company, preserving the Imperial–Ogden balance in London. A pivotal figure in this founding group of directors was BAT Co.'s first company secretary—Harry Wills' brother-in-law and assistant at Wills—Hugo Cunliffe-Owen, whom Duke seems to have earmarked at an early stage as a suitable candidate for leadership within the fledgling company. One other figure who was to feature prominently in the organization's early history was Ogden's solicitor Joseph Hood who joined the board in place of Harold Roberts, the manager of ATC's export department, during the company's first year in operation. With the appointment of Hood the three founding companies of BAT Co.—ATC, Imperial, and Ogden—each had six representatives on the company's board of directors.

The creation of the new company as a combination of previously independent elements was virtually certain to induce tensions at managerial level, particularly given the circumstances of enduring hostility that had characterized the tobacco war. In particular, the relations between Wills' and Ogden's

TABLE 4.5. The eighteen founder directors of BAT Co.

Name	Original affiliation	Exit date
Duke, J. B.	ATC	July 1923
Wills, Sir W. H. Bt.	Imperial	June 1911
Cobb, J. B.	ATC	January 1909
Harris, W. R.	ATC	January 1913
Lambert, C. E.	Imperial	May 1910
Fuller, W. W.	ATC	June 1906
Wills, H. H.	Imperial	August 1904
Ogden, W. B.	Ogden	June 1906
Player, W. G.	Imperial	August 1904
Ogden, T.	Ogden	June 1906
Cunliffe-Owen, H. v. R.	Imperial	February 1945
Hill, P. S.	ATC	January 1912
Gracey, T.	Imperial	January 1918
Dula, C. C.	ATC	June 1905
Walters, R. H.	Ogden	August 1916
Walters, P. R.	Ogden	June 1905
Ogden, P.	Ogden	July 1917
Roberts, H.	ATC	March 1903

Source: BAT Co. Annual Report 1902; Notices of Change of Directors.

representatives on the BAT Co. board were already strained as a result of the earlier failed negotiations between the two firms, and could not have been improved when the very high debts incurred by the Liverpool-based organization became apparent after this business was sold to Imperial. In return for the transfer of the Ogden business ATC had received 14 per cent of Imperial's total shareholding, making Duke's firm the largest single shareholder in the company after the Wills family itself, and yet after inspecting the Liverpool firm's books Imperial discovered that between December 1901 and September 1902 the company had run up losses of £376,000 on total sales of only £1,850,000. Not only was Imperial saddled with these costs, which had been generated in the assault against its own business, but the cancellation of the American-inspired Ogden bonus scheme led a group of 4,670 participating traders to initiate legal proceedings against Imperial, the new owners of Ogden, in an effort to claim money which they argued was due to them. This set in motion a train of legal actions that became known collectively as the 'Ogden Litigation' and which continued through the courts (and was even debated in the House of Lords) until September 1906 when terms of settlement were agreed.[16]

The tensions between the Imperial and Ogden factions in London were compounded by the deep gulf which existed between Imperial's (particularly Wills' and Player's) paternalistic management philosophy, on the one hand, and the far more competitive approach which had been the hallmark of Duke's business regime, on the other. To a certain extent, the problem of conflicting corporate cultures between the British and American sides of the company could be managed through the simple expedient of partitioning, allowing the two sides of the organization to manage their own business affairs with relative autonomy. Such an approach could not be applied in dealing with all BAT Co.'s problems, however, since certain critical decisions, which affected the method of operation of the company as a whole, needed to be treated consistently across the organization. In these matters, where Duke and his American colleagues held the strongest hand, conflict could not easily be avoided.

Soon after Duke's return to New York, Imperial's elder statesman and founding director of BAT Co., Sir William Henry Wills, sent the American

[16] Corina, *Trust in Tobacco*, pp. 103–4. The fact that all of these costs had been generated by Duke and the management of Ogden's, but were ultimately borne by Imperial, seems certain to have damaged the prospects of a harmonious accord between the two sides of BAT Co.'s London management. It also helps to explain why Imperial's directors attempted to use Duke's absence from the company's AGM to (unsuccessfully) eject him from their board. Letter from J. B. Duke to the directors of the Imperial Tobacco Co., dated 6 March 1903 (Box 5, No. 280), J. B. Duke Papers.

tycoon a drawing of himself made by 'Spy' the well-known political cartoonist of the English magazine *Vanity Fair*. Duke appreciated the gesture of conciliation and wrote by hand to Sir William offering his thanks.[17] The cordial nature of this exchange, however, contrasted sharply with Duke's attitude towards the more volatile Harry Wills, one of BAT Co.'s two London-based vice-chairman. The two clashed in October 1903 over the question of patent control relating to machinery used to manufacture Russian-type mouthpiece cigarettes in Japan. Harry Wills questioned the rationale of the company incurring a great deal of expense in order to gain the rights to use these machines if ATC's Japanese subsidiary, the Murai Brothers Tobacco Co., was to be given exclusive control of them. Duke was clearly irritated by Wills' letter, feeling that the matter had been dealt with perfectly adequately by Harris and Cunliffe-Owen in New York and that the appropriate information had been relayed to the directors in London.[18] Quite possibly Harry Wills had been further aggrieved by Duke's decision to bring BAT Co.'s secretary, Cunliffe-Owen, to America at this time, since Owen had previously acted as Harry Wills' own personal assistant.

In any case, matters came to a head early in 1904. On 16 March, Harry Wills wrote to Duke setting out the circumstances of a BAT Co. employee, a Mr Schwalm, whose failing health necessitated his retirement from business.[19] Harry Wills proposed that BAT Co. should pay a pension to Schwalm in view of the services that he had rendered the company. Duke was not prepared to be at all sympathetic to this request. In his reply to the BAT Co. vice-chairman, he made the following points:

> while I would prefer to agree with you in judgement about any matter, I cannot see any obligation resting on BAT Co. to pension [Mr Schwalm]. It is true that I am not familiar with a pension system, because it has never been adopted in any of the companies with which I have been associated, nor in others of which I have known . . . It strikes me that it is scarcely to be expected that BAT Co. should begin a pension list when it is scarcely more than a year old . . . Our expectation is that our employees will, from their salaries, make savings sufficient to take care of them when they become old or disabled. At any rate, in as much as there is not a single person carried on the pay-rolls of any of our American companies who is not actively engaged in the service of that company, I do not see how I could

[17] Letter J. B. Duke to W. H. Wills, dated 7 January 1903 (Box 5, No. 277), J. B. Duke Papers.

[18] Letter J. B. Duke to H. H. Wills, dated 30 October 1903 (Box 5, No. 316), J. B. Duke Papers.

[19] Schwalm had been transferred to BAT Co. from Wills. He was taken back on to the Imperial staff after the request for a pension had been turned down by Duke. *BAT Bulletin*, 17 (73) (1926), 18.

favour the inauguration of a pension system in the B-A, especially in its infancy . . . I know you wanted me to write you frankly my views on the subject, and I have therefore done so.[20]

The response could hardly have demonstrated a greater division in the philosophies of the two businessmen. For Harry Wills, brought up in a tradition where employees' welfare was a central concern of business, Duke's rejection of his appeal seems to have represented the final straw.

On 14 May, Harry Wills wrote to Duke informing him of his desire to retire from business life and thus of his decision to tender his resignation as a director of BAT Co. a mere eighteen months after having assumed the position of vice-chairman. Wills' counterpart in London, William Ogden, also wrote to Duke expressing his deep regret at the ex-Imperial man's decision but Duke, in his reply to Harry Wills, made no effort to induce a change of mind. Rather, Duke's concern lay with Wills' proposal that his successor at Cecil Chambers should be Lawrence Hignett, a man with whom the BAT Co. chairman was not at all familiar.[21] Thus on 6 August, whilst still only in his late 40s, Harry Wills formally resigned from the board of BAT Co. The man who had contributed so much to the phenomenal success of the Wills company through, among other things, his development of the 'Woodbine' cigarette brand, now turned his back on business life and devoted his time to shooting, walking, and charitable activities.[22] Only under the changed circumstances engendered by the First World War was he persuaded to return to management, by which time his failing health made the period of office a brief one.

Harry Wills' retirement from the board of BAT Co. was coupled with that of another Imperial stalwart, William G. Player, who stood down on the same day. The double loss was a blow to the status of the London office, and the pair were replaced as directors by two members of the smaller branches of Imperial, Arthur C. Churchman of the firm of W. A. & A. C. Churchman of Ipswich, and, in deference to Harry Wills' request, Lawrence Hignett of Hignett, Bros. & Co. whose Liverpool-based export business, the Richmond Cavendish Co., had been transferred into the control of BAT Co. Harry Wills' position as vice-chairman, however, remained vacant. William Ogden's suggestion that the post should be offered to Cunliffe-Owen was

[20] Letter J. B. Duke to H. H. Wills, dated 29 March 1904 (Box 5, No. 331), J. B. Duke Papers.

[21] Letter J. B. Duke to H. H. Wills, dated 26 May 1904 (Box 5, No. 346), J. B. Duke Papers.

[22] Alford, *W. D. & H. O. Wills*, p. 329. According to Alford, Harry Wills had first announced his intention of retiring in 1900. Idem., pp. 275–6.

endorsed with alacrity by James Duke who wrote to Ogden, 'I entirely agree with you about the propriety of the election of Mr Cunliffe-Owen to succeed Mr H. H. Wills as Deputy Chairman, and also the proposed increase in his salary.'[23] However, the idea seems to have been scotched by Harry Wills, who felt that the post should be offered to Sir William H. Wills or, in the event of his declining the position, to Charles Lambert (of the Lambert & Butler branch of Imperial). Only in the event that both of these directors turned down the office was Harry Wills prepared to consent to the post being offered to Cunliffe-Owen. When William Ogden put Harry Wills' proposal to Duke it was grudgingly accepted, and in December 1904 Sir William H. Wills, the chairman of Imperial, was duly elected to join William Ogden as BAT Co.'s joint vice-chairman in London.[24]

These changes of key personnel in London were soon mirrored by changes of an even greater magnitude originating from New York. In June 1905, two new, young American directors were appointed. George Garland Allen, whose position as director in the American side of the organization was to become a central feature of BAT Co.'s management structure, was promoted from ATC's export department to replace Caleb C. Dula.[25] At the same time, an ex-employee of Liggett's, Albert G. Jeffress, became the first American director to serve at BAT Co.'s London office when, at the age of 30, he was appointed to replace Ogden's Percy Walters.[26]

Duke, meanwhile, continued to travel back and forth between London and New York as he attempted to push ahead with BAT Co.'s international business. It was while Duke was based in London, in January 1905, that news reached him of a sudden deterioration in his father's health. He immediately returned to the family home in Durham where, after rallying briefly, Washington Duke passed away on 8 May 1905.[27] Duke's deep regard for his father made his death a devastating blow for the American tycoon. Moreover, its impact on his state of mind was considerably worsened by a breakdown of the turbulent marriage into which he had entered the previous November, largely at the behest of his father. With the divorce proceedings scheduled to commence in September 1905, and with the popular press poised to generate the maximum

[23] Letter J. B. Duke to W. B. Ogden, dated 20 June 1904 (Box 5, No. 361), J. B. Duke Papers.

[24] Letter J. B. Duke to W. B. Ogden, dated 5 July 1904 (Box 5, No. 364), J. B. Duke Papers.

[25] J. K. Winkler, *Tobacco Tycoon: the Story of James Buchanan Duke* (1942), pp. 137–9.

[26] Walters seems to have moved in the opposite direction, becoming a director of BAT Co.'s Canadian subsidiary.

[27] R. F. Durden, *The Dukes of Durham, 1865–1929* (1975), p. 162.

possible coverage of the affair, Duke decided to stand down as chairman of BAT Co., passing over the role to W. R. Harris in August of that year.

In addition to the distractions from the tobacco business generated by the divorce proceedings, other business concerns began to intrude on Duke's time. In June 1905, Duke and his family launched the Southern Power Co., the first of a number of schemes designed to generate electricity for North Carolina. In subsequent years, the Dukes began to step up their investments in textile mills and other industries which used hydroelectric power.[28] With ATC beginning to attract strong criticism in America for its reputed exploitation of local tobacco farmers,[29] the opportunity to promote initiatives which supported the economic development of the region was one that greatly appealed to Duke. For a number of years, therefore, his involvement in tobacco-related affairs waned.

Thus the appointment of Allen and Jeffress, in the few weeks before his decision to stand down, can be seen as an important step taken by Duke to delegate his own authority within BAT Co. to a new generation of managers. The most significant development from this point of view, however, was Duke's success in promoting Cunliffe-Owen into a position of authority within the organization. With Harry Wills formally retired, Sir William H. Wills was persuaded to stand down as vice-chairman and on 10 August 1905, exactly one week after Duke relinquished his position as chairman, Hugo Cunliffe-Owen officially joined William Ogden as the new BAT Co. vice-chairman. When, six months later, William Ogden himself died whilst on a visit to Ceylon (Sri Lanka), Cunliffe-Owen found himself in the position of BAT Co.'s second in command.[30]

Initial Operations Abroad

By 1906, as BAT Co.'s new chairman and deputy assumed control, the bulk of the company's foreign investments were located in three political/geographical regions: the British Dominions, western Europe, and the

[28] Durden, *Dukes of Durham*, pp. 183–6.

[29] J. C. Robert, *The Story of Tobacco in America* (1949), pp. 154–60.

[30] Cunliffe-Owen's position as BAT Co.'s Secretary was taken by an American, Charles T. Hill, who moved to the London headquarters to join up with his compatriot Albert Jeffress. William Ogden's place on the board of directors was also taken by an American, Samuel J. Gillchrest, who had earlier managed ATC's London depot. Following William Ogden's death, however, no further vice-chairmen were appointed until 1909. For an obituary of William Ogden, see *Tobacco (London)*, 26 (303) (1906), 131.

potentially huge markets formed by the Chinese and British Indian empires. Outside of these areas operations had been acquired since 1902 in Mexico, Trinidad, and Jamaica as an outcome of the purchase of the three American-based export firms—T. C. Williams, David Dunlop, and the Camerons—and in addition two companies had been purchased in Cairo which were involved in the export of Turkish cigarettes to India and continental Europe. Set against these acquisitions was the loss through nationalization of the Murai Brothers subsidiary in Japan. A complete list of foreign operating companies controlled by BAT Co. as at 30 September 1906 is provided in Table 4.6.

The British Dominions

Investments in the white settler economies of the British Empire had for the most part been initiated prior to the formation of BAT Co. In each of these markets, BAT Co.'s strategy involved the incorporation of local firms into a jointly owned subsidiary enterprise which was then granted a good deal of operational autonomy. Thus in Canada, BAT Co.'s main operating subsidiary, the American Tobacco Co. of Canada (ATCC), had been set up by Duke's American organization in Montreal in September 1895, as a joint enterprise with the local firm D. Ritchie & Co. The key personnel in the Ritchie organization were the Davis family, three of whom were appointed as directors of the newly formed venture, including the president of the company, Mortimer B. Davis.[31] In 1898 ATCC acquired part of the share capital of the Empire Tobacco Co. of Quebec and in 1903 it took control of a second Quebec-based firm, B. Houde Co.

The main development in Canada, however, occurred in 1908 when a new subsidiary company called the Imperial Tobacco Co. of Canada was incorporated in Ottawa at the much higher capital value of $11 million.[32] In addition to producing its own brands of tobacco and cigarettes, the Imperial concern

[31] In fact, ATCC was a joint venture more in the managerial sense than in terms of ownership, since American interests controlled 99.75 per cent of the share capital. S. Mercier, 'A Brief History of Tobacco In Canada', unpublished typescript (111 pp.), n.d., BAT Co. Southampton Archive, Box 42, see p. 19. Mortimer Davis was knighted in 1917.

[32] This $11 million in shares was divided into 60,000 ordinary shares of $100 each ($5.4 million of which were taken up by BAT Co.) and 1 million preference shares of $5 each. Of the preference shares 821,918 were offered for public subscription converted into 1,027,397 sterling-denominated shares of £1 each. In April 1912, a new company of the same name was incorporated in Ottawa with an increased share capital of 6 million ordinary shares of $5 each ($27 million owned by BAT Co.) and 1,999,995 preference shares of £1 each. No changes occurred in the management of the organization as a result of this restructuring. Mercier, 'Tobacco in Canada', pp. 33–9.

TABLE 4.6. BAT Co. operating subsidiaries outside the UK and USA, 30 Sept. 1906

Name & location	Character of business	Capital value ($US)	BAT Co. share (%)
The American Tobacco Co., of Canada (Ltd.), Montreal.	Cigarettes and smoking	1,000,000	89.7
The Empire Tobacco Co. (Ltd.), Granby, Quebec.	Plug and smoking	600,000	56.0[a]
The B. Houde Co. (Ltd.), Quebec, Canada.	Cigarettes, smoking and snuff	500,000	73.0[a]
British Tobacco Co. (Australia) Ltd., Sydney.	Holding company	16,912,562	44.5[b]
The American Tobacco Co., of Australasia (Ltd.), Sydney.	Cigarettes and smoking	1,338,287	100.0[c]
The British Australasian Tobacco Co. Prop. (Ltd.) Melbourne.	Plug and smoking	4,963,611	100.0[c]
Kronheimer (Ltd.), Sydney.	Selling company	2,490,723	56.9[c]
States Tobacco Co. (Ltd.) Melbourne.	Cigars	437,985	100.0[c]
W. D. & H. O. Wills (Australia) Ltd., Sydney.	Plug and smoking	486,650	100.0[c]
The British Empire Trading Co. (Ltd.), Wellington, New Zealand.	Selling company	583,980	75.0
The United Tobacco Companies (Ltd.), Cape Town, South Africa.	Holding company	3,893,200	65.6
United Tobacco Co. (North), Ltd., Johannesburg.	Cigarettes and smoking	656,977	100.0[d]
United Tobacco Co. (South), Ltd., Cape Town.	Cigarettes and smoking	1,338,287	100.0[d]
British–American Tobacco Co. (India), Ltd., Calcutta, India.	Selling company	194,660	100.0
Peninsular Tobacco Co. (Ltd.), Karachi, India.	Cigarettes	48,665	100.0
The Empire Bioscope Co. (Ltd.), India.	Advertising	2,433	100.0
British–American Tobacco Co. (Ceylon), Ltd., Colombo.	Selling company	36,498	100.0
British Cigarette Co. (Ltd.), Shanghai, China.	Cigarettes	2,490,000	97.1
Mustard & Co., Shanghai, China.	Selling company	575,000	81.3
Maspero Frères (Ltd.), Cairo, Egypt.	Cigarettes	145,995	100.0
African Cigarette Co. (Ltd.) Cairo.	Cigarettes	97,330	100.0[e]
The American Tobacco Co. of Denmark, Copenhagen.	Selling company	26,800	100.0
British–American Tobacco Co. (Norway), Ltd., Christiania.	Cigarettes	9,733	100.0

TABLE 4.6. (*cont.*)

Name & location	Character of business	Capital value ($US)	BAT Co. share (%)
Nya Aktiebolaget Cigarett-fabriken, Stockholm, Sweden.	Cigarettes and smoking	536,000	95.0
Emil Boussard (Ltd.), Belgium.	Cigarettes	97,330	100.0
Georg A. Jasmatzi, Akt. Ges., Dresden, Germany.	Cigarettes and tobacco	1,190,000	80.0
Cigarettennfabrik Josetti, Berlin.	Cigarettes and smoking	113,050	98.0[f]
Jamaica Tobacco Co., Kingston, Jamaica.	Cigarettes and cigars	200,000	51.0
Black Horse Tobacco Co., Monterrey, Mexico.	Manufacturer of black leaf tobacco	200,000	94.0[g]
West Indian Tobacco Co., Trinidad.	Manufacturers of black leaf tobacco	40,000	75.0[h]

Notes:
[a] Owned by the American Tobacco Co. of Canada.
[b] Includes shares held by T.C. Williams Co.
[c] Held through the British Tobacco Company (Australia), Ltd.
[d] Held through the United Tobacco Companies Ltd.
[e] Entire capital stock held by Maspero Frères.
[f] All but $238 of stock held by G. A. Jasmatzi, Akt. Ges.
[g] Held by W. S. Mathews & Sons, Louisville, Kentucky.
[h] Includes $24,000 of stock held by W.S. Mathews & Sons.
Source: US Bureau of Corporations, *Report on the Tobacco Industry*, Table 34.

acquired an agency for sale in Canada of certain brands of the British-based Imperial Tobacco Company.[33] The fifteen directors of the new concern included eight BAT Co. directors, with Hugo Cunliffe-Owen as vice-president and Percy Walters as BAT Co.'s director in residence. However, the management team were effectively local tobacco people, under the presidency of Mortimer Davis, with David C. Patterson, a close associate of James Duke, as treasurer and auditor. Naturally, this huge enterprise dominated the Canadian tobacco industry and over time it began to procure a greater proportion of its raw material requirements (notably tobacco leaf) from domestic Canadian producers.

The market which had absorbed the most investment from BAT Co. by 1906 was Australia. Here, the events of the tobacco war in Britain were par-

[33] In 1909 Imperial launched Player's Navy Cut on the Canadian market with great success. Mercier, 'Tobacco in Canada', p. 36. BAT Co.'s own records indicate that it was not until 1921 that BAT Co. assigned to the Canadian Imperial company all the goodwill and trade marks that it had acquired in 1902, in exchange for some 400,000 ordinary shares. BAT Co. Corporate Index, BAT Co. Southampton Archive, Box 114.

ticularly dramatic because by 1901 ATC, Imperial (through Wills), and Ogden had all made significant investments there. In addition, a number of other American firms, such as the Cameron group of companies, T. C. Williams, and David Dunlop, had made substantial progress in the Australian tobacco market. One of Duke's first acts following the formation of BAT Co., therefore, had been to acquire control of the US-based plants of these American firms before rival Australian manufacturers were able to do so. By 1904, the various competing groups in the Australian tobacco industry had arranged to pool their operations into a single holding company.

The holding company used to effect this merger was the British Tobacco Co. (Australia) Ltd., which was registered in England on 8 April 1904 with an authorized share capital of £4.2 million.[34] Into this company were transferred the assets of the five operating companies listed in Table 4.6: (i) the American Tobacco Co. of Australasia which represented an amalgamation of Duke's ATC interests dating from 1894; (ii) W. D. & H. O. Wills (Australia) which comprised the manufacturing company set up by Wills in 1901 in collaboration with their Australian agents Heyde, Todman & Co.; (iii) the British Australasian Tobacco Co. (Ltd.) which had been created in 1903 through a merger of two large domestic cigarette manufacturers, the Dixson Tobacco Co. and Wm. Cameron Bros. & Co. (part of the American-owned Cameron group); (iv) the States Tobacco Co., which had been formed as a cigar manufacturing enterprise by the local firms of Dixson and Jacobs, Hart & Co. in 1902; and (v) 56.9 per cent of the shares of Kronheimer Limited, a group of tobacco merchants which had been formed earlier in 1904 and which operated as the sole importer of British and American tobacco products. BAT Co. held a substantial minority interest in this holding company, and was represented on the board of directors by Hugo Cunliffe-Owen and William B. Ogden.[35] The first chairman of the British Tobacco Company (Australia) was Mr W. E. Shaw, and Mr A. J. Warry seems to have acted as BAT Co.'s local representative on the board.[36] In New Zealand, meanwhile, where ATC had been forced to close its factory before 1902, BAT Co. held the controlling interest in a distribution company, the British Empire Trading Co.[37]

[34] 'British Tobacco Company (Australia) Limited History', unpublished typescript, 1970, BAT Co. Southampton Archive, Box 51, p. 5. The authorized capital of this company was therefore over two-thirds that of BAT Co. itself.

[35] R. Walker, *Under Fire: a History of Tobacco Smoking in Australia* (1984), pp. 45–7.

[36] A. J. Warry had earlier acted as the Australian-based director of W. D. & H. O. Wills (Australia) Ltd., Alford, *W. D. & H. O. Wills*, p. 220.

[37] According to an in-house account of its export business, the New Zealand government's policy of discouraging local manufacture in order to secure its customs revenue from tobacco necessitated the closure of ATC's factory in that country. American Tobacco Co., 'A few facts', p. 4.

The third of these Dominion markets, South Africa, had been one of the early successes for British firms such as Wills and Player as they sought overseas outlets for their manufactured tobacco products. Indeed, by 1894 Wills had granted a licence to the South African firm of Holt & Holt to manufacture certain of its brands directly. Whilst this latter move was prompted mainly by a desire to protect its trade marks from imitators, the development of local production facilities through licensing also acted to strengthen Wills' hand against American competition. During the early 1890s ATC had set up its own depot in Cape Town, under the management of Alfred I. Hart,[38] and the American firm also granted Holt & Holt a licence to manufacture its cigarette brands. However, around the turn of the century Wills' position in South Africa relative to ATC was significantly boosted by the outbreak of the Boer War. American merchant shipping was discriminated against in favour of British transports containing military supplies, including English cigarettes and tobacco for the troops. Moreover, the military authorities placed controls on the movement of goods within the region, making it much more difficult to supply the market with American cigarettes from Holt & Holt's factory in Johannesburg. Between 1899 and 1902, therefore, British military involvement in South Africa enabled Wills and Player to gain an improved market position against their American rivals.[39]

With the formation of BAT Co. in 1902 ownership of ATC's Cape Town depot, together with the licensing arrangements entered into with the Holt & Holt company by ATC and Wills, became the property of the new organization. In 1903 BAT Co. consolidated its South African assets when it established a new holding company, the British Tobacco Company (South Africa) Ltd. Soon after, BAT Co. and the Holt family agreed to amalgamate their interests in the region, and another company was formed in England on 22 July 1904 called the United Tobacco Companies Ltd. (UTC), with a capital value of £800,000, which defined its market territory as being 'that portion of the mainland which lies below the tenth degree of South latitude'.[40] BAT Co. took control of two-thirds of the issued capital of this company and appointed six of the nine founding directors. The remaining three directors, Hillier,

[38] Hart was interviewed in 1893 by the trade press whilst serving as ATC's South African representative. *Tobacco (London)*, 13 (152) (1893), 90.

[39] American Tobacco Co., 'A few facts', p. 4. Player took the opportunity to consolidate its position by dispatching complimentary supplies of their 'Drumhead' cigarettes to the troops fighting in South Africa as a Christmas present. See E. G. C. Beckwith, 'A History of John Player & Sons, 1877–1939'. Unpublished typescript (1949), 18 pp., John Player & Sons Archive, Nottingham Record Office, File No. DD Pl 7/5/1.

[40] BAT Co. Corporate Index, BAT Co. Southampton Archive, Box 114.

Albert, and David Holt, formed the management team, with a Mr G. W. Hawley acting as BAT Co.'s local representative.[41] The following year BAT Co. sent its director Thomas Gracey to South Africa to oversee the setting up of two wholly owned, locally registered operating subsidiaries, UTC (South) based in Cape Town and UTC (North) with headquarters in Johannesburg.[42] Almost immediately the UTC organization began purchasing raw leaf from growers in Southern Rhodesia (modern-day Zimbabwe) although it was not until 1918 that this arrangement was put on a formal, contractual basis.[43]

The willingness of BAT Co.'s leading competitors in Australia, Canada, and South Africa to collaborate with the new Anglo-American giant concern was not always matched by the attitude of other elements in the trade. In both Australia (1906) and Canada (1902) Royal Commissions were established in response to complaints that the tobacco industry had become the victim of monopolistic control.[44] However, in neither case was punitive action taken against the subsidiary firm in question, and subsequently these three Dominions of the British Empire emerged as the principal bedrock of BAT Co.'s international cigarette business, their inherent stability being enhanced by the fact that they operated effectively as national firms under local management control. In other regions of the world, BAT Co.'s early subsidiaries found the local environment much more threatening.

Initiatives in Asia

Prior to the formation of BAT Co. the cigarette business in Asia had been developed principally on the basis of an export trade. The major exception to this rule had occurred in Japan when in 1899 the Meiji government had imposed a tariff on imported cigarettes of 100 per cent. This decision had persuaded ATC to adopt a strategy of foreign direct investment in Japan via its acquisition of a majority shareholding in the Kyoto-based Murai Brothers tobacco firm. As this operation began to expand its production capacity, the Murai Brothers' director appointed by ATC, E. J. Parrish, began to develop an export trade in its cigarettes to Shanghai, Hong Kong, and the British

[41] *Tobacco (London)*, 24 (287) (1904), 514. Wills' domination of the South African market is reflected in the fact that none of the six BAT Co. directors appointed were Americans: H. H. Wills, W. B. Ogden, H. Cunliffe-Owen, T. Gracey, J. Hood, and L. Hignett.

[42] *Tobacco (London)*, 28 (336) (1908), 58. UTC (South) was set up under the laws of the Cape colony, with its headquarters and a newly built factory at 32 Kloof Street, Cape Town. UTC (North) was set up in Pretoria under the laws of the Transvaal, taking over Holt's Acme Tobacco factory in Johannesburg and in 1906 opening a pipe tobacco factory in Rustenburg. 'History of UTICO Holdings Limited and its Associated Companies', BAT Co. Southampton Archive, Box 90.

[43] *Tobacco International*, 187 (1985), 58.

[44] Mercier, 'Tobacco in Canada', pp. 22–6; Walker, *Under Fire*, p. 46.

Indian empire (an area which, from an American perspective, embraced the Straits Settlements as well as India, Burma, and Ceylon). Encouraged by the expansion of the cigarette market in Asia, Duke had appointed ATC's own representatives to oversee sales in Shanghai, Hong Kong, Singapore, and Calcutta. In contrast to Wills and other purely export-based firms, which used local agencies to distribute their products and which treated each market as an independent entity, ATC had begun to view south and east Asia as a regional market which could be developed from production facilities located in both the United States and Japan.

Thus before the creation of BAT Co. in 1902, Duke had allowed Parrish a good deal of leeway in developing ATC's operations in Japan, although Parrish himself had always maintained close communication with William Harris in New York. Upon the formation of BAT Co., however, Parrish was instructed to advise the new London headquarters of all matters pertaining to the manufacturing business in Japan. In the other Asian markets, directors of BAT Co. soon began to take a far more direct interest in the development of business strategies, arranging visits in order to gauge progress and advise on policy. For example, within six weeks of the formation of the alliance, and the consequent cessation of competition between the American and British manufacturers in Asian markets, the management of BAT Co. in London telegraphed Parrish to inform him of a rise in prices of the company's products in China, India, and Singapore, including brands of cigarettes that Murai were exporting there.[45] Parrish himself clearly believed this strategy to be in error, since he argued that other Japanese firms would be able to export their products to these markets at significantly lower prices.[46] Parrish was also concerned that, if Murai's export trade was undermined by BAT establishing local manufacturing plants in China and elsewhere, a major bulwark against full nationalization of the tobacco industry in Japan would be lost. However, his views seem to have made little impression in London.

In Calcutta, control over BAT Co.'s affairs soon became consolidated under the British side of the organization when the ex-Ogden director Percy Walters was given initial responsibility for the Indian market.[47] The management in London had followed up the imposition of price increases on imports to India by stipulating that the Indian trade should be focused on three lines: ATC's 'Pedro' brand, Murai's 'Top' cigarettes, and Wills' established brand

[45] Letter E. J. Parrish to BAT Co., London, dated 27 November 1902, papers of E. J. Parrish, Special Collections Department, Perkins Library, Duke University, hereinafter Parrish Papers.

[46] Letter E. J. Parrish to BAT Co., London, dated 30 December 1902, Parrish Papers.

[47] Notes from letter by R. G. Baker dated 30 September 1957, BAT Co. Southampton Archive, Box 188.

of 'Scissors'.[48] This move was coupled with the decision to retain the Liverpool-based merchant house Atherton & Co. as the company's main agent for the Indian market, and this firm continued to utilize the Bukhsh Ellahie enterprise as its Indian distributor. The impact of this seems to have worked to the advantage of the Wills brand, since the Atherton agency had been dropped by both ATC and Murai shortly before the outbreak of the tobacco war in Britain, and thus their brands were no longer being distributed to Bukhsh Ellahie's clients.[49]

For a brief period, around 1903–4, James Thomas took up the managerial reins for BAT in Calcutta, where he had earlier worked for ATC.[50] This may have been an attempt by Duke to reassert American influence in India but, if so, the effort failed because Thomas contracted malaria and was forced to pass over control to Atherton's local manager Nicholas Jellico. Following this disruption, in 1905 two of BAT Co.'s London directors, William B. Ogden and Lawrence Hignett, travelled to Calcutta in order to reorganize the operations in India from a branch to a subsidiary company. Jellico was appointed as the local managing director with Percy Walters in charge of the India office of BAT Co. in London which supervised the affairs of this new subsidiary. At the time of Duke's resignation as chairman in 1905, therefore, BAT Co.'s Indian operation was effectively under the control of British personnel.

In China, by contrast, Americans dominated the management of BAT's operations. Prior to 1902, the distribution arrangements of Wills and ATC in Shanghai had been vested in different agents, with the American firm having utilized the services of Mustard & Co., under the supervision of ATC's local representative C. E. Fiske, and the British firm having engaged Rex & Co. for the same purpose. To begin with, these arrangements were continued, and BAT Co.'s import trade from its factories in Britain and America was handled separately. This dual arrangement was clearly considered to be unnecessary in

48 Parrish complained that this policy, together with the price rise, would lead to a collapse of Murai Brothers' market share in India. Letter E. J. Parrish to BAT Co., London, dated 30 December 1902, Parrish Papers.

49 In fact, Atherton & Co. had only ever acted as a guarantor for Murai, who had invoiced their goods directly to Bukhsh Ellahie for distribution. When ATC set up its own depot in Calcutta, these arrangements were summarily cancelled by Parrish. Letter E. J. Parrish to E. A. Woodward, Calcutta, dated 19 June 1901. Subsequently, with Bukhsh Ellahie reinstated as distributor, Parrish noted to London that when 300,000 'Top' cigarettes had been shipped to Calcutta in November 1903 Murai had been forced to record a net loss on the deal. Letter E. J. Parrish to BAT Co., London, dated 25 January 1904.

50 According to Thomas, he was first transferred to India upon joining ATC, after that company had acquired his existing employers, the Liggett & Myers Tobacco Co. in 1899, and was posted there again in 1903 after the formation of BAT Co. J. A. Thomas, *A Pioneer Tobacco Merchant in the Orient* (1928), pp. 9–10 and 24.

the longer term, however, and was revised in favour of ATC's former agency. In 1903 BAT Co. bought the controlling interest in Mustard & Co., and Laurits Andersen, its previous manager, became part-owner of the reconstituted firm with 10 per cent of the authorized share capital.[51]

Having created Mustard & Co. as its own distributor in Shanghai, it was a logical step to dispense with the services of Rex & Co. During 1904, as Hugo Cunliffe-Owen briefly took charge of the company's affairs in China, Alfred Rex agreed to comply with BAT's wish to discontinue his firm's agency, in return for an immediate payment of £750, followed by further annual remittances of £500 over a five-year period. For its part, Rex & Co. covenanted not to undertake operations in the tobacco business in China for a period of fifteen years. Following Rex's withdrawal, the agency for the British brands was turned over to Mustard & Co., who thus managed the distribution of all BAT Co.'s imported goods for the Shanghai area.[52] In addition to these operations centred in Shanghai, the company also operated an import branch in Hong Kong which remained under the direct control of the London headquarters, and covered the south of China.

On the formation of BAT Co., James Thomas was selected to manage the company's affairs in Hong Kong, before being transferred to Calcutta in 1903. In Shanghai, C. E. Fiske maintained supervisory control over the group of Chinese dealers who distributed BAT's products into the north of China and Korea. Fiske's handling of this business, however, seems to have raised problems and in August 1904 Parrish wrote from Tokyo imploring him to improve relations with his compradors and the associations of Chinese and Korean dealers with whom they dealt. The following month, Parrish warned Fiske that the Japanese government-controlled tobacco company was about to launch a major assault on the cigarette market in Korea.[53] Soon after this the management of BAT Co. decided to place James Thomas in charge of their operations in Shanghai, following his return from India in 1904, and in June 1905 he took over from Fiske as the manager of BAT's distribution and marketing operation for north China. One month later a boycott of American products broke out in Shanghai which targeted the company's products and spread rapidly to other treaty ports.[54]

[51] Papers of BAT Co. held at the Center for Chinese Business History of the Shanghai Academy of Social Sciences, hereinafter BAT Archive (SASS), Documents 2-E-56–59.

[52] This was formally agreed on 28 June 1905. BAT Archive (SASS), Document 2-C-59; *Ying Mei Yien Kung Ssu Yeuh Pao* [British American Tobacco Co. Monthly Journal], September 1923, 10.

[53] Letters from E. J. Parrish to C. E. Fiske, Shanghai, dated 24 August 1904 and 9 September 1904, Parrish Papers.

[54] S. Cochran, *Big Business in China: Sino-Foreign Rivalry in the Cigarette Industry, 1890–1930* (1980), p. 46.

The boycott was an important factor in encouraging BAT to step up local production of cigarettes in China. The company had already taken control of the factory in Pootung (Pudong), Shanghai, which Wills had purchased from the American Cigarette Company shortly before the formation of BAT. In July 1903 the American Cigarette Company was put into liquidation and a new company of the same name was incorporated under the Hong Kong Ordinances to serve as BAT's manufacturing arm in China, and this was placed under the management of Henry A. Keily who had been posted to Shanghai from England for the purpose.[55] In support of Keily, a number of senior Japanese staff were also transferred to the Pootung factory from the Murai Brothers' factory in Tokyo as local production was stepped up.[56]

Expansion of production in China was also partly a response to the deteriorating political climate that the Murai Brothers' subsidiary began to experience in Japan. During the summer of 1903 Parrish had travelled back to the United States and had discussed the political developments in Japan with James Duke and William Harris. On his return in September, Parrish wrote to Duke that 'the air [is] full of rumours relating to "Government Monopoly of Manufacturing".'[57] These rumours quickly transpired into hard facts. In October 1903, Japanese officials informed Parrish that a Bill was being prepared to create a government monopoly on all tobacco manufacturing activities within Japan and outlined the terms on which compensation to his firm would be based. In response, Parrish attempted to generate resistance to the policy of nationalization whilst, at the same time, manoeuvring for best advantage in terms of compensation.

Outright resistance to the policy quickly proved futile. In the wake of escalating nationalism within Japan, stimulated by the impending conflict with Russia, a Bill creating a state tobacco monopoly in Japan was duly passed by the Diet in the spring of 1904. At the same time the Murai company received a second blow when it learned that the terms of compensation, which already failed to include any allowance for goodwill and trade marks, had been altered from a sum calculated on the basis of three years' average earnings to one based on 20 per cent of average annual sales revenue. The impact of the change was to reduce the level of compensation from just under ¥4 million to less than ¥2 million, whilst the effect of the change on one of Murai's main Japanese rivals, the Chibu company, worked in the opposite direction.[58]

Faced with the potential of a disastrous loss of assets in Japan, Duke posted

55 *Yeuh Pao*, September 1923, pp. 8 and 18.

56 Letter E. J. Parrish to H. Cunliffe-Owen, Shanghai, dated 17 June 1904, Parrish Papers.

57 Letter E. J. Parrish to J. B. Duke, New York, dated 9 September 1903, Parrish Papers.

58 R. F. Durden, 'Tar Heel Tobacconist in Tokyo, 1899–1904', *The North Carolina Historical Review*, 53 (1976), 361.

William Harris to Tokyo in an effort to gain an improved settlement. In May 1904, Duke sent the following telegram to Parrish from Washington DC, where he was engaged in discussions with the American authorities:

> Protest against excluding Oriental plant [a printing company owned by Murai], depots or any assets. If any inadequate payment tendered and accepted, take it only under protest, so as to save all our rights to claim further sums. We are in conference here, and rely on American and British Governments to protect us. Repeat to Harris.[59]

In its efforts to obtain a more favourable settlement, therefore, BAT Co. utilized the diplomatic channels of both the American and British government representatives, using its British registration to petition the support of the British Minister to Japan, Sir Claude MacDonald. This tack proved very successful. Following diplomatic representations from MacDonald and the American Minister to Japan, Lloyd C. Griscom, the Japanese government reassessed the level of compensation to be awarded to the shareholders of the Murai company who finally received a sum which much more accurately reflected the losses involved.[60] Moreover, BAT Co. retained control of the brand trade marks that it had issued to the Murai Company, such as 'Pin Head', 'Cameo', and 'Old Gold' which were being marketed with much success in the rapidly growing market of China.[61]

[59] Telegram from J. B. Duke to E. J. Parrish, c/o Murai, Tokyo, dated 3 May 1904 (Box 5, No. 337), J. B. Duke Papers.

[60] Part of the reason for the leverage which the British and American consular representatives held over the Japanese government lay in the latter's desire to raise finance from these countries to prosecute the war against Russia in Manchuria. According to an internal BAT Co. source, the nationalization of the Murai Bros. operation allowed the Japanese government to float a war loan of ¥150 million against which it pledged the receipts of the new tobacco monopoly. American Tobacco Co., 'A few facts', p. 3. Note also correspondence between MacDonald and Grey at the Foreign Office in which the former states that, 'It would . . . be the most suicidal policy for Japan to alienate the sympathies of the two nations [Britain and the United States] from whom she got the money to fight Russia.' See FO 371/180/22969, MacDonald (Tokyo) to Grey (London), dated 7 June 1906.

[61] Two years later, following complaints to the Foreign Office by Joseph Hood concerning the lack of official support afforded to the company in China, MacDonald wrote the following note to Lord Grey in London: 'At the time of the establishment of the Tobacco Monopoly in Japan (1904) the Company's representative in Tokio, a certain Col. Parish [*sic*], was enabled to make the most advantageous terms with the Japanese Government, when withdrawing the Company's business, entirely owing to the very strong pressure brought to bear on the said Government by Mr Griscom, American Minister, and myself, working in accord. I have no hesitation in saying that had it not been for the energetic steps we took on that occasion, and the activity we displayed in guarding the company's interests, their representatives would have been absolutely helpless, and their interests would have suffered most severely.' FO 371/180/22968, letter MacDonald to Grey dated 6 June 1906. Joseph Hood later acknowledged the legitimacy of MacDonald's argument. See FO 371/180/24772, letter Hood to Grey dated 19 June 1906.

European-based Investments

As with the British Dominions, western Europe provided BAT with a region in which both the level of purchasing power and the existing demand for tobacco products was sufficiently great to allow for the development of a mass market in machine-made cigarettes. Unfortunately for the Anglo-American concern many of these potential European markets for cigarettes were administered by the national government, either directly through a state tobacco monopoly or by a system of licensing local firms, and could not be penetrated through foreign direct investment. The main exceptions to this rule of state control were the countries of Scandinavia, the Low Countries, Switzerland, and Germany. It was from this group of nations, therefore, that the company attempted to expand its range of direct investments in Europe during the years after 1902.

Before the formation of BAT Co., ATC had acquired productive capacity only in the relatively large market of Germany. However, in 1901 ATC had also formed a subsidiary in Copenhagen to promote its sales in Denmark and the surrounding region. Activities in these markets were stepped up after the foundation of BAT Co. In Norway, a sales subsidiary was set up in 1905 and the following year, in order to diminish the effect of an increase in the tariff on imported tobacco goods, a manufacturing operation was added. Also in 1906, a Swedish subsidiary was formed which took over the business of Aktiebolaget Cigaretfabriken and became BAT Co.'s second largest investment in Europe after Germany.[62] Two years later a subsidiary was set up in Finland called Orientaliska Cigarettfabriks Aktiebolaget and also at this time manufacturing commenced in Denmark.[63]

These developments in Scandinavia were coupled with new investments in Holland and Belgium during 1906. In Belgium the assets of a local company, Emil Boussard, were transferred into a holding company called BAT Co. (Belgium) and this subsidiary operated a factory in Antwerp, whilst in Holland the activities of its subsidiary BAT Co. (Holland) were limited to the operation of a sales depot in Rotterdam. In Germany, where Duke's ATC had begun a substantial investment programme in 1901 with the purchase of

[62] The Swedish company also took over businesses owned by F. L. Hansen and C. A. Lundblad. BAT Co. Corporate Index, BAT Co. Southampton Archive, Box 114.

[63] BAT Co. Corporate Index, BAT Co. Southampton Archive, Box 114. See also H. W. Nordvik, 'Conflict and Cooperation: Competitive Strategies and the Struggle for Control over the Norwegian Tobacco Market, 1905–1930', in R. P. Amdem and E. Lange (eds.), *Crossing the Borders: Studies in Norwegian Business History* (1994), p. 134, n. 10; *Tobacco (London)*, 34 (407) (1914), xi.

the Georg A. Jasmatzi company of Dresden,[64] BAT Co. experienced a great deal of organized resistance from within the trade.

In many respects, the response of rival firms to the sales promotion campaigns initiated by the new management of the Jasmatzi concern paralleled the response of the Imperial group of companies in Britain to the Ogden schemes. Towards the end of 1902, opposing tobacco and cigarette manufacturers formed themselves into a 'Defence Committee' and ran a campaign in which they cautioned dealers and consumers against purchasing products 'contaminated with American capital'.[65] These attempts to resist the incursion by foreign capital received support from the German state, which refused to accept the products of the Jasmatzi firm in army canteens and urged all its soldiers to withdraw their custom from any retailers who dealt in these goods.[66] In fact, the publicity generated for cigarettes as a result of this conflict was one factor which helped to fuel a rapid expansion in sales of the new product in Germany, as Table 4.7 demonstrates.

Some of the progress which BAT was able to achieve in Germany, where cigarettes made from Turkish tobacco were more popular than American Bright tobacco cigarettes, was a result of its purchase in 1905 of the Cairo-based cigarette manufacturer Maspero Frères.[67] Egypt had, of course,

TABLE 4.7. Estimated consumption of cigarettes in Germany (million sticks), 1893–1913, selected years

Year	Cigarettes
1893	690
1903	3,650
1908	6,510
1911	9,947
1913	13,136

Source: Blaich, *Der Trustkampf*, p. 15.

[64] *Tobacco (London)*, 22 (253) (1902), 16. This programme included the purchase of the firm Cigarettennfabrik Josetti in Berlin, who sold a popular brand of Egyptian cigarettes. F. Blaich, *Der Trustkampf (1901–15)* (1975), p. 68.

[65] *Tobacco (London)*, 23 (266) (1903), 65.

[66] *Tobacco (London)*, 24 (277) (1904), 54.

[67] American Tobacco Co., 'A few facts', p. 2. In 1913, BAT Co. set up in London two export companies designed, presumably, to deal in this type of leaf; Export Tobacco Co. (Orient) and Export Tobacco Co. (Russia). The disruptions caused by the First World War and the loss of the German market (whose factories were the main consumer of the Turkish-type leaf) seems to have led to these companies being wound up.

emerged as an important centre for cigarettes made from Turkish Latakia tobacco during the 1880s and the firm of Theodoro Vafiadis in particular had developed a significant export trade, notably to India.[68] During 1903, Vafiadis had built a new factory in Cairo with a view to pushing its export trade further, and BAT Co.'s objective in purchasing the Maspero Frères concern may well have been to counter this source of competition directly.[69] In contrast to its other foreign investments, therefore, the company's operations in Egypt before the First World War were driven more by the export trade to India and Europe than by a desire to develop sales in the domestic market.

Between 1906 and 1911, following Duke's resignation as chairman, the management of the company under Harris and Cunliffe-Owen essentially consolidated BAT Co.'s position in those countries where it had established its main investments. BAT Co.'s financial records show that, after a modest beginning, the joint venture soon began to yield substantial profits. Although no dividend was declared at the end of the company's first year in business, the British vice-chairman William Ogden wrote to Duke in January 1904

TABLE 4.8. BAT Co. reported profits and ordinary dividends, 1903–19

Year to 30 September	Audited profits (£'000)	Ordinary dividend (%)
1903	148,541	Nil
1904	406,857	6.0
1905	711,483	12.0
1906	751,780	14.0
1907	1,031,325	23.0
1908	1,062,729	23.0
1909	930,647	19.5
1910	1,358,384	31.0
1911	1,655,880	37.5
1912	1,981,159	26.5
1913	2,151,836	27.5
1914	2,177,022	24.5
1915	1,850,059	22.5
1916	2,733,361	30.0
1917	3,105,002	30.0
1918	3,140,174	30.0
1919	3,776,507	30.0

Source: BAT Co. Annual Report and Accounts.

[68] O. Goswami, 'Then Came the Marwaris', *Indian Economic and Social History Review*, 22 (1985), 225.

[69] *Tobacco (London)*, 23 (266) (1903), 95.

proposing to pay the first interim dividend to ordinary shareholders of 2 per cent. Duke replied in the affirmative, complimenting Ogden on the company's financial position and indicating that he could see 'no reason why your proposed course is not wise and conservative'.[70] In the years that followed, BAT Co. saw its annual profits rise rapidly above the £1 million mark and was able to pay an increasingly generous return to its parent companies. In the financial year which ended in September 1911, BAT Co.'s last as a majority-owned subsidiary of ATC, the annual dividend remitted against its ordinary shares provided a return of 37.5 per cent (see Table 4.8). By this time the value of BAT Co.'s balance sheet assets stood at one and a half times the nominal share capital of the company (cf. Appendices 1 and 2), and the company stood poised for a period of fresh expansion as Duke resumed leadership.

[70] Letter J. B. Duke to W. B. Ogden dated 4 February 1904. Business papers of J. B. Duke (Box 5, No. 323), J. B. Duke Papers.

5

The Impact of Conflict

Introduction

BETWEEN 1911, when the US Supreme Court ordered the dissolution of ATC, and the end of the First World War, the identity and character of BAT Co. was fundamentally transformed. This transformation was not a smooth process, but rather involved two distinct stages. To begin with, the terms of the anti-trust action meant that the company was no longer controlled by ATC and the bulk of its equity passed into the hands of British shareholders. In line with this shift in ownership, moves were made to locate its core management expertise at the London headquarters under Duke's chairmanship. Within a few years, however, this process of managerial consolidation was temporarily disrupted by the outbreak of the war in Europe and by Duke's consequent decision to reside permanently in America. During the course of the war it became necessary once again to manage the company's business from two operational centres, London and New York, but with the balance of power now tilted decisively towards Britain.

Following the armistice of November 1918, the London-based directors were in a position to assert control over the management of BAT Co.'s affairs world-wide, and from this point onwards the company functioned unambiguously as a British-based multinational, even allowing for the continued importance of Americans within the company's management team. Perhaps the most important aspect of the changes wrought between 1911 and 1919, however, was the formation of a distinct corporate culture which served to define BAT Co.'s identity throughout the inter-war years and beyond. The war provided BAT's workforce with a common cause—one through which many employees from different parts of the organization were actively linked by military service—and acted to fuse together the different elements of the organization, facilitating a sense of unity between the main operating companies. Capitalizing on this spirit of adventure and sense of mission, BAT Co. was able to build an international cigarette manufacturing business between the wars which, in terms of its geographical scope, had no contemporary equal in the field of branded consumer goods.[1]

The Dissolution of ATC

Duke's business activities in the American tobacco industry had been an issue for anti-trust proponents in the United States long before the formation of BAT Co. Indeed, within months of the five-firm merger that created ATC in January 1890, the anti-trust measures contained in the Sherman Act had become law and quickly led to a number of restraint of trade suits being brought against the tobacco combine using anti-trust legislation enacted at the state level.[2] However, these attempts to control the activities of ATC bore little fruit and this, together with an apparent unwillingness of the federal government to use the provisions of the Sherman Act against the abuse of monopoly power nationally, had led to a good deal of public unease over the continued growth of big business at the beginning of the twentieth century.

Certainly the question of the growth of trusts provided a major issue in the 1900 presidential election campaign, and both the Democratic and Republican platforms were committed to opposing the growth of private monopolies. Following his election, the Republican President McKinley had resolved to press the issue with the Senate, but was assassinated before he was able to do so.[3] Hence the matter fell into the hands of the Vice-President, and McKinley's successor, Theodore Roosevelt. It was during Roosevelt's administration that the first successful anti-trust measure was implemented as the result of a suit against the Northern Securities Company.[4] The immediate importance of this case from the point of view of ATC was that it questioned the legality of using holding

1 The most geographically extensive manufacturing multinational to compare with BAT Co. seems to be Lever Brothers which around 1914 operated thirty-three factories outside of Britain in at least nine countries. G. Jones, *The Evolution of International Business: an Introduction* (1996), Table 4.1. However, the extent of its geographical expansion after the First World War does not match that of BAT Co. See D. K. Fieldhouse, *Unilever Overseas: the Anatomy of a Multinational* (1978).

2 R. B. Tennant, *The American Cigarette Industry* (1950), p. 58.

3 G. Kolko, *The Triumph of Conservatism* (1963), p. 65.

4 The case against Northern Securities was politically highly popular and was instrumental in gaining Roosevelt a reputation as a 'trustbuster' and led to the interpretation of this period of American political history as the 'Progressive Era'. This interpretation has been strongly criticized by Kolko as a misrepresentation of the forces at work at this time, and particularly as a misunderstanding of Roosevelt's role. See Kolko, *Triumph of Conservatism*, pp. 65–9, ch. 5 and *passim*.

companies as a vehicle for take-overs.[5] Duke responded speedily to its implications by reversing the merger of 1901 in which the American Tobacco and Continental arms of the business had been placed under the giant Consolidated Tobacco holding company.[6] Nevertheless, the Supreme Court ruling against Northern Securities in 1904 had served to illustrate that a suit could be brought successfully against corporations which used acquisition as a means of exerting market power, and ATC was quickly identified as a candidate for future action.

Late in 1906, the American Justice Department began taking the necessary steps required to introduce litigation against ATC. Despite an attempt by one of ATC's directors, Thomas F. Ryan, to pre-empt legal action by offering to dispose of the trust's holdings in BAT Co., R. J. Reynolds, and other subsidiaries, in July 1907 a grand jury inquiry was convened to examine the activities of Duke's tobacco trust under the prosecution of the assistant Attorney-General, James C. McReynolds. Ryan's political influence, however, was successful in blunting some of the more extreme proposals, such as the creation of a receivership over ATC or the instigation of criminal action against James Duke.[7]

The formal action against ATC was directed against the operations of a subsidiary company, the MacAndrews and Forbes Company, which operated an almost complete monopoly of liquorice paste. Appearing before the Circuit Court for the Southern District of New York, ATC, as the parent company, was found guilty of criminal violations of Sections One and Two of the Sherman Act. In 1908, before the same court, a government suit against twenty-nine named individuals and sixty-five corporations sought to dissolve the tobacco trust or to prevent it from engaging in interstate commerce. The court found ATC to be in violation of the Act—although not BAT Co. and Imperial or the United Cigar Stores who were also party to the suit—and the ATC-controlled firms in the combination were debarred from interstate trade by the ruling 'until conditions existing before the illegal contracts or combinations were entered into are restored'.[8] Both sides appealed against the verdict and the proceedings moved up to the Supreme Court.

After a further series of hearings, the Supreme Court judged in May 1911 that all the companies in the combination, including BAT Co. and Imperial, were acting in restraint of trade and should be held liable within the judgment. However, it ruled that the effect of enforcing a ban on interstate trade would be

[5] J. W. Aarts, *Antitrust Policy Versus Economic Power* (translated by L. Scott) (1975), p. 22.

[6] P. G. Porter, 'Origins of the American Tobacco Company', *Business History Review*, 43 (1969), 76.

[7] Kolko, *Triumph of Conservatism*, pp. 126–7. Apparently International Harvester had succeeded in preventing anti-trust action by a similar scheme involving distribution of stock among shareholders.

[8] Court ruling cited in Tennant, *American Cigarette Industry*, p. 59.

detrimental to the interests of stockholders and the general public as a whole, and ordered instead that the directors of ATC should draw up a plan for the dissolution of the combination into a group of independent companies. A period of eight months was allowed for the completion of this process of division, with failure to provide a satisfactory arrangement leading to the implementation of the lower court's interstate trade restriction or, possibly, the appointment of a receiver. A scheme for the dissolution of the trust was duly drawn up, principally by Duke himself, and this was approved in the formal decree issued by the Supreme Court on 16 November 1911.[9]

From BAT Co.'s point of view, the court's decision had two major ramifications. First, it ruled that the agreement between ATC and Imperial which created BAT Co. was unlawful and thus, as a consequence, invalidated the division of markets between ATC, Imperial, and BAT Co. which had been part of that agreement.[10] Second, the court ordered ATC to divest its institutional shareholding in BAT Co. (together with other relatively independent subsidiaries) and distribute it between ATC's stockholders.[11] Obviously, an implication of this condition was that Imperial's 33 per cent holding in BAT Co. now became the largest single concentration of ownership. The twenty-nine individual defendants in the case were also forbidden to increase their collective shareholdings in the American successor companies beyond a specified ceiling level for a period of three years. However, since this condition did not apply to holdings in BAT Co. it may explain why Duke chose to resign from the ATC board and become more closely connected once again with the Anglo-American organization. His position as president of ATC was taken by one of the American directors of BAT Co., Percival S. Hill, who now stood down and was replaced on the board by Peter Arrington, the head of BAT Co.'s American leaf-purchasing operation.

The Financial Development of BAT Co.

The ruling of the Supreme Court provided the impetus for a rapid expansion in the share capital of BAT Co. Before the events of 1911, the initial authorized capital of £6 million had remained largely unchanged. At the end of 1903 the

[9] Tennant, *American Cigarette Industry*, p. 60. For the full proceedings and final ruling in the case, see US Senate Documents, vol. 25, No. 111, Federal Anti-Trust Decisions 1890–1912, vol. IV (1912), pp. 168–251.

[10] Thus BAT Co. was now free to enter the US market if it so wished—although this would require the company to redraft its Memorandum of Association, which it only did in July 1927. The validity of the market-sharing arrangements between Imperial and BAT Co. was not affected by the ruling since, being British registered, neither company fell within the immediate jurisdiction of the American Supreme Court.

[11] Tennant, *American Cigarette Industry*, p. 60.

total issued capital amounted to £5,220,021, divided into 3,720,021 ordinary shares and 1,500,000 preference shares each of £1. With the exception of the twenty-one ordinary shares allocated to named directors, this entire share issue was held by ATC and Imperial at the agreed ratio of 2:1. A resolution dated 1 November 1907 converted 500,000 unissued ordinary shares to 5 per cent preference shares and these were distributed in 1908, along with a fresh issue of 100,000 5 per cent preference, bringing the total authorized share capital to £6.1 million and the total issued to £5,820,021 at which it remained until 1912 (see Appendix 1). During that time, a small number of ordinary shares were allocated to key directors and employees of the company, including some residing abroad (see Table 5.1), but throughout its first decade in operation the preponderance of BAT Co.'s shares continued to be held by ATC and Imperial, and the company formally remained a majority-owned subsidiary of Duke's ATC empire.

The asset base on which BAT Co.'s share capital rested was made up in roughly equal proportions of the working assets in plant and materials which comprised BAT Co.'s export business, and the shares held in, and loans made to, its subsidiary companies. Between 1903 and 1911 this asset base had expanded gradually in nominal terms, as is illustrated in Figure 5.1 (see also Appendix 2), and by the latter date had attained a value of £9.12 million, funded by a combination of outside borrowing and retained profits. In fact, BAT Co.'s balance sheet undervalued the company's holdings in its subsidiary companies whose share capital was carried in the parent company's books at only some two-thirds of its true worth.[12] Thus, when Duke resumed

Table 5.1. BAT Co. shareholders located overseas, 1911

Name	Location	Occupation	Shares
J. A. Thomas	Shanghai	Merchant	5000
P. R. Walters	Montreal	Tobacco manufacturer	2000
A. J. Warry	Sydney	Tobacco manufacturer	2000
G. W. Hawley	Cape Town	Tobacco manufacturer	2000
A. Christensen	Copenhagen	Merchant	2000
R. J. Templeton	Rotterdam	Merchant	1000
C. P. Page	Calcutta	Merchant	1000

Source: BAT Co. Shareholders List, Companies House.

[12] It was a hallmark of BAT Co.'s financial conservatism under Cunliffe-Owen that the value at which the assets of subsidiary companies was carried in the parent company's books was always well within the true value of these assets. The two-thirds ratio has been calculated using the book value of BAT Co. subsidiaries as at 30 September 1906 (see Table 4.6) compared with the valuation of the shares in associated companies recorded in BAT Co.'s balance sheet at the same time. The valuation of the shares in associated companies has been calculated after allowing for the problem of double-counting the share value of the company's Australian

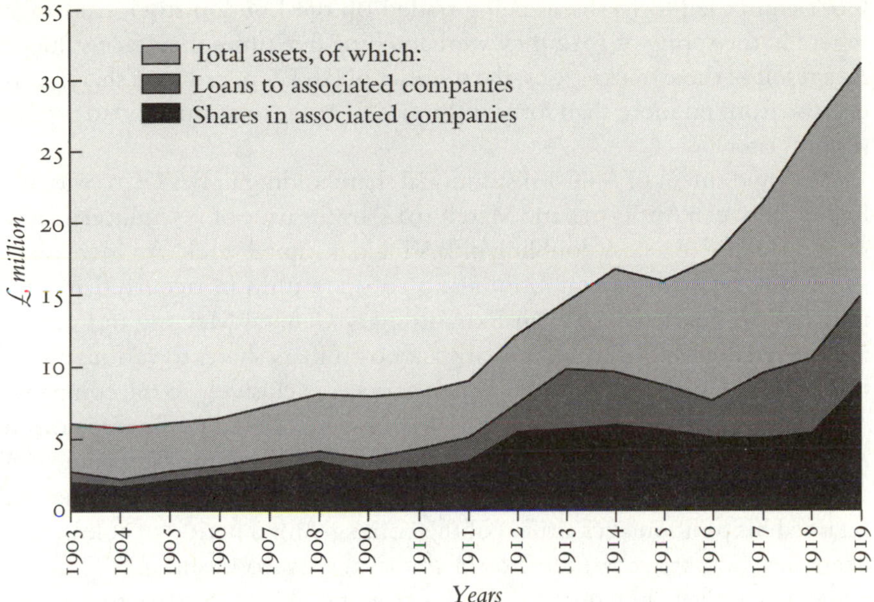

FIGURE 5.1. BAT Co. balance sheet assets, 1903–19
Source: BAT Co. Annual Report and Accounts.

his position as chairman of BAT Co. in 1911, plenty of scope existed for a fresh issue of the parent company's stock.

One of Duke's first tasks on assuming control, therefore, was to organize a new issue of share capital for the company. Before this was put in hand, however, ATC fulfilled its obligations under the Supreme Court ruling by divesting its institutional shareholding in BAT Co.[13] Of the £2.48 million in ordinary shares held by Duke's organization, £1.25 million were purchased directly by ATC's own shareholders[14] whilst the remainder were sold off to the general public for cash.[15] The decision to market this portion of BAT

subsidiaries which also constituted the asset base of BAT Co.'s main Australian holding company, The British Tobacco Co. (Australia) Ltd.

[13] Under the terms of the Supreme Court ruling the twenty-nine individual defendants were forbidden for three years to hold stock in the successor companies beyond a specified quota; however, this prohibition did not apply to the securities of BAT Co., for which the terms merely required the divestment of ATC's institutional shareholding. Tennant, *American Cigarette Industry*, p. 63.

[14] *Tobacco (London)*, 32 (375) (1912), 61.

[15] In September 1912, ATC made a distribution to its shareholders in the form of a cash dividend based on 20 per cent of the proceeds from the sale of half of its holdings in BAT Co., half of its holding in Imperial, and all of its holdings in the United Cigar Stores. The total amount of cash received for these securities was reported to be in excess of $8 million. *Tobacco (London)*, 32 (381) (1912), 39. Shortly after the sale of the Imperial equity, Duke stood down from Imperial's board of directors. *Tobacco (London)*, 33 (387) (1913), 24.

Co.'s equity led to its shares being traded on the London stock exchange where in the spring of 1912 they were fetching five times their face value.[16] As a result of these transactions, the number of BAT Co. ordinary shareholders rose from no more than forty at the end of 1911, to around 3,750 twelve months later.[17]

The divestment of ATC's institutional shareholding in BAT Co. was followed, between April 1912 and March 1914, by the issue of £5 million in new shares, leading to a near doubling of BAT Co.'s capital stock. An increase in the ordinary share capital amounting to £2.5 million occurred in two tranches. In February 1912, an Extraordinary General Meeting in London authorized the issue of an additional 500,000 ordinary shares to various directors of BAT Co. in order to secure their services exclusively to the company. Altogether, 449,728 of these ordinary shares were offered to the directors in April 1912 at a rate of 30s. each (i.e., one and a half times the face value). Of these shares, 280,228 were issued to Duke himself on condition that he retained his position as chairman of the company for a period of at least five years and did not act as a director of any rival tobacco business.[18] Thus the agreement obliged him to resign as a director of ATC in return for the opportunity to purchase shares in BAT Co. at a price which, at the current trading values, left him £1 million richer.[19]

The second batch of £2 million in ordinary shares was authorized in July 1912 and issued at par value to shareholders on the basis of one for every two held, maintaining Imperial's holding of around one-third of BAT Co.'s voting stock.[20] The following year another £3.5 million in ordinary shares was authorized, bringing the total ordinary share capital to £10 million, but these were not actually issued until the company was in a position to resume normal operations after the First World War. In addition to this expansion

[16] *Tobacco (London)*, 32 (378) (1912), 87–9.

[17] These figures are taken from the speech made by Joseph Hood at the 1912 BAT Co. AGM and reported in *Tobacco (London)*, 33 (385) (1913), 44–5.

[18] Letters Joseph Hood to J. B. Duke dated 11 April 1912 and C. T. Hill to J. B. Duke dated 12 April 1912; Indenture between BAT Co. and J. B. Duke dated 12 April 1912, J. B. Duke Papers, Box 6.

[19] The other BAT Co. directors who signed similar share contracts binding themselves to the company were Cunliffe-Owen, Hood, Lawrence Hignett, Churchman, Jeffress, Allen, Gracey, Gillchrest, Arrington, Percy Ogden, Hallward, Charles Hill, and Gilliam. They are named in the Indenture agreement signed by Duke (see previous note).

[20] Allowing for the issue of 500,000 shares to directors, the subsequent issue of 2 million ordinary shares to existing shareholders left Imperial with control of just under 30 per cent of BAT Co. ordinary shares, a proportion which was maintained until the 1970s. According to the company, by the end of 1914 the total number of ordinary shareholders had risen to 5,400. *Tobacco (London)*, 35 (410) (1915), 38.

of BAT Co.'s ordinary share capital, in May 1912 an additional £2.4 million worth of 5 per cent preference shares was authorized, and these were also issued in two tranches. The first distribution of £1 million took place in October 1912, and was offered initially to existing shareholders, but eventually £700,000 were taken up by public subscription at a premium of 1s. 6d. In March 1914, the remaining £1.4 million were sold in a single tranche to investment trusts controlled by John Phillipps (Viscount St Davids) at a premium of just 9d.[21] Thus the geographical distribution of BAT Co.'s shareholding had been transformed by the ruling of the Supreme Court. By the time of the outbreak of the war, around 70 per cent of the company's registered shares were held in the United Kingdom, and slightly less than 25 per cent in the United States.[22]

The Shift to London

Throughout the course of the anti-trust proceedings against Duke's ATC, the management of BAT Co. had remained under the nominal control of Duke's successor as chairman, William Harris, based at the company's New York office.[23] In November 1910, an American management committee of BAT Co. had been reappointed which comprised Harris, Duke, Percival Hill,

[21] John Wynford Phillipps, the first Viscount St Davids, was a loyal supporter of Lloyd George who from 1890 became involved in various investment trusts in the City of London. See J. P. Scott, 'John Wynford Phillipps', in D. Jeremy (ed.), *Dictionary of Business Biography: A Biographical Dictionary of Business Leaders Active in Britain in the Period 1860–1980* (1984), vol. 4, pp. 865–9.

[22] Refuting the charge of American control of BAT Co., the company's secretary, A. M. Rickards, stated that of 10,128,890 registered shares only 2,411,989 were held in America whilst 7,074,379 were held in Great Britain and Ireland, and the remainder throughout the world, principally in British colonies. Reported in *Tobacco (London)*, 35 (411) (1915), vii. The proportion of BAT Co.'s shares held in Britain at this time will have been slightly exaggerated by the fact that Duke's own shareholding was deposited partly in London as security against the shares which were issued to him in 1912 but which were allocated in five equal tranches between 1912 and 1917. See letter from J. Hood to J. B. Duke, London, dated 11 April 1911, J. B. Duke Papers, Box 6. The international and fragmented nature of the company's shareholders led BAT Co. to change its Articles of Association in 1913 allowing shareholders to exchange their registered shares for bearer share warrants which could be traded directly without the consent of the board, facilitating ease of transfer particularly for foreign shareholders. At the same time, another change enabled the company to dispense with the requirement that 51 per cent of the shares be represented at meetings for fear that such a quorum would seldom be achieved. See *Tobacco (London)*, 33 (390) (1913), 83–5.

[23] To begin with, BAT Co. shared offices with ATC at 111 Fifth Avenue. It then moved temporarily to 200 Fifth, before settling at 511 Fifth around the time of the First World War.

Cunliffe-Owen, and George Allen.[24] The last-named seems to have been responsible for much of the general management of the company's American production capacity, communicating between the factories in Petersburg and Durham and the sales operations abroad. The decision to transfer Cunliffe-Owen to New York seems to have been made by Duke during the first half of 1910, as an experiment for one year. The transfer caused consternation among the directors of Imperial, who were concerned that Duke might have plans to engage him outside of the management of their international affiliate, but he wrote to assure them that he had no intention of detaching Cunliffe-Owen from BAT Co.[25] In London, meanwhile, Cunliffe-Owen's departure was preceded by the appointment of three new vice-chairmen in November 1909. These were Arthur Churchman, Lawrence Hignett, and Joseph Hood, all of whom became key figures in the company's management until the early 1920s.

As soon as the dissolution of ATC had been completed, and the final decree issued in November 1911, Duke turned his attention towards consolidating the management of BAT Co. in London. His arrival in London early in 1912 provoked great anticipation in tobacco trade circles, and he immediately set about boosting the company's British production capacity. Exports of cigarettes from America had ceased their upward trajectory after Duke's resignation in 1905 (see Table 5.2) and as part of the process of reorganizing the production capacity in America following the dissolution, Duke's factories at Durham, which had been pressed into service for BAT Co.'s export trade, were transferred to the newly independent Liggett & Myers Tobacco Co.[26] As Table 5.3 indicates, the loss of output from the Durham factory was compensated for by an expansion of production capacity at the Petersburg plant. In contrast to the situation in America, British tobacco exports had grown rapidly and consistently during the early years of the twentieth century. By 1910

[24] An American committee of directors had been set up originally on 6 October 1902 following the formation of BAT Co. in London. The committee seems to have lapsed following Duke's resignation as chairman in 1905. Its reappointment coincides with Duke's return to active business matters following a period of rest and recuperation. BAT Co. Corporate Index, BAT Co. Southampton Archive, Box 114. On Duke's need for a period of rest see *Tobacco (London)*, 29 (338) (1909), 29.

[25] Letter J. B. Duke to G. A. Wills, Imperial Tobacco Co., Bristol, dated 10 November 1910, J. B. Duke Papers, Box 3, vol. 2, No. 13.

[26] As part of the reorganization, the firm of W. Duke, Sons & Co. became a branch of the Liggett & Myers Tobacco Co. and the Durham factories seem to have been among the twelve plants transferred to them from ATC. See letter from F. A. Wilson to J. A. Thomas, dated 4 February 1913, papers of James Augustus Thomas, Special Collections Department, Perkins Library, Duke University, Box 1 (hereinafter Thomas Papers); Tennant, *The American Cigarette Industry*, p. 61.

TABLE 5.2. US exports of cigarettes ('000 sticks), 1901–11

Year	Europe	N. America	S. America	Asia	Oceania	Africa	Total
1901	99,352	8,938	528	681,965	153,266	108,341	1,052,390
1902	220,342	23,593	156	807,572	108,597	113,354	1,273,614
1903	188,543	15,064	216	1,030,347	126,381	95,901	1,456,452
1904	90,538	8,965	46	1,237,667	126,157	65,033	1,528,406
1905	60,484	9,555	404	1,538,045	142,543	86,772	1,837,803
1906	50,630	9,665	381	1,446,899	154,239	49,125	1,710,939
1907	40,787	14,342	560	1,821,797	120,274	335	1,998,095
1908	38,080	22,763	818	1,423,366	51,200	3,137	1,539,364
1909	12,850	17,204	507	1,511,405	37,037	165	1,579,168
1910	13,860	26,116	1,340	1,493,544	47,583	5,514	1,587,957
1911	13,963	55,316	1,469	1,133,323	23,142	5,975	1,233,188

Source: Foreign Commerce and Navigation of the US.

TABLE 5.3. Value of machinery and fixtures at BAT Co.'s main American and British factories as at September, 1909–12

Factory	1909 (£)	1910 (£)	1911 (£)	1912 (£)
British-based				
Ashton Gate	90,291	108,102	116,408	142,618
Liverpool	9,304	11,121	12,303	12,794
Cornwallis Street	6,558	7,672	9,297	9,261
East Smithfield				2,253
American-based				
Durham, NC	30,166	27,100		
Durham Stemmery			5,321	4,404
Rochester, NY	4,070	4,070	4,070	4,070
Cameron	139	36	36	
Petersburg, VA	9,736	5,784	30,455	39,328

Source: BAT Co. Archive.

British factories were exporting approximately three times the volume of cigarettes compared with their American counterparts, and British brands (notably 'Pirate' and 'Ruby Queen') dominated the rapidly growing market in China. Thus Duke now sought to consolidate this success by expanding production within England.

BAT Co.'s cigarette output in Britain had been based initially at the factory inherited from Wills at Ashton Gate in Bristol, and the value of this plant continued to be enhanced during the period of the anti-trust action against ATC (see Table 5.3). In September 1907, the ex-Richmond Cavendish factory at Roberts Street in Liverpool had been pressed into service and in June 1910 production began at Ogden's Cornwallis Street factory which was also located in Liverpool.[27] Further production capacity was added in London during 1910 with a manufacturing company incorporated under the title of the St James's Tobacco Co., but which was re-registered as the Westminster Tobacco Co. later that year.[28] Following Duke's arrival in London, the company's capacity was extended in Liverpool, through the erection of a new factory at Commercial Road, which began production in January 1913, and a factory at Southampton, which was also put in hand during 1913. The Commercial Road plant at Liverpool, which was placed under the control of H. A. Keily, BAT Co.'s first factory manager in Shanghai, was a substantial investment and was claimed by the company to represent the most complete

[27] J. Jones, 'Cigarettes—Liverpool 5: the Story of the Liverpool Branch of the British–American Tobacco Company Ltd', p. 7.

[28] BAT Co. Corporate Index, BAT Co. Southampton Archive, Box 114.

and up-to-date bonded cigarette factory in the world.[29] On the strength of these investments, the annual sales of British cigarette exports practically doubled in volume between 1911 and 1913 (see Appendix 3).

This expansion in the production capacity of BAT Co.'s British-based factories was complemented by a major new investment in a London headquarters. On land leased from the London County Council at Millbank, adjacent to the Houses of Parliament in Westminster, the company erected an impressive office block to house the organization's rapidly expanding head office departments. Duke himself laid the foundation stone for Westminster House in 1913, and his periods of residence in London began to become more extended. In May 1913 he wrote enthusiastically from England to his brother Benjamin N. Duke, 'The British AT Co. are doing a flourishing business they are 500 million cigarettes behind orders. The profits are showing up well.'[30] As the tobacco trade press began to speculate on the possibility of Duke settling permanently in London,[31] the man himself appeared to substantiate the rumours when, in January 1914, he took out a six-month lease on Crewe House in Curzon Street, Mayfair, in an arrangement which also carried an option to buy the property.[32]

Whatever had been his intentions in this respect, however, they were immediately transcended by the outbreak of hostilities in August 1914. Within days of the declaration of war, Duke had secured a berth on a transatlantic liner and was steaming away from England and back towards his native land. In abandoning war-beleaguered Britain, which was now home to most of BAT Co.'s production capacity as well as its newly built headquarters, and returning to the secure neutrality of the United States, it was clear that Duke could not fulfil his commitments as chairman. Although Corina's contention that Duke's contract with BAT Co. required him to spend six months a year overseas (i.e., outside America) is not substantiated, it is nevertheless clear that he had effectively abdicated his responsibility for managing the company's affairs by turning his back on Britain.[33] Once again, Cunliffe-Owen seems to have played an important mediating role by spending much of the war deputizing for Duke in both London and New York. For his part, Duke seems to have adhered to his contractual obligations with BAT Co. only insofar as they obliged him to remain independent of the tobacco industry in America, concentrating his energies instead on other aspects of his business empire. The

29 Report of BAT Co. AGM for 1914 in *Tobacco (London)*, 35 (410) (1915), 38.

30 Letter J. B. Duke to B. N. Duke, dated 28 May 1913, J. B. Duke Papers, Correspondence Box No. 1.

31 *Tobacco (London)*, 33 (390) (1913), 51.

32 M. Corina, *Trust in Tobacco: the Anglo-American Struggle for Power* (1975), 132; R. F. Durden, *The Dukes of Durham* (1975), p. 189.

33 Corina, *Trust in Tobacco*, p. 133.

outbreak of the First World War, therefore, effectively marks the end of Duke's executive control of BAT Co., even if it did not represent the conclusion of his period of office as the company's chairman or terminate his influence over company affairs. His opinions continued to be sought, and the reputation he possessed among investors made his nominal position as chairman a tangible benefit to the company.

International Growth 1905–14

During the period of William Harris's chairmanship the geographical dimensions of BAT's foreign direct investments remained quite static and the organization concentrated mainly on the consolidation of its existing areas of production. The loss of the subsidiary in Japan led to substantial investment in new plant in China between 1905 and 1910, and a similar, but more limited, investment programme was also undertaken in India at this time. In the British Dominions, the subsidiary companies were allowed to develop their production capacity in line with market conditions. Only in western Europe did the company expand the range of its direct investments into new countries during these years. Duke's resumption as chairman heralded a more active phase in BAT Co.'s foreign direct investment. The share issues of 1912–14 were designed partly to fund the expansion of factory output in Britain, and to support the construction of the company's new headquarters. However, they also allowed BAT to expand the scope of its international production, and to step up its efforts to secure a substantial share of the cigarette market in Germany.

The region which emerged as a primary target of BAT Co.'s expansion plans at this time was South America. Many South American economies had undergone a period of rapid economic growth during the export boom of the late nineteenth century, and the large, growing markets of Argentina and Brazil in particular presented appealing locations for British and American cigarette manufacturers looking to expand abroad.[34] Indeed, BAT may have chosen this moment to invest in Latin American in order to counter the potential threat posed by the successor firms to the tobacco trust in America. Moreover, the London trade journal *Tobacco* had noted during 1913 that a new company called the Argentine Tobacco Co., Ltd. had recently been

[34] The average annual rate of growth of exports for the thirty-year period between 1883 and 1913 had been 4.5 per cent in Brazil and 7.6 per cent in Argentina (the highest in the subcontinent). B. Albert, *South America and the World Economy from Independence to 1930* (1983), Table II. Similar figures (4.3 per cent for Brazil and 6.7 per cent for Argentina) for the period 1890–1912 are given by V. Bulmer-Thomas, *The Economic History of Latin America since Independence* (1994), Table 3.4.

formed in London to operate in Buenos Aires and that this clearly constituted a direct rival to BAT Co.[35]

The Argentine Tobacco Co., Ltd. constituted a type of foreign direct investment that was frequently found in Britain and other parts of Europe during the late nineteenth and early twentieth century, although generally it was confined to sectors such as primary production and utilities rather than manufacturing.[36] Such investments, termed free-standing companies,[37] took the form of joint stock companies which were promoted either by established mercantile investment groups or simply as autonomous overseas companies.[38] The Argentine Tobacco Co. took the latter form, being essentially an autonomous company promoted by the London banking house of Emile Erlanger & Co., which was incorporated in October 1911 with an authorized capital of £1,380,580. The board of directors in London comprised two members of the Erlanger family, Baron Emile Beaumont d'Erlanger, chairman of the company, and Baron Frederick Alfred d'Erlanger, together with four other directors. The identity of the four remaining directors perfectly illustrates the way in which free-standing companies such as the Argentine Tobacco Co. drew together merchants who had country-specific knowledge with bankers capable of raising finance for such foreign investments. These four directors comprised a Paris-based banker, Pierre Girod, two British capitalists with existing interests in free-standing companies operating in Argentina, John Gibson, the vice-chairman of the Argentine Tobacco Co. who was also vice-chairman of the Argentine Navigation Co., and George Kitchen, chairman of the Buenos Aires Port and City Tramways Co., together with another Paris-based merchant banker, Baron Frederic Portalis, whose company Portalis & Co. acted as the local agent for the Argentine Tobacco Co. in Buenos Aires.[39]

[35] The report notes that at the first ordinary general meeting of this company the chairman, Baron Emile B. d'Erlanger, had confided in shareholders that BAT Co. did seem to be planning to establish itself in Buenos Aires. *Tobacco (London)*, 33 (389) (1913), 53.

[36] For a recent discussion see T. A. B. Corley, 'Britain's Overseas Investments in 1914 Revisited', *Business History*, 36 (1994), 71–88.

[37] See M. Wilkins, 'The Free-Standing Company, 1870–1914; an important type of British Foreign Direct Investment', *Economic History Review* (2nd series), 41 (1988), 259–82; M. Wilkins and H. Schröter (eds.), *The Free-Standing Company in the World Economy, 1830–1996* (1998).

[38] C. Jones, 'Institutional Forms of British Foreign Direct Investment in South America', *Business History*, 39 (1997), 21–41.

[39] The d'Erlanger brothers were born in Paris during the 1860s of a German father and an American mother, but had renounced both German and French citizenship to become naturalized British subjects. They are members of an international group who were an important force behind the growth of international capital movements between 1870 and 1914 and have been aptly named by Charles Jones as a cosmopolitan bourgeoisie. See C. Jones, *International Business in the Nineteenth Century: The Rise and Fall of a Cosmopolitan Bourgeoisie* (1987).

The prospectus issued by the Argentine Tobacco Co. on 1 November 1911 indicated that its main objective was to enter the tobacco market in Argentina by purchasing twelve cigarette manufacturers in Buenos Aires and operating them as a single integrated concern.[40] The directors argued that the benefits of consolidation in cigarette manufacturing had been amply demonstrated in both Britain and America, and that their initiative was designed to apply the same procedures in the case of Argentina. Local management was to be undertaken by a board of directors located in Buenos Aires, comprising of nine members, of whom six would be drawn from the acquired firms and three would be appointed by the main board in London.

In July 1912, the capital of the company was raised to £1,963,330 in order to acquire a further seven Argentine cigarette manufacturing companies and to fund the building of a new central factory in Buenos Aires. The new company issued its first balance sheet for the twelve months to October 1913 which showed that of the Argentine Tobacco Co.'s total asset value of £2.96 million almost one half (£1.4 million) was attributed to the goodwill paid to the owners of the nineteen companies whose businesses had been purchased. During the course of the First World War the company was able to pay dividends to its shareholders, but by October 1918, in its final balance sheet, the asset value of the Argentine Tobacco Co. had fallen by almost 20 per cent, despite the fact that the proportion of goodwill remained virtually unchanged. In July 1919, the company called an Extraordinary General Meeting to gain approval from its shareholders to sell the business to Piccardo & Co., BAT's main rival in Argentina, and a liquidator was subsequently appointed in February 1920 to wind the company up.

BAT Co. had not been slow to react to the threat posed by the Argentine Tobacco Co. and on 9 August 1913 it had incorporated its own operating subsidiary directly in Buenos Aires, Cia Nacional de Tabacos SA, with an authorized capital of £5 million. This company was then used to acquire Bozetti & Co., one of the surviving independent tobacco businesses that operated a tobacco factory in Buenos Aires, and its owner, Snr Héctor Bozetti, stayed on with the new company after BAT Co. had taken control.[41] In 1914, Nacional de Tabacos formed a separate subsidiary, SA 'El Fénix' Fábrica de Cigarillos, for the purpose of owning cheaper local brands that could be manufactured and marketed by Cia Nacional along with established BAT Co. brands. During the First World War this investment remained rel-

[40] A copy of this prospectus can be found in the files of dissolved companies held at the Public Record Office (PRO), London, under BT31/20255.

[41] Nobleza Piccardo, 'Hacia Un Siglio De Historia [Towards a Century of History]', 1987, BAT Co. Southampton Archive, Box 67.

atively undeveloped, but after 1918 further expansion was undertaken in a move which probably helped to precipitate the decision of the Argentine Tobacco Co. directors to sell up their interests in Argentina.

In the case of Brazil, BAT Co. began the process of market entry in May 1913 when it incorporated in London the Cia Continental de Cigarros Ltd. to act as its Brazilian subsidiary.[42] This company was authorized to deal in all types of tobacco goods, but not permitted to engage in exports from Brazil (other than to the United States) without the consent of BAT Co.[43] Although the company quickly organized the construction of its own manufacturing plant in Rio de Janeiro, this facility was transferred the following year to a newly acquired operating subsidiary called Souza Cruz with factories in Rio de Janiero, Bahia, and Santa Cruz. This latter company was a domestic Brazilian firm, founded in 1903 by a Portuguese immigrant Sr Albino Souza Cruz, which had been identified by Cunliffe-Owen as a suitable operation for BAT Co. to acquire.[44] On 14 March 1914 BAT Co. re-registered this company in Rio de Janeiro with an authorized capital of Cr.4,000,000 of which 75 per cent was subscribed for by BAT Co.'s Continental de Cigarros holding company. Souza Cruz then began to develop a market based on its own brands of cigarettes, most notably 'Sonia', rather than established Imperial or ATC Marks.[45] Since no goodwill was sold to the subsidiary by BAT Co., the territorial constraints which had been placed on the holding company were not applied to the operating subsidiary.

These early developments by BAT Co. in South America were supervised by Montague Law Whishaw, a British subject who had been born in St Petersburg and recruited by BAT Co. in Russia during 1912 at the age of 22. His engagement had initially been made with a view to developing the company's operations in Tsarist Russia, but these seem to have been thwarted by a group of Russian banks who, led by the Russo-Asiatic Bank of St Petersburg, formed a company in London during September 1913 called the Russian Tobacco Company. This organization was then used to buy up the equity of eleven Russian-based tobacco factories in St Petersburg, Moscow, and Rostov-on-Don.[46]

42 Another free-standing company called the Brazilian Tobacco Co. was set up in London on 13 March 1912, but its capital value remained at a nominal £100 and no business was ever entered into. It was not connected with the Argentine Tobacco Co. initiative. See PRO BT31/13848/120818.

43 *Tobacco (London)*, 33 (390) (1913), 41.

44 Transcript of an interview with Mr J. Banks, 12 April 1972, Windsor House Papers, p. 2.

45 The 'Sonia' brand was a low-price version of a brand sold by Souza Cruz prior to its purchase by BAT called 'No. 17'. Banks transcript, p. 8.

46 For a list of the companies purchased by the Russian Tobacco Co., including two more that were purchased in 1916, see N. Gurushina, 'British Free-Standing Companies in Tsarist Russia', in Wilkins and Schröter, *The Free-Standing Company*, p. 191.

The failure to make progress in Russia led to Whishaw's transfer to Argentina and may have been a factor in persuading Duke to step up the company's operations in Germany, where the earlier decision to begin a programme of acquisitions provoked a major backlash from within the domestic tobacco trade. By 1906 BAT Co. already held a significant share of the German market through its control of subsidiaries in Dresden and Berlin, the Jasmatzi and Josetti companies respectively. A further advance had been made in October 1910 when the Jasmatzi subsidiary purchased a majority of the shares of another Dresden-based company, a cigarette and cigar manufacturer called Sulima, when that establishment was converted into a public company.[47]

When ATC had first purchased its controlling interest in the Jasmatzi concern during 1901 Duke had appointed the previous owner Georg A. Jasmatzi as the managing director alongside E. F. Gutschow who had been transferred from ATC's business in the United States. In 1903, however, Herr Jasmatzi was persuaded to relinquish his managerial position on terms that forbade him to re-enter the tobacco business for a period of ten years. Jasmatzi later bitterly regretted agreeing to these conditions and it became clear that, as soon as he was able to do so, he would recommence an independent trade again.[48] It may well have been with an eye to this eventuality that Duke decided to make further acquisitions in order to strengthen the company's position in Germany. In early 1912, BAT Co. acquired control of two other Dresden-based rivals, Delta and Adler, and all of BAT Co.'s German subsidiaries were then placed under the umbrella of a new holding company, registered in Dresden, called the Tabakhandelsgesellschaft GmbH.

This enterprise was put under the control of Gutschow, the managing director of Jasmatzi, with two BAT Co. trustees, Messrs Godsey and Neale, as directors. Through this holding company, BAT Co. acquired 70 per cent of the share capital of Delta GmbH in March 1912 and 75 per cent of the share capital of Adler GmbH two months later.[49] Whilst these acquisitions involved firms which produced mainly cheap cigarettes, BAT Co. also attempted to acquire a share of the market for higher quality cigarettes by purchasing, through its trustees Godsey and Neale, 40 per cent of the share capital of the cigarette manufacturer Batschari of Baden-Baden. These shares were purchased in August 1912, and in March the following year the

[47] F. Blaich, *Der Trustkampf (1901–15)* (1975), p. 69.

[48] In 1913 Jasmatzi set up the firm of Georg A. Jasmatzi and Sons and began to compete with BAT for a share of the cigarette market in Germany. *Tobacco (London)*, 42 (496) (1922), i.

[49] Blaich, *Der Trustkampf*, pp. 68–70.

Batschari board passed a resolution requiring 70 per cent support by shareholders for any new decisions—hence giving BAT Co.'s trustees effective power of veto.[50]

By 1912, the companies in which BAT Co. held an interest accounted for roughly 25 per cent of German cigarette output,[51] a fact which deeply perturbed domestic firms. Early in 1913, an Anti-Trust Association was formed which embraced manufacturers, tobacco retailers and other retail outlets, tobacco workers' groups, and other regional groups of industrialists and chambers of commerce throughout Germany. Boycotts of the products of BAT-controlled firms were demanded and anti-trust rallies were organized at which speakers condemned the use of American advertising devices (particularly redeemable coupons) and urged dealers to combat the foreign trust in order 'to preserve the middle class and small retailers'.[52] The impact of advertising was frequently commented upon by groups hostile to the BAT Co. enterprises, who argued that the high levels of expenditure by the foreign-owned firms made it difficult for many of the smaller domestic enterprises to survive.[53] A less critical account in the German tobacco press still warned of the ultimate danger of monopoly:

> At present the Trust occasions no financial loss to Germany, for many millions of marks have flowed into German coffers through the buying up and financing of big German cigarette factories. The Trust employs German workers, and pays in Germany big direct and indirect taxes and duties. But it will be a very different state of things if the Trust succeeds in buying up and controlling more big factories.[54]

The activities of the trust also attracted the attention of the German authorities. Early in 1914, the police in Dresden made searches of twenty-three tobacco firms in an attempt to determine whether they had links with foreign companies. The search of the Jasmatzi factory occupied more than ten hours and led to disquiet in the British tobacco trade press.[55]

BAT at War

The company's operations in Germany were brought to an abrupt end by the declaration of war in August 1914. The hostilities also dislocated BAT Co.'s

[50] Blaich, *Der Trustkampf*, p. 70.

[51] *Tobacco (London)*, 33 (394) (1913), 28.

[52] *Tobacco (London)*, 33 (391) (1913), 53.

[53] *Tobacco (London)*, 34 (402) (1914), 43.

[54] Reported in *Tobacco (London)*, 33 (396) (1913), 88.

[55] *Tobacco (London)*, 34 (398) (1914), 25.

operations in Belgium where the company's Antwerp factory became a victim of the military conflict. Whilst the loss of the Antwerp plant was of marginal significance to the company, the size of the company's investment in Germany, and the fact that these assets now lay in enemy territory, made the loss of the plants there a far more serious problem. The response of the company was to seek to dispose of these assets to one of the major German banks, having first gained permission from the British government's Committee on Trading with the Enemy. After a period of negotiation, a sale agreement was reached with the Deutsche Bank under which BAT Co. were to be paid £1.5 million for their German assets. The terms of the sale meant that the sum was not payable until five years after the declaration of peace, although interest was to be paid at 5 per cent per annum from that date. Having made the agreement, BAT Co. set aside the full sum against their own reserves, which could then be written off if the assets were eventually seized without compensation. In fact, the company received full payment for their German assets towards the end of 1921 and were able to write the sum back into their accounts.[56]

In operational terms, the outbreak of war created both problems and opportunities for BAT Co. The most important problems were those generated by the loss of productive resources and the dislocation of raw material supplies, with the departure of staff members into the forces and the disruption of merchant shipping being the most significant. Opportunities were presented primarily as a result of the emergence of a new customer in the shape of the British government. This aspect of BAT Co.'s production was to become particularly important from the beginning of 1916, when the War Office began to invite tenders from firms for the supply of duty-free tobacco and cigarettes to the troops abroad. The Wills branch of the Imperial Tobacco Company successfully applied for a large segment of this trade, the bulk of which it contracted out to BAT Co. who possessed the necessary distribution network.[57] Thus the huge quantities of 'Woodbine', 'Player's Navy Cut', and 'Gold Flake' cigarettes that were the mainstay of this trade, and which became such a distinctive feature of trench warfare during the 1914–18 war, were produced primarily by BAT Co.'s factories in Bristol, Liverpool, and Southampton; the

[56] See *Tobacco (London)*, 36 (422) (1916), 37; 37 (434) (1917), 39; 41 (491) (1921), 111. Among the papers of James Thomas is a press clipping which reports that he was involved in the negotiations over the German companies. It is certainly true that Thomas was in Germany at the time the war broke out, so the story has some credence. However, the negotiations seem to have extended over a period of some months and it is not conceivable that Thomas alone could have conducted these. Much more probable is that Herr Gutschow, the manager of BAT Co.'s German company Jasmatzi, took the leading role. See press cutting from *Evening News* (Shanghai) n.d., Thomas Papers (Box 3).

[57] B. W. E. Alford, *W. D. & H. O. Wills and the Development of the UK Tobacco Industry, 1786–1965* (1973), p. 321.

latter factory in Blechynden Terrace being augmented by another in Albert Road during 1916 as a direct result of increasing orders for the services.[58] The phased expansion of the Liverpool factory also continued during this time. Even with this extra capacity, however, the heavy demand from the War Office made it necessary during 1916 for BAT Co. to transfer the bulk of production for the Chinese market to America, where the company built a new factory in Richmond, Virginia, for the purpose.[59] By the end of 1917, 80 per cent of the output from the company's English factories was destined for the Army or Navy.[60]

The impact of the war on BAT Co.'s manpower resources accelerated during the course of the conflict. By January 1915, between 600 and 700 of BAT Co.'s male employees, including some at director level,[61] had volunteered for the forces and by the end of 1916 this had increased, across the company as a whole, to over 2,200.[62] By the end of the war, a total of 353 members of staff from BAT Co. and its associated companies had lost their lives in the conflict. The impact was obviously felt most acutely in England, where by 1917 8,000 of the company's 9,000 total employees were women. Speaking at the company's AGM in 1917, Joseph Hood referred to 'the splendid way the women whom we have trained in the offices and factories have risen to the occasion and done excellent work'.[63] Notwithstanding such praise, most of the women employed by BAT Co. lost their places to men when the war ended, partly as a result of the company's policy of holding open the jobs of all the male employees in Britain who enlisted.[64] The employment of women in BAT Co.'s British factories as machine-minders, however, did continue after the war.[65]

58 L. A. Batchelor Smith, *Loom of Memories: A History of Southampton Branch of British–American Tobacco Co., Ltd.* (1969), p. 19.

59 According to Cunliffe-Owen, the new American factory doubled the company's production capacity in the United States. This factory now operated in tandem with the original one located in Petersburg. *Tobacco (London)*, 37 (434) (1917), i.

60 *Tobacco (London)*, 38 (446) (1918), 56.

61 Arthur Churchman, a retired Army officer, was appointed as Lieutenant-Colonel of the 6th Suffolk (Cyclist) Regiment on the outbreak of the war. *BAT Bulletin*, 1 (1915), 1–2. Another director, Percy Ogden, died whilst in service. *Tobacco (London)*, 38 (446) (1918), 56.

62 *Tobacco (London)*, 37 (434) (1917), 41.

63 *Tobacco (London)*, 37 (434) (1917), 41.

64 Allowances were paid to staff who volunteered or, later, were conscripted to the forces during the war as follows: married men—half salary (up to a maximum of £100 p.a.) plus £10 for each child; single men who were sole supporters of parent(s)—one-third salary (maximum of £75 p.a.); single men who were part supporters of parent(s)—one-quarter salary (maximum of £50 p.a.); other single men—one-tenth salary (maximum £25 p.a.). These rates, which were agreed in March 1916, did not apply to subsidiary company employees, although some of these companies made their own provision for employees who joined the allied war effort. See memorandum J. Hood to J. A. Thomas, dated 23 March 1916, Thomas Papers, Box 3.

65 Batchelor Smith, *Loom of Memories*, p. 8.

The expansion of their English factories and the replacement of men by women in the workforce enabled BAT Co. to overcome two of the constraints which the advent of the war had placed on the company's productive capacity. More intractable were the shortages of material supplies. Some of these, such as packing cases, cardboard boxes, printing materials, and tins were still being supplied by associated companies, but other inputs, notably machinery, were affected by the transfer of such trades to munitions work. In respect of tobacco leaf supplies, the initial problem faced by the company was the increase in freight and insurance required to obtain tobacco from America. In addition, as with raw material supplies generally, high demand for leaf amongst producers in Britain and the disruptions in supply caused by the war quickly raised the price. These problems were compounded in January 1916 when the Board of Trade, in an attempt to free up tonnage for vital supplies, prohibited the import of leaf tobacco into Britain except under licence. The allocation of licences became an extremely contentious issue in the tobacco trade.

The controversy was particularly acute in relation to BAT Co. When the Board of Trade came to the decision to introduce licences, it was as part of a scheme to reduce the overall level of tobacco imports in 1916 to one-third of the 1915 level. In an attempt to placate the industry, an Advisory Committee was convened, drawing on experts from within the industry, in order to organize a fair method of allocation. The chairman of the committee was H. C. Archer, a well-respected member of the Tobacco Section of the London Chamber of Commerce. The two other members were D. M. McLeod, representing the importers of tobacco, and BAT Co.'s director Joseph Hood, representing the tobacco manufacturers. The appointment of Hood to the committee was extremely unpopular within the tobacco trade, principally due to the overwhelming scale of the BAT–Imperial organization and the close connections that BAT Co. had held with the American tobacco trust.

The inherent unpopularity of the decision to reduce imports of tobacco through the issue of licences was exacerbated by two decisions which the committee reached while framing the rules governing imports under the new regulations. The first decision concerned the method of allocating licences. Essentially, a simple choice confronted the committee in this respect. Either the individual manufacturers could be granted a licence to import one-third of the amount of tobacco which they had used in 1915 or, alternatively, the tobacco importers could be granted the licences directly. It had been widely felt in the trade that Archer's preference was to adopt the former approach but, in the event, the committee ultimately came down in favour of granting licences to the importers. Obviously such an outcome suited McLeod, who represented the importers, and the impression was thus widespread that Hood had been the decisive voice in determining the outcome. Deep resentment surfaced in the tobacco trade press that, 'By granting licences to importers instead of to the manufacturers, the latter are placed at the mercy of the former.'[66]

The second controversial aspect of the committee's deliberations created even greater outcry. Because of the need to supply tobacco goods to the troops, the committee decided that manufacturers, in addition to the one-third allowance, should also be permitted to continue to import all the tobacco that they required for their export trade. While this obviously enabled a number of firms to import more tobacco than would have been the case under the original restrictions, critics were not slow to point out that, '. . . in the case of exporters doing no home trade, they are given the privilege of importing one third more than they actually use. To take an extreme case, the British–American Tobacco Co. will be able to import an enormous quantity of tobacco they do not require, say, eight million pounds.'[67] The government, it was claimed, were bowing to big interests.

Joseph Hood's influence on this aspect of government policy was of great benefit to BAT Co. In its annual report of 1916, the company was at pains to stress the mutual advantage which the additional import capacity gave to exporting firms, but it could not disguise the benefits bestowed on BAT Co. in particular. After suffering a dip in profits during 1915, BAT Co.'s earnings during 1916 set new records as their sales soared—increasing by 20 per cent in the space of a year.[68] Expansion of production capacity in the United States allowed the company to service the rapidly expanding Chinese market which the English factories could no longer cope with (see Table 5.4), and by the end of that year its American factories were producing at over three times the pre-war level.[69] In 1917, Cunliffe-Owen was reporting to the American tobacco press that the number of employees on the company's payroll had roughly doubled since the outbreak of the war, from 25,000 to 50,000.[70] Overall, the war in Europe provided BAT Co. with a tremendous stimulus in its sales and, particularly after 1916, sharply rising profits.

As well as the material benefits provided by the increased demand for cigarettes, the war helped BAT Co. to establish a corporate identity which encompassed the company's various affiliated concerns. Before 1914, even

66 *Tobacco (London)* 36 (428) (1916), 26.

67 *Tobacco (London)* 36 (428) (1916), 27.

68 *Tobacco (London)*, 37 (434) (1917), 41. The 20 per cent figure compares the three months October–December 1915 with the same period in 1916.

69 *Tobacco (London)*, 38 (446) (1918), 56.

70 *Tobacco (London)*, 37 (434) (1917), i. This figure, of course, would have included the men at the front and their temporary female replacements.

TABLE 5.4. Cigarettes imported into China ('000 sticks), 1908–19

Year	United States	Great Britain	Total imports
1908	578,480	967,113	2,762,724
1909	677,403	1,336,696	3,147,529
1910	532,112	2,122,566	3,782,114
1911	244,274	2,493,681	3,905,476
1912	207,164	2,819,317	4,400,991
1913	381,685	4,248,729	6,262,745
1914	162,500	4,480,957	6,155,994
1915	378,868	3,771,016	5,284,098
1916	1,613,106	3,082,344	6,686,228
1917	3,784,218	872,343	7,974,072
1918	4,563,129	234,914	9,305,898
1919	4,239,735	153,433	7,895,056

Note: Total imports include imports from Hong Kong.
Source: Cochran, *Big Business in China*, Table 1.

with the greater focus on London for its top management, the organization remained one of largely independent elements with little sense of collegiality to link them together. BAT Co.'s subsidiary companies in countries such as Canada, Australia, South Africa, China, and India had origins which were quite different from one another and thus would have been, for the most part, only dimly aware of the ties of common ownership which bound their operations together. The war provided these disparate groupings of BAT Co. staff with a compelling unifying cause. The decision to sell off the company's German concerns coupled, later, with the entry into the war of America on the side of the allies, meant that BAT Co. was a multinational corporation whose individual national elements, particularly its core grouping of British Empire nations, found themselves facing a common adversary. It remained true, however, that the mere existence of this war-inspired coalition was of limited significance to the company unless it could be utilized in some tangible form to provide a link between the subsidiary concerns. The initiative which effectively captured this sudden climate of mutual interest, and harnessed it to a medium which could give expression to the evolving company's identity, was an in-house journal called the *BAT Bulletin*.

The stimulus which provoked the publication of the *BAT Bulletin* was provided by those members of staff who had been posted abroad by the armed forces and who wrote to head office with snippets of news to be passed on to colleagues or requests for information. Since these employees were simply on extended leave from the organization, they retained a sense of affiliation which, given the inevitable periods of inactivity associated with immobile warfare, encouraged them to engage in correspondence. Meanwhile, in London, the company had moved into its newly built headquarters at Westminster House in February 1915, provoking both a sense of optimism and a period of upheaval which boded well for the taking of fresh initiatives. Hence, under the management of Frank D. Shepherd, a member of staff at the company's head office, a four-page weekly publication was launched in April 1915 'in honour of the staff of BAT Co. who have joined His Majesty's Forces', the principal objective of which was to receive and disseminate news of the company's employees engaged in military service. In so doing, the publication served to update staff across the whole organization of newsworthy items from all quarters. The *Bulletin* immediately struck a harmonious chord within BAT Co., and its initial requests for financial support to cover the costs of production received the support of staff from the directors downwards.[71] Within the space of a few months, weekly editions of the publication had expanded from four to eight to sixteen pages, and H. S. Wheatley, a recently recruited employee with twenty-five years' experience of journalism, was invited to assume the role of editor.[72] The directors quickly appreciated the value of the *Bulletin* for promoting an *esprit de corps* among the staff and absorbed the publishing costs involved in the exercise.[73]

After the war, in April 1920, the *Bulletin* changed format to become a monthly house journal reporting newsworthy company events and publishing short accounts of commercial life abroad in BAT Co.'s expanding cigarette empire. It continued to perform this function throughout the 1920s, providing some telling insights into the company's operations as seen through the eyes of those in the field, before ceasing publication in June 1930 following another change of format to a quarterly magazine one year previously. By this time the flow of articles from abroad had largely ceased as BAT Co.'s post-war expansion reached maturity and the company experienced its first general downturn in business as its sales became affected by the economic depression. During its fifteen-year lifespan, however, the *BAT Bulletin* played a pivotal role in drawing together the many operating elements within the company and providing them with a common corporate image and an ongoing channel of communication with the organization's managerial apex.

The outbreak of war, and the vast increase in domestic cigarette production required to supply the troops, certainly disrupted BAT Co.'s programme

[71] James Thomas in Shanghai was among the first of the foreign-based staff to send a contribution to the editor of the *Bulletin*. See letter from H. H. Neale to Thomas dated 13 July 1915, Thomas Papers, Box 2.

[72] *BAT Bulletin*, 2 (35) (1915), 129.

[73] *Tobacco (London)*, 37 (434) (1917), 41.

of foreign investment. Indeed, in addition to the withdrawal from Germany, two of BAT Co.'s other existing foreign manufacturing initiatives were temporarily abandoned. A factory in Palestine, at Jaffa (Tel Aviv), which had been put into operation during 1911 by the company's Egyptian subsidiary, Maspero Frères, was closed down when the controlling Ottoman administration joined the war on the side of the Central Powers in November 1914.[74] Another factory, in Batavia (Jakarta) on the island of Java, which the company had bought in 1908 from its Dutch owners, Anton Justman Tabak Maatschappij, was also closed down in 1914, presumably due to general operating difficulties caused by the hostilities.[75]

Throughout the duration of the war no further significant investments were made by BAT Co. in its foreign subsidiaries, although in some cases it was necessary to make loans to existing affiliates to help cover the purchase of increasingly expensive supplies of leaf tobacco and other materials. The only fresh investments that were undertaken during the period 1915–18 were directed at increasing the productive capacity of the company's English and American factories. Expansion of their factories at Liverpool and Southampton during the war was coupled with investments in plant, machinery, and buildings in America, where the company leased an additional factory in Norfolk, Virginia, in order to help cope with the transfer of export production from Britain.[76] Even after the war ended, production of cigarettes for the market in China remained predominantly based in the United States factories. This export trade provided BAT Co.'s two American-based directors (aside from Duke), George G. Allen in New York and Edgar S. Bowling in Petersburg, with their main preoccupation in the immediate post-war years, although the New York office also held a watching brief over developments in Central America and the Caribbean.

Managing an International Business

Between 1912 and 1918 two more American directors were appointed to the BAT Co. board in London, joining Albert Jeffress, Samuel Gillchrest, James Thomas, and the secretary, Charles Hill, who were already based there. In March 1912, James D. Gilliam, whose earlier career was spent with the Maspero Frères subsidiary in Egypt where he gained experience in the use of Turkish leaf, was appointed as a director with responsibility for that region,

74 *BAT News* (Autumn 1986), 20–1.

75 BAT Co. Corporate Index, BAT Co. Southampton Archive, Box 114.

76 *Tobacco (London)*, 37 (434) (1917), i; 38 (446) (1918), 56; BAT Co. Corporate Index, BAT Co. Southampton Archive, Box 114.

TABLE 5.5. BAT Co. board of directors at December 1918

Name	Nationality	Residence
Duke, J. B.	American	New York, USA
Cunliffe-Owen, H.	British	Berks., UK
Churchman, A. C.	British	Ipswich, UK
Hood, J.	British	Frinton, UK
Hignett, L.	British	Harrow Weald, UK
Jeffress, A. G.	American	Middx., UK
Allen, G. G.	American	New York, USA
Bowling, E. S.	American	Petersburg, VA, USA
Gillchrest, S. J.	American	Hampstead, UK
Gilliam, J. D.	American	Hampstead, UK
Hallward, L.	British	Maidenhead, UK
Hill, C. T.	American	Harrow, UK
Stericker, W. P.	British	Surrey, UK
Thomas, J. A.	American	Shanghai, China
Whedbee, M. M.	American	London, UK
Whishaw, M. L.	British	London, UK
Wills, G. A.	British	Bristol, UK

Note: Throughout his period in London, Thomas's residence was given as Shanghai.
Source: BAT Co. Annual Report and Accounts.

although his later responsibility was with UK-based production.[77] In 1917 Matthias M. Whedbee, who had previously been involved with the company's operations in Belgium, joined the board following the death of Percy Ogden. By the end of the war, therefore, BAT Co.'s directors featured eight British and eight Americans, excluding Duke, but fourteen of these were now based in the United Kingdom, including James Thomas (see Table 5.5).

As BAT Co.'s links with ATC were severed, so its relationship with Imperial became markedly closer. Although the resignation of Harry Wills and William Player from the BAT Co. board in 1904 had sharply reduced Imperial's direct involvement in the management of its international affiliate,[78] as soon as ATC's shareholding in BAT Co. ceased, Imperial and BAT began to develop a collaborative partnership in areas of common interest. These invariably involved vertical integration. This first surfaced in the field of packaging, an industry

[77] J. G. Lisman, 'For Ever Flows the River Nile'. Unpublished typescript, n.d., 14 pp. Account of author's experience working for BAT in Egypt. BAT Co. Southampton Archive, Box 27.

[78] After 1905, the only seat on the BAT Co. board of directors assigned to Imperial was the one held by the Imperial company's current chairman. After the death of Lord Winterstoke in 1911, this was held by Harry Wills' brother George A. Wills. He was succeeded in 1928 by Gilbert A. H. Wills (Lord Dulverton).

which had witnessed increased mechanization during the early 1900s.[79] In 1912 the two companies, together with G. H. Williamson & Sons Ltd., invested in the Bristol Tin Case Co., Ltd.,[80] and the following year they became partners in the St Anne's Board Mill Co., Ltd., an initiative designed to reduce their dependence on foreign suppliers of carton packaging materials.[81]

Collaboration of this kind between BAT Co. and Imperial was undoubtedly strengthened by the need for BAT to manufacture Wills' and Player's cigarettes for the armed forces and it continued after the war, particularly in their joint ownership of companies producing machinery. In 1919, as demand from the British government fell drastically, BAT Co. agreed to sell the Ashton Gate factory in Bristol back to the Wills branch of Imperial.[82] The factory had been concerned mainly with manufacturing cigarettes for the forces during the war, combined with production of goods for ships' stores. The additional capacity was most welcome for Imperial at this time, since the returning troops boosted cigarette sales in Britain from 57 million lb. in 1918 to 80 million lb. in 1919. As a result of the transfer, a number of employees were relocated from Bristol to the main factory in Liverpool. The decline in orders, however, obliged BAT Co. also to cease manufacturing at its two smaller factories in Liverpool, at Roberts Street and Cornwallis Street; so severing its last links with the factories that it had inherited from the founding companies.[83] After the war, the company adopted a policy of increasing its cigarette production in factories located directly within its primary foreign markets. This meant that locally manufactured products rapidly eclipsed the volume of BAT Co.'s export sales, and that the company's investments in buildings, plant, and machinery in the 1920s were directed overwhelmingly towards its overseas operating subsidiaries.

As the manufacturing operations of BAT became more dispersed into enterprises based outside of Britain and America, a managerial structure was developed which enabled the headquarters to maintain control over the organization's critical decision-making processes. Policy decisions relating to the majority of foreign subsidiaries became the role of the board of directors in London whose managerial responsibilities were either functional or regional. Those directors designated with regional responsibilities administered two types of foreign subsidiary organization: those based both on production and

[79] Monopolies Commission, *Report on the Supply of Cigarettes and Tobacco and of Cigarette and Tobacco Machinery* (1961), p. 15.

[80] Monopolies Commission, *Report on Cigarettes and Tobacco*, pp. 48–9.

[81] Corina, *Trust in Tobacco*, p. 131.

[82] *BAT Bulletin*, 8 (208) (1919), 2529–30.

[83] In fact the company continued to use these two factories in Liverpool but for purposes other than tobacco manufacturing. Jones, 'Cigarettes—Liverpool 5', p. 18.

sales, and those concerned with managing sales depots only. This latter type of operation could be set up as a BAT Co. majority-owned subsidiary company or could operate simply as a branch of the London headquarters. The main subsidiary operations however, constituted the primary core of BAT Co.'s business and were managed through directors' regular tours of inspection which kept the majority of them abroad for months at a time.

Beneath these managing directors were a large group of expatriates with function-specific roles covering accounting, sales, and production activities, who constituted the mainstay of BAT Co.'s international management staff. After a period of initial orientation at home, these enterprising men were given foreign postings within an organization that operated throughout much of the globe. Once abroad they would serve as part of a team organized under the local No. 1, the most senior expatriate grade, of the region to which they had been posted. The local No. 1 would normally hold the position of managing director of the subsidiary or associated company which had been created for the purpose of managing the operations there. Not surprisingly, the relatively common background of these expatriate managers created a particular type of corporate culture within the BAT organization which, like the sporting activities in which many engaged, featured both competitive rivalry and corporate-centred group loyalty. By the time of the outbreak of the Second World War BAT Co. had a total of 740 such expatriate managers on its books.[84]

The management structure developed by BAT Co. between the wars therefore took the form of a hierarchy in which certain day-to-day managerial responsibilities were devolved to local territorial managers or boards of subsidiary companies, but in which ultimate authority was vested in the directors of the parent company in London. In subsidiaries which engaged in local production it was obviously necessary to delegate certain of the functional tasks of the London head office to staff based locally, and consequently those subsidiaries engaged in large-scale manufacturing were manned by a group of expatriate staff who held a greater range of managerial responsibilities. Where subsidiaries operated as sales organizations only, many fewer of these functional responsibilities needed to be devolved to local management teams. In all cases, whether a subsidiary or a branch, and whether manufacturing or sales only, scrutiny by head office through travelling auditors and directors' tours of inspection constituted a central feature of the international management process. To succeed, this structure required appointments to be made to the London board which provided the necessary experience in

[84] *BAT News* (Autumn 1989), 26–7.

operational matters. Thus over time, the BAT Co. directorate developed largely as a group of long-serving employees who held vast experience of the industry and, even more so, of the company. An appointment as a company pupil between the wars thus held out the real prospect of rising to achieve a place on the board of directors of a subsidiary company and, possibly, of BAT Co. itself.[85]

By 1919, therefore, the establishment of a distinct corporate culture within BAT Co. as an autonomous organization was taking a clear shape. Freed from the control of its erstwhile American parent, and independent of but still allied to its minority owner Imperial, the company was now in a position to chart its own course. With a vast potential terrain of market opportunities beckoning it, BAT Co. began the 1920s with a burst of investments which by 1926 had seen its share capital rise from £10 million to £28 million and set its world-wide sales curve heading inexorably towards the level of 100 billion cigarettes per annum. Presiding over this period of massive expansion and great affluence was BAT Co.'s first appointed secretary, James Duke's own nominated heir, Hugo Cunliffe-Owen, for whom the old American tobacco baron finally stepped down from his post of chairman in 1923. Thereafter, Sir Hugo—he was made a baronet in the 1920 New Year Honours—set about building a tobacco empire of his own.

[85] The term 'pupil' was used to mean management trainee.

Part Three

Commerce and Colonialism in Asia

6

BAT in China

Introduction

The vast Chinese economy provided BAT with a major challenge, as the company sought for the first time to extend the production of machine-made cigarettes into regions of the world which were neither industrialized nor westernized. At the beginning of the twentieth century, the direct impact of foreign trade and investment on the conduct of Chinese commercial life was largely confined to the small enclaves which had been designated as treaty ports and, of these, only Shanghai had achieved any significant level of industrial growth.[1] However, by 1900 a number of developments during the preceding decade had raised the prospect of improved conditions for foreign business in China during the twentieth century. In Peking (Beijing) the Imperial government had initiated a programme of reforms designed to accommodate at least some limited forms of economic modernization, and these had included the granting of mining and railway construction rights to foreign investors. Such developments, particularly the building of a railway network linking the major cities of China, suggested to contemporary observers that the country stood on the verge of a period of rapid economic growth.[2]

[1] J. Osterhammel, 'British Business in China, 1860s–1950s', in R. P. T. Davenport-Hines and G. Jones (eds.), *British Business in Asia since 1860* (1989), p. 192; R. F. Dernberger, 'The Role of the Foreigner in China's Economic Development, 1840–1949', in D. H. Perkins (ed.), *China's Modern Economy in Historical Perspective* (1975), p. 37. As well as Shanghai, a certain amount of industrial development had occurred in Manchuria, mainly as a result of investment from Russia.

[2] Transport accounted for nearly a third of direct foreign investment in China in 1914, the bulk of which was invested in railways. J. K. Fairbank (ed.), *Cambridge History of China*, vol. 12, part 1 (1983), p. 204.

As a result of these favourable conditions, in the period before the revolution of 1911 a small group of western firms were able to make inroads into the potentially vast Chinese markets for mass consumer goods such as kerosene, soap, and cigarettes. Of these commodities, the distribution network created by Standard Oil of New York to market its kerosene preceded that created by BAT for manufactured cigarettes, but was quickly surpassed in its extent by the tobacco firm during the early twentieth century.[3] American firms such as Standard Oil were well equipped to make headway in a market of large physical dimensions such as China by employing the same organizational structures that had been constructed to distribute such goods across the United States. The architect of BAT's organization in China, James Thomas, utilized the same system of functionally specialized departments and a nation-wide system of depots that had underpinned ATC's successful conquest of the market for cigarettes in America. In reproducing this marketing structure in China, however, Thomas was confronted with both a novel problem and a potential advantage. The difficulty lay in the fact that foreign firms such as BAT were unable to hold legal title to property outside of the treaty ports, and were thus unable to build a system of their own depot facilities for the purpose of distributing goods in China. On the other hand, the Chinese themselves had already created distribution systems capable of channelling goods to markets throughout China, based on networks featuring merchants with a common place of origin.[4] Thomas' main achievement on behalf of BAT lay in his ability to utilize these Chinese merchant networks to overcome the problems posed by the lack of property rights.

The distribution structure which Thomas masterminded from his office in Shanghai featured both a growing number of Chinese merchants who were employed directly by BAT to act as dealers and depot-keepers, and a still larger group who operated in the same fashion as agents under contract. Thomas's ability to engage in commerce with the Chinese on their own terms, and to infuse this facility across BAT's China organization as a whole, found its ultimate expression in the creation of two joint ventures with Chinese firms. The second of these partnerships, with the Cantonese-originated Wing Tai Vo organization, developed into an important, semi-autonomous arm of

[3] On Standard Oil in China see Chu-Yuan Cheng, 'The United States Petroleum Trade with China, 1876–1949', and M. Wilkins, 'The Impacts of American Multinational Enterprise on American–Chinese Economic Relations, 1786–1949', both in E. R. May and J. K. Fairbank, *America's China Trade in Historical Perspective: The Chinese and American Performance* (1986).

[4] G. G. Hamilton, 'The Organizational Foundations of Western and Chinese Commerce: A Historical and Comparative Analysis', in G. G. Hamilton (ed.), *Business Networks and Economic Development in East and Southeast Asia* (1991), pp. 48–65.

the company's operation in China between the wars. The company's distribution system provided the platform upon which, by the 1930s, BAT had built up an impressive network of factories covering Shanghai, Hankow (Wuhan), Tientsin (Tianjin), Mukden (Shenyang), Harbin, Tsingtao (Qingdao), and Hong Kong.

By the time of Thomas's departure from BAT in 1919, the company had in place an extensive distribution network across China. This facility served them well during the 1920s as the political conditions under which foreign firms were obliged to operate grew increasingly complex and uncertain. Within this environment, the position of cigarettes as a revenue-raising tool placed BAT at the centre of a struggle to influence China's fiscal structure which became a preoccupation of the leading colonial powers. As the Chinese polity became increasingly fragmented following the revolution of 1911, provincial governments attempted to raise taxation on the movement of cigarettes across the boundaries of the territories they controlled. The levying of transit taxes on cigarettes disrupted the free movement of goods and acted to undermine the financial position of the central authorities in Peking, making the achievement of an integrated market for foreign products within China much more difficult to achieve. Throughout most of the 1920s, BAT became deeply involved in the diplomatic efforts of Britain and the United States to reinforce the power of the central authorities in China, as they sought to prevail on the Chinese government to abolish provincial transit taxes in return for the benefits of greater tariff autonomy. Only with the accession to power of Chiang Kai-shek's Kuomintang (KMT) government after 1927, however, were conditions of relative stability restored for BAT's cigarettes in China as the company struck a deal with the regime's Western-educated Finance Minister, T. V. Soong, to make advance payments of cigarette taxes in order to support Chiang's campaign of national unity.

After 1928 sales of BAT's cigarettes in China boomed. Although some Chinese manufacturers continued to compete effectively with the Western company—notably small-scale firms who copied BAT's brands using hand-rolled products—the main large-scale competition to BAT came from Japanese manufacturers based initially in Manchuria. In fact, to begin with, the Japanese invasion of China's three north-eastern provinces in 1931 acted to stabilize conditions in the region and enabled the market for cigarettes there to grow rapidly to both the Western and Japanese firms' advantage, and by 1937 BAT annual sales had reached the level of 55 billion sticks across the China market as a whole. However, this proved to be the high-water mark of the company's sales operations there. With the invasion of the Chinese mainland by Japanese forces in 1937 operating conditions became increasingly difficult for BAT until, following the outbreak of the Pacific War in

BAT Co. operational locations in China, 1902–45

Note: Places with a date attached show the locations of BAT Co.'s cigarette manufacturing facilities and commencement of production.

1941, the company's assets in China were sequestrated by the occupying forces and the staff who remained were interned for the duration of the conflict. After the war, attempts by the company to re-establish their market in China quickly collapsed after the accession to power of the communist regime.

Managing a Chinese Distribution Network

Although BAT and its predecessors had been marketing machine-made cigarettes in China since the early 1890s, it was following the nationalization of its Japanese subsidiary in 1904 that the company seems to have stepped up its operations there. The critical development occurred in June 1905, when James Thomas was posted to Shanghai by Duke to take over the management of BAT's interests in northern China from C. E. Fiske. On his arrival Thomas took control of BAT Co.'s branch headquarters in Shanghai and assumed managerial responsibility for the company's various other sales offices in northern China. At this time, BAT's direct ownership of business enterprises within China was limited to its Shanghai factory, which it had inherited from Wills, and the sales operation run by Mustard & Co. This latter organization had initially acted as ATC's agent in Shanghai but in 1903 BAT Co. registered its own Mustard & Co. subsidiary in New Jersey and this latter firm purchased the assets of the original agency. In 1905, BAT Co. formally granted this new Mustard & Co. sole rights to distribute its products for a radius of 100 miles around Shanghai. The distribution system operated by Mustard & Co. utilized the services of various Chinese merchant houses organized around the local Shanghai Tobacco Guild. Elsewhere in northern China BAT Co.'s Shanghai headquarters directly appointed dealers in important towns to act as the company's distributors, whilst arrangements for the south of China were handled separately by the Hong Kong office where Thomas himself had been based for a period during 1903.

Thomas's long-term objective was to develop a distribution structure across the provinces of China which would replicate the system of company-controlled warehouses that Duke and his colleagues at ATC had created in America. To do this, Thomas required native Chinese to work as BAT employees and agents. Thus the company hired compradors or interpreters to help its Western managers establish links with the indigenous mercantile community. Through these compradors, the company began to employ local merchants directly to act as their depot managers. They also drew up sole agency contracts with suitable independent dealers who were able to pass BAT's cigarettes through their existing sales networks. In this respect,

Thomas's task was facilitated by the well-developed mercantile structure which existed in China at the start of the twentieth century.[5]

To be appointed as BAT dealers, Chinese merchants were required to demonstrate that they possessed both sufficient capital resources to cover the requirements of stock, and suitable premises for dealing in the company's products. Additionally, distributors who wished to obtain stocks of cigarettes on credit needed to be able to offer BAT two supporting guarantors drawn from other merchants in the community, each of whom operated from a permanent place of business.[6] Naturally, these conditions limited the company's scope in expanding its network of dealers. Moreover, expansion of its distribution system in China was complicated by the fact that, as a foreign company, BAT was not permitted to own depots beyond the confines of the treaty ports. Thus Thomas faced the problem of creating secure channels through which cigarettes could pass from the foreign enclaves into the economy of China itself, without contravening the terms of the formal treaties through which the company was obliged to operate.

The system which Thomas devised to extend the company's distribution facilities beyond the treaty ports was based around two contracts, forms 15A and 16A, which depot managers and dealers respectively were obliged to sign before being permitted to handle BAT's products. Form 15A enabled BAT to furnish depots run by independent merchants with adequate stocks by retaining BAT's ownership of the goods until such time as they were released to the dealers.[7] This arrangement was supported by form 16A, a Guarantee Bond signed by all of BAT's dealers, which acted as a means of security against the value of the stocks held. By signing the 16A agreement, each dealer pledged a fixed amount of compensation to the company in the event of losses, calculated in relation to the dealer's maximum level of monthly stock.[8]

These contracts provided BAT with the security they needed to extend credit to their dealers, who were then allocated goods on a consignment basis of no more than thirty days after they had been drawn from the depot. In areas too remote for the company to set up depot facilities, the company's main dealers were permitted to draw stocks on behalf of sub-dealers, under similar

[5] On the operation of Chinese mercantile networks at this time see G. W. Skinner, 'Marketing and Social Structure in Rural China', *Journal of Asian Studies*, 24 (1964), 3–43.

[6] Chen Ren Jie, 'Ying Mei yan gong si mai ban Zheng Bo Zhao' [The Compradore of the BAT Co.: Cheang Park Chew], *Wenshi ziliao xuanji* [Selection of material relating to culture and history], Zhong guo renmin zhengzhi xieshang huiyi (ed.) [Consultative Political Conference of the Chinese People], Shanghai (1978), p. 159.

[7] This system paralleled that used by ATC in America during the 1890s (see Chapter 3).

[8] History of YTTC, papers of BAT Co. held at the Centre for Chinese Business History of the Shanghai Academy of Social Sciences, hereinafter BAT Archive (SASS), Doc. Nos. 13-D-1–2.

guarantee arrangements, thus effectively performing the wholesaling function.[9] The flow of stocks was monitored both by BAT's own territorial managers and by the accounting department at the headquarters in Shanghai which controlled all the financial transactions across the entire Chinese market. Thus Thomas's distribution strategy in China involved the cultivation of strong links with the indigenous mercantile community, underpinned by explicit contracts and guarantees, which allowed BAT to operate effectively beyond the limits of the treaty ports.

As Thomas consolidated BAT's position in China, he developed a particularly close relationship with two members of the native Chinese community who worked for the company. In Shanghai, where sales and distribution were managed by Mustard & Co., arrangements had been developed with a group of wholesale merchants who operated through the offices of the Shanghai Tobacco Guild. Prominent among these was the firm of Wing Tai Vo, a partnership of Cantonese merchants led by Cheang Park Chew, who had been granted the rights to distribute Wills' 'Ruby Queen' cigarettes in Shanghai by the English firm's agency in China, Rex & Co., sometime during the late 1890s.[10] When Rex's contract was terminated by Cunliffe-Owen in 1904, Cheang's Wing Tai Vo company continued their relationship with BAT through its Mustard & Co. subsidiary. Cheang made a favourable impression on James Thomas soon after the American's arrival in Shanghai in 1905 when, in the midst of a severe boycott of American products, he was able to maintain sales of BAT's 'Ruby Queen' cigarettes by cleverly exploiting their British origins.[11] Thereafter, Thomas and Cheang formed a close and trusting relationship upon which BAT was able to build an important element of its cigarette distribution system after the First World War.

In establishing a market for the company's goods in China, Thomas also found a valuable ally in Wu Ting Seng.[12] Wu, who was employed by Thomas as an interpreter on his arrival in Shanghai, had been instrumental in developing Mustard & Co.'s links with the Shanghai Tobacco Guild through which it had come to dominate the trade in cigarettes in the city. During the 1905 boycott of American products, as BAT came under a volley of criticism

[9] The system operated by BAT is described in detail in an internal 'Memorandum on Consignment Delivery System' in the BAT Archive (SASS), Doc. Nos. 13-D-21–25.

[10] The names Wing Tai Vo and Cheang Park Chew are the Cantonese transliterations used by BAT in their references to the firm in legal documents, internal memoranda, etc. The conventional transliterations from Mandarin Chinese using the Wade–Giles system are Yung-t'ai-ho and Cheng Po-chao respectively.

[11] Chen Ren Jie, 'Ying Mei', p.157; M.-C. Bergère, *The Golden Age of the Chinese Bourgeoisie 1911–1937* (1989), p. 145.

[12] Wu Ting Seng is the Cantonese transliteration. The more conventional Wade–Giles transliteration is Wu T'ing-sheng.

for its foreign monopoly of the trade and as Chinese rivals exploited the opportunity by producing their own cigarettes in opposition to BAT's brands, Wu gained Thomas's appreciation by speaking out in favour of the Western company at a meeting of the Shanghai Chamber of Commerce called to announce the boycott of American goods.[13]

Unlike Cheang, who was a member of the mercantile class that had gained from the rapidly expanding trade based around the treaty ports, Wu was part of the urban gentry whose political influence was expanding as the Imperial regime attempted to modernize the institutions governing China. In Wu, Thomas recognized the potential for building a new type of alliance between BAT and Chinese merchants based on a joint venture company managed by an influential Chinese entrepreneur. The fact that this business was a Chinese-run enterprise meant that, unlike BAT, it would be able to operate freely beyond the treaty ports. Thus in 1912 Thomas and Wu travelled to London together in order to develop the scheme further. In July of that year a new company, wholly owned by BAT Co., called the Enterprise Tobacco Co. was registered in London and given control over a number of BAT's brands. The following November Thomas registered a second company, this time in Shanghai, called the Union Tobacco Co. This company was also majority controlled by BAT Co., but it was a joint venture managed by Wu Ting Seng who was made a principal shareholder. The Union Tobacco Co. was thus a Chinese-run business, partly owned by a respected member of the Chinese gentry, which could operate as a selling company within China on BAT's behalf. The joint venture was then allocated by the Enterprise Tobacco Co. the sole right to distribute two BAT brands—'Purple Mountain' and 'New York'—across the whole of China.

Initially the partnership was a resounding success. As a subsidiary company BAT allowed Union to take goods on extended credit, thus allowing the organization to deal in much greater volumes of cigarettes than had previously been possible for the credit-constrained Chinese agents. In 1916, Thomas wrote to Wu congratulating him for the Union Co.'s sales performance with 'Purple Mountain' cigarettes and advising him to 'push the sale of "Purple Mountain" cigarettes for all they are worth'.[14] In an effort to assist the sales campaign and to overcome production shortages caused by the war in Europe, production of the brand was transferred to the Pootung plant,

13 S. Cochran, *Big Business in China: Sino-Foreign Rivalry in the Cigarette Industry, 1890–1930* (1980), p. 46.

14 Letter J. A. Thomas to Wu Ting Seng, Shanghai, dated 4 February 1916, papers of James Augustus Thomas, Special Collections Department, Perkins Library, Duke University, Box 2, hereafter Thomas Papers.

although the 'New York' brand continued to be imported from the United States.[15]

The experiment with the Union joint venture in 1912 was coupled with a more systematic development of the company's distribution system throughout China. Following the revolution of October 1911, the unstable political conditions in China encouraged Thomas to abandon a centralized selling organization covering the whole of northern China and to develop a regionally based structure featuring relatively autonomous sales divisions. Towards the end of 1912 the geographical scope of Mustard & Co.'s sole distribution rights was extended beyond the radius of 100 miles around Shanghai, as its dealer network expanded.[16] A still more significant change was initiated in 1914, however, when the Chinese market was divided by Thomas into five huge regions.

To begin with operations in the south of the country were still organized under separate control from Hong Kong, and supervision of the company's affairs in the three provinces which comprised Manchuria continued to be undertaken from Shanghai. Elsewhere, the sales organization for China was restructured into three divisions with headquarters in Shanghai, Tientsin, and Hankow, and these became Southern, Northern, and Central Divisions respectively. Under these new arrangements, BAT's expatriate territory managers reported to newly created divisional managers, who then reported to the Shanghai headquarters. Thus another tier of management was added to help streamline communication within the organization and improve territorial supervision.[17]

In 1915 a separate sales division was set up in Manchuria, with its headquarters based in Mukden. In this part of China, especially around Harbin in the north, Russian cigarette manufacturers had been operating since the turn of the century, popularizing their own type of tobacco product featuring a mouthpiece, and BAT's main established rival in Manchuria was the Russian firm of A. Lopato & Sons, which had first set up manufacturing operations at Harbin in 1898. In 1913, BAT gained a financial interest in the Lopato company's factory, but it was not until five years later that a more co-ordinated

[15] Letters E. S. Bowling, Petersburg, to J. A. Thomas, Shanghai, dated 21 September 1915, J. A. Thomas, New York, to T. Cobbs, Shanghai, dated 10 February 1916, Thomas Papers, Box 2.

[16] BAT Archive (SASS), Doc. No. 2-C-41.

[17] *Ying Mei Yien Kung Ssu Yueh Pao* [British American Tobacco Co. Monthly Journal], September 1923. The Yueh Pao was BAT's house journal in China and the edition of September 1923 was a special commemorative issue to mark the twenty-first anniversary of the formation of BAT Co. This edition contained a detailed account of BAT's development in China during the preceding two decades, and synopses of the company's many Chinese dealers.

approach to operations in Manchuria began to be developed when the two companies formed a joint venture, majority owned by BAT but under the chairmanship of E. A. Lopato, called the Alliance Tobacco Co. Although Alliance was still nominally independent of BAT, with a separate board of directors, the two companies began to work more closely together during the 1920s when the distribution arrangements for Alliance's products were placed under the control of BAT.[18]

The creation of a regional management structure based on sales divisions devolved a good deal of authority away from the Shanghai headquarters, and proved to be Thomas's parting shot as managing director in China. At the end of 1915 Thomas, who had been appointed to the board of BAT Co. in 1909, was transferred to the company's London headquarters as director responsible for China. From the company's point of view, this move can be seen as a counterbalance to the need to transfer much of the production for China from factories in Britain to the United States during the latter part of the war. Thomas was replaced in Shanghai by his long-standing American deputy Thomas F. Cobbs, another experienced Asia hand.

Although Thomas spent the next three years based in London, he never really settled there and soon begun to hanker for a return to China. By now in his mid-fifties, however, his age ruled out any new posting on behalf of BAT. Thus when in 1919 he was offered the opportunity to act as managing director of a new initiative, the Chinese–American Bank of Commerce, he requested leave of absence from BAT and took up the new challenge.[19]

Production and Marketing

Under Thomas's guidance BAT's operations in China experienced a period of sustained growth and by 1916 the company's Chinese sales were running at almost 10 billion cigarettes (*c.*200,000 cartons of 50,000 cigarettes) per annum (see Table 6.1). Of these cigarettes, about 40 per cent were imports drawn from the United States and Britain (cf. Table 5.4), and the remainder were produced directly by the company in its Chinese factories (see Table

[18] Minutes of a meeting between the directors of the Alliance Tobacco Co. and BAT Co. (China) held on 20 September 1922, BAT Archive (SASS), Doc. Nos. 13-C-51–54.

[19] On the bank, and Thomas's work for it, see N. Pugach, 'Keeping an Idea Alive: the Establishment of a Sino-American Bank, 1910–1920', *Business History Review*, 26 (1982), 33–53; idem., *Same Bed Different Dreams: a History of the Chinese–American Bank of Commerce, 1919–1937* (1997), pp. 60–8.

TABLE 6.1. Cigatette sales in China (BAT v. rival firms), 1902–41 (various years)

Year	BAT Sales		Rival Firms	
	(Cartons of 50,000)	(% Share)	(Cartons of 50,000)	(% Share)
1902	12,682	–	n.a.	–
1909	80,353	–	n.a.	–
1910	105,548	–	n.a.	–
1911	129,933	–	n.a.	–
1912	142,933	–	n.a.	–
1914	187,969	–	n.a.	–
1915	179,127	–	n.a.	–
1916	192,975	–	n.a.	–
1918	267,202	–	n.a.	–
1919	309,028	–	n.a.	–
1920	340,419	–	n.a.	–
1921	355,610	–	n.a.	–
1922	405,707	–	n.a.	–
1923	509,478	79.3	132,643	20.7
1924	634,624	82.1	138,704	17.9
1925	587,950	77.1	174,886	22.9
1926	580,413	70.4	244,032	29.6
1927	562,690	67.7	268,497	32.3
1928	516,419	61.1	328,439	38.9
1929	820,431	68.4	379,027	31.6
1930	877,905	65.3	466,813	34.7
1931	823,764	60.1	545,962	39.9
1932	797,146	62.3	482,811	37.7
1933	791,953	59.9	529,844	40.1
1934	708,162	54.9	581,212	45.1
1935	752,777	56.9	569,464	43.1
1936	877,376	63.3	509,558	36.7
1937	1,118,616	67.2	546,471	32.8
1938	901,939	73.0	333,819	27.0
1939	871,943	64.1	487,943	35.9
1940	885,518	58.5	627,005	41.5
1941	894,909	59.8	602,725	40.2

Note: Sales for BAT include Wing Tai Vo sales.
Source: Shanghai (ed.), *Ying Mei*, pp. 512, 733.

TABLE 6.2. Output of manufactured cigarettes by BAT in China by factory location, 1912–25, 1931–2, 1936–41 (50,000 cartons)

Year	Shanghai	Hankow	Tientsin	Tsingtao	Mukden	Hong Kong	Total
1912	57,700	38,480			6,520		102,700
1913	65,180	40,160			9,120		114,460
1914	56,360	15,400			5,860		77,620
1915	66,520	25,580					92,100
1916	75,220	34,040					109,260
1917	83,120	31,900					115,020
1918	122,820	28,600			2,300		153,720
1919	183,220	47,720			9,500		240,440
1920	188,800	55,120			23,400		267,320
1921	185,320	64,920			27,700		277,940
1922	183,040	62,420	23,720		38,700		307,880
1923	212,680	70,760	57,360		59,080		398,880
1924	285,460	116,020	99,720	2,000	54,440		557,640
1925	187,120	105,060	119,820	16,000	61,160		489,160
1931	252,011	114,779	131,653	98,698	58,132	5,808	661,081
1932	306,526	658	120,652	78,966	45,107	8,778	560,687
1936	329,503	144,560	123,769	95,120	191,424	11,380	895,756
1937	368,995	190,733	177,434	134,716	232,337	20,339	1,124,554
1938	229,887	150,425	140,060	87,397	214,323	36,431	858,523
1939	357,037	16,262	132,749	121,638	199,667	29,944	857,297
1940	344,932	37,131	143,742	118,695	185,700	38,965	869,165
1941	362,871	35,500	160,765	131,038	164,476	65,203	919,853

Note: Output figures do not include production at Lopato's factory in Harbin.
Source: Shanghai (ed.), *Ying Mei*, Table 4, pp. 1635–6.

6.2).[20] The company's production capacity within China had been steadily increased during the early 1900s, particularly after the loss of the Japanese factories in 1904. To begin with the company built up its existing American Cigarette Co. plant in Pootung which it re-registered as the British Cigarette Co. (BCC) during the boycott of American products in 1905. This Shanghai plant provided cigarettes for distribution throughout China, in particular for the markets around the treaty port of Tientsin in the north, and the Yangtze River (Chang Jiang) basin trade. Sales in both of these markets were

[20] In 1916 China imported around 4.7 billion cigarettes from Britain and the United States (see Table 5.4), to which should be added the estimated output of BAT's Chinese factories of 5.4. billion cigarettes (see Table 6.2). This accords quite well with the estimated sales of BAT in China of about 9.6 billion cigarettes (see Table 6.1), especially allowing for the fact that the sales are calculated for the year ending September and, given the growth trend, will normally have been higher for the twelve months of the corresponding calendar year.

experiencing rapid growth as the company's distribution network expanded under Thomas's management, and in 1906 BCC built a new factory in the strategic Yangtze port of Hankow which was located on the main railway line linking Canton with the north of China. The factory at Hankow was further extended in 1911 and this together with Shanghai, where a second production compound was built in 1914, became the major focal points for the company's production in China until the 1920s (see Table 6.2).

The only other region of China in which BAT developed production capacity before the First World War was Manchuria. The company had set up its first office in this region at Newchwang (Yingkou) in 1905, following the end of the Russo-Japanese war, and began to compete fiercely for the custom of tobacco smokers in the region. In 1906, the London trade journal *Tobacco* noted that, 'The Americans appear to have determined on capturing the Manchurian market at all costs, and have sent their agents into the country with parcels of all sorts of tobacco, and these they are selling at obvious losses.'[21] Three years later the company built its first production facility within Manchuria at the provincial capital of Mukden with the support of the resident US Consul-General, Willard Straight, who obtained the necessary land titles on the company's behalf.[22] The factory in Mukden gave BAT much greater scope to compete against Japanese manufacturers who were busily expanding their operations in Korea at this time.[23] In 1914, however, the Mukden plant burned down and it was not until the end of the First World War that production was resumed at this site.[24] Further north in Manchuria, the company developed a joint venture with the Russian cigarette manufacturers Lopato & Sons at Harbin. As with the factory in

[21] *Tobacco (London)*, 26 (311) (1906), 573.

[22] J. A. Thomas, 'Selling and Civilization: Some Principles of an Open Sesame to Big Business Success in the East', *Asia* (December 1923), 949.

[23] BAT's operations in Korea, where it had established sales outlets through local dealers under Thomas's predecessor C. E. Fiske, came under increasing pressure from Japanese competitors as the country was brought under Japan's imperial yoke between 1905 and 1910. In 1904 E. J. Parrish had written to Fiske to warn him that the newly formed Japanese Tobacco Monopoly was about to make a big push in Korea, stating that 'large orders for Japanese cigarettes, from our old jobbers in Korea, are in the hands of the government'. Letter E. J. Parrish to C. E. Fiske, Shanghai, dated 9 September 1904, papers of E. J. Parrish, Special Collections Department, William R. Perkins Library, Duke University, hereinafter Parrish Papers. In 1914, the authorities imposed a new tax on tobacco products in Korea which led BAT to cease its operations there. Letter from A. M. Rickards to Secretary of State for Foreign Affairs, dated 6 October 1931, FO 371/15491/5415.

[24] *Yueh Pao*, p. 79. An account of BAT's factories in China contained in the Shanghai archive states that the company began to rebuild the factory at Mukden the same year but the figures in Table 6.2 do not record any fresh output from this source until after the end of the First World War. BAT Archive (SASS), Doc. Nos. 2-G-1–13.

Mukden, this production site was also expanded following the end of the First World War.

The creation of production and distribution facilities for machine-made cigarettes by BAT in China was coupled with impressive support in terms of marketing. Although an article of mass production, cigarettes were by no means the cheapest way of consuming tobacco and a pricing strategy needed to be developed which both encouraged consumers to adopt this form of smoking and allowed dealers a reasonable profit margin. Thomas's approach to pricing cigarettes, both in China and in India, was to offer them for sale at a price which was convenient in terms of the local currency. Thus during his time in Hong Kong Thomas reduced the price of BAT's cigarette brands to 5 cents, enabling them to be purchased by a single coin which could not be done at the prevailing price of 6 cents.[25] Thomas felt that this strategy of tying the price of cigarettes to a specific coin had the advantage of fixing the price in the mind of consumers and made it difficult for dealers to engage in profiteering.

In his memoirs, Thomas has stated that he tried to place more emphasis on customer service than on salesmanship in his approach to marketing cigarettes in China. His principal concern was to provide the customer with a reliable product at a reasonable price, and this required a well-organized system of distribution. He recruited salesmen from the tobacco-growing states of America to introduce cigarettes into the furthest reaches of the Chinese empire, and paid a bonus to those who learned to speak commercial Chinese. These salesmen travelled into the Chinese hinterland with consignments of cigarettes in an effort to publicize the new product. In effect, these teams of salesmen and their supporting retinue of Chinese guides and carriers acted as missionaries for the new product. Thomas explained how they operated:

> Our caravans were fitted out completely—carts, tents, cooks, 'chow', medicines. They were as self-sufficient as an exploring expedition. These caravans penetrated from the farthest head of navigation or rail-head all over interior China, beyond the gorges of the Yangtze, across the Mongolian desert to Urga (Ulaan Baator) and to far-away Langchow (Lanzhou) in Kansu (Gansu) Province, forty-five days by mule-back from Kalgan (Zhangjiakou). With every convoy went two foreigners, one of whom was pretty sure to be a young American from the tobacco-growing states of [the US].[26]

Some of the extreme conditions which these salesmen experienced in China

[25] Thomas, 'Selling and Civilization', p. 948; idem., *A Pioneer Tobacco Merchant in the Orient* (1928), p. 34.

[26] Thomas, 'Selling and Civilization', p. 948.

have been documented in their own recollections.[27] One described a fairly typical tour, covering the area around Peking in 1912, as follows.

> In May I took a ten day trip covering the small towns lying on the outskirts of the city. My crew consisted of an interpreter, a cook-boy, and a number one and number two coolie . . . All of the towns were alike, small market villages supported by the surrounding farmers. The average population was about 1,000, of which at least two-thirds were children and babies.
>
> As soon as the coolies had made up their hot paste we set out and, starting with the inn, plastered posters all over the town. Then we loaded up with cartons and handbills and started our sampling campaign. I walked in front and handed out the sample packets, followed by the interpreter distributing handbills and the coolies carrying our supplies in the rear. After a rest the interpreter and I called on all the cigarette shops. A shopkeeper would usher us into one of the little rooms; we sipped tea and after discussing the weather and the rotten exchange, we expressed our amazement at his lack of stock, sold him a few cartons and left. Later the dealers called at the inn with their bags of coppers and took up the stocks we had sold them. Thus was the company's business being built up in every village, town and city throughout the country.[28]

Thomas used these roving salesmen to do more than merely peddle and publicize the existence of BAT's cigarettes. He also created a system through which conditions in the different markets could be recorded and relayed back to Shanghai for processing. To do this Thomas created a system based on form 163, which the travelling salesmen were required to complete at regular intervals, that set out the prevailing conditions for each town in terms of population, number of dealers operating, depot facilities available, stock levels by brand, the local currency exchange rate, and the general income levels of the inhabitants. This information provided BAT's management in Shanghai with the best possible picture of the company's sales performance, allowing them to synchronize production and distribution with relative accuracy. In this way, the markets concerned could be provided with a reliable flow of products through a distribution system modelled on that developed by ATC in America.

Although Thomas tended to place the role of service above that of promotion, it is nevertheless clear that the company used printing factories, which were attached to its cigarette plants, to manufacture advertising materials the

[27] W. A. Anderson, *The Atrocious Crime (of being a young man)* (1973); R. Easton, *Guns, Gold and Caravans* [*China Caravans* (UK version)] (1978); J. L. Hutchison, *China Hand* (1936); L. Parker and R. D. Jones, *China and the Golden Weed* (1976). For accounts by British recruits in China at a somewhat later period see also J. Stericker, *A Tear for the Dragon* (1958); N. Burnett, *On the Edge of Asia* (1995); R. P. Dobson, *China Cycle* (1946); J. Logan, *China: Old and New* (1982).

[28] Hutchison, *China Hand*, pp. 101–2.

like of which had never previously been seen in China, and the company's salesmen were entreated to utilize these materials to the maximum effect. Occasionally this task was undertaken with excessive zeal, as when a massive billboard advertising 'Pirate' cigarettes was erected in the Yangtze gorges. Thomas was forced to provide a written apology for this indiscretion to the wife of the British Consul in Chengtu (Chengdu), General Fox, remarking that, 'It is not the policy of the Company to spoil the beautiful scenery of the Yangtze Gorges.'[29] Nevertheless, promotion through poster displays was the most common form of marketing used by BAT in China, and few opportunities were missed to exploit these materials to the full. Somewhat later, an even more extravagant publicity mechanism was generated by the company when it created a modern film studio in Shanghai, producing feature films designed to promote BAT cigarette brands and to record newsworthy events.[30]

Post-war Expansion

By the end of the First World War BAT employed a workforce in China of close to 10,000 people, of whom between 500 and 600 were foreign.[31] However, this huge enterprise lacked a well-defined corporate structure in China itself, since there was no single holding company which controlled operations there. The London parent company held a majority stake in the three manufacturing companies: BCC, Lopato & Sons, and the Alliance Tobacco Co., the first of which controlled the factories in Shanghai and Hankow, whilst the latter two both operated production facilities in Manchuria. In addition to these manufacturing enterprises, two other subsidiaries had been created to oversee distribution in China; Mustard & Co., to which BAT Co. had granted sole distribution rights to certain of its brands in the region surrounding Shanghai, and the Chinese-run Union Tobacco Co., which had been allocated through a BAT Co. brand-holding subsidiary company (Enterprise Tobacco Co.) a small number of brands to market across the whole of China. Elsewhere, the company's sales offices were effectively branches of the main BAT Co. parent company, which reported to the

[29] Letter J. A. Thomas to Mrs Fox, dated 30 September 1914, Thomas Papers, Box 1.

[30] The motion picture facility, headed by William H. Jansen, was found to be particularly useful in developing close relations with provincial governors by filming their ceremonial events, etc. See letter from A. Rose to Wang Hsien, Secretary to H. E. the Governor of Shansi, dated 23 May 1924; letter from F. C. Jordan, Nanking, to Departmental Manager, BAT Co. (China) Ltd., Shanghai, dated 14 October 1925, BAT Archive (SASS), Doc. Nos. 21-A-20 and 21.

[31] Letter from J. Hood (BAT Co.) to Amery (Colonial Office) dated 6 January 1920, FO 371/5324/117.

Shanghai headquarters. Not surprisingly, therefore, at the end of the war the directors of BAT Co. in London sought to create a more coherent corporate structure in China by forming a locally registered holding company as they had done in other major markets.

Up until 1915, foreign businesses that wished to register a company in China could do so under the Ordinances set down by the British colonial regime in Hong Kong.[32] By the turn of the century, however, a growing number of these Hong Kong-registered companies, including BAT Co.'s own manufacturing arm BCC, were actually operating entirely outside of Hong Kong—in Shanghai and other treaty ports. Provision had been made for such a state of affairs in 1911, when the Companies Ordinances were amended to allow firms operating elsewhere in China to officially register their enterprises in Hong Kong. However, the British authorities in the Crown Colony became increasingly concerned that companies registered in Hong Kong, but actually operating elsewhere in China, would be able to claim immunity from Chinese laws by virtue of their Hong Kong registration, but still be beyond the effective control of the colonial authorities. Thus in 1915 additional legislation was enacted to extend the scope of the Ordinances and allow companies that were based elsewhere in China to register directly in their place of business.

The effect of this new legislation, The China (Companies) Order in Council, was thus to create two separate types of British-registered company in China: 'Hong Kong China Companies', the operations of which were directed from Hong Kong, and 'China Companies', whose operations were directed from other parts of China where the principle of extraterritoriality was in force. The new Order of 1915 stipulated, amongst other things, that 'the majority of the Directors of a China Company shall be British subjects resident within the limits of this Order' in an effort to minimize the extent to which these provisions could misused.[33] The effect, however, was to create a minefield of bureaucratic confusion.

In February 1919, BAT Co. registered a new holding company for its Chinese operations in Shanghai, under the terms of the 1915 Order, called BAT Co. (China) Ltd. In line with the regulations governing such China Companies, a number of British directors were appointed to the board of BAT Co. (China). Hugo Cunliffe-Owen became the designated chairman of the holding company, with the American Thomas Cobbs continuing in his role as

[32] For a summary of the development of British jurisdiction in China see P. H. Ch'en, 'The Treaty System and European Law in China: A Study of the Exercise of British Jurisdiction in Late Imperial China', in W. J. Mommsen and J. A. de Moor, *European Expansion and Law: The Encounter of European and Indigenous Law in 19th- and 20th-Century Africa and Asia* (1992), pp. 83–100.

[33] See FO 371/5324/F181.

successor to James Thomas as local managing director. This newly created operation was a vast financial enterprise, with an authorized capital of Mex.$225 million of which Mex.$161.8 million was immediately issued.[34] BCC became the manufacturing arm of the organization, and the distribution arrangements with Mustard & Co. were transferred to the new company. One benefit of restructuring its Chinese assets in this way was that it allowed BAT some financial leverage in its negotiations with the Chinese government. BAT Co.'s management in London were particularly anxious to ensure that the organization would not be subject to discrimination in terms of the level of taxation of its products, and to offset the ongoing threat of a Japanese-sponsored government monopoly of the industry. In line with this thinking, one-third of BAT Co. (China)'s authorized capital took the form of 8 per cent cumulative preference shares, one-third of which were to be offered in exchange for an equivalent amount of Chinese government 6 per cent bonds and an agreement by BAT to buy back a fixed proportion of these shares for cash at par value at any time over the following ten years.[35]

As these negotiations were under way, however, the management of BAT Co. found themselves deflected by the decision of Sir John Jordan, the British Minister in Peking, to amend the China (Companies) Order in Council in an attempt to strengthen British commercial influence in China. Under the terms of the amendment, it was stipulated that companies registered under the 1915 Order should now have a British subject in the position of managing director. Such a revision created consternation within BAT since the company's Chinese operations at that time were still largely under the management of Americans, notably Thomas Cobbs and William Morris, or a Russian in the case of the business in Manchuria.[36] In an effort to overcome the difficulties raised by the amendment, the company dispatched one of its vice-chairmen, Arthur C. Churchman, to China to engage in discussions with the authorities there. In the meantime, Joseph Hood and BAT Co.'s secretary A. M. Rickards engaged in a frantic dialogue with representatives at the Foreign Office in London.[37]

Ultimately, BAT were able to solve the problem by exploiting the fact that Jordan's amendment to the legislation related to the registration of China Companies only, and did not apply to companies registered in Hong Kong.

[34] Given the fact that, around 1919, the Chinese Mexican dollar (the Yuan) was trading more or less at parity against the American dollar, the issued capital of BAT Co. (China) was roughly equal to the current value of BAT Co.'s entire balance sheet assets.

[35] Letter J. A. Thomas to G. G. Allen, dated 20 August 1919, Thomas Papers, Box 3. The offer was never taken up by the Chinese government.

[36] See letter from J. Hood (BAT Co.) to L. S. Amery (Colonial Office), dated 6 January 1920, FO 371/5324/F117.

[37] This correspondence can be found in Foreign Office files FO 371/5324 and 5325.

Thus in 1920 BAT Co. (China) was re-registered in Hong Kong and its head office in China was formally transferred to the British colony. The move required a majority of the company's resident directors to live in Hong Kong and, as a result, fourteen BAT Co. (China) directors were instructed to tender their resignations, including James Thomas.[38] In spite of its inconvenience, it nevertheless enabled Thomas Cobbs as an American citizen to maintain his position as managing director.

The incident served to emphasize the pre-eminent position which the London directors now held over the Chinese operation. When James Duke protested to the British Ambassador in Washington, Sir Auckland Geddes, that the new measures discriminated unfairly against the American employees of the company, the Foreign Office merely retorted that the London directors of the company were perfectly satisfied with the move to Hong Kong.[39] The episode also brought home to the top management of BAT Co. in London the importance of building close links with the Foreign Office and consular service in relation to the business in China. Shortly after the shift in headquarters from Shanghai to Hong Kong, BAT Co. recruited a long-standing member of the British diplomatic service in China, Archibald Rose, to act as their advocate in matters of a political nature. One of his first tasks was to secure the rescinding of the amendment to the Order in Council, allowing the re-registration of BAT Co. (China) in Shanghai and the restoration of its headquarters there in 1922.

The post-war expansion of BAT's operations in China extended across production facilities, local tobacco leaf processing, and an expanded system of distribution and marketing. Major investments were made in cigarette manufacturing and printing facilities in the northern city of Tientsin between 1919 and 1921, and in Tsingtao during 1924. The plant in Tsingtao, in Shantung (Shandong) province, was designed to take advantage of the expanding supply of locally grown flue-cured tobacco leaf from the company's Ershihlipu (Ershilipu) plant. Under the supervision of R. H. Gregory, BCC had recruited over fifty Americans to work in its leaf department between 1916 and 1920 in an effort to support the local cultivation of tobacco from Ameri-

[38] Letter T. F. Cobbs to J. A. Thomas, dated 27 July 1920, Thomas Papers, Box 4. Thomas had by this time already gone on leave of absence from BAT to work for the Chinese–American Bank of Commerce. The other directors who were requested to resign from the China company at this time were R. Bailey, S. Trumper, V. J. S. Rumble, W. C. Foster, C. F. Wolsiffer, A. T. Hueckendorff, P. H. Millard, T. E. Skidmore, C. E. Harber, A. Bassett, W. W. England, H. B. Emerson, and H. Thomas.

[39] Duke's protest to Geddes was followed up by George Allen who wrote directly to the British Ambassador on the matter. See letter from G. G. Allen to Sir A. Geddes, dated 6 December 1920, FO 371/5325/3334. The popular press in the United States generally played up the amendment as a typical case of British high-handedness.

can seed. During this period it built facilities for processing leaf in Honan (Henan) and Anhwei (Anhui) provinces as well as in Shantung. It was the latter site which proved to be the most successful; the Honan plant on the other hand was an inauspicious initiative, costing the company both money and lives.[40] Table 6.3 illustrates the growth in local leaf procurement for cigarette manufacturing in China between 1915 and 1940.

The period after 1919 also saw further refinements made to the regional distribution system which had been introduced by Thomas. Under BAT Co. (China) the distribution structure based around five sales departments was further strengthened, with four of the departments (Shanghai, Hankow, Tientsin, and Manchuria) served by their own factories and only Hong Kong in the south still completely reliant on outside supplies. These five regional departments were then subdivided into divisions which, for the most part, were based on China's provincial structure. Divisions were segmented into territories, based on county boundaries, and each territory was divided into districts using China's postal system. These districts were the primary unit of the sales organization, and were managed by district salesmen who provided the links with the local Chinese retailers and reported back to their territorial managers. The basic sales structure, as it operated in 1924, is shown in Figure 6.1.

The five sales departments constituted relatively independent entities and provided the company with an organizational structure which was well suited to cope with the dislocations from political upheavals, warfare, and natural disasters that China suffered between the wars.[41] At the top of this structure were British or American departmental and divisional managers who supervised the passage of cigarettes through the various layers of the company's dealerships. At the territorial and district level, however, Chinese employees were used to manage the process of distribution and to engage in selling. During the 1920s BAT also developed franchising arrangements whereby responsibility for the sales performance of certain territories was given over to trusted

[40] BAT was forced to abandon its operation in Honan during the Chinese civil war of 1925. In 1933, it set up the Hsuchang Leaf Tobacco Co. under the management of Wu Ting Seng, assisted by an American, G. H. Newsome, and attempted to resume its support for the cultivation of flue-cured leaf in Honan. However, by purchasing leaf directly from the cultivators the operation worked against the interests of local groups who were acting in the capacity of tobacco brokers. In 1935 Wu Ting Seng was assassinated by professional gunmen and the following year Newsome was also murdered, causing BAT to abandon the initiative. BAT Archive (SASS), Doc. Nos. 14-E-65–76; *BAT News* (Spring 1988), 10–13.

[41] James Hutchison noted on his return to China in 1929 that each department operated its own advertising, accounting, and traffic offices and thus were effectively self-contained units. Hutchison, *China Hand*, p. 180. See also S. Cochran, 'Economic Institutions in China's Interregional Trade: Tobacco Products and Cotton Textiles, 1850–1980'.

TABLE 6.3. Purchases of flue-cured leaf tobacco by BAT in China ('000 lbs.), 1915–40

Year	Shantung	Honan	Anhwei	Total
1915	490			490
1916	2,323			2,323
1917	8,620		212	8,832
1918	24,883	1,940	623	27,446
1919	22,454	7,579	8,544	38,577
1920	27,611	14,331	7,115	49,057
1921	13,636	8,306	28	21,970
1922	6,742	5,598	3,361	15,701
1923	19,969	9,468	5,747	35,184
1924	21,957	23,509	12,330	57,796
1925	20,810	7,636	10,108	38,554
1926	5,916		3,069	8,985
1927	5,194			5,194
1928	16,307		468	16,775
1929	17,327		3,922	21,249
1930	20,575		2,898	23,473
1931	17,854		161	18,015
1932	26,935		4,419	31,354
1933	46,036		11,492	57,528
1934	37,499	43	16,004	53,546
1935	58,012	17,394	15,080	90,486
1936	47,515	6,814	20,017	74,346
1937	18,149			18,149
1938	15,750			15,750
1939	20,023			20,023
1940	8,521			8,521

Notes: Shantung = Ershihlipu plant constructed 1917–20; 1915–16 processed at Fangtse plant; Honan = Hsuchow plant constructed 1918–20: 1917–21 also processed at Hankow plant; Anhwei = Mentaitze plant constructed 1918–19: 1917 processed at Pengpu plant. BAT also operated: Tsingtao re-ordering plant built 1935; Whashing Road leaf plant (Shanghai) constructed 1930–1; Hankow leaf plant, machines installed in 1936–7.
Source: BAT Archive (SASS), Doc. Nos. 14-D-130–136: 14-D-232–233.

Chinese employees. These distributors were allocated a Western supervisor and removed from the BAT payroll, being remunerated instead through profit-sharing arrangements.[42] Distribution arrangements such as these gave the Chinese a much more prominent role in developing BAT's sales operations, although the scope of their managerial discretion was limited by the

[42] An example of the appointment of a Chinese distributor within the Hong Kong department can be found in the case of Si King Sun, who had earlier been employed as an assistant to the divisional manager for Yunnan, J. H. Crocker. In July 1923 Mr F. H. Parkinson, the man-

Tientsin Department: Manager Mr W. B. Christian	
Northern Division	(Twelve territories)
Peking Division	(Three territories)
Frontier Division	(Nine territories)
Luhan Division	(Twelve territories)
Shantung Division	(Thirteen territories)
Hankow Department: Manager Mr H. B. Emerson	
Hupeh Division	(Twenty-six territories)
Hunan Division	(Thirteen territories)
Honan Division	(Fifteen territories)
Kiangsi Division	(Six territories)
Hong Kong Department: Manager Mr H. E. Parkinson	
South China Division	(Fifteen territories)
Kwangsi Division	(Four territories)
Yunnan Division	(Six territories)
Shanghai Department: Manager Mr V. S. J. Rumble	
Eastern Division	(Twenty-three territories)
Nanking Division	(Forty-six territories)
Manchurian (Moukden) Department: Manager Mr V. L. A. Fairley	
S. Manchurian Division	(Thirty-four territories)
N. Manchurian Division	(Twenty-one territories)

FIGURE 6.1. BAT Co. (China) Ltd. sales structure, April 1924
Source: Cox, 'Creating a Distribution Network for Cigarettes in China', Figure 1.

agreements into which they entered. For example, an agreement allocating two Chinese distributors responsibility for the twelve territories comprising the Luhan division of the Tientsin department stipulated that, 'Distributors will not sell any cigarettes at a lower price than the Company's current price without the consent in writing of the Company.'[43]

ager of the Hong Kong sales department, wrote to Crocker inviting him to place Si in control of three territories in Yunnan division on a commission basis, with the understanding that he would assume responsibility for any losses sustained. Crocker was told that he was to be appointed as Mr Si's advisor and that Si would no longer appear on the company's payroll as an employee. Si was invited to make any changes that he felt necessary to the depot arrangements in the three territories before assuming control of them. BAT Archive (SASS), Doc. Nos. 13-C-346–347. In his memo, Parkinson makes it clear that this type of arrangement had already been implemented in other departments.

43 Agreement between BAT Co. (China) Ltd. and Tsui Tsun San and H. L. Kung, BAT Archive (SASS), Doc. Nos. 13-D-67–71. See also letter from H. L. Kung to J. A. Thomas, dated 5 October 1920, Thomas Papers, Box 5 in which he explains that he and Tsui have set up a separate organization called the San Ho Cigarette Co. to handle 'Rooster' and 'Kingfisher' cigarettes in the Luhan division on the same basis as Wing Tai.

The appointment of distributors was part of a general move on behalf of the company to increase the involvement of Chinese merchants in their business affairs. Thomas's first major attempt to do this had been through the Union Tobacco Co. joint venture with Wu Ting Seng, but by the time of his departure from BAT Co. in 1919 this initiative had foundered. Nevertheless, Thomas' close relations with Wu were matched by his faith in Cheang Park Chew, the managing director of the Wing Tai Vo Tobacco Co., whom he had taken to London with Wu Ting Seng in 1912 in an effort to strengthen his loyalty to the company.[44] On his return to Shanghai, Cheang had been given the franchise for the imported 'Ruby Queen' brand of cigarettes for the whole of China. At this time BAT simply sold the goods to Cheang at a standard price and allowed him to add on whatever profit margin he felt appropriate. In November 1917, a more formal arrangement was drawn up whereby BAT paid all expenses in connection with the distribution of 'Ruby Queen' and a fixed commission on each 50,000 case sold.[45] Eighteen months later, by an agreement dated 16 May 1919, Cheang was instructed to set up a sales network of distributors which exactly paralleled BAT's China-wide depot system.[46] In addition to the 2 per cent commission payable to Cheang himself, Wing Tai Vo's distributors were to be paid a commission of 1 per cent. These distributors were given exclusive rights to deal in the brands of 'Ruby Queen' and 'Vanity Fair' (a lower grade brand) within the limits of each specified sales division, and were themselves to appoint association dealers and sub-dealers in each of the villages, towns, and districts served by the sub-depot within their designated division. In November 1919, Cheang cabled Thomas to exclaim that his Wing Tai Vo organization had sold over 5,000 cases of 'Ruby Queen' cigarettes during the month of October, and another 444 cases of 'Vanity Fair'.[47]

Cheang's ability to rapidly expand BAT's cigarette sales lay in his willingness to offer more generous credit terms to his large network of dealers. Whereas BAT, in order to safeguard itself, had been obliged to place stringent conditions on its Chinese distributors in terms of guarantees, the regional solidarity which characterized Wing Tai Vo's network of Cantonese merchants allowed him to adopt much less restrictive conditions.[48] Cheang required

44 Chen Ren Jie, *Ying-Mei*, p. 158.

45 BAT Archive (SASS), Doc. No. 2-E-32.

46 Agreement between Mr Cheang Park Chew and BAT Co. (China) Ltd., dated 16 May 1919, Thomas Papers, Box 3.

47 Letter Cheang Park Chew, Shanghai, to J. A. Thomas. London, dated 18 November 1919, Thomas Papers, Box 3.

48 The regional links which were so important to the success of Wing Tai Vo were a characteristic feature of the capitalist bourgeoisie that had emerged in Republican China at that time. These groups, including Cheang Park Chew (Zheng Bo Zhao) are discussed by Bergère, *Golden Age*, ch. 4, esp. pp. 141–52.

much less in terms of the capital value of distributors; he extended credit on the strength of only one guarantor and on a much more lenient basis, and he even paid interest on money that was lodged with him as security. As a result, Wing Tai Vo was able to push a greater volume of sales through its network of distributors.[49] By September 1920, sales of 'Ruby Queen' had set a new monthly record for the company in China of 11,462 cases of 50,000 cigarettes and BAT began to supplement American production of their China brands with output from the factory in Liverpool.[50]

During 1920 Cheang Park Chew's position within BAT had been strengthened still further by the departure of Wu Ting Seng. In March 1919 Wu's interest in the Union Tobacco Company as a shareholder was terminated, and in June the following year Wu resigned from BAT altogether and transferred his affiliation to the rival Nanyang Brothers Tobacco Company. In response, BAT awarded the franchise for those brands handled by Union within the Shanghai area to Wing Tai Vo.[51] The sales performance of Cheang's organization was by now crucial to the success of the company's operation in China, particularly in the area around Shanghai, and during 1921 BAT reached an agreement with Cheang to form a new joint venture called the Wing Tai Vo Tobacco Corporation.[52]

Using capital resources derived from sales commissions, Cheang and his two main business partners, Cheang Gong Xia, his eldest son, and Huang Yi Cong, his brother-in-law, were able to put up 49 per cent of the agreed capital of the new corporation of 1 million Yuan. BAT Co. (China) put up the remaining 51 per cent, thus retaining voting control of the partnership, and to the three Chinese directors BAT added three of their own senior staff, William Morris, Joseph Daniel, and Arthur Bassett.[53] Bassett, who was made vice-chairman of the Wing Tai Vo Tobacco Corporation, had earlier been appointed by Cobbs as Cheang's business adviser and foreign associate as part of the agreement of May 1919.[54] In addition, one Chinese shareholder, Chin Chong Yin, and one British representative, Robert Bailey, were appointed as inspectors. In order to maintain financial control of the Wing Tai Vo Corporation, BAT required that all dealers settled accounts through payment to

[49] Chen Ren Jie, 'Ying Mei', pp. 160–1.

[50] Letter C. W. Pettitt, BAT Co.'s China Department, London, to Thomas dated 5 October 1920, Thomas Papers, Box 5.

[51] Letter H. C. Tan, BAT Co. (China), Shanghai, to Thomas dated 10 June 1920, Thomas Papers, Box 4.

[52] BAT Archive (SASS), Doc. Nos. 2-E-32–43.

[53] Chen Ren Jie, 'Ying Mei', p. 159.

[54] BAT Archive (SASS), Document No. 3-A-6. Bassett was also responsible for appointing Chen Ren Jie as Cheang's secretary. Chen had worked under Bassett for the BAT organization and was used to monitor the operations at Wing Tai. He was one of only two 'outsiders' who worked for the Wing Tai Vo organization. Chen Ren Jie, 'Ying Mei', p. 163.

Plate 16. James A. Thomas who created BAT's nation-wide distribution system in China between 1905 and 1915.

Plate 17. BAT Co. staff pose outside Mustard & Co.'s main office in Shanghai around 1905. Thomas (third from left) is standing alongside his predecessor, C. E. Fiske.

Plate 18. Chinese street-vendor selling 'Pin Head' and 'Atlas' cigarette brands, *c.*1900. The Chinese symbols for 'Pin' and 'Head' were recognized in many parts of China at this time as the generic name for cigarettes.

Plate 19. BAT office in Korea *c.*1905. Note the advertisement for the popular 'Pirate' brand of cigarettes on the roof of the building.

PLATE 20. Camels loaded with cases of cigarettes bound for Urga (Ulaanbaatar) in Mongolia.

PLATE 21. Promoting cigarettes in Yunnan province using gramophone records, 1908.

Plate 22. A BAT Co. selling-cart salesman at work in China, *c.*1910.

Plate 23. The British Cigarette Co. factory in Pootung (Pudong) Shanghai, *c.*1920.

Plate 24. Young girl packing cigarettes in the Pootung factory.

Plate 25. Handling hogsheads of tobacco at BAT's Ershilipu leaf-processing plant in Shantung (Shandong) province, *c.*1920.

Plate 26. Chinese farmers delivering tobacco leaf to a company buying station.

Plate 27. A company-owned railway carriage, probably in Hankow (Wuhan), with sales team displaying promotional materials.

Plate 28. Wills' Calcutta distributor promoting the company's 'Scissors' brand of cigarettes during the 'Tobacco War' of 1901.

Plate 29. Charles Percy Page who managed BAT's operations in India from 1906 until his death in 1923.

Plate 30. Unloading a 30-foot Lancashire boiler for BAT Co.'s cigarette factory in Monghyr (Munger), India, during 1924.

PLATE 31. A Bombay (Mumbai) tobacconist promoting Ardath's 'State Express 555' cigarette brand, 1929.

PLATE 32. The Imperial Tobacco Co.'s cinema car and sales team kitted-out to promote 'Red Lamp' cigarettes, 1922

PLATE 33. A cup-winning hockey team drawn from staff of the Imperial Tobacco Co.'s Bangalore factory, 1922.

Plate 34. Ardath's offices in Penang, *c.*1930.

Plate 35. A street hawker in Singapore, 1931.

the parent company's banks. Thus Wing Tai Vo had no independent accounting records; the sales generated were recorded by the accounting division of the parent company at its Shanghai headquarters and all accounts were receivable by that company. Commission was then paid to Wing Tai Vo in due course on the value of cigarettes that were sold through its distribution mechanism. In addition Wing Tai Vo received an annual bonus of 20,000 Yuan and, of course, 49 per cent of the dividends generated by the profits of the Wing Tai Vo Corporation were paid to Cheang and his relatives on the board of directors.

By the early 1920s, therefore, BAT had two distinct distribution structures operating across China. First, the company's own integrated, but regionally based distribution system in which the role of managing the company's distribution network was delegated as far as possible to non-salaried Chinese agents working on commission, overseen by a monitoring system using salaried Westerners in the capacity of foreign inspectors. Secondly, the joint venture with the Wing Tai Vo Tobacco Corporation which managed its own China-wide distribution network, presided over by Cheang Park Chew, but under BAT (China)'s financial control. This latter organization directly employed over 200 staff, all of whom were linked together by the native place association based on their Cantonese heritage.[55] Figure 6.2 illustrates the importance of the Wing Tai Vo operation to the company's sales in China between 1923 and 1941.

Operating as a Foreign Enterprise

Cobbs' tenure as managing director in China lasted for a little over five years before his retirement in 1921.[56] His position was taken by another American, William Morris, whose term of office continued until his transfer to London in 1927 where he became director with responsibility for Chinese affairs.[57] Morris's period of control in Shanghai was marked by increasingly chaotic

55 Chen Ren Jie, 'Ying Mei', pp. 160–1; Bergère, *Golden Age*, pp. 150–1.

56 Cobbs' impending retirement is noted by C. W. Pettitt of the China office in London in a letter to Thomas and confirmed in Thomas's reply. See letter from C. W. Pettitt to J. A. Thomas dated 30 July 1920 and reply dated 20 November 1920, Thomas Papers, Boxes 4 and 5. His actual retirement is noted in FO 371/9205/127.

57 Morris had joined BAT from ATC in November 1903 and was appointed manager of the company's factory in Durham. He had been transferred to Shanghai in 1910 as manager of the company's factories there following the departure of Henry Keily to Liverpool. *BAT Bulletin*, 18 (94) (1928), 313.

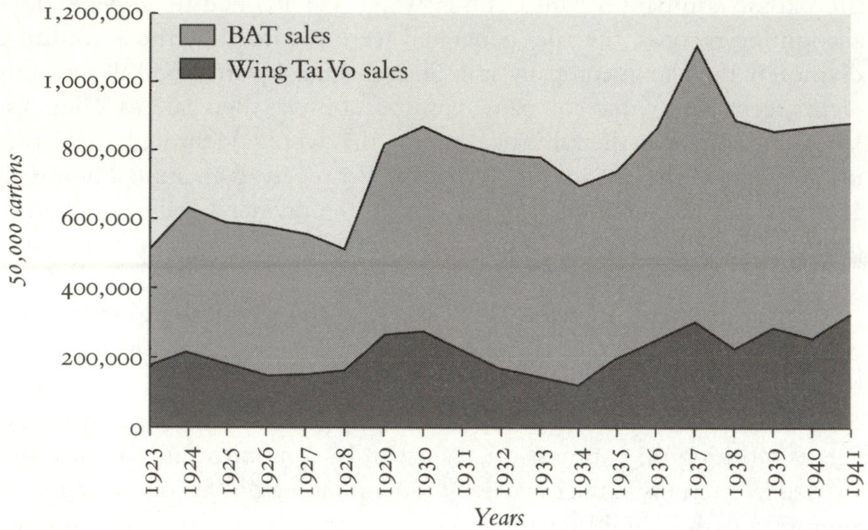

FIGURE 6.2. Sales of manufactured cigarettes in China (BAT v. Wing Tai Vo), 1923–41
Source: Shanghai (ed.), *Ying Mei*, pp. 512, 630.

political conditions. The overthrow of the Imperial Dynasty by Sun Yat-sen's Nationalists in 1911 had failed to establish a stable government and succeeded only in plunging the country into a complex civil war. Sun and his supporters in the Kuomintang (KMT) retreated to the south of the country and were gradually able to build up a new base in Canton (Guangzhou) where they enlisted military support and advice from the Soviet Union after 1922. In the north, meanwhile, the machinery of government in Peking fell under the control of various provincial warlords whose fortunes ebbed and flowed, principally in relation to their ability to extract tax revenues from any available source.[58] Naturally, the facility of exploiting the production and trade in cigarettes as a source of such tax revenue became a major objective of both national and provincial governments and brought BAT into conflict with various Chinese authorities.

During the early 1920s the question of cigarette taxation also became a crucial issue for the foreign powers as they attempted to protect their economic interests in China and, at the same time, bolster the authority of a national government in Peking. BAT's negotiations concerning the taxation of cigarettes

[58] For a summary of the political background to this period see J. K. Fairbank, *China: A New History* (1992), pp. 235–93.

centred on two issues. One concerned the levying of local taxes (principally a transit tax called likin) by provincial governments which were increasingly becoming a burden on internal trade and acted to divert revenues away from central government, thereby adding to the degree of political instability in China. The other was the attempt by the central government in Peking to levy taxation on tobacco goods at the point of production through the creation of a central tobacco tax bureau.

After 1918, these two tax issues became linked, as BAT sought to negotiate with the central government for the abolition of likin in return for a fixed level of duty imposed on all cigarettes produced in China. The success of such a strategy required the generation of sufficient revenues in Peking to enable the central government to compensate provincial authorities for the loss of their likin tax receipts. It was precisely this type of scheme that interested the foreign powers who were engaged in their own discussions with the authorities in Peking. They felt that a similar approach could be adopted to abolish likin on all internal trade, which was threatening to disrupt the continued development of China as an export market, in return for greater autonomy over the tariff levels which the central government could levy on its external trade. The abolition of likin and its substitution by a higher national import tariff would also serve the purpose of strengthening central government, and allow for greater political stability in China.

BAT had plenty of experience in such negotiations. The company had first engaged in discussions with the authorities in Peking regarding cigarette taxation in 1904 when the manager of BCC, Henry Keily, struck a deal with the chief Foreign Minister of the Imperial government which allowed the company's locally manufactured cigarettes to be taxed on a par with native goods. This gave its cigarettes manufactured in Shanghai the advantage of avoiding customs duties of 5 per cent *ad valorem*, as well as a reshipment tax of 2.5 per cent for those which left the treaty ports, but it left them exposed to a variety of local levies including likin.[59]

Further negotiations took place when, following the failure of Sun Yat-sen to establish his authority in the wake of the 1911 revolution, the governance of China fell under the control of the military leader Yuan Shih-k'ai. In 1913 his government had solicited BAT's support for a state tobacco monopoly, but the company had been warned off engaging in such discussions by the British Minister Sir John Jordan.[60] The following January the

[59] See letter from Satow to Grey, dated 7 April 1906 and other correspondence in FO 371/180/18884; see also Cochran, *Big Business*, pp. 42–3 for tax negotiations surrounding the Mukden factory.

[60] See letter from Jordan to Grey, dated 5 March 1914, FO 371/1945/12596.

company was again approached on the question. This time James Thomas and Arthur Bassett travelled to Peking for discussions on the setting up of a government tobacco bureau which would levy a stamp tax on all manufactured cigarettes in exchange for the abolition of likin. This was a far more acceptable idea to the company than that of a state monopoly, and Joseph Hood in London wrote to Earl Grey at the Foreign Office to explain why BAT was prepared to pursue negotiations in this respect.[61] Thomas sent Wu Ting Seng to negotiate in Peking on BAT's behalf during the spring of 1914, and in the meantime Cunliffe-Owen travelled to China to oversee the process and make the final arbitration. However, when Cunliffe-Owen saw the terms Wu had agreed with Yuan Shih-k'ai's government he turned them down flat.[62] As a result BAT's goods continued to be subjected to likin and other provincial taxes and their local managers became involved in countless disputes as to the validity of these levies.[63]

Following the failure of these negotiations with Yuan Shih-k'ai's government in 1913–14, the finance ministry in Peking had set up a Wine and Tobacco Administration with a view to controlling the domestic trade. Without the participation of BAT the experiment had not been a success and late in 1918 the newly installed President of the Chinese Republic, Hsu Shih-ch'ang, decided that the Wine and Tobacco Administration should be made an independent concern.[64] In January 1919, Chang Shou-lin, formerly vice-Minister of finance and ex-head of the Salt Administration, was appointed as director-general of the reformed Wine and Tobacco Administration and began an effort to expand upon the annual tax revenue received from tobacco sales. Two months later Archibald Rose, still at this point based at the British Legation in Peking, wrote to BAT's legal department in China explaining that he had arranged for an interview with the newly appointed director-general of the Wine and Tobacco Administration. In his letter Rose stated that Chang 'hoped to have foreign assistance in the Tobacco Administration' and urged BAT's representatives to 'establish pleasant personal relations' with him.[65]

[61] Letter Hood to Grey, dated 4 March 1914, FO 371/1945/9864.

[62] Letter Jordan to Grey, dated 28 July 1914, enclosing Cunliffe-Owen's response, FO 371/1945/56433.

[63] See for example letters from A. T. Heuckendorff to Statistical Department, Shanghai, dated 31 October 1915 and J. N. Jordan to Lu Cheng Hsiang, Minister for Foreign Affairs, dated 10 November 1915, BAT Archive (SASS), Doc. Nos. 24-B-47–50.

[64] A. Nathan, *Peking Politics* (1976), p. 77; H. K. Tong, 'Development of China's Wine and Tobacco Administration', *Millard's Review*, 8 (1919), 197–200.

[65] Letter from A. Rose to W. B. Kennett, Peking, dated 5 March 1919, BAT Archive (SASS), Doc. No. 24-B-21.

During the months that followed the British authorities increasingly recognized the advantages that could be gained from allowing the Chinese government greater tariff autonomy in exchange for the abolition of likin, and continued to encourage BAT to participate in tax negotiations with the Chinese government in Peking.[66] In April 1921, Sir Beilby Alston of the British Legation in Peking cabled the British Consulate General in Shanghai requesting BAT to send representatives to the capital 'for [the] purpose of negotiating [a] settlement of [the] taxation question throughout China with [the] W[ine] and T[obacco] authorities'. BAT's management was strongly urged to take up the invitation on the grounds that their China-made goods were not covered by the terms of the existing trade treaties and hence could not be afforded consular protection from increased taxes levied by provincial governments.[67]

For BAT, the benefits of reaching an agreement with the central authorities lay in stemming the growing burden of provincial taxes which were increasingly disrupting the firm's sales in China and had led to a complete suspension of business in Shantung Province. Thus a series of negotiations between BAT (assisted by a Foreign Office diplomat from the British Legation) and the Chinese government ensued which extended over a three-month period.[68] When a settlement was finally reached, in August 1921, BAT agreed to pay 2.5 per cent *ad valorem* tax on all goods shipped into the interior, whether imported or manufactured in China, and in addition, cigarettes manufactured within China (and thus not subject to import tax) would be levied with a factory tax of Mex.$2.00 per case of 50,000 cigarettes. In return, the company's goods would be exempt from paying all likin and other provincial duties, and in any cases where such duties were levied and paid by the company, these would be deducted from the amount of inland tax paid to the central government.[69] It was estimated that the effect of the agreement

[66] The issue of China's tariff reform was an important element in the discussions of the Washington Conference, held in November 1921, which was designed to restore the military balance of power in the Far East among the principal powers. By early 1921, the diplomatic approach to these discussions had become an overriding concern of the Foreign Office staff in Peking. On the discussions and outcome of the Washington Conference, see W. R. Louis, *British Strategy in the Far East, 1919–1939* (1971), ch. 3.

[67] Letter from HMB Consulate General, Shanghai, to BAT General Manager, Shanghai, dated 27 April 1921, containing transcript of telegram from Sir B. Alston, BAT Archive (SASS), Doc. No. 24-C-45.

[68] During the course of the negotiations, the company repeatedly expressed concern to the Foreign Office that the Japanese were attempting to earmark the new tax revenues for security against earlier loans, and possibly to gain outright control of the Wine and Tobacco Administration. See letter A. M. Rickards (Secretary BAT Co.) to FO, dated 30 April 1921 and letter A. Rose to E. Teichman (Peking), dated 18 May 1921, FO 371/6654/1623.

[69] Agreement between BAT Co. (China) and Wine and Tobacco Monopoly Tax Bureau, dated 3 August 1921, BAT Archive (SASS), Doc. Nos. 24-C-63–66.

would be to raise the total amount of agreed tax payable by BAT in China by as much as Mex.$800,000 per year.[70] However, the compensating advantage of free movement for their goods helped to raise the company's sales in China between 1921 and 1924 from 18 billion to 32 billion cigarettes per annum.

At almost the same time that the agreement with the Wine and Tobacco Administration was reached, Archibald Rose left the British diplomatic service and became a director of BAT Co. (China). Rose's demeanour has been well described by one interviewee, the author Graham Greene, as having:

> the appearance of a senior army officer, perhaps a brigadier, in plain clothes. He was correctly dressed in dark capitalist uniform, with a well-tied bow tie, a well-groomed moustache; he had the politeness of a man speaking to his equal in age and position. He would have made a good Intelligence officer, and I have little doubt now that he belonged, however distantly, to the Secret Service. A man in his position, recruiting and controlling men for the Chinese hinterland, could hardly have escaped contact with the 'old firm', and perhaps for that reason he was not scrupulously accurate about the details of the employment. The end justified the means.[71]

Under Cunliffe-Owen, therefore, it is clear from the appointment of Rose that the company increasingly tended to see its political interests in China as lying squarely behind those of British imperialism rather than, as had been the case under Thomas, through a process of direct relations undertaken by influential Chinese such as Wu Ting Seng.

One major weakness of the agreement made between BAT and the Wine and Tobacco Administration in August 1921 was that its terms did not extend to the five provinces in the south which were under the control of the KMT regime in Canton. Immediately upon the agreement between BAT and the Wine and Tobacco Administration being put into force, therefore, the authorities in Canton imposed a 20 per cent levy on tobacco goods. BAT's secretary in China, W. B. Kennett, wrote to protest against this new tax to the British Consul-General in Canton, who lodged a formal complaint to the commissioner for foreign affairs of the Canton government.[72]

In fact, BAT's sales in these provinces were not great and it was not a region in which the company had built a factory (and hence the Canton government would have no recourse to any of the taxes levied on factory output). Reporting to the directors in Shanghai, one of BAT's principal officials wrote:

[70] Letter Sir B. Alston to Lord Curzon, Peking, dated 4 November 1921, FO 371/6670/4838.

[71] Initially attracted by the idea of a posting to China, Greene soon became disenchanted at the prospect of working for BAT following his brief period as a pupil at the Liverpool factory and resigned after two weeks. G. Greene, *A Sort of Life* (1971), p. 148.

[72] Letter W. R. Kennett to J. W. Jamieson, dated 30 September 1921; letter J. W. Jamieson to Li Chin-lu, dated 3 October 1921, BAT Archive (SASS), Doc. Nos. 24-D-1–6.

> The tax, which is being put on at present in Canton city only, has not had much effect on our business up to the present. It is not of course, paid by the company, but by the retailers, and has been put on all competition brands as well as our own. Between you and me I think Mr Yik Fuman has already discovered a way of getting round the payment of this tax, but I thought it wise not to inquire too deeply into his methods.[73]

The most significant aspect of this episode was that BAT and the British government's representatives in China acted in accord, principally to ostracize the rebel Canton regime.

In the company's main markets of northern China the provisions of the 1921 agreement with the Peking government initially worked well. During 1922, from a gross payment of the new tax stamps of Mex.$726,717, BAT were obliged only to deduct Mex.$17,277 in respect of unauthorized provincial taxation. Optimism proved ill-founded, however, as the political structure of China became increasingly fragmented. In April of 1923 Sir Ronald Macleay, the British Minister in Peking, wrote to the Foreign Secretary Lord Curzon in London expressing concern that the provinces of Fukien (Fujian) and Chekiang (Zhejiang), both now effectively independent of Peking, had followed the lead given by Canton and introduced a 20 per cent consumption tax on tobacco goods. In spite of diplomatic pressure brought to bear in Peking, the political disintegration of China continued during 1923 and threats to impose a similar tax were made in a number of provinces during the months that followed.[74] By the beginning of 1925, the new taxes had spread to most of the provinces and the central authorities began to attempt to justify them, as consumer taxes, rather than oppose them.[75] The impact on the company's sales by this time had become apparent and both BAT's management and the British authorities realized that the success of British enterprise in China now depended critically upon the emergence of a strong central government which was willing and able to enforce its laws in favour of business.

The Impact of Chinese Nationalism

The years during which the tax agreement with Peking held sway witnessed a period of rapid growth in sales for the company, whose partnership with the

73 Letter E. B. Macnaghten to W. Morris, dated 24 October 1921, BAT Archive (SASS), Doc. No. 24-D-7.

74 A detailed discussion of the introduction of these taxes is contained in FO 371/9217/832.

75 Letter A. L. Dickson to Director of National Cigarette Bureau, Shanghai, dated 16 January 1925, BAT Archive (SASS), Doc. Nos. 24-D-185–190.

Wing Tai Vo organization proved to be a great success.[76] In the early 1920s, BAT's brands accounted for around 80 per cent of all cigarette sales in China and few rival firms were able to compete effectively. However, as the political situation began to deteriorate seriously so opportunities for Chinese firms began to expand, especially with the rise of nationalist sentiment among Chinese consumers during the mid-1920s. Between 1925 and 1928, BAT's performance in China was badly hit by a combination of consumer boycotts and workers' strikes, as well as by competitive pressure stemming from a growing number of Chinese cigarette manufacturers.

The success of Chinese cigarette companies waxed and waned in direct relation to the strength of pro-nationalist and anti-foreign sentiment in China. The boycott of American goods in 1905, which Wing Tai Vo had so effectively helped BAT to evade, afforded Chinese firms the first such opportunity for a brief period of competitive success.[77] One company which established operations at this time was the Hong Kong-based firm, the Kwantung (Canton) Nanyang Tobacco Company, Ltd. The company was set up by two brothers, Chien Chao-nan and Chien Yü-chieh, with relatives among the overseas Chinese, and its initial success was founded on its sales in South-East Asia, notably through Singapore. In common with many other such small companies which set up at this time, the Nanyang concern began to experience financial difficulties as the boycott of foreign products receded and in 1908 it ceased production and attempted to sell up. A lack of buyers meant that the capital assets of the company were in fact retained and during 1909 the brothers decided to recommence production. In 1911, following another upsurge of nationalist sentiment in the wake of the Republican revolution, the company's sales began to expand rapidly.[78] Building on the strength of its Chinese origins, and the greater support for the Republican movement around Canton, Nanyang began to have some success against BAT within China itself. Although its cigarettes were undoubtedly inferior in quality to those manufactured by BAT, consumers were persuaded to

[76] By 1923, Wing Tai Vo accounted for 35 per cent of all BAT's sales in China. Shanghai (ed.), *Ying Mei*, pp. 512 and 630.

[77] Bergère, *Golden Age*, pp. 50–1, notes that the campaign of May 1905 was the first occasion in which boycotting had been used for explicitly political purposes and that it had spread to all the merchant communities of the treaty ports; Cochran, *Big Business*, pp. 45–53, suggests that around twenty new Chinese companies were formed during this time, but that few survived much beyond the duration of the boycott. For an example of such a rival concern, the Pei-yang Tobacco Company, set up in Tientsin in 1905 and wound up in 1908, see W. K. K. Chan, *Merchants, Mandarins, and Modern Enterprise in Late Ch'ing China* (1977), pp. 104–6.

[78] For statistics on the Nanyang company's sales and profits, 1912–48, see Cochran, *Big Business*, Table 6.

patronize its brands in preference to those of the foreign company through the use of clever advertising campaigns and acts of benevolence such as support for flood relief. By 1917 the Nanyang company had gained sufficient strength to establish a plant in Shanghai in direct competition with its Western rival, and the following year it transferred its headquarters there from Hong Kong.[79]

During the course of the First World War the capital assets of the Nanyang company expanded twentyfold, and in 1918 the enterprise was transformed into a joint stock company[80] as indigenous Chinese businesses in general underwent a period of expansion.[81] As BAT found itself obliged to shift its headquarters from Shanghai to Hong Kong, the threat posed by Nanyang was acknowledged by Cobbs in a letter written to Thomas during November 1920:

> I left Hongkong on the 9th instant against [the] advice of some of our Legal friends there to come to Shanghai on account of serious competition which we have got in Shanghai and the Yangtsze [*sic*] Delta, and I want you to know that this competition is serious. I have particular reference to Canton-Nanyang 'Ngai Kuo' [brand]. They are trying to the utmost limit to influence public sentiment in their favour. Their 'China for the Chinese' slogan is, in my opinion, becoming stronger throughout China today.[82]

As the success of the Nanyang company in China gathered pace BAT adopted various strategies to undermine the Chiens' credibility, most notably by drawing attention to Chien Chao-nan's Japanese citizenship following Japan's annexation of Shantung and the subsequent issuing of the Twenty-One Demands in May 1915.[83]

One of the strategies adopted by the management of BAT in an attempt to neutralize competition from Nanyang was amalgamation. The Western company had first approached the Chiens regarding a possible merger in 1914, when Wu Ting Seng had acted as an intermediary. In 1917 they had raised the question of co-operation again when James Thomas attempted to persuade the Chiens to join BAT in the type of joint venture later used with

[79] On the development of the Nanyang company, see Cochran, *Big Business*, pp. 54–61 and *passim*; Y. C. Wang, 'Free Enterprise in China: The Case of a Cigarette Concern, 1905–1953', *Pacific Historical Review*, 29 (1960), 395–414; *Tobacco (London)*, 46 (551) (1926), xvii.

[80] Cochran, *Big Business*, pp. 96–102; the Chiens began to offer Nanyang's stock for public subscription in May 1919, idem., p. 115.

[81] Rawski has argued that a variety of Chinese-owned businesses were stimulated by the activities of foreign firms, citing examples of industrial activities such as processed foods, chemicals, machinery, and cigarettes. T. G. Rawski, *Economic Growth in Prewar China* (1989), p. 6.

[82] Letter T. F. Cobbs to J. A. Thomas, Peking, dated 17 November 1920, Thomas Papers, Box 5.

[83] Wang, 'Free Enterprise', p. 402; Cochran, *Big Business*, pp. 63–5.

Wing Tai Vo. Although Thomas seems to have convinced Chien Chao-nan of the benefits to be gained from such an arrangement, the other partners in the firm held out against such a move.[84] A third attempt at a merger was initiated in 1919 by Chien Chao-nan himself, who travelled to the United States to hold discussions with George Allen. These negotiations continued through 1920 and in 1921 appeared to have reached a successful conclusion when Albert Jeffress struck a deal with Chien Chao-nan in Shanghai. At the last moment, however, the remaining directors of Nanyang, who had come from Hong Kong in order to ratify the deal, were unwilling to accept the terms and refused to sign—much to the frustration of Jeffress.[85]

In fact, the economic climate for business in China improved sufficiently during the early 1920s to allow both BAT and Nanyang to expand their cigarette sales. Following its failure to reach an agreement with BAT, the Nanyang management revived their strategy of appealing to nationalism as a competitive weapon and gradually began to develop direct links with the KMT. Although this policy created certain difficulties for the Chinese firm, as it temporarily became embroiled in factional disputes between the moderate and militant arms of the KMT, after 1925 the strategy began to deliver Nanyang a major source of advantage over BAT.[86]

The factor which proved decisive in allying the interests of Nanyang with those of the KMT was the advent of the May Thirtieth movement. In May 1925 a group of Chinese, protesting against the shooting of a fellow worker by a supervisor at a Japanese-owned mill, were themselves fired upon by British troops. The incident provoked a wave of nationalist protests against British enterprises which in relation to BAT took the form of a boycott of the company's products and strikes at their Shanghai and Hankow factories. For the first time, the 15,000 workforce at Shanghai acted in unity to confront BAT's management. In doing so they were assisted by financial support from the Nanyang company which helped to prolong the dispute for four months.[87] The protest also brought together the opposing wings of the KMT as the two factions turned their attention towards the common struggle against imperialism. This consolidation of the KMT leadership around the cause of nationalism persuaded the Chiens to give the regime their full support; a decision

[84] Cochran, *Big Business*, pp. 84–96.

[85] Letter A. G. Jeffress, Shanghai, to J. A. Thomas, dated 13 March 1921, Thomas Papers, Box 5; Cochran, *Big Business*, pp. 145–50.

[86] Initially the Nanyang managers had appointed two representatives of the KMT as supervisors at their Shanghai factory in order to ally themselves more closely with the moderate wing of the organization's labour leadership. Cochran, *Big Business*, pp. 172–6.

[87] Perry has noted that there were three main factions within BAT's Shanghai workforce: skilled mechanics, semi-skilled cigarette machine-minders, and unskilled leaf strippers and cigarette packers. E. J. Perry, *Shanghai on Strike: The Politics of Chinese Labor* (1993), pp. 148–51.

which was further encouraged by the emergence of a new leader, Chiang Kai-shek, who appeared to be purging the leftist elements within the leadership in Canton and held out the promise of a government of national unity which would favour indigenous businesses.[88]

Meanwhile, BAT's sales were being severely disrupted by the May Thirtieth boycott. Demand for Wing Tai Vo's 'Ruby Queen' brand in Shanghai completely collapsed in the summer of 1925, and the product needed to be disguised as an American brand under the name of 'Red Pack' before sales could be restored. As a result of the boycott, BAT's cigarettes became officially designated as contraband goods. In Honan division, for example, BAT dealers were fined by the local magistrate for selling British cigarettes.[89] As the protest spread, the boycott of BAT's cigarettes received support from all sections of the Chinese business establishment. The Chinese Newspapers Association refused to carry BAT advertising, and the chairman of the Ningpo Steamship Company, who was also the president of the Shanghai General Chamber of Commerce, refused to allow his vessels to transport BAT's goods. As a result, the company's sales were decimated—in Canton where a blockade on British trade was in force, no sales were made at all during the month of September[90]—and many new rival Chinese firms sprang up which were able to establish their goods in the market.[91] The problems in Canton territory were exacerbated by the introduction of a 40 per cent surtax on foreign cigarettes by the KMT government there.

BAT responded to these nationalist pressures by attempting to forge its own political alliances through links with influential Chinese officials. To this end Cunliffe-Owen devised a scheme whereby the number of Chinese shareholders in BAT Co. (China) could be increased without diluting the parent company's control.[92] To do this, a public company called the British–American (China) Tobacco Securities Co., Ltd. was formed in 1926, capitalized at a value of Mex.$2 million, in which each $100 share corresponded to an equivalent share in BAT Co. (China) Ltd. Divisional managers were then requested to suggest names of appropriate Chinese nationals who should be

[88] The key development in this respect was the assassination of a high-ranking KMT official, Liao Chung-k'ai in August 1925, which signalled the beginning of Chiang Kai-shek's attempt to purge the communists from the leadership. Liao had been responsible for organizing a boycott of Nanyang's products in Canton between October 1924 and January 1925. See Cochran, *Big Business*, p. 175.

[89] BAT Archive (SASS), Doc. No. 26-B-160.

[90] BAT Archive (SASS), Doc. Nos. 26-B-365–367.

[91] Cochran, *Big Business*, pp. 176–85; Chen Ren Jie, *Ying Mei*, pp. 163–6; Hou Ching-ming, *Foreign Investment and Economic Development in China, 1840–1937* (1965), p. 152.

[92] Cablegram from Hugo Cunliffe-Owen to William Morris, BAT Archive (SASS), Doc. No. 3-G-71.

offered the opportunity to buy shares in the new company at a discounted price of $85 each. The manager of the company's Nanking Division, Mr M. I. Hartigan, thus wrote to his manager at the Shanghai Department suggesting named individuals in each of his territories to whom shares in the Securities company should be offered. In the Wuhu territory, for example, those identified were:[93]

Ho Ru Pu	Superintendent of Wuhu Customs and Commissioner for Foreign Affairs
Hsu Erh Feng	Chief of Police
Liu Tiao Shih	Manager of Bank of China
Wu Hsing Chao	Assistant to Chairman of Chamber of Commerce and Chief Manager of Wuhu Electric Light Company
Tung Shan Foh	Chairman of Chamber of Commerce
Tang Ming Ching	Owner and Manager of Wuhu Wan Kiang Yih Pao
Li Tsong (illegible)	Lord Li's son, Manager of Wuhu China Merchant Steamer Company
Hsia Su Tang	Chief of Chekao Volunterr [*sic*] Corps
Chu Chih Fu	Luchowfu 20 per cent Tax Official

This effort by BAT to use its political influence as a competitive strategy reached its critical stage between 1927 and 1928 when the business community in Shanghai came under the control of Chiang Kai-shek's KMT government.

During the course of the KMT's military campaign to provide China with a unified government—the Northern Expedition which started out from Canton in July 1926—sales of BAT's cigarettes came under increasing pressure from anti-foreign boycotts. Following the capture of Hankow by KMT forces in November 1926, an anti-British boycott was initiated and BAT's two plants were closed down for months whilst the company's management negotiated with union leaders acting on behalf of the 3,500 workforce.[94] The boycott in the region continued to disrupt sales and in Hunan the BAT divisional manager reported in February 1927 that all other British companies in Changsha had closed down their offices, which had subsequently been occupied by workers' representatives.[95]

[93] Memo from M. I. Hartigan to Departmental Manager BAT Co. (China) Ltd. dated 4 September 1926, BAT Archive (SASS), Doc. Nos. 3-G-80–81.

[94] See reports from *North China Daily News* dated 11 February and 15 March 1927, and *North China Herald* dated 19 March 1927, BAT Archive (SASS), Doc. Nos. 34-E-61–64.

[95] Letter J. N. Joyner, Hunan Division Manager, Changsha, to the Directors, BAT Co. (China), Shanghai, dated 28 February 1927, BAT Archive (SASS), Doc. Nos. 26-A-51–52. BAT intelligence suggests that Nanyang subsidized this boycott of their products. Letter A. S. Kent, BAT (China) to Sir S. Barton, HBM Consulate-General, Shanghai, dated 20 October 1927, BAT Archive (SASS), Doc. Nos. 24-E-179–180.

As the KMT advance approached Shanghai, workers at BAT's factories there staged a series of armed uprisings, culminating on 21 March 1927 in the expulsion from the Pootung district of troops supporting the regime of warlord Sun Chuan-fang, coinciding with the arrival of the KMT army.[96] Chiang Kai-shek himself arrived in Shanghai five days later and immediately entered discussions with Chinese business leaders who implored him to prevent the communist forces within the nationalist movement from asserting control. In April 1927, supported by funds raised by these businessmen, Chiang used his underworld connections with Shanghai's Green Gang to launch a bloody coup against communist elements within the labour movement that subsequently became known as the 'White Terror'.[97]

The support for indigenous business which Chiang Kai-shek's breakthrough promised to Chinese businessmen such as the Chiens, however, was quickly undermined as the regime he established at Nanking (Nanjing) sought at any cost to obtain the revenues required to perpetuate its control. A tax on all tobacco products was quickly introduced across Kiangsu (Jiangsu) and Chekiang provinces and by July 1927 the amount of this levy had been raised to 50 per cent *ad valorem*, creating major problems for Nanyang's financial viability and threatening rapid bankruptcy for many of the small Chinese manufacturers who had emerged as competitors to BAT in Shanghai during the boycott of 1925.[98]

When the decision to impose the new 50 per cent tax was made, BAT immediately closed down its factories in Shanghai in an effort to put pressure on the authorities in Nanking.[99] In the meantime, Archibald Rose attempted to marshal support from Sir Miles Lampton of the Peking Legation and Sir Sydney Barton, the British Consulate-General in Shanghai, for the company's decision not to pay the tax.[100] During the stand-off between BAT and the Chiang Kai-shek regime, the Nanyang company attempted to gain advantage by co-ordinating the various Chinese cigarette manufacturers based in Shanghai around a newly established public godown to which only non-foreign firms could subscribe. By acting in concert through the offices of this co-operative organization, the Chiens were then able to negotiate on behalf of all Chinese cigarette manufacturers a 30 per cent reduction in the tariff levied by the

96 Perry, *Shanghai on Strike*, pp. 151–3.

97 P. M. Coble, Jr, *The Shanghai Capitalists and the Nationalist Government, 1927–1937* (1980), pp. 28–31.

98 Cochran, *Big Business*, pp. 188–92.

99 Letter BAT Co. (China) to Sir S. Barton, HBM Consulate-General, Shanghai, dated 30 July 1927, BAT Archive (SASS), Doc. Nos. 24-E-29–30.

100 Letters A. Rose to Sir S. Barton, dated 5 August 1927, and to Sir M. Lampton, dated 19 August 1927, BAT Archive (SASS), Doc. Nos. 24-E-32–39.

Nanking authorities, giving the domestic firms a permanent price advantage over BAT. In response, BAT requested the British Consulate-General in Shanghai to lodge an official protest.[101]

Throughout the latter part of 1927, BAT and the nationalist government in Nanking were at loggerheads as the company maintained its opposition to the new tax. Pressure was placed on the company by the authorities to re-open its factories in Shanghai, to which BAT acquiesced on 15 August. Within weeks, however, a fresh dispute over working conditions saw the entire workforce walk out. Once again, the workers were supported financially through donations made by Nanyang and another Chinese firm, the Huacheng Tobacco Co., with funds being drawn from the discounts allowed to the public godown. This funding allowed the protest to continue throughout the remainder of the year, with the workforce now adding to its other demands a call for BAT to pay the new tax as part of any deal to settle the strike.[102]

BAT's only means of escape from this predicament lay in the ability of its well-managed business organization to generate a vast potential source of revenue for the Nanking regime in the form of cigarette taxes. From 1925, the financial affairs of the KMT had been handled by their Harvard-educated Finance Minister T. V. Soong, who had already negotiated a levy on tobacco of 12.5 per cent directly with the management of BAT when the regime had taken control of Hankow.[103] However, when Soong arrived in Shanghai in April 1927 and tried to assert his authority as Minister of Finance, Chiang perceived the move as a threat to his own position and forced Soong out. Chiang then began to suffer setbacks of his own, through a combination of military reverses against the troops of warlord Sun Chuan-fang and opposition from the KMT government in Hankow (the Wuhan regime), forcing him to stand down in August 1927. During his absence a coalition government took shape in Nanking, but it lacked the strength to maintain its grip over the business community in Shanghai from which Chiang had drawn the majority of his revenues. Chiang, meanwhile, travelled to Japan and was married to Soong Mei-ling, the youngest sister of T. V. Soong and sister to Madame Sun Yat-sen. The alliance helped Chiang Kai-shek's position within the leadership of the KMT and in January 1928 he returned to Nanking and resumed control of the government. One of Chiang's first acts was to reinstate T. V. Soong as Finance Minister, and it was this development

[101] Letter A. S. Kent to Sir S. Barton, dated 18 November 1927; memorandum of a meeting between A. Bassett, A. S. Kent, and Sir S. Barton on 30 November 1927, BAT Archive (SASS), Doc. Nos. 24-E-54–61.

[102] Perry, *Shanghai on Strike*, pp. 154–6.

[103] Letter A. S. Kent, Shanghai, to H. Cunliffe-Owen, London, dated 20 July 1928, BAT Archive (SASS), Doc. No. 24-E-109.

which allowed BAT an opportunity to reassert its leading position in the Chinese cigarette industry.[104]

As early as 1925, the Foreign Office in London had begun to recognize that a policy of reconciliation towards the nationalists might be expedient in order to prevent the KMT falling under the influence of Bolshevism. In December 1926 the official policy of the British government towards Chinese nationalism was revised, explicitly recognizing China's right to tariff autonomy and pledging the abandonment of foreign tutelage over China's affairs.[105] This shift in policy was designed to encourage the moderate wing of the KMT and was actively supported by the big business interests in China.[106] Once T. V. Soong had resumed his position as Finance Minister in January 1928, BAT quickly set about reaching an accommodation with Chiang's regime in Nanking.

The company had already engaged in discussions with the Nanking government, soon after the imposition of the 50 per cent tax in July 1927, with a view to the introduction of an inclusive duty of 27.5 per cent on all its imported cigarettes. The idea had been to bring the tariff on imported cigarettes into line with the revised treaty agreements, but in Soong's absence the discussions had stalled.[107] In the negotiations of January 1928, however, BAT's management and T. V. Soong achieved a resolution of the tax issue, based on a reduced tax rate of 22.5 per cent on all native manufactured products and a composite tax of 27.5 per cent on imported cigarettes.[108] T. V. Soong's offices were also utilized to bring to a conclusion the strike at the company's Pootung factory when a number of new working conditions were agreed by BAT's management at a round table conference held at Soong's own residence in Shanghai on 16 January. Production recommenced two days later and the British military authority withdrew its guard from the factory compound on 21 January.[109]

[104] Coble, *Shanghai Capitalists*, pp. 28–46.

[105] E. S. K. Fung, 'The Sino-British Rapprochement, 1927–1931', *Modern Asian Studies*, 17 (1983), 79–105; S. L. Endicott, *Diplomacy and Enterprise: British China Policy, 1933–1937* (1975), p. 9.

[106] J. Osterhammel, 'Imperialism in Transition: British Business and the Chinese Authorities', *China Quarterly*, 98 (1984), 260–86; P. J. Cain and A. G. Hopkins, *British Imperialism: Crisis and Deconstruction, 1914–1990* (1993), pp. 235–62.

[107] Letter A. S. Kent to Sir S. Barton, Shanghai, dated 16 August 1927, BAT Archive (SASS), Doc. Nos. 24-E-34–35.

[108] This 27.5 per cent comprised a 20 per cent *ad valorem* rate, levied specifically on manufactured tobacco imports, together with the regular 5 per cent import duty and a surtax of 2.5 per cent. See report of new tax arrangements in *North China Herald*, dated 27 January 1928, reproduced in BAT Archive (SASS), Doc. No. 24-E-154.

[109] Report in *North China Herald*, dated 18 January 1928, reproduced in BAT Archive (SASS), Doc. Nos. 34-F-42–44; letter A. S. Kent to China Department of BAT Co., London, dated 20 January 1928, BAT Archive (SASS), Doc. Nos. 24-E-150–151; Perry, *Shanghai on Strike*, pp. 156–7; Cochran, *Big Business*, pp. 192–5.

With the tax settlement in place, and the establishment of a sympathetic leadership in Nanking now assured, BAT actively subscribed to the new arrangements. Soong introduced a policy of allowing discounts for advance payment of the tax and was quickly in a position to use the new revenues generated by the tobacco duties to float government securities that could be used to fund the continuation of the Northern Expedition to Peking.[110] Nanyang and other rival firms were dismayed that the KMT leadership had abandoned its policy of favouring national firms over foreign manufacturers, and stories circulated in the press that BAT had made an advanced payment of Mex.$5 million in tax to secure the deal and had paid a personal bribe to T. V. Soong to the tune of Mex.$70,000, which the company strenuously denied.[111] The higher taxes which the Chinese firms had been forced to pay had severely damaged their profitability and many small companies simply ceased production between 1928 and 1929. The Nanyang Brothers also accumulated heavy losses during these years and, although the company's management persevered in its efforts to compete with BAT, throughout the early 1930s the company's financial position remained precarious. Eventually, in 1937 the surviving partner, Chien Yü-chieh, sold the controlling interest in the Nanyang company to none other than T. V. Soong.[112] Ironically, therefore, Soong ended the decade as the managing director of BAT's only major Chinese-owned cigarette manufacturing rival. During these years the tax on tobacco goods emerged as the third most valuable source of income for the Nanking government and, by the mid-1930s, BAT had become its single largest taxpayer.[113]

Under the new conditions of the 1930s, the most important competition for BAT from amongst the Chinese producers came from small-scale businesses which had developed cigarette manufacture by the traditional method of hand-rolling. As these small enterprises became more experienced and began to incorporate some rudimentary forms of mechanization it became possible for them to manufacture products which were hardly distinguishable in appearance from factory-made goods.[114] During the

[110] Wang, 'Free Enterprise in China', p. 404; Coble, *Shanghai Capitalists*, pp. 70–3; letter A. S. Kent to H. Cunliffe-Owen, London, dated 20 July 1928, BAT Archive (SASS), Doc. Nos. 24-E-108–113.

[111] Reply by A. S. Kent to item in *Republican Daily News*, dated 16 August 1928, BAT Archive (SASS), Doc. Nos. 24-F-18–19.

[112] Cochran, *Big Business*, p. 197; Wang, 'Free Enterprise in China', p. 407. Further negotiations between BAT and Nanyang regarding a possible merger had taken place in 1932. Details are given in the Minutes of the Chairman's Daily Committee of 28 and 29 June 1932, BAT Co. Secretarial Dept.

[113] Osterhammel, 'Imperialism in Transition', p. 283.

[114] Letter A. Rose to Sir A. Cadogan, dated 3 September 1934, FO 371/18086/6164.

early 1930s, these producers made serious inroads into BAT's market share in northern China and the Yangtze basin. Sales of hand-rolled cigarettes were boosted by the rapid rises in taxation on manufactured cigarettes which the Nanking regime implemented. Between 1930 and 1934, as Chiang Kai-shek's regime desperately sought to raise its revenue-generating capacity, the level of consolidated tax levied on the cheapest grade of factory-made cigarette rose from $32 per case to $80 per case.[115] However, the tax raised on hand-rolled cigarette manufacturers—a trade which in 1928 had been of little consequence—was levied by provincial governments and set at only $10 per case, even when it was collected at all. By 1934, hand-rollers were able to sell a case of their cigarettes to dealers at a price of $60, which was $20 less than the amount of tax imposed on BAT's cheapest grades of cigarettes.

While Cunliffe-Owen complained to shareholders in London about the use of 'unscientific taxation' employed by various taxing authorities,[116] the management in Shanghai sought to galvanize the Finance Ministry in Nanking, now under H. H. Kung, to prevent the huge losses in tax revenues caused by the growth of hand-rolled cigarettes. With assistance from Sir Alexander Cadogan at the British Legation in Peking, Kung was persuaded to implement a system of controls designed to phase out the entire hand-rolling cigarette industry in China. From an estimated market share of 25 per cent in 1934, the output of the hand-rollers was systematically reduced as their licences were revoked in quarterly blocks determined by the simple expedient of a quota system based on the drawing of lots. As the controls began to

[115] The system of consolidated cigarette taxation under the Nanking government was not a simple *ad valorem* system and was continually revised from the time of its initial introduction in January 1928. To begin with, a seven-grade system operated which divided cigarettes into classes based on their sales value and imposed a fixed levy per case on each class along a sliding scale. This meant that the value-added component was roughly equal as between different grades of cigarettes. However, in October 1930, the number of grades of cigarettes was reduced from seven to three, and in October 1932 from three to two. This process of reclassification was helpful to BAT *vis-à-vis* the larger Chinese firms because all the cheaper grades of cigarettes had the same amount of tax levied on them, whereas under the seven-grade system the Chinese firms' cheap goods paid less tax than BAT's cheapest brands. Indeed, when in 1934 the Nanking government proposed replacing the two-grade system with a four-grade system, BAT lobbied the British Consular-General in Shanghai to lodge a protest with the Ministry of Finance to prevent such a change. See correspondence between British Consulate at Shanghai and A. Cadogan at the Peking Legation, FO 371/18086/6448/6696; Chen Hang-seng, *Industrial Capital and Chinese Peasants* (1939), pp. 37–41.

[116] By which he meant that the rate of tax levied on cigarettes was so high that it reduced consumption at the margin sufficiently to outweigh additional revenue raised (i.e., to the point where demand had become price elastic). Speech by H. Cunliffe-Owen to shareholders at the BAT Co. AGM, 5 January 1934, *Tobacco (London)*, 54 (638) (1934), 67.

bite in 1936, BAT's sales recaptured the levels of the early 1930s before surging still further in 1937 to reach the highest levels ever recorded by the company in pre-communist China.

Competition from American and Japanese Firms

Indigenous Chinese firms were not the only source of competition that BAT had to face in China. Following the nationalization of the tobacco manufacturing industry in Japan in 1904, Japanese manufacturers established operations in those regions of China where Japan's political influence was most pronounced. By the 1930s, the expansion of Japanese imperialism into mainland China meant that these manufacturers were emerging as the most serious rivals to BAT. Before this, however, the company had been forced to fend off competition from American firms who saw the Chinese market as a growth opportunity after the end of the First World War.

Of the four main firms who succeeded ATC after its dissolution in 1911 only one, Liggett & Myers, made a serious attempt to challenge BAT's hegemony in China. Around 1920, this company opened depots in Hong Kong and Shanghai in an effort to establish an import trade in its 'Chesterfield' cigarettes. In addition, the company also selected a low-price cigarette brand called 'Red House' around which they mobilized a strong marketing campaign in the Shanghai area.[117] BAT's response was to license a new brand to Cheang Park Chew's Wing Tai Vo organization called 'Victory' specifically to nullify the threat posed by Liggett's 'Red House'. Cheang's close links with local dealers provided the BAT brand with a massive advantage and Liggett & Myers were able to make only very limited headway in the market.[118]

A second source of competition from America also arose in the early post-war years from a company called the Tobacco Products Corporation (TPC) which had been set up in 1912 by members of the same group of businessmen that had been involved in the financing of ATC (see Chapter 8). The principal objective of TPC had been to acquire control of as many of the remaining independent American tobacco firms as possible in order to compete with the successor firms to ATC. Initially, therefore, its focus had been the United States market, but in 1919 it formed the Tobacco Products Export Corporation (TPEC) as a vehicle through which it could manage the various foreign operations that it had acquired. These business enterprises

[117] Letter J. A. Thomas to A. G. Jeffress, London, dated 24 August 1920, Thomas Papers, Box 4.

[118] Chen Ren Jie, 'Ying Mei', p. 158.

included a factory at Yulin Road in Shanghai which TPC had set up in 1917.[119]

TPEC made some progress in establishing a market for its cigarettes in China, mainly under the guidance of its vice-president Gray Miller, but by 1925 the business seems to have been losing money and was spun off from TPEC into a separate company called TPC (China). As an American firm, TPC's brands were less affected at this time by the anti-British boycott inspired by the May Thirtieth campaign, but it was experiencing difficulties purchasing leaf tobacco due to the fact that, as one TPC executive put it, 'every Chinaman in Shanghai is trying to break into the cigarette business'.[120] With the TPC operation in China making a loss, and with the TPEC parent company also struggling to maintain financial viability, William Morris recognized an opportunity to gain a new sales outlet for BAT in the Chinese market. In June 1925 Morris cabled George Allen at BAT's New York headquarters to suggest that, if the boycott of British goods in Shanghai persisted, it would make sense to buy out TPC (China) but to continue to operate it as a separate manufacturing and selling organization. In turn, Allen cabled Jeffress at BAT's London headquarters to seek authority to pursue the matter with Tom Yuille, president of the main holding company of TPC (China) in New York.[121] Within weeks Allen was reporting to Jeffress that terms had been settled for the transfer of TPC's Shanghai business to BAT for US$3 million plus $1 million goodwill.[122] It was agreed that Gray Miller should remain in charge of TPC (China), so that its separate identity could be maintained as

[119] The decision by TPC to set up a factory in China was reported in the trade journal *Tobacco (London)*, 37 (436) (1917), 47. For the origins of TPC cf. Chapter 8 of the present volume. A history of TPEC in China can be found in BAT Archive (SASS), Doc. Nos. 2-D-112–115; 128–131; 160–166.

[120] Letter W. R. Johnson, TPC (China), Shanghai, to R. M. Ellis, TPEC, New York, dated 29 July 1925, BAT Co. Secretarial Department File No. MA 85.

[121] Yuille was already well acquainted with the set-up at ATC, having joined the leaf department of that firm at the time of its formation in 1890. By 1901 he headed the leaf-purchasing department of the trust, and remained as vice-president in charge of leaf tobacco purchasing and manufacturing until 1916. M. Duke and D. P. Jordan, *Tobacco Merchant: The Story of Universal Leaf Tobacco Company* (1995), p. 15.

[122] The transfer of TPC (China) to BAT was effected partly through a transfer of shares in BAT (China) rather than entirely in cash since the shareholders in TPC (China) wished to retain a direct interest in the cigarette business in China. The final amount paid for goodwill was US$750,000. As part of the deal, BAT Co. agreed to purchase 160,000 shares in TPEC (about one-third of the total shares issued) and hold them for at least one year. The TPEC was considered to be in such poor shape by BAT's management that they wrote off the cost of these shares from the following year's profits as a dead loss. Cunliffe-Owen attempted to interest Gilbert Wills in buying TPEC's business in Britain, which included a factory in Brixton, London, to use as a semi-independent competitive weapon, but Wills declined. Correspondence contained in BAT Co. Secretarial Department File No. MA 85.

a way of helping BAT to overcome the problems caused by the boycott of British goods.[123]

Two years after the purchase of TPC (China), as conditions in the Chinese market continued to pose difficulties for foreign firms, BAT (China) also bought control of Liggett & Myers' business and trade marks in China and Indo-China. The deal, arranged between Cunliffe-Owen, Morris, and Liggett & Myers' representative C. B. Arthur, involved the payment of $100,000 gold to Liggett & Myers annually for fifteen years, the issue of $2.5 million in ordinary shares in BAT (China) and the sale of a further $7.5 million ordinary shares to Liggett. The contract itself was consummated outside of the United States to avoid possible complications connected with the Sherman and Clayton Acts. After completion of the deal, the Chinese sales force of Liggett & Myers was amalgamated with that of TPC (China), and the latter company undertook to manufacture Liggett's brands. As with the TPC purchase, BAT's role in the amalgamation was kept secret so that the American identity of the organization could be maintained.[124] By the end of 1927, therefore, BAT controlled all the important Western interests in the Chinese cigarette market,[125] although the American shareholders of TPC and Liggett & Myers maintained a financial involvement through their ownership of a block of BAT Co. (China) shares.

From the second half of 1928, as the company took advantage of the new tax agreement with the KMT government to boost its market, BAT's sales in China surged to new heights. With the two American rivals now under its control, and Nanyang still recovering from losses incurred during its campaign to oust BAT from the market, the company stood in its strongest position for half a decade. However, one competitive threat lurking on the horizon was that posed by the expanding Japanese tobacco industry. Following the occupation of Manchuria by Japanese troops in 1931, Japanese cigarette manufacturers began to emerge as BAT's main large-scale rival in China.

Competition to BAT from Japanese-manufactured cigarettes in China and Korea had developed immediately following the imposition of state control over tobacco manufacturing in Japan at the beginning of the century, when

[123] BAT (China) actually sold to TPC (China) one of its factories in Shanghai (at Dixwell Road) in order to allow its business to expand at this time. BAT's ownership of TPC (China) was not revealed even to the two companies' own staff until 1935.

[124] Correspondence relating to the purchase of Liggett & Myers' business in China is contained in BAT Co. Secretarial Department File No. MA 48.

[125] At least two tobacco companies manufacturing Oriental-style cigarettes were operating in Tientsin during the early 1920s. These were the Galatis Tobacco Association and the Tientsin Tobacco Co., *Rea's Far Eastern Manual (2nd Edn)* (1924), p. 314. After resigning from Nanyang, Wu Ting Seng bought control of a Greek tobacco company called the Souter Tobacco Co., personal communication with Mr Wu Sing Pang, 30 August 1995.

the rights to distribute the government monopoly's brands in Korea and China was granted to a company called the Tōa Tabako Kabushiki Kaisha (also known as the East Asia Tobacco Company). This organization set up its head office in Tokyo, and established three factories in Korea between 1908 and 1912 following the extension of Japanese rule there. In China itself the main factory of the Tōa company was based in Manchuria, at Newchwang, on a site that fell under the jurisdiction of the Japanese-controlled South Manchuria Railway Authority.[126] During the First World War, further investments in production capacity were made by the Tōa within China. In May 1917 the company purchased control of a small firm in Shanghai which had been operating under Greek supervision as the An Li Tai Tobacco factory, and the following year it commenced production in Tientsin.[127] Also in 1917, following the assumption of control of German possessions in Shantung province by Japan, two other Japanese tobacco concerns set up production facilities in Tsingtao, although neither appear to have manufactured cigarettes. According to one source, the Tōa's Newchwang factory produced over 2 billion cigarettes in 1917 and 3.75 billion in 1921, although an unspecified proportion of these were destined for consumers in Japan.[128]

During the 1920s the progress of Japanese-made cigarettes in the Chinese market was relatively limited, partly because Japan's products suffered even more than BAT's from the effects of nationalist boycotts. BAT's main concern with Japan at this time was its fear that the Chinese government's Wine and Tobacco Administration would fall under Japanese influence or control.[129] This problem never actually transpired and, in fact, Japan's main impact on the Chinese tobacco industry as a whole at this time was its role as the principal foreign purchaser of Chinese-grown tobacco leaf for its factories in China, Korea, and Japan.[130] However, after the annexation by Japanese troops of Manchuria between 1931 and 1933, and the creation of the

[126] The rights over the land bordering the railway (about 20 km. either side of the track) were granted to Japan by the Treaty of Portsmouth in 1905 and the area was governed by the SMR company quite independently of the rest of Manchuria. T. Wright, *Coal Mining in China's Economy and Society, 1895–1937* (1984), pp. 121–2.

[127] G. Hershatter, *The Workers of Tianjin, 1900–1914* (1986), p. 49, n. 13.

[128] *Rea's Far Eastern Manual* (1923), pp. 310–17. This report states that the Tōa factory in Newchwang operated 100 cigarette-making machines, whilst BAT's Mukden plant contained only fifteen.

[129] For example, see H. K. Tong, 'Japan Seeking China's Tobacco Monopoly', *Millard's Review*, 5 (1918), 49–52; correspondence between A. M. Rickards, secretary of BAT Co., and E. Teichman, Foreign Office, between April and June 1921, FO 371/6654/1623.

[130] *Rea's Far Eastern Manual*, p. 310; Cochran notes that the Tōa was at this time the third largest purchaser of Chinese flue-cured leaf tobacco behind BAT and Nanyang, Cochran, *Big Business*, p. 196.

Japanese puppet state of Manchukuo, the impact of Japanese competition became a much more pressing matter for BAT.

The Japanese Advance in China

The initial impact of the Japanese advance into Manchuria in September 1931 was a disruption of BAT's market there sufficient to cause a 25 per cent decline in its cigarette sales during the subsequent twelve-month period (see Table 6.4). Of more concern to the company than the short-term dislocation brought about by the invasion, however, was the long-run impact of Japanese political control over the region. On 6 October BAT Co.'s secretary A. M. Rickards wrote to Sir John Pratt at the Foreign Office demanding an assurance from the Japanese that they would not extend their tobacco monopoly into Manchuria, and a pledge that no discriminatory legislation would be imposed in respect of the tobacco business there. In doing so, Rickards took the opportunity to remind the Secretary of State of the difficulties that BAT had faced following the Japanese annexation of Korea some twenty years earlier.[131]

In fact, BAT had already made some provision for the possible separation of its operations in Manchuria in 1930 when it promoted a new corporate identity in Shanghai called the Chi Tung Tobacco Co., Ltd. This organization was set up to operate as BAT's distribution arm in Manchuria on a commission basis and on 12 January 1931 it formally took over the godowns, staff, and selling organization previously supervised by BAT Co. (China).[132] Thus the company already had in place an organization enabling it to operate in Manchuria independently from its other business interests in China. During 1933, after the creation of the Japanese-sponsored state of Manchukuo, Chi Tung assumed control of the company's business in Manchuria on its own account, as a subsidiary of BAT Co. (China), with H. V. Tiencken appointed as managing director in Mukden, under the supervision of A. S. Kent at the headquarters in Shanghai.

Japan's objective in Manchuria was to create an economically autonomous region which could be placed under the administration of a nominally independent government but which would, in effect, be a Japanese colony. Immediately following the occupation, therefore, the Japanese authorities created a finance bureau to take control of, among other things, the consolidated tobacco tax revenues that accrued from cigarettes manufactured within

[131] Letter from A. M. Rickards to J. Pratt dated 6 October 1931, FO 371/15491/5415.

[132] BAT Co. Secretarial Department Legal History File.

TABLE 6.4. Breakdown of BAT and Wing Tai Vo (WTV) sales in China by regional market (50,000 cartons), 1931–41

Year	Manchuria		Tientsin		Hankow		Shanghai		Hong Kong	
	BAT	WTV	BAT	WTV	BAT	WTV	BAT	WTV	BAT	WTV
1931	118,639	1,052	203,312	57,928	129,608	52,543	118,459	112,475	41,011	1,623
1932	87,017	695	202,809	42,160	127,049	44,780	156,123	89,343	39,762	1,253
1933	129,381	985	177,911	33,179	141,201	33,372	149,268	87,135	37,734	1,582
1934	150,834	1,523	138,152	24,725	124,353	26,321	116,958	79,363	47,449	–
1935	174,759	–	143,227	24,935	121,166	20,808	115,557	105,819	47,119	94
1936	178,242	–	164,506	26,969	143,750	24,404	120,033	154,213	56,536	–
1937	219,950	–	209,794	31,818	196,907	43,684	143,265	177,901	80,970	994
1938	217,557	–	178,821	21,837	145,562	19,977	53,735	159,024	88,586	3,080
1939	180,688	–	222,043	31,353	38,275	12,992	77,242	201,075	90,235	4,584
1940	180,669	–	283,049	33,274	41,680	23,113	127,296	180,268	66,499	890
1941	165,927	–	235,658	44,520	26,903	9,154	62,822	235,415	80,899	2,312

Note: Sales statistics are for year ending September.

Source: Shanghai (ed.), *Ying Mei*, pp. 734–46.

the region. BAT's main Japanese rival, the Tōa company, quickly fell into line by purchasing its tax stamps from this Fengtien Bureau of Finance. Chi Tung was put under pressure to follow suit and, following the seizure of part of its stock for non-payment of tax, Archibald Rose informed the Foreign Office that the company had fallen into line—warning at the same time that 'Japanese Authorities are . . . trying to secure control of the Customs and Tariffs in Manchuria.'[133]

Rose engaged in a period of active diplomacy over the question of BAT's operations in Manchuria, where formal diplomatic ties with Britain had been severed by the crisis of 1931. The issue which first generated concern for BAT was the differential tax situation between Manchuria proper and the autonomous Railway Zone within it. The fact that the factory operated by the Tōa Company in Newchwang was located within the Railway Zone, meant that it was not obliged to pay the consolidated Chinese tax on any of its products that were sold within the boundaries of the zone. In contrast, BAT's cigarettes manufactured in Mukden were all liable for tax regardless of whether they were sold inside or outside the Railway Zone, thus leaving them at a price disadvantage. During March 1932, Kent and Tiencken engaged in a series of fruitless discussions with Dr Kanai, a senior Japanese government official, in an effort to rectify the discrepancy.[134] Kanai's only advice was that BAT should build a factory of its own within the zone, thus prompting a further series of negotiations with the Japanese authorities. Eventually permission was gained to lease a small factory at Liaoyang under the supervision of an existing BAT Co. (China) subsidiary, the Keystone Tobacco Co., but not before fresh concerns regarding a Japanese tobacco monopoly in Manchuria had been raised.[135]

As these negotiations dragged on, Archibald Rose took steps in London to enlist support from the Department of Overseas Trade to set up a meeting with the relevant parties in Japan. Initially, attempts were made to include a representative from the tobacco industry in a delegation of Japanese cotton textile businessmen who were visiting Britain for high-level discussions, but

[133] Letter from A. Rose to Foreign Office dated 24 March 1932 enclosing text of agreement reached between Chi Tung and the Fengtien Bureau of Finance regarding the purchase of tax stamps. FO 371/16203/3039.

[134] See letter from A. S. Kent to A. Bassett in Shanghai, dated 8 March 1932 and memorandum of interview with Japanese official Dr Kanai dated 21 April 1932, BAT Archive (SASS), Doc. Nos. 24-G-15–21; reports of the negotiations are also contained in FO 371/16203/4540/4566.

[135] Initially BAT were given permission to open a factory in Mukden but despite five months of negotiations between March and September 1933 this proved impossible. The Liaoyang factory was eventually opened in the autumn of 1933. Various papers relating to this question are contained in FO 371/17110 and 17111.

this ploy was rejected by the British Embassy in Tokyo who felt that a widening of the agenda would be counter-productive.[136] Instead Rose visited Japan directly in September 1933 and held discussions with various influential politicians and military officials, which helped to smooth the path and enabled the Liaoyang factory to commence operations. Rose also managed to gain an interview with the president of the Tōa Company, Mr Tsuneo Kanemitsu, with whom he raised the possibility of a pooling arrangement between his company and BAT to cover the market in Manchuria. Rose then travelled to Manchuria from where he wrote to Cunliffe-Owen expressing his optimism over future developments in Manchukuo.[137]

Rose's optimism was well-founded. As the Japanese regime in Manchuria consolidated its control over the region, transportation was afforded greater security and trading conditions improved markedly. After an initial dip in sales following the dislocations caused by the invasion itself, BAT's Manchurian Department began to thrive. Despite competition from the Tōa Company, BAT managed to maintain its market share in the region at around 75 per cent and saw its sales there practically double between 1931 and 1937 (see Table 6.4). Indeed, the relative importance of Manchuria to the company's sales in China actually increased after the creation of Manchukuo. Whereas before the invasion of Manchuria the region had accounted for 20 per cent of the company's overall sales in China, by 1935 this proportion had increased to 30 per cent.

In other parts of China operating conditions were subject to disruption from continued political instability and banditry, with sales in northern China bearing the brunt of these difficulties during the mid-1930s. Industrial strife also continued to present BAT with problems, as the large factory workforce employed by the company provided the focal point of political struggles within the nationalist movement, and in May 1934 the company took the decision to close down its original factory in Shanghai, the Pootung No. 1 plant, because of the highly politicized nature of the workforce there. The decision provoked a strike at the No. 2 plant which lasted for ninety-six days, although the company was able to maintain production at its other factories in Shanghai.[138] The disruptions in Shanghai highlighted the increasing

[136] Letter from A. Rose to Sir E. Crowe dated 8 May 1933 and his reply dated 9 May 1933 together with other correspondence related to the visit, FO 371/17111/3127/3220/3431.

[137] See letter from A. Rose to H. Cunliffe-Owen dated Mukden 17 October 1933 contained in FO 371/17111/6757/6789/6961.

[138] For contemporary papers relating to the strike and its settlement see FO 371/18085/4417 and FO 371/18086/4690/5518; an account by one of BAT's British managers at Pootung can be found in Burnett, *On the Edge of Asia*, pp. 32–5; for the political background to the strike, see Perry, *Shanghai on Strike*, pp. 153–9.

difficulties which the company now faced as a foreign enterprise in China and persuaded BAT's management in London to adopt a new identity as it had done in Manchuria. In September 1934, all of BAT's production and distribution rights in China outside of Hong Kong were transferred to a pair of new subsidiary companies called respectively the Yee Tsoong Tobacco Co., Ltd. (YTT) and Yee Tsoong Tobacco Distributors Ltd. (YTTD), with the latter being a fully owned subsidiary of the former. As well as giving the company more of a local identity, BAT also used the change as an opportunity to encourage greater participation from local investors in the subsidiary.

The local connections of YTT were enhanced by the appointment for the first time of a Chinese director, C. S. Shen. Meanwhile, in an effort to engage more investment from the Chinese—and in Manchuria from the Japanese—Archibald Rose continued his round of diplomatic negotiations. Shortly before the creation of YTT, Sir Alexander Cadogan at the Foreign Office provided Rose with a letter of introduction to Madame Chiang Kai-shek whom he visited in July 1934. In her interview with Rose, Madame Chiang pronounced it unlikely that the Chinese government would feel able to invest in a British company, but suggested he approach the Chinese banking community. This led to further discussions with a leading Shanghai banker, S. L. Hsü, and then with T. V. Soong, but the discussions do not seem to have resulted in any fresh investment from this source.[139]

BAT's efforts to obtain investment from Japanese sources in Manchuria also proved unsuccessful, but for a quite different reason. The authorities in Manchukuo were very interested in making investments in the tobacco business there, but with a view to economic control rather than merely financial participation. In 1934 a company named the Manchu Tobacco Co. was founded in Tokyo whose licence to operate from the Manchukuo authorities was granted on the proviso that it could be purchased by the government at any time.[140] Although this organization made little initial investment of its own, it nevertheless represented a serious threat to Chi Tung's position in Manchuria in the longer term. During 1935, the management of the Tōa Company approached BAT Co. (China) through a representative of Uni-

[139] The correspondence between Rose and Cadogan, including reports of the meetings with Madame Chiang, S. L. Hsü, and T. V. Soong, are recorded in FO 371/18086/F5051/F5640/F6164. Soong raised the possibility of investing via his recently formed China Development Finance Corporation which BAT Co.'s directors had earlier declined an invitation to invest in themselves, Minutes of the Chairman's Daily Committee dated 24 April 1934, BAT Co. Secretarial Department.

[140] Discussions between W. P. Stericker, F. F. Macnaghten, and the Foreign Office in July 1934, FO 371/18114/4771/4819/4834.

versal Leaf, offering to buy out its Chi Tung subsidiary.[141] It was argued that the pooling arrangement which had been proposed by Archibald Rose to the Tōa's president would not be permitted by the authorities in Manchukuo and that the formation of the Manchu Tobacco Co. provided a clear signal that competition was about to become intensified. BAT, who were in the process of trying to gain permission for additional production capacity in Manchuria through the construction of a new factory in Newchwang, interpreted the Tōa's bid as a direct threat to its continued existence in Manchuria and demanded that the Foreign Office lodge a protest through the British Ambassador in Tokyo.[142] The management of the Tōa Company later denied making the approach and BAT were subsequently granted permission to build a factory in Newchwang, although this latter agreement was made conditional on the Chi Tung subsidiary being reformed as a company under Manchukuo law.[143]

The obligation to re-incorporate Chi Tung in Manchukuo was symptomatic of the pressures that BAT found itself under in Manchuria as the Japanese-controlled regime tightened its grip on the economy there. Following the outbreak of war between Japan and China in 1937, these pressures became acute as the Manchukuo authorities began to wrest complete control of the tobacco industry in Manchuria. This control was effected by the same means as had been used at the turn of the century in Japan itself; namely through a government monopoly of leaf tobacco. To begin with, exchange controls were imposed to reduce imports and a quota imposed on the amount of leaf that could be purchased from outside the Yen currency bloc. Then a state-sponsored company called the Manchu Leaf Tobacco Kabushiki Kaisha was created in November 1938 which was given control over the purchase and distribution of all domestic and imported tobacco leaf. The principal objective of the new company was stated to be the improvement of conditions for the cultivation of leaf tobacco in Manchuria, and the Chi Tung company was invited to put up capital in the organization. However, BAT's management doubted that this would give them any effective influence over the company's

141 The Universal Leaf Tobacco Company set up a substantial buying operation in China during the mid-1920s, see Duke and Jordan, *Tobacco Merchant*, pp. 32–45.

142 This episode is related in the Foreign Office papers contained in FO 371/19236/7. It was originally considered that the protest, lodged by Britain's Ambassador to Japan, Sir R. Clive, should contain a threat of retaliation. However, the Secretary of State for Foreign Affairs, Sir Samuel Hoare, felt that such an approach would be inadvisable given that the Japanese actions in Manchuria had merely paralleled British discrimination against Japanese interests in Egypt, FO 371/19237/5238.

143 Chi Tung was duly re-incorporated in Mukden on 29 July 1936 with a capital denominated in Manchurian Yuan. At the end of 1936, BAT Co. (China) was also re-registered in the British colony of Hong Kong.

affairs and, since it was already unable to remit dividends from Chi Tung, further investment in Manchukuo seemed futile.[144] With the loss of control over leaf supplies, Chi Tung saw its market share in Manchuria decline precipitously from 1938 (see Table 6.5).

The Japanese invasion of mainland China after 1937 led to a severe disruption of BAT's operations and a sharp decline in the company's sales. In northern China these problems were less acute because the transfer of authority had occurred more rapidly and the attitude of the Japanese military authorities towards foreign business had been less aggressive, according to a report by the British Ambassador. In Shanghai and the surrounding districts, however, his report pointed out that there had been an almost complete breakdown of the company's Chinese selling organization during 1938.[145] As the war progressed, greater disruption still was experienced in the Middle Yangtze region, centred on Hankow. In May 1939 Rose wrote to the Foreign Office pointing out that Japanese control of all transport in the Yangtze valley meant that the Hankow factory was effectively cut off and that sales in the Hankow Department had virtually collapsed.[146]

By 1939, all of BAT's production capacity in China outside of Hong Kong lay in Japanese-controlled territory. Moreover, the main leaf-producing areas of China, notably the areas in Anhui and Shantung, were also Japanese-occupied and an organization called the Central China Tobacco Association was sponsored to oversee the distribution of tobacco leaf. BAT was prevented from using its traditional methods of leaf procurement and put under pressure to use foreign exchange to buy its tobacco in spite of the fact that the company held large cash balances in local currency.[147] By 1941 it was felt by Cunliffe-Owen that a tobacco leaf monopoly covering the whole of Japanese-occupied China was inevitable.[148]

The period after the invasion of 1937 also witnessed large-scale investment in occupied China by Japanese tobacco manufacturing firms. In 1939 the Manchu Tobacco Co. took control of the operations of the Tōa Company and set up a corporate structure which was designed to create a China-wide

[144] Getting money out of Manchukuo became a major preoccupation for BAT after 1937. This could only be done by using financial resources held in Manchukuo to purchase supplies within Japan which were then shipped out, enhancing the exports and foreign earnings of the Yen bloc. BAT Co. Archive (SASS), Doc. Nos. 7-B-37–40.

[145] Report from Sir A. Clark-Kerr, Shanghai, to the Foreign Office in London dated 9 November 1938, FO 371/22099/13328.

[146] Letter from A. Rose to Sir A. Cadogan dated 8 May 1939, FO 371/23474/4411.

[147] Letter from A. Rose to R. G. Hoare dated 26 April 1939 and various other correspondence, FO 371/23474/4067.

[148] Letter H. Cunliffe-Owen to Under Secretary of State for Foreign Affairs, dated 10 February 1941, FO 371/27686/746.

Table 6.5. Market share of BAT and Wing Tai Vo (WTV) in regional markets of China (per cent), 1931–41

Year	Manchuria		Tientsin		Hankow		Shanghai		Hong Kong		All China	
	BAT	WTV	BAT	WTV	BAT	WTV	BAT	WTV	BAT	WTV	BAT	WTV
1931	77.1	0.7	66.0	18.8	57.1	23.2	22.7	21.6	23.8	0.9	44.2	16.3
1932	71.7	0.6	70.9	14.7	59.6	21.0	33.2	19.0	20.8	0.7	47.8	13.9
1933	73.4	0.6	67.4	12.6	63.6	15.0	32.2	18.8	19.8	0.8	48.3	11.9
1934	70.3	0.7	62.1	11.1	56.5	12.0	25.8	17.5	27.0	0.0	45.0	10.3
1935	71.9	0.0	65.7	11.4	55.9	9.6	26.2	24.0	27.5	0.1	46.6	11.8
1936	69.1	0.0	70.6	11.6	61.1	10.4	25.5	32.7	32.6	0.0	48.4	15.0
1937	74.1	0.0	71.0	10.8	62.5	13.9	26.2	32.6	42.5	0.5	51.8	15.5
1938	67.2	0.0	72.4	8.8	73.6	10.1	18.3	54.1	58.3	2.0	56.3	16.8
1939	53.2	0.0	67.0	9.5	50.2	17.1	17.9	46.5	60.3	3.1	45.8	18.8
1940	49.9	0.0	67.9	8.0	29.5	16.4	25.2	35.7	56.6	0.8	45.3	15.4
1941	45.6	0.0	59.0	11.2	27.6	9.4	14.3	53.5	58.2	1.7	39.7	20.2

Notes: Sales statistics are for year ending September.
Figures for market share of BAT and WTV for all China are calculated from regional subtotals and differ slightly from those given in Table 6.1.
Source: Shanghai (ed.), *Ying Mei*, pp. 734–46.

tobacco business. In addition to this, a number of independent Japanese tobacco firms established and expanded their operations in China via acquisition and expropriation of Chinese firms. Most notable amongst these independent firms was the Toyo Tobacco Co., based in Shanghai and Hankow, which was reputed to be the largest Japanese company in central China and was one of a number of such firms financed by the vast Mitsui trading conglomerate. Taken together, BAT's management calculated that by 1941 Japanese firms held 40 per cent of the total cigarette production capacity for China and Manchuria combined.[149]

This estimate is consistent with the sales figures calculated by BAT for the year ending September 1941, which indicate that BAT and Wing Tai Vo had a combined market share of 60 per cent across China as a whole. In spite of the many difficulties, therefore, the company had been able to hold its position relatively well in all its markets outside of Manchuria other than the Hankow region. By now, however, the last vestiges of competitive pressure had turned to political compulsion. In August 1941, in response to the freezing of Japanese assets abroad, BAT's management received instructions from the Japanese authorities that its funds in Shanghai were to be frozen until effective control of its operations had been surrendered to the Japanese and armed guards admitted to the factories. Rose relayed the details to the Foreign Office in a letter dated 11 August, and three days later the issue was considered at a meeting of Britain's War Cabinet which concluded that:

> From the wider point of view of British interests in occupied China as a whole, a yielding by the BAT on this issue would encourage the Japanese to exercise similar pressure on other British firms and to carry out more openly and ruthlessly their policy of squeezing out of China all British interests in the areas under their control.[150]

Thus the management of BAT in China were instructed to hold firm against this attempt by the Japanese to assume control over the company's assets in Shanghai. However, on the outbreak of the Pacific War in December 1941 the occupying Japanese forces placed their own officials in command and, after a period of transition lasting around a year, Japanese managers took full operational control of all BAT's factories and the company's expatriate staff were interned for the remainder of the war. Ironically, over 100 of these staff were imprisoned in the factory compound built by BAT at Pootung which had been converted into an internment camp.

149 These estimates placed Japanese firms' annual production capacity in China at 34.1 billion cigarettes and in Manchuria at 10.6 billion cigarettes. BAT Co. Archive (SASS), Doc. Nos. 2-A-105–116.

150 Letter A. Rose to Foreign Office dated 11 August 1941 and other papers in FO 371/27687/7971.

The outbreak of the Pacific War brought BAT's sales in China to an end for a period of over four years. In 1945, successful negotiations with the restored government of Chiang Kai-shek enabled the company to resume control of its assets there, and between 1946 and 1949 the Chinese market regained its position as one of BAT's most important, even though sales reached little more than one-third of their pre-war peak. Following the communist take-over, however, conditions quickly became impossible as the regime imposed controls on wages and prices which had the effect of bankrupting the company's China subsidiary. No further sales were made after 1951. With the company's assets in China now subsumed by back-taxes calculated by the authorities, and with a number of its leading executives effectively held as hostages, BAT's managers in London were faced with demands to continue paying a redundant workforce. Eventually, in 1953, a deal was struck which allowed BAT to surrender its Chinese assets in return for the release of its remaining foreign staff, and the company's once mighty business empire in China was reduced to a small operation in the British Crown Colony of Hong Kong.

7

BAT in India

Introduction

THE feature which marks out BAT's operations in India from those undertaken in most other regions before the Second World War was the detailed attention given to the process of leaf cultivation and trade. Although the company did support the growing of tobacco in other parts of its international organization, notably in China, Brazil, and parts of Africa, it was in India that this aspect of the business took on its highest profile. In 1912, BAT Co. set up a subsidiary company called the Indian Leaf Tobacco Development Co. (ILTD) whose responsibility it was to secure supplies of leaf for the two factories that had already been set up in the British Indian Empire. Operating initially in Bihar Province, close to the company's first permanent factory at Monghyr (Munger) near Calcutta, ILTD provided advice and support for tobacco cultivators, particularly those who were prepared to experiment with the growing of American Bright leaf tobacco. Over the course of the next few years, the centre of gravity of ILTD moved to the south of the country, around Guntur in the Madras Presidency, and during the 1920s the company's leaf activities were given a further boost when ILTD succeeded in developing an export trade to Britain in its Guntur tobacco. As a result tobacco cultivation became a major aspect of BAT's operations in India between the wars as the policy of Imperial Preference in Britain served to encourage such efforts to refocus the country's international trade more directly towards the needs of the British Empire.

The creation of ILTD itself had been largely a response to a change in policy, stemming from the fiscal requirements of the Government of India. During 1909, as the authorities in Calcutta sought a means of raising revenue to replace the diminishing income from sales of opium, the decision was taken to introduce a specific tariff on the import into India of both tobacco products and tobacco leaf. These increased tobacco duties gave BAT a strong incentive to speed up the development of manufacturing within India and, along with it, advance the promotion of local sources of leaf tobacco. In fact, BAT responded to the Government of India's trade policy initiative by adopting a much higher profile in India generally through the setting up of an Indian-registered, Rupee-denominated subsidiary called the Imperial Tobacco Co. of India (ITC) in 1910. During the years that followed ITC became the main BAT Co. operating subsidiary in India and blossomed into a major Indian-based business enterprise between the wars, with a head office in Calcutta modelled on BAT Co.'s own world-wide headquarters at Millbank in London. As late as 1950, ITC's capitalization of over Rs.40 million made it the largest subsidiary of any multinational company operating in India.[1] However, in spite of its dominance of this most industrialized arm of the tobacco industry in India, ITC's market position was based predominantly on sales of cigarettes which, as a whole, accounted for only about 2 per cent by weight of Indian tobacco consumption during the 1930s.[2]

Developing Local Production

An export market for tobacco goods in India had first been developed by BAT's predecessors as early as 1881,[3] but it was not until 1905 that direct investment in cigarette manufacturing capacity was undertaken there. The initial demand for imported machine-made cigarettes stemmed from the expatriate population, who had already become familiar with the product at home, and typical sales outlets were the regimental messes and gentlemen's clubs which served this group of consumers.[4] By the early 1890s cigarettes had gained a position at the luxury end of the tobacco goods market in India, and the imported hand-rolled Turkish cigarettes of Theodoro Vafiades & Co. of

[1] B. R. Tomlinson, 'Foreign Private Investment in India', *Modern Asian Studies*, 12 (1978), 676–7. This study suggests that the next largest foreign subsidiary in India by 1950 was Glaxo's Bombay-based operation, Glaxo Laboratories (India) Ltd., which had been set up in 1947 with a starting capital of Rs.20 million.

[2] This figure is based on estimates of tobacco consumption in India and Burma from a report by the Government of India published in 1939 (see Table 7.6). Naturally, the value of cigarette sales would have been more than 2 per cent of the total.

[3] According to Alford's account of W. D. & H. O. Wills, the Bristol firm sent a salesman to India in 1881 to gather orders and by 1886 had drawn up a schedule of discounts for overseas trade including cigarettes. B. W. E. Alford, *W. D. & H. O. Wills and the Development of the UK Tobacco Industry, 1786–1965* (1973), p. 164.

[4] Even by 1910 British soldiers stationed in India still accounted for a significant proportion of the sales of imported cigarettes. *Tobacco (London)*, 30 (352) (1910), 47.

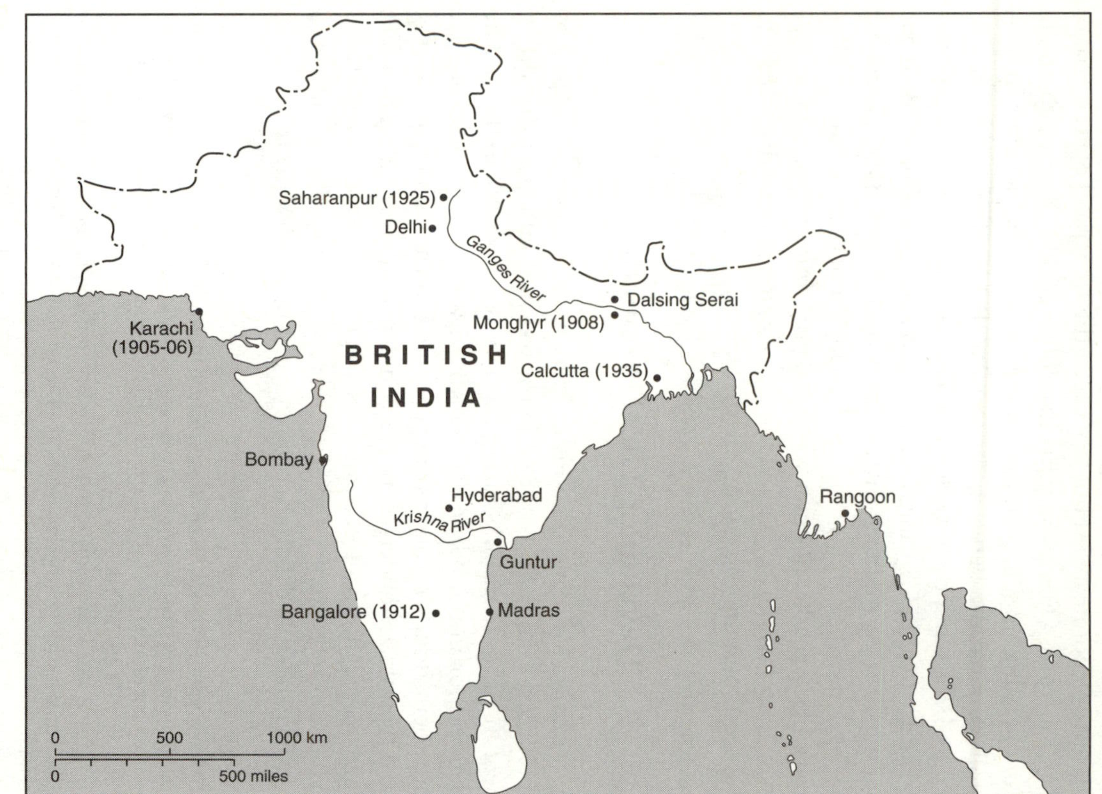

BAT Co. operational locations in British India, 1902–45

Note: Places with a date attached show the locations of BAT Co.'s cigarette manufacturing facilities and commencement of production.

Cairo had been adopted as a fashionable status symbol by the expatriate businessmen of Calcutta—the burra sahibs.[5]

The indigenous population of India, in contrast, continued to consume their tobacco in traditional forms such as through pipes (hookahs), taken orally, or smoked in the form of bidis and cheroots.[6] Bidi manufacturing was a handicraft occupation of village Indians in which imperfectly cured tobacco was rolled up using the leaves of other plants and tied with thread to produce a crude form of cigarette. The production of cheroots and small cigars, on the other hand, developed during the late nineteenth century into a minor industry in the south of India, with both indigenous and expatriate-owned factories having been set up by the turn of the century.[7] The most prominent of these cigar manufacturers was a group of expatriate merchant houses based around Madras—Spencer & Co., McDowell & Co., and Oakes & Co.—who retailed their own products in India and also developed a market for the highest quality Indian cigars in Britain. These merchants also dealt in the cigarettes and other tobacco products of English firms such as W. D. & H. O. Wills.

In Calcutta, machine-made cigarettes from both Britain and America were initially marketed through the Liverpool-based agents George Atherton & Co., who also had experience of manufacturing their own cigarettes and tobacco goods.[8] By 1896 Atherton's resident manager in Calcutta, Nicholas C. Jellico, had granted an agency to a local tobacco merchant, Bukhsh Ellahie & Co., to act as sole distributor for the products of both Wills and the American Tobacco Co. (ATC) in India and Burma (Myanmar).[9] The arrangement provided these cigarette manufacturers with greater access to the indigenous markets of India, enabling imports of American cigarettes, for example, to rise fiftyfold over the course of the 1890s.[10] In 1901, with a significant market in place, ATC ended its association with the Atherton agency, and terminated

[5] O. Goswami, 'Then Came the Marwaris', *Indian Economic and Social History Review*, 22 (1985), 225–49.

[6] J. Goodman, *Tobacco in History: The Cultures of Dependence* (1993), p. 12.

[7] Report by the Finance Department of the Government of India to the Secretary of State for India, dated 12 January 1911, IOR/L/E/7/687; R&S Dept. File No. 234/11.

[8] The first record of Atherton's involvement as an importer of tobacco goods can be found in the 1892 edition of Thakar's Indian Directory. This indicates that Atherton was dealing in cigarettes on behalf of the London-based Thomas Bear & Son and two branches of ATC, Allen & Ginter and W. S. Kimball. Two years later, W. D. & H. O. Wills appear as a client of Atherton for the first time. *Thakar's Indian Directory*, IOL/ST/1215.

[9] *Thakar's Indian Directory*, 1896 edn., p. 32, IOL/ST/1215.

[10] American cigarette exports to the British East Indies grew from 2.8 million in 1891 to 144.2 million in 1899. The export figures for British East Indies included the Straits Settlements as well as British India, and no separate figures were made available for the two markets before 1904, at which time exports to British India accounted for 88 per cent of the total. Cf. Table 2.2.

its distribution arrangements with Bukhsh Ellahie, setting up instead its own depot in Calcutta at 95 Clive Street under the management of a salaried employee, E. A. Woodward.[11]

Following the incorporation of BAT Co. in September 1902 direct competition between Wills and ATC in India ended and Atherton's agency was temporarily restored. The depot which had been set up by ATC at Clive Street now became BAT Co.'s branch headquarters in India, and during 1903 James Thomas was installed as the company's manager in Calcutta. This arrangement was soon disrupted, however, when Thomas suffered a bad bout of malaria in 1904 and was forced to leave India. A projected visit there by Cunliffe-Owen, on his return journey from China that year, was also prevented when the BAT Co. secretary himself fell ill whilst in Ceylon (Sri Lanka).

Thus at the beginning of 1905 two BAT Co. directors, vice-chairman W. B. Ogden and Lawrence Hignett, sailed to India in order to review the management arrangements there. During the course of this visit the Indian operation was upgraded from a branch to a fully fledged subsidiary, BAT Co. (India), which was registered in London in March 1905. This move precipitated the termination by BAT Co. of Atherton's agency—in just the same way that the company had ended Rex & Co.'s contract in Shanghai the year before—but the expertise of the Atherton organization was maintained through the appointment of N.C. Jellico as the new subsidiary's managing director.[12] In turn, Jellico continued to utilize the services of Bukhsh Ellahie as sole agent in India (but not Burma).[13]

[11] It is clear from the correspondence of E. J. Parrish, manager of ATC's joint venture with the Murai Brothers Co. in Japan, that ATC had decided by 1901 to dispense with agents in China, India, and the Straits in favour of their own representative. The Murai Brothers had made an arrangement with Atherton & Co. during the latter part of 1899 to grant a sole agency in India and Burma for their brands to Bukhsh Ellahie, on condition that Atherton guaranteed payment for their goods in return for a commission of 2 per cent. In April 1901, Atherton wrote to Murai Brothers cancelling this agreement, 'Owing to arrangements we have made since we had the pleasure of meeting your representative some eighteen months ago', and advised Murai that it should now deal directly with Bukhsh Ellahie. Parrish used this change in circumstances as an excuse to terminate Ellahie's sole agency and to transfer it to ATC's representative. Letter E. J. Parrish to E. A. Woodward, Calcutta, dated 19 June 1901, papers of E. J. Parrish, Special Collections Department, Perkins Library, Duke University.

[12] An account by R. G. Baker of his time in India working for BAT recalls a meeting with George Atherton in 1917. According to this account, Atherton retained the agency in India for a short period after BAT took over the Imperial's export trade, but as the trade began to grow the agency agreement was bought out. R. G. Baker, 'Redried Leaves and Tobacco Bugs'. Unpublished typescript (1967), BAT Co. Southampton Archive, Box 27.

[13] This tobacco wholesaler operated from a headquarters at Colootollah Street, Calcutta, and is also referred to in accounts of the period as Hajee Bux Elahi and Haji Allah Bux. The Calcutta headquarters of the firm was used to induct new recruits into the company's selling system. Notes on the history of ITC, BAT Co. Southampton Archive, Box 188.

Jellico's deputy in Calcutta was C. Percy Page who had been posted to India in 1903 at the age of 23 and had made a favourable impression on the Atherton man with his flair for marketing. When Jellico died suddenly in 1906, Page took over his role as local managing director of BAT Co. (India) and remained in control of the company's selling organization in India until his own death in 1923.[14] Under the direction of Page, Bukhsh Ellahie's sole agency was limited to distribution within eastern India and new selling depots were set up by BAT in Bombay (Mumbai), Madras, Karachi, Delhi, and Rangoon (Yangon), each managed by a company employee.[15]

Sales of imported cigarettes continued to rise during these early years with Bukhsh Ellahie putting much effort behind the Wills' 'Scissors Army Grade' brand which had been designated by London as the main British-made cigarette for India. Between 1901 and 1905, the volume of cigarette imports into India as a whole doubled, while the value of this export trade from Britain's factories tripled to reach £150,000.[16] Efforts were now being made to extend the market beyond the expatriate community and to encourage the better-off local consumers to adopt the practice of cigarette smoking. As in Shanghai, however, this scheme was quickly disrupted in Calcutta by a nationalist-inspired boycott. This action formed part of the Swadeshi movement through which the educated middle classes in Bengal attempted to galvanize support for the development of Indian-owned industries. A boycott of British products was sanctioned by nationalist leaders in August 1905, and this led to a reversal of the expansion in cigarette imports that had been evident since the turn of the century.[17]

The boycott of 1905–6 provided the initial spur for BAT Co. to set up production facilities within the Indian market, and in November 1905 it formed the Peninsular Tobacco Company in London to operate as its manufacturing arm in India. A temporary factory was put together at Karachi under the management of J. T. Wilkie and was provided with ten Bonsack machines and 250,000 lb. of locally procured tobacco leaf, selling its first cigarettes in June 1906. More land was purchased nearby, at Anand Junction, on which it was planned to build more permanent premises together with facilities for redrying

[14] Obituary of C. P. Page, *BAT Bulletin*, 14 (43) (1923), 982.

[15] Depot managers in 1908 were J. M. C. Austin, Calcutta; R. J. Brown, Bombay; R. L. Hoare, Rangoon; E. B. Mills, Madras; R. A. McKie, Karachi; C. B. Nicholls, Delhi. *Thakar's Indian Directory*, 1908 edn., IOL/ST/1215.

[16] These figures are contained in a report prepared for a parliamentary debate on the question of tobacco duties in India during 1910, IOR/L/E/7/687; R&S Dept. File No. 2437/10.

[17] The Swadeshi movement began as a protest against the Viceroy Lord Curzon's decision to partition Bengal in an effort to ease difficulties over the administration of the province. S. Sarker, *Modern India, 1885–1947* (1983), pp. 111–25.

locally grown tobacco leaf. However, after a short period of time it became evident that the climate around Karachi was not suitable for working and storing tobacco leaf and the location was abandoned as a centre for manufacturing. Thus in 1907, construction was put in hand on a site closer to the headquarters of the sales company in Calcutta. This plant was built for BAT by Martin & Co. at Monghyr, around 150 miles north-east of Calcutta on the Ganges River in Bihar Province, with a view to utilizing the locally grown tobacco leaf.[18] F. A. Parkinson was brought over from Ceylon to assume the role of Peninsular's first managing director.[19]

As well as spurring BAT to manufacture cigarettes within India, the Swadeshi boycott also gave encouragement to Indian firms to develop their own production facilities. By the time the Peninsular Tobacco Co. opened its factory in Monghyr in 1908 a number of indigenous cigarette manufacturing concerns had sprung up in Calcutta and East Bengal.[20] Of these, the most serious rival to BAT appears to have been the East India Tobacco Company which had been launched in 1907 with a capital value of Rs.500,000 and an estimated output of 20 million cigarettes a month.[21] Another Indian rival, which set up in the south of India at Bangalore during the time of the Swadeshi boycott, was the City Tobacco Company. In 1907 this company opened a steam-driven cigarette manufacturing plant at Bowringpet which exported both cigarettes and cured tobacco to several parts of India.[22]

As the boycott of British goods subsided, BAT was able to regain its market share and restore its competitive advantage over these domestic rivals. With the cost of the cheapest grades of imported cigarettes from Britain and

[18] Notes on the history of ITC, BAT Co. Southampton Archive, Box 188; R. G. Baker, 'Redried Leaves and Tobacco Bugs'. Unpublished typescript (1967), BAT Co. Southampton Archive, Box 27; C. Basu, *Challenge and Change: The ITC Story, 1910–1985* (1988), pp. 23–4.

[19] Parkinson, who had earlier managed one of the two distributors of Imperial Tobacco's goods in Colombo, Ceylon, had become acquainted with Cunliffe-Owen during his brief stay there in 1904. These two distributors, Cargills Ltd. and Miller & Co., were retained by BAT Co. when it took over this trade. In 1905, a sales subsidiary was registered in London called BAT Co. (Ceylon) and was made the company's sole agent there, but in 1911 it reached an agreement with Cargills and Miller, appointing them once again as distributors. BAT did not manufacture cigarettes in Ceylon until 1927. BAT Co. Corporate Index, BAT Co. Southampton Archive, Box 114.

[20] A study by Sarkar mentions three Swadeshi units which had been set up in Calcutta by 1907 to manufacture cheap cigarettes (the Globe Cigarette Company, the East India Cigarette Company, and the Bengal Cigarette Manufacturing Company), and another in East Bengal (the Rangpur Tobacco Company). S. Sarkar, *The Swadeshi Movement in Bengal, 1903–1908* (1973), pp. 129–30.

[21] Report by the Finance Department of the Government of India to the Secretary of State for India, dated 9 February 1911, IOR/L/E/7/687; R&S Dept. File No. 501/11.

[22] *Indian Trade Journal*, 12 (150) (1909), 134.

America running between Re.1-0-0 and Rs.1-8-0 per 1000,[23] local manufacturers were faced with a stiff price constraint and even BAT's Peninsular factory was forced to operate at a loss during its early years. The company had invested nearly £50,000 in land, buildings, plant, and machinery at Monghyr and was employing a workforce of around thirty senior staff on monthly wages ranging from Rs.95 to Rs.1350. In addition, by 1910 some 663 factory hands were employed on daily wages which varied from Re.1-0-0 for machine-minders and Rs.0-8-0 for male coolies, down to Rs.0-4-0 for female packers. Given a daily output at this time of 1 million sticks, the cost per 1000 cigarettes in wages alone ran to perhaps one-third of the lowest price that could be charged to dealers on the cheapest imported cigarettes.[24] Thus, whilst local production would prove cost effective in the long-term, especially once the volume of output could be raised to a more efficient level and locally grown tobacco employed in place of costly American leaf, it was first necessary to build up a sufficiently large market using cheap imported cigarettes. However, within two years of commencing production at Monghyr, BAT found its strategy in India jeopardized due to the fiscal requirements of the Indian government.

The Tobacco Duties Debate

The opening decade of the twentieth century had heralded a period of rapid growth in the Indian cigarette market. The upward trend in imports of the product had reached a plateau following the boycott of 1905–6, but this in turn had given way to a sharp rise in the import of unmanufactured tobacco following the construction of the first Peninsular factory in Karachi (see Table 7.1). The principal beneficiaries of the rising trade in manufactured cigarettes were BAT Co.'s factories in Bristol and Liverpool. In value terms, the United Kingdom accounted for 77 per cent of all the cigarettes landed in India during 1908–9,[25] whilst these exports accounted for 21 per cent of all Britain's outward trade in the product (see Appendix 3). Only the vast Chinese market was of greater importance than India to Britain's cigarette exports before the First World War.

[23] One rupee, which exchanged for 1s. 4d. in sterling at this time, was divided into 16 annas. Thus 1 anna was worth 1d.

[24] These figures are given in a report by the Finance Department of the Government of India to the Secretary of State for India, dated 9 February 1911, IOR/L/E/7/687; R&S Dept. File No. 501/11. By 1916 the Monghyr factory was producing an annual output of 2.4 billion cigarettes and 126,000 lb. of smoking tobacco. IOR/L/E/7/687; R&S Dept. File No. 3747/17.

[25] *Indian Trade Journal*, 13 (162) (1909), 126.

TABLE 7.1. Export of cigarettes and unmanufactured tobacco from the UK and US to India, and total imports into India, 1901–39

Year	UK exports to India			US exports to India		All imports to India		
	Unmanufactured tobacco ('000 lb.) [1]	Cigarettes ('000 lb.) [2]	Cigarettes ('000 sticks) [3]	Unmanufactured tobacco ('000 lb.) [4]	Cigarettes ('000 sticks) [5]	Unmanufactured tobacco ('000 lb.) [6]	Cigarettes ('000 lb.) [7]	Cigarettes ('000 sticks) [8]
1901	59	n.a.	n.a.		226,367	514	1,165	459,010
1902	39	n.a.	n.a.		237,812	927	1,510	594,940
1903	39	n.a.	n.a.		323,463	505	1,724	679,256
1904	13	n.a.	n.a.	3	450,305	558	2,240	882,560
1905	38	n.a.	n.a.		432,052	801	2,519	992,486
1906	71	1,477	581,938	205	320,613	679	3,119	1,228,886
1907	79	2,044	805,336	171	479,483	1,350	2,913	1,147,722
1908	116	1,857	731,658	584	401,690	1,225	3,634	1,431,796
1909	467	1,952	769,088	968	324,263	1,213	2,996	1,180,424
1910	141	1,149	452,706	470	253,757	2,703	3,084	1,215,096
1911	23	1,230	484,620	114	4,076	251	1,113	438,522
1912	87	1,211	477,134	47	9,525	157	1,415	557,510
1913	13	1,514	596,516	95	3,755	287	1,451	571,694
1914	13	1,230	484,620	168	2,532	282	1,591	626,854
1915	38	1,605	632,370	29	275	165	1,440	567,360
1916	43	2,175	856,950	18	2,532	136	1,686	664,284
1917	14	3,574	1,408,156	22	67,555	210	2,403	946,782
1918	4	2,933	1,155,602	30	301,027	616	3,491	1,375,454
1919	20	2,294	903,836	37	217,230	500	4,094	1,613,036
1920	22	3,285	1,294,290	38	1,289,732	880	4,160	1,639,040
1921	6	1,714	675,316	412	270,253	712	6,206	2,445,164
1922	25	3,655	1,440,070	685	85,375	1,050	2,739	1,079,166

	[1]	[2]	[3]	[4]	[5]	[6]	[7]	[8]
1923	15	3,378	1,330,932	3,978	30,925	1,228	4,087	1,610,278
1924	15	2,702	1,064,588	7,226	4,774	4,557	3,453	1,360,482
1925	24	3,161	1,245,434	4,762	1,415	7,082	2,748	1,082,712
1926	29	4,033	1,589,002	4,920	2,406	4,907	3,412	1,344,328
1927	29	5,546	2,185,124	3,835	2,727	5,703	4,175	1,644,950
1928	18	5,070	1,997,580	6,476	3,532	3,985	5,596	2,204,824
1929	21	5,114	2,014,916	4,734	5,350	6,761	4,952	1,951,088
1930	14	3,408	1,342,752	1,372	12,315	4,552	5,283	2,081,502
1931	55	1,847	727,718	2,663	8,252	1,608	3,060	1,234,991
1932	165	697	274,618	4,633	6,291	2,845	1,436	570,059
1933	1,648	581	228,914	2,083	5,823	5,116	832	332,494
1934	1,133	613	241,522	2,081	5,510	4,187	593	225,672
1935	691	824	324,656	1,535	11,788	2,977	614	239,231
1936	81	1,002	394,788	2,765	10,596	1,921	831	321,625
1937	1	1,138	448,372	2,898	13,688	3,283	919	353,047
1938	814	1,420	559,480	3,588	19,458	6,598	993	378,629
1939	918	1,565	616,610	3,827	18,066	6,371	1,218	461,060

Notes: Column [1], [2], and [3] figures are for calendar year; column [4] and [5] figures for 1901–18 are for year ending June, thereafter for calendar year; column [5] figures for 1901–3 relate to British East Indies which includes British India and Straits; column [6], [7], and [8] figures are for year ending March. n.a. = not available.

Sources: Columns [1], [2]: Annual Statement of the Trade of the UK with Foreign countries and British possessions; column [3]: calculated from column [2] using conversion factor 1 lb. tobacco = 394 cigarettes; columns [4], [5]: Foreign Commerce and Navigation of the United States; columns [6], [7]: Annual Statement of the Sea-borne Trade and Navigation of British India; column [8]: 1900–29 calculated from column [7] using above conversion factor; 1930–39 as [7].

In both China and India, the duty on cigarette imports stood at a nominal 5 per cent *ad valorem*, and in the Indian market no taxes at all were levied on the import of unmanufactured tobacco. This very accommodating tariff regime meant that there was no strong incentive for BAT to engage in local production, and the timing of the decision to embark on manufacturing in Karachi had clearly been the result of agitation directed against imported cigarettes. Following the incorporation of its Peninsular manufacturing subsidiary Peter Arrington, a BAT Co. director and American leaf expert, was posted to Karachi in order to set up a leaf department.[26] However, the poor quality of the locally grown leaf and the absence of any duty on imports meant that BAT was still inclined to rely on American-grown leaf for most of its tobacco requirements. Thus, although the decision to shift production to Monghyr had been taken primarily in order to utilize the tobacco which was being grown by cultivators in Bihar Province, by the end of 1909 Peninsular had still to develop a successful product based predominantly on native tobacco.[27]

As the market for cigarettes expanded in India, the authorities in Calcutta also recognized the potential benefits that could accrue in its wake. In 1906, the Government of India's Commercial Intelligence Department launched a weekly publication called the *Indian Trade Journal* which was soon reporting developments in the tobacco industry in India. Two aspects of cigarette production were of particular interest. First, the product provided a potential outlet for the capital of middle-class Indians who were anxious to develop Swadeshi industries, and in 1907 the journal informed its readers that, 'photographs, catalogues and [a] price list of a British-made, high power cigarette machine; particulars of a patent tobacco cutting machine; and details of a type of modern packing for mechanical and chemical purposes . . . may be inspected at this office'.[28] Second, the industry heralded a new opportunity for the commercialization of Indian agriculture if the appropriate form of tobacco could be cultivated. Thus, also in 1907, the journal published an item outlining experiments that had been undertaken

[26] On Arrington see *BAT Bulletin* 3 (75) (1916), 354.

[27] It is difficult to estimate precisely the proportion of locally grown tobacco which was used in the cigarettes manufactured at Karachi. It is stated in BAT Co.'s own records that the board of directors of Peninsular authorized the purchase of 250,000 lb. of local leaf in April 1906 which would have made approximately 100 million cigarettes. Imports of unmanufactured tobacco in the year commencing April 1906 were approximately 650,000 lb. greater than the average level of imports over the preceding six years. These could have been used to make roughly 260 million cigarettes, giving a total of 360 million, which was easily within the annual production capacity attainable with ten Bonsack machines. (A state-of-the-art Bonsack could produce 600 cigarettes per minute at this time, compared with output capacity of 200 which the first Bonsack could handle.) This rough calculation therefore suggests that the cigarettes made at Karachi featured two and a half times as much imported leaf as they did locally grown tobacco.

[28] *Indian Trade Journal*, 7 (80) (1907), 64.

by the Agricultural Department of the Indian Civil Service at its Rangpur Agricultural Station designed to cultivate a form of tobacco which would be suitable either for use as cigar wrapper or for cigarettes.[29]

In October 1909 the journal devoted an editorial to the subject of India's tobacco trade in which it noted that the modern cigarette factory recently set up (by BAT) in Bengal would provide a growing source of demand for native tobacco leaf, but only if a better class of tobacco plant were to be cultivated and up-to-date methods of curing introduced. In regard to this latter question, the journal suggested that, 'what would seem to be required is a sort of central curing factory in certain tobacco tracts, such factories to be controlled by experts who know their business thoroughly and who have had long experience in such factories in America'.[30] This was clearly a task for which BAT was well equipped and one that it had, to a small extent, begun to put in hand through the formation of Peninsular's leaf department. However, a great deal of further investment would be required in order to put in place the extensive system envisaged by the Department of Commercial Intelligence, and with the existing structure of tariffs favouring imported tobacco goods over domestically produced varieties BAT Co. had little incentive to engage in such an investment programme. Only if these economic conditions were to be significantly altered would BAT need to undertake a capital investment in the Indian tobacco industry. Perhaps not surprisingly then, it was just such a change that the Government of India implemented in March 1910.

One of the major problems confronting the Government of India at this time was the structure of its revenue base. During the opening years of the twentieth century the majority of its income continued to be derived from the land, but the scope for expansion from this source was strictly limited.[31] Another traditionally important source of income was that provided by the sale of opium destined for China. However, these sales were being gradually phased out[32] and an estimate by the Revenue Department of the India Office around this time suggested that the total loss in revenue from the diminishing sales of Bengal opium between 1908 and 1917 would amount to between £4 and £5 million.[33] The most convenient alternative source of revenue was customs duties, but any increase in these was fiercely resisted by Whitehall before the First World War on free-trade grounds.

[29] *Indian Trade Journal*, 5 (65) (1907), 701–3.

[30] *Indian Trade Journal*, 15 (187) (1909), 82–3.

[31] D. Kumar, 'The Fiscal System' in D. Kumar (ed.), *The Cambridge Economic History of India* (1982), pp. 905–44.

[32] R. K. Newman, 'India and the Anglo-Chinese Opium Agreements, 1907–14', *Modern Asian Studies*, 23 (1989), 525–60.

[33] IOR/L/E/7/668; R&S Dept. File No. 2604/10.

In 1908–9, the declining revenues from opium sales led the Government of India to register a budget deficit of almost £4,000,000 which the authorities in Calcutta proposed to rectify through an increase in the general revenue tariff from 5 to 7.5 per cent.[34] Although this proposal was rejected by the India Office, as a tax on British exports, the financial situation continued to demand new fiscal measures. On the 6 January 1910 the Indian government forwarded a financial statement to the Secretary of State for India, Lord Morley, with figures which projected a small deficit, or at best a nominal surplus, for 1909–10 and a major deficit for the year 1910–11 in the absence of fresh taxation.[35] The prospect of three consecutive budget deficits provoked deep anxiety at the India Office in London.

Finding their proposals for an increase in the general tariff rate rebuffed, the Government of India proposed a new solution to the revenue shortages which was to substantially increase the customs duties on imported tobacco. At 5 per cent *ad valorem*, the existing general tariff rate on manufactured goods was extremely low; amounting to as little as 4 annas (4d.) per 1000 on the cheapest brands of cigarettes. The India Office was certainly willing to consider some advance on this rate (the newly elected Liberal government in Britain had raised import duties on tobacco sharply during its own 'people's budget' of 1909) but baulked at the rates requested by Calcutta. These measures proposed flat rate duties of Rs.2-0-0 (2s. 8d.) per lb. on unmanufactured tobacco, against which no duty at all had previously been levied, and Rs.2-8-0 (3s. 4d.) per lb. on cigarettes. It was argued by Calcutta that these proposed rates were not unreasonable, compared with the duties in force in Britain at this time (Table 7.2).

Within Whitehall the strongest opposition to the implementation of such a dramatic rise in the import duties on tobacco came from the Financial Secretary at the India Office, L. Abrahams. In January 1910, Abrahams had noted to Secretary of State Morley that the size of the increase in duties would be such as to raise the price of cheap cigarettes by up to 250 per cent which 'would probably give rise to violent criticism, and might almost destroy the import trade in cigarettes (and in other kinds of tobacco), and defeat the hope of deriving a large revenue from them'. In addition, Abrahams argued that the proposed duties were open to objection 'as being likely to protect the Indian tobacco growing and tobacco manufacturing industries'. Whilst he accepted that, for the present time, India possessed neither tobacco of sufficiently high

34 B. R. Tomlinson, 'India and the British Empire, 1880–1935', *Indian Economic and Social History Review*, 12 (4) (1975), 345.

35 Confidential dispatch from the Government of India Finance Dept. to Secretary of State for India, No. 15 of 1911, IOR/L/E/7/687; R&S Dept. File No. 234/11.

TABLE 7.2. Tobacco duties in India and the UK, 1910 (per lb. in s. d.), 1910

	Duty in UK	Duty in India	
		Proposed	Adopted
Unmanufactured tobacco	3 10[a]	2 8	2 0
Cigars	7 0	4 0	3 4
Cigarettes	5 8	3 4	2 8[b]
Other manufactured tobacco	5 4	3 0	2 2

Notes: [a] average; [b] subject to a minimum of 6s. 8d. per lb.
Source: IOR L/E/7/687.

quality, nor the necessary manufacturing facilities to take advantage of the potential protection afforded by the duties, he urged caution: 'it is necessary to have regard to the possibility that the growth and manufacture of tobacco in India might be developed on new lines if very high duties, such as the Government of India recommend, are suddenly imposed'.[36]

Morley, a disciple of the *laissez-faire* school of thought,[37] was undoubtedly influenced by Abrahams' arguments and sought a reduction in the level of duty. Eventually, a compromise was reached and, as Table 7.2 shows, the duties which were finally adopted were a little below those originally proposed. In the case of cigarettes, a rather complicated formula was applied which meant that, for the majority of cheap cigarettes weighing less than 3 lb. per 1000 the rate of duty would be set at Rs.5 (6s. 8d.) per 1000 compared with 4 annas (4d.) per 1000 before the change. Cigarettes which had previously been sold to dealers at Re.1 per 1000 would therefore now cost Rs.6.

The announcement of the new duties caused outrage within the British tobacco industry, whose leaders had not been consulted or advised in any way of their impending introduction. Three days after the new duties were imposed, Morley received a deputation at the India Office of four Members of Parliament from Bristol constituencies who sought an assurance that the duties would be reduced if their impact on tobacco exports to India was severe. The Secretary of State agreed to explore the possible advantages of

36 Minute from L. Abrahams, Financial Secretary at the India Office to the Secretary of State, 24 January 1910, IOR/L/E/7/687; R&S Dept. File No. 234/11.

37 Dewey points to Morley's commitment to *laissez-faire* in discussing his unwillingness to sanction the creation of a Department of Industries in Madras when he felt that intervention at the provincial level was in danger of extending into State ownership of industry. See C. J. Dewey, 'The Government of India's "New Industrial Policy", 1900–1925: Formation and Failure', in K. N. Chaudhuri and C. J. Dewey (eds.), *Economy and Society; Essays in Indian Economic and Social History* (1979), pp. 215–57.

imposing a countervailing excise to ameliorate the protective effect of the duties and to review their impact on the level of tobacco imports into India after a trial period. A series of questions were raised in the House of Commons regarding the purpose and likely effect of the duties, and both Joseph Hood in Bristol and Percy Ogden in Liverpool made statements to the press outlining the likelihood of redundancies at these two factories due to the impact of the new tax on the cigarette export trade.[38]

The opposition which BAT voiced to the Indian tobacco tariff was, however, tempered with caution because the traditional remedy to the protectionist impact of such measures, based on the imposition a countervailing excise levied on domestic producers, threatened to compound the company's difficulties by increasing the costs of production for the Peninsular initiative. As a fledgling multinational enterprise with direct investments in India, BAT's best policy in the medium term was simply to bypass the duties through local manufacturing utilizing native leaf. In fact, the most effective measure that BAT could take in opposition to the tariff was to undermine its revenue-generating power by ceasing to export cigarettes and tobacco to India, and by diverting to other destinations those which had already been consigned there. In May the manager of BAT's Calcutta depot, J. Austin, reported to the press that the company had redirected 35 million cigarettes which had just landed in India on to their subsidiary in China, and had returned a further 25 million to the factory at Bristol.[39] The impact of this strategy was dramatic. Between March and September 1910, the average monthly imports of cigarettes fell to barely 70,000 sticks compared with the 250,000 which had been recorded over the preceding two years. Meanwhile, imports of unmanufactured tobacco, which had soared the previous year as the Monghyr factory expanded production (cf. Table 7.1), practically ceased as the company placed all its emphasis on developing native leaf. BAT's actions therefore badly damaged the avowed strategy of the Government of India to use the tariff to raise revenue, but it could do this only by fulfilling the administration's ulterior objective of forcing the company to undertake a substantial investment in Indian agriculture.

During the latter part of 1910, the Government of India reported to the new Secretary of State at the India Office, Lord Crewe, that the introduction of a countervailing duty on tobacco goods produced within India was considered to be an impractical method of providing a counterbalance to the protective impact of the higher import duties. In his return, Crewe therefore insisted that a lower schedule of duties be drawn up and implemented with

[38] *Tobacco (London)*, 30 (352) (1910), 46–7. In fact no redundancies were made at the main Ashton Gate factory in Bristol.

[39] *Pioneer Mail*, 6 May 1910, p. 13.

immediate effect. On 14 February 1911 the Secretary of State sent a telegram to Calcutta, informing them that the duties on unmanufactured tobacco were to be halved to Re.1 per lb. and that other duties were to be adjusted in line with this 'before vested interests were able to spring up under protection of the existing high duty'.[40] For BAT, however, the die had already been cast. The potential of India as a location for manufacturing cheap machine-made cigarettes now required the provision of low-cost locally grown tobacco, and over the next few years a major push was made to develop sources of domestic tobacco leaf within British India.

Empire Tobacco

BAT Co. served formal notice of its intention to process more locally grown leaf in India by registering a new company, the Indian Leaf Tobacco Development Co. (ILTD), in Calcutta on 3 July 1912. This company was placed under the supervision of an American, Robert C. Harrison, who had originally been transferred to India in 1909 as an assistant to Peter Arrington in the Peninsular Tobacco Co.'s leaf department.[41] During these formative years Harrison had been one of a group of American experts brought over to India in order to assess the quality of the tobacco grown by local farmers, in the same way as R. H. Gregory and his team had done in China.[42] Among the earliest tasks undertaken by Harrison had been to encourage the farmers in the region around the Monghyr factory to grow tobacco that would be suitable for use in cigarettes and to give advice regarding techniques of cultivation.[43]

The processes that were employed by local cultivators for curing tobacco leaf in Bihar remained extremely crude, with the leaf merely being left on the ground to dry out in the sun. This made storage of the leaf problematic, since the high moisture content left the tobacco susceptible to mould, and between 1908 and 1910 two leaf redrying plants were set up by the Peninsular company in disused indigo factories at Shahpur Patory and Khajauli.[44] After the higher import duties on unmanufactured leaf had been promulgated, a much larger redrying plant was constructed by Peninsular at Dalsing Serai 80 miles

[40] Telegram from Secretary of State for India, Lord Crewe, to Government of India dated 14 February 1911, IOR/L/E/687; R&S Dept. File No. 234/11.

[41] *BAT Bulletin*, 14 (37) (1923), 827.

[42] A diary of Gregory's early experience studying patterns of tobacco leaf cultivation in China between June and August 1906 can be found in the papers of Richard Henry Gregory, Special Collections Department, Perkins Library, Duke University.

[43] *Wealth of India*, 4 (4) (1915), 307–8.

[44] On the process of tobacco cultivation and preparation, see D. Tucker, *Tobacco: An International Perspective* (1982), pp. 1–29.

north of Monghyr.[45] By 1912 a variety of cheap cigarette brands, such as 'Red Lamp', 'Battleaxe', and 'Madari', were being produced at the Monghyr factory based entirely on locally grown leaf tobacco.[46]

As the company continued to survey the tobacco producing regions of India it discovered that the leaf grown in the south-east of the country, around the district of Guntur in Madras Presidency (now Andhra Pradesh), was subjected to a superior curing process which enabled the cured leaf to be stored without further redrying prior to manufacture. The area was explored further around 1910 by Donald Murdoch, an English BAT Co. pupil who had been transferred from Ashton Gate to the Peninsular Tobacco Co. in 1907.[47] Murdoch soon discovered that a severe barrier to effecting transactions with the ryots (peasant cultivators) who grew the tobacco lay in the absence of a common language. The local Telugu dialect was difficult to master and Murdoch was forced to engage the services of a tobacco broker, K. L. Naidu, before the company could begin purchasing tobacco leaf in this part of India.[48] ILTD set up offices in Guntur around 1911, and Murdoch collaborated with a local firm in order to learn the vernacular and understand local business practices.[49] To take advantage of this new source of leaf, Peninsular began building its first cigarette manufacturing factory in the south of India during 1912 at Bangalore, which was well placed to receive supplies of tobacco from Guntur by rail.[50] In 1914 BAT posted Murdoch to the United States to become more familiar with the method of handling leaf, before returning the following year in order to take over from Harrison as manager of ILTD.[51]

Around 1916 the company transferred its headquarters in the south from Guntur to the town of Chirala where it set up a buying centre close to the railway station.[52] Subsequently the company became a major operator in this region, but as the leaf itself required no further processing prior to storage, ILTD's investment here remained quite limited. The factor which boosted the importance of Guntur tobacco leaf was the introduction in Britain of a policy

[45] By 1921 this redrying plant at Dalsing Serai employed a local workforce numbering between 300 and 350. *BAT Bulletin*, 12 (20) (1921), 440–4.

[46] Baker, 'Redried Leaves', pp. 19 and 40–1.

[47] *BAT Bulletin*, 12 (22) (1922), pp. 486 and 523.

[48] The firm of Messrs. Naidu was already purchasing local leaf on commission for an English tobacco manufacturer, N. G. Ranga, 'Some Facts Concerning the Development of the Tobacco Trade of the Madras Presidency', *Indian Journal of Economics*, 7 (July 1926), 34.

[49] Basu, *Challenge and Change*, p. 48.

[50] The Bangalore factory commenced production during 1913. Basu, *Challenge and Change*, p. 38.

[51] Harrison returned to America as a director of the Export Leaf Tobacco Co., BAT Co.'s US tobacco purchasing arm. *BAT Bulletin*, 14 (37) (1923), 827.

[52] ILTD Co., 'Indian Tobacco Leaves: Story of Co-operation in India', p. 2.

of Imperial Preference in September 1919. This provided a measure of protection for raw materials procured from within the British Empire, and the effect of the new policy on tobacco leaf imports from India was to reduce duty from 8s. 2d. (more than double the rate in force at the outbreak of the First World War) to 6s. 1½d.[53] Suitably encouraged, ILTD dispatched a sample of their Bihar tobacco to manufacturers in Britain during 1920 to see whether an export trade could be established, but the response was disappointing.[54] The following year, however, sample shipments were made of Guntur leaf and these were found to be acceptable by manufacturers of pipe tobacco who were able to mix the cheaper Indian leaf with other types to reduce costs without detriment to the flavour.[55] Thus in 1922, arrangements were made to build a new factory at Chilara in which the leaf could be redried prior to export.[56]

The increased demand for Guntur leaf which the export trade stimulated brought a new difficulty to bear on ILTD's management. As tobacco farming had become more commercialized during the 1910s some of the bigger ryots began to buy up large quantities of leaf directly from the cultivators. In doing so, these dealers formed a producer cartel that pushed the price of Guntur tobacco up towards the cost of the imported leaf which it was designed to substitute.[57] To overcome this problem, ILTD set up four buying depots and encouraged the cultivators to bring their tobacco directly for purchase.[58] The price set at these depots quickly emerged as a ceiling for the market in Guntur tobacco, enabling the company to purchase as much leaf as it required.[59] During the mid-1920s the volume of leaf processed by ILTD expanded, and two more drying machines were installed at Chirala between 1925 and 1926, with a further eight sub-depots set up in 1927 to collect the leaf. The entire enterprise was run by a staff of Europeans numbering a mere twenty-four.[60]

[53] On the background to the policy of Imperial Preference see M. Havinden and D. Meredith, *Colonialism and Development: Britain and its Tropical Colonies, 1850–1960* (1993), esp. pp. 148–52.

[54] In 1920 another colonial BAT Co. subsidiary, UTC in South Africa, set up a leaf export operation in Rhodesia called the Tobacco Development Co. (Rhodesia) Ltd., *BAT News* (Autumn 1985), p. 20.

[55] The differential in duty levied on Empire tobacco was reduced again in July 1925 to three-quarters of the rate for American leaf. By 1927 over 250 brands of smoking mixtures were on sale in Britain which featured colonially grown leaf. M. Corina, *Trust In Tobacco: The Anglo–American Struggle for Power* (1975), p. 156; *Tobacco (London)*, 53 (626) (1933), iv.

[56] ILTD Co., 'Indian Tobacco Leaves', p. 5.

[57] Ranga, 'Madras Tobacco Trade', p. 36.

[58] An attempt by BAT to cut out such dealers in their tobacco-purchasing operations in Hsuchang, China, during the 1930s ended disastrously, with the murder of two employees, Wu Ting Seng and G. H. Newsome. BAT Archive (SASS), Doc. Nos. 14-E-65–76.

[59] Ranga, 'Madras Tobacco Trade', p. 35; ILTD Co., 'Indian Tobacco Leaves', pp. 5–6.

[60] *BAT Bulletin*, 17 (81) (1927), 284–6.

As the company's buyers began to learn the local dialect and establish closer relations with the ryots, ILTD moved to a new stage by initiating the growing of American Virginian leaf around Guntur. A small group of ryots were chosen by the company to plant the new seeds and were provided with support and advice by newly recruited agricultural graduates from England. In return, the growers contracted with the company to sell the entire standing crop to ILTD at a predetermined price.[61] Thus although the company never owned the land upon which tobacco leaf was grown, nor employed cultivators directly, by guaranteeing to purchase the crop at the time of planting ILTD had effectively engaged in backward vertical integration into tobacco cultivation via bonded contracts linked to a system of close managerial supervision.

As the area under cultivation of Virginia tobacco continued to expand, ILTD began to introduce flue-curing of the leaf. Initially the company had encouraged farmers to adopt the system of rack-curing their tobacco by hanging it up on bamboo structures, but this remained a slow and unpredictable method of curing tobacco, extending over a period of at least three, and possibly up to six weeks, and requiring dry weather. In 1928, therefore, two brick-built flue-curing barns were erected at the Guntur depot and two American staff were brought over to experiment with the locally grown leaf. The trials proved successful, and in 1929 more barns were built in seven of the company's buying depots and a total of 500,000 lb. of tobacco was flue-cured.

The long-term objective of ILTD, however, seems to have been to replicate the American system of cultivation under which the farmers took full responsibility for the flue-curing process. Since this transfer required a significant capital investment on behalf of the ryots, ILTD developed a scheme whereby the necessary inputs were provided directly by the company and the costs recouped when the tobacco was purchased. This enabled efficient farmers of limited means the opportunity to upgrade their operations and produce the flue-cured type of tobacco which sold at anything up to five times the value of the indigenous crop (see Table 7.3). Although these capital investments served to bind cultivators to ILTD—at least until the costs of the capital equipment were recouped—the company also demonstrated how such facilities could be constructed at a lower cost using bamboo and mud rather than brick. By 1932, the Guntur region was producing sufficient flue-cured leaf to allow sales to be made to dealers from other firms.[62] As the range

[61] ILTD Co., 'Indian Tobacco Leaves', p. 7.

[62] ILTD Co., 'Indian Tobacco Leaves', pp. 20–2; ILTD continued its practice of using bonded contracts with ryots throughout the 1930s, *Report on the Marketing of Tobacco in India and Burma* (1939), p. 202.

TABLE 7.3. Average prices for leaf tobacco at Guntur, Madras, 1930–7

Year	Virginia flue-cured	Country tobacco
	(price per candy of 500 lb., in Rupees)	
1930	128	n.a.
1931	128	n.a.
1932	154	57
1933	148	30
1934	127	30
1935	143	54
1936	150	43
1937	187	50

Source: Government of India, *Report on the Marketing of Tobacco*, pp. 114, 117.

of cultivators expanded, so the acreage and crop of flue-cured tobacco grew (see Table 7.4) and other firms set up their own redrying facilities in the region. In 1936 ILTD opened its first buying depot north of the Krishna River in the Godavari district where the cultivation of Virginia tobacco leaf spread extremely quickly. With this development the lines of communication to the factory at Chirala were considerably lengthened and a second redrying plant was built at Anaparti. By 1941 the company was operating fourteen buying depots in southern India, covering a belt of tobacco-growing land over 200 miles in length.

The 1930s saw the main fruits of ILTD's investments in terms of the Indian export trade. Although the trade depression of the 1930s led to an overall decline in India's exports of tobacco leaf, that part of the trade stemming from the areas around Guntur in Madras continued to expand in volume terms, even though the unit value of tobacco exports declined slightly.[63] This trade was, however, rather narrowly based on the UK market which accounted for upwards of 66 per cent of the unmanufactured tobacco exports originating from Madras (see Table 7.5). ILTD's own trade seems to have been largely responsible for this. The company, which purchased over one-half of all the cigarette tobacco produced in India during the 1930s,[64] focused its own

[63] The average value of India's tobacco exports (including both manufactured and unmanufactured taken together) fell from around Rs.350,000 per million lb. in the mid-1920s to around Rs. 320,000 per million during the 1930s, *Marketing of Tobacco in India*, p. 55. Note that unmanufactured tobacco dominated Indian exports throughout this period.

[64] *Marketing of Tobacco in India*, p. 320.

TABLE 7.4. Acreage and output of flue-cured tobacco leaf in Guntur District, 1928–41

Year	Acreage for flue-curing (acres)	Crop of flue-cured leaves ('000 lb.)
1928	80	42
1929	920	500
1930	2,500	1,400
1931	3,750	2,000
1932	6,000	3,300
1933	22,000	11,000
1934	33,000	16,500
1935	39,100	21,000
1936[a]	39,800	21,500
1937	85,600	43,000
1938	99,000	49,000
1939	101,000	50,500
1940[b]	78,000	39,000
1941	126,000	55,100

Notes: [a] Cyclone year; [b] Floods led to shortage of seedlings.
Source: ILTD Co., 'Indian Tobacco Leaves', p. 22.

exports on the requirements of the Imperial Tobacco Co. in Britain.[65] It had, nevertheless, more than satisfied the objectives set out by the Government of India during the tobacco duties debate of 1910 by creating a vibrant tobacco leaf export industry in Britain's leading colonial possession.

Competing in the Indian Cigarette Market

The decision to set up the Peninsular Tobacco Company as its Indian manufacturing arm in 1905 gave BAT Co. the distinction of being Britain's first manufacturing multinational to invest in production capacity within India. Five years later, during the upheavals caused by the imposition of the tobacco tariff, the company moved a step further by registering its first Rupee-denominated company in Calcutta. The Imperial Tobacco Company of India, Ltd. (ITC), a wholly owned BAT Co. subsidiary, was incorporated on 24 August 1910 with an initial capital of just Rs.1,000. By the end of the following month, however, the new company's issued capital had been expanded to Rs.3 million and it had taken control of all BAT Co.'s interests

[65] Basu, *Challenge and Change*, p. 174.

TABLE 7.5. Exports of unmanufactured tobacco from India and Burma by port of origin, and UK imports of unmanufactured tobacco from India (million lb.), 1925–38 (annual averages)

Port of origin	1925–6 to 1929–30	1930–1 to 1934–5	1935–6 to 1937–8
Bengal	4.33	2.86	0.77
Madras	13.35	15.79	21.78
Bombay	5.85	5.2	7.63
Sind	0.05	0.02	0.02
Burma	7.03	2.1	0.87
Total exports	30.61	25.97	31.07
UK imports	10.56	10.58	21.8

Note: UK imports are averages for calendar years (1926–30, 1931–35, 1936–38).
Sources: Indian exports: Government of India, *Report on the Marketing of Tobacco*, p. 59; UK imports: Monopolies Commission, *Report on the Supply of Cigarettes and Tobacco*, Appendix 7, Table 1.

in India, Aden, and Burma, apart from the Peninsular Tobacco Co. It was also assigned the selling and distribution rights to BAT brands in India which had originally been vested in the London-registered BAT Co. (India) subsidiary.[66] ITC began its operations based in a rented office at 14 Radha Bazar Lane from where the local managing director, C. Percy Page, supervised a small European management team with functional responsibilities covering sales, accounting, advertising, supply, and legal affairs. Below the offices was the company's warehouse, or godown, which was supervised by an ex-Indian Army contractor.

The Imperial concern thus became BAT Co.'s selling arm in India, and operated in tandem with the Peninsular manufacturing company. To these two entities were added a third in 1912 through the registration of ILTD in Calcutta as the group's local tobacco leaf procurement organization. The pivotal position of Calcutta in the lines of communication between India and Britain meant that ITC's offices were effectively the administrative centre of the group, and its role as BAT Co.'s India headquarters was formalized at the end of the First World War when the company's investment in India was stepped up. Between September 1919 and November 1921 the issued capital of ITC was raised from Rs.3 million to Rs.41.6 million and the manufacturing and leaf-procurement businesses of Peninsular and ILTD were brought under its direct control.

66 In 1913, BAT Co. also registered the Arcadian Tobacco Co. Ltd. in London which was designed to create high-class brands that were manufactured on its behalf by the Peninsular Tobacco Co. BAT Co. Corporate Index, BAT Co. Southampton Archive, Box 114.

Page continued as chairman of the expanded ITC concern and retained control until his death on return from home leave in 1923. He was succeeded briefly by R. McNeil, who himself died whilst on home leave the following year, after which the chairmanship passed to Harry Abbott who presided until 1935. The 1920s were a successful period for the company in India, with cigarette sales rising from 3.5 billion to 8.8 billion per annum over the course of the decade. This growth in business was mirrored by an expansion in the size of ITC's management headquarters. For a period in the early 1920s the company moved its offices to the National Bank building at 5 Fairlie Place,[67] but in 1926 the decision was made to commission the building of an impressive new headquarters, Virginia House, located away from the traditional business centre of Calcutta in a more residential area at 37 Chowringhee. On its completion in 1928, this new four-storey office was in many respects an Indian version of BAT Co.'s headquarters at Millbank; the third floor of the building contained the advertising, supply, leaf, and factory departments; the second floor housed the directors' offices and the general sales department; the general accounts and legal departments shared the first floor leaving the ground floor to be divided between the traffic department and records office, and a branch of Lloyds Bank who also operated a similar arrangement out of Westminster House in London.[68]

Between the commissioning and occupation of Virginia House, however, the corporate structure of BAT's Indian operations again underwent a change. In an effort to reduce the incidence of Indian taxation, all of the operating companies in India were re-registered in the Isle of Man with the exception of ITC itself. This latter entity ceased to act as a holding company and received only the profits derived from the selling side of the business. The profits in India from manufacturing (now transferred from the Peninsular company to a new subsidiary, Tobacco Manufacturers (India)) and leaf dealing now accrued to the companies registered in the Isle of Man and these, together with Imperial, were placed under the ultimate ownership of a new holding company, the Raleigh Investment Company Ltd., which was itself a Manx-registered corporation capitalized at £12.5 million. The arrangements gave BAT Co. much greater financial flexibility over its Indian operations and also provided Cunliffe-Owen with a revenue stream capable of funding his wider business objectives through the Tobacco Securities Trust (cf. Chapter 9). However, the changes seem to have had little impact on the functioning of BAT's Indian business which continued to be man-

67 According to the address given for Imperial in *Thakar's Indian Directory* the company moved to the National Bank building in 1921.

68 Basu, *Challenge and Change*, pp. 66–80.

aged from Calcutta by the board of ITC under the ultimate supervision of the London directors.

ITC's business success during the 1920s was based on the company's ability to rapidly expand the market for its locally manufactured, low-priced cigarettes among the native population of India. This in turn required the creation of an integrated system of sales, marketing, and distribution which could both stimulate demand for the new product and put in place the appropriate sales infrastructure to satisfy that demand. Even more than in China, the success of ITC's marketing effort depended upon salesmen drafted in from the company's home country. These salesmen worked through a regional sales network which in the early 1920s operated through five depots located in Calcutta, Delhi, Karachi, Bombay, and Madras. Each of these depots was divided into districts (five in the case of Calcutta depot for example) and these districts (later known as circles) were in turn further broken down into three or four sections. Each district was staffed by a salesman posted from England, and these district salesmen were supported by a group of section salesmen recruited from the local population, and who reported on their activities each month. The task of the district salesmen was simply 'to sell cigarettes' and this engaged their time for a full twenty-five days per month. Travelling their territory with a section salesman and a posting peon (foot-soldier), these district salesmen would visit bazaars and set up stalls from which samples of cigarettes would be distributed and competitions such as lucky-dips and cigarette-shies organized. Bazaars were plastered with posters by these teams, and an efficient salesman was expected to sample (i.e., distribute free of charge to consumers) up to 100,000 cigarettes personally per month. The supporting paperwork was relatively simple at this stage; each day a standardized report form would be completed and returned to the depot manager, giving particulars of the work done.[69]

This marketing system was supported by a distribution structure in which Indian wholesalers were given sole agency for certain brands across the region in which they operated. These supplies were ordered from the central depot serving the area, but the process was poorly co-ordinated and the delays in transit often meant that markets were left short of stocks for periods of time. The difficulties in these supply arrangements were tackled by the introduction of a new system shortly after Harry Abbott assumed the chairmanship of ITC. The revised method involved a switch from a brand-centred approach, in which wholesalers were given control of certain lines of cigarettes throughout the territory, to one based on the exclusive control of distribution

[69] Notes on the history of ITC, BAT Co. Southampton Archive, Box 188; *BAT Bulletin*, 12 (22) (1922), 488.

arrangements for all brands within a particular town. The 'one-town/one-distributor' approach was the brainchild of J. E. Brookes, who had been transferred to India in 1922 from managing the company's sales in South Manchuria. After Abbott took control, Brookes' new distribution system was put in place in the Calcutta depot with encouraging results. Distributors were now obliged to complete a 'weekly stock position return' and the process of co-ordinating supply and demand became much more exact.[70] As a result, a much greater proportion of a district salesman's time was devoted to stock control and associated paperwork, rather than the day-to-day process of selling. One aspect of the new system which gave the company's cigarettes an advantage over those produced by smaller rivals was the company's pledge to take back at full value any stocks which were not moving or were old, thus ensuring that dealers would not lose out if a brand declined in popularity. This change was accompanied with a shift from unsecured to secured credit arrangement to dealers, with 4 per cent interest allowed against cash security, and a move towards cash sales wherever possible. The changes proved most beneficial to the wholesalers themselves as their turnover increased, and appointment as a distributor of ITC's products became much sought after by local firms.

Between the wars, ITC constituted the dominant player in the cigarette market in India, but rival firms were not without influence especially through the export trade. Imported cigarette sales, which had fallen back after the imposition of the import duty in 1909, began to rise during the First World War when BAT received requisitions to supply tobacco goods to the Indian Army. As in China, a significant proportion of these cigarettes were exported from the company's American factories (cf. Table 7.1), and the American brand of 'Eagle' became quite popular in India at this time. However, at the end of the war, the trade was handed back to the English factories, and a concerted effort was made to boost the popularity of the traditional Wills brand 'Scissors' by holding a competition in which a total of Rs.50,000 was given away in prizes.[71]

Most of the competition to ITC in India before 1930 stemmed from British rivals. Some time before the First World War the London-based company Thomas Bear & Sons began sales operations in India with particular emphasis on its 'Elephant' brand. However, this company was bought out in 1920 by the Imperial Tobacco Co. (of Great Britain and Ireland) and its overseas interests were taken over by BAT Co. who continued to market their 'Elephant' cigarettes in India. Thomas Bear & Sons took a minority share in ITC,

[70] *Ying Mei Yien Kung Ssu Yueh Pao* [British American Tobacco Co. Monthly Journal] (September 1923), p. 79.

[71] *BAT Bulletin*, 12 (2) (1921), 435–6.

and Thomas Bear & Sons (India) became a brand-owning subsidiary of ITC in India.

Other British tobacco manufacturers who developed an export trade in India between the wars were Carreras, Rothmans (who briefly operated a factory in Ceylon), and Godfrey Phillips. Carreras had emerged as a particularly successful competitor to the Imperial group in Britain following the introduction of 'Black Cat' cigarettes in 1904 which, from 1905, featured gift coupons and other prize-giving schemes. Together with their equally successful 'Craven A' brand, Carreras had managed to raise their market share in Britain to over 13 per cent by the beginning of the 1930s.[72] Using the output from the company's huge Arcadia Works at Mornington Crescent in north London, Carreras had cultivated an export trade in its cigarettes which established them as a strong competitor brand to BAT's products in a number of foreign markets, including India. Following the trade depression of the early 1930s, however, the company's profits suffered a sharp fall, and its sales in India were damaged by nationalist boycotts of British products. In an effort to arrest the decline in sales, Carreras' chairman Sir Louis Baron drew up plans during 1932 to open a factory within India. In response Sir Hugo Cunliffe-Owen—no doubt concerned that the additional capacity would serve merely to make trading conditions in India yet more difficult—opened discussions with Baron about the possibility of reaching an agreement between the two firms there. Baron reported Cunliffe-Owen's idea to the board of Carreras who felt that any such arrangement should not be limited to India but should embrace all the territories outside of Great Britain and Ireland apart from Australia.[73] At the time, similar discussions were already taking place in Britain designed to end coupon trading and create a situation of profit pooling between the largest tobacco firms which eventually led to the signing of the Martin Agreement in 1933 (cf. Chapter 8).

The dialogue between Cunliffe-Owen and Baron must have lapsed for a period of time because in 1934 Carreras registered an Indian subsidiary in Calcutta and leased a property in the Kidderpore district of the city from the Port Commissioners which it converted into a modern cigarette factory. Not until the following year was an agreement finally reached between BAT and Carreras to introduce a series of pooling arrangements in various parts of the world. In India, BAT Co. registered a new subsidiary, Cigarette Manufacturers (India), specifically for the purpose of operating Carreras' Calcutta factory, and the acquisition gave ITC control over some three-quarters of the

72 Corina, *Trust in Tobacco*, pp. 112 and 164.

73 Minutes of the Chairman's Daily Committee (hereafter CDC Minutes), 16 November 1932.

total cigarette manufacturing capacity in India.[74] The decision came as a severe blow to the prestige of the chairman of Carreras' Indian branch, but the collaboration was symptomatic of the times and the following year BAT also reached a pooling arrangement in Ceylon with Godfrey Phillips who had taken over Rothmans' factory there.[75] By the end of 1935, therefore, BAT interests had taken control of practically all the trade of British firms in India. However, in 1936 Godfrey Phillips registered a new subsidiary company in Calcutta, Godfrey Phillips (India) Ltd., with a starting capital of Rs.3.3 million and constructed a factory there which began production in 1938. This company later acquired a second plant in Bombay during 1944.[76]

Competition to ITC from local Indian firms took two forms. On the one hand, ITC consistently attempted to expand the market for their cigarettes among those smokers who favoured the indigenous bidi type of cigarette. During the 1920s a number of very low-priced brands such as 'Gem' were developed which retailed for as little as ten for 1 pice (one-twelfth of a British penny). However, even though these cheap brands accounted for 70 per cent of all cigarettes sold in India by the 1930s,[77] the company found bidi smokers difficult to convert to cigarettes and sales of these indigenous products still outnumbered those of cigarettes by a factor of ten to one. Table 7.6 illustrates that cigarette smoking was far more evenly spread throughout the country than bidi consumption, indicating that the latter product continued to meet the requirements of local consumers whilst the former found its main adherents within a gradually emerging middle-income, national market.

Competition from indigenous manufacturers of machine-made cigarettes, on the other hand, remained quite limited, at least until the nationalist boycotts of the 1930s. A brief period of competition from a local manufacturing concern arose shortly after the end of the First World War when the expatriate jute-based managing agency Howeson & Co. refloated the East India Tobacco Co. in 1919 as the British India Tobacco Co. This organization had originally been formed during 1909 under the managing directorship of M. Omari with a factory at Dum Dum outside the centre of Calcutta. The owner

74 *Report on Marketing of Tobacco*, p. 320; Basu, *Challenge and Change*, p. 92. According to this account, it was not until 1943 that Carreras (India) completed the sale to Imperial of all its business, goodwill, brands, trade marks, and other assets in India and Burma.

75 Baker, 'Redried Leaves', pp. 63–9. BAT had also by this time acquired a small factory in Bombay from A. & J. Green.

76 J. N. Gupta *et al.* (eds.), *Directory of Foreign Collaborations in India* (1966), vol. 2, p. 694; Tomlinson, 'Foreign Private Investment in India', pp. 655–77. A press report in the *Pioneer Mail* of 12 June 1912 indicated that Godfrey Phillips had been planning to build a factory in Calcutta around this time, due to the higher level of duties, but there is no evidence that this plant was actually built. IOR/L/E/7/687; R&S Dept. File No. 2028/12.

77 *Report on the Marketing of Tobacco*, p. 85.

TABLE 7.6. Estimated per capita consumption of cigarettes and bidis in India and Burma, 1934/5

Province or state	Cigarettes		Bidis		All tobacco
	lb.	No.	lb.	No.	lb.
Assam	0.125	44	0.062	62	3.103
Bengal	0.054	19	0.133	133	2.997
Bihar & Orissa	0.042	15	0.126	126	2.888
Bombay	0.118	41	0.477	477	3.069
Central Provinces & Berar	0.044	15	0.179	179	0.937
Madras	0.028	10	0.218	218	3.147
North-West Frontier Province	0.083	29	0.001	1	6.411
Punjab	0.058	20	0.005	5	2.034
Sind	0.155	54	0.687	687	3.126
United Provinces	0.029	10	0.07	70	4.504
Baroda	0.111	39	0.66	660	1.97
Nizam's Dominions	0.087	30	0.664	664	1.838
Kashmir	0.044	15	0.068	68	1.182
Mysore	0.107	37	0.572	572	1.977
Travancore	0.009	3	0.137	137	1.977
Other areas	0.075	26	0.217	217	2.554
All India	0.057	20	0.197	197	2.915
Burma	0.127	45	0.476	476	6.383

Source: Government of India, *Report on Marketing of Tobacco*, Appendix XXVIII.

of the Howeson agency, John Howeson, was well acquainted with Cunliffe-Owen (cf. Chapter 9) and may have been advised of the potential market for cigarettes in India by the then deputy chairman of BAT Co. in a characteristic attempt to generate some competitive stimulus for his own company's subsidiary.[78] Despite the investment of Rs.3 million, and some successful attempts to lure existing ITC staff to work in the factory at Dum Dum, the British India Tobacco Co. initiative foundered in the wake of the nationalist boycotts of 1920–1, eventually being wound up in 1922.[79]

By 1923 only eleven cigarette factories were operating in India, falling to a mere nine by 1929,[80] and of these, the Peninsular company operated three. The factory at Monghyr had been expanded to the point where its output was reported to have exceeded 2 billion cigarettes per annum by the end of the

78 Reginald Baker, chairman of ITC from 1935 to 1945, held a suspicion that Cunliffe-Owen may have been financially involved in the Howeson initiative. Baker, 'Redried Leaves', p. 43.

79 *The Investors India Yearbook*, Nos. 9, 10, and 11, Calcutta, 1921, 1922, 1923.

80 *Report on the Marketing of Tobacco*, p. 320.

First World War.[81] By 1923 this plant had been supplemented by the operation in Bangalore, designed to take advantage of the tobacco leaf grown in Guntur, and a newly built factory in Saharanpur, north of Delhi, to supply the fast-growing market in northern India. In addition the company developed its own printing facilities at Monghyr during the early 1920s, training local operatives in the use of the machinery and, inadvertently, creating the company's first industrial dispute by paying these employees higher rates than the tobacco machinery operatives.[82]

ITC's advanced production technology, marketing expertise, and scale of operation made it very difficult for local firms to compete effectively with their products. Nevertheless, during the 1920s one such firm managed to develop a cigarette with a level of local consumer appeal which, for all their efforts, ITC were unable to match. The company was a small concern based in the Princely State of Hyderabad, and the name of this cigarette was 'Charminar'.[83] The brand had been created by an Indian tobacco producer named Abdul Sattar who had earlier run the factory in Bowringpet which had manufactured cigarettes under the title of the City Tobacco Company. This operation had been unable to compete effectively against the products of BAT, and sometime during the early 1920s Sattar had been engaged by Vazir Sultan & Sons, a group of Sultans in Hyderabad, to manage a small cigarette factory which they had set up in a designated government excise area.

For a number of years during the mid-1920s Sattar's 'Charminar' brand held its market around Hyderabad despite concerted attempts by ITC to break its appeal. Unlike other small Indian cigarette manufacturers, who simply dumped cigarettes on to dealers with very little consideration of the long-term prospects of the brand, Sattar carefully nurtured the sales of 'Charminar' by ensuring that stock levels closely reflected demand and that the dealers were never left holding stale cigarettes. This policy seems to have allowed Vazir Sultan's cigarettes to reach consumers in better condition even than those distributed by ITC.[84] Inevitably, the detrimental impact that this firm's competition was having on ITC's sales in the region prompted questions regarding a possible take-over of the Vazir Sultan concern. Although the chairman Harry Abbott and the majority of the board in Calcutta were not

81 S. Reed (ed.), *Indian Year Book*, Times of India (1920), p. 461.

82 Baker, 'Redried Leaves', pp. 48–9.

83 The name refers to a prominent feature of the city of Hyderabad: a huge triumphal arch built in 1591 to commemorate the end of a plague.

84 This explanation of 'Charminar's' success was put forward by A. C. Acree, who was involved in negotiations with the Sultans in 1928. Letter H. Abbott, ITC, Calcutta, to H. Gough, BAT Co., London, dated 13 June 1928, BAT Co. Legal Dept. Papers, File MA 92 FC0241/2.

enthusiastic, and felt that the company would be acting from a position of weakness, another director, Reginald Baker, favoured this course of action, arguing that it would make good financial sense. On home leave in London during 1928, Baker had mentioned the advantages of purchasing Vazir Sultan during a chance meeting with Cunliffe-Owen in one of the lifts at Millbank. With his own acquisitive instincts being given free rein through the Tobacco Securities Trust at this point, Sir Hugo was quick to provide his blessing for such a scheme and on returning to Calcutta Baker informed his fellow directors that Cunliffe-Owen was in favour of buying out this successful Indian competitor.[85]

A take-over bid for a firm registered in Hyderabad was complicated due to the fact that the legal arrangements fell under the jurisdiction of the Princely State rather than the laws of British India. ITC's initial strategy was to make separate agreements with the owners of Vazir Sultan on the one hand, and with Abdul Sattar as its manager on the other, fearing that reaching a deal with the Sultans alone would leave them exposed to continued competition with any new initiative launched by Abdul Sattar. However, since neither ITC not Sattar held residential status within Hyderabad, no contract could be drawn up between these two parties which would have been legally binding under the laws of the Princely State. Months passed with little substantive progress being made, other than the registration of a BAT Co. subsidiary in Hyderabad which could be used as a future take-over vehicle and to undertake manufacturing of its own brand of cigarettes, 'S.Y.A.', on a temporary licence.[86]

It was only at the beginning of 1930 that Reginald Baker and the management of Vazir Sultan reached an agreement over the sale and purchase of the business in Hyderabad. The deal was brokered by Mr B. A. Collins, a member of the Indian Civil Service who acted as Director of Commerce and Industry for the government of Hyderabad, and supervised by BAT Co.'s London director, Harold Gough. Two conditions were specified at the time of the agreement: that the residents of the state of Hyderabad, including the Sultans, should be allowed to hold 25 per cent of the capital of the new company; and that the company furnished the government of Hyderabad with the services of a tobacco leaf cultivation expert for a period of two years. Before the transfer of the operating licence could be arranged, however, it required

85 Baker, 'Redried Leaves', pp. 55–7.

86 The company was registered as the Hyderabad Tobacco Company. Letter A. C. Acree, ITC, Hyderabad, to H. Gough, BAT Co., London, dated 12 June 1928; letter W. G. Ryan, ITC, Calcutta, to F. F. Macnaghten, BAT Co., London, dated 23 January 1929, BAT Co. Legal Dept. papers, File MA 92 FC0241/2.

approval by the Council of State and this served to delay the completion of the process until November. This pause in the proceedings allowed Abdul Sattar an opportunity to set up another small factory even whilst he continued to manage the Sultans' concern. Despite the efforts of ITC's management to persuade him to come over to the new company, Sattar could not be tempted and launched a new brand, 'Golconda', immediately the transfer was effected. Within a few months, however, Sattar died and the threat posed to 'Charminar' by his new brand disappeared.[87]

The acquisition of Vazir Sultan was effected through the creation of a subsidiary of the Raleigh holding company, called the Vazir Sultan Tobacco Company Ltd., with a capital of 100,000 shares of Rs.10 each. Of these shares, 10,000 were allocated to the government of Hyderabad and 7,000 put up for purchase by local residents. The bulk, 65,000, were held by BAT Co.'s new Indian holding company, Raleigh Investment Co., and the remaining 18,000 were issued to the Sultans along with Rs.667,649 in cash which together made up the agreed purchase price.[88] In terms of the physical assets purchased from the Sultans—which comprised two very old cigarette-making machines and one Legg tobacco cutter, all accommodated in a dilapidated factory—the price was relatively high. However, this rudimentary plant had been generating monthly sales of around 16 million sticks and profits estimated by ITC's management at Rs.200,000 per month.[89]

The decision to push ahead with the purchase of Vazir Sultan may have been stimulated by the increasingly difficult political and economic environment which ITC faced in India at this time. The campaign of civil disobedience initiated by the Indian Congress in 1930 was coupled with a boycott of British goods for which cigarettes were a primary target.[90] Between March and May of 1930, the average monthly sales of BAT's cigarettes in India fell from just over 700 million to barely 300 million. Only from 1934 did sales begin to recover in earnest, and not until the outbreak of the Second World War did they return to the levels of the late 1920s. The Vazir Sultan brands

[87] Letter W. G. Ryan, ITC, Calcutta, to F. F. Macnaghten, BAT Co., London, dated 24 January 1930; letter H. Gough, Calcutta, to F. F. Macnaghten, London, dated 20 February 1930; letter W. G. Ryan, ITC, Calcutta, to F. F. Macnaghten, London, dated 3 April 1930; BAT Co. Legal Dept. papers, File MA 92 FC0241/2; Baker, 'Redried Leaves', pp. 55–60.

[88] Note that these sums were denominated in the local Rupee (Hyderabad State) rather than in the British India Rupee, although these exchanged at a value close to parity.

[89] Memorandum relating to the conditions of formation of Vazir Sultan Tobacco Co. Ltd. for the purposes of acquiring the business of Vazir Sultan & Sons, dated 12 March 1930, BAT Co. Legal Dept. papers, File MA 92 FC0241/2.

[90] One source notes that from May to August 1930 the British Trade Commissioner's office was flooded with panic-stricken reports and complaints from Imperial Tobacco, Dunlop, and other 'white' firms. Sarkar, *Modern India*, p. 293.

were of some help to BAT in this respect, since its identity gave its brands the appearance of being under Indian control.[91]

BAT in China and India: a Comparison

A study of BAT's activities in the tobacco markets of China and India provides a number of valuable insights regarding the way in which the internationalization of the cigarette industry varied in its impact on host economies. Although the ultimate objective of BAT in each case was to promote the widespread adoption of machine-made cigarettes as a new form of tobacco consumption, the actual approach employed in each market was strongly influenced by the prevailing economic and social conditions. Moreover, the contrasting colonial experiences of these two nations before the Second World War meant that the political environment played a decisive role in shaping the conditions under which BAT was constrained to operate. Thus the economic impact of BAT's investment in the cigarette industries of China and India was by no means identical in each of the two cases under review.

Differences in BAT's performance were also an outcome of the specific circumstances relating to the company's own formation and early development. As an Anglo-American alliance, the composition of the company's management team in each market had a strong bearing on the shape of subsequent developments. During the early years American influence prevailed in Shanghai as ATC's managing agency, Mustard & Co., were granted the right to distribute BAT's products there in preference to Wills' former agent Rex & Co. Until the end of the First World War Americans provided the driving force behind BAT's sales expansion in China, and Duke strongly resented the diminution in American managerial influence which the changes in British-enacted company law in Hong Kong threatened to bring about. Notwithstanding this legislation, and the fact that London's control over the Chinese operation began to strengthen markedly after Thomas' departure in 1916, the legacy of its American roots continued to be a strong feature of the management there. In India, by contrast, the appointment of Nicholas Jellico as James Thomas's replacement in 1904 served to consolidate the links between Calcutta and London. Thereafter, the bulk of the staff

[91] Indeed, Harry Abbott wrote to admonish BAT Co.'s solicitor, F. F. Macnaghten, who had written to the Vazir Sultan company care of ITC in Calcutta. Abbott's letter noted that, 'The Vazir Sultan Co. is supposed to be a company—so far as the public are aware—formed in Hyderabad, running in competition against the Imperial Co.'. Letter H. Abbott, ITC, Calcutta, to F. F. Macnaghten, BAT Co., London, dated 25 May 1932, BAT Co. Legal Dept. papers, File MA 92 FC0241/2.

posted to Britain's principal colony by BAT Co. were drawn from the UK. The relative importance of American versus British business culture which featured in these two subsidiary concerns—taken in conjunction with the prevailing political environment—meant that the management approach adopted by BAT in China was one driven primarily by commercial imperatives, whilst that in India, although it never lost sight of the profit motive, increasingly took on many paternalistic features of the colonial administration under whose auspices it operated.

Both China and the British Indian Empire provided BAT with huge potential markets for their products, amongst populations where tobacco consumption was already well established. In each case an export market was initially developed among the expatriate groups in the major cities, first by BAT's predecessors and, later, the company's own export factories, using existing brands from the home market such as 'Pin Head' and 'Sweet Caporal' (cf. Table 4.1). This approach was supplemented by the development of export brands, such as Wills' 'Ruby Queen' in China and 'Scissors' in India, which could be franchised to local distributors on a sole agency basis. The critical move, however, was the decision to manufacture cigarettes locally through subsidiaries who could develop their own brands which more accurately reflected local tastes and customs. In both cases, the timing of this step towards local manufacture seems to have been determined by the advent of popular resistance to foreign cigarettes which took the form of consumer boycotts. Such pressures, which were manifest not only in a colonial context, meant that the product ranges offered to smokers in China and India soon bore little resemblance to one another. The export-based cigarette trade endured in both countries, nevertheless, as part of an overall strategy of product differentiation which was used to segment and expand the market.

The importance of the Chinese market to BAT's sales and profits was reflected in the fact that the factories there were supplied with the most up-to-date machinery, whilst the early Indian plants were equipped with second-hand machines which were surplus to requirements in China.[92] The engineering department attached to the factory at Shanghai in fact developed into an important centre of technical expertise within the BAT organization world-wide, and in the 1920s the department assembled Standard cigarette-making machines locally under licence for use in the company's factories in China, India, and elsewhere in the Far East. During the late 1920s the department's chief engineer, T. E. Skidmore, also developed a superior mechanism for cutting the continuous cigarette rod made by these machines into individual sticks. This machine, named the 'Felstead' cutter after Cunliffe-

[92] Baker, 'Redried Leaves', p. 23.

Owen's Derby-winning horse of 1928, was patented by BAT Co. and produced at Pootung for use in conjunction with the Standard machines. It was subsequently adopted for use in many of BAT's factories including the leading-edge Liverpool and Southampton plants.[93] The management of BAT in China were desperate to maintain the local skilled engineering workforce during the crisis period of 1925–8, and BAT Co.'s London office urged both the India- and Java-based manufacturing operations to avail themselves of the facilities in Shanghai for obtaining machine spares in order to prevent redundancies there.[94]

The spatial location of the company's cigarette manufacturing factories in China reflected the logistical requirements of distribution in a country with a relatively undeveloped transport infrastructure and a high incidence of natural disasters, such that by the end of the 1920s each of the five regional markets of China had been equipped with a plant of its own. Of the cigarette manufacturing plants built by BAT in China, only the Tsingtao factory seems to have been located with regard to leaf procurement from the tobacco-growing region of Shantung as its principal consideration. In India, however, a more dense network of transport facilities meant that the choice of both Monghyr and Bangalore as the first two locations for manufacturing was made with the objective of leaf procurement uppermost in mind.

In both countries, the factories and leaf-processing plants set up by BAT provided a means of employment for many thousands of workers, male and female. In terms of factory labour, the workforce in China became increasingly politicized after 1925 and the company became embroiled in a series of strikes and industrial actions over the course of the following decade as the urban labour force became the focal point of the struggle for political influence.[95] The situation in India, by contrast, was far more sanguine. Although various industrial disputes did emerge over the course of the 1930s, it was not until 1940 that a concerted programme of industrial action was undertaken at ITC's factories which received the political backing of the Indian Congress.[96] In general, however, the company seems to have succeeded in building a good working climate in India, much along the lines of the factories in England, using sport as a bonding mechanism.[97] Certainly at

93 *BAT News* (Spring 1988), 37–8.

94 BAT Archive (SASS), Doc. Nos. 12-C-106–107.

95 E. J. Perry, *Shanghai on Strike: The Politics of Chinese Labor* (1993), pp. 135–66.

96 Basu, *Challenge and Change*, pp. 105–7. Notes by J. L. Bowring, a factory manager in India, mention a sit-in strike at the Bangalore factory over incentive rates in 1936 as the first such incident in the Indian company's experience, BAT Co. Southampton Archive, Box 188.

97 The colonial experience clearly made it easier for the company to develop a sporting ethos among its Indian factory staff. The *BAT Bulletin* provides examples of sporting activities in both China and India, but in the former this seems to have been rather more limited to the

the leaf-processing plants of ILTD the company paid higher wages to the staff than other employers engaged in similar activities and began to introduce the kind of benefits which were granted to factory staff in Britain such as sick leave, some paid leave, a superannuation fund, and an athletic association which organized, among other things, an annual sports day (including musical chairs for the ladies!).[98]

The rather paternalistic attitude which ITC and ILTD took towards their factory staff tended to reveal itself among upper- and middle-class Indians more in the form of condescension. ITC's own history notes that, 'The British in the early days were uniformly kind and protective to the young Indian clerks who joined ILTD, provided, of course, that they knew their place and showed proper respect for their "betters".'[99] Only very gradually in the 1930s were educated Indians assimilated into management grades within ITC; a process which was speeded up by the onset of the Second World War. All the same, even this slow rate of progress placed ITC at the forefront of Indianization among British companies with subsidiary concerns in India. Unlike the situation in China, where partnerships and collaboration with Chinese firms on something close to an equal basis had been an important characteristic of BAT's distribution operation since the involvement of Wu Ting Seng in 1912, in India the company's only similar partnership at this level followed the acquisition of the Vazir Sultan Tobacco Co., and this constituted a situation of majority ownership over members of the ruling élite of a nominally independent Princely State!

These contrasting relations with indigenous personnel were undoubtedly the result, in part, of the contrasting political environments in which BAT found itself operating. Links with Chinese merchants and gentry were necessary for BAT to circumvent the limitations imposed by the treaty port arrangements under which foreign firms were forced to operate in China. These difficulties were greatest in relation to the tobacco procurement side of the company's business, and in December 1920 a separate Chinese company called the Hung An Land Investment Co. was set up under Wu Ting Seng's management to enable the company to purchase the land it required for its leaf-processing facilities.[100] As a result of the chaotic political conditions in China between the wars, BAT's ability to control the cultivation of tobacco

Western staff (e.g., a tennis tournament) whilst in the latter there are examples such as a hockey team made up mainly (but not exclusively) of native factory workers. *BAT Bulletin*, 16 (69) (1926), 270–1; 13 (29) (1922), 647.

98 ILTD Co., 'Indian Tobacco Leaves', p. 50.

99 Basu, *Challenge and Change*, p. 136.

100 S. Cochran, *Big Business in China: Sino-Foreign Rivalry in the Cigarette Industry, 1890–1930* (1980), pp. 140–5.

leaf was quite limited, and of the three sites in which flue-cured tobacco was procured in China, only Shantung provided a consistent supply of leaf. In contrast, the cultivation of leaf tobacco in India was a factor in the Government of India's decision to impose a tariff on imports of cigarettes and tobacco in 1910, and in pioneering the establishment of an export industry in the commodity ILTD played a developmental role in British Indian economic policy between the wars.[101]

The aspect of the company's performance which varied least between the two countries was the process of marketing cigarettes. In each case, sales teams led by Western BAT staff travelled the length and breadth of the country introducing not only cigarettes, but forms of marketing hitherto unknown. With little in the way of local media, advertising and promotion mainly took the form of brightly coloured posters and the setting-up of cigarette stalls from which the product could be sampled. The most pioneering element in the company's marketing armoury was the new medium of film, and in both cases this was enlisted to help with the promotional effort. In India, a travelling cinema was used, which traversed the country showing company-made movies such as 'The Cigarette Bride' in an effort to entice consumers to adopt cigarettes as their preferred form of tobacco consumption.[102] Yet more extravagant, in China, was the decision to set up the company's own movie studio in Shanghai which was reputedly the most advanced to be found anywhere outside of the United States.[103]

In both cases, too, the role of the Western salesmen changed over time. After a period of promotion and mass marketing, the fundamental task of these salesmen became the management of the distribution networks and the collection and dissemination of sales intelligence. Once a demand for cigarettes had been stimulated, the primary consideration became the management of the flows of stocks, and the matching up of supply with prevailing patterns of demand. Increasingly, the Western sales staff of BAT became engaged in the various forms of paperwork which were needed to turn a high volume of sales into a reliable source of revenue. Whilst the image of BAT's legacy in China and India may have been most apparent to outside observers in terms of their role as pioneers of marketing practices, the ultimate success of the enterprise resided in the successful transfer from Britain and the United States of the rather more prosaic business skills of financial and management accounting.

[101] Publicizing the benefits of the work undertaken by ILTD Co. in this respect was almost certainly the reason behind the publication of the history of the organization by BAT Co. in 1941.

[102] *BAT Bulletin*, 13 (31) (1922), 706–8.

[103] Cochran, *Big Business in China*, p. 130.

Part Four

International Business in an Unstable World

8

Maintaining Global Leadership

Introduction

AFTER the dislocations brought about by the dissolution of ATC and the outbreak of the First World War, the 1920s represents a period in which BAT Co. consolidated its position as the world's pre-eminent manufacturer in the international cigarette market. By the end of the decade, the company had emerged as a major force in practically all of the national tobacco markets outside of Britain and America in which access via an export trade or foreign direct investment was a feasible strategy. However, the path to global leadership was not straightforward. At the end of the First World War BAT Co.'s top management was divided between Britain and America and only Hugo Cunliffe-Owen, who had spent much of the war in the United States, was in a position to effectively mediate between the two camps. Although the balance of power clearly favoured London, the activities of Duke and other American tobacco interests continued to have significant ramifications for BAT Co. in the immediate post-war years.

After the dissolution of ATC, various individuals connected with the tobacco industry in the United States saw an opportunity to compete in foreign markets against BAT Co. In one particularly significant case, that of the Tobacco Products Export Corporation, Duke himself—although still nominally chairman of BAT Co.—became financially involved and hence found himself holding a key position in two opposing international tobacco enterprises. This dilemma ultimately precipitated Duke's retirement from the chairmanship of BAT Co. in 1923 and his replacement by Cunliffe-Owen. Duke's departure from the scene meant that the new chairman of BAT Co. took charge of the London headquarters at a time when it had clearly established its hegemonic position within the BAT organization. Far from marginalizing the US-based management, however, Cunliffe-Owen sought to strengthen it, first through expanding BAT Co.'s interests in Latin America and then delegating much of the managerial responsibility for this region to the New York office, and subsequently by taking BAT Co. directly into the US market through the acquisition in 1927 of the North Carolina-based Brown & Williamson Tobacco Company.

By the end of the 1920s, as well as having established BAT Co.'s leading position in a range of cigarette markets across the globe, and having successfully defended its leadership of the international tobacco industry against American challengers, Cunliffe-Owen's management had also succeeded in re-establishing the company as a true Anglo-American alliance. Thus by the time events on Wall Street signalled the end of a decade of rapid expansion for BAT Co., Hugo Cunliffe-Owen had securely established his personal control over the management of a company whose international operations spanned more than forty countries.

The Retirement of Duke

In early 1918 Hugo Cunliffe-Owen returned to London from New York, and joined up with Joseph Hood, Arthur Churchman, and Lawrence Hignett, who had taken charge of BAT Co.'s affairs at Millbank following Duke's departure in 1914. Of these latter three, it was Hood who had emerged as the key actor in BAT Co.'s London-based headquarters during the war and he undoubtedly represented a plausible candidate to succeed Duke as chairman of BAT Co. However, it is clear that Duke's own nominated successor was Cunliffe-Owen, and after the war Hood elected to develop his ambitions in the political sphere rather than in business. During the war years, as well as his involvement in the Board of Trade's Tobacco Advisory Committee discussed in Chapter 5, Hood served on the Tobacco Control Board which had been set up to regulate retail and wholesale prices in the tobacco industry as part of the government's attempt to curb war-time price inflation. The war years had also seen the BAT Co. vice-chairman acting as Assistant Controller for a section of the Ministry of Information, and serving as a member of the Merchandise Marks Committee of the Board of Trade. Thus Hood had clearly begun to acquire a high profile in government circles and when, immediately after the war had ended, he stood as the Conservative Party candidate for Wimbledon he was duly elected to serve as a Member of Parliament in the Lloyd George coalition government of 1918–22. He nevertheless remained a director of BAT Co. until 1921.[1]

[1] Hood was awarded a peerage in the New Year Honours of 1922. *Tobacco (London)*, 42 (494) (1922), xxix.

Once the war in Europe was over, BAT Co.'s management began to put into operation the planned increase in the company's share capital which the outbreak of the conflict had disrupted. At an Extraordinary General Meeting in May 1919, chaired by Hood, the board of directors obtained authorization for the issue of £2.3 million of the remaining ordinary shares to be allocated *pro rata* to existing shareholders at the rate of one new share for every three held. In addition, the meeting supported the sale of a block of 141,000 ordinary shares to thirteen of the company's eighteen directors and to the President of the Export Leaf Tobacco Co., R. C. Harrison, at a price of £2 each.[2] As with the earlier share scheme, which had allocated almost 500,000 shares to the BAT Co. directors in 1912, these shares were offered on condition that the director in question bound himself to the company's service for a period of five years. Hood pointed out that neither himself nor Lawrence Hignett would avail themselves of the offer since neither felt prepared to bind themselves to the company for such a period of time. Significantly, James Duke was one of the other three BAT Co. directors who also did not feel able to participate in the share offer, thus confirming his essentially honorary status as chairman. Another four years were to pass, however, before circumstances arose which caused Duke to resign from this position.

The timing of Duke's resignation from BAT Co. was almost certainly linked to events in the tobacco industry in America. The dissolution of ATC in 1912 created four main manufacturing concerns as successors to the old trust—a reformed American Tobacco Co., Liggett & Myers, Lorillard, and R. J. Reynolds—but also left the trust's main retailing arm, the United Cigar Stores Co., free to continue its operations under the control of George J. Whelan. Whelan soon came to the conclusion that the success of his retailing organization depended on a restoration of its direct links with the tobacco manufacturing side of the business. With this objective in mind, Whelan joined forces with a group of financiers who had earlier been involved with the Duke tobacco trust, and with their help launched a company called the Tobacco Products Corporation (TPC). The TPC was incorporated in Virginia towards the end of 1912 with Whelan listed as a stockholder although not, at this point, as a director.[3] Placed under the management of George L. Storm, the TPC initially seems to have focused its

[2] The issue of these shares to directors created some opposition amongst the company's smaller shareholders. However, at the EGM Lord St Davids, whose various investment trusts were major shareholders in BAT Co., spoke in support of the scheme and it was passed unanimously. *Tobacco (London)*, 39 (462) (1919), 78–9.

[3] R. B. Tennant, *The American Cigarette Industry: A Study in Economic Analysis and Public Policy* (1950), pp. 74–5. The financiers involved in the TPC initiative included William H. Butler, formerly of the Kinney Tobacco Co., who was a director of the new organization.

attention on the manufacture of cigars.[4] However, this policy was quickly revised as Storm and his allies began to target the small group of independent cigarette and tobacco manufacturers that had survived competition from Duke's ATC but whose profits had been adversely affected by the post-dissolution surge of competition between the successor companies. Thus between 1912 and 1919 the TPC bought control of ten such companies.[5] Among the first of these was a well-established Cairo-based manufacturer of Turkish cigarettes called M. Melachrino which operated a successful factory in New York and had also developed a market for its cigarettes in Europe, notably in Britain and Germany. In 1919, TPC purchased the American interests of Philip Morris & Co., a high-class cigarette manufacturer of English origin which had incorporated a manufacturing operation in New York in 1902.[6] These acquisitions gave TPC an important share of cigarette sales in the United States, centred on the Turkish segment of the market which had grown rapidly in popularity during the first decade of the twentieth century.[7] In 1917 the TPC made itself sole selling agent for these manufacturing subsidiaries and its links with the United Cigar Stores became public knowledge when, around this time, George Whelan took over as president of the corporation from Storm.[8] By this time, also, it was clear that Duke had become heavily involved in the stock of the TPC [9] and, fearing a restoration of monopolistic practices, an anti-trust complaint was filed by the Federal Trade Commission in 1918.[10]

Partly due to its relatively small scale of operation, and partly as a result of

[4] Storm had resigned from the General Cigar Co. to become vice president of TPC. R. Cox, *Competition in the American Tobacco Industry 1911–1932: A Study of the Effects of the Partition of the American Tobacco Company by the United States Supreme Court* (1933), p. 328.

[5] The firms in which interests were acquired by the TPC are as follows: 1912—Surbrug Co., M. Melachrino & Co., Booker Tobacco Co., and Stephano Bros.; 1915—Standard Tobacco Co. and Nestor Gianaclis Co.; 1916—Schinasi Bros.; 1917—Prudential Tobacco Co.; 1918—Falk Tobacco Co. (Herbert Tareyton cigarettes); 1919—Philip Morris. Tennant, *American Cigarette Industry*, p. 75.

[6] R. Kluger, *Ashes to Ashes: America's Hundred-Year Cigarette War, the Public Health, and the Unabashed Triumph of Philip Morris* (1996), pp. 49–51.

[7] In 1910, shortly before the dissolution of ATC, manufacturers outside the trust had accounted for around 14 per cent of cigarette sales in the United States. These were concentrated mainly in the Turkish segment of the market. Tennant, *American Cigarette Industry*, Table 3.

[8] Tennant, *American Cigarette Industry*, p. 75. Cox gives the date at which Whelan succeeded Storm as 1918. Cox, *Competition in the American Tobacco Industry*, p. 328.

[9] Tennant, *American Cigarette Industry*, p. 75. By 1917 Duke's original five-year share agreement with BAT Co. of 1912 had expired, enabling him to obtain a financial interest in TPC.

[10] This anti-trust complaint was never successfully pursued. Tennant, *American Cigarette Industry*, p. 75.

the successful marketing of Burley-blend cigarettes by the main successor companies to the old trust, the attempt by TPC to enlarge its share of the American cigarette market soon foundered.[11] In 1919, therefore, Whelan handed control of TPC to James M. Dixon—another protégé of Duke—and concentrated his own efforts on the development of retailing by setting up the United Retail Stores Corporation, again with Duke's financial backing.[12] So closely involved did Duke become with this initiative that in May 1920 James Thomas wrote to Albert Jeffress at BAT Co.'s headquarters in London expressing his understanding that Duke had stood down from the position of chairman of BAT Co. in order to give his full attention to the United Retail Stores Corporation. Thomas seems to have been sufficiently convinced of the accuracy of this information regarding Duke's departure to offer his own resignation from the BAT Co. board if Cunliffe-Owen, whom he understood had succeeded Duke, so wished. In his reply Jeffress was careful to quash the rumour of Duke's resignation, but it is clear from the correspondence that Duke's involvement with the American interests had antagonized certain BAT Co. directors.[13]

Duke's growing ties with Whelan also coincided with the decision by TPC to launch the Tobacco Products Export Corporation (TPEC) as a holding company for the group's non-American tobacco businesses.[14] Between 1912 and 1919 TPC had gained control of a number of productive assets outside of the United States, including two factories in Canada, one in Egypt, and

[11] The relatively small scale of TPC's operations meant that the costs of transportation could not be spread over sufficient units to compete with the successor companies. Indeed TPC and its Melachrino subsidiary filed a complaint against the Southern Pacific railroad company during 1920 in an unsuccessful attempt to force them to reduce their freight charges on less-than-carload shipments of cigarettes from New York to the markets on the Pacific coast. See Tobacco Products Corporation *et al.*, v. Southern Pacific Company *et al.*, Case No. 10368, Interstate Commerce Commission Reports, vol. 55 (1919), pp. 69–70.

[12] *Tobacco (London)*, (463) (1919), 93–4. Rumours in the tobacco press indicate that in the latter half of 1919 there was talk of an amalgamation between the United Retail Stores and ATC whose president, Percival S. Hill, had earlier been a director of BAT Co. *Tobacco (London)*, 39 (468) (1919), v.

[13] See letter J. A. Thomas to A. G. Jeffress, dated 15 May 1920 and reply dated 5 July 1920, Thomas Papers, Box 10.

[14] In addition to TPEC, Whelan also made use of the newly sanctioned Webb–Pomerene Act to launch a venture called the American Foreign Trade Corporation which involved collaboration between a diverse group of American manufacturers who were willing to trade their products in the markets of the Near East in exchange for leaf tobacco supplies used in the production of Turkish-type cigarettes. The venture seems to have made very little substantive progress however. Cox, *Competition in the American Tobacco Industry*, p. 330; *Tobacco (London)*, 39 (463) (1919), 93–4. On the implications for American international business of the Webb–Pomerene Act, passed in 1918, see M. Wilkins, *The Maturing of Multinational Enterprise: American Business Abroad from 1914 to 1970* (1974), pp. 49ff.

one in China.[15] In addition, during 1919 the group secured a factory in Brixton, South London, which it used to manufacture the Turkish cigarettes of its Melachrino subsidiary directly in Britain.[16] In the early 1920s, therefore, the TPEC emerged as the leading American rival to BAT Co. in the international tobacco industry, with Whelan, Duke, and Thomas Ryan playing a critical supporting role.[17] The main problem for the directors of TPEC was that in many foreign markets—most obviously China—BAT Co. had stolen a march on them and was already well established. Thus in 1920, with the assistance of Duke and Ryan, Whelan targeted one of the few markets in which BAT Co. had a minimal involvement by making an audacious bid to buy up the French government tobacco monopoly.[18] Although these negotiations seem to have extended over a substantial period of time they ultimately failed to bear fruit, and overall the progress of TPEC was extremely limited.

In 1922, therefore, Whelan turned his attention back towards the United States tobacco market. There he began by amalgamating the TPC with the United Retail Stores Corporation, subsequently dissolving the latter entity, and then using TPC's control of the Philip Morris Corporation to set up a new subsidiary, called Philip Morris International. Philip Morris International then purchased from the American Tobacco Co. (ATC) the US rights to the Imperial Tobacco Co.'s brands, which it began to manufacture and distribute through TPC's United Cigar Stores chain of retail outlets.[19] The decision to

[15] Cox, *Competition in the American Tobacco Industry*, p. 330. A report of the decision by TPC to set up operations in China in 1917 can be found in *Tobacco (London)*, 37 (436) (1917), 47. Note that this report also mentions the TPC factory in Cairo which, it states, supplied markets outside of the United States and Canada.

[16] TPC had first established operations in Great Britain on 6 August 1913 when it formed the Globe Tobacco Co. This organization changed its name to the Tobacco Products Corporation of Great Britain and Ireland on 2 February 1919. On 30 October 1916 TPC had also taken control of a company which operated under the name of Henry Scholey. This firm had acted as the sole wholesale agent in Britain for the Melachrino company since before the turn of the century and on 26 January 1923 its identity was changed to that of M. Melachrino & Co. BAT Co. Corporate Index, BAT Co. Southampton Archive, Box 114. The acquisition by TPC of the factory in Brixton, and its plan to use it to manufacture the cigarettes of the Melachrino brand is reported in *Tobacco (London)*, 39 (465) (1919), 93.

[17] In addition to George J. Whelan, George L. Storm, and James M. Dixon, the founding directors of TPEC included Reuben M. Ellis and Leonard B. McKitterick, who had joined TPC from the Melachrino concern and who subsequently became leading figures in the Philip Morris Corporation, and Gray Miller, a future chairman of BAT Co. On Ellis and McKitterick see Kluger, *Ashes to Ashes*, pp. 73–4.

[18] Cox, *Competition in the American Tobacco Industry*, p. 332.

[19] In discussing this episode, Cox merely refers to the sale of 'a number of brands of the Imperial Tobacco Co.', whilst Tennant's account specifies that only the Player's brands were involved. However, a contemporary report in the tobacco trade press indicates that Philip Morris International gained the American rights to all the Imperial brands that ATC had inher-

market Imperial's brands in America, which elsewhere in the world belonged to BAT Co., was perhaps undertaken with a view to re-establishing TPC as the American arm of BAT Co. Given these circumstances it is not surprising to find that, in the summer of 1923, rumours were circulating in New York of a proposed merger between the TPC and BAT Co. A director of the American company had visited London, apparently to engage in merger talks, but on his return had refused to comment on the matter, implying that the scheme had come to nothing.[20]

Within a few days of this disclosure, Duke stood down as chairman of BAT Co. and handed control to his designated successor, Hugo Cunliffe-Owen. Comments made by Cunliffe-Owen upon his accession to the chairmanship of BAT Co. imply that Imperial may, understandably, have wished to block a merger between BAT Co. and TPC which would have effectively turned TPC into Imperial's transatlantic alter-ego.[21] Duke himself, interviewed on his return from a trip to Europe, effectively admitted that the story of a merger between BAT Co. and TPC was not without foundation.[22] Moreover, his strenuous denial of any pressure to resign his post as chairman of BAT Co., or of any discord between BAT Co., Imperial, TPC, and himself, served only to fuel speculation that a state of acrimony had developed between the parties.

Shortly after this event, TPC ceased its active involvement in the American tobacco industry by selling off its American-based manufacturing assets to ATC and leasing the Imperial brand rights back to the same organization.[23] Meanwhile TPEC continued to operate as an international competitor to BAT Co., for example in China, for a few years during the mid-1920s. For Duke, however, the failure to establish a link between the two elements of his international tobacco empire appear to have represented his parting shot. In his account of the American tobacco industry published in 1933, Cox concluded that Duke 'resigned the post [of chairman of BAT Co.] under circumstances which indicated that he had been forced out by British interests now in control but which he preferred to interpret as a voluntary move preliminary to retiring from business'.[24] There certainly seems to be little doubt that the timing of his departure was directly related to the strategy of the TPC to seek a merger with BAT Co. What has never been revealed is whether the

ited. Cox, *Competition in the American Tobacco Industry*, p. 333; Tennant, *American Cigarette Industry*, p. 83 (n. 26); *Tobacco (London)*, 42 (501) (1922), 73.

[20] *Tobacco (London)*, 43 (513) (1923), xv.

[21] *Tobacco (London)*, 43 (512) (1923), 71.

[22] *Tobacco (London)*, 43 (515) (1923), 53.

[23] The TPC organization ultimately folded in 1929, shortly before the stock market crash, and at this point Philip Morris was sold off as an independent enterprise. Kluger, *Ashes to Ashes*, p. 74.

[24] Cox, *Competition in the American Tobacco Industry*, p. 73.

decision to retire was Duke's own response to the failure of the proposed merger, or whether his continued involvement with the rival TPC organization soured his relationship with the board of BAT Co. sufficiently for his retirement to be forced upon him, as Cox seems to suggest.[25] Whatever the truth of the matter, for the international tobacco industry as a whole, and for BAT Co. in particular, Duke's retirement constituted the end of an era.

Duke's departure and Hood's decision to retire from active involvement in BAT's affairs in favour of British party politics left Cunliffe-Owen with a free rein to shape the company's future development in his own way, and from his office in Millbank he came to dominate the company between the wars.[26] In contrast to Duke, who was prepared to leave a good deal of the responsibility for the day-to-day management of the foreign branches to the man on the spot, Cunliffe-Owen favoured a much greater degree of centralized control with directors spending a significant proportion of their time in direct management of their allocated territories. As a corollary, he believed that the most appropriate qualification for a place on BAT Co.'s board was a thorough knowledge of the tobacco trade and his appointees were almost invariably men of long-standing experience—usually gained within the BAT organization itself. Consequently, between the wars the company became increasingly introspective under his essentially patriarchal style of leadership.[27]

Operations in the Western Hemisphere

At the time of Duke's resignation from the chairmanship of BAT Co. in 1923 the company's operations in the markets of the western hemisphere were relatively limited, accounting for only around 12 per cent of the company's total sales volume. In the Canadian market—the company's largest in the western hemisphere at the end of the war—the Imperial Tobacco Co. of Canada maintained its steady development as a relatively autonomous enterprise

[25] The notice of Duke's retirement in the *BAT Bulletin* naturally avoids any reference to disharmony, indicating only that the move had been anticipated for some time. *BAT Bulletin*, 14 (1923), 873–5. Duke died a little over two years after his retirement from BAT Co.'s chairmanship in October 1925.

[26] Hood's two fellow vice-chairmen also retired around this time, Lawrence Hignett in June 1921 and Arthur C. Churchman in June 1923, shortly before Cunliffe-Owen's accession to the position of chairman.

[27] For brief biographies of Cunliffe-Owen see R. P. T. Davenport-Hines, 'H. v. R. Cunliffe-Owen', in D. Jeremy (ed.), *Dictionary of Business Biography: A Biographical Dictionary of Business Leaders Active in Britain in the Period 1860–1980* (1984), vol. 1, pp. 865–9; and *BAT News* (Autumn 1988), 8–11.

under the continuing leadership of Mortimer B. Davis.[28] In the United States itself, the principal manufacturing facilities operated by BAT Co. were the factories of the David Dunlop and T. C. Williams subsidiaries at Petersburg, Virginia, which Duke had purchased soon after the formation of the company in 1902, and the plant in Richmond, Virginia, which had been opened during the war to allow the British factories to take on government war orders.[29] Both of these American factories supplied cigarettes and tobacco purely for export markets, predominantly to China and South-East Asia, and this export business was supervised by George G. Allen from the company's New York office at 511 Fifth Avenue. BAT Co.'s other US-based operation was the Export Leaf Tobacco Co. headquartered in Danville, Virginia, which also operated a factory in Richmond. Since 1915 this organization had been under the supervision of Robert C. Harrison, who had assumed the responsibility for co-ordinating BAT Co.'s various leaf tobacco procurement needs in America following the departure of Peter Arrington.[30] In 1912 the Export Leaf Tobacco Co. also set up a branch in Greenville, North Carolina, for the purchasing, redrying, and shipping of leaf tobacco.

The First World War had disrupted the tobacco leaf trade between Britain and America, resulting in shortages that needed to be made good at the war's conclusion.[31] In consequence, 1919 saw both Imperial and BAT Co. as major purchasers of American tobacco leaf, with the two organizations accounting for 47 per cent of the sales of southern Bright crop in that year.[32] The affairs

[28] BAT Co. also had a subsidiary operating in Newfoundland by this time under the name of the Imperial Tobacco Co. (Newfoundland) Ltd. In spite of the similarity of the title to the Canadian company it appears that the two were operating independently until after Newfoundland elected to become the tenth province of the Dominion of Canada in 1949 when the two combined their operations. See S. Mercier, 'A Brief History of Tobacco in Canada', 111 pp. typescript, n.d., BAT Co. Southampton Archive, Box 42, pp. 78–9.

[29] According to the company's own records, the cigarette factory at Richmond was actually owned by the Export Leaf Tobacco Co. who leased it to BAT Co. BAT Co. Corporate Index, BAT Co. Southampton Archive, Box 114. Of BAT Co.'s other US manufacturing plants, the Durham factory was transferred to Liggett & Myers at the time of the dissolution, whilst the old Kimball factory in Rochester was finally disposed of in 1921. On the latter see *Tobacco (London)*, 42 (494) (1922), vii. On BAT Co.'s Richmond factory, which came into operation in 1916, see *Tobacco (London)*, 37 (434) (1917), i.; *BAT Bulletin*, 13 (36) (1923), 801–2; *Tobacco (London)*, 46 (541) (1926), 96.

[30] Arrington died in 1916. His place on the BAT Co. board was taken by another American, Edgar S. Bowling, who was based at Petersburg. *BAT Bulletin*, 3 (75) (1916), 354.

[31] The outbreak of the First World War also encouraged BAT Co.'s American headquarters to engage in some degree of vertical integration as a result of the shortage of supplies and difficulties with shipping space. Hence in 1917 the company bought out the Smith Paper Co., of Lee, Massachusetts, and also during the war it founded the Garland Steamship Corporation. This latter organization was bought out by BAT Co.'s shareholders in the 1920s.

[32] US Federal Trade Commission, *Report on the Tobacco Industry* (1921), p. 52.

of both of these companies were subjected to detailed scrutiny at the end of the war when the Federal Trade Commission decided to investigate complaints of monopsonistic buying on behalf of the large manufacturers. These complaints had become particularly vociferous following the formation of the Universal Leaf Tobacco Co. in January 1918 as a holding company combining together twenty-four separate concerns involved in some aspect of the tobacco leaf-purchasing trade. The findings of the FTC investigation obliged the Export Leaf Tobacco Co. to purchase leaf directly, rather than through intermediaries such as Universal. In general, however, BAT Co. increasingly adopted the policy after the war of stimulating local leaf growing directly in many of their overseas markets, hence gradually reducing their dependence on American-grown leaf.

Thus, although both the American cigarette export trade and leaf-procurement business continued after the end of the war, Duke's resignation in 1923 had the effect of further marginalizing the role of the American-based management. Following Duke's departure, BAT Co. listed only three of its seventeen directors as being based in the United States: George Allen and Robert Harrison in New York, and Edgar Bowling in Petersburg. Allen's New York office, whilst it still supervised the cigarette export trade to Shanghai had, by this time, ceded overall control of the operations in China to directors based at Westminster House. However, the New York office did have one area of increasing responsibility in the post-war years because it oversaw the company's expanding activities in Central America.

In Latin America as a whole, BAT's two largest markets at the end of the war were those of Argentina and Brazil where in each case the company had earlier acquired a local tobacco manufacturer. Although the original owners had retained an interest in the business, the main management responsibility had been assumed by staff transferred to South America by the BAT Co. board in London. Between the wars, overall supervision of these two markets was retained at Millbank and territorial directors of BAT Co. paid regular visits to review developments there.

Local management of the company's Souza Cruz subsidiary in Brazil was vested in an experienced employee, Ernest Carthagh Gillon, who had joined BAT Co. on its inception in 1902 and had then enjoyed management postings covering India, China, Belgium, and Sweden before his transfer to Brazil in 1916.[33] Gillon, whose style of management seems to have earned him the nickname 'Napoleon' in certain quarters, was supported by William Thompson, who was transferred from BAT Co.'s Argentine subsidiary in 1918, and by a small group of expatriate staff recruited mainly from the banking sector

[33] On Gillon, see *BAT Bulletin*, 18 (96) (1928), 373–4.

in Rio de Janeiro, which was passing through a difficult period during the war.[34] The Souza Cruz firm had set up its original factory in Rio and to this were added further plants in São Paulo, Bahia (Salvador), Pôrto Alegre, Belo Horizonte, Santa Cruz, and Para (Belém).

Outside of the urban areas, smoking in Brazil at the beginning of the twentieth century mainly took the form of tobacco fermented with molasses and other ingredients and was smoked either rolled in a corn-cob straw or using a simple clay pipe. Cigarettes, which were smoked exclusively in the towns, were crudely made affairs using very raw tobacco, and Souza Cruz was one of a number of firms that had set up to manufacture cigarettes of this kind. The relatively poor state of the Brazilian economy meant that cigarettes and other tobacco products were sold by general stores and cafes rather than specialized tobacco distributors. Consequently, Souza Cruz's success in Brazil was founded upon the creation of a distribution system which carried the company's goods directly to these small-scale dealers, whilst its profitability began to rise when the system of credit sales was replaced by one based on direct sales for cash.[35]

Early brands of Bright tobacco cigarettes introduced by Souza Cruz into Brazil included 'Jockey Club' in 1921,[36] and with other successful brands such as 'Sonia' and 'Liberty', Souza Cruz's cigarette sales in Brazil expanded steadily from just under 2 billion in 1921 to a little over 5 billion per annum by 1929, pressing hard on domestic competitors. During the economic downturn of the early 1930s, however, these rival firms began to introduce brands which featured redeemable coupons, and were able to wrest some market share from Souza Cruz whose managers were unwilling to respond in kind. Instead, BAT used its technological leadership in packaging to introduce a brand on to the Brazilian market in 1931 called 'Hollywood', which featured the type of soft-cup pack seen in many American movies of the time. The innovation was not a great success to begin with, as impoverished smokers in the early 1930s sought greater economy rather than sophistication, and ultimately Souza Cruz was forced to compete directly in the coupon segment of the market by buying out a struggling rival manufacturer called Castelloes and continuing to operate it independently as a manufacturer of coupon

34 Transcript of an interview with Mr J. Banks, 12 April 1972, Windsor House Papers, p. 2. Banks himself was hired by Souza Cruz in 1916 as an accountant having been working for a bank in Rio de Janeiro.

35 Transcript of an interview with Mr D. Tailby, 13 April 1972, *Windsor House Papers*, p. 3. Tailby was transferred to Brazil in the early 1930s, having joined BAT Co. in England during the 1920s and been posted earlier to Norway and Germany. Banks (see previous note) refers to this system of direct sales as the 'peddling' system.

36 *BAT News* (Spring 1986), 21.

brands such as 'Adelphi', 'Classicos', and 'Hippicos'. However, the company did not abandon the soft-cup initiative in Brazil, and in 1935 Souza Cruz introduced another cigarette packaged in this form called 'Continental' which met with greater short-term success.[37] Also around this time Souza Cruz managed to persuade its competitors in Brazil to abandon coupon brands as economic conditions began to recover. After suffering a dip during the early 1930s, therefore, BAT's sales in Brazil accelerated thereafter and had reached a level of 10 billion per annum by the time of the outbreak of the Second World War.

The development of a cigarette manufacturing industry in Brazil was accompanied by the cultivation of tobacco crops suitable for use in the new product. Souza Cruz introduced Bright tobacco in the region around Santa Cruz do Sul in Rio Grande do Sul, using American-trained experts to support the local farmers, mainly immigrants of German origin, who then began to cultivate the crop and to deliver their leaf to the company's redrying plant in Santa Cruz by mule-cart. Later, the growing region spread north into Santa Caterina, and a number of further leaf-processing plants were built by the company in order to handle the strains of Virginia, Burley, and domestic Amarelinho leaf which together were developed into a distinctive Brazilian-blend of cigarette tobacco.[38]

In Argentina, where BAT Co. registered its own subsidiary concern in Buenos Aires under the title Cia Nacional de Tabacos SA in 1913, initial progress was made via the acquisition of a local firm named Bozetti & Co. This company already operated a cigarette manufacturing plant in Buenos Aires, and marketed their products under the 'Misterio' brand name.[39] To begin with, this operation focused its efforts on the capital of Argentina, building a new factory as well as offices and warehouses there and during this initial phase the subsidiary in Argentina was placed under the management of Montague L. Whishaw. After the war, Whishaw was made a director of BAT Co. in London with special responsibility for the South American region and his place in Argentina was taken by John Armstrong Anderson, who had joined BAT Co. as a manager at the Ashton Gate factory in November 1902. After a brief spell in Buenos Aires between 1913 and 1915, Armstrong was transferred to London before returning to Argentina in 1919 as manager.[40]

[37] *BAT News* (Spring 1988), 14.

[38] G. Brooks, 'Recipes for Success', *BAT Industries Outlook*, 14 (Autumn 1991), 6–9; Economist Intelligence Unit, *Leaf Tobacco: Its Contribution to the Economic and Social Development of the Third World* (1981), pp. 3 and 11–13.

[39] Nobleza Piccardo, 'Hacia Un Siglo De Historia' [Towards a Century of History], 1987, BAT Co. Southampton Archive, Box 67.

[40] On Anderson, see *BAT Bulletin*, 18 (96) (1928), 373–4.

It was mainly under Anderson's guidance that BAT's operations in Argentina began to flourish and grow. During 1918 the company had set up its first subsidiary outside Buenos Aires, in Rosario, and this was rapidly followed by the opening of operations in Tucumán, Mendoza, and Córdoba between 1920 and 1922. As a result, BAT's sales in Argentina accelerated rapidly during the early 1920s to reach a level in excess of 2 billion cigarettes per annum by 1925. As in Brazil, an important factor behind the success of BAT's operations in Argentina was Nacional's ability to deliver cigarettes reliably to its many dealers, using a fleet of 400 vans, which needed to be renewed every two years due to the appalling state of the country's roads.[41]

The expansion of sales in Argentina was based partly on traditional cigarettes made from dark tobacco, such as the brands 'Embajadores' and 'Senadores', but even more on the growing popularity of cigarettes which featured American Bright tobacco. These cigarettes became popularized as 'blondes', and by 1927 Nacional was producing a wide variety of such products under brand names such as 'Flag', 'American Club', 'Jockey Club', 'Columbia', and 'Belmont'. To support this development, after 1925 the company also promoted the growing of American strains of leaf, including Maryland tobacco, initially in the Misiones region of the country. This activity had developed sufficiently by the outbreak of the Second World War to allow cigarette manufacturers in Argentina to be self-sufficient.

The period of rapid growth in output during the early 1920s in Argentina gave way to a period of stagnation. At the beginning of the 1930s Nacional's sales began to experience a sharp decline as consumers' incomes fell, and in 1932 BAT Co. was forced to write off losses that its Argentine subsidiaries had incurred on advertising expenditure. Whishaw was ordered by Cunliffe-Owen to travel to Argentina in order to investigate the problems, and he reported back that two rival manufacturers had rapidly brought out cheap 20-cent brands which Nacional had failed to match. The response marshalled by Whishaw, with the consent of the London board, was to move the organization over to direct selling, as had already been done in Brazil, and to set up a pooling arrangement with two other Argentine cigarette manufacturers; Falcón Calvo & Co. and the Piccardo group of companies, and to extend this further if at all possible.[42] In the meantime, Cunliffe-Owen issued an order that any established subsidiary making losses should cut its running expenses by reducing the wage bill. Ultimately, such measures were able to stabilize the

41 Nobleza Piccardo, 'Siglo De Historia'.

42 Discussions had been held with a view to an amalgamation between Nacional and Piccardo. This eventually took place in 1977. See minutes of BAT Co.'s Chairman's Daily Committee dated 24 May 1932, 30 August 1932, 7 November 1932, 16 November 1932, 3 February 1933, and 8 February 1933.

situation in Argentina and restore BAT's fortunes there after 1936 as other firms were drawn into Nacional's distribution system.[43]

The situation in Chile, the only other South American market in which BAT Co.'s London board took direct managerial control, was somewhat different to Argentina and Brazil because in this case the company entered via a green-field investment rather than through acquisition. An independent subsidiary concern was set up, based at the coastal town of Valparaiso, under the title of BAT Co. (Chile) Ltd. This operation comprised offices and a factory, and began selling its products during April 1922 in competition with the main domestic tobacco manufacturer Chilena de Tabacos.[44] The Chilean subsidiary made gradual progress until, in 1936, the two firms merged through an exchange of shares. At this point, BAT Co.'s recorded sales in Chile doubled from 1.5 billion to over 3 billion cigarettes per annum.

Elsewhere in South America,[45] the activities of BAT Co.'s subsidiaries were overseen by the company's headquarters in New York. In British Guiana a company named the Demerara Tobacco Co. was set up in 1919 and sales in this market were recorded until May 1923 at which point the company seems to have ceased trading. Not until 1930, when the company established a new depot in Georgetown, were further sales registered in British Guiana.[46] More enduring progress was experienced in neighbouring Venezuela. In this market BAT Co. established Cigarrera Bigott Sucs on 7 January 1921 in order to take over the business of Luis Bigott, who retained control of a block of shares. Initially the operations of this subsidiary were restricted solely to Venezuela itself, but later in 1921 it was granted permission to trade in Curaçao and this was extended in 1923 to include the nearby island of Trinidad.

[43] In 1935 BAT began to distribute the products of Manufactura de Tabacos Mitjans, Colombo & Cia. Two years earlier, in a sign of the political times, a decree was passed in Argentina forbidding the use of the word 'national' in the corporate name of any company. As a result, the title of BAT's Argentine subsidiary was changed to Compañia Nobleza de Tabacos.

[44] *BAT Bulletin*, 13 (33) (1923), 751.

[45] In Peru, where the government exercised a state monopoly over tobacco goods, BAT Co. expressed an interest during 1924 in taking on the role of concessionaire which was being offered for a period of thirty-three years in return for a cash payment. The scheme's primary objective was designed to support railway building in Peru, but BAT Co.'s interest in managing the operation was not pursued. *Tobacco (London)*, 44 (528) (1924), 75. In addition to BAT Co.'s lack of success in Peru, Shepherd notes that the company was unable to gain a permanent foothold in Colombia where a small number of cigarettes were sold by the company between May 1937 and May 1940. P. L. Shepherd, 'Transnational Corporations and the International Cigarette Industry', in R. Newfarmer (ed.), *Profits, Progress and Poverty* (1985), p. 88.

[46] A cigarette manufacturing unit was installed in Georgetown four years later and the Demerara Tobacco Co. was re-incorporated on 14 June 1934 with an authorized capital of £40,000 as the operating subsidiary. Demerara Tobacco Co., 'Thirty Years', BAT Co. Southampton Archive, Box 86.

In Central America BAT Co. had already made investments in four markets prior to the outbreak of the war in Europe. Two of these interests, in Mexico and Trinidad, first fell into BAT Co.'s possession in 1903 as a result of its purchase of two-thirds of the share capital of the Louisville-based firm of W. S. Mathews & Sons, a firm engaged in the buying, rehandling, and export of dark Kentucky and Tennessee tobacco leaf.[47] The Mathews concern had developed commercial links with two of the firms that it supplied with this dark type of tobacco leaf. One was a company operating a factory in Monterrey, Mexico, called the Black Horse Tobacco Co., and the other was the West Indian Tobacco Co. based in Trinidad and operating a small cigarette manufacturing plant at Port-of-Spain. Between 1904 and 1911, BAT Co. purchased majority control over both of these companies.[48]

The West Indian Tobacco Co. continued to develop under the management of its original owner John Phillips, who had set up the business in 1896, and created the highly successful 'Anchor' brand in 1914 which it sold to smokers in Trinidad at a price of 4 cents for a packet of eight cigarettes.[49] In 1925, Phillips expanded BAT Co.'s interests into Barbados by setting up BAT Co. (Barbados) in partnership with both BAT and a distribution company called T. S. Garraway & Co.[50]

In Mexico, the Black Horse Tobacco Co. was incorporated by BAT Co. in New Jersey in 1904 and the following year responsibility for the management of its operations in Monterrey was passed to George Cooper. Cooper had come into the employment of BAT Co. as a result of Duke's acquisition of the Petersburg-based tobacco manufacturer, T. C. Williams & Co. in 1903. After being posted briefly to Australia, he began managing the Black Horse Tobacco Co. in 1905 and continued in that post throughout the troubled period of the Mexican civil war, before returning to work under George Allen in the New York sales department in 1919.[51] Unlike the West

47 Initially in 1903 the ownership of the capital stock of W. S. Mathews was divided into equal thirds between the original owners, BAT Co., and the American Snuff Co. However, in September 1906, BAT Co. bought out the latter company's share and thus became the majority owners. US Bureau of Corporations, *Report of the Commissioner of Corporations on the Tobacco Industry* (Part I), (1909), pp. 307–8.

48 When BAT Co. purchased its interest in W. S. Mathews in 1904, these two small-scale tobacco manufacturers in Trinidad and Mexico were given support by BAT Co. and Mathews to incorporate their businesses as limited liability companies and, as a result, they both became part-owned subsidiaries of BAT Co. Later, when BAT Co. sold its interest in W. S. Mathews & Sons during 1911, it received in return additional shares in both the Black Horse and West Indian Tobacco companies, becoming the majority shareholder in both.

49 'The West Indian Tobacco Company Limited 1904–1964', BAT Co. Southampton Archive, Box 86, p. 2.

50 'British–American Tobacco Co. (Barbados) Ltd., 1925–1965', BAT Co. Southampton Archive, Box 86.

51 *BAT Bulletin*, 16 (70) (1926), 277.

Indian Tobacco Co., which had manufactured cigarettes from its inception in 1896, the Black Horse Tobacco Co. seems to have dealt in tobacco products other than machine-made cigarettes.[52]

The location of BAT Co.'s two other pre-war investments in Central America and the Caribbean were Costa Rica and Jamaica. The cigarette market in Jamaica had been cultivated by British and American manufacturers since the late nineteenth century, with W. Duke, Sons & Co. having registered its 'Cameo' brand there as early as 1889 and Wills' marketing 'Capstan' and 'Three Castles' there from 1898. During the period of the tobacco war between ATC and Imperial in Britain, the market in Jamaica had been a focal point of the war's international dimension.[53] After the formation of BAT Co., the company's various interests in Jamaica were incorporated together under the title of the Jamaica Tobacco Co. which, like the Black Horse organization, was registered in New Jersey.[54] In 1922, following a fire the previous year which had destroyed its Jamaican factory, the Jamaica Tobacco Co. merged its interests with that of a local firm formed by Cuban émigrés, B. & J. B. Machado Tobacco Co. Ltd. This company already produced its own machine-made cigarettes under brand names such as 'White Seal', 'Lily', and 'Rosebud' using locally grown tobacco leaf, and it now became BAT Co.'s operating subsidiary in Jamaica. As well as cigarettes, the cigar trade remained an important aspect of BAT Co.'s operations in Jamaica, notably the 'Golofina' brand.

In Costa Rica the company operated through another New Jersey-registered subsidiary called the Republic Tobacco Co. which had been set up in April 1912.[55] From the outset this company engaged in the manufacture of cigarettes directly within Costa Rica, although its status remained that of a branch until 1920 when it was re-incorporated directly in Costa Rica.[56] In 1926 the Republic Tobacco Co. was granted permission by BAT Co. to conduct its trade beyond the borders of Costa Rica, into Nicaragua, Aruba, and the Netherlands West Indies, and to sell to the Panama Railroad Co.[57]

[52] BAT Co. monthly sales statistics do not record any cigarette sales in Mexico before 1924.

[53] During the period of the tobacco war, Imperial's interests in Jamaica were overseen by the Lambert & Butler branch, cf. Chapter 3.

[54] US Bureau of Corporations, *Report on the Tobacco Industry* (Part 1), pp. 306–8.

[55] According to BAT Co.'s corporate records, it held $325,000 of the Republic Tobacco Company's authorized capital of $375,000 at this time. BAT Co. trial balance as at 30 September 1912, BAT Co. Southampton Archive, Box 87.

[56] However, the company continued to hold its board meetings in the United States. 'Historical Background of Republic Tobacco Co.' Unpublished typescript (1970), 6 pp., BAT Co. Southampton Archive, Box 67.

[57] Like the initial development in Costa Rica, the company also operated a branch in Panama and this form of operation was maintained there until 1942. The Panama branch, however, did not manufacture its own products but was supplied from the company's New York depot.

Direct investments in Central America were stepped up significantly after Cunliffe-Owen succeeded Duke as chairman in 1923. The first, and most important, of these investments was undertaken early in 1924 when BAT Co. acquired control of a company based in Mexico City called La Fábrica de Cigarros 'El Aguila' SA. As a prelude to the take-over, BAT Co. registered its own operating subsidiary company in Mexico City on 29 April 1924 which it called Cie. Manufacturera de Cigarros 'El Aguila' SA, and then used the share capital of this new corporate entity to buy out the original 'El Aguila' company. On completion of the deal, BAT Co. owned 75 per cent of the 'El Aguila' share capital and the remaining 25 per cent was held by the shareholders of the old concern which was subsequently wound up. The following year another Mexican firm by the name of Cia. Industrial del Centro SA was purchased, with operations at Irapuato, and this acted as a branch of the 'El Aguila' company under the continuing direction of its existing manager Leopoldo Caraballo.

Despite efforts to integrate itself into the Mexican economy through the development of products utilizing locally grown leaf,[58] the 'El Aguila' subsidiary met with increasing hostility during the 1930s. Its position as a near monopoly producer of cigarettes, coupled with its foreign ownership and expatriate management, left the subsidiary vulnerable to populist agitation. In an effort to deflect these problems, BAT Co.'s management decided to implement the strategy of self-generated competition in Mexico. In 1936 its existing interests in the Black Horse Tobacco Co. at Monterrey were extended through the formation of a new subsidiary, Cie. Cigarrera 'La Moderna', which was designed to provide meaningful competition to the 'El Aguila' concern. The ploy was successful, as 'La Moderna' captured an increasing share of the Mexican market whilst its links with BAT Co. were kept deliberately opaque.[59]

BAT Co.'s interests in Central America were further extended between 1926 and 1928 by the creation of subsidiary companies in El Salvador, Honduras, and Guatemala. In El Salvador, the Salvador Tobacco Co. was incorporated on 3 December 1926 and then expanded through a series of acquisitions. In 1929 it purchased the Egyptian Tobacco Co. from Messrs. Sansur and Abularach and followed this with the acquisitions of Tabacalera La Morena and Fábrica Morazán from Messrs E. Soler and P. Soler, at which point the BAT Co. changed the name of its subsidiary in El Salvador from the

58 In 1936, 'El Aguila' began to operate its own leaf-purchasing subsidiary in Mexico called Tabaco En Rama S.A., which it set up on 31 December 1935.

59 Rivalry between the two groups became increasingly fierce and by the late 1960s, 'La Moderna' had achieved a dominant position in the Mexican market. Personal correspondence with Mr E. J. Symons, 3 January 1998.

Salvador Tobacco Co. to Cigarrería Morazán Sucesores SA. Another rival manufacturer, the Pyramid Cigarette Co., was acquired from its owner Mr Gadala Maria in 1932.

In Honduras, a subsidiary was formed in February 1928 called Tabacalera Hondureña SA which acquired first the business of a cigarette manufacturer operating under the name Tabacalera La Bohemia SA and then another rival firm called Fábrica La Cigarillos La Competidor later the same year. Also in 1928 a subsidiary company was formed in Guatemala to assume control of a group of domestic cigarette manufacturers who had merged their interests the previous year in an effort to resist the continued advance of BAT in Central America. The ploy failed to prevent BAT Co.'s entry and negotiations for the take-over were completed in the autumn of 1928. At this point the Tabacalera Nacional SA began operating as BAT Co.'s Guatemala subsidiary, recording its first sales there for the company in November of that year.[60]

Thus BAT Co.'s New York office took the leading role in supervising the interests acquired by the company in Central America after the First World War. The career of BAT Co. employee Lewis Newbill, who was appointed as general manager of the Guatemala concern in 1928, illustrates quite well the evolving pattern of BAT Co.'s business interests which were served from the United States. Newbill had been brought up on a tobacco farm in Virginia and in 1913 he joined BAT Co.'s American leaf-procurement subsidiary, the Export Leaf Tobacco Co. A few years later he was transferred to the company's new cigarette factory in Richmond where he helped to manage the production and shipment of the company's 'New York', 'Pin Head', and other brands for the market in China. After a spell in the US Army during the latter part of the war, Newbill was re-employed in the company's New York office in 1920 where he trained in accountancy and was appointed to act as a travelling auditor. In this capacity he undertook audits in territories such as Mexico, Venezuela, Trinidad, Jamaica, and Panama on behalf of the New York office. In May 1928, together with Caleb White, a senior manager from New York,[61] Newbill carried out an audit of those businesses in Guatemala which BAT Co. was in the process of purchasing. On completion of the deal, White departed for New York and Newbill was instructed to remain in Guatemala to act as the local manager—a task he continued to perform until his retirement in the early 1950s.[62]

60 Background information on BAT Co. subsidiary companies in Central America has been drawn from the BAT Co. Corporate Index, BAT Co. Southampton Archive, Box 114.

61 In 1952, Caleb White was appointed as BAT Co.'s sole distributor in Venezuela.

62 This account of Lewis Newbill's career with BAT Co. was written by Mr C. Burton, a successor to the post of general manager in Guatemala, and published in *BAT News* (Autumn 1987), 30–1.

By the time that Cunliffe-Owen assumed the role of chairman, therefore, the focus of the company's New York office was shifting away from its earlier orientation towards China and instead was having its attention turned increasingly towards the management of BAT Co.'s interests in Latin America. This process of creating a pan-American management structure based in the US was given further impetus in 1927 when Cunliffe-Owen made the controversial decision to re-enter the huge, but fiercely competitive, American cigarette market.

Establishing the Louisville Orbit

The American market had been thrown into disequilibrium by the dissolution of ATC in 1912. The decision to make Duke responsible for the restructuring of the industry into smaller organizations created a good deal of unease amongst those who had brought the anti-trust action in the first place. These concerns appeared well-founded when the terms of the dissolution were announced and it became apparent that the same twenty-nine individuals named in the original anti-trust suit remained in control of a large portion of the shares of the successor companies.[63] Moreover, the method of dividing the physical plant of the ATC business between the four main successor companies seemed to many observers to have had the effect of simply partitioning the industry into a number of well-defined segments, each dominated by one of the newly created firms. In fact, this latter concern proved to be unfounded because it quickly became evident that the product that would dominate the industry in its post-dissolution phase was the machine-made cigarette. Thus most of the competitive activity which followed the break-up of ATC centred on the cigarette market.

The cigarette trade in America at this time was segmented into those products which utilized domestically grown flue-cured Bright Virginia and Burley leaf and those using imported Turkish tobacco. This latter type of cigarette had witnessed a revival in popularity in the early years of the twentieth century and as a result a number of blended cigarette brands, featuring some portion of Turkish leaf, had been developed to exploit this growing fashion. Thus the cigarette market in America could be divided into domestic, Turkish, and

[63] The percentage of the voting stock held jointly by the twenty-nine individual defendants in the action after the break-up was 35 per cent in the reformed ATC, 41 per cent in the Liggett & Myers and Lorillard companies, and 38 per cent in R. J. Reynolds. However, the whole of the institutional shareholding of ATC in these companies was distributed away, and a ceiling placed on these individuals' total shareholding in the successor companies. Tennant, *American Cigarette Industry*, pp. 62–3.

'pseudo-Turkish' brands, with each of these divisions further segmented by price.

The division of the ATC cigarette brands among the main successor companies had been based on the allocation of the factories that had formerly produced them. Given the existing plant specialization which ATC had operated, this method of allocation had distributed the cigarette business of ATC in a way which gave three of the successor companies a predominant role in certain segments of the cigarette market, whilst allocating no cigarette brands at all to the fourth. Thus Liggett & Myers was allocated a total of 27.8 per cent of the cigarette market by volume, including all the cheap domestic brands such as 'Piedmont', all the mouthpiece brands, and the only expensive 15-cent Turkish blend, 'Fatima'. American Tobacco, with 37.1 per cent of the market, retained all the cheap 5-cent 'pseudo-Turkish' blended cigarettes such as 'Mecca', and together with Liggett & Myers shared the medium-priced 10-cent domestic brands. Finally Lorillard, with a 15.3 per cent share of the cigarette market, was allocated all the 10- and 15-cent Turkish brands except one ('Egyptian Straights' which American retained).[64] The R. J. Reynolds company was not allocated any cigarette brands.

This well-ordered distribution of the cigarette market rapidly broke down after 1912 as the rival firms outbid one another with extravagant marketing schemes featuring the usual paraphernalia of gifts and redeemable coupons for their many brands. However, the decisive marketing move proved to be the decision by R. J. Reynolds to experiment with the production of its own brand of cigarettes.[65] Reynolds' approach to competing in the cigarette market concentrated on the development of a single, nationally advertised brand, which placed the emphasis on quality and value for money and eschewed the use of coupons and free gifts. In developing the new product Reynolds chose as a model the Liggett & Myers' 15-cent Turkish blended brand 'Fatima', which was the most popular cigarette in the Eastern urban sector of the market. However, Reynolds sought to create a version of the product which was based predominantly on a mixture of domestic flue-cured Bright and Burley leaf to which flavourings could be applied, adding only a sufficient quantity of imported aromatic leaf to allow the brand to be legitimately promoted as a Turkish-blend cigarette. Positioned in the middle of the price range at 10 cents for twenty, and thus better value than 'Fatima', Reynolds devised an

[64] Tennant, *American Cigarette Industry*, p. 64 and Table 9. In terms of the allocation of the most popular brands, American retained Pall Mall, Egyptian Straights, Hassan, Mecca, and Sweet Caporal, Liggett & Myers received Fatima, Piedmont, American Beauty, Imperiales (a Turkish-blend mouthpiece cigarette), Home Run, and King Bee, while Lorillard were given Helmar, Murad, Mogul, Turkish Trophies, and Egyptian Dieties.

[65] N. M. Tilley, *The R. J. Reynolds Tobacco Company* (1985), pp. 203–25.

entirely novel brand name for the product, which they called simply 'Camel'. This new brand was then launched with an extensive advertising campaign, co-ordinated by the N. W. Ayer advertising agency, which featured a clever three-part promotional strategy based around the theme, 'the Camels are coming'.[66]

The successful launch of 'Camel' in 1913 took the other American cigarette manufacturers by surprise. Eventually both Liggett & Myers, with 'Chesterfield' (1915), and American Tobacco, with 'Lucky Strike' (1916), mounted a response based on a similar strategy. Their impact was diminished, however, by the outbreak of the First World War and the decision of the American military authorities to requisition cigarette supplies based upon market shares in the immediately preceding years, during which time the 'Camel' brand had captured one-third of the entire American cigarette market. By 1920, the tobacco market in America had been transformed by the 'Camel' revolution. The three brands were established leaders with practically all other brands rendered obsolete, and all the earlier coupon schemes were abandoned as promotional devices in favour of national advertising campaigns. During the 1920s, cigarette retail prices of the three leading brands were harmonized, with Reynolds playing the role of price-leader, whilst Lorillard, the only one of the four main successors to ATC which failed to successfully develop its own version of 'Camel', was reduced to the role of a marginal player in the industry.[67]

The response to Reynolds' new marketing departure in America was led by two executives who had figured among the original eighteen directors of BAT Co. in 1902. At Liggett & Myers, Caleb C. Dula was placed in control and quickly recognized the threat posed by 'Camel' to his firm's leading brands. Under Dula's prompting, Liggett introduced 'Chesterfield' as a similar Bright and Burley blended cigarette, but infused the Burley component with less flavourings, to produce a more sophisticated blend which appealed to the targeted 'Anglophile' smokers.[68] By the mid 1920s 'Chesterfield' had emerged clearly as the nation's second most popular cigarette behind Reynolds' exotic offering.

In contrast, the reformed ATC, under the direction of Percival S. Hill, had struggled to come to terms with the new state of affairs. Hill was relatively conservative in his approach to the management of American Tobacco and it was his son, George Washington Hill, who as the company's sales manager

66 Kluger, *Ashes to Ashes*, p. 57.

67 Lorillard did make a belated attempt to introduce 'Old Gold' as a direct competitor to 'Camel' in 1926 but it made only limited headway before the depression altered the composition of the American cigarette market. Tennant, *American Cigarette Industry*, p. 87.

68 Kluger, *Ashes to Ashes*, p. 61.

selected 'Lucky Strike' as a plausible candidate to compete against 'Camel' and who coined the phrase 'It's toasted!' as an advertising slogan. Notwithstanding the success of Luckies however, by the early 1920s American still trailed in third place in the industry's pecking order. Only after Percival Hill's death in 1925, and the assumption of control by his dynamic offspring, did American's sales of 'Lucky Strike' begin to acquire the upward trajectory which would see them sweep ahead of both 'Chesterfield' and 'Camel' by 1930. A critical reason for this success, however, lay in George Washington Hill's willingness to accept, albeit somewhat reluctantly, his own limitations as a marketing man and his appointment of Albert D. Lasker of the Lord & Thomas advertising agency to lead the brand's campaign.[69]

The deaths of both James Duke and Percival Hill in 1925 severed the most important remaining links between BAT Co. and its American founding fathers. Early the following year, with his eye clearly fixed on the American market, Cunliffe-Owen appointed George Cooper as a fourth US-based BAT Co. director.[70] Since returning from Mexico in 1919 Cooper had been instrumental in assisting BAT Co.'s expansion elsewhere in Latin America, and Cunliffe-Owen now co-opted his support as he sought to expand the company's interests in the US market. Since none of the brands inherited by BAT Co. on its inception were available for them to use in the US—where the TPC had begun to vigorously market the Imperial brands they had purchased from American Tobacco—entry by acquisition represented the only realistic avenue open to the company.[71]

The firm identified by Cunliffe-Owen as a potential target for acquisition was the Brown & Williamson Tobacco Co. of North Carolina. One of the founders of this company, George Brown, had died in 1913 and the firm was now managed by his partner Robert Williamson, who was himself on the verge of retirement. Since the turn of the century Brown & Williamson had

[69] Lasker introduced some of the most startling advertising campaigns ever seen in the United States, including an endorsement of the product by 20,679 American physicians, and by 1930 'Lucky Strike' had assumed the position of market leader. Kluger, *Ashes to Ashes*, pp. 75–9.

[70] Cooper had started his career in the tobacco industry with the Allen & Ginter branch of ATC in 1898 at the age of 17. *BAT Bulletin*, 16 (70) (1926), 277–8.

[71] The 1911 Decree effectively ended the restrictive covenant that BAT Co. had entered into with ATC not to trade in the US market. In June 1927, a meeting was held between BAT Co.'s solicitor, Fred Macnaghten, and Imperial's solicitor, Sowerby, at which it was agreed that BAT Co. would not claim any rights to market post-Decree Imperial brands in the United States, or to describe itself as successors to W. D. & H. O. Wills or any other branch of Imperial. BAT Co. also agreed not to engage in any import trade into the United Kingdom. At the same time BAT Co. agreed that, contrary to the position in other foreign markets, Imperial were free to trade in or export to the United States. BAT Industries, Secretarial Department Papers.

traded in cut tobacco and plug, showing no inclination to expand either its range of products or its geographical market scope. However, just around the time that Cunliffe-Owen started to develop the idea of expanding BAT Co.'s activities into the US, Brown & Williamson suddenly made two important new acquisitions within North Carolina. In 1925 it bought out the J. G. Flynt Tobacco Co. of Winston-Salem, which produced a well-established brand of pipe tobacco called 'Sir Walter Raleigh', and the following year it purchased the R. P. Richardson Co. of Reidsville which had just started to market cigarettes under its 'Old North State' brand name. With these new lines in hand, and with its operations focused on the factories at Winston-Salem and Reidsville, Brown & Williamson now presented BAT Co. with the foundations they required to enter the American market.

In October 1926, Cunliffe-Owen and other representatives of BAT Co. began formal negotiations with a group of executives from Brown & Williamson to discuss the terms of a take-over.[72] An accord was reached between the parties in March 1927 when BAT Co. agreed to pay $3,312,677 for the North Carolina concern and it subsequently registered the Brown & Williamson Tobacco Corporation at Wilmington, Delaware on 16 March 1927 as its new American operating company with headquarters based in Winston-Salem. At this point Robert Williamson stood down and Mr C. A. Kent briefly took control of Brown & Williamson's management before, in August 1927, George Cooper was appointed to replace Kent as chief executive of the Brown & Williamson Tobacco Corporation; a position he was to hold for twenty years.[73] Almost at once construction work began on a factory for the company in Louisville, Kentucky and in 1931 this town, rather than New York, became the general headquarters for BAT Co. in the US, and the management of the company's interests in Latin America was transferred to this location. This part of the BAT Co. organization thus became known in the 1930s as the 'Louisville Orbit'.

Competition in the British Market

Cunliffe-Owen's decision to enter the American cigarette market through the acquisition of Brown & Williamson posed two main risks for BAT Co. On the one hand, the move required not only a substantial initial investment in physical plant and goodwill, but it also obliged the company to engage in massive promotional expenditures if it was to make an impression on the market share

[72] Brown & Williamson Tobacco Corporation, *The First Hundred Years, 1893–1993* (1993), p. 15.

[73] Brown & Williamson, *First Hundred Years*, p. 59.

of three leading brands. Advancing this objective would inevitably require a subsidy from the profitable elements of BAT Co.'s operations until such time as the Brown & Williamson enterprise could be put on a sound financial footing. These financial risks in the United States were compounded, on the other hand, by the obvious danger of a counter-offensive by the main American manufacturers in those foreign markets where BAT Co. at present faced only limited competition from domestic firms.

To a certain extent, both of these problems were actually experienced in the late 1920s. From the point of view of BAT Co.'s profitability, the most significant adverse affect of the Brown & Williamson deal arose from the high direct costs that competing for a share of the American cigarette market entailed. Following the launch of its first major cigarette brand—'Raleigh'—in the autumn of 1928, the Brown & Williamson operation immediately began to rack up substantial losses and it became necessary to cross-subsidize these costs from out of its other American businesses. Consequently, in March 1929, BAT Co. set up in Delaware the Pocahontas Corporation as a holding company for all its American-based businesses.[74] This move allowed the revenues from BAT Co.'s profitable American operations to be set against Brown & Williamson's losses, albeit at the cost of cutting off the flow of dividends that BAT Co. in London had previously received from this quarter.

Thus, the risk of losses from BAT Co.'s invasion of the American market bore out the company's worst fears and, despite some improvement in Brown & Williamson's market share from 1932, these American losses continued to worry the BAT Co. board throughout the remainder of the 1930s. The problem of retaliation by the large American manufacturers in other markets, however, was felt most keenly not by BAT Co. but by its British associate Imperial. This was because the primary response of the US tobacco firms to BAT Co.'s invasion was ATC's decision to re-enter the British market.

Clearly BAT Co.'s move into America constituted a breach of the agreement between Imperial, BAT Co., and ATC in 1902 not to enter each other's markets. Although this agreement had been invalidated by the Dissolution Decree of the Supreme Court in 1911, the three companies who had been the

[74] The Pocahontas Corporation operated as BAT Co.'s holding company for David Dunlop, Brown & Williamson Tobacco Corporation, the Export Leaf Tobacco Co., the Smith Paper Co., David M. Lea & Co., and T. C. Williams & Co. Pocahontas also took over the debts owing to BAT Co. from Brown & Williamson in return for the issue of a promissory note. The only element of BAT Co.'s American operations which seem to have been carried on independently of this new holding company was the export trade in various non-cigarette tobacco goods produced at the Dunlop factory in Petersburg. This trade, and the machinery at Petersburg, were purchased by another BAT Co. subsidiary, the Maclin-Zimmer McGill Tobacco Co., in June 1929. BAT Co. Corporate Index, BAT Co. Southampton Archive, Box 114.

original signatories continued to respect the agreement in practice until BAT Co.'s acquisition of Brown & Williamson. From BAT Co.'s point of view, of course, the terms of the agreement had already been broken outside of America by successor companies to the old ATC. Soon after the dissolution ruling had taken effect both the Liggett & Myers Company and TPC had taken steps to compete with BAT Co. in China and elsewhere. In fact by 1927, as BAT Co. acquired control of Brown & Williamson, competition from these American firms in China had already been largely repulsed and thus the danger posed to its operations in other parts of the world—particularly in its important Asian markets—by the ATC successors was of limited significance. This was particularly true in the case of ATC whose leading American brand, 'Lucky Strike', was actually owned by BAT Co. in practically all the other markets of the world by virtue of the 1902 brand allocation agreement; an agreement which was not affected by the 1911 ruling since it fell outside the jurisdiction of the US Supreme Court.[75]

American Tobacco's response to the invasion of the US market by BAT Co. was therefore to adopt the same strategy with respect to the British market. In 1927 ATC's new president, George Washington Hill, concluded a deal which saw the New York firm acquire the entire share capital of J. Wix & Sons Ltd. and, by so doing, add another twist to the growing degree of competitiveness that was a feature of the UK tobacco market in the latter half of the 1920s.[76]

During the 1920s, J. Wix & Sons had emerged as one of a group of fringe firms that had begun to compete effectively with the various branches of the Imperial Tobacco Co. in Britain. Between 1902 and the end of the First World War, the Imperial Tobacco Co. had significantly strengthened its position as the predominant force in the British tobacco industry by increasing its share of the market for tobacco goods from 47 per cent in 1903 to 73.5 per cent by 1920. At this latter date, the federation of branches which made up the Imperial group accounted for 91 per cent of all Britain's cigarette sales; and of these W. D. & H. O. Wills alone counted for 60 per cent, and John Player & Son 24 per cent.[77] It was this virtual monopoly over the cigarette

75 It must be seen as a gross oversight by ATC to develop as its response to the 'Camel' revolution a brand for which it did not own the overseas rights, perhaps reflecting a post-dissolution inward-looking mentality by American firms other than TPC.

76 At the time of its acquisition J. Wix and Sons controlled less than 2 per cent of the cigarette market. M. Corina, *Trust in Tobacco: the Anglo-American Struggle for Power* (1975), p. 152. Following the purchase of Wix by American Tobacco the existing owner Mr Julius Wix and his two sons left the company. Monopolies Commission, *Report on the Supply of Cigarettes and Tobacco and of Cigarette and Tobacco Machinery* (1961), p. 66.

77 Monopolies Commission, *Report on the Supply of Cigarettes*, pp. 17–18, 39.

business which was responsible for winning Imperial its increased share of the tobacco market as a whole, as cigarettes continued to grow in popularity compared with other tobacco products.[78]

Imperial's competitive advantage over rival producers lay in its stronger position with regard to inputs; vertical integration gave the company direct access to supplies of both packing materials and raw tobacco, for which it alone among British operators controlled its own leaf-purchasing company. In addition, the company operated a bonus scheme that provided it with a significant weapon with which to capture the loyalty of tobacco distributors and retailers. The bonus scheme had been introduced by Imperial as part of its campaign against ATC and was retained after the conflict had ended. It rewarded distributors who were prepared to sign a written agreement by paying them a bonus which was directly related to their sales of the company's products. In exchange for receiving the bonus, distributors were obliged to 'make all proper and reasonable efforts to extend the sale of Imperial's goods and promote Imperial's interests, to conform to the company's prices, terms and conditions of sale and not knowingly to sell Imperial's goods to anyone who does not so conform'.[79]

The preponderant position of Imperial in the British tobacco industry, and in particular their use of the bonus scheme, was one of the factors which helped to place the issue of monopoly power on the political agenda in Britain, just as the case of ATC had done earlier in the United States. Soon after the end of the war a Standing Committee on Trusts was set up by the British government under the provisions of the Profiteering Act (1919), and a sub-committee was formed to investigate the degree of Imperial's control over the tobacco industry. Reporting in December 1919, the sub-committee, under the chairmanship of Sidney Webb, found that although Imperial had power to dictate prices it had not exercised this power to secure full monopoly control.[80] This conclusion was much as had been predicted in the tobacco press,[81] and was in common with the findings of the Standing Committee's investigations across a range of industries.[82]

[78] In 1905 cigarettes accounted for 26.1 per cent of tobacco sales in the United Kingdom (by weight), whilst by 1920 they accounted for 52.5 per cent. G. H. Todd, *Statistics of Smoking in the UK* (6th edn.), (1972).

[79] Monopolies Commission, *Report on the Supply of Cigarettes*, p. 83.

[80] *Tobacco (London)*, 40 (471) (1920), 130.

[81] *Tobacco (London)*, 39 (468) (1919), 56.

[82] Hannah points out that Beveridge judged the Standing Committee on Trusts to be an exercise in window-dressing designed primarily to placate the left. As well as Sidney Webb, the members also embraced J. A. Hobson and Ernest Bevin. L. Hannah, *The Rise of the Corporate Economy* (2nd edn.) (1983), p. 44. See also B. W. E. Alford, *W. D. & H. O. Wills and the Development of the UK Tobacco Industry, 1786–1965* (1973), p. 331.

Plate 36. An elderly James Duke (front row, second from left) poses with colleagues aboard the SS James B. Duke in the early 1920s. On Duke's left is George Allen, manager of BAT Co.'s New York office, and to Allen's left is Robert Harrison, a tobacco leaf expert who pioneered the growing of cigarette tobacco in India. Behind Duke are George Cooper (extreme left) who took charge of Brown & Williamson in 1927 and Edgar S. Bowling (next but one to Cooper) who managed BAT's factory in Petersburg.

Plate 37. Westminster House, BAT Co.'s London headquarters from 1915. Duke laid the foundation stone in 1913.

PLATE 38. Ardath cigarettes begin their journey to markets in the British Empire from the company's Worship Street factory in London. Destinations shown on the cases include Nairobi, Singapore, Calcutta, Auckland, Sydney, and Freemantle.

PLATE 39. 'State Express 555' cigarettes in stock awaiting consignment to China, *c.*1920.

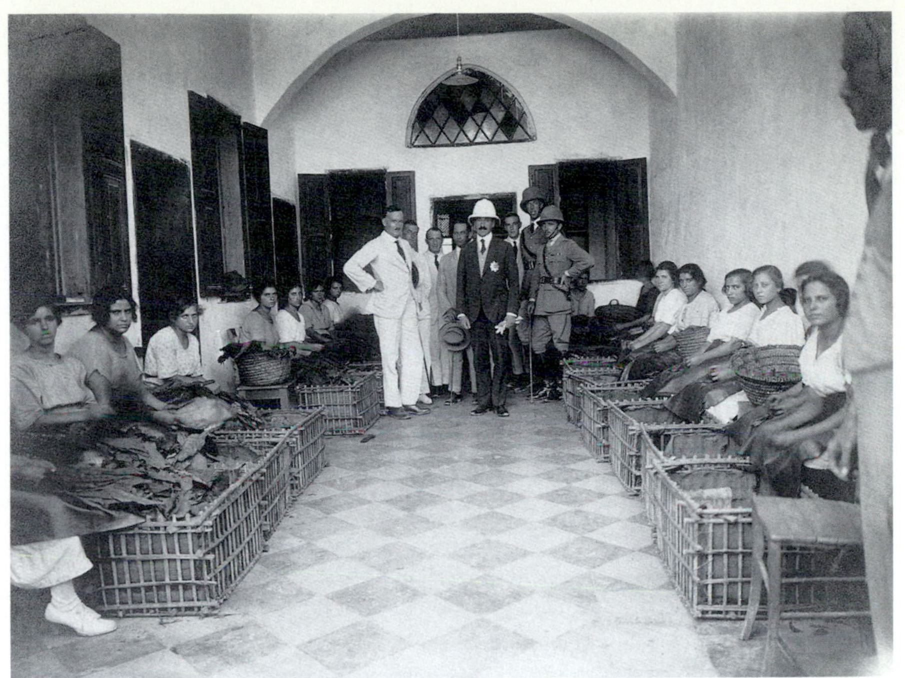

PLATE 40. The British High Commissioner for Palestine, Sir Herbert Samuel, visiting BAT's Maspero Frères factory in Jaffa (Tel Aviv) in 1922.

PLATE 41. A BAT Co. territorial director, K. Stanley Smith (seated centre), visiting the newly acquired cigarette manufacturing plant of Karaman, Dick & Salti Ltd. in Haifa, 1928. Sitting on Smith's right is Jacques O. Matossian, an Armenian director of BAT Co.'s Eastern Co., and standing directly behind Smith is Arthur Fieldsend, the local manager for Palestine.

PLATE 42. A German BAT sales representative, Emil Winckler, sampling cigarettes in German East Africa around 1910. Winckler was engaged by BAT through the German East Africa Company and was taken prisoner by the British during the First World War.

PLATE 43. A cigarette safari in East Africa, *c.*1910. The bearers travelled 13–15 miles per day.

PLATE 44. Transporting cigarettes in Uganda, *c.* 1920.

PLATE 45. BAT's office in Broad Street, Lagos, photographed soon after the company commmenced operations there in 1911.

Plate 46. A BAT sales team about to embark on a promotion of 'Compadre' cigarettes in Chile, 1928. The stunt involved parachuting cigarettes from an aeroplane with the supporting advertising message delivered through a loud-hailer.

Plate 47. Tiger-skin-clad salesmen of the Black Horse Tobacco Co. in Monterrey, Mexico, promoting 'Black Tiger' smoking tobacco in 1928. The cover on the mule reads, 'Everybody smokes "Black Tiger" but me—and you know what I am.'

PLATE 48. The Brown & Williamson factory complex in Petersburg, Va., advertising the company's new 'Wings' cigarettes, *c.*1930.

PLATE 49. Brown & Williamson's office staff about to begin their journey from Winston-Salem, NC to Louisville, KY, on 20 January 1929.

Plate 50. Sir Hugo Cunliffe-Owen at work in London …

Plate 51. … and at play in Southampton during an English summer, 1929.

In fact, the conclusions of the sub-committee were quickly borne out by subsequent events in the industry. During the 1920s, as overall demand for tobacco products fell in the wake of the post-war economic depression, a marked revival of price cutting and other forms of competition occurred as firms new to the cigarette business attempted to carve out for themselves a share of the most dynamic segment of the tobacco market.[83] In an effort to compete with Imperial, certain rival firms also began to introduce retailer bonus schemes of their own. Two companies that were successful in gaining a modest share of the cigarette business by such means were Godfrey Phillips, notably with its 'Army Club' brand, and Carreras who successfully launched 'Craven A' in 1921 and followed this with 'Black Cat' cigarettes featuring gift coupons. Although all of the Imperial branches resisted the use of coupons in their cigarettes, the tactic began to grow in importance and J. Wix & Sons had introduced a coupon brand in 1926 shortly before selling out to ATC.[84]

ATC's entry into the British market thus occurred at a time when the branches of Imperial were experiencing a more difficult commercial climate. Since the cause of the American firm's entry had been BAT Co.'s decision to purchase Brown & Williamson, the effect seems to have been to fracture relations between BAT Co. and Imperial, especially between Cunliffe-Owen and Gilbert Wills (Lord Dulverton) who had succeeded to the chairmanship of Imperial in 1924. By the 1930s, the two chairmen were scarcely on speaking terms with one another.

Prior to the Brown & Williamson purchase, relations between Imperial and BAT Co. had been quite close and the two firms had collaborated in a number of areas of common interest. Of particular significance had been the two companies' joint investments in the cigarette machinery field. In 1920 they became majority shareholders of Brecknell, Munro, and Rogers Ltd., a Bristol-based firm that had obtained a licence from the American Machine and Foundry Co. to produce the Standard cigarette manufacturing machine which had emerged as the main successor to the Bonsack around this time.[85] More importantly, in 1927 the two companies bought a 49 per cent share in the Molins Machine Co. whose factory in Deptford, London, had just produced the Molins Mark I cigarette machine. This had raised the speed of production from the existing level of around 600 cigarettes per minute to over

[83] Between 1920 and 1924 the volume of cigarette sales in the United Kingdom fell by 6.5 per cent, whilst the volume of pipe and hand-rolling tobacco fell by 17.5 per cent. P. N. Lee (ed.), *Tobacco Consumption in Various Countries* (4th edn.) (1975), p. 80.

[84] Monopolies Commission, *Report on the Supply of Cigarettes*, pp. 19–20.

[85] When R. J. Reynolds began manufacturing cigarettes in 1913 it had chosen to use the Standard machine. Tilley, *R. J. Reynolds*, p. 206.

1000. Thereafter Molins remained at the forefront of the cigarette machinery engineering trade and Imperial and BAT Co. were able to maintain a technological advantage over all their manufacturing rivals for a considerable period of time.[86]

This pattern of collaboration between Imperial and BAT Co. had been extended further in 1926 when the two companies secretly purchased control of the Ardath Tobacco Co. Ardath had been one of the few British tobacco firms that competed effectively with BAT Co. in the expanding post-war export markets for cigarettes and by 1925 the firm was selling an estimated 84 per cent of its output abroad.[87] It had been particularly successful in the markets of Singapore and British Malaya and it was as a consequence of its rivalry with BAT Co. in this market that Cunliffe-Owen persuaded Imperial's chairman Gilbert Wills that the two firms should jointly purchase Ardath in 1926. The following year, Imperial used its control of the British rights to Ardath's brands to compete in the growing coupon segment of the British cigarette market without overtly altering the company's hostile stance towards this form of promotion.

By the late 1920s, then, Imperial's virtual monopoly of the British cigarette market had been eroded by competition from firms such as Carreras, Gallaher, and Godfrey Phillips. These manufacturers began by using lower prices to gain a foothold for their brands in the market before shifting the basis of competition towards product promotions and non-price competition. Thus the second half of the 1920s witnessed an expansion in competition based on cigarettes containing gift coupons, led by Carreras and Wix, and between 1925 and 1930 the coupon brands' share of the market grew from 4 per cent to 16 per cent. The acquisition of Ardath's brands enabled Imperial to enter this rapidly expanding market segment in a small way, but such was the coupon strategy's success with the smoking public that by 1932 Imperial's executive committee agreed that Wills should directly launch its own gift coupon brand.[88]

[86] The Triumph machine, produced by the United Cigarette Co., had a model on the market in 1925 which was capable of producing 1000 cigarettes per minute, but the quality of the cigarettes produced was very erratic. Later developments of the Molins machine, notably the Mark 5 and Mark 6 increased the reliability of the output, and its effectiveness in different climatic conditions, more than the speed. Not until the development of the Mark 8 did the speed of production increase markedly again, to 1600 per minute in 1959 and 2000 per minute in 1964. R. Hill, *The Making of Molins: The Growth and Transformation of a Family Business, 1874–1977* (1978), pp. 19–25, 30, 63–71.

[87] Monopolies Commission, *Report on the Supply of Cigarettes*, p. 60. A rough estimate based on figures given in the Monopolies Commission report and by Corina, *Trust in Tobacco*, p. 150, suggests that Ardath had captured around one-eighth of total UK cigarette exports by 1925.

[88] Alford, *W. D. & H. O. Wills*, pp. 330–55.

Imperial's entry into the coupon segment of the market had only a very marginal effect on its overall sales, since it mainly led Wills' customers to substitute the new 'Four Aces' coupon brand for their traditional 'Woodbine' offering. However, it did allow the company to move into a position from where it could broker a deal with the other leading manufacturers to withdraw all coupon brands from the market. This collusive arrangement was drawn up towards the end of 1933 between Imperial and the six next largest manufacturers, including American Tobacco's Wix subsidiary. Under the terms of this agreement, each of the firms in question withdrew from the use of coupons as a means of promotion and those manufacturers whose trade suffered a decline would be compensated by the companies which gained.[89] This agreement was overseen by Martin's Bank, which managed the compensation fund, and therefore became known as the Martin Agreement. As well as curtailing the use of coupons, the agreement set out the terms at which goods would be supplied to the trade and specified maximum permitted trade discounts. Effectively, the Martin Agreement ushered in a period of collusive oligopoly extending across Britain's most important tobacco manufacturers that lasted until after the end of the Second World War.[90]

Expansion in South East Asia and the Middle East

The 1920s was a period of extremely rapid growth for BAT Co., during which time the output of its cigarettes practically trebled. In order to finance this post-war expansion the directors obtained the agreement of shareholders to raise additional capital by means of two issues of ordinary shares. Already, in March 1919, the company had made a rights issue from its existing authorized share capital of £2.1 million (see Table 8.1). Then, at the company's seventeenth Annual General Meeting in January 1920, it was agreed that the ordinary share capital of BAT Co. should be increased by £5.5 million, bringing the total

89 This agreement provides a perfect example of the use of lump-sum compensation as a way of moving from a sub-optimal to an optimal outcome within the context of a simple model of oligopolistic competition using the prisoners' dilemma concept of game theory. In effect, Imperial used their higher profits to bribe the smaller firms into agreeing to end the destabilizing competitive activity of coupon trading.

90 The six manufacturers who signed the Martin Agreement with Imperial were Ardath, Carreras, Gallaher, Godfrey Phillips, J. Wix, and the International Tobacco Co. This latter enterprise had been developed by the members of the Wix family who had quit their original firm after having sold out to American Tobacco. In 1935 it set up a subsidiary in Cape Town. Altogether, the Martin Agreement lasted until 1945, by which time Imperial had paid into the compensation fund a total of £13.5 million. On the Martin Agreement see Corina, *Trust in Tobacco*, pp. 161–76; Alford, *W. D. & H. O. Wills*, pp. 352–3; Monopolies Commission, *Report on the Supply of Cigarettes*, pp. 20–1.

TABLE 8.1. BAT Co. new capital issues between 1919 and 1940 (£'000)

	Date	Ordinary shares		Preference shares	
		Authorized	Issued	Authorized	Issued
As at	1.1.19	10,000	6,254	4,500	4,500
	19.3.19[a]		8,378		
	27.1.20[b]	15,500	12,644		
	1.5.20[c]		15,844		
	10.5.20	18,000			
	21.6.26	25,500			
	1.7.26[d]		19,895		
	1.7.26[e]		23,135		
	2.9.29[f]			10,500	10,500
As at	1.1.40[g]	25,500	23,759	10,500	10,500

Notes:

[a] Rights issue: 2,124,123 ordinary shares issued at par to shareholders in ratio of 1 for 3.

[b] Rights issue: 4,265,458 ordinary shares issued at par to shareholders in ratio of 1 for 2.

[c] Bonus issue: 3,200,073 ordinary shares issued as a bonus to shareholders in ratio of 1 for 4.

[d] Bonus issue: 4,051,241 ordinary shares issued as a bonus to shareholders in ratio of 1 for 4.

[e] Rights issue: 3,239,246 ordinary shares issued at par to shareholders in ratio of 1 for 5.

[f] Issue of 6 per cent preference shares for cash.

[g] Includes 623,900 ordinary shares issued to directors and employees between 1919 and 1940.

Source: BAT Co. Secretarial Dept. Records.

authorized capital (ordinary and preference) to £20 million. The bulk of these ordinary shares were issued to shareholders in the form of a rights issue, the new shares being offered at par value in the ratio of one share for every two held. A few months later, in May 1920, the authorized ordinary share capital was raised by another £2.5 million. On this occasion, the funds were obtained from the company's own accumulated reserves and as a result a distribution of ordinary shares was made to shareholders in the form of a bonus issue of one new share for every four existing shares held. Thus between March 1919 and May 1920 the issued ordinary share capital of BAT Co. was increased from £6.2 million to £15.8 million.

These resources were rapidly absorbed, and in June 1926 a further £7.5 million increase in the company's ordinary share capital was authorized. Of these shares, just over £4 million represented capitalized profits and these were allocated to shareholders as a bonus in the ratio of one for every four shares held. The remaining £3.2 million of ordinary shares issued at this time took the form of a rights issue and were allocated in the ratio of one for every five shares held. Remarkably, three years later, another £6 million of capital was raised through the issue of a new tranche of 6 per cent preference shares.

The effect of the additional investments made by BAT Co. during the 1920s was to extend the scope of the company's operation and make it less reliant for its sales and profitability on a small number of markets. As Table 8.2 illustrates, the Chinese market remained of great importance throughout the 1920s, but its relative contribution to the company's cigarette sales did decline. The relative importance, too, of the markets of the British Dominions and India was reduced over the course of the decade. In contrast, the region where BAT's cigarette sales expanded most rapidly was Latin America, whose share of the company's annual sales rose from 7 per cent to 17 per cent over the course of the 1920s. The two other regions which assumed greater significance for the company during these years were South East Asia, based principally in Singapore and Java, and the Middle East, centred on the Egyptian market.

Singapore and Malaya

Unlike the situation in India and China, BAT Co.'s initial expansion in the South East Asian markets of Malaya and the Dutch East Indies was founded to a much greater degree on exports of cigarettes from its factories in Britain and China rather than foreign direct investment and local production.[91] This was particularly true in the case of Singapore and Malaya, and was an important reason why the Ardath Tobacco Co. had been able to mount a serious challenge to BAT there. By the early 1920s the South East Asian markets had begun to assume a good deal of significance to BAT Co.—accounting for 10 per cent of the company's total sales volume by 1921, all of which were imported into the region (Table 8.3).

Singapore constituted an ideal location from which to develop the trade in South East Asia generally, the island having emerged as a major entrepôt following the opening of the Suez Canal in 1869. Together with the island of Penang, a few nearby coastal possessions, and the ex-Portuguese trading port of Malacca, Singapore had been established as a British Crown Colony—the Straits Settlements—in 1867.[92] From these small enclaves, British political influence had spread in stages to subsume all of the nine states which made up the Malay peninsula, culminating in the formation of the protectorate of British Malaya after 1909.[93]

[91] Exports of cigarettes from BAT's British Cigarette Company factories in China to the Straits Settlements and Java began during the First World War. See BAT Archive (SASS), Doc. No. 24-C-120.

[92] M. Havinden and D. Meredith, *Colonialism and Development: Britain and its Tropical Colonies, 1850–1960* (1993), pp. 39–41.

[93] Four of the states—Perak, Selangor, Negri Sembilan, and Pahang—which had entered treaty arrangements with Britain after 1874, allied themselves into the Federated Malay States in 1895; Johore, the state at the southern end of the peninsular bordering Singapore, signed a

TABLE 8.2. BAT Co. cigarette sales by region, 1920/1 and 1929/30

Region	1920/1		1929/30	
	(million sticks)	(%)	(million sticks)	(%)
British Dominions	5,976	16	9,590	10
British India	3,653	10	7,122	7
South-East Asia	3,642	10	11,291	11
China	18,683	51	44,037	45
Middle East	393	1	4,569	5
Colonial Africa	77	neg.	1,351	1
South America	2,221	6	9,341	10
Central America	396	1	6,891	7
USA	Nil		259	neg.
Europe	1,804	5	3,759	4
Total (subsidiaries & depots)	36,845	100	98,210	100
BAT Co. direct sales	1,149		926	
Total sales	37,994		99,136	

Source: BAT Co. Monthly Sales Returns.

During the late nineteenth century, the economy of Malaya began to experience a significant upturn. Tin mining had emerged as the main economic activity on the peninsular, and this was largely under the control of immigrants from southern China. Also by this time a number of British trading houses had been set up, both in Singapore and in Penang, and had developed a substantial business on the strength of the consignment trade from Britain, and as agents for banks and shipping lines. One of the longest established of these trading houses, Guthrie and Co., whose origins dated back to the 1820s, had been used by W. D. & H. O. Wills to market its cigarettes in this region during the 1890s.[94] Following the formation of BAT Co., however, Guthrie and Co.

treaty of protection with Britain in 1885; finally, in 1909, Thailand ceded suzerainty over the four remaining Malay states in the north—Kelantan, Trengganu, Kedah, and Perlis—and these together with Johore became known as the Unfederated Malay States. J.-J. van Helten and G. Jones, 'British Business in Malaysia and Singapore since the 1870s', in R. P. T. Davenport-Hines and G. Jones (eds.), *British Business in Asia since 1860* (1989), p. 159.

94 C. J. A. Dally, 'Singapore Tobacco Co. Ltd.: A Short History'. Unpublished typescript (56 pp.), n.d., BAT Co. Southampton Archive, Box 51. This source indicates that, as well as Guthries, Wills had used another agent in Singapore called Huttenback Brothers & Co. The latter firm operated in both Singapore and Penang and seems to have continued for a period to act as BAT Co.'s agent in the latter location. The company's own records suggest that Huttenback and Messrs Clarke & Co. acted as BAT's first agents in Singapore. BAT Co. Corporate Index, BAT Co. Southampton Archive, Box 114.

TABLE 8.3. BAT Co. cigarette sales in South-East Asia (million sticks), 1921–41

Year	Singapore	Java	Siam	Indo-China	Total
1921	3,153.6	488.2	[b]		3,641.8
1922	3,374.5	605.1	[b]		3,979.6
1923	3,142.5	907.1	543.0		4,592.6
1924	3,677.9	1,556.2	591.7		5,825.8
1925	4,505.6	1,589.7	786.6		6,881.9
1926	7,737.3	[a]	1,083.3		8,820.6
1927	8,754.6	[a]	1,202.6		9,957.2
1928	9,330.2	[a]	1,195.2		10,525.4
1929	10,281.3	[a]	1,816.1		12,097.4
1930	9,524.0	[a]	1,767.1		11,291.1
1931	2,658.3	4,835.3	1,351.0		8,844.6
1932	2,274.1	4,307.1	1,471.0	139.7	8,191.9
1933	2,278.4	5,143.3	1,349.0	640.8	9,411.5
1934	3,288.8	5,512.6	1,113.5	763.7	10,678.6
1935	3,061.9	5,066.5	1,140.6	948.7	10,217.7
1936	2,615.1	4,715.9	1,260.2	636.5	9,227.7
1937	2,891.6	5,811.8	1,308.3	788.9	10,800.6
1938	3,476.0	6,096.2	1,636.0	823.4	12,031.6
1939	3,188.6	5,954.9	1,633.3	780.1	11,556.9
1940	3,328.0	6,211.0	1,938.0	885.0	12,362.0
1941	4,109.0	5,889.0	2,515.0	1,154.5	13,667.5

Notes: Singapore sales figures include peninsular Malaya, Penang, Sumatra, Borneo, Celebes, and all the Dutch East Indies except for Java.

[a] Sales for Java 1926–30 are included in figures for Singapore.

[b] Sales for Siam 1921–2 are included in figures for Singapore.

Source: BAT Co. Monthly Sales Returns.

relinquished its agency for Wills' brands and the company set up its own sales office in Singapore at 94 Robinson Road.

The company's first manager in Singapore was H. W. Davies, who operated under the general supervision of James Thomas in Calcutta. Before his posting to Shanghai in 1905, Thomas acted for a few years as BAT Co.'s 'Great Eastern Representative' and seems to have been given a general brief by Duke to oversee the establishment of the company's operations in India and South East Asia.[95] In the Straits Settlements the market for imported cigarettes was very limited to begin with, being confined mainly to the small European population, the military, and any trade which could be secured

[95] According to his own recollections, Thomas had been sent by Duke to Singapore in 1900 as ATC's manager in the Straits Settlements. J. A. Thomas, *A Pioneer Tobacco Merchant in the Orient* (1928), p. 24.

from the provisioning of ships' stores. Nevertheless, a potentially substantial market existed among the Chinese immigrants, who made up about 70 per cent of the population of Singapore, since most of these inhabitants already smoked a rough tobacco called 'ang hoon' which they fashioned into a crude type of cigarette. As in China itself, the development of a market for machine-made cigarettes among the Chinese in the Malay peninsular was promoted through the establishment of links with Chinese merchants. Two such dealers, who were operating on the company's behalf in 1903 and who eventually became BAT Co.'s largest agents in the Malayan market, were the firms of Chin Wah Hin and Kwang Yang Hin. This latter firm also operated branches in Bangkok, Hong Kong, and Canton.[96]

In 1906, responsibility for the management of the Singapore branch passed from H. W. Davies to G. W. Hawley, who had connections with the UTC operation in South Africa and in 1909, Hawley handed over to C. E. D. Warry.[97] As business in Singapore began to gather pace, BAT Co.'s management in London took the decision to set up a subsidiary company to oversee this market and, on 26 January 1911, a company was incorporated in London called BAT Co. (Straits) Ltd. This entity, capitalized at £30,000, was then granted exclusive rights to import BAT Co.'s brands of tobacco into Malaya, Penang, Sumatra, Borneo, Celebes, and all the Dutch East Indies except for Java where alternative arrangements already existed. Separate arrangements also existed in Siam (Thailand) at this time, where BAT Co. operated a depot in Bangkok.[98] Following the creation of BAT Co. (Straits), K. Stanley Smith was posted to the new subsidiary as Warry's assistant, and L. R. Daines as his sales manager. Over the course of the next two years the operation expanded into the Federated Malay States by opening offices in Kuala Lumpur (9 MacArthur Street), Penang, and Ipoh. The Singapore office itself also expanded by setting up a separate sales department.

The new Straits subsidiary promoted a variety of brands of cigarettes, including Wills' 'Three Castles', 'Capstan', 'Gold Flake', 'Embassy', 'Pirate', 'Peacock', and 'Cycle'. A boycott of American products in Singapore during 1912 created problems, but the company's two main Chinese dealers continued to trade in its goods and no permanent decline in sales was suffered. Nevertheless, competition from low-priced Chinese tobaccos selling at 5 cents for 3 oz. made selling conditions difficult for the more expensive cigarettes which were priced at 5 or 6 cents for twenty. In addition to the pressure from Chinese tobacco

[96] Dally, 'Singapore Tobacco Co.', p. 5. For Chinese cigarette firms operating in Thailand see R. A. Brown, *Capital and Entrepreneurship in South East Asia* (1994), Table 12 .8.

[97] C. E. D. Warry was most probably linked with A. J. Warry who had earlier acted as Wills' agent in Australia, and who now helped to manage BAT's affairs in Sydney.

[98] BAT Co. Corporate Index, BAT Co. Southampton Archive, Box 114.

goods, BAT Co. also faced direct competition from the rival British company, Ardath, which in 1912 had began to distribute its 'State Express 555' brand in the Federated States through a Kuala Lumpur-based firm called Chow Kiat. Only the cheaper brands of 'Pirate' and 'Cycle' made much progress for BAT Co. in Singapore and Malaya before the war, although the introduction of a brand called 'Double Eagle' in 1913 demonstrated the potential for expanding sales via the medium of coupon brands.[99] However, by 1913, in spite of a period of growth, the Straits Settlements still accounted for only 6 per cent of Britain's cigarette exports.

Inevitably, the outbreak of the First World War adversely affected the progress of BAT Co.'s Straits subsidiary. Supplies into Singapore were disrupted as shipping was diverted around the Cape of Good Hope, and in 1916 an excise tax of 30 cents per lb. was levied on all tobacco products in order to raise revenues for the war. As with China, exports of cigarettes from Britain to South-East Asia declined precipitously after the fighting in Europe had begun, and although the company's factories in America took up some of the responsibility for supplying the Straits Settlements, it was in a far more modest way than in the case of the Chinese market. During the war, increasing supplies of cigarettes began to reach Singapore from China and BAT Co.'s chief Chinese rival, the Nanyang Brothers Tobacco Co., began to step up exports from its factory in Hong Kong. In 1918, Nanyang took a further step by setting up its own office in Singapore and distributing directly its own imported brands of cigarettes such as 'Golden Horse' and 'Great Wall'.[100]

Thus when the war ended and normal trading conditions resumed, BAT Co.'s Straits subsidiary found itself facing much more intense competition from both Nanyang and Ardath. The latter firm adopted an expansionist policy of exporting its cigarettes to any trading company that was prepared to purchase a specified minimum quantity, rather than limiting supplies to a small number of import wholesalers. The strategy boosted sales of Ardath's cigarettes in Malaya, but also acted to destabilize the market. In 1920, therefore, Ardath came to an agreement with the five largest import houses, to whom it granted exclusive terms, and soon after the company set up its own office in Singapore to handle the trade.[101]

The various sources of competition which BAT Co. (Straits) faced at this time did not prevent the company from expanding sales of its imported cigarettes

[99] Dally, 'Singapore Tobacco Co.', p. 9.

[100] Dally, 'Singapore Tobacco Co.', p. 11. Dally also mentions that one of BAT's Chinese agents, Chop Lim Hoe Chiang, had been appointed after having experienced success in marketing a brand of cigarettes called 'Chye Choo Siew' which were brought in from China. These may well have been one of Nanyang's brands. Dally, op. cit., p. 13.

[101] Ardath's office in Singapore was set up in 1922. Dally, 'Singapore Tobacco Co.', p. 12.

steadily during the early 1920s. Cigarette sales in general benefited from the suppression of opium by the authorities in Malaya, and from a greater willingness among second-generation Chinese to adopt the machine-made product. Operating a sales strategy based on imported cigarettes remained viable as long as the tariff rate on manufactured tobacco goods remained low, and even a rise in the rate of duty from its war-time level of 30 cents per lb. to 70 cents in 1921 did not persuade the company to deviate from its approach to Singapore as an export-based market. However, when a further rise was imposed in 1925, the company did feel compelled to act, and moved ahead on two fronts.

The first step towards setting up local production facilities in Singapore involved the acquisition of its main British-based rival. During 1925 BAT Co. had succeeded in obtaining an option to purchase in Britain the entire share capital of the Ardath Tobacco Co. but the acquisition was complicated by the terms of its agreement with Imperial which precluded the Anglo-American firm from trading in the British home market. Rather than purchase the Ardath business outright by themselves, therefore, and then sell off its home trade to Imperial, Cunliffe-Owen persuaded Gilbert Wills that the two companies should jointly set up a holding company, the Universal Tobacco Co. Ltd., to act as a take-over vehicle. Having floated the new subsidiary in December 1925, BAT Co. and Imperial then provided Universal with the necessary funds to buy out the entire share capital of Ardath from its owners Mr Albert Levy and the British, Foreign and Colonial Corporation. This deal was completed on 30 December 1925, and six months later, on 22 June 1926, a new company named the Ardath Tobacco Co. Ltd. (Great Britain) was established and the original concern was wound up. Through their ownership of Universal, BAT Co. and Imperial each controlled 50 per cent of the share capital of Ardath, with Imperial assuming control of the company's brands in Britain, and BAT Co. taking over its foreign business. With the share capital of Ardath divided evenly between BAT Co. and Imperial, the profits generated by its business were paid in dividends to the Universal Tobacco Co. and then shared equally between the two parent firms, even though Ardath's export trade continued to represent easily the bulk of its sales. [102]

By arranging to secure control of Ardath's business indirectly through the Universal holding company, and thus continuing to operate the company as a semi-autonomous concern, both BAT Co. and Imperial were able to use the Ardath brands as an independent element in their business strategies. In the case of Imperial, as noted previously, ownership of Ardath's brands enabled them to obtain a share of the British market for cigarettes containing

[102] Monopolies Commission, *Report on the Supply of Cigarettes*, p. 60.

gift coupons without appearing to compromise their stance of opposing such promotional schemes. BAT Co., meanwhile, continued to develop Ardath's foreign business in direct competition with its own subsidiaries whose staff in Malaya remained unaware of the ties of common ownership between themselves and their principal British rivals. Throughout the latter half of the 1920s, Ardath's cigarettes out-competed those of BAT (Straits) in Malaya, with one brand in particular, 'Double Ace', winning practically total control in large sections of the Malayan market to the great frustration of BAT Co.'s local management team.[103]

Having secured control of by far the bulk of the British cigarette export trade to Malaya through its purchase of Ardath, BAT Co. then implemented the second part of its response to the higher level of duties on manufactured tobacco imports into Singapore. In 1926 BAT (Straits) took over a building which had previously been used as a depot by the soft-drinks company of Fraser & Neave and set up its first manufacturing facility in Malaya. New brands were developed, such as 'Golden Egg', 'Elephant', and 'White Stork' and these were allocated on an exclusive basis to the company's various selling agencies who were thereby encouraged to actively compete against one another to expand their market share. Also, by inviting them to assist in the process of selecting a brand name and designing the packet, the creation of new brands was a useful way of promoting closer links with the Chinese sales agencies.[104]

During the following years, as these local brands began to establish their market share, the level of manufacturing in Malaya was stepped up. On 18 June 1928 the company paid $289,653 for just over two acres of land between Hoe Chiang Road and Kee Seng Street and over the course of the next two years it built a new factory and warehouse on this site to serve as the base for its manufacturing activities in Singapore. This factory commenced production in 1930, when local manufacture was transferred from the old depot to

[103] According to Dally's account of the Malayan market in the late 1920s, 'BAT (Straits) continued to grow, but Ardath grew quicker.' From BAT Co.'s point of view, of course, this was the perfect outcome. Dally, 'Singapore Tobacco Co.', p. 22.

[104] Difficulties sometimes emerged over copyright in such cases however, if the chosen brand name could be shown to infringe upon any existing mark of a rival company. One case in point involved the brand 'Twenty-One' (a packet depicting an ace and a king playing card) which was developed in conjunction with a sales agent called Ban Leong. This was claimed to be an infringement of an existing brand marketed by the United Kingdom Tobacco Co. which also had the words 'Twenty One' on the packet (even though the brand name of this company's product was actually 'Golden Sword'). The dispute led to a series of court cases in Britain before it was eventually settled in BAT Co.'s favour on an appeal to the House of Lords. In the meantime, however, BAT (Straits) took the precaution of renaming the brand 'Ace King'. Dally, 'Singapore Tobacco Co.', p. 17.

the new purpose-built site. Also at this time the company set up its first manufacturing facility in the Federated Malay States, at Jalan Sungei Besi in Kuala Lumpur.[105]

The expansion of BAT's sales in Malaya was put into reverse during the early 1930s, however, when the world recession crippled international trade and led to a collapse in the prices of raw materials which severely curtailed purchasing power in export-based economies such as Singapore and Malaya. The company's difficulties in these markets were compounded when, in September 1931, the authorities in Singapore raised the duty on imported raw tobacco leaf from 30 cents to 70 cents per lb. The decision by BAT Co. to set up a factory to manufacture cigarettes directly within Singapore had naturally reduced the revenue derived by the British colonial authorities from tobacco taxes, and the increase in raw tobacco import duties was designed to restore some of this income.

BAT Co.'s management in London responded to the changes by implementing a complete reorganization of its activities in South East Asia. During 1932, the use of separate sales organizations for the products of Ardath and BAT Co. in Malaya was abandoned and a unified distribution system was introduced called the Malayan Tobacco Distributors. BAT (Straits) continued to operate as a manufacturer, but its factory in Singapore faced severe cost pressure as a result of the increased duty on imported leaf tobacco. As these duties were limited to Singapore, cigarettes manufactured elsewhere in Malaya were considerably cheaper and a thriving trade in contraband tobacco goods sprang up as cigarettes were smuggled across the border with Johore. For a short period, BAT (Straits) set up its own factory in Johore Bahru in an effort to stem the decline in sales suffered by its Singapore factory. This experiment did not continue for very long, however, and during 1933 the company abandoned the manufacture of cigarettes in Singapore and Malaya and reverted to an export-based trade. The main factory at Hoe Chiang Road was converted into a printing house, the Kuala Lumpur factory became a depot for the Malayan Tobacco Distributors, and BAT (Straits) ceased to operate.[106]

[105] BAT/MTC Perspective History, BAT Co. Southampton Archive, Box 49.

[106] The Hoe Chiang Road factory premises were converted into the London and Eastern Printing Co. Ltd., which was incorporated in Singapore on 21 August 1933, and provisioned with machines supplied by Capitol Lithographers Ltd., a BAT Co. printing subsidiary company in Shanghai. The company produced packaging for brands that were marketed in Singapore but which were actually manufactured in England. Thus the raw material (board) was imported into Singapore from Britain and Canada, processed, and then shipped out to the British cigarette manufacturing factories using the same cases in which the finished products were to be subsequently shipped back to South East Asia—now packaged in their Singapore-made cartons. The combination of low costs of production in Singapore and the Imperial Preference scheme of import duties seems to have made this roundabout method of production

The policy of the colonial authorities towards tobacco import duty therefore acted to discriminate against the development of an import-substituting cigarette manufacturing industry in Singapore and Malaya during the 1930s.

Dutch East Indies

Along with its base in Singapore, BAT Co.'s other main location in South East Asia before the First World War was provided by Batavia (Jakarta) on the island of Java—then part of the Dutch East Indies (Indonesia). Before 1914, direct exports from Britain to Java were negligible, and the location was mainly provisioned through the re-export trade centred on Singapore, although in 1908 BAT Co. did buy out the firm of Anton Justman, a rival Dutch tobacco manufacturer. This acquisition brought BAT Co. a factory in Batavia which was utilized as a production facility until its closure in 1914.[107] There is, however, no evidence to suggest that this factory was used to produce cigarettes.[108]

Tobacco cultivation had originally been stimulated by the Dutch imperial system which required the peasants of Java and, to a lesser extent, Sumatra to grow commercial crops for export, one of which was tobacco. As this system broke down in the second half of the nineteenth century the growing of tobacco was undertaken by private interests, including Dutch planters who developed cigar-leaf tobacco for export to Europe and America.[109] In parallel with the export trade, native farmers began to grow tobacco for their own consumption. This tobacco was usually smoked in the form of a cigarette in which the strong tobacco leaf was rolled up in a maize sheath (klobot) and became known as a strootje (a Dutch word meaning straw cigarette).[110] An

perfectly profitable. The London and Eastern Printing Co. also made packages (hulls) for BAT Co.'s Indian and Siamese associated companies, printed calendars for Malayan Tobacco Distributors and outside concerns such as National Carbon, and also printed calendars for the Philippines. It even printed pineapple tin labels. During the Second World War it was used by the Japanese to print maps. The factory was managed by H. E. Darville and W. T. Mulvey, assisted by technicians from Shanghai and about 200 local staff who were paid around 35 cents per day. Dally, 'Singapore Tobacco Co.', pp. 26–7.

107 H. G. Verkerk, 'A short note of the beginning of business carried on by B.A.T. in Indonesia under its own name', BAT Co. Southampton Archive, Box 42.

108 Castles argues that until 1925, when BAT Co. began to operate its factory in Cheribon (Cirebon), all Western-style cigarettes consumed in Java were imported. L. Castles, *Religion, Politics, and Economic Behaviour in Java: the Kudus Cigarette Industry* (1967), pp. 32–5. The account of tobacco in Java in the trade journal *Tobacco* corroborates this assertion. *Tobacco (London)*, 46 (549) (1926), xxvii.

109 By the outbreak of the First World War the Dutch East Indies were reckoned to be the world's second largest exporters of tobacco leaf. J. Goodman, *Tobacco in History: the Cultures of Dependence* (1993), p. 211.

110 Castles, *Kudus Cigarette Industry*, p. 32.

indigenous cottage industry began to develop around this product from the 1880s, with hand rollers employed in a putting-out system of production, particularly around the region of Kudus in Central Java. These local manufacturers found that strootjes containing a mixture of tobacco and crushed cloves proved to be highly popular, and this variant of the product became known as a kretek.[111] Kreteks were later produced using paper as well as the maize-sheath wrapping, and after the First World War production of kreteks expanded to comprise a substantial portion of the market for tobacco products in Java.[112]

Thus as BAT Co. set about re-establishing its business in Java after the war, kreteks emerged as an important source of low cost competition to imported cigarettes. During the early 1920s, therefore, whilst the company was still operating in Java under the Anton Justman identity, BAT Co. began to implement a much more extensive sales promotion campaign. This effort included sending salesmen in vans around the countryside, supported by an interpreter and a 'boy', to engage in sampling and selling of the products and the posting of advertising materials, in much the same way as had been done in China and India. The Western salesmen, often First World War veterans, performed the task with the self-deprecating humour of those who had experienced more exacting conditions and who had followed the commands of more onerous battle orders. Applying fictitious identities to the supporting members of their sales team, the hard-pressed salesmen recounted their exertions somewhere in Java thus:

> On approaching the village of —— we halted, and, as in Flanders, advanced in single file, our two selves, wearing very short shorts and ingratiating smiles, formed the skirmishing patrol, whose primary duty it was to thrust relevant advertising material under the nose of a slightly skeptical market: behind us, in a strong and urgent support, came Lady Lil [the Ford van], Simos [the interpreter] discreetly directing her energies, while in the rear, faint but pursuing, plodded a miscellaneous troupe of camp followers, with the oldest inhabitant at the head.
>
> On reaching the village green, or its equivalent, Lady Lil emitted a gasp, and came to rest, and, while the crowd gathered round, a turn of the key revealed her vasty depths. From there emerged popular brands, advertising matter, and, finally, Zimmerman [the boy] himself, a combination which could have excited no

[111] The word kretek was evidently an onomatopoeic reflection of the tendency of the cloves to crackle and explode as they burned. A. Reid, 'From Betel-Chewing to Tobacco Smoking in Indonesia', *Journal of Asian Studies*, 44 (1985), 529–47.

[112] Reid, 'From Betel-Chewing', p. 539. By 1930, it is estimated that the annual output of kreteks had reached around 7 billion. In 1931, by comparison, BAT Co. recorded sales of 4.8 billion cigarettes in Java. The figures for kretek sales are drawn from reports by the colonial government of the Dutch East Indies and are summarized in Castles, *Kudus Cigarette Industry*, Table 11.

> greater wonder had it heralded the arrival of King Tutankhamen's Tomb . . . on wheels.
>
> Enthusiasm having been registered, our proceedings were both speedy and simple; money and cigarettes changed hands, health and friendship were plighted, and so on to the road again.[113]

As these efforts began to push annual sales of BAT Co.'s cigarettes towards the 1 billion mark in Java, so the company set about reducing the cost of the product further by engaging in local manufacturing.

In 1923 BAT Co. acquired a company under the name of the Indo-Egyptian Cigarette Co. and on 29 January 1924 this was re-registered as BAT Manufacturers (Java) Ltd. (BATM (Java)). This new company then purchased the share capital of Anton Justman and became BAT Co.'s manufacturing subsidiary in Java. A modern cigarette factory was constructed at Cheribon (Cirebon) in Central Java, some distance east of Batavia. The impact on sales of this initiative was sufficient to encourage the company to build a second factory, at Soerabaya (Surabaya) in Eastern Java, giving the company production capacity which straddled the main kretek-producing town of Kudus.[114] In 1927, BATM (Java) acquired the business of the BAT Co. subsidiary, the Westminster Tobacco Co. in Java, and the following year set up BAT Co. (Java) as a separate selling organization there.[115]

As well as the local kretek manufacturers, BAT (Java) faced competition from other manufacturers of 'white' cigarettes (the term used to distinguish them from kreteks). According to one source, the main opposition came from a Belgian company called Faroka who operated a factory at Malang in Eastern Java, and a Dutch trading corporation Jacobson van den Berg, who operated a factory in Batavia.[116] Figures in this study indicate that, by 1931, 6 billion cigarettes were manufactured in Java and another 1 billion were imported. Given BAT Co.'s own sales statistics, this would suggest that BAT controlled about 70 per cent of the market for conventional cigarettes in Java at the time.

As in the case of Singapore and Malaya, the impact of the world trade depression on local prosperity during the early 1930s hit cigarette sales in Java and BAT responded by cutting the price of its brands, bringing it still

[113] *BAT Bulletin*, 14 (41) (1923), 930.

[114] *Tobacco (London)*, 46 (549) (1926), xxvii. This item mentions that BAT was experimenting with the cultivation of Bright tobacco in Java at the time, and a leaf tobacco development company was later formed in Indonesia.

[115] BAT Co. Corporate Index, BAT Co. Southampton Archive, Box 114.

[116] Castles, *Kudus Cigarette Industry*, pp. 27, 37. Castles also mentions the Dutch-owned firm Industria, but it is not clear whether this was simply the operating identity of the van den Berg's Batavia factory.

more closely into competition with the native kreteks.[117] During the latter half of the 1920s, in response to the competitive pressures created by the local manufacture of 'white' cigarettes, a number of the kretek manufacturers had begun to organize production in factories in an effort to improve productivity. However, kretek production remained a handicraft industry and thus highly labour intensive. In 1932, as the depression began to bite into the government's revenues from import duties, the Dutch authorities in Java levied an excise of 20 per cent on the retail value of all manufactured tobacco products, and all packets of cigarettes were obliged to be sealed with a paper 'banderol' showing that the tax had been paid and stating the retail value of the pack. Local kretek manufacturers responded by arguing that, because the hand-rolled articles provided far higher levels of employment, the authorities should grant them a tax preference. These arguments were favourably received, and a lower rate of duty was subsequently levied against kreteks. In 1935, the government of the Dutch East Indies further extended the level of protection afforded to the kretek manufacturers by implementing a minimum retail price for 'white' cigarettes and by restricting the installation of new capacity for machine-made cigarettes through the imposition of a licensing system.[118] This group of measures helped the kretek manufacturers to remain viable and continue to hold a significant market share. Although the effect of these government policies was not sufficiently restrictive to curtail the local manufacture of cigarettes in Java, as it had been in Singapore and Malaya, they nevertheless acted to constrain the growth of this segment of the tobacco industry in the Dutch East Indies during the 1930s.

Malaya and Java therefore comprised the main centres of BAT Co.'s trade in South-East Asia during the inter-war period, although, as Table 8.3 illustrates, some progress was also made in Siam (Thailand) and Indo-China (Vietnam). In Siam, sales were organized through a depot in Bangkok until 1933, when a subsidiary company BAT Co. (Siam) Ltd. was incorporated in Singapore. Around 1936 a factory was set up in Bangkok using equipment transferred from Shanghai and a tobacco leaf growing programme was initiated in an effort to develop lower cost local brands. As a result of these developments sales in Siam accelerated sharply in the years leading up to the outbreak of the Pacific War. The operation in Siam constitutes a fairly typical example of a small BAT Co. subsidiary, with the key management functions handled by a team of expatriates numbering around a dozen. The No. 1 was supported by managers who supervised the functions of production,

117 Reid, 'From Betel-Chewing', p. 539.

118 Castles, *Kudus Cigarette Industry*, pp. 36–7.

sales, and accounting, with the production manager taking responsibility for both the factory supervisors and the leaf development specialists.[119]

BAT's trade in Indo-China began as an outgrowth of the China company's expansion into the south-western province of Yunnan. Organizing the distribution of its products into this remote region of China was the responsibility of the Hong Kong depot, and was undertaken with the assistance of French trading companies who transshipped the company's goods from the port of Haiphong in Annam (Northern Vietnam) into Yunnan.[120] A more significant step was taken in 1931 when negotiations between the management of BAT Co. (China) in Shanghai and the French business magnate Gaston Rueff saw BAT Co. acquire a 20 per cent stake in a cigarette manufacturing company called Les Manufactures Indochinoises de Cigarettes (MIC) which had been incorporated in Saigon (Ho Chi Minh City) in 1929 by Rueff's trading company Les Messageries Fluviales de Cochinchine (MFC). On 31 December 1931, BAT Co. set up a wholly owned selling company in Indo-China (COTAB), and BAT Co. and MFC used their jointly owned MIC subsidiary to purchase an independent tobacco factory called Trung Hue which was then leased to COTAB. Thus BAT Co. was able to conduct its own manufacturing operation within Indo-China, but using productive assets that were actually majority owned by Rueff's MFC firm.[121]

Egypt and the Middle East

Another region which received a major push from BAT Co. during the 1920s was the Middle East. Activities here centred on Egypt and Palestine, both of which were British-administered territories between the wars. In Egypt, between 1900 and 1930, the cigarette business was transformed from an export-oriented industry to one which focused almost exclusively on the internal market.[122] BAT Co. had made some progress here between 1905 and 1906 when it acquired control of two companies in Cairo, the first of which

[119] Interview with Mr P. Tindley, 22 October 1997.

[120] The earliest evidence of the company's links in Indo-China with a French company constitutes an agreement between the Hong Kong depot of BAT Co. (China) and Cie. Franco-Asiatique des Petroles whose Saigon office undertook to arrange for the transshipment of BAT's cigarettes into Yunnan via Haiphong in October 1923. See BAT Archive (SASS), Doc. No. 23-3.

[121] BAT Co.'s initial 20 per cent interest in MIC was increased to 45 per cent in 1935. BAT Corporate Index, BAT Co. Southampton Archive, Box 114.

[122] By the late 1920s Egyptian manufactured exports were confined largely to cotton-seed oil and cattle cake. R. Owen, 'Egypt in the World Depression: Agricultural Recession and Industrial Expansion', in I. Brown (ed.), *The Economies of Africa and Asia in the Inter-war Depression* (1989), pp. 137–51.

was Maspero Frères, which was run by an American, James D. Gilliam,[123] and the second was the African Cigarette Co. After the war the company set about the task of expanding its business in Egypt, purchasing control of two other firms, namely Nicolas Soussa Ltd., and Gamsargan Frères.[124] Also after the war, moves were made to develop markets elsewhere in the Middle East. These took the form of a new depot in Mesopotamia (Iraq), which the company opened in March 1920 but closed down two years later,[125] and the re-opening of Maspero Frères' factory in Jaffa which had originally started up in 1911.[126] By the beginning of 1923 this factory was reported to be producing 4 million cigarettes a month.[127]

The bulk of BAT Co.'s production capacity in this region, however, was located in Egypt which had developed into a fiercely competitive cigarette market by the early 1920s. This market featured a full range of BAT Co.'s cigarette brands, including imported British brands such as 'Flag' (Ardath also exported 'State Express' to Egypt), high quality Egyptian-style cigarettes[128] for the officers' messes of the British military (some featuring the appropriate regimental crest), as well as popular low priced local brands for the mass market (such as 'Rodah'), which the company made in its factory at Cairo.[129] Competition in this latter market segment came from a variety of Greek and Armenian tobacco manufacturers, the most important of which was the well-established Armenian firm Tabacs et Cigarettes Matossian SA which had been incorporated at Alexandria in 1899. During the mid-1920s, cigarettes were

[123] Gilliam was appointed as a director of BAT Co. in London in 1912. His early career as manager of Maspero Frères in Cairo is mentioned in J. G. Lisman, unpublished typescript, BAT Co. Southampton Archive, Box 27, p. 5.

[124] The Nicolas Soussa operation was acquired by BAT Co. in 1910; BAT Co.'s acquisition of Gamsargan Frères is noted in *Tobacco (London)*, 34 (400) (1914), 48. It is possible that both of these companies were subsequently incorporated into Maspero Frères, which was BAT Co.'s main operating company in Egypt.

[125] After the closure of this depot in 1922, BAT Co. appointed Frank G. Strick & Co. (Busrah) Ltd. as its sole customer in the region on 22 January 1923.

[126] BAT News (Autumn 1986), 20–1.

[127] *Tobacco (London)*, 43 (506) (1923), xix.

[128] Cigarettes manufactured in Egypt before the First World War used tobacco leaf imported mainly from Turkish-controlled territories in the Ottoman Empire, since tobacco growing in Egypt itself was forbidden. In the United States, these types of cigarette became generally known as Turkish cigarettes, due to the origins of the leaf, whilst in Britain they were termed Egyptian cigarettes as a result of the location of their manufacture.

[129] According to an account written by an employee of Maspero Frères who worked as a sales representative for the company in Egypt from 1923, the Cairo factory employed over 1,000 Egyptians together with a number of Greek blenders and was engaged in producing good cigarettes from Greek and Turkish tobaccos. The account does not state whether these cigarettes were hand-rolled or machine-made. Lisman, BAT Co. Southampton Archive, Box 27, p. 1.

extensively promoted in Egypt through the use of coupons and free gifts, and various companies, including the Matossian concern, gave away vouchers which could be used in places of entertainment. BAT Co.'s Maspero Frères' subsidiary ran coupon schemes and also operated their own Universal chain of tobacco shops at which they gave away free Czechoslovakian matches to their customers.[130]

This burst of competitive activity led to a rapid expansion in BAT Co.'s turnover in Egypt, and cigarette sales increased fivefold between 1921 and 1926 to reach over 1 billion sticks per year. Part of this growth was obtained through the acquisition of two firms based in Alexandria. First, in 1921, they acquired the tobacco business of Stamelis Douras which was then incorporated as a subsidiary of BAT Co. under the title SA des Tabacs et Cigarettes Papatheologou. Then, in 1924, Maspero Frères bought out the business previously carried on by Kevork Ipekian, forming Kevork Ipekian Ltd. Throughout this period, however, BAT Co.'s principal target for acquisition was its main rival in Egypt, the Matossian company, and ongoing negotiations continued with its owners during the mid-1920s in an effort to secure an amalgamation. Terms for a merger were finally agreed in May 1927, and under the aegis of a holding company called Eastern Co. SA, BAT Co. became joint owners with the three Matossian brothers (Jacques, Joseph, and Victor) of the total £E5 million ordinary share capital of Eastern Co. split on a 50:50 basis.[131] The impact of the merger was to raise sharply BAT Co.'s production capacity in Egypt, which by 1928 featured factories at Cairo, Alexandria, Ghizeh (El Giza), and Zagazig, and which boosted the company's sales there to a level approaching 5 billion sticks per annum by this date giving them, according to a contemporary report, 90 per cent of the market.[132]

BAT Co. had also expanded further in the Middle East during the late 1920s. In Palestine (Israel) the company had incorporated a new subsidiary at Haifa under the title of Karaman, Dick & Salti Ltd. in January 1927, which took over the existing business enterprise of Société de Tabacs et Cigarettes et Watania. Two further enterprises were acquired and operated through the Karaman, Dick & Salti subsidiary: the business of Baddour Brothers in Jerusalem was bought out in April 1929 and incorporated as Baddour Ltd., the majority of whose shares were purchased by Eastern Co., and another in

[130] *Tobacco (London)*, 43 (508) (1923), iii.

[131] BAT Corporate Index, BAT Co. Southampton Archive, Box 114.

[132] This figure for Eastern Co.'s market share is attributed in the report to the company's new general director. The report also indicates that, in addition to Matossian and Maspero Frères, Eastern Co. also absorbed the assets of K. & G. Melkonian, Papatheologou Frères, Gamsaragan Frères, Kevork Ipekian, Nicolas Soussa, and E. Mavrides. *Tobacco (London)*, 47 (564) (1927), vii.

Amman, Transjordan (Jordan), called Osman Sharabati, which was incorporated in March 1931 as the National Tobacco and Cigarette Co., Ltd.

In 1930 the Eastern Co. had decided to push still further into the Middle East by mounting a challenge in the market for cigarettes and tobacco goods in Syria. Before the First World War the market in this region had been run as a monopoly by the Turkish government but in 1919, when it had fallen under a French mandate, the trade had been thrown open to competition. The assets of the former monopoly were acquired by a Parisian group, Compagnie Libano-Syrienne des Tabacs (CLST) who by 1930 were well entrenched. Eastern Co. set up a subsidiary called Société des Tabacs et Cigarettes de Syrie et du Liban in an effort to wrest a share of the market, but it quickly ran into problems. By November 1932, BAT Co.'s director with responsibility for the Eastern Co., K. Stanley Smith, was reporting to the board in London that the subsidiary was making losses in the region of £E2,500 per month and detailing his discussions with the CLST who were seeking to gain an official monopoly concession for the Syrian market. A few months later, Smith was in a position to propose to the directors in London that the Syrian subsidiary be sold to CLST in exchange for a 28.5 per cent share of that company and the deal was duly approved. In 1935 the monopoly was re-imposed by the French government and CLST together with four local manufacturers formed a Regie company to administer it. Through its shares in CLST, BAT Co. continued to hold a financial interest in the Syrian monopoly.[133]

At the time of the creation of the Eastern Co. in 1927, Egypt had assumed the position of one of BAT Co.'s leading markets. However, the effect of the world depression reversed the growth in consumption there to such an extent that from 1932 onwards only about 2.8 billion sticks were being sold by the Eastern Co. in Egypt annually. As a result of this decline in sales, the 1930s witnessed a period of rationalization of the company's plants in Egypt and by May 1932 the Cairo factory had been closed down and production transferred to factories of the Matossian branch.[134]

As well as suffering a decline in sales as a result of falling incomes caused by the depression, it was clear that the Eastern Co. was losing market share

[133] Smith's discussions are reported in the Minutes of the Chairman's Daily Committee (hereinafter CDC Minutes) of 16 November 1932 and 10 February 1933, BAT Industries Secretarial Department files. Information on the CLST is contained in the BAT Co. Corporate Index, BAT Co. Southampton Archive, Box 114.

[134] According to Lisman's account, the closure of the factory in Cairo led to the paying off of 12,000 Egyptian factory workers. Lisman himself was allocated this task before being transferred from Maspero Frères to work for BAT Co. in East Africa. Lisman, BAT Co. Southampton Archive, Box 27, p. 9.

to its main rival in Egypt, the Coutarelli Co. During 1932, therefore, a senior BAT Co. director, Samuel Gillchrest, was sent to Egypt to investigate the situation and report back to the chairman and directors at Westminster House. Paradoxically, Eastern Co.'s loss of market share had arisen partly as a result of their control of wholesalers who were proving unreliable. Their rivals Coutarelli, who had been unable to gain access to the wholesale trade, had been forced to sell directly to the retail trade and this had actually led to their products being pushed more effectively. Thus during his visit Gillchrest oversaw the reorganization of Eastern Co.'s distribution system to one which sold directly to the retail trade—a policy recommended by Cunliffe-Owen. During the visit, an attempt had also been made to arrange an informal meeting between Mr Coutarelli, Gillchrest, and K. Stanley Smith, in order to discuss the possibility of a merger between the two companies. However, Coutarelli had indicated that he and his family would be unwilling to sell their business to any company with which the Matossian family were connected. An alternative proposal for collaboration between the two enterprises which Coutarelli put forward, involving a partition of the Egyptian market into two territories that could be divided between the companies, was felt by Gillchrest to be liable to work against BAT's interests even if the agreement was adhered to by Coutarelli which, in Gillchrest's view, was doubtful.[135]

Gillchrest's attempt to improve matters made little difference to Eastern Co.'s sales and in March 1933 Cunliffe-Owen wrote to K. Stanley Smith in Alexandria pointing out that, even after allowing for economies in the operations in Egypt, the subsidiary appeared likely to make a loss of about £E14,000 per month. He therefore instructed Smith to press the Matossians to provide proposals as to how these losses would be dealt with and how the ordinary shareholders (effectively BAT Co.) would be compensated for the need to make additional cash available to keep the business afloat.[136] Ultimately, as the financial problems continued to mount and BAT Co. were forced to fund the losses, a series of transfers were made of the Matossians' shareholding in Eastern Co. to the parent company in London, followed in July 1937 by the writing down of the ordinary share capital of the Egyptian subsidiary from £E5 million to £E2 million.[137] The process of plant rationalization also continued during the 1930s in Egypt and by 1938 manufacture of all Eastern Co.'s brands had been concentrated into a single factory at Ghizeh, with the company's administrative offices also being transferred

135 CDC Minutes, 18 November 1932.

136 CDC Minutes, 31 March 1933.

137 CDC Minutes, 5 October 1936 and 5 July 1937.

to this location and away from the Matossians' original base in Alexandria.[138]

The deal struck in Egypt between BAT Co. and Matossian in 1927 carries certain parallels with the company's arrangements undertaken with Cheang Park Chew's jointly owned Wing Tai Vo Corporation in China. The Matossian organization seems to have established very close relations with the wholesale distribution trade in Egypt which seemed to make it an effective ally to BAT Co.'s technical and marketing expertise. However, whereas in China Wing Tai Vo was supervised financially by BAT Co. (China), the Eastern Co. had no similar arrangements with an Egyptian-based operating parent company. The difficulties in effectively supervising the management of the Egyptian operation after 1927, especially after the recession led to the need for much tighter financial management, are apparent from the discussions of the chairman's committee in London. Compared with the profitability of the operations in China, BAT Co.'s Egyptian investments merely seem to have added to the financial pressures that weighed upon the firm as the golden years of the 1920s turned into the depressed decade of the 1930s.

[138] In 1938, to avoid the imposition of Egyptian taxation on the company's businesses in Palestine and Transjordan, a separate holding company was set up to acquire all of Eastern Co.'s shares in companies operating outside of Egypt and all the assets located in Palestine and Transjordan. This subsidiary was registered in Hong Kong and was originally called Hong Kong Holdings but its name was changed to Near East Holdings in 1947. BAT Co. Corporate Index, BAT Co. Southampton Archive, Box 114.

9

Sir Hugo's Empire

Introduction

IN the period between the wars, even prior to the resignation of J. B. Duke from his position as chairman in 1923, Sir Hugo Cunliffe-Owen assumed the dominant role within BAT. Upon his accession to the chairmanship he imposed a style of management on the company which accurately reflected his own autocratic personality. Within the BAT organization he exerted dictatorial control, and his influence over the company's international affairs was all-pervasive.

Cunliffe-Owen's authority was based upon his long-standing experience in the tobacco industry. He had trained initially as an engineer and was therefore well acquainted with the production side of the business. At the same time, he seems to have been blessed with an intuitive grasp of marketing, and fully appreciated the vital role that it played. More than anything, however, he was an exceptionally talented businessman and he used this strength to create a complex international business empire which could be managed to a large extent by a systematic set of procedures that he was able to retain under his control. As a leader, his chosen strategy was to build up the company by creating within BAT a meritocracy that nurtured and rewarded experience. Consequently, all but a handful of the company's senior managers attained their position only after many years of loyal service.

His primary concern was to promote the financial strength of BAT through a policy of continual expansion, and between the wars the company extended its operations into as many foreign tobacco markets as possible. The bold decision to enter the American market via the purchase of Brown & Williamson created consternation among many of Sir Hugo's fellow directors when the early results proved to be adverse, but he retained faith in the correctness of the decision and his conviction was, ultimately, well rewarded. Similar steadfastness was demonstrated by his decision to persevere with the market in Germany despite the difficulties the company faced there in the 1930s. Once again, the policy brought long-term benefits to the company.

By the 1930s, Cunliffe-Owen's activities had begun to expand beyond the management of BAT's core product through his decision to set up the Tobacco Securities Trust (TST) in 1928. TST was designed primarily to provide investment capital for a range of independently operated business ventures, but Cunliffe-Owen also used it as a vehicle for more speculative purposes. When one such scheme backfired badly during the mid-1930s, however, the Trust became involved in a financial scandal and Cunliffe-Owen found himself obliged to curtail drastically the scope of TST. The early 1930s also saw Cunliffe-Owen briefly adopting a higher political profile as he allied himself publicly with Lord Beaverbrook's Empire Crusade and its attempt to revive the political fortunes of the Conservative Party following its defeat in the 1929 election.

Certainly his style of leadership did not endear him to all of his colleagues, and a deep rift developed between himself and Imperial's chairman, Lord Dulverton. On more than one occasion Cunliffe-Owen initiated legal proceedings against the company that still held practically one-third of BAT Co.'s share capital and was its partner in a number of ventures. Despite their shareholding and representation on the board of directors, Imperial's management held no effective control whatsoever over the international affairs of BAT Co. under Cunliffe-Owen's regime.

As for the fortunes of BAT Co. itself, the chairmanship of Sir Hugo provided a period of prosperity which was diminished less than might have been expected by the world recession that broke after 1929. Although both sales and profits declined during the early 1930s, in general the company adapted well to the new circumstances by cutting costs and maintaining market share through a series of cartel-like pooling arrangements and alliances. A more serious blow for the company than the Great Crash was the outbreak of the Second World War which, at least temporarily, wiped out many of BAT's most important markets in Europe and the Far East. It was precisely at this critical point that many of Cunliffe-Owen's initiatives brought their greatest return; in particular his decision to increase the company's activities in the western hemisphere during the 1920s. Thus the greatest blow of all to BAT was the loss of Sir Hugo himself. As the company struggled to come to terms with the difficult challenges of the post-war world, Cunliffe-Owen's failure to effectively groom a suitable successor left the company in a state of dangerous drift following his sudden death late in 1947.

The Cunliffe-Owen Regime

Speaking at BAT Co.'s twenty-fifth Annual General Meeting, held in January 1928, Sir Hugo Cunliffe-Owen outlined the transition which the company had witnessed during its first quarter century:

> Whilst when the company was incorporated its operations consisted mainly—although not entirely—in the export of goods from England and America to foreign countries, today the most important end of the company's business is its shareholding in companies operating in other countries. Today we have upwards of 120 allied undertakings in which we are large shareholders, and we and those companies employ upwards of 75,000 people.[1]

Whilst Sir Hugo's description presented a perfectly accurate picture of the BAT organization, his portrait of the firm as a group of allied undertakings did rather tend to underplay the degree of centralized control that was exercised from the company's Westminster House headquarters, and in particular from his own third-floor office. Unlike the early days under Duke, when a largely export-based business had relied upon the use of trusted employees to run the main overseas operations, Cunliffe-Owen's BAT featured a level of central control over the operation that reflected the Englishman's autocratic inclinations. Although he was perfectly prepared to listen and act upon advice that he considered to be sound, Sir Hugo brought his influence to bear on every aspect of BAT's vast international business during his time as chairman. Indeed, rarely can the influence of a single individual have expressed itself over such a wide geographical compass.

By 1927, as BAT Co. celebrated its silver jubilee, Cunliffe-Owen represented the only surviving director from the group of eighteen that had formed the company's first board in 1902. The directors who now attended to BAT Co.'s affairs had worked their way up through the company and held vast collective experience with respect to the tobacco industry. A small group of these men participated with Sir Hugo in the Chairman's Daily Committee which constituted the main decision-making forum in BAT Co. The directors in question were Samuel J. Gillchrest (Cunliffe-Owen's deputy), Walter P. Stericker (production), Montague L. Whishaw (sales), Hon. Sir Frederick F. Macnaghten (legal), and Harry H. Neale (finance). Both Gillchrest and Neale had originally been employed in the London branch of ATC, thus joining BAT Co. on its formation. Stericker was introduced to BAT by Arthur C. Churchman around 1905 and was appointed as chief engineer, Whishaw had been recruited in 1912 in St Petersburg before pioneering BAT Co.'s expansion

[1] *BAT Bulletin*, 18 (93) (1928), 285.

into Argentina the following year, and Macnaghten, the most recent recruit among all the directors at the time, had joined the company in 1917 as a solicitor in order to free Joseph Hood of that responsibility. Of these men, only Macnaghten ever seems to have seriously challenged Cunliffe-Owen's dictatorial control over crucial BAT policy decisions at this time.[2]

The remaining members of BAT Co.'s board of directors were allocated territorial responsibilities. Some, such as George G. Allen at the New York office, George Cooper the chairman of Brown & Williamson in Louisville, and Robert C. Harrison, the chairman of the Export Leaf Tobacco Co., were based in the United States. The others divided their time roughly equally between the London office and tours of inspection of their allocated territories where they advised the local No. 1s who were stationed abroad. These latter men usually held the post of managing director of a foreign subsidiary company for whose affairs they were responsible—although occasionally in smaller markets they were simply branch managers of the BAT Co. organization. Cunliffe-Owen's influence on the affairs of BAT Co.'s foreign operations was thus mediated through the control exercised by his fellow BAT Co. directors over the decisions of the local No. 1s. In turn, the directors of BAT Co. were themselves constrained by Cunliffe-Owen's ability to award or withhold annual bonuses, in the form of share allocations, based on his appraisal of their performance. Through this structure, Sir Hugo was able to exert considerable leverage over the conduct of BAT Co.'s international empire of subsidiaries.

Along with the reports that his committee received from the directors as they returned from their visits to foreign territories, a variety of other mechanisms were put in place to monitor and manage BAT Co.'s operations abroad. Short-term scrutiny of performance in each market was achieved via the requirement to cable to Westminster House monthly reports of sales volumes. Over the medium term, the financial performance of each BAT Co. subsidiary was carefully monitored. In order to generate consistent financial performance, detailed instructions were issued from Westminster House to guide those responsible for the keeping of subsidiary company accounts, and these accounting procedures were used consistently across all of BAT's international markets. [3] These accounting instructions, drawn up in the early 1920s, were sometimes referred to as the 'cookery book' and were considered sufficiently important by some subsidiaries to be kept secure in a safe. Their implementation by individual subsidiaries was continually monitored by a

[2] Interview with Sir Duncan Oppenheim, 7 March 1997.

[3] Classification of Accounts of a Subsidiary Manufacturing and Selling Company, June 1923, BAT Co. Southampton Archive, Box 49.

group of travelling auditors who toured BAT Co.'s various territories on tours of duty from London, or from Louisville in the case of the Central American territories.

In addition to sales and financial monitoring, strategic control over the subsidiaries was also effected by means of the allocation of trade marks. Development of a market through the addition of brands drawn from BAT Co.'s portfolio involved the transfer of goodwill to a subsidiary and was therefore expected to result in a consequential rise in performance. Local No. 1s would normally require a strong case to be put forward from their sales teams before raising the question of launching a new brand on to their market with the director responsible. Again, the ultimate authority in such matters rested with Cunliffe-Owen himself.

From time to time Cunliffe-Owen visited an overseas territory which required managerial reorganization. Following the purchase of Brown & Williamson in 1927, he frequently travelled to the United States to offer advice to George Cooper, and sometimes he continued his journey to appraise developments in the company's huge and complex Chinese market. Strangely he never visited India, apparently for superstitious reasons, and by the 1930s he was limiting his direct overseas involvement to the United States market.[4] For the most part, therefore, the travelling directors took the leading role abroad and, where necessary, they were given instructions and authority to dismiss local directors whose performance was considered to be unsatisfactory.[5] On the other hand, those executives who excelled in their foreign postings were given the incentive of a possible directorship within BAT Co. as their long-term and genuinely achievable objective. Thus for the many management trainees taken on by BAT Co. between the wars in a financial capacity and as production or sales pupils—almost invariably introduced to the firm by virtue of an existing contact within the company itself—Cunliffe-Owen's regime provided the opportunity of life-time employment and a career path which potentially stretched to the highest positions within the organization. As a result staff loyalty at management level became an ingrained feature of the BAT Co. corporate culture, a trait which continued well beyond the period of Sir Hugo's reign.

[4] Cunliffe-Owen had a highly superstitious nature and he seems to have taken his illness in Ceylon during 1905 as a sign that he should never visit India. Personal communication with Sir Duncan Oppenheim, dated 21 October 1998.

[5] Various cases of dismissal are detailed in the minutes of the Chairman's Daily Committee. For example, a Mr Daines was instructed by Cunliffe-Owen to resign from his post in Singapore and the Dutch East Indies following reports from the director responsible for that territory, Mr N. J. Sweeney. Minutes of the Chairman's Daily Committee (hereafter CDC Minutes), 24 April 1932.

One relationship which was undoubtedly damaged by virtue of Sir Hugo's drive to strengthen and expand the operations of BAT Co., however, was the link with the Imperial Tobacco Co. Gilbert Wills—created Lord Dulverton in 1929—had taken over from George Wills as chairman of Imperial in 1924. Already under pressure from domestic rivals in the British tobacco industry, there can be little doubt that Dulverton was angered by Cunliffe-Owen's decision to invade the American market since it led, almost inevitably, to a response from ATC which was directed against the UK, damaging Imperial's market share still further. By the time that Gilbert Wills succeeded George Wills as Imperial's representative on the BAT Co. board—following the latter man's death in 1928—he and Cunliffe-Owen had become bitter adversaries.

The antagonistic nature of the relationship between the two men was brought sharply into relief in 1932 when Imperial purchased control of one of its main UK rivals, the Belfast-based firm of Gallaher. Imperial's decision to buy a 51 per cent share of Gallaher was itself prompted by fears that ATC was poised to follow its initial acquisition of J. Wix with the purchase of the Northern Ireland-based firm. Gallaher agreed to the merger on the understanding that its management would remain independent from that of Imperial, whose directors gave assurances to this effect.[6] However, immediately following Imperial's purchase of the controlling interest in Gallaher, Cunliffe-Owen invoked the terms of the 1902 agreement to claim possession of Gallaher's export business and overseas brand rights. The demand caught both Imperial and Gallaher's management off-guard, since the latter firm had developed scarcely any export trade in their brands up to this point. Gallaher were understandably upset that Imperial had neglected to consider this aspect of the take-over, and Lord Dulverton was sufficiently angered by BAT's approach to rebuff Cunliffe-Owen's initial attempt to assume control of the Irish firm's overseas brand rights. However, when Cunliffe-Owen took steps to obtain legal counsel concerning BAT's rights under the agreement, the deal was allowed to go through.[7] Gallaher were obliged to create a separate export department which was managed directly by BAT Co. and their 'Torchlight' brand was pushed in the Far East export trade when the

[6] Monopolies Commission, *Report on the Supply of Cigarettes and Tobacco and of Cigarette and Tobacco Machinery* (1961), p. 59. Note that one recommendation of this 1961 report was that Imperial should divest itself of its shareholding in Gallaher. Although this recommendation was not, in fact, enforced by the British government, the publicity generated by the finding of the Commission persuaded Imperial to sell off its shares in Gallaher anyway. M. Corina, *Trust in Tobacco: the Anglo-American Struggle for Power* (1975), pp. 218–21.

[7] CDC Minutes, 28 April and 6 May 1932.

company's established Ardath brand 'Double Ace' was facing a consumer boycott.[8]

The strained relations between Cunliffe-Owen and Dulverton continued throughout the 1930s, but did not prevent collaboration between the two companies where it served their mutual interests. When the world depression struck, for example, BAT Co.'s recently expanded Millbrook factory in Southampton suffered from excess capacity. Fortunately for BAT Co., Imperial's use of Ardath as its coupon brand from 1927 led to a dramatic rise in its sales and by 1930 the volume of demand for the product had outstripped the capacity of Ardath's Worship Street factory in London.[9] In the early 1930s, therefore, a substantial amount of production capacity at BAT's Southampton plant was switched to manufacture Ardath cigarettes for the British market. Owing to the restrictions contained in the 1902 agreement, these cigarettes could only be produced by BAT Co. indirectly, under a manufacturing contract from Imperial. Hence the Millbrook factory operated under the identity of the Universal Tobacco Co. which was the name of the joint venture concern that BAT Co. and Imperial had set up when they originally purchased Ardath in 1925.[10] Whilst Lord Dulverton was clearly happy for BAT Co. to take up production of the Ardath gift coupon brand for British consumers, he dismissed outright Cunliffe-Owen's suggestion that Ardath should also put out a new plain cigarette to compete with Wix and Carreras in the non-coupon market, and was unmoved when Sir Hugo threatened legal action.[11]

The opportunity to produce Ardath cigarettes for the British market allowed BAT to retain many more staff at its English factories than would otherwise have been possible.[12] The depression led to a sharp fall in the company's

[8] L. A. Batchelor-Smith, *Loom of Memories: A History of Southampton Branch of British–American Tobacco Co., Ltd.* (1969), p. 70.

[9] Ardath's share of the British cigarette market rose from 1.4 per cent in 1928 to 6.2 per cent in 1930, and remained high for the next three years until the signing of the Martin Agreement. Monopolies Commission, *Report on the Supply of Cigarettes*, p. 61.

[10] Batchelor-Smith, *Loom of Memories*, pp. 60–7.

[11] CDC Minutes, 29 November 1932. Cunliffe-Owen and Dulverton also fell into dispute during 1938 when the BAT Co. chairman accused Imperial of allowing Ardath's sales in Britain to collapse in the wake of the Martin Agreement. Cunliffe-Owen argued that BAT's sales of Ardath cigarettes in Malaya were being detrimentally affected by this policy, but Lord Dulverton merely pointed out that the Ardath brands were suffering from the cessation of coupon trading in the same way that other such brands had done since the Martin Agreement. However, with Ardath's sales in Britain declining from almost 3 billion per annum in 1931 to less than one-sixth of that total by 1936, the BAT Co. chairman was not impressed by this line of argument and felt that Ardath's goods were being deliberately neglected by Imperial in favour of their other brands. BAT Co. Legal Dept. File No. MA 148B.

[12] In the early 1930s production of Ardath cigarettes accounted for at least one-half of the Millbrook factory's daily output. Batchelor-Smith, *Loom of Memories*, p. 67.

overseas sales which the new home production went only part way towards replacing. Between 1930 and 1932, BAT's overseas sales fell by around 10 per cent and short-term working in the factories gave way in the autumn of 1932 to redundancies. Recruitment of management trainees also ceased in 1931 for a period of time, and many existing managers and pupils were made redundant.

The impact of the depression caused BAT Co.'s reported profits to decline sharply after 1930. In consequence of this, the company's management cut the final dividend paid on ordinary shares from 1s. 8d. to 8d. from 1932. In an effort to restore the company's sales volume, a deliberate policy of aggressive price competition was implemented in overseas markets[13] and, as sales volumes recovered during the mid-1930s, Cunliffe-Owen admitted that:

> While we are doing a larger volume of business, we do not make the same ratio of profit per 1,000 cigarettes, and, consequently, while our profits continue to climb, they do not climb in proportion to the sales, as the business as a whole is done on a smaller margin of profit, and though this is in some ways a pity, there is, in my judgement, the compensation that it renders our business sounder and less open to attack.[14]

Cunliffe-Owen's willingness to cut profit margins in order to secure higher sales volumes was a strategy which proved to be of the utmost importance for the firm's development in the United States, and from 1932 this market was to provide BAT Co. with an important element in its sales recovery.

Brown & Williamson Takes to the Wing

When BAT Co. purchased Brown & Williamson in 1927, the US cigarette market was dominated by three brands: R. J. Reynolds's 'Camel', ATC's 'Lucky Strike', and Liggett & Myers' 'Chesterfield', which together accounted for around 88 per cent of total sales of manufactured cigarettes. The high profile launch into this market of 'Raleigh' by Brown & Williamson's management late in 1928 made relatively little impression and

[13] Thus in relation to the market in Malaya where BAT Co. faced competition from low-priced Chinese tobacco goods, for example, Cunliffe-Owen recommended that, 'due to lower purchasing power there, efforts should be concentrated on increasing sales of cheaper lines of cigarettes and to reduce advertising expenses on the more expensive lines for the time being'. CDC Minutes, 10 May 1932.

[14] *Tobacco (London)*, 56 (662) (1936), 73. For example, profit on cigarettes exported to Malaya fell from just under 4s. 10d. per 1000 in 1931 to less than 2s. 0d. per 1000 in 1934 and 1935 before gradually recovering to just over 3s. 0d. by 1937. BAT Co. Legal Dept. File No. MA 148B.

had achieved a mere 0.5 per cent market share by 1929, dwindling thereafter. With the recession hitting BAT Co.'s foreign markets, the company was forced to close down its main American export plant in Petersburg[15] and the picture which greeted Cunliffe-Owen when he visited the United States in January 1931 was bleak indeed.

The summer of that year, however, witnessed a tactical error on behalf of the dominant group of cigarette manufacturers that opened the way for rival firms to expand their share of the market. Under the leadership of R. J. Reynolds, the American cigarette industry had developed into a classic three-firm oligopoly based on informal collusion. Competition for market share focused on a variety of sales campaigns, with prices held constant across the three leading brands. In spite of the fact that leaf prices had collapsed following the onset of the depression, R. J. Reynolds raised the retail price of its 'Camel' brand from 14 to 15 cents during June 1931; a move which both ATC and Liggett & Myers immediately followed.[16] Compounded by the diminishing spending power of American consumers, the effect of the rise in price was to reduce the aggregate level of cigarette consumption by 6 billion in 1931 and a further 10 billion in 1932—the first serious setback in the growth of cigarette sales in twentieth-century America.[17]

With the depressed price of leaf tobacco keeping down the cost of the principal raw material, and with many consumers severely pressed to maintain their expenditure on cigarettes, the potential emerged for manufacturers who were willing to cut profit margins and forgo high marketing costs to secure market share on the back of a lower-priced product. The first firm to successfully exploit this opportunity was a Richmond-based enterprise called Larus and Brother who in the autumn of 1931 brought on to the market a cigarette called 'White Rolls' selling at the bargain price of 10 cents for twenty. Other firms soon followed the lead. A few months later the recently independent Philip Morris & Co., whose 'Marlboro' brand had been one of the few successes of the Tobacco Products Corporation before its collapse in 1929, dropped the price of their 'Paul Jones' brand to match that of Larus' 'White Rolls'. By the end of 1931, therefore, the 10 cents for twenty concept led to an important new segment being established in the American cigarette market, although the expansion of Philip Morris was not to begin in earnest until the introduction of its more expensive 'Philip Morris English Blend' two years later.[18]

[15] Brown & Williamson Tobacco Corporation, *The First Hundred Years, 1893–1993* (1993), p. 52.

[16] R. Kluger, *Ashes to Ashes: America's Hundred-Year Cigarette War, the Public Health, and the Unabashed Triumph of Philip Morris* (1996), p. 82.

[17] H. B. Rowe, *Tobacco Under the AAA* (1935), Appendix A, Table 4.

[18] On the successful launch of Philip Morris, see Kluger, *Ashes to Ashes*, pp. 93–102.

Faced with this new form of competition the leading producers decided to hold prices at 15 cents and expand their marketing expenditures in a bid to stifle the expansion of the 10-cent products. By now, however, other firms had begun to appreciate the potential of a marketing breakthrough using the 10-cent ploy, and the pioneering brands were joined by a variety of others. None of these new 10-cent brands, however, were backed by the level of support which BAT offered to George Cooper, the chairman of Brown & Williamson, as he bid to engineer the crucial breakthrough for the company in America. In March 1932 Cooper took the company's recently launched 15-cent 'Wings' brand and cut its price to match that of the other new low-price entrants. The impact on Brown & Williamson's sales, illustrated in Table 9.1, was sensational. 'Wings' quickly emerged as the market's leading 10-cent brand and BAT Co.'s American export factory in Petersburg was brought back into operation to help the company cope with the burgeoning domestic demand.

In September 1932 Cunliffe-Owen travelled to the United States in order to assess the situation and advise on strategy. On his return to London the following month he outlined to the other members of his Daily Committee the measures that had been put in place. Louisville was to have its own leaf department, and marketing support for 'Wings' was to be stepped up. In spite of the wafer-thin profit margins in the 10-cent market, Cunliffe-Owen had authorized expenditure on shop displays for 'Wings' cigarettes to be raised to 5 cents per 1,000 sold. Other measures were introduced in an effort to keep down costs elsewhere in America. A proposed expansion of paper manufacturing at the group's Smith Paper Co. factory was put on hold. In addition, the chairman of the Export Leaf Tobacco Co., Robert C. Harrison, was instructed to explore whether cheaper, Chinese-grown, flue-cured tobacco could be substituted for American leaf whose price fall was now being reversed by virtue of Roosevelt's Agricultural Adjustment Act.[19] Cunliffe-Owen sensed the possibilities offered by the success of 'Wings' and ordered that a confidential report on the activities of rival firms in the American market was to be forwarded to London by the Brown & Williamson management every fortnight so that he could keep abreast of developments.[20] By the end of 1932, the 10-cent brands as a whole held a 10 per cent share of the American cigarette market and 'Wings' alone accounted for over 6 per cent (Table 9.2).

[19] A. J. Badger, *Prosperity Road: The New Deal, Tobacco, and North Carolina* (1980), p. 59; P. R. Johnson, *The Economics of the Tobacco Industry* (1984), p. 32. For a detailed contemporary assessment of the impact of the Agricultural Adjustment Act on the leaf tobacco growers in the United States, see Rowe, *Tobacco Under the AAA*, esp. ch 4.

[20] CDC Minutes, 18 and 31 October 1932.

TABLE 9.1. Brown & Williamson monthly cigarette sales in the USA, February–August 1932

Month	Cigarette sales (million sticks)
February	10.4
March	49.6
April	254.7
May	358.5
June	646.9
July	811.8
August	1185.3

Source: BAT Co. Monthly Sales Figures.

TABLE 9.2. US cigarette sales, standard brands and Brown & Williamson brands (billion sticks), 1925–40

Year	Camel	Lucky Strike	Chesterfield	Brown & Williamson brands		
				Raleigh	Wings	Kool
1925	34.2	13.7	19.7	–	–	–
1926	38.0	14.8	25.1	–	–	–
1927	38.4	19.1	27.8	–	–	–
1928	36.7	27.4	26.1	–	–	–
1929	37.2	37.0	28.1	0.5	–	–
1930	35.3	43.2	26.4	0.2	–	–
1931	33.3	44.2	22.8	0.1	0.1	–
1932	23.9	36.7	20.9	0.2	7.1	–
1933	25.6	36.7	29.3	0.2	5.1	0.5
1934	33.3	32.1	31.9	0.6	5.6	2.4
1935	39.4	30.7	31.8	1.4	6.4	2.9
1936	46.4	33.1	34.4	2.4	8.0	3.0
1937	47.7	34.5	34.7	4.2	7.2	2.8
1938	43.7	36.4	33.7	6.7	4.9	2.8
1939	42.8	38.3	33.0	8.2	5.0	3.0
1940	44.5	42.0	33.5	9.4	6.0	2.5

Sources: John C. Maxwell, Jr, *Historical Sales Trends in the Cigarette Industry*, Lehman Brothers, Kuhn Loeb Research; Tennant, *American Cigarette Industry*, Table 18.

Of course, the expanding sales of 'Wings' did little to improve Brown & Williamson's short-term financial performance, but the brand had crucially provided the company with a platform from which it could expand its more profitable lines, and this it now sought to do. The strategy adopted by Brown & Williamson to consolidate the progress achieved by 'Wings' was to engage in product differentiation in an effort to further segment the market for cigarettes. As a first step, it picked up on an idea that had been pioneered by its main local rival manufacturer in Louisville, the Axton–Fisher Tobacco Co., which in 1927 had pioneered the development of mentholated cigarettes. Axton–Fisher called their new product 'Spud' and marketed it at a premium price of 20 cents a pack.[21] Such a high-margin product was precisely what Brown & Williamson needed and in February 1933 the firm put out its own mentholated cigarette using the rather more appropriate brand name 'Kool'. Supporting the launch with advertising campaigns that used national magazines, the brand quickly built up a solid market and provided the company with an important source of revenue.

The launch of 'Kool' was accompanied by two other attempts by Brown & Williamson to widen the range of cigarettes on the market during the 1930s. The firm's main 'Raleigh' brand was repositioned at a price that allowed it to compete directly with the leading popular brands and in 1932 on-pack redeemable coupons were introduced offering consumers free gifts such as playing cards. Later, as demand for the product accelerated, the range of gifts was extended to take in consumer goods such as toasters and electric irons for which the depression had now created excess production capacity.

The coupon scheme developed for 'Raleigh' cigarettes was extended to 'Kool' and, in 1936, to another innovative Brown & Williamson product, a cigarette with a cork-tipped filter made from cellulose acetate called 'Viceroy'. The main benefits of this brand were to be reaped after the Second World War, but the strategy of product differentiation employed by Brown & Williamson succeeded in establishing the company as a major player in the American tobacco industry. Even though the leading manufacturers had recovered from their pricing error by the mid-1930s, by the outbreak of the Second World War in 1939 Brown & Williamson were the fourth largest competitor in the American cigarette industry,[22] and the US market accounted for 13 per cent of BAT Co.'s total sales world-wide. Ultimately, Cunliffe-Owen's decision to target the markets of the western hemisphere would prove to be of vital importance for the company's financial viability after the 1930s.

[21] W. F. Axton, *Tobacco and Kentucky* (1975), pp.110–11. Early in 1936, the Axton–Fisher Tobacco Co. put forward a proposal to BAT Co. to merge its concern with Brown & Williamson, but the idea did not find favour in London. Ultimately, the company sold out to Philip Morris in 1941. Op. cit., p. 113.

[22] Tennant gives the market share of the leading six cigarette manufacturers in the United States in 1939 as follows: R. J. Reynolds, 23.7 per cent; ATC, 23.5 per cent; Liggett & Myers, 21.6 per cent; Brown & Williamson, 10.6 per cent; Philip Morris, 7.1 per cent; Lorillard, 5.8 per cent. Figures are based on production data, except for Brown & Williamson, which are based on sales. R. B. Tennant, *The American Cigarette Industry: A Study in Economics Analysis and Public Policy* (1950), Table 19, p. 94.

European Tobacco Monopolies and Cigarette Cartels

In contrast to the competitive conditions found in the US tobacco industry between the wars—albeit oligopolistic in nature—the situation in much of mainland Europe was one of monopoly and formal cartels. For the majority of Europe's markets, the production of cigarettes and tobacco was controlled by national governments either directly, through the operation of an appointed authority, or indirectly, through the allocation of a monopoly concession to a private firm.[23] Under the latter type of scheme, BAT Co. occasionally became involved in the negotiations to manage a country's tobacco monopoly when the concession came up for renewal.[24]

Such a situation had arisen in Portugal during 1926, when Cunliffe-Owen was invited to Lisbon by the Minister of Foreign Affairs for discussions. BAT had earlier been approached by a London finance house who were interested in the idea of using the company's prospective management of the country's tobacco tax receipts as security for a large loan to the Portuguese government. [25] For his part, Cunliffe-Owen was prepared to consider the provision of management expertise to the Portuguese government—in return for a share of the profits—but he was quite unwilling for BAT to operate a state monopoly. Thus he stated that a precondition for BAT's involvement in Portugal was that the industry should be opened up to outside competition; a proposal which proved unacceptable to the Portuguese government.

Elsewhere in Europe between the wars BAT Co. did a small amount of business with state-controlled monopolies through direct sales, normally via an agent. In France—easily the most important market in terms of sales volume—BAT Co. was represented by the firm of G. & R. Anspach which acted

[23] Between the wars, State-run tobacco monopolies operated in France, Italy, Austria, Hungary, Rumania, and Yugoslavia, whilst government concessions were granted to private firms in Spain, Turkey, Greece, Portugal, and Sweden. The operation of these monopoly systems before the First World War, compared with the free-market systems prevalent elsewhere, is considered in A. W. Madsen, *The State as Manufacturer and Trader: An Examination of Government Tobacco Monopolies* (1916). This book contains detailed case studies of the monopolies of France, Italy, Austria, Spain, and Sweden in Europe, as well as Japan.

[24] The possibility of BAT Co. managing the Turkish tobacco monopoly concession was raised at the Chairman's Daily Committee by a director with responsibility for the Near East, Mr K. Stanley Smith, in May 1932. It was emphasized that the scheme would definitely not involve any capital investment on behalf of BAT Co. CDC Minutes, 10 May 1932.

[25] See FO 371/11927/W3535 on the question of raising loans to the Portuguese government and BAT Co.'s possible role. After the Second World War BAT were appointed by the British Military Administration to take over a monopoly concession in Libya, where an Italian-run industry had earlier operated. The arrangement was brought to an end following the revolution of 1969. *BAT News* (Autumn 1986), 2–4.

as the company's liaison office with the Régie and arranged for such advertising as the firm undertook there. In Spain, where a state monopoly was operated by Tabacalera, BAT Co.'s affairs were handled by Snr R. J. Thiebaut, whilst in Sweden the company dealt directly with the Svenska Tobakmonopolet. BAT Co.'s records show that between 1936 and 1939 the company sold its cigarettes in a total of sixteen different state-controlled markets within Europe.[26] This included Norway, where the company had been effectively forced into selling its subsidiary to a local company when the Norwegian government's Trust Control Authority supported a boycott of the company's products by domestic tobacco firms.[27]

As the situation in Norway makes clear, BAT faced problems even in those European markets where the tobacco industry was not subject to active state involvement. In Switzerland, for example, where the company registered a subsidiary concern in Geneva in August 1920 called Bramtoco SA, BAT found its operations hampered by a boycott engineered from within the trade, where the company's use of coupons to promote its 'Star' brand of cigarettes generated particular hostility.[28] Given these prevailing circumstances, it is perhaps surprising to discover that during the 1930s BAT Co.'s turnover in European markets actually increased as a proportion of the company's total world-wide sales (Table 9.3). The reason for this growth was almost exclusively due to the company's expansion in Germany.

BAT Co.'s original dealings in Germany, before the First World War, had been focused on its control of the Jasmatzi company in Dresden. After war had broken out, an arrangement was arrived at by which the Deutsche Bank agreed to purchase all of the assets of BAT Co.'s German subsidiaries and to take over the loans which these companies had contracted with the parent company in London.[29] BAT Co. received payment for these assets in 1921,[30] and from April 1922 the company ceased to record any sales of cigarettes in the German market. BAT Co.'s decision to dispose of its German operations led the Jasmatzi company to fall back under the control of its original Greek

[26] In order of importance for sales volume these markets were: France, Spain, Sweden, Portugal, Italy, Austria, Norway, Rumania, Czechoslovakia, Hungary, Greece, Yugoslavia, Turkey, Poland, Albania, and Bulgaria. BAT Co. Southampton Archive, Box 112.

[27] BAT Co. sold its interests in Norway to J. L. Tiedmann. For a discussion of these developments in the Norwegian market, see H. W. Nordvik, 'Conflict and Cooperation: Competitive Strategies and the Struggle for Control over the Norwegian Tobacco Market, 1905–1930', in R. P. Amdam and E. Lange (eds.), *Crossing the Borders: Studies in Norwegian Business History* (1994), pp. 131–60.

[28] *Tobacco (London)*, 42 (497) (1922), xxix.

[29] *Tobacco (London)*, 34 (422) (1916), 37 and 35 (434) (1917), 39.

[30] *Tobacco (London)*, 42 (494) (1922), ix.

TABLE 9.3. BAT Co. cigarette sales by region, 1930/1 and 1938/9

Region	1930/1		1938/9	
	(million sticks)	(%)	(million sticks)	(%)
British Dominions	8,827	9.9	12,647	8.9
British India	5,195	5.8	8,643	6.1
South-East Asia	8,845	9.9	13,047	9.2
China	42,184	47.1	43,903	30.9
Middle East	3,914	4.4	3,407	2.4
Colonial Africa	1,177	1.3	2,133	1.5
South America	8,531	9.5	18,470	13
Central America	6,847	7.7	12,826	9
USA	224	0.3	18,754	13.2
Europe	3,748	4.2	8,359	5.9
Total sales (depots & subsidiary companies)	89,492	100	142,188	100
Direct sales (UK factories)	646		1,063	
Direct sales (US factories)	99		500	
Grand total	90,237		143,751	

Source: BAT Co. Monthly Sales Figures.

owner, Georg A. Jasmatzi, who once again built the firm up until his death in 1922.[31]

During the first half of the 1920s the German cigarette industry underwent a process of rapid concentration as many of the country's small tobacco firms were crippled by high levels of taxation and the effects of hyperinflation.[32] By 1925, the three main cigarette manufacturers in Germany—Kiazim Gonn, Jasmatzi, and Reemtsma—controlled almost 50 per cent of the industry's output.[33] During this period, the Deutsche Bank helped the Jasmatzi company to organize a leaf tobacco purchasing cartel, in which a group of a dozen German cigarette manufacturers participated, called the Standard Commercial Tobacco Co. of New York.[34] The Standard company was controlled

[31] *Tobacco (London)*, 42 (496) (1922), i.

[32] Citing a report in the German tobacco trade press, the London journal *Tobacco* reported that: 'At a tobacconist's in Muhldorf (Bavaria) cigarettes are wrapped up for customers in thousand mark notes, not with the object of attracting buyers, but because the cost of a little paper bag is now 4,800 Marks.' *Tobacco (London)*, 43 (515) (1923), 95.

[33] *Tobacco (London)*, 45 (533) (1925), i.

[34] Although the Standard company was based in New York, it was primarily engaged in purchasing tobacco leaf grown in the Levant rather than in the United States. As a result of the large Turkish segment in the American cigarette market, New York was a major market for this type of leaf. By 1925 Standard were reported to be in control of one third of the trade. *Tobacco (London)*, 45 (533) (1925), i.

jointly by the Jasmatzi and Reemtsma concerns and in October 1925, in an effort to restore their profitability,[35] these two groups combined their cigarette manufacturing operations, taking control of around 45 per cent of all German cigarette output.[36] From this point onwards the managing director of the newly enlarged Reemtsma concern, Herr Philipp Reemtsma, became the leading figure in the German cigarette industry. During the depression of the early 1930s, he took the main role in organizing the cartel of German cigarette manufacturers which operated a system of market quotas within Germany.

Throughout this period the German market was heavily protected from foreign-manufactured tobacco goods by means of tariffs which, together with domestic duties, served to make the price of English pipe tobacco in Germany ten times that charged in Britain during the mid-1920s.[37] In 1926 BAT attempted to regain an interest in the German market by setting up a subsidiary company in Hamburg—the British–American Tobacco Co. (C.E.) GmbH—to manufacture cigarettes locally. In spite of various difficulties that the company experienced in Hamburg,[38] a small factory was put into operation using four elderly machines to produce traditional English brands such as 'Gold Flake', 'Player's Navy Medium Cut', and 'Capstan Navy Cut' under licence from BAT Co. Since the popular cigarettes in Germany at this time featured oriental tobacco leaf, these Virginia leaf products were marketed as high-price, luxury niche products. Such were the limitations of this segment of the market, however, that in 1929 the company began to use their Near Eastern cigarette operations to provide them with Turkish brands by incorporating a company in Germany to manufacture their Egypt-based Melkonian subsidiary's cigarette brands in a small factory near Hamburg.[39] Also around this time, BAT Co. bought out another small Hamburg-based manufacturer of lower-priced oriental-style cigarettes, the AZET-Zigarettenfabrik.

[35] In 1925 the Jasmatzi company's financial position was such that it was able to pay dividends only to its preference shareholders, the ordinary dividend being deferred. *Tobacco (London)*, 45 (537) (1925), vii.

[36] *Tobacco (London)*, 45 (538) (1925), xxii.

[37] *Tobacco (London)*, 46 (550) (1926), v.

[38] FO 371/11333, correspondence between the British Consulate General in Berlin and the Foreign Office, 3 and 11 December 1926 relating to the difficulties that expatriate BAT Co. staff were experiencing in their efforts to obtain long-term visas to work in Hamburg. Apparently the problems were the result of complaints by the local Chamber of Commerce.

[39] This company was originally registered as Zigarettenfabriken Melkonian GmbH but changed its name to Zigarettenfabriken Melachrino GmbH in 1930 after BAT Co. acquired the London branch of this manufacturer of Turkish cigarettes from the Tobacco Products Corporation. BAT Cigaretten Fabriken GmbH, *BAT Magazin zum 50 jährigen Bestehen, 1926–1976* (1976), p. 6.

Thus between 1926 and 1932 BAT Co. gradually expanded its position in the German cigarette market. In this latter year, however, a significant expansion of the German operation was undertaken. In December 1931 BAT Co. had granted a loan of £250,000 to the brothers Karl and Sigmund Bergmann, Jewish owners of a tobacco firm registered in Essen with a factory in Dresden, who were seeking to sell up and move to Holland. The loan was secured against the entire shareholding of their company, Haus Bergmann. As part of the deal BAT Co. were granted an option to purchase 60 per cent of the Bergmann company at a specified date. Unknown to BAT Co., however, a similar option was already held by Reemtsma. When Philipp Reemtsma discovered the Bergmann's arrangements with BAT, he quickly exercised the option to buy control of the Jewish enterprise. At this point BAT Co. demanded the full repayment of their loan to the Bergmanns from Reemtsma, together with the interest which had accrued on the debt. Unwilling to pay, Philipp Reemtsma first attempted to persuade Cunliffe-Owen to operate Haus Bergmann as a joint venture but, when it became clear that no satisfactory settlement would be reached along these lines, he agreed to sell the Bergmann business to BAT Co. for 4.5 million Reichsmark. The deal reached with Reemtsma allocated Haus Bergmann a fixed 10 per cent share of the German cigarette market as part of the pooling arrangements of the manufacturers' cartel.[40]

The purchase of Haus Bergmann was scheduled to take place on 1 January 1933 but a few days before the completion of the deal Karl and Sigmund Bergmann were arrested by the German authorities for failing to disclose details of their loan from BAT Co. Subsequently the two brothers were charged with obtaining foreign exchange on fraudulent invoices for leaf tobacco purchases. BAT Co.'s solicitor, Fred Macnaghten, immediately wrote to the Foreign Office in London outlining the situation that had arisen and requesting consular support for BAT Co.'s representatives in Germany.[41] The charges against the Bergmanns were only dropped when BAT Co. provided guarantees to the German customs authority that it would respect the regime of foreign exchange controls which were in force, and confirmed their intention to continue the operation of the Bergmann brothers' factory in Dresden.[42] Once these matters had been finalized, BAT Co. registered a new subsidiary under the name of BAT (Deutschland) GmbH on 21 December 1932, and this became the holding company for Haus Bergmann.[43]

40 CDC Minutes, 13 September and 9 November 1932.

41 FO 371/15955, letter F. F. Macnaghten to Foreign Office, 28 December 1932.

42 CDC Minutes, 23, 28, 29, 30 December 1932 and 2 January 1933.

43 This new subsidiary was actually a re-registration of the Melachrino company which BAT Co. already operated in Germany.

The pooling agreement that the Bergmann company subscribed to in Germany was based on a group of eighty depots located around the country, for which the members of the cartel shared the operating costs and through which they reaped benefits of scale economies in the distribution process. These eighty depots served a total of approximately 6,000 accredited wholesalers. Each month these wholesalers were allocated a specified quantity of different goods on which they received a discount, provided they agreed to purchase the full amounts allocated to them. Thus the distribution arrangements were controlled directly by the cartel at the depot level, and indirectly, via price incentives, at the wholesale level.[44] Before the Bergmann concern was formally brought into the pool, however, the newly installed National Socialist regime in Berlin expressed a desire to form its own national cartel of cigarette manufacturers. Consequently, after 1934 90 per cent of the German cigarette manufacturing capacity was brought under the control of the government. Philipp Reemtsma's own influence on the industry was further strengthened by his willingness to work in collaboration with the authorities in Berlin, and BAT's operations in Germany fell increasingly under his sway. By 1938, for example, staff were being transferred directly between the Reemtsma and Bergmann organizations.[45] When war broke out the main management of BAT in Germany had been placed under a Mr Parsons, and he was supported by a solicitor, Dr Buch, and a cousin of Cunliffe-Owen's who was resident in Germany, Ernst von Reitzenstein.[46]

The cartel arrangements that Reemtsma had co-ordinated in Germany were symptomatic of the inward-looking mentality which characterized the international cigarette industry as a whole during the 1930s. Confronted by depressed consumer incomes and facing an increasingly difficult international trading and financial environment, national cartels emerged as an obvious and effective method of tailoring excess capacity to diminished demand without the need to cut prices. Minutes of the Chairman's Daily Committee in 1932 make Cunliffe-Owen's views on the matter perfectly clear:

> Sir Hugo Cunliffe-Owen referred to the possibility of introducing some species of pooling or cartel arrangements in various territories in which BAT or its Associated Companies were interested. Sir Hugo emphasised that in the existing circumstances of trade depression, manufacturers were inclined to give more to their customers, with a consequent continual decrease in profits, and stated that his belief was that the remedy lay in some comprehensive scheme of co-operation and rationalization.[47]

[44] CDC Minutes, 18 January 1933.

[45] CDC Minutes, 3 June 1938.

[46] Cunliffe-Owen's mother, Jenny von Reitzenstein, had come from a minor German aristocratic family. *BAT News* (Autumn 1987), 8.

[47] CDC Minutes, 23 December 1932.

These ideas were soon being put into practice in Belgium where BAT Co. had recently acquired the controlling interest in a local firm, Odon Warland SA. Following a visit to Belgium early in 1933, Cunliffe-Owen reported to the committee that he felt BAT should try and come to some arrangement with their main rival cigarette manufacturer in Belgium, Tobacofina, but in the meantime make life as difficult as possible for them. He also felt that, in view of the growing national feeling in Belgium in favour of home industries, it was essential to exploit the name 'Odon Warland' and the Belgian nature of the Odon Warland Co. as much as possible. At the same time he recommended a sharp drop in advertising expenditure on behalf of the subsidiary in order to reduce costs, although his review of staff salaries did not lead him to believe that any savings could be made in that respect.[48] Soon afterwards, the Odon Warland organization reached an agreement with Tobacofina and another leading Belgian tobacco firm, Gosset, to create a cartel in which the pooled profits would be shared between the three firms in fixed proportions.[49]

Economic Instability and the Empire Crusade

The desire to blend into local markets as discretely as possible—a policy which the company had already adopted in the majority of its operations in Latin America—was a logical response to the growth of economic nationalism and autarky that typified the world economy in the 1930s. As Kindleberger has pointed out, the financial collapse which followed the 1929 stock exchange crash in America led to the adoption of beggar-thy-neighbour policies in which national governments sought to bring comfort to their own economies by damaging those of other nations.[50] The decision by the Hoover administration in the United States to engage in extended tariff protection through the passage of the Smoot–Hawley Act in 1930, coupled with the repatriation of foreign loans by the many American banks suffering a crisis of liquidity following the crash, served to throw the international trading system into a violent disequilibrium. The result was to destabilize the carefully reconstructed international exchange rate mechanism in which most currencies had traded in fixed relation to their gold value.

Even before the decision was taken to remove sterling from the Gold Standard in 1931, BAT Co. had experienced problems from the British

48 CDC Minutes, 13 January 1933.

49 The shares agreed were: Tobacofina, 47 per cent; Gosset, 30 per cent; BAT, 23 per cent. Cunliffe-Owen had earlier instructed Mr Odon Warland to bid for a share amounting to 25 per cent but, if Tobacofina and Gosset would not agree to this, to accept a share of 23 per cent or if necessary 22 per cent. CDC Minutes, 18 April and 12 May 1933.

50 C. P. Kindleberger, *The World in Depression, 1929–1939* (1986).

government's operation of the fixed exchange rate system. These difficulties revolved around the decision to tie the value of the Indian rupee to sterling at the fixed rate of 1s. 6d. under the Currency Act of 1927. This overvalued rate of exchange for the Indian currency, which was retained even after sterling was withdrawn from the Gold Standard, could only be supported in the long term by means of continued deflation of the Indian economy. In order to engineer this deflation, silver coins were withdrawn from circulation by the Government of India and only partially replaced by paper currency. The surplus silver was then sold off on the open market, depressing the value of the metal world-wide.[51] Households in India that predominantly held their assets in this form therefore found their purchasing power in continuous decline throughout the period. For BAT Co., the decline in the value of silver not only damaged the purchasing power of many Indian consumers, it also adversely affected the profitability in sterling terms of their operations in those markets in which silver remained the basis of the currency, most notably China. The need to restore and stabilize the relative value of silver became a recurring theme in Cunliffe-Owen's speeches during the early 1930s.[52]

Naturally, the fracturing of international economic stability after 1931 posed new difficulties for a multinational company like BAT. For one thing, the growth in nationalism made the use of expatriate managers more difficult to maintain in a number of countries,[53] and in Nazi Germany it made the continued employment of Jews in any prominent position impossible after 1933.[54] More generally, the imposition of exchange controls and the volatility of exchange rates made international financial management far more problematic in the 1930s. As Cunliffe-Owen explained to shareholders at the end of 1933:

> In many countries the exchange rate is nominal; in other countries you cannot remit at all, and in some countries you can only remit under the most stringent government regulations for the purchase of supplies.[55]

[51] Rothermund states that between 1922 and 1938 approximately 2,310 million rupee coins were taken out of circulation. D. Rothermund, *India in the Great Depression, 1929–1939* (1992), p. 36. The rate of 1s. 6d. imposed in 1927 was 12.5 per cent higher than the pre-war sterling exchange rate of 1s. 4d.

[52] *Tobacco (London)*, 51 (602) (1931), 65; 52 (614) (1932), 71; 53 (626) (1933), 73.

[53] During the 1930s, the Brazilian government introduced the Two Thirds Law which required this minimum proportion of Brazilian nationals to be represented in every category of every establishment operating in the country. *BAT News* (Spring 1990), 35.

[54] As a result of this situation the solicitor of Haus Bergmann, a Dr Kaufmann, was obliged to resign from the board of directors. He was paid a retainer by BAT Co. to work for them in London instead. CDC Minutes, 6 September 1933, 23 October 1935, and 15 December 1936.

[55] Speech made at the 1933 BAT Co. Annual General Meeting, reported in *Tobacco (London)*, 54 (638) (1934), 67.

Thus in Argentina, where funds could only be remitted in exchange for supplies, BAT Co. arranged for machinery to manufacture mouthpiece cigarettes to be shipped from Finland, drawn against the Argentine subsidiary Cia Nacional de Tobacos for the full price. It is not clear whether any mouthpiece cigarettes were ever actually made in Argentina, but the scheme was conceived as a direct response to exchange control considerations.[56] In Brazil, meanwhile, a small paper manufacturer called Pirahy was purchased as a means of consolidating profits which could not be remitted from the country.[57]

The company's international transactions in leaf tobacco also provided them with a possible means of coping with exchange restrictions. This could be achieved by manipulating the price at which intra-firm transactions were accounted for between subsidiaries, or through the purchase and shipment of leaf from regions in which currency restrictions did not hold, to other parts of the organization. The main decisions concerning leaf purchases in the US and subsequent transactions seem to have been co-ordinated by BAT Co. in London.[58] These purchases were then undertaken on behalf of BAT Co. by its American-based tobacco procurement organization, the Export Leaf Tobacco Co.

The normal procedure for leaf transactions seems to have been for BAT Co.'s head office to act as intermediary between the Export Leaf Tobacco Co. and the operating subsidiary by settling accounts on the subsidiary's behalf and then reclaiming the outstanding sum.[59] Where exchange controls were a problem however, as in the above case of Argentina, the Export Leaf Tobacco Co. would be instructed to draw on the subsidiary company's account directly.

As international trading conditions became more difficult in the 1930s, so these leaf transactions grew in complexity. After the Japanese invasion of Manchuria, remitting any funds from this part of the Chinese operation became increasingly problematic. Financial transfers could be made most easily by indirect means via leaf tobacco transactions. Thus profits generated in Manchukuo were used to purchase leaf tobacco from the Japanese Tobacco Monopoly which was then shipped for use in the company's plants in Egypt—thereby fulfilling the economic objective of the Japanese government of helping to boost the country's export earnings.[60]

56 CDC Minutes, 24 November 1932.

57 Transcript of an interview with Mr J. Banks dated 12 April 1972, p. 10.

58 Thus, for example, a decision was taken by the Chairman's Daily Committee to purchase 10 million lb. of Burley tobacco for BAT's associated companies outside of the United States. CDC Minutes, 29 January 1934.

59 BAT Archive (SASS), Doc. Nos. 14-A-38–39.

60 BAT Archive (SASS), Doc. Nos. 7-B-37–40.

In Germany, the requirement to purchase oriental tobacco from Turkey and Bulgaria following the acquisition of Haus Bergmann in 1932 also presented difficulties in terms of foreign exchange transactions. In this case, the company used the international banking system to provide financial guarantees to the local firms who undertook the purchases on BAT Co.'s behalf in the local currency. Thus in 1933 Midland Bank, jointly with the Deutsche Bank, agreed to guarantee a loan of 5 million Levas made by the Kreditbank of Sofia to the Bulgarothracian Tobacco Co. who then drew on the Sofia bank in order to purchase the required tobacco leaf for BAT in Germany.[61] This arrangement obviated the necessity for BAT Co. to actually hold financial balances in the foreign currency concerned, since the tobacco supplies could be purchased directly from the Bulgarian company through the Deutsche Bank using German Marks. At the same time, it avoided the unnecessary foreign exchange transactions which purchasing such tobacco on the New York market involved.

Under the prevailing conditions of uncertainty and dislocation in international commodity markets, direct control of sources of leaf tobacco became increasingly desirable. The company had, in any case, encouraged and supported the growing of American tobacco in the large markets of China, Brazil, and India in order to keep down costs and increase flexibility of supply sources. Between the wars a variety of tobacco growing and procurement initiatives were also undertaken in British colonies in Africa.

The first steps in this process had in fact been undertaken by BAT's British partner, the Imperial Tobacco Co., which had used experts drawn from its American leaf-purchasing organization to set up operations in Nyasaland (Malawi) in 1907.[62] BAT Co.'s South African subsidiary, the United Tobacco Cos., had begun purchasing tobacco leaf from growers in Southern Rhodesia (Zimbabwe) as early as 1905, but this was only placed on a formal basis after the First World War with the incorporation of a BAT Co. subsidiary in Salisbury (Harare) called the Tobacco Development Co. (Rhodesia) Ltd. in March 1920 as a marketing depot and a leaf tobacco buying agency.[63] In East Africa, where the company had set up its first depot to distribute imported cigarettes in Mombasa in 1908,[64] leaf growing experts were

[61] Midland Bank Archives, Records of Central Hall Branch, Westminster, Reference Book 361/17, 10 August 1933.

[62] W. Twiston-Davies, *Fifty Years of Progress: An Account of the African Organisation of the Imperial Tobacco Company* (*c.*1958), p. 68.

[63] History of UTICO Holdings Limited and its Associated Companies, BAT Co. Southampton Archive, Box 90. Of the authorized capital of £100,000 in shares of £1 each, £20,007 were issued to the United Tobacco Cos. for cash. BAT Co. Corporate Index, BAT Co. Southampton Archive, Box 114.

[64] *BAT Bulletin*, 13 (36) (1923), 809–13.

dispatched in 1927 to collaborate with the Ugandan Agricultural Department in a scheme to assist local farmers to engage in the cultivation of fire-cured tobacco leaf. The following year a cigarette manufacturing factory was set up at Jinja in Uganda.[65]

A similar pattern of development occurred in West Africa, where the first import depot had been set up in Lagos in 1911.[66] With the encouragement of the Nigerian colonial government, who granted BAT Co. a three-year excise-free holiday as an incentive, a factory was set up at Oshogbo and began to manufacture 'Bicycle' cigarettes in 1933.[67] This venture was supported by the arrival of an experienced American leaf expert, Mr E. H. Mathewson, who helped to pioneer the growing of Virginia tobacco at Ogbomosho (dark air-cured), Zaria (Bright air-cured), and Arikinkin near Oshogbo (flue-cured) during the remainder of the 1930s.[68]

The development of colonial sources of tobacco as a substitute for American-grown leaf can be seen to have played a role that reflected Cunliffe-Owen's growing preoccupation with the British Empire as an international trading bloc. These ideas found their political expression through Sir Hugo's links with Lord Beaverbrook's Empire Crusade, launched on 8 July 1929, for which he acted as treasurer.

Lord Beaverbrook, then plain Max Aitken, had come to Britain from Canada in 1910 where he had made a fortune from his corporate dealings in the cement industry. Within a short period of time he obtained a seat in Parliament as a Conservative MP and was appointed as private secretary to Bonar Law. At the same time he purchased shares in a variety of business enterprises, most notably the controlling interest in Rolls-Royce which he subsequently sold on to James Duke in 1913.[69] In 1912 he acquired control of the Colonial Bank and in 1917 he appointed Cunliffe-Owen to the bank's board of directors. This link between the two men was consolidated in 1918 following

[65] 'A History of BAT Group in Kenya', n.d., BAT Co. Southampton Archive, Box 39. BAT cigarette sales in East Africa peaked in 1930 at 450 million, falling back until a further period of growth after 1935 took them beyond 1 billion per annum during the early 1940s.

[66] *BAT Bulletin*, 12 (18) (1921), 398.

[67] J. H. Maslen, 'A Nigerian Narrative', *BAT News* (Spring 1984), 3–5. The factory was a converted cotton ginnery and was able to produce up to five million 'Bicycle' cigarettes a month using American leaf. F. Foord, 'Early Days in Nigeria', *NTC Magazine*, 3 (4) (1967), 3–6. Between 1933 and 1937 cigarette sales in West Africa increased from 500 million to slightly over 1 billion per annum. On conditions in West Africa at this time, seen from the perspective of an expatriate BAT employee, see J. H. Maslen, *Beating About the Nigerian Bush* (1994).

[68] J. H. Maslen, 'Nigerian Tobacco Co. Ltd.: History', typescript, 16 pp. BAT Co. Southampton Archive, Box 87.

[69] A. J. P. Taylor, *Beaverbrook* (1972), pp. 43 and 78.

Beaverbrook's appointment as Minister of Information in Lloyd George's War Cabinet. Cunliffe-Owen was delegated to act as Controller of Eastern Propaganda for the new Ministry (with Joseph Hood appointed as his deputy) in which capacity he organized the production and dissemination of allied propaganda directed at Turkey.[70]

At the end of the war Beaverbrook sold his interest in the Colonial Bank to Barclays and began to develop his media interests, taking control of the *Daily Express* in 1919 and the *Sunday Express* two years later.[71] For a period of time the two men rather fell out of touch, and contact between them only resumed in earnest during 1925 when Cunliffe-Owen sought to encourage both Beaverbrook and James Duke to participate in a scheme to process bauxite from British Guiana in Canada. Although this scheme was unsuccessful, the contact served to awaken a mutual interest among the two men in Imperial business matters.[72]

Beaverbrook's own economic and political ambitions came together in his Empire Free Trade Crusade. The principal motivation for this campaign was to engineer a revival in the political fortunes of the Conservative Party following its election defeat in 1929.[73] The Crusade, spearheaded by Beaverbrook's *Express* and *Evening Standard* newspapers, was designed as a populist response to the electorate's support of the Labour Party's socialist-inclined policies. At its core was an appeal to patriotism and the potential economic benefits offered by the British Empire as a protected trading bloc.[74]

Cunliffe-Owen formally publicized his support for the campaign in a pamphlet entitled 'Industry and the Empire Crusade: a statement to manufacturers' towards the end of 1929.[75] The economic crux of Cunliffe-Owen's argument was that if British manufacturers were to emulate the success of American business enterprises, it was necessary for them to fully embrace the techniques of mass production.[76] This required the support of a large, secure

70 House of Lords Record Office (HLRO), Beaverbrook Papers, BBK/E/3/9.

71 Cunliffe-Owen had also been a director of another Beaverbrook concern, Provincial Cinematograph Theatres, but resigned in 1921. His letter of resignation, dated 23 May 1921, can be found in the HLRO Beaverbrook Papers, BBK C/106.

72 Letter from Cunliffe-Owen to Beaverbrook, 25 February 1925; note from Beaverbrook to Cunliffe-Owen, 9 July 1925; letter Cunliffe-Owen to Beaverbrook, 13 July 1925, HLRO, Beaverbrook Papers, BBK C/106.

73 A. Chisholm and M. Davie, *Beaverbrook: A Life* (1992), p. 278.

74 I. M. Drummond, *British Economic Policy and the Empire, 1919–1939* (1972), pp. 31–4.

75 HLRO, Beaverbrook Papers, BBK C/106.

76 As part of this philosophy, Cunliffe-Owen became one of the first British industrialists to adopt the American system of scientific management in his factories when he introduced the Bedaux system at the Liverpool factory in 1926. J. Jones, 'Cigarettes—Liverpool 5: the Story of the Liverpool Branch of British–American Tobacco Company Ltd', p. 55. On the Bedaux system see J. Wilson, *British Business History, 1720–1994* (1995), pp. 163–4.

market for their manufactures in the same way that American firms had benefited from the huge domestic market of the United States. Thus the Empire Crusade proposed the adoption of protectionist policies against the products of America and Europe—particularly foodstuffs—as a means of strengthening the reciprocal trading potential of Empire countries for British manufacturing industries. In addition, it was envisaged by Cunliffe-Owen that a system of cartels would manage industrial output across the Empire, enabling the manufacturers in the Dominions to gain a share of orderly, managed markets for manufactured goods.

The ideas found very little favour with the opinion-makers of the Dominions—especially in Canada where Cunliffe-Owen's pamphlet was greeted with outright hostility.[77] In Britain, the campaign created temporary excitement in by-election contests, but generated little enthusiasm among industrial leaders.[78] The Crusade lost its political impetus after the collapse of the Labour government in 1931, and its economic objectives were to a certain extent satisfied by the adoption of Empire Preference at the Ottawa Conference in 1932.[79]

On the face of it, Cunliffe-Owen's support for a campaign based on protectionism seems somewhat inconsistent with his position as chairman of a multinational company, especially given the fact that it faced no serious international competition from American or European cigarette manufacturers in its main markets. In economic terms, his willingness to subscribe to the ideas of Empire Trade did reflect the belief he held in the efficacy of cartel arrangements to prevent excess supply in industries of mass production. The prime motive for his support, however, seems to have been a fear of the spread of socialism in Britain—which had been heightened by the advent of the General Strike in 1926—and the desire at all costs to prevent state ownership of industry.[80] After 1932 his interest in the campaign began to wane and when

[77] See correspondence between Cunliffe-Owen and Beaverbrook, 27 and 29 December 1929, HLRO, Beaverbrook Papers, BBK C/106.

[78] Cunliffe-Owen was unsuccessful in his attempts to solicit support for the campaign from Lord Kylsant and Dudley Docker. Those who were prepared to donate funds usually did so only on the understanding that their support was to remain anonymous. HLRO, Beaverbrook Papers, BBK C/107.

[79] Preferential rates of duty for Empire-produced tobacco were first introduced at the end of the First World War when, from 1 September 1919, a preferential rate of five-sixths of the full duty was introduced. On 1 July 1925 this was increased to three-quarters, and the maintenance of this differential was guaranteed at the Ottawa Conference. However, the degree of protection afforded to Empire-produced tobacco was reduced by the introduction of flat-rate increases which were applied to both the full and preferential rates equally in 1927 and 1931. Drummond, *British Economic Policy*, p. 131.

[80] Given the numerous state tobacco monopolies in Europe it is perhaps not surprising that this exhortation against state ownership continued as a theme of Cunliffe-Owen's speeches.

Beaverbrook invited him in 1934 to give his name to a book supporting the ideas of Empire Trade he replied:

> As you know, my company has got a world-wide business—not only in the Colonies—but in many foreign countries, and I thought it well to take up with my colleagues the question of my authorship of this book. They are very much opposed to it because they fear that it might place us in an embarrassing position in a non-Empire country.[81]

Thus with the immediate threat of socialism no longer pressing, Cunliffe-Owen's economic philosophy seems to have reverted to a stance based more on free trade.

The Tobacco Securities Trust

By the 1930s BAT's geographical expansion had largely run its course. The company now operated directly in almost fifty separate markets, ranging in size from British Guiana and the Channel Islands, selling 5–20 million cigarettes a year, to the huge markets of China, India, and Latin America in which the bulk of the company's annual sales of almost 100 billion cigarettes were located. Since many of these operating companies took the form of nominally independent concerns in which BAT Co. was the major (often only) shareholder, most of its income was derived from dividends. Thus, before the advent of consolidated company accounts, the profits which BAT Co. declared in its annual return consisted of the amounts which Cunliffe-Owen felt it appropriate for the subsidiary companies to remit, together with profits earned by BAT Co.'s own factories in Britain.[82] Indeed, when the furore concerning the use of secret accounts erupted in the British press following

See, for example, his speech to BAT Co. shareholders towards the end of the war published in *Tobacco (London)*, 64 (759) (1944), 47–9. However, his opposition towards the Labour Party moderated after the Second World War and he made concerted efforts to encourage the Labour administration under Atlee to become more involved with BAT Co.'s affairs.

[81] Letter Cunliffe-Owen to Beaverbrook, 11 May 1934, HLRO, Beaverbrook Papers, BBK C/108.

[82] Even the dividends paid by the publicly quoted Canadian subsidiary seem to have been controlled by Cunliffe-Owen. In 1933, the Imperial Tobacco Co. of Canada had attempted to resist the influence of the London board of BAT Co. over the level of dividends paid out by stating the opinion of their legal advisors that all dividends should be declared by the directors of the company (i.e., the board in Montreal) rather than the shareholders (the majority of the shares were held by BAT Co.). Cunliffe-Owen concurred with this. However, when Imperial's directors suggested an increased interim dividend to be paid in the first quarter of 1934, Cunliffe-Owen would not give the matter his approval. CDC Minutes, 1 May 1933 and 8 February 1934.

the Royal Mail case of 1931, Cunliffe-Owen was perfectly happy to admit to shareholders at BAT Co.'s AGM that their company's subsidiaries also held 'secret' reserves which were not shown in the parent company's balance sheet, since he felt that this underlined the financial strength of BAT.[83]

Cunliffe-Owen's approach to BAT's financial affairs tended to be extremely conservative, therefore, always ensuring that the financial performance of subsidiaries was properly monitored and that they retained adequate reserves wherever possible and appropriate. In his private affairs, however, he was far more willing to gamble (he owned and bred a string of racehorses) and he was perfectly prepared to be financially adventurous, bordering on the reckless, in his dealings outside of BAT. Furthermore, he seems to have held a penchant for associating with unorthodox entreprenuers and financial mavericks. This side of his business character helps to explain why, towards the end of the 1920s, Sir Hugo developed a scheme which enabled him to use part of BAT Co.'s vast dividend income to engage in more speculative dealings through the medium of an investment company called the Tobacco Securities Trust (TST).

The initial inspiration for this manoeuvre seems to have arisen from a decision to restructure the company's Indian-based subsidiaries under the aegis of a holding company, registered outside of India, in an effort to gain tax advantages from corporate consolidation.[84] For this purpose, the Raleigh Investment Co. Ltd. was registered in the Isle of Man on 8 August 1927 as a holding company for the various interests of BAT Co. in India.[85] The share capital of the Raleigh Investment Co. was set at £12.5 million, an amount far in excess of the book value of the corporate assets that were transferred into it but one which, it could be argued, more accurately reflected the true earning power of the company's Indian businesses.[86]

[83] *Tobacco (London)*, 52 (614) (1932), 71. For a summary of the Royal Mail case, in which the profits of the holding company were sustained by the running down of secret reserves held in the accounts of subsidiaries, see E. Jones, *Accountancy and the British Economy, 1840–1980* (1981), pp. 149–52.

[84] C. Basu, *Challenge and Change: The ITC Story, 1910–1985* (1988), p. 67.

[85] The Indian-based distribution and sales operation remained under the ambit of the Calcutta-registered ITC but this now became a subsidiary of the Raleigh Investment Company, while the cigarette manufacturing and leaf operations were transferred to new, Manx-registered companies, called respectively Tobacco Manufacturers (India) Ltd. and the Indian Leaf Development Company Ltd. Two further subsidiaries of Raleigh were created in 1927: Printers (India) Ltd. was formed to embrace the printing factory that had been set up alongside the Monghyr cigarette factory in 1925, and the Dominion Tobacco Co. Ltd. became registered as brand owners.

[86] In a list of Britain's 200 largest industrial enterprises for the year 1930, Raleigh's share value of £12.5 million would have placed it in twenty-fifth position. See A. D. Chandler, *Scale and Scope: The Dynamics of Industrial Capitalism* (1990), Appendix B2.

This method of using the income streams from its overseas businesses to support fresh capital assets continued the following year when BAT Co. set up two new holding companies, the Abbey Investment Co. Ltd. and Tobacco Investments Ltd., with capital values of £1.5 million and £2 million respectively. The Abbey Investment Co. was formed to consolidate a proportion of the income that BAT Co. received from its South-East Asian export business. In return for a cash consideration of £1.5 million (the capital value of Abbey) BAT Co. agreed to give Abbey a perpetual 40 per cent share of its net annual profits from the shipments of goods to the Straits Settlements and 40 per cent of the net annual profits (in excess of £25,000) that were derived from shipments of its goods to the Dutch East Indies.

Tobacco Investments Ltd. (originally called International Investments) was incorporated in order to hold shares in various associated companies of BAT Co. which were not quoted on any recognized stock exchange, thereby holding a fixed percentage of BAT Co.'s interest in each of these territories. Table 9.4 provides a breakdown of those interests which BAT Co. sold to Tobacco Investments for £2 million, including 50 per cent of its equity holding in the Abbey Investment Co. Through the formation of these two holding companies, therefore, BAT Co. effectively hived off around 20 per cent of the income from its main overseas subsidiaries and 40 per cent of its earnings on exports to South East Asia into separate concerns.

The next step in this process of corporate restructuring was the formation in London of TST. This was floated in September 1928 with an authorized share capital of £5 million, divided into 4 million ordinary shares of £1 and 4 million deferred shares of 5s. 0d. At the time of the flotation, BAT Co. subscribed for £1 million of the ordinary share issue and 50,000 of the deferred shares. The bulk of the remainder of the shares were issued to BAT Co.'s ordinary shareholders (which of course included the Imperial Tobacco Co.) at a rate of one £1 ordinary unit of stock and one 5s. 0d. deferred unit of stock for every eight BAT Co. shares held. As a result of this rights issue, BAT Co. ordinary shareholders received a total of 3 million £1 ordinary units of stock in TST and 3 million 5s. 0d. deferred units of stock in TST worth £750,000.[87] This total of £3.75 million was made up of a proportion of the shares in the publicly quoted companies based in Australia, Canada, and South Africa, together with the entire £2 million share capital of Tobacco Investments (Table 9.5).

[87] The transfer of these assets of £3.75 million was accounted for in BAT Co.'s own balance sheet for September 1929 by the writing down of £1.166 million. Cunliffe-Owen pointed out to shareholders at the following AGM in January 1930 that the value at which the shares of subsidiary companies were carried in BAT Co.'s books was considerably below their true asset value. Clearly, therefore, the creation of TST partly involved an expansion of BAT Co.'s share capital. For Cunliffe-Owen's speech see *Tobacco (London)*, 50 (590) (1930), 72.

TABLE 9.4. BAT Co. operating subsidiaries' shareholdings sold to Tobacco Investments Ltd.

% of BAT holding	No. of shares	Description	Market
15	3,600	$25 shares in Imperial Tobacco Co. (Newfoundland) Ltd.	Newfoundland
20	48,684	£1 ordinary shares in B. & J. B. Machado Tobacco Co. Ltd.	Jamaica
20	8,923	WI$ 5 shares in West Indian Tobacco Co. Ltd.	Trinidad
20	20	£1 shares in British Cigarette Co. (E) Ltd.	China
20	18,603	Florins 100 shares in BAT Co. (Java) Ltd.	Dutch East Indies
20	10,000	Florins 100 shares in BAT Co. (NI) Ltd.	Dutch East Indies
20	10,000	Florins 100 shares in Java Leaf Tobacco Development Co. Ltd.	Dutch East Indies
20	12,000	£1 shares in Thomas Bear & Sons Ltd.	India
26	2,343,750	£1 ordinary shares in The Raleigh Investment Co. Ltd.	India
25	1,875	£1 shares in BAT Co. (Ceylon) Ltd.	Ceylon
20	6,000	£1 shares in BAT Co. (Straits) Ltd.	Straits Settlements
50	750,000	£1 shares in Abbey Investment Co. Ltd.	South-East Asia
15	8,982	Kr.100 shares in American Tobacco Co. Ltd.	Denmark
10	167	£30 shares in Black Horse Tobacco Co. Ltd.	Mexico
10	6,096	Ps100 common shares in Cia. Manufactura de Cigarros 'El Aguila' SA	Mexico
15	9,000	AP$100 shares in Cia. Nacional de Tabacos	Argentina
15	4,499	Bol. 100 common shares in Cia. Anonima Cigarrera Bigott Sucs	Venezuela
20	20,000	£1 ordinary shares in Cia. Continental de Cigarros Ltd.	Brazil
17.5	187,939	Mex$ 100 ordinary shares in BAT Co. (China) Ltd.	China
5	1,250	£E100 ordinary shares in Eastern Co. SAE.	Egypt
5	194	£E100 participating bonds in Eastern Co. SAE.	Egypt

Source: BAT Co. Secretarial Dept. Records.

TABLE 9.5. BAT Co. subsidiaries' shares sold to Tobacco Securities Trust

% of BAT holding	No. of shares	Description
20	724,394	$1 ordinary shares in British Tobacco Co. (Australia) Ltd.
25	1,136,160	$5 ordinary shares in Imperial Tobacco Co. of Canada Ltd.
20	356,160	£1 ordinary shares in United Tobacco Cos. (South) Ltd.
100	2,000,000	£1 ordinary shares in International Investments (Tobacco Investments) Ltd.

Source: BAT Co. Secretarial Dept. Records.

The share structure of TST was unusually complex, with BAT Co.'s original shareholding being given greater voting weight in order to ensure that it retained effective control. The breakdown of share ownership in TST after the rights issue had taken place is shown in Table 9.6. The division of the capital into ordinary and deferred stock was deliberately designed in order to permit speculative investments over and above the tobacco-based assets. The company agreed to pay a preferential dividend to the ordinary shareholders of 15 per cent. This, it was felt, would be the return which could be anticipated on the tobacco-based assets. Any residual profits were to be paid as dividends to the ordinary and deferred shareholders in equal proportion; thus each 5s. 0d. deferred share would earn the same as each £1 ordinary share in respect of these additional profits. Hence the deferred shares were high risk, but would pay high dividends if the speculative investments proved to be successful. As Table 9.6 shows, in addition to the 750,000 deferred stock issued to BAT Co. ordinary shareholders, an additional 112,000 had been issued by 1 November 1928, and it seems certain that these had been purchased by the leading protagonists in the TST initiative.

Given the relative financial sophistication of the TST scheme, it is not surprising to find that one of Britain's top financial experts played a central role in its development. The individual who was appointed as chairman of TST was Reginald McKenna, chairman of the Midland Bank and a former Chancellor of the Exchequer. Cunliffe-Owen, who had also been a director of Midland Bank since 1924, was appointed vice-chairman and he, McKenna, and BAT Co.'s solicitor, Fred Macnaghten, took the main responsibility for its policy decisions. Thus by the beginning of the 1930s, Cunliffe-Owen's business empire effectively included control over a small investment bank as well as a vast multinational tobacco company.

The central objectives of TST were to provide venture capital for new business initiatives within Britain and, at the same time, to utilize its financial resources with a certain degree of opportunism in the face of other

TABLE 9.6. Share capital of the Tobacco Securities Trust Co. Ltd. at 1 November 1928

Ordinary shares and stock					
Shares of £1 each (No.)			Stock in £1 units (value)		
Issued	Owned by	Number	Issued	Owned by	Value
1,000,000	BAT Co.	850,000	3,000,000	BAT Co.	£222,741
	I.T.Co.	150,000		I.T.Co.	£684,259
				Sundry	£2,092,000
Deferred shares and stock					
Shares of 5/- each (No.)			Stock in 5/- units (value)		
Issued	Owned by	Number	Issued	Owned by	Value
50,000	BAT Co.	36,000	£862,000	BAT Co.	£9,183
	I.T.Co.	14,000		I.T.Co.	£205,814
				Sundry	£646,703

Source: BAT Co. Secretarial Dept. Records.

profitable openings. During the early 1930s TST became involved in the support of a number of important businesses in Britain. Two companies which TST helped to develop were the construction-related businesses of Taylor Woodrow and Marley Tile.[88] The latter company retained especially close links with BAT for a number of years.[89] More important in generating profits for TST, however, were short-term, speculative transactions.[90] One such transaction occurred in 1933 when TST, in partnership with the second Lord Trent, helped to finance the purchase of 1 million shares in Boots the chemist from the US combine, Drug Inc., to whom Jesse Boot had sold out in 1928.[91]

In 1934 however, TST's financial opportunism overreached itself when a subsidiary of Tobacco Investments called the Dean Finance Co. became involved in an attempt to corner the markets for pepper and shellac in Britain. TST's involvement in this scheme seems to have stemmed from Reginald McKenna's connection with one of the parties engaged in the transactions, John Howeson.[92] The episode ultimately earned Howeson a term in prison

[88] *BAT News* (Spring 1988), 18.

[89] F. Wellings, *The History of Marley* (1994).

[90] *Tobacco (London)*, 55 (649) (1935), xvi.

[91] S. Chapman, *Jesse Boot* (1973).

[92] On Howeson's links with McKenna, see J. Hillman, 'The Impact of the International Tin Restriction Scheme on the Return to Equity of Tin Mining', *Business History*, 39 (3), (1997), 65–80.

and served to damage the reputations of both McKenna and Cunliffe-Owen when the scandal broke in the popular press.

The events in question began towards the end of 1933 when a firm of merchants, Williams, Henry & Co., contracted to buy substantial quantities of both shellac and pepper for forward delivery in the hope of holding up the market in each commodity long enough to create a shortage and thus make a profit from the price increase. A finance company led by Garabed Bishirgian had acted as broker for the deal. Also around this time the Dean Finance Co. had themselves purchased a small quantity of shellac and had provided a loan to Williams, Henry & Co. which was secured against a bill of sale for more shellac. Problems began to arise when it became clear that, in spite of a further loan from the Dean Finance Co. in August 1934, Williams, Henry & Co. lacked the full funds required to cover their position on shellac due for delivery in September. At this point, Bishirgian, Howeson, and another merchant, Louis Hardy, issued a prospectus to increase the capital of a partner firm, James & Shakspeare, which could be used to acquire an interest in Williams, Henry & Co. and thus finance the shellac contract. This prospectus omitted to mention the outstanding commitments that Williams, Henry & Co. held in relation to the contracted shellac deliveries.

During the last quarter of 1934, the funding for the pepper and shellac scheme fell apart. The Dean Finance Co. had put up funds, together with John Howeson, to finance the next consignment of shellac which was due for delivery in December, but prior to this a member of the underwriting firm for the James & Shakspeare flotation learned of Williams, Henry & Co.'s outstanding commitments on the September consignment of shellac. Still worse, at this point it was also revealed that the latter firm had accrued commitments against pepper deliveries to the extent of £1.6 million. On discovering this situation the Dean Finance Co. refused to proceed with their loan to Williams, Henry & Co. and that firm defaulted on its commitments and was served with a compulsory winding-up order in February 1935.[93] Bishirgian, Howeson, and Hardy were all charged under the Larceny Act with publishing a prospectus known to be false in a material particular, and a first-class financial scandal met the full glare of publicity. Howeson's eventual fate of imprisonment was avoided by Bishirgian only through the recourse of taking his own life.

Cunliffe-Owen faced the wrath of his fellow directors on the board of TST because the entire scheme to speculate on the price of shellac via the Dean Finance Co. had been undertaken without any reference to them whatsoever. Imperial's two representatives on the TST board, Lord Bradbury and Sowerby, Imperial's solicitor, were absolutely furious at Cunliffe-Owen's

[93] *Economist*, 30 November 1935, pp. 1078–9.

recklessness in the matter. The impact of the shellac losses on the profitability of TST in 1935 was substantial, reducing net revenues by approximately one-third to £527,103. Nevertheless a full 15 per cent dividend was paid to ordinary shareholders. In certain respects, TST had been rather fortunate to escape with such limited financial consequences. The bills of sale which served as security for the loans made to Williams, Henry & Co. against the shellac had never been registered on TST's behalf by BAT Co.'s solicitor Fred Macnaghten and were, consequently, quite worthless.[94] Fortunately for the shareholders, BAT Co. had taken physical possession of the shellac. Huge stocks of the commodity were stored at the company's Southampton plant where they remained for several years before being gradually sold off as the price recovered.[95]

The affair effectively brought to an end the speculative activities of TST. At the following year's Annual General Meeting it was announced that Reginald McKenna had resigned as chairman of the company and his place had been taken by Lord Catto, formerly Governor of the Bank of England,[96] who immediately announced that TST from now on would limit its field of investment solely to tobacco-related concerns.[97]

An Empire in Retreat

As the 1930s wore on, the international political environment in which BAT operated began to grow increasingly hostile. A foretaste of the problems to come was provided by the Japanese annexation of Manchuria in 1931, whilst the full-scale invasion of China six years later began the process of decline in BAT's operations in South-East Asia as a whole during the 1940s. As BAT fought its rearguard action in China during the late 1930s, so events in Europe continued their slide towards full-scale war. At the Chairman's Daily Committee meeting of 1 September 1939, as German troops began their invasion of Poland, it was recommended that provision should be made to increase facilities for the manufacture of BAT's goods in the UK. A floor of the Southampton factory which had been used for the storage of bonded goods was now to be utilized for manufacturing, and all machinery not required for immediate use elsewhere was collected together for use in the

94 Interview with Sir Duncan Oppenheim, 7 March 1997.

95 Batchelor-Smith, *Loom of Memories*, p. 68.

96 See *BAT News* (Autumn 1987), p. 10.

97 *Tobacco (London)*, 57 (673) (1937), 51.

English factories.[98] A few weeks earlier, following the requisition of Westminster House by the Ministry of Fuel and Power,[99] 400 members of staff from BAT Co.'s headquarters and their equipment had been relocated to Rusham House in Egham, Surrey, with the help of a fleet of Marley Tile platform lorries and a few of Sir Hugo's horseboxes.[100]

The declaration of war against Germany immediately led to the loss of control of the company's plants in Hamburg and Dresden, and the German companies were placed under the supervision of a Dr Zarnack who had been appointed as Custodian of Enemy Property. Fortunately the company's solicitor, Dr Buch, attended loyally to BAT's interests throughout the duration of the war and was able to thwart an attempt by Reemtsma to have the BAT properties amalgamated with his own.[101] The loss of the German subsidiary was followed in 1940 by similar reverses in Denmark (March), Holland (April), Belgium and the Channel Islands (June), and Finland in August 1941, as Europe continued to be overrun. After the loss of the Finnish operation, Switzerland constituted the only market in Europe where BAT Co. retained local operations.

These setbacks in Europe were soon dwarfed by events in BAT's markets in the Far East. In occupied China, BAT's sales were suspended by the authorities in August 1941 following the American government's decision to freeze Japanese credits. Thereafter, operating conditions in the Chinese market became subject to continual disruption and the imposition of financial controls by the Japanese.[102] The parent company in London lost all influence over its activities in China during December 1941, following the declaration of war against Japan by the United States government. After this, for around a year, the expatriate personnel based in China were obliged to assist in the operation of BAT's plants under Japanese supervision before being interned for the remainder of the conflict.[103]

A similar fate soon befell BAT operations elsewhere in South-East Asia. French Indo-China was fully occupied by the Japanese in July 1941, and in Siam the local managing director negotiated the sale of the company's assets

98 CDC Minutes, 1 September 1939.

99 L. Dennett, 'BAT Industries: a historical note'. Unpublished typescript (1987), p. 14.

100 *Tobacco (London)*, 61(727) (1941), 43; *BAT News* (Spring 1988), p. 19. BAT Co.'s headquarters was to remain in Egham until October 1953.

101 As a result of the work of Dr Buch, no scheme for compensation was ever put forward by BAT Co. against the loss of control over these assets. At the end of the war Reemtsma was imprisoned by the Allies for supplying a squadron of aircraft to the Luftwaffe, and BAT was able to negotiate an increased share of the German market. Interview with Sir Duncan Oppenheim, 7 March 1997.

102 BAT Archive (SASS), Document Nos. 20-B-3–9 and 32–33.

103 For a personal account written by P. Whitting see *BAT News* (Spring 1987), pp. 37–40.

there to the government just two days before the arrival of Japanese troops in December 1941.[104] Within the first few months of 1942 the company's main territories in the rest of the Far East had fallen under Japanese control. The islands of the Dutch East Indies, whose oil installations were a major target of the Japanese military expansion, were captured in February 1942 and the same month witnessed the surrender of Singapore and the end of British control in Malaya. Japanese troops then moved forward into Burma where BAT sales ceased to be recorded. The effect of these losses on BAT Co.'s sales statistics was dramatic, with the company's foreign subsidiaries and overseas depots as a whole experiencing a decline in volume from 149 billion sticks in 1940/1 to 98 billion sticks in 1941/2.

As a consequence of these setbacks, by 1942/3 two-thirds of BAT's sales were located in the western hemisphere and the largest single market for its cigarettes had become the United States, where consumption of Brown & Williamson's products now exceeded 25 billion sticks. The massive contribution that Brown & Williamson made to BAT Co.'s sales performance during this traumatic period, however, was not matched by an equivalent flow of profits from its American subsidiary. The reason for this lay in Britain's desperate need for US dollars to finance imports of American supplies and munitions in the period before the signing of the Lend–Lease Bill by President Roosevelt in March 1941.

Attempts by the British government to obtain aid from the United States in its war effort against the Axis powers met various obstacles before 1941. Although the incumbent Roosevelt administration was sympathetic towards Britain's cause, it faced the problem of maintaining popular support among the American electorate as it fought out the final stages of the presidential campaign of 1940. Roosevelt was aware that much public opinion in the United States simply failed to appreciate the vulnerability of Britain's economy at this time. Many Americans who wanted the country to retain its neutral stance in relation to the European conflict felt that Britain, with its huge empire, already had the resources it needed to purchase its war needs and should be required to trade normally with America. Giving aid to Britain would, it was argued, simply drag the United States into the conflict. Moreover, two pieces of legislation served to prevent the American government from extending credit to the British state. The Johnson Act proscribed the making of monetary loans to foreign governments, and the Neutrality Act of 1939 required the full payment for all goods traded to belligerent countries before they left the United States.

[104] Unlike Shell, who abandoned its distribution activities in Siam before the Japanese invasion, BAT had a vested interest in the leaf development scheme and negotiated its withdrawal with reluctance. Personal communication with P. Tindley, 16 August and 22 October 1997.

In response to these difficulties, the British Treasury considered a variety of methods which might be used to expand the country's gold and US dollar reserves during the latter part of 1940. One obvious way in which this could be achieved was through the liquidation of foreign investments, most especially those actually held in the United States itself. The main responsibility for attending to this matter seems to have fallen to Sir Frederick Phillips for whom a number of papers were prepared in the autumn of 1940.[105] From BAT Co.'s point of view the most significant of these was a note from Lord Catto, the chairman of TST. Catto considered the feasibility of raising dollars for the British war effort by means of selling off the US-registered subsidiaries of British corporations to American investors, and he identified fifty-five such British-owned subsidiary enterprises. The note began by highlighting the less liquid nature of such direct investments compared with simple marketable securities, and then turned to the practical difficulties of raising funds by means of the sale of these assets. In this respect he noted that many such subsidiary concerns were of limited value unless they continued to operate as part of an integrated enterprise linked to the parent company in Britain. Thus simply selling the subsidiaries to American investors as independent operations would be highly inefficient. In addition, he added, many of the concerns in question were not profitable. Faced with these difficulties, therefore, Catto suggested that the only method whereby dollars might be raised in a way that would give real security to an American investor would be in the form of a prior charge (such as a bond or preferred stock) on the American subsidiary's property and business.[106]

The points made by Lord Catto were taken up in a secret memorandum from the Treasury to the Chancellor of the Exchequer dated 4 November 1940. This memo began as follows:

> Mr [Henry] Morgenthau [US Treasury Secretary and the British government's main point of contact in the Roosevelt administration] had asked that Sir Frederick Phillips should pay a further visit to Washington about 1st December. The Marquis of Lothian [British Ambassador in Washington] has confirmed previous views that the United States Administration will be willing to give us substantial financial assistance, but he has added:-
>
> i. that it may take them some time, perhaps six months, to get the necessary legislation through Congress;

[105] These papers included contributions from two eminent British economists of the time, J. M. Keynes and D. H. Robertson. See PRO Treasury papers T 160/995/F19422.

[106] T 160/995/F19422. The concerns which are explicitly mentioned by Lord Catto in his note are the Distillers Co., Dunlop, Courtaulds, and Shell Oil. Unfortunately, the full list of the fifty-five companies with important subsidiaries in the United States is not included in the file.

ii. that, in order to forestall public and Congressional criticism, they will require us to show that we have exhausted our available resources, including, in particular, our direct investments in the United States and our investments in South America.[107]

Sir Frederick Phillips then departed for negotiations in the United States and he was followed, early in 1941, by Sir Edward Peacock armed with a list of British direct investments in the form of US subsidiary corporations that could be used to raise dollars.[108] The first British company to suffer the consequences of this policy was the textile firm Courtaulds who, in March 1941, was forced to sell off its US subsidiary, the American Viscose Corporation.[109]

One month earlier, in February 1941, Cunliffe-Owen had been summoned to the Treasury for a meeting with Frederick Leith-Ross and informed that his company must sell off its Brown & Williamson subsidiary in order to raise dollars. With little choice in the matter, Cunliffe-Owen reluctantly acquiesced to the Treasury's demand and the company's finance director, David Melville, was immediately dispatched to New York in a Royal Navy destroyer. In the meantime, the sale of the American Viscose Corporation had generated publicity in America which helped to evoke greater sympathy towards Britain's plight and Cunliffe-Owen was able to persuade the British government to allow BAT Co. scope for raising dollars without actually handing over control of Brown & Williamson.[110]

On his arrival in New York, Melville met up with Brown & Williamson's lawyer, Colonel Hartfield, with a view to formulating a plan by which BAT Co. could use the assets of Brown & Williamson to raise dollars without the company surrendering control of its American subsidiary. Within a few days the two men, along with Sir Edward Peacock, began to engage in loan negotiations with Jesse Jones of the Reconstruction Finance Corporation (RFC)—a US government sponsored financial institution.[111] On 4 April 1941 Sir Frederick Phillips telegraphed to the Treasury in London the news that; 'Jones had offered American management of Brown [&] Williamson a loan to enable them to buy out British interests.' Twelve days later, Phillips relayed the following message from Melville to Cunliffe-Owen: 'Loan of

[107] T 160/995/F19422.

[108] FO 371/28797/W3574.

[109] FO 371/28797/W4284.

[110] *Tobacco (London)*, 62 (735) (1942), 43.

[111] The RFC had been established in January 1932 with a capital endowment of $500 million and was empowered to extend extraordinary loans to banks in need. During 1933, it had been used by Roosevelt and Morgenthau to purchase stocks of gold as part of the Warren plan to reverse the decline in agricultural prices. B. Eichengreen, *Golden Fetters: the Gold Standard and the Great Depression, 1919–1939* (1992), pp. 323–47; Kindleberger, *The World in Depression*, pp. 198 and 221–4.

$40,000,000 [forty million dollars] completed. Will cable full details tomorrow, through Peacock.'[112]

The scheme to raise dollars through the Brown & Williamson subsidiary, which Melville and Hartfield had developed with the RFC, exactly mirrored that proposed in Lord Catto's earlier memorandum. The loan of $40 million made to Brown & Williamson was used partly to repay a $15 million overdraft with the Guaranty Trust Company of New York. The remaining $25 million was used to redeem the outstanding bond and preference share issues held by the parent company in London.[113] As a result of this arrangement, BAT Co. received $25 million which it paid over to the British Treasury in return for an equivalent amount of sterling. Crucially, however, the deal allowed BAT Co. to retain the whole of the common shares of Brown & Williamson, in return for an agreement to forgo any dividends on these s hares for a period of five years or until at least $10 million had been repaid.[114] Thus BAT Co.'s earnings from the Brown & Williamson subsidiary were forfeited in return for the sterling equivalent of $25 million. Importantly, however, the company had retained control of its prime American asset at a time when its operations were beginning to generate positive returns.

As the war continued, a rising share of the company's business became focused on sales to the military authorities. In America, sales by Brown & Williamson to the military between 1943 and 1945 were an important factor in raising the profitability of BAT Co.'s American subsidiary. By the end of the war, BAT Co.'s direct sales (i.e., goods that were not sold through a subsidiary or foreign depot) accounted for almost 15 per cent of the total, whilst in 1939 they had amounted to barely 1 per cent. The longer-term impact of the war, however, was less favourable. The dispatching of American troops to Europe and Asia brought with it the type of American blended cigarettes which had not previously played a significant role in the international market. After the war, the American manufacturers seized the opportunity to cut into BAT Co.'s market share in countries where, before 1940, the bulk of the competition for BAT brands had come from domestic manufacturers. The international cigarette industry which emerged in the post-war world was rather more in the nature of a global oligopoly as American firms such as R. J. Reynolds and Philip Morris and, later, the Rembrandt Group of South Africa, challenged BAT Co.'s dominant position.[115]

[112] FO 371/28797/W3953.

[113] A full breakdown of the assets used to secure the loan of $25 million, which included all the preference shares and 15,000 common shares in Smith Paper Inc., Mass., are detailed in a letter from D. G. M. Bernard of the Bank of England to T. K. Bewley of the Treasury dated 18 April 1941 in FO 371/28797/W3953.

[114] *Tobacco (London)*, 62 (735) (1942), 43.

[115] For background on the international development of these rivals to BAT Co. see UNCTAD, *Marketing and Distribution of Tobacco* (1978), pp. 33–52.

The political changes wrought by the war also acted against BAT Co.'s interests in many cases. The rise of communist regimes, most particularly in China, allied to the fact that most of the markets of Europe remained under state control, meant that the geographical boundaries of the international tobacco market receded after 1945. Moreover, the process of decolonization brought various problems of market dislocation in its wake which in some cases—such as in Egypt under Nasser—proved more than just temporary setbacks.

Unfortunately for BAT, the organization was soon forced to confront these post-war challenges without the experience of Sir Hugo Cunliffe-Owen to guide them. During the war, at a time when a German invasion of Britain appeared highly probable, steps had been put in place to transfer the company's headquarters to the United States. One of the BAT Co. directors, Gray Miller, who had served for many years as the chairman of the Canadian subsidiary, was sent to Brown & Williamson's headquarters in Louisville with the necessary papers to re-register BAT Co. as a company under US law. Although this scheme was never put into practice, during the war Cunliffe-Owen began to consider the question of his successor and eventually settled his mind on appointing Gray Miller as the next BAT Co. chairman.[116]

On 20 February 1945, six months before Cunliffe-Owen's 75th birthday, Gray Miller was officially appointed to the position of chairman of BAT Co., with Sir Hugo adopting the title of president. However, Cunliffe-Owen does not seem to have considered Gray Miller's appointment as curtailing his own activities within the company. Thus when, on hearing news of the succession, Lord Beaverbrook wrote to his friend expressing the hope that the changes would not bring to an end Sir Hugo's active involvement in business affairs, the latter replied:

> I am, by no means, retiring from active participation in the business of British–American Tobacco Company; in fact, beyond the change in title, the new step will make no difference in my activities.

He continued:

> I feel that the years are running on and that, sooner or later, Gray Miller would actively have to take my place. I, therefore, thought it well that he should do so

[116] Cunliffe-Owen had two sons from his first marriage, Hugo and Dudley, and two daughters. Sir Hugo was fiercely opposed to the idea of BAT Co. becoming a family dynasty in the way of traditional British tobacco firms, and there was never any possibility of either of his sons taking on a role within the company. In fact the eldest son, Hugo Leslie, was killed on active service during the war, which was a devastating blow to Sir Hugo. The younger son, Dudley, did take on a role in Cunliffe-Owen's aircraft company after the war. *BAT News* (Autumn 1987), pp. 8–11.

> whilst I am still here, so that I could help and guide him, particularly, as to his becoming better known, which, of course, will be one of his difficulties.[117]

Sadly for Cunliffe-Owen's plans, Gray Miller lapsed into ill health shortly after succeeding to the chairmanship and died a little over two years later. Cunliffe-Owen continued to act as effective chairman of the company from his position as president, and appointed the long-serving but ailing Harold Gough to succeed Gray Miller in May 1947.

At the age of 77, however, the strain on Sir Hugo's health of the many difficult problems that faced BAT Co. in the immediate post-war era now became acute. To compound matters, another aspect of Sir Hugo's business life began to throw up severe problems. During the 1930s Cunliffe-Owen had become involved in the civil aircraft industry and, with the onset of the war, the range of activities undertaken at his company's factory in Eastleigh were greatly extended. When the war ended, and orders fell away, maintaining the aircraft company's viability became another factor pressing upon Sir Hugo's mind. A new ten- to fourteen-seater aircraft had been developed after the war, but its performance at the Radlett flying display in September 1947 failed to impress and the continued financial viability of the company was placed in jeopardy. Production of the aeroplane was suspended in November and, on 14 December 1947, Sir Hugo Cunliffe-Owen died of a heart attack at his home in Sunningdale.[118]

The loss of Cunliffe-Owen was a severe blow to BAT Co. at a crucial time in its corporate history. Gough was able to continue as chairman only for another two years before his health collapsed, and his successor, the production manager Thomas Field Winmill, found adjusting to the role of chairman well-nigh impossible. Not until Winmill's death in 1953, and the succession of Duncan Oppenheim, did the company seriously embark upon a process of reorganization and managerial delegation which was able to fill some of the many gaps left by the loss of Sir Hugo's leadership.

117 Letter from Cunliffe-Owen to Beaverbrook dated 2 March 1945, BBK C/108.

118 R. P. T. Davenport-Hines, 'Sir Hugo von Reitzenstein Cunliffe-Owen' in D. J. Jeremy (ed.) *Dictionary of Business Biography* (1984), vol. 1, pp. 865–9.

Conclusion

10

The Global Cigarette

Introduction

THE cigarette industry provides a particularly enlightening case study of international business development in the period before the Second World War because it represents one of the first lines of business in which manufacturing firms attempted to expand their foreign sales by means of a transfer of production and management technology directly to the markets concerned. The thrust behind this burst of international growth was provided by the competitive rivalry that developed between tobacco firms based in Britain and America as they increasingly attempted to expand the sales of mass-produced cigarettes beyond their home markets from the late 1880s.

A feature of this international expansion is that it coincided with the evolution in America of new type of industrial and organizational enterprise: the professionally managed corporation. In contrast to the traditional family firm which hitherto had dominated manufacturing activity in industrialized countries, the modern corporation was designed to cope with rapid advances in the volume of production and developed organizational structures that were capable of diffusing management expertise across a previously inconceivable breadth of commercial activity. Such organizational structures enabled these American corporations to grow extremely rapidly during the closing decade of the nineteenth century, expanding both organically and by means of acquisition and merger. In seeking to exploit markets abroad, such corporations were well equipped to move beyond the simple export-based method of operation, in which products were dispatched for distribution by independent import agents, and were able to extend their organizational compass directly into foreign economies, supervising their own systems of production and distribution. A study of the early evolution of the international cigarette industry therefore provides an opportunity to explore questions regarding the benefits of such a direct approach to serving customers abroad compared with the more conventional arm's-length strategies employed by traditional family-based firms.

Moving beyond this initial phase, a detailed study of the subsequent growth of cigarette manufacturing during the first half of the twentieth century also permits an exploration of international expansion as it was affected by changing economic conditions. As outlined in Chapter 1, the international cigarette industry experienced four broad phases of competition between the 1880s and the Second World War: an initially competitive phase (*c.*1880–1902) during which the expanding trade in cigarette exports was supplemented, and in some cases superseded, by direct investment; a monopoly phase (1902–*c.*1918) when the creation of the Anglo-American joint venture BAT Co. led to a general cessation of competition in international markets between the leading cigarette manufacturers in Britain and the United States; a period of renewed competition (*c.*1918–29) following the dissolution of the tobacco trust in America and the emergence of new competitors in Britain; and finally an era of cartels (1929–*c.*1945) as declining incomes, trade dislocation, and the increasingly restrictive policies of nationalism encouraged the replacement of market-based competition with collusive agreements and price controls. During each of these phases, the form of competition within the global cigarette industry took on a different complexion.

The willingness of some American cigarette manufacturers to adopt a strategy of foreign direct investment during the 1890s also meant that the industry provided one of the first examples of a market-driven multinational corporation (MNC)—the business institution which came to dominate international economic transactions during the second half of the twentieth century. Although a number of manufacturing firms from Europe and America had made foreign investments by 1914,[1] what made the cigarette industry particularly remarkable was the fact that, in BAT Co., the industry spawned a company whose very survival depended upon its ability to develop into a successful MNC. This feature of the company's history stems from the fact that the agreement between the British and American firms which brought BAT Co. into existence on 27 September 1902 also denied it access to the two countries' markets in which both its shareholders and its headquarters were located. With an almost complete absence of organizational models available

[1] For an overview see H. Cox, 'The Evolution of International Business Enterprise', in R. John (ed.), *Global Business Strategy* (1997), pp. 9–46; G. Jones, *The Evolution of International Business: an Introduction* (1996), pp. 99–146.

for it to emulate, BAT Co. was thus obliged to develop systems of international management that were essentially its own creation, but which naturally drew on elements of both its American and British progenitors. The present study therefore provides an opportunity to explore the evolution of a pioneering MNC and to assess the strengths and weaknesses of the international management system that it created.

The Changing Nature of Internationalization in the Cigarette Industry

The emergence of cigarette manufacturing as an export-based form of international business actually predated the mechanization of the production process. Hand-rolled cigarettes manufactured in the factories of American firms such as Allen & Ginter were being exported to Britain during the early 1880s as a novel form of tobacco smoking and, with their colourful packaging and innovative advertising, they represented the first of a number of American fads to find a market within Europe. A little later, a combination of Greek, Egyptian, and Armenian tobacco manufacturers produced hand-rolled cigarettes in Cairo which were exported to a growing number of depots around the world. As relatively expensive luxury items, however, the export market for these products was largely confined to the upper classes and cigarettes remained a peripheral element within the range of manufactured tobacco products. Nevertheless, the experience gained by these firms helped to prepare the ground for the rapid expansion in the cigarette export trade that occurred in the 1890s.

The decisive breakthrough for the cigarette industry really occurred around 1885 when the successful mechanization of the hand-rolling process allowed for huge gains in productivity and thus a dramatic fall in the average price of the product. Machine-made cigarettes selling at affordable prices and marketed using the popular media and strong brand images quickly demonstrated the potential which the new product held as an item of mass consumption. Having already established their products in foreign markets during the 1880s, the group of five leading American cigarette manufacturers who joined together to form the American Tobacco Company (ATC) in 1890 made strenuous efforts to further develop their international sales and by 1900 this part of the business accounted for around one-third of the sales of all cigarettes manufactured by ATC in its American factories.

Although mechanization drastically reduced production costs, cigarettes remained a relatively expensive form of tobacco consumption and most of these early exports were sold to customers in the higher income markets of

Canada and Europe—especially Britain and Germany—and to settlers, expatriates, and military elements in the markets of Australia, South Africa, India, and the West Indies. The main region in which cigarettes were first successfully marketed to non-Western consumers was in East Asia. In Japan and China the new product found immediate favour with indigenous consumers and by the beginning of the twentieth century Asian markets accounted for over 50 per cent of American cigarette exports. In Japan, acceptance by consumers of cigarettes was helped by the fact that a similar type of tobacco product, featuring a mouthpiece, had already gained popularity. The same was true in parts of north China, and cigarette smoking in some parts of the country also provided a substitute for the diminishing trade in opium.

Initially, international trade in cigarettes was developed through the formation of links with importers abroad who handled the marketing of the product and used their connections with wholesalers to manage the distribution of the goods to retailers. This system provided a useful mechanism for developing a base in foreign markets but it also created a variety of problems for the exporting firm. The English firm W. D. & H. O. Wills, for example, found that one of their main importers in South Africa was using the company's 'Three Castles' brand of smoking tobacco to manufacture cigarettes which it then marketed under the 'Three Castles' name despite the fact that the tobacco actually used by Wills in this brand of cigarettes was quite different to its packet tobacco of the same name. Worse still for the British firm was the discovery that other South African firms were marketing imitations of their cigarettes on a completely independent basis using their own tobacco. This left Wills with little choice other than to license its most trustworthy distributor to manufacture its products directly within South Africa and instruct them to invoke legal measures to protect the integrity of the company's trade marks. In general however, despite the difficulties of management inherent in the agency-based export trade, British tobacco manufacturers showed a marked reluctance to transfer production abroad in any form.

By contrast, ATC and its precursors had quickly appreciated the importance of transferring key skills abroad through the relocation of personnel from their export department to act as local representatives. Having created a system of marketing and distribution for their products which spanned the vast market of the United States, James Duke moved during the 1890s to set up similar depots in a number of its foreign markets using salaried staff whom he felt able to trust. Equally critical for success in international markets, however, was the ability to provide retailers with a reliable supply of low-priced cigarettes. The rival American cigarette manufacturer Cameron & Cameron, for instance, who attempted to compete with Duke's firm in the Japanese export market by hiring one of ATC's former employees to act as its representative, found the strategy backfired because the cigarettes it attempted to sell there were simply too expensive.

The price at which cigarettes were put on the market constituted a crucial variable in the formula that determined the success of overseas sales. Initially, the use of exports allowed ATC to derive full benefit from the high volume output of its American factories but, in those economies where tariffs on cigarettes were high, such a price advantage was likely to prove temporary compared with local manufacturing. As the domestic firms in countries with established tobacco industries began to develop their own cigarette manufacturing capacity, it became imperative for ATC to obtain direct control over local production facilities. During the mid-1890s, therefore, foreign direct investments were undertaken by ATC in the markets of Canada, New Zealand, and Australia, in each case through a merger with local manufacturers. A similar combination of tariffs and local competition persuaded Duke to expand ATC's direct operations through acquisition into Japan, Germany, and Britain between 1899 and 1901.

Even as late as 1899 most British firms, as well as some of ATC's remaining American rivals, were reluctant to adopt a strategy of foreign direct investment. Hence, when the Meiji government in Japan raised tobacco tariffs sharply on 1 January of that year, Wills attempted to minimize its effect on the price of their goods by invoicing cigarettes to its Japanese distributor at cost price in return for a share of the profits. The strategy was viewed as a temporary manoeuvre by the Wills management, and both the British firm and the American business of Cameron & Cameron soon withdrew from the Japanese market following the promulgation of the tariff. In contrast, ATC acquired control of the leading Japanese cigarette manufacturer and, for a period of time, actually strengthened its position in Japan under the management of Duke's appointed representative Edward J. Parrish.

Such a tentative approach to international competition by Wills was not so evident, however, when rivalry with ATC focused on its home market. Duke's attempt to acquire a dominant share of the market in Britain through the purchase of Ogden's in 1901 was met by a well-conducted defensive amalgamation of the leading cigarette manufacturers, led by Wills, into the Imperial Tobacco Company. The decision by Duke to invade the British market, and the spirited resistance offered by the Imperial group of firms, represents the first of two events which were to decisively shape the pattern of development in the international cigarette industry during the twentieth century. The most enduring legacy stemming from the outcome of this struggle—the formation of BAT Co.—also led to the manufacturing rights for all of Wills', Players', and ATC's cigarette brands to be divided across three separate firms. By the agreement of 27 September 1902, these brand rights were allocated to ATC for the United States, Cuba, and the Philippines, to Imperial for the United Kingdom and Ireland, and to BAT Co. for the rest of the world. This proved a valuable endowment for BAT Co., particularly in the markets of the British Dominions and in China where Wills' 'Ruby Queen' brand achieved astonishing levels of popularity in the early twentieth century. But this division of ownership also created a situation in which none of these leading brands could be marketed globally by any of the three organizations.

Having been created as the pre-eminent international cigarette manufacturer by the agreement of September 1902, BAT Co.'s main activity during its first decade was concerned with consolidating its position in those markets where it had acquired production capacity and with the stepping up of its export trade. No serious international rivals came to the fore at this time and for the most part the company concentrated its efforts on the relatively high income markets of Europe and the British Dominions, and the potentially vast Asian markets made up of the Chinese Empire and the British Empire, particularly in the Indian subcontinent. In both China and India, BAT expanded its local production capacity and began to encourage the growing of tobacco leaf suitable for use in its cigarettes.

The stability of BAT's opening decade contrasts sharply with the situation confronting the company after 1911. The dissolution of ATC by the Supreme Court in the United States during that year represents the second major event that served to determine the shape of the international tobacco industry. Two main consequences followed from this action. The first affected BAT Co. whilst the second influenced the competitive situation in the international tobacco industry generally. The effect on BAT Co. stemmed from the Supreme Court's ruling that ATC should divest its institutional equity interest in the concern that it jointly owned with Imperial, and this led to many of BAT Co.'s shares being traded on the London stock exchange. As a result, Imperial became the largest minority shareholder in BAT Co., by virtue of its initial one-third share allocation, and ownership of the company's stock as a whole tilted heavily towards Britain. By 1915, BAT Co.'s secretary was able to report that practically 70 per cent of the company's registered shares were held in Britain and less than 25 per cent in America.

The dissolution of ATC also created a group of successor firms in America that constituted potential rivals to BAT in its foreign markets. The four main manufacturing companies which were formed from the assets of ATC were Liggett & Myers, R. J. Reynolds, P. Lorrillard, and a reformed ATC but, in fact, none of these companies pursued an extensive international strategy between the wars. The American business historian Mira Wilkins has put forward a set of hypotheses to explain why these companies displayed such reticence to engage in direct competition with BAT during the 1920s, positing that: '(1) British–American Tobacco was well entrenched abroad, while in Britain, the former affiliate of the old American Tobacco, Imperial Tobacco, reigned supreme; (2) the boom in cigarette demand at home kept the businessmen occupied; (3) much of the overseas demand for US-made cigarettes could be filled by exports; and (4) in the 1890s, when the US cigarette industry had invested overseas in a massive manner, cigarettes were a new product; by the 1920s they were so no longer; thus the *need* for investments to introduce the product was not imperative.'[2]

Each of these hypotheses can be seen to have held some importance for explaining the muted competitive response of the successor firms to BAT Co.'s international position. The role of the American domestic market was certainly important, although to begin with less as a source of growth than as a forum of intense competition. The four successor companies fought a long struggle for market share in the US cigarette market after R. J. Reynolds successfully launched its 'Camel' brand of cigarettes in 1913, and this undoubtedly deflected their attention from the international market. BAT Co.'s entrenched position, in particular its investments in Latin America either side of the First World War, was also a factor that must have weakened the resolve of these firms to engage in business abroad, although it clearly did not preclude such a strategy. The notion that foreign sales could be organized through exports once a market abroad had been established for the product also carries a degree of credibility. Certainly the one successor firm that did challenge BAT in its main Chinese market, Liggett & Myers, did so on the strength of an export division and a locally based sales team, rather than through relocating production abroad. A number of British firms, such as Ardath, Carreras, and Godfrey Phillips, also joined battle against BAT in foreign markets on the strength largely of exports. The strategy was not without success, but lacked the durability of one based on the broad range of international production facilities employed by BAT. Whenever trading conditions became more difficult these export-based initiatives faltered and by the early 1930s BAT Co. either owned or controlled through management agreements each of these firm's foreign operations. Conceptually an export strategy may have been a feasible alternative to local production but under the prevailing conditions of the world economy between the wars it could rarely be sustained.

Where Wilkins' four hypotheses are found wanting is in their implicit assumption that the only source of US-based competition to BAT Co. was derived from the four main successor companies to ATC. In fact, one

[2] M. Wilkins, *The Maturing of Multinational Enterprise: American Business Abroad from 1914 to 1970* (1974), pp. 152–3. Author's own emphasis.

American-based company did present a serious threat to BAT's hegemonic position in the international cigarette industry between the wars, and this was the Tobacco Products Export Corporation (TPEC). This company had been formed in 1919 as an outgrowth of an initiative called the Tobacco Products Corporation (TPC) set up in 1912 by the same group of financiers who had helped to fund the growth through acquisition of Duke's ATC and in which Duke himself became financially involved from 1917. The rationale of TPC had been to acquire control of the remaining independent tobacco companies in America, and thereby to compete directly with the successor companies for a share of the domestic cigarette market. As an incidental part of this strategy, TPC had gained control of various overseas assets from the companies they acquired and, from around 1918, the management of TPC began to seriously develop these foreign assets into an international company called TPEC. Factories were operated by the company in Canada, China, Egypt, and Britain, and an unsuccessful bid was launched to take over the French government tobacco monopoly. In America meanwhile, where TPC had acquired the rights through its Philip Morris subsidiary to produce Imperial's brands, the idea seems to have developed around 1923 that this company could function as the American arm of the Imperial–BAT group. By the summer of that year, rumours of a merger between BAT Co. and TPC began to circulate in New York following a visit to London by an American director of TPC. Nothing ultimately came of these rumours, which were strenuously denied by the management of TPC, but soon after this episode James Duke tendered his resignation as chairman of BAT Co. giving no obvious reason for the timing. TPEC continued to operate its factory in Shanghai until trading conditions there became difficult in 1927, when it sold out to BAT Co. Two years later the entire TPC enterprise foundered and BAT Co. acquired more assets from TPEC, including the business of the Melachrino company which gave BAT an important share of the market for Turkish cigarettes in Germany.[3]

Certainly during the 1920s, therefore, American tobacco firms were by no means completely dormant with respect to the international cigarette industry, and Shepherd's assertion that British and American manufacturers operated a '*de facto* cartel', and that '[t]he *quid pro quo* US cigarette firms obtained for not entering the [international] market was protection in exploiting the large, rapidly-growing US market' misrepresents the true position of these firms.[4] Not only did some American tobacco manufacturers compete inter-

3 TPC leased all its American manufacturing rights to ATC in 1923, and in 1929 Philip Morris & Co. was the subject of a management buy-out.

4 P. L. Shepherd, 'Transnational Corporations and the International Cigarette Industry', in R. Newfarmer (ed.), *Profits, Progress and Poverty* (1985), p. 87.

nationally throughout the 1920s, but BAT Co. entered the US market directly in 1927 through the purchase of the Brown & Williamson Tobacco Co. of Winston-Salem. This bold and costly adventure led the reformed ATC to retaliate through the acquisition of the British manufacturer J. Wix & Sons. In both cases, these moves did not constitute mere competitive posturing, but were long-term investments with which both companies persevered and which ultimately both paid good returns. However, the large losses that BAT Co. incurred as a result of the Brown & Williamson purchase during the late 1920s and early '30s make it clear that the American cigarette manufacturers, with their heavy marketing expenditure, did not require a great deal of protection from foreign invaders in their domestic market.[5]

The Great Depression of the 1930s ushered in a new phase for the industry by reducing spending power in many markets and severely disrupting international trade and the free movement of capital and dividends. During this period, BAT was forced to operate on significantly lower profit margins, but also attempted to forestall mutually destructive price cutting by forming a series of pooling (market sharing) arrangements both with its remaining British rivals (notably Carreras and Gallaher) and with domestic rivals in a series of foreign markets including Europe, the Middle East, South America, and various parts of Asia. In an effort to placate the growing strength of nationalism in many markets, BAT operated closely with domestic firms and made their international identity as invisible as it could. By the time of the outbreak of the Second World War, therefore, whilst BAT Co. remained as the only genuine example of a multinational corporation operating within the tobacco industry, its constituent parts operated in each market as close to the ground as possible. Given the extremely dislocated nature of the international economy during the 1930s, such a multi-domestic form of operation would seem to have constituted the most appropriate form of global organization under the prevailing circumstances.

Managing a Multinational Corporation before the Second World War

The main thrust into foreign markets had been undertaken by ATC following its formation in 1890. Two features of the development of Duke's company during the 1890s were of particular significance for the subsequent

[5] It was reported that ATC were planning to spend $12.3 million on advertising their products in America during 1929, just as Brown & Williamson were attempting to make an initial impact on the cigarette market there. *Tobacco (London)*, 49 (578) (1929), 43.

growth of its international activities. First, by adopting a managerial structure which delegated operational decision-making to functionally specialized departments (the so-called U-form structure), ATC was able to readily channel some of its high-volume production in America to foreign markets by grafting an export department on to its existing administrative system. Thus during the course of the 1890s, ATC's export department operated effectively as the company's international division and was able to supply low-priced machine-made cigarettes to a wide range of foreign markets. Second, ATC's continued expansion within the United States involved the purchase of a series of rival firms. This corporate acquisition provided Duke with a strategic tool that he could use to prise open foreign markets where tariffs and other obstacles made an export strategy problematic. Between 1894 and 1895 ATC purchased control of tobacco firms in Australia, New Zealand, and Canada, and in each case set up an ATC-owned subsidiary to manage the company's affairs in these markets. To these were added controlling interests in the Murai Brothers' company in Japan and the Jasmatzi firm in Germany before, in 1901, Duke acquired control of the Ogden tobacco manufacturing firm in Britain.

The assault on the British market led ATC's chief international rival, the English family firm of Wills, to also employ the tactic of amalgamation as a means of effectively combating Duke's initiative. The creation of the Imperial Tobacco Co. was spearheaded by Wills through a merger of thirteen British tobacco firms in a move that superficially appeared to parallel the formation of ATC itself a decade before. As Chandler[6] has explained, however, the logic of such amalgamations in Britain lay more with co-operation and price control than with rationalization and unit cost reduction, and no plant closures were made following the establishment of the integrated concern.

Duke's willingness to employ acquisition as a market entry strategy in the international sphere was of vital importance as a means of accelerating the growth of a global cigarette industry. The purchase of Ogden's gave rise to a period of heightened competition not merely in Britain, but in all the markets where the constituent companies of Imperial were engaged in competitive rivalry with ATC. Although, at the outset, Duke almost certainly intended to engage in a long campaign within the British market, it soon became clear that the strategy of resistance developed by the Imperial group would impose too great a cost for such a policy to be sustained. Thus Duke made the price for his withdrawal from Britain the signing of an agreement which would allow ATC's international expansion to continue unfettered by

[6] A. D. Chandler, Jr, *Scale and Scope: The Dynamics of Industrial Capitalism* (1990), pp. 286–91.

competition from the major British tobacco companies. The creation of BAT Co. was the instrument through which this objective was achieved. By negotiating for ATC to receive two-thirds of BAT Co.'s share capital, largely on the strength of the much more extensive foreign assets that ATC transferred to the new organization, Duke ensured that the American parent company was in a position to exert control over BAT's strategic decision-making. In practice, however, the management of BAT Co.'s affairs was more complex and ambiguous than this ownership structure suggests.

The formation of BAT Co., with its registered office in London beyond the reach of the US anti-trust authorities, actually created a strange hybrid of an organization. The export factories of Imperial and Ogden in Britain and those of ATC in America were transferred to the new company and these plants continued to manufacture and supply orders for their traditional brands. Thus the company managed two export departments, each of which continued to produce cigarettes in competition with the other, but within an organizational structure that allowed such production capacity to be rationalized if necessary. In addition, BAT Co. acquired control of ATC's foreign subsidiaries, together with the overseas assets of Wills and Ogden's, which were now formally managed from the London headquarters.

Duke's imprint on the operation of BAT Co. was reflected in the creation of an organizational structure based around functional departments which mirrored that of ATC. The company also quickly abandoned the use of agents to run its overseas operations and replaced these with newly recruited salaried staff in the way that Duke's concern had developed abroad. In other respects, however, the company more closely resembled the federated structure of Imperial insofar as its foreign subsidiaries, particularly those in Canada, Australia, Germany, and the Far East, held a good deal of responsibility for their own conduct, under the general supervision of BAT Co.'s board of directors.

The composition of BAT Co.'s board of directors also reflected the hybrid nature of the organization. Imperial's one-third share of BAT Co.'s capital was faithfully reflected in its allocation of six of the company's eighteen initial directors. However, the remaining twelve places were filled by directors drawn not only from ATC but also from Ogden's, with the five places allocated to directors drawn from the Liverpool firm all based in England. Duke, as BAT Co.'s chairman, headed a committee of directors based in New York which comprised himself and four executives drawn from ATC but the bulk of BAT Co.'s directors were British and were based in England. Some of the English-based directors were delegated to supervise the company's factories in Liverpool and Bristol, with the majority based in London charged with overseeing the company's foreign businesses. Indeed, the American-based committee of directors was charged merely with the responsibility of supervising BAT Co.'s American-based activities, notably tobacco procurement (which was soon consolidated into a separate subsidiary) and the export factories that were transferred from ATC to BAT Co. in 1903. Thus even though Duke's influence over the organization at this point was undoubtedly the decisive one, much of the day-to-day decision-making lay outside of his direct control and no mechanism was ever put in place whereby the directors of BAT Co. were obliged to report formally to, or receive instructions from, the board of ATC. In this respect, the company was an autonomous decision-making entity and cannot be characterized as the overseas arm of ATC.[7]

The creation of a dual headquarters in London and New York soon began to generate friction within the organization. In 1904 both Harry Wills—Duke's vice-chairman—and William G. Player resigned from BAT Co.'s board and when, the following year, Duke himself stood down as BAT Co.'s chairman the core of the company's decision-making gained still greater independence. Duke's successor as chairman was William Harris who, as ATC's financial director, had been instrumental in creating that company's system of cost accounting. More significant at that time was the promotion of BAT Co.'s secretary Hugo Cunliffe-Owen to the position of vice chairman under Harris. Duke had clearly identified Cunliffe-Owen as his ultimate successor and took steps to ensure that he was exposed to management roles on both sides of the Atlantic, as well as spending time abroad in other parts of the BAT organization. As Cunliffe-Owen consolidated his position within BAT, Duke became embroiled in the anti-trust action which led to ATC's dissolution in 1911 and to the forced transfer of its institutional shareholding in BAT Co. into the hands of private stockholders (including the company's own directors). Duke's decision in 1912 to resume the chairmanship of BAT Co. led him to spend more time in London where a new headquarters was commissioned and built at Westminster. Before this new building was ready for occupation, however, the outbreak of war led Duke to return permanently to the United States and meant that, whilst the American remained as BAT Co.'s nominal chairman, Cunliffe-Owen's influence over the company now became the decisive one.

The war led to a clear division of responsibilities between the American and British sides of the organization. Whilst the factories in England turned towards supplying war contracts for the British government, those in America now dealt with the export trade to China and the Far East. During the war Cunliffe-Owen travelled between London and New York and oversaw the expansion of production in both countries that the changed conditions neces-

[7] Chandler, *Scale and Scope*, p. 247.

sitated. The company's foreign subsidiaries, meanwhile, seem to have been allowed to continue to operate on a relatively loose rein as BAT's managers in London concentrated on the massive increase in war-related production. In particular, around 1915 James Thomas was able to undertake a major reorganization of the China operation that devolved key aspects of management responsibility away from Shanghai and placed the rapidly growing business there on a more regional footing. One impact of the war on the development of BAT was to bind together the various elements of the organization behind a unified cause, and in many respects it was during these years that the company's cultural identity was effectively formed.

Shortly after completing his restructuring of the Chinese organization, Thomas was transferred to London as BAT Co. director responsible for the company's China department. Thomas's relocation to London in 1917 served as a prelude to the more active management of subsidiaries that the conclusion of the war in Europe allowed, and following the cessation of hostilities BAT's management gave much greater emphasis to international expansion via foreign direct investment. Spurred by the growing financial returns from its Chinese manufacturing investments, Cunliffe-Owen recognized that this approach provided the way ahead for the company, and ploughed the company's profits from the war, together with fresh capital raised in Britain, back primarily into investments in Asia and Latin America during the 1920s.

Cunliffe-Owen's formal accession to the chairmanship of BAT Co. following Duke's resignation in 1923 served merely to confirm his control over the organization, and between the wars the company was shaped in large measure by the force of his dominant personality. There is no doubt that his earlier experience in America inclined him towards aspects of management that prevailed in the United States. He was, for example, adamant that BAT Co. would not revert to the type of family dynasty that characterized the domestic tobacco industry in Britain and his two sons, Hugo and Dudley, were actively discouraged from a career within BAT in order to consolidate the culture of the company as a genuine meritocracy. More generally, the company's trail-blazing approach to international markets reflected far more readily the aggressive character of Duke, and his financial adventurism, than the more conservative approach that generally prevailed within the tobacco trade in Britain. Methods of American scientific management were also introduced into BAT's English factories during the 1920s, via the importation of the Bedaux system of task management.[8]

The importance that Cunliffe-Owen attached to BAT's American origins

[8] I am grateful to Matthias Kipping for drawing my attention to this aspect of BAT's operations.

helped persuade him to take the highly risky step of entering the domestic market in the United States in 1927 through the purchase of the small firm of Brown & Williamson. Although this move reduced BAT Co.'s overall profitability for a period of years, as the initial investment struggled to earn a return in the fiercely competitive American market, it served to restore the company's position as an Anglo-American alliance and took the fight against the successor companies to ATC for market share in international markets into their own backyard. In the long-run, Cunliffe-Owen's determination to make the American investment a success provided BAT with its most important legacy from his period of management in the difficult post-Second World War years.

Another of Cunliffe-Owen's bold initiatives between the wars was to restore BAT Co.'s position as a major force in the German cigarette market from which it had been forced to withdraw during the First World War. Whereas the main thrust of BAT's investments in the 1920s had concentrated on the pre-industrial regions of Asia, Africa, and Latin America at this time, Cunliffe-Owen was perfectly prepared to purchase assets in more mature markets where these became available. Operations in Germany had been resumed in a small way during 1926, but the main expansion there occurred during the early 1930s. Having acquired the operations of the Melachrino company from TPC in 1929, BAT then purchased in 1932 the assets of the much larger firm of Haus Bergmann, whose Jewish owners were seeking to sell up and relocate to Holland. As with the Brown & Williamson initiative, in the short run BAT's expansion in Germany gave the company a number of headaches, although in this case they were less to do with profitability than with the severe operating constraints imposed on it by the Nazi regime. Once again, however, the decision proved its worth in the long run as sales and profits grew rapidly during the post-Second World War boom.

Under Cunliffe-Owen, BAT Co. developed a relatively simple organizational system to manage a corporate structure which was, for its time, extremely complex. By the 1920s BAT Co., whilst continuing to operate its own export factories in Britain and America, acted as the holding company for a myriad of subsidiaries scattered around the globe. These subsidiaries provided BAT with its operating identities in the different markets in which it operated, and their profits generated the dividends that supported the parent company's international expansion. The history of BAT is therefore, in effect, the history of a great many individual corporate entities, each of which performed some function as part of the overall operation. This highly complex corporate structure was a source of pride to Cunliffe-Owen, and he used it to project a public persona of the company in Britain that was as mysterious and enigmatic as the image of the man himself.

In fact, the highly fragmented structure of the company enabled Cunliffe-Owen to maintain a vice-like grip over the organization by preventing an accumulation of power in any given regional market. Up until 1918, for example, the market in China was sufficiently large to give the American management there a degree of autonomous power within the organization, but after the end of the war the management in London carefully asserted its control over affairs in Shanghai. The centralization of strategic management within the BAT empire under Cunliffe-Owen took the form of a small committee, of which he was the chair, that received intelligence from each of the subsidiary companies regarding sales performance and profitability. This committee was made up of the finance and legal directors, together with the deputy chairmen responsible for sales and production. The remaining directors of BAT Co. were allocated territorial responsibilities and, for periods of months at a time, these directors would embark on tours of inspection covering their designated regions of the BAT empire. Thus a simple hierarchical management structure evolved in which Cunliffe-Owen's authority relied on regular, detailed information submitted by subsidiaries regarding their performance and was implemented through a group of territorial directors who formed the link between his strategic management committee and the expatriate managing directors of the overseas subsidiaries. As a general rule, subsidiary companies were given a period of time to establish themselves, often being able to trade at a loss to begin with, but once this phase was completed an appropriate return on investment was expected to be remitted to the parent company in London.

The disintegrated nature of BAT's international structure made the process of managing the company through the recession of the 1930s somewhat easier to achieve, since problems experienced in one market did not disturb the performance of the group as a whole. Naturally, the profitability of the company as a whole declined during this period of difficult trading and the widespread implementation of exchange controls made the remittance of profits from many markets—for example in South America—problematic. But with most of its subsidiary concerns well-established by this time, the company was able to ride out the turbulent conditions and, in many markets, used links with local firms to organize systems of market sharing to avoid competitive price cutting. Indeed, like Duke before him, Cunliffe-Owen recognized that a monopoly of production within a single organization removed the competitive drive that was required to stimulate sales performance. Thus BAT opposed the establishment of sales monopolies, favouring partnerships with rivals rather than complete rationalization, and occasionally deliberately set out to create competition for its own subsidiaries. In a number of markets, sales personnel working for different subsidiaries of BAT Co.

were kept ignorant of the fact that they were actually engaged by the same parent company.

The recession therefore increased the advantages of adopting a country-by-country approach to the management of its international cigarette empire. The structure also allowed BAT some respite from nationalist sentiments that in many cases increased in hostility towards foreign-owned enterprises during the 1930s, and Cunliffe-Owen actively sought to deflect such criticism by emphasizing the identity of local business enterprises that the company had acquired in many of its markets. In China, during the 1930s, the identity of BAT Co.'s operating company was changed from the British Cigarette Company to the Yee Tsoong Tobacco Corporation in an effort to reinforce the fact that all the company's cigarettes for this market were produced in Chinese factories.

By the time of the outbreak of the Second World War therefore, and despite Cunliffe-Owen's predilection towards American systems of management, BAT's international organizational structure had evolved into the classic European style of parent/daughter company.[9] Strategic control emanated from the centre but most functional decision-making was undertaken by expatriate staff in the foreign locations under the control of a local managing director. This multi-domestic structure dispersed production facilities into most of the markets that the company served but still permitted a degree of international co-ordination. A significant proportion of the tobacco leaf and other raw materials which the subsidiary companies used was procured on an international basis and provided the company with opportunities to engage in transfer pricing in order to redistribute profits. The company also exerted direct control over production machinery via vertical integration with the Molins machinery company.

Thus the multi-domestic approach adopted for production and distribution in most of its markets did not prevent the company from gaining benefits from its transnational organization. Indeed, whilst individual subsidiaries exhibited a great deal of variety in terms of their brand portfolios, the systems of financial management which they employed were consistent across the entire organization, allowing the key decision-makers to identify changes in relative performance with the maximum speed. It was in this operational aspect of its performance, perhaps even more than in marketing, that the company achieved its greatest source of competitive advantage over domestic firms.

However, the organizational structure that BAT Co. developed contained

[9] S. Humes, *Managing the Multinational: Confronting the Global–Local Dilemma* (1993), pp. 18–54.

certain weaknesses as well as strengths. By developing a portfolio of largely market-specific brands, the company was able to side-step the problem that arose from its lack of control over important brand-names in the markets of Britain and America, but after the Second World War it did leave BAT without a product that could be targeted towards the new market segment opened up by international brands such as 'Rothmans' and 'Marlboro'. Indeed, the company's expanding direct sales trade based on the duty free market after the war saw it in many cases supplying the brands of its British and American rivals for which BAT owned the international rights.

The chief weakness of the organizational structure that BAT Co. developed between the wars, however, was that it concentrated far too much strategic decision-making power into the hands of a single individual. The system worked as long as the central figure in the organization had both the skill and natural authority to carry this weight of decision-making upon his shoulders, and as long as such a concentration of decision-making across such a vast operation could feasibly be handled by one individual. Neither of these conditions could possibly endure indefinitely. It is perhaps ironic, therefore, that a company which had actively eschewed the model of the family firm ultimately faced a crisis of succession. When Cunliffe-Owen's chosen heir, Gray Miller, predeceased him shortly after the end of the Second World War, the company desperately required managerial reorganization. Within a matter of months, however, Cunliffe-Owen himself died, leaving the company ill-equipped for a number of years to deal with the managerial challenges that lay ahead. Like BAT itself, the global cigarette industry had been decisively shaped by the influence of Cunliffe-Owen; upon his passing the stage was set for the industry to develop into a new, oligopolistic phase in which BAT would be merely one among a small group of competing multinational tobacco firms.

Bibliography

Primary Sources

A. Interviews and Correspondence with BAT Co. Employees

(i) Oral Interviews with Retired BAT Co. Staff

Sir D. M. Oppenheim, 21, 28 February, and 7 March 1997.
Mr E. J. Symons, 15 December 1997.
Mr P. Tindley, 22 October 1997.

(ii) Written Transcripts/Correspondence

Mr M. Anderson, 27 March 1990.
Mr J. Banks, 12 April 1972.
Mr A. Basu, 8 January 1988.
Mr T. R. Bates, various dates.
Mr C. L. Breeze, 24 March 1972.
Mr G. H. J. Clarke, 23 March 1972.
Mr R. G. Davies, various dates.
Mr P. A. Etheridge, 13 April 1972.
Mr N. K. Ghoshal, 25 February 1988.
Mr A. R. Holliman, 29 November 1996 and 25 March 1998.
Mr D. S. F. Hobson, 16 January 1998.
Mr J. H. Maslen, 11 December 1997.
Mr J. Palmer, 13 January 1972.
Mr B. G. Pearson, March 1972.
Sir P. Rogers, 27 March 1972.
Mr D. Tailby, 13 April 1972.
Mr J. Turner, 27 March 1972.
Mr Wu Sing Pang, 30 August 1995.

B. Archive Collections

(i) British–American Tobacco Co., London, Staines, and Southampton, UK

(ii) Special Collections Department, Perkins Library, Duke University, NC, USA

W. R. Erwin, 'The papers of the British–American Tobacco Co., Ltd., Petersburg, Virginia', catalogue and summary.

Papers of the British–American Tobacco Co., Ltd.
Papers of James Buchanan Duke.
Papers of Richard Henry Gregory.
Papers of Edward James Parrish.
Papers of James Augustus Thomas.
Papers of Richard Harvey Wright.

(iii) Centre for Chinese Business History, Shanghai Academy of Social Sciences, Shanghai, China

Papers of the British–American Tobacco Co. (China) Ltd.

(iv) Public Record Office, Kew, London, UK

Foreign Office Papers, FO series.
Treasury Papers, T series.

(v) House of Lords Record Office, London, England

Beaverbrook Papers, BBK series.

(vi) India Office Library and Records, London, England

Papers of the Revenue and Statistics Department, R&S series.

(vii) Companies House, Cardiff, Wales

British–American Tobacco Co. Ltd. Annual Report and Accounts.

(viii) Hong Kong and Shanghai Bank Archives, Poultry, London, UK

Records of the Midland Bank, Central Hall Branch, Westminster.

(ix) Bristol Public Record Office

W.D. & H. O. Wills Archive.

(x) Nottingham Record Office

John Player & Sons Archive.

C. Company Publications

American Tobacco Company, ' "Sold American!"—The First Fifty Years'. American Tobacco Co. 1954.

BAT Cigaretten Fabriken GmbH, 'BAT Magazin zum 50 jährigen Bestehen, 1926–1976'.

L.A. Batchelor Smith, *Loom of Memories: A History of Southampton Branch of British–American Tobacco Co., Ltd.*, BAT Co., Southampton, 1969.

'British–American Tobacco Co. (Barbados) Ltd., 1925–1965'.

G. Brooks, 'Recipes for Success', *BAT Industries Outlook*, No. 14, Autumn 1991.

Brown & Williamson Tobacco Corporation, 'The First Hundred Years, 1893–1993'.

Demerara Tobacco Co. 'Thirty Years'.

ILTD Co., 'Indian Tobacco Leaves: Story of Co-operation in India', BAT Co., London, n.d.

J. Jones, 'Cigarettes—Liverpool 5: the Story of the Liverpool Branch of British American Tobacco Company Ltd'. Liverpool Hugh Evans & Sons, n.d.
Nobleza Piccardo, 'Hacia Un Siglio De Historia' [Towards a Century of History].
W. Twiston-Davies, 'Fifty Years of Progress: An Account of the African Organisation of the Imperial Tobacco Company', Imperial Tobacco Co., Bristol, n.d.
'The West Indian Tobacco Company Limited 1904–1964'.

D. Newspapers and Periodicals

(i) British–American Tobacco Periodicals

BAT Bulletin.
BAT Industries Outlook.
BAT News.
NTC Magazine [Nigerian Tobacco Co.].
Ying Mei Yien Kung Ssu Yeuh Pao [British American Tobacco Co. Monthly Journal].

(ii) Other newspapers and periodicals

Cigar and Tobacco World.
Economist.
Indian Trade Journal.
Indian Year Book.
Investors India Yearbook.
Millard's Review.
North China Daily News.
North China Herald.
Pioneer Mail.
Rea's Far Eastern Manual.
Thakar's Indian Directory.
Tobacco (London).
Tobacco International.
Wealth of India.

Secondary Sources

Books and Articles

Aarts, J. W., *Antitrust Policy Versus Economic Power* (translated by L. Scott). Leiden: H. E. Stenfert Kroese B.V., 1975.
Albert, B., *South America and the World Economy from Independence to 1930*. London: Macmillan, 1983.
Alford, B. W. E., *W. D. & H. O. Wills and the Development of the UK Tobacco Industry, 1786–1965*. London: Methuen & Co., 1973.
——, 'Penny Cigarettes, Oligopoly, and Entrepreneurship in the UK Tobacco Industry in the Late Nineteenth Century', in B. Supple (ed.), *Essays in British Business History*. Oxford: Oxford University Press, 1977, pp. 49–68.

ANDERSON, W. A., *The Atrocious Crime (of being a young man)*. Philadelphia, PA: Dorrance & Co., 1973.

ASHE, S. A. (ed.), *Biographical History of North Carolina, Vol V*. Greensboro, NC: Charles L. Van Noppen, 1906.

AXTON, W. F., *Tobacco and Kentucky*. Lexington, KY: University Press of Kentucky, 1975.

BADGER, A. J., *Prosperity Road: The New Deal, Tobacco, and North Carolina*. Chapel Hill, NC: University of North Carolina Press, 1980.

BASU, C., *Challenge and Change: The ITC Story, 1910–1985*. Calcutta: Orient Longman, 1988.

BERGÈRE, M.-C., *The Golden Age of the Chinese Bourgeosie 1911–1937*. Cambridge, UK: Cambridge University Press, 1989.

BLAICH, F., *Der Trustkampf, 1901–15*. Berlin: Duncker & Humblot, 1975.

BROWN, R. A., *Capital and Entrepreneurship in South East Asia*. London: St Martin's Press, Macmillan, 1994.

BULMER-THOMAS, V., *The Economic History of Latin America since Independence*. Cambridge, UK: Cambridge University Press, 1994.

BURNETT, N., *On the Edge of Asia*. Ringwood, Hants: Navigator Books, 1995.

BURNS, M. R., 'Outside Intervention in Monopolistic Price Warfare: The Case of the "Plug War" and the Union Tobacco Company', *Business History Review*, 56 (1) (1982), 33–53.

——, 'New Evidence on Predatory Price Cutting', *Managerial and Decision Economics*, 10 (1989), 327–30.

CAIN, P. J. and HOPKINS, A. G., *British Imperialism: Innovation and Expansion, 1688–1914*. London : Longman, 1993.

——, ——, *British Imperialism: Crisis and Deconstruction, 1914–1990*. London: Longman, 1993.

Cartophilic Society of Great Britain, *Tobacco War and BAT Co. Booklets* (Reference Booklets Nos. 18 and 21, originally issued 1951 and 1952), Newport, Gwent: Starling Press, 1978.

CASTLES, L., *Religion, Politics, and Economic Behaviour in Java: the Kudus Cigarette Industry*. Cultural Report Series No. 15, Southeast Asia Studies. New Haven, CT: Yale University, 1967.

CHANDLER, A. D., Jr, *Strategy and Structure: Chapters in the History of the Industrial Enterprise*. Cambridge, MA: MIT Press, 1962.

——, *The Visible Hand: The Managerial Revolution in American Business*. Cambridge, MA: Harvard University Press, 1977.

——, *Scale and Scope: The Dynamics of Industrial Capitalism*. Cambridge, MA: Harvard University Press, 1990.

CHAN, W. K. K., *Merchants, Mandarins, and Modern Enterprise in Late Ch'ing China*. Cambrige, MA: Harvard University Press, 1977.

CHAPMAN, S., *Jesse Boot*. London: Hodder & Stoughton, 1973.

CHEN HANG-SENG, *Industrial Capital and Chinese Peasants*. Shanghai: Kelly and Walsh, 1939.

CH'EN, P. H., 'The Treaty System and European Law in China: A Study of the Exercise of British Jurisdiction in Late Imperial China', in W. J. Mommsen and J. A. de Moor, *European Expansion and Law: The Encounter of European and Indigenous Law in 19th- and 20th-Century Africa and Asia*. Oxford: Berg Publishers, Inc., 1992, pp. 83–100.

CHEN REN JIE, 'Ying Mei yan gong si mai ban Zhen Bo Zhao' [The Compradore of the BAT Co.: Cheang Park Chew], *Wenshi ziliao xuanji* [Selection of material relating to culture and history] Zhong guo renmin zhengzhi xieshang huiyi (ed.) [Consultative Political Conference of the Chinese People], Shanghai, 1978, pp. 156–64.

CHISHOLM, A., and DAVIE, M., *Beaverbrook: A Life*. London: Hutchison, 1992.

CHU-YUAN CHENG, 'The United States Petroleum Trade with China, 1876–1949', in E. R. May and J. K. Fairbank (eds.), *America's China Trade in Historical Perspective: The Chinese and American Performance*. Cambridge, MA: Harvard University Press, 1986, 205–36.

COBLE, P. M., Jr, *The Shanghai Capitalists and the Nationalist Government, 1927–1937*. Cambridge, MA: Harvard University Press, 1980.

COCHRAN, S., *Big Business in China: Sino-Foreign Rivalry in the Cigarette Industry, 1890–1930*. Cambridge, MA: Harvard University Press, 1980.

——, 'Economic Institutions in China's Interregional Trade: Tobacco Products and Cotton Textiles, 1850–1980', paper prepared for Conference on Spatial and Temporal Trends and Cycles in Chinese Economic History, 980–1980, Bellagio, Italy, August 1984.

CORINA, M., *Trust in Tobacco: the Anglo-American Struggle for Power*. London: Michael Joseph, 1975.

CORLEY, T. A. B., 'Britain's Overseas Investments in 1914 Revisited', *Business History*, 36 (1) (1994), 71–88.

COX, H., 'Growth and Ownership in the International Tobacco Industry: BAT 1902–27', *Business History*, 31 (1) (1989), 44–67.

——, 'International Business, the State and Industrialisation in India: Early Growth in the Indian Cigarette Industry, 1900–19', *Indian Economic and Social History Review*, 27 (3) (1990), 289–312.

——, 'Creating a Distribution Network for Cigarettes in China, 1900–1941', University of Reading, Department of Economics, Discussion Papers in International Investment and Business Studies, Series B, Vol. 8 (196), 1995.

——, 'The Evolution of International Business Enterprise', in R. John (ed.), *Global Business Strategy*. London: International Thompson Business Press, 1997, pp. 9–46.

——, 'Learning to do Business in China: The Evolution of BAT's Cigarette Distribution Network, 1902–41', *Business History*, 39 (3) (1997), 30–64.

——, and SMITH, R., 'An Assessment of BAT Co.'s Profitability between the Wars'. Paper presented to the Accounting, Business, and Financial History First Annual Conference held at Cardiff Business School, 26–27 September 1990.

COX, R., *Competition in the American Tobacco Industry 1911–1932: A Study of the Effects of the Partition of the American Tobacco Company by the United States Supreme Court.* New York: Columbia University Press, 1933.

Davenport-Hines, R. P. T., 'Sir Hugo Von Reitzenstein Cunliffe-Owen (1870–1947)', in D. Jeremy (ed.), *Dictionary of Business Biography: A Biographical Dictionary of Business Leaders Active in Britain in the Period 1860–1980*. Vol. 1. London: Butterworths, 1984, pp. 865–9.

——, and Jones, G., 'British business in Japan since 1868', in idem, *British Business In Asia since 1860*. Cambridge, UK: Cambridge University Press, 1989, pp. 217–44.

Dernberger, R. F., 'The Role of the Foreigner in China's Economic Development, 1840–1949', in D. H. Perkins (ed.), *China's Modern Economy in Historical Perspective*. Stanford, CA: Stanford University Press, 1975, pp. 19–47.

Dewey, C. J., 'The Government of India's "New Industrial Policy", 1900–1925: Formation and Failure', in K. N. Chaudhuri and C. J. Dewey (eds.), *Economy and Society: Essays in Indian Economic and Social History*. Delhi: Oxford University Press, 1979, pp. 215–57.

Dobson, R. P., *China Cycle*. London: Macmillan & Co., 1946.

Drummond, I. M., *British Economic Policy and the Empire, 1919–1939*. London: George Allen & Unwin, 1972.

Duke, M., and Jordan, D. P., *Tobacco Merchant: The Story of Universal Leaf Tobacco Company*. Lexington, KY: University Press of Kentucky, 1995.

Durden, R. F., *The Dukes of Durham, 1865–1929*. Durham, NC: Duke University Press, 1975.

——, 'Tar Heel Tobacconist in Tokyo, 1899–1904', *The North Carolina Historical Review*, 53 (4) (1976), 347–63.

Easton, R., *Guns, Gold and Caravans* [*China Caravans* (UK version)]. Santa Barbara, CA: Capra Press, 1978.

Economist Intelligence Unit, *Leaf Tobacco: Its Contribution to the Economic and Social Development of the Third World*, EIU, London, 1981.

Eichengreen, B., *Golden Fetters: the Gold Standard and the Great Depression, 1919–1939*. New York: Oxford University Press, 1992.

Endicott, S. L., *Diplomacy and Enterprise: British China Policy, 1933–1937*. Manchester, UK: Manchester University Press, 1975.

Fairbank, J. K., (ed.) *Cambridge History of China*. Vol. 12, Part 1. Cambridge, UK: Cambridge University Press, 1983.

—— , *China: A New History*. Cambridge, MA: Harvard University Press, 1992.

Fieldhouse, D. K., *Unilever Overseas: the Anatomy of a Multinational*. London: Croom Helm, 1978.

Francks, P., *Japanese Economic Development: Theory and Practice*. London: Routledge, 1992.

Fung, E. S. K., 'The Sino-British Rapprochement, 1927–1931', *Modern Asian Studies*, 17 (1) (1983), 79–105.

Goodman, J., *Tobacco in History: the Cultures of Dependence*. London: Routledge, 1993.

GOSWAMI, O., 'Then Came the Marwaris', *The Indian Economic and Social History Review*, 22 (3) (1985), 225–49.

Government of India, *Report on the Marketing of Tobacco in India and Burma*. Simla: Government of India Press, 1939.

GREENE, G., *A Sort of Life*. London: The Bodley Head, 1971.

GUPTA, J. N., *et al.* (eds.), *Directory of Foreign Collaborations in India*. Vol. 2. Delhi: Indiana Overseas Publications, 1969.

GURUSHINA, N., 'British Free-Standing Companies in Tsarist Russia', in M. Wilkins and H. Schröter (eds.), *The Free-Standing Company in the World Economy, 1830–1996*. Oxford: Oxford University Press, 1998, pp. 160–201.

HAMILTON, G. G., 'The Organizational Foundations of Western and Chinese Commerce: A Historical and Comparative Analysis', in G. G. Hamilton (ed.), *Business Networks and Economic Development in East and Southeast Asia*. Hong Kong: Centre for Asian Studies, University of Hong Kong, 1991, pp. 48–65.

HANNAH, L., *The Rise of the Corporate Economy* (2nd edn.). London: Methuen, 1983.

HAVINDEN, M., and MEREDITH, D., *Colonialism and Development: Britain and its Tropical Colonies, 1850–1960*. London: Routledge, 1993.

HAWKS POTT, F. L., *A Short History of Shanghai*. Shanghai: Kelly and Walsh, 1928.

HERSHATTER, G., *The Workers of Tianjin, 1900–1914*. Stanford, CA: Stanford University Press, 1986.

HILL, R., *The Making of Molins: The Growth and Transformation of a Family Business, 1874–1977*. London: Molins Ltd., 1978.

HILLMAN, J., 'The Impact of the International Tin Restriction Scheme on the Return to Equity of Tin Mining', *Business History*, 39 (3) (1997), 65–80.

HILTON, M., 'Retailing History as Economic and Cultural History: Strategies of Survival by Specialist Tobacconists in the Mass Market', *Business History*, 40 (4) (1998), 115–37.

HOU CHING-MING, *Foreign Investment and Economic Development in China, 1840–1937*. Cambridge, MA: Harvard University Press, 1965.

HUMES, S., *Managing the Multinational: Confronting the Global-Local Dilemma*. Hemel Hempsted, Herts: Prentice Hall International, 1993.

HUTCHISON, J. L., *China Hand*. Boston: Lothrop, Lee and Shepard Co., 1936.

Interstate Commerce Commission Reports, Tobacco Products Corporation *et al.*, v. Southern Pacific Company *et al.*, Case No. 10368, Vol. 55, 1919, Washington: Government Printing Office, 1920, pp. 69–70.

JOHNSON, P. R., *The Economics of the Tobacco Industry*. New York: Praeger, 1984.

JONES, C., *International Business in the Nineteenth Century: The Rise and Fall of a Cosmopolitan Bourgeoisie*. Brighton: Wheatsheaf, 1987.

——, 'Institutional Forms of British Foreign Direct Investment in South America', *Business History*, 39 (2) (1997), 21–41.

JONES, E., *Accountancy and the British Economy, 1840–1980*. London: Batsford, 1981.

JONES, G., *The Evolution of International Business: an Introduction*. London: Routledge, 1996.

KINDLEBERGER, C. P., *The World in Depression, 1929–1939*. Harmondsworth: Penguin, 1986.

KLUGER, R., *Ashes to Ashes: America's Hundred-Year Cigarette War, the Public Health, and the Unabashed Triumph of Philip Morris*. New York: Alfred Knopf Inc., 1996.

KOLKO, G., *The Triumph of Conservatism*. New York: The Free Press, 1963.

KUMAR, D., 'The Fiscal System' in D. Kumar (ed.), *The Cambridge Economic History of India*. Delhi: Orient Longman/Cambridge University Press, 1982, pp. 905–44.

LEE, P. N. (ed.), *Tobacco Consumption in Various Countries*, Tobacco Research Council Paper 6, 4th edn. London: Tobacco Research Council, 1975.

LOGAN, J., *China: Old and New*. Hong Kong: South China Morning Press, 1982.

LOUIS, W. R., *British Strategy in the Far East, 1919–1939*. Oxford: Clarendon Press, 1971.

MACKENZIE, C., *Sublime Tobacco*. London: Chatto & Windus, 1957.

MADSEN, A. W., *The State as Manufacturer and Trader: An Examination of Government Tobacco Monopolies*. London: Unwin, 1916.

MASLEN, J. H., *Beating About the Nigerian Bush*. Ringwood, Hants: Navigator Books, 1994.

Monopolies Commission, *Report on the Supply of Cigarettes and Tobacco and of Cigarette and Tobacco Machinery*. London: HMSO, 1961.

MULLEN, C., *Cigarette Pack Art*. London: Gallery Press, 1979.

NATHAN, A., *Peking Politics*. London: University of California Press, 1976.

NEWMAN, R. K., 'India and the Anglo-Chinese Opium Agreements, 1907–14', *Modern Asian Studies*, 23 (3) (1989), 525–60.

NORDVIK, H. W., 'Conflict and Cooperation: Competitive Strategies and the Struggle for Control over the Norwegian Tobacco Market, 1905–1930', in R. P. Amdem and E. Lange (eds.), *Crossing the Borders: Studies in Norwegian Business History*. Oslo: Scandinavian University Press, 1994, 131–60.

OSTERHAMMEL, J., 'Imperialism in Transition: British Business and the Chinese Authorities', *China Quarterly*, 98 (1984), 260–86.

—— , 'British Business in China, 1860s–1950s', in R. P. T. Davenport-Hines and G. Jones (eds.), *British Business in Asia since 1860*. Cambridge: Cambridge University Press, 1989, pp. 189–216.

OWEN, R., 'Egypt in the World Depression: Agricultural Recession and Industrial Expansion', in I. Brown (ed.), *The Economies of Africa and Asia in the Inter-war Depression*. London: Routledge, 1989, pp. 137–51.

PARKER, L., and JONES, R. D., *China and the Golden Weed*. Ahoskie, North Carolina: Herald Publishing Co., 1976.

PERRY, E. J., *Shanghai on Strike: The Politics of Chinese Labor*. Stanford, CA: Stanford University Press, 1993.

PORTER, G., and LIVESAY, H. C., *Merchants and Manufacturers: Studies in the Changing Structure of Nineteenth Century Marketing*. Baltimore, MD: Johns Hopkins Press, 1971.

PORTER, P. G., 'Origins of the American Tobacco Company', *Business History Review*, 43 (1) (1969), 59–76.

PORTER, P. G., 'Advertising in the Early Cigarette Industry: W. Duke, Sons & Company of Durham', *The North Carolina Historical Review*, 48 (1), 1971, 31–43.

PUGACH, N., 'Keeping an Idea Alive: the Establishment of a Sino-American Bank, 1910–1920', *Business History Review*, 56 (1) (1982), 33–53.

——, 'Second Career: James A. Thomas and the Chinese–American Bank of Commerce', *Pacific Historical Review*, 56 (1987), 195–229.

——, *Same Bed Different Dreams: a History of the Chinese–American Bank of Commerce, 1919–1937*. Hong Kong: Centre for Asian Studies, University of Hong Kong, 1997.

RANGA, N. G., 'Some Facts Concerning the Development of the Tobacco Trade of the Madras Presidency', *Indian Journal of Economics*, 7 (July 1926), 34–40.

RAWSKI, T. G., *Economic Growth in Prewar China*. Berkeley, CA: University of California Press, 1989.

REID, A., 'From Betel-Chewing to Tobacco Smoking in Indonesia', *Journal of Asian Studies*, 44 (3) (1985), 529–47.

ROBERT, J. C., *The Tobacco Kingdom: Plantation, Market, and Factory in Virginia and North Carolina, 1800–1860*. Durham, NC: Duke University Press, 1938.

——, *The Story of Tobacco in America*. Chapel Hill, NC: University of North Carolina Press, 1949.

ROBERTS, B. W. C., and KNAPP, R. F., 'Paving the Way for the Tobacco Trust: From Hand Rolling to Mechanized Cigarette Production by W. Duke, Sons and Company', *The North Carolina Historical Review*, 69 (3) (1992), 257–81.

ROTHERMUND, D., *India in the Great Depression, 1929–1939*. New Delhi: Manohar, 1992.

ROWE, H. B., *Tobacco Under the AAA*. Washington, DC: Brookings Institute, 1935.

SARKAR, S., *The Swadeshi Movement in Bengal, 1903–1908*. New Delhi: People's Publishing House, 1973.

——, *Modern India, 1885–1947*. New Delhi: Macmillan India, 1983.

SCHMITZ, C. J., *The Growth of Big Business in the United States and Western Europe, 1850–1939*. London: Macmillan, 1993.

SCOTT, J. P., 'John Wynford Phillipps', in D. Jeremy (ed.), *Dictionary of Business Biography: A Biographical Dictionary of Business Leaders Active in Britain in the Period 1860–1980*, Vol. 4. London: Butterworths, 1984, pp. 865–9.

Shanghai shehui kexueyuan jingji yangjiusuo [Economic Research Institute at the Shanghai Academy of Social Science] (ed.), *Ying Mei Yan Gongsi zai Hua qiye ziliao huibian* [Documents on the Enterprises of BAT in China], 4 volumes, Beijing, 1983.

SHEPHERD, P. L., 'Transnational Corporations and the International Cigarette Industry', in R. Newfarmer (ed.), *Profits, Progress and Poverty*. Notre Dame, IN: Notre Dame Press, 1985, pp. 63–112.

SKINNER, G. W., 'Marketing and Social Structure in Rural China', *Journal of Asian Studies*, 24 (1) (1964), 3–43.

SOBEL, R., *They Satisfy: the Cigarette in American Life*. New York: Anchor Press/Doubleday, 1978.

STERICKER, J., *A Tear for the Dragon*. London: Arthur Baker Ltd., 1958.

TAYLOR, A. J. P., *Beaverbrook*. London: Hamish Hamilton, 1972.

TENNANT, R. B., *The American Cigarette Industry: A Study in Economic Analysis and Public Policy*. New Haven, CT: Yale University Press, 1950.

THOMAS, J. A., 'Selling and Civilization: some principles of an open sesame to big business success in the East', *Asia* (December 1923), 896–9, 948–50.

——, *A Pioneer Tobacco Merchant in the Orient*. Durham, NC: Duke University Press, 1928.

TILLEY, N. M., *The Bright Tobacco Industry, 1860–1929*. Chapel Hill, NC: University of North Carolina Press, 1948.

——, *The R. J. Reynolds Tobacco Company*. Chapel Hill, NC: University of North Carolina Press, 1985.

TODD, G. H., *Statistics of Smoking in the UK* (6th edn). Tobacco Research Council, Research Paper No. 1, 1972.

TOMLINSON, B. R., 'India and the British Empire, 1880–1935', *Indian Economic and Social History Review*, 12 (4) (1975), 337–80.

——, 'Foreign Private Investment in India', *Modern Asian Studies*, 12 (4) (1978), 655–77.

TONG, H. K., 'Japan Seeking China's Tobacco Monopoly', *Millard's Review*, 5 (8) (1918), 49–52.

——, 'Development of China's Wine and Tobacco Administration', *Millard's Review*, 8 (6) (1919), 197–200.

TUCKER, D., *Tobacco: An International Perspective*. Euromonitor Publications, London: 1982.

UNCTAD, *Marketing and Distribution of Tobacco*. UNCTAD Report TD/B/C.1/205, Geneva: United Nations, 1978.

US Bureau of Corporations, *Report of the Commissioner of Corporations on the Tobacco Industry*, Parts I–III. Washington: US Department of Commerce and Labor, Government Printing Office, 1909.

US Federal Trade Commission, *Report on the Tobacco Industry*. Washington: Government Printing Office, 1921.

US Senate Documents, Vol. 25, No. 111, Federal Anti-Trust Decisions 1890–1912, Vol. IV. Government Printing Office, Washington: 1912.

VAN HELTEN, J.-J. and JONES, G., 'British Business in Malaysia and Singapore since the 1870s', in R. P. T. Davenport-Hines and G. Jones (eds.), *British Business in Asia since 1860*. Cambridge: Cambridge University Press, 1989, pp. 157–88.

WALKER, R., *Under Fire: A History of Tobacco Smoking in Australia*. Carlton, Vic: Melbourne University Press, 1984.

WANG, Y. C., 'Free Enterprise in China: The Case of a Cigarette Concern, 1905–1953', *Pacific Historical Review*, 29 (4) (1960), 395–414.

WELLINGS, F., *The History of Marley*, Cambridge: Woodhead Publishing, 1994.

WILKINS, M., *The Maturing of Multinational Enterprise: American Business Abroad from 1914 to 1970*. Cambridge, MA: Harvard University Press, 1974.

——, 'The Impacts of American Multinational Enterprise on American–Chinese Economic Relations, 1786–1949', in E. R. May and J. K. Fairbank, *America's*

China Trade in Historical Perspective: The Chinese and American Performance. Cambridge, MA: Harvard University Press, 1986, pp. 259–92.

WILKINS, M., 'The Free-Standing Company, 1870–1914: an Important Type of British Foreign Direct Investment', *Economic History Review* (2nd Series), 41 (2) (1988), 259–85.

——, and SCHRÖTER, H., (eds.), *The Free-Standing Company in the World Economy, 1830–1996*. Oxford: Oxford University Press, 1998.

WILSON, J., *British Business History, 1720–1994*. Manchester: Manchester University Press, 1995.

WINKLER, J. K., *Tobacco Tycoon: The Story of James Buchanan Duke*. New York: Random House, 1942.

WRIGHT, T., *Coal Mining in China's Economy and Society, 1895–1937*. Cambridge, UK: Cambridge University Press, 1984.

Appendix 1

BAT Co. Sources of Funding and Profit–Loss Account, 1903–46: Year ending 30 September

	1903 (£m.)	1904 (£m.)	1905 (£m.)	1906 (£m.)	1907 (£m.)	1908 (£m.)	1909 (£m.)	1910 (£m.)	1911 (£m.)	1912 (£m.)	1913 (£m.)	1914 (£m.)
Profit & loss account												
Opening profit		0.149	0.255	0.445	0.601	0.777	0.886	0.968	1.124	1.261	2.159	2.412
To (from) reserves												1.289
Less capitalized profits												
Less dividends												
5% preference		0.077	0.075	0.075	0.075	0.097	0.105	0.105	0.105	0.105	0.117	0.188
6% preference												
ordinary final						0.074	0.074	0.056	0.112	0.093	0.500	0.438
ordinary interim		0.223	0.446	0.521	0.781	0.781	0.670	1.042	1.302	0.885	1.282	1.063
Add profits for year	0.149	0.406	0.711	0.752	1.032	1.061	0.931	1.359	1.656	1.981	2.152	1.965
Closing profit	0.149	0.255	0.445	0.601	0.777	0.886	0.968	1.124	1.261	2.159	2.412	1.399

	1903 (£m.)	1904 (£m.)	1905 (£m.)	1906 (£m.)	1907 (£m.)	1908 (£m.)	1909 (£m.)	1910 (£m.)	1911 (£m.)	1912 (£m.)	1913 (£m.)	1914 (£m.)
Total funds												
Share capital												
5% preference	1.500	1.500	1.500	1.500	1.500	2.100	2.100	2.100	2.100	2.100	3.100	4.500
6% preference												
ordinary	3.720	3.720	3.720	3.720	3.720	3.720	3.720	3.720	3.720	6.252	6.254	6.254
premium										0.225	0.225	0.225
Add reserves		0.007	0.068	0.058	0.079	0.087	0.093	0.115	0.119	0.140	0.173	1.719
Add closing profit	0.149	0.255	0.445	0.601	0.777	0.886	0.968	1.124	1.261	2.159	2.412	1.399
Net worth	5.369	5.482	5.733	5.879	6.076	6.793	6.881	7.059	7.200	10.876	12.164	14.097
Add outside credit	0.541	0.230	0.267	0.466	1.094	1.276	1.056	1.060	1.926	1.412	2.372	2.750
Total funds	5.910	5.712	6.000	6.345	7.170	8.069	7.937	8.119	9.126	12.288	14.536	16.847

Appendix 1. *(cont.)*

	1915 (£m.)	1916 (£m.)	1917 (£m.)	1918 (£m.)	1919 (£m.)	1920 (£m.)	1921 (£m.)	1922 (£m.)	1923 (£m.)	1924 (£m.)	1925 (£m.)	1926 (£m.)
Profit & loss account												
Opening profit	1.399	1.617	2.093	2.902	3.381	4.913	3.077	3.171	4.721	4.978	5.521	6.156
To (from) reserves			0.257	0.560				−1.222				−0.755
Less capitalized profits						3.673	0.002					4.048
Less dividends												
5% preference	0.225	0.225	0.225	0.225	0.225	0.225	0.225	0.225	0.225	0.225	0.225	0.225
6% preference												
ordinary final	0.469	0.469	0.313	0.375	0.375	0.512	1.440	1.281	1.444	1.446	1.607	1.809
ordinary interim	0.938	1.563	1.501	1.501	1.644	2.305	2.561	2.567	2.568	2.652	2.679	2.999
Add profits for year	1.850	2.733	3.105	3.140	3.776	4.879	4.322	4.401	4.494	4.866	5.146	6.196
Closing profit	1.617	2.093	2.902	3.381	4.913	3.077	3.171	4.721	4.978	5.521	6.156	4.026

	1915 (£m.)	1916 (£m.)	1917 (£m.)	1918 (£m.)	1919 (£m.)	1920 (£m.)	1921 (£m.)	1922 (£m.)	1923 (£m.)	1924 (£m.)	1925 (£m.)	1926 (£m.)
Total funds												
Share capital												
5% preference	4.500	4.500	4.500	4.500	4.500	4.500	4.500	4.500	4.500	4.500	4.500	4.500
6% preference												
ordinary	6.254	6.254	6.254	6.254	8.502	16.003	16.016	16.046	16.071	16.071	16.071	23.481
premium	0.225	0.225	0.225	0.227	0.368	0.391	0.401	0.417	0.445	0.462	0.462	0.540
Add reserves	1.760	1.807	2.205	3.153	3.261	3.385	3.295	1.804	1.807	1.828	1.909	2.270
Add closing profit	1.617	2.093	2.902	3.381	4.913	3.077	3.171	4.721	4.978	5.521	6.156	4.026
Net worth	14.356	14.879	16.086	17.515	21.544	27.356	27.383	27.488	27.801	28.382	29.098	34.817
Add outside credit	1.637	2.692	5.466	9.218	9.919	5.679	6.240	5.162	4.645	4.922	4.756	4.433
Total funds	15.993	17.571	21.552	26.733	31.463	33.035	33.623	32.650	32.446	33.304	33.854	39.250

APPENDIX 1. (*cont.*)

	1927 (£m.)	1928 (£m.)	1929 (£m.)	1930 (£m.)	1931 (£m.)	1932 (£m.)	1933 (£m.)	1934 (£m.)	1935 (£m.)	1936 (£m.)	1937 (£m.)	1938 (£m.)
Profit & loss account												
Opening profit	4.026	4.277	4.736	3.813	3.765	2.619	2.756	2.857	2.999	3.147	3.368	3.656
To (from) reserves				0.100							0.150	0.100
Less capitalized profits	0.003	0.001	1.166									
Less dividends												
5% preference	0.225	0.225	0.225	0.225	0.225	0.225	0.225	0.225	0.225	0.225	0.225	0.225
6% preference				0.330	0.360	0.360	0.360	0.360	0.360	0.360	0.360	0.360
ordinary final	1.958	1.958	1.962	1.965	1.965	0.786	0.786	0.786	0.789	0.789	0.789	1.086
ordinary interim	3.917	3.921	3.928	3.930	3.930	3.930	3.930	3.940	3.947	3.947	3.948	3.949
Add profits for year	6.354	6.564	6.358	6.502	5.334	5.438	5.402	5.453	5.469	5.542	5.760	5.591
Closing profit	4.277	4.736	3.813	3.765	2.619	2.756	2.857	2.999	3.147	3.368	3.656	3.527

	1927 (£m.)	1928 (£m.)	1929 (£m.)	1930 (£m.)	1931 (£m.)	1932 (£m.)	1933 (£m.)	1934 (£m.)	1935 (£m.)	1936 (£m.)	1937 (£m.)	1938 (£m.)
Total funds												
Share capital												
5% preference	4.500	4.500	4.500	4.500	4.500	4.500	4.500	4.500	4.500	4.500	4.500	4.500
6% preference				6.000	6.000	6.000	6.000	6.000	6.000	6.000	6.000	6.000
ordinary	23.500	23.540	23.574	23.583	23.583	23.583	23.584	23.677	23.682	23.682	23.688	23.703
premium	0.540	0.560	0.577	0.581	0.581	0.581	0.581	0.621	0.623	0.623	0.626	0.634
Add reserves	2.278	2.506	2.534	2.667	2.712	2.748	2.779	2.831	2.862	2.859	3.035	3.162
Add closing profit	4.277	4.736	3.813	3.765	2.619	2.756	2.857	2.999	3.147	3.368	3.656	3.527
Net worth	35.095	35.842	34.998	41.096	39.995	40.168	40.301	40.628	40.814	41.032	41.505	41.526
Add outside credit	4.083	5.724	7.733	6.599	8.012	8.816	7.883	8.145	7.353	8.071	8.874	8.567
Total funds	39.178	41.566	42.731	47.695	48.007	48.984	48.184	48.773	48.167	49.103	50.379	50.093

Appendix 1. *(cont.)*

	1939 (£m.)	1940 (£m.)	1941 (£m.)	1942 (£m.)	1943 (£m.)	1944 (£m.)	1945 (£m.)	1946 (£m.)
Profit & loss account								
Opening profit	3.527	3.367	2.597	2.635	2.442	2.506	2.501	2.572
To (from) reserves		0.500			0.100	0.250	0.250	0.550
Less capitalized profits								
Less dividends								
5% preference	0.225	0.225	0.225	0.225	0.225	0.225	0.225	0.225
6% preference	0.360	0.360	0.360	0.360	0.360	0.360	0.360	0.360
ordinary final	0.790	0.593	0.297	0.693	0.594	0.594	0.693	1.188
ordinary interim	3.950	3.957	3.168	1.980	1.980	1.980	1.980	2.178
Add profits for year	5.165	4.865	4.088	3.065	3.323	3.404	3.579	4.975
Closing profit	3.367	2.597	2.635	2.442	2.506	2.501	2.572	3.046

	1939 (£m.)	1940 (£m.)	1941 (£m.)	1942 (£m.)	1943 (£m.)	1944 (£m.)	1945 (£m.)	1946 (£m.)
Total funds								
Share capital								
5% preference	4.500	4.500	4.500	4.500	4.500	4.500	4.500	4.500
6% preference	6.000	6.000	6.000	6.000	6.000	6.000	6.000	6.000
ordinary	23.703	23.758	23.758	23.758	23.758	23.758	23.758	23.758
premium	0.634	0.114	0.114	0.114				
Add reserves	3.184	4.241	4.261	4.675	5.710	5.973	6.317	7.253
Add closing profit	3.367	2.597	2.635	2.442	2.506	2.501	2.572	3.046
Net worth	41.388	41.210	41.268	41.489	42.474	42.732	43.147	44.557
Add outside credit	11.492	9.672	12.231	16.742	15.083	17.680	22.550	21.578
Total funds	52.880	50.882	53.499	58.231	57.557	60.412	65.697	66.135

APPENDIX 1. (*cont.*)

Notes

1. The increase in reserves of £1.289 million in 1914 was maintained as a general reserve to provide against losses arising from the company's German investments. The majority of this was added back to profits in the 1922 accounts. A similar contingency reserve was created during Second World War, although more gradually.
2. The capitalized profits of £3.67 million in 1920 were primarily used to support the increase in ordinary share capital from £8.5 million to £16 million at the end of the First World War. Some of this was used to purchase shares in the Garland Steamship Co.
3. The capitalized profits of £4 million in 1926 were used to support another increase in the ordinary share capital from £16 million to £23.5 million.
4. The capitalized profits of £1.16 million in 1929 were used towards the setting up of the Tobacco Securities Trust, whose shares were distributed to BAT Co. ordinary shareholders.

Appendix 2

BAT Co. Balance Sheet Assets, 1903–46

Year	Buildings & plant[a] (£m.)	Goodwill & trade marks (£m.)	Shares in assoc. Cos[b] (£m.)	Loans to assoc. Cos[b] (£m.)	Stocks in leaf & final goods (£m.)	Debtors & debit bal's (£m.)	Cash & other investments[c] (£m.)	Total assets (£m.)
1903	0.397	1.497	1.945	0.581	0.760	0.148	0.583	5.911
1904	0.370	1.342	1.494	0.619	1.014	0.475	0.398	5.712
1905	0.395	1.098	2.103	0.554	1.005	0.623	0.221	5.999
1906	0.363	1.021	2.450	0.602	1.225	0.569	0.115	6.345
1907	0.370	1.021	2.777	0.821	1.640	0.463	0.077	7.169
1908	0.416	1.011	3.320	0.722	1.965	0.506	0.130	8.070
1909	0.415	1.000	2.713	0.958	1.970	0.323	0.558	7.937
1910	0.446	0.884	3.034	1.280	2.029	0.220	0.225	8.118
1911	0.487	0.883	3.353	1.643	1.992	0.316	0.450	9.124
1912	0.507	0.879	5.423	1.926	1.086	0.712	1.755	12.288
1913	0.689	0.879	5.674	4.230	1.670	0.593	0.801	14.536
1914	0.916	0.879	5.987	3.592	3.493	0.451	1.529	16.847
1915	1.043	0.879	5.592	3.118	3.708	0.449	1.204	15.993
1916	1.068	0.879	5.093	2.631	4.517	2.310	1.075	17.573
1917	1.150	0.879	5.081	4.456	5.561	2.723	1.702	21.552
1918	1.166	0.879	5.256	5.278	8.654	3.229	2.271	26.733
1919	0.936	0.505	8.692	6.068	8.197	2.773	4.291	31.462
1920	0.961	0.505	11.356	7.195	7.021	2.531	3.464	33.033
1921	1.027	0.200	15.341	5.548	6.873	2.108	2.526	33.623
1922	1.020	0.200	15.266	4.696	4.850	1.659	4.961	32.652
1923	1.005	0.200	15.620	4.812	5.466	1.095	4.247	32.445
1924	0.986	0.200	16.033	6.460	6.149	0.652	2.826	33.306
1925	1.058	0.200	16.155	5.913	5.726	1.877	2.926	33.855
1926	1.120	0.200	16.919	8.589	5.023	5.200	2.197	39.248
1927	1.148	0.200	20.136	5.391	5.653	3.812	2.838	39.178

APPENDIX 2. *(cont.)*

Year	Buildings & plant[a] (£m.)	Goodwill & trade marks (£m.)	Shares in assoc. Cos[b] (£m.)	Loans to assoc. Cos[b] (£m.)	Stocks in leaf & final goods (£m.)	Debtors & debit bal's (£m.)	Cash & other investments[c] (£m.)	Total assets (£m.)
1928	1.346	0.200	20.931	5.434	6.269	4.353	3.032	41.565
1929	1.522	0.200	21.718	6.832	8.809	2.430	1.220	42.731
1930	1.766	0.200	21.959	7.488	8.117	3.669	4.496	47.695
1931	1.682	0.200	22.097	6.836	6.739	2.533	7.919	48.006
1932	1.460	0.200	23.507	7.918	4.797	2.095	9.006	48.983
1933	1.429	0.200	24.400	6.326	3.866	2.235	9.729	48.185
1934	1.350	0.200	24.351	9.372	3.489	1.700	8.310	48.772
1935	1.332	0.200	28.313	4.910	3.946	1.553	7.914	48.168
1936	1.308	0.200	30.819	4.299	3.469	1.720	7.287	49.102
1937	1.348	0.200	31.250	5.768	3.812	1.323	6.679	50.380
1938	1.362	0.200	31.480	5.213	4.389	1.436	6.012	50.092
1939	1.417	0.200	31.549	7.101	4.778	2.433	5.401	52.879
1940	1.434	0.200	32.103	6.564	5.144	2.044	3.394	50.883
1941	1.453	0.200	26.906	7.528	4.843	3.858	8.709	53.497
1942	1.453	0.200	27.259	3.940	7.258	3.767	14.355	58.232
1943	0.485	0.200	27.303	3.583	9.893	5.337	10.755	57.556
1944	0.442	0.200	26.138	7.877	10.587	8.362	6.804	60.410
1945	0.414	0.200	26.449	12.076	11.884	8.896	5.777	65.696
1946	0.388	0.200	26.437	12.770	17.612	7.100	1.628	66.135

[a] The accounting convention of cost less depreciation was used to value fixed assets. In 1943, a significant portion of fixed assets was written off the balance sheet against depreciation. The comparable depreciated figure for fixed assets in 1942 was £0.579 million.

[b] From 1929 onwards the figures for investments in and loans to subsidiary companies are detailed separately from the associated companies in the annual accounts.

[c] From 1931 onwards the annual accounts specify that this figure includes balances in overseas bank accounts. These are not itemized separately.

Source: BAT Co. Annual Report and Accounts.

Appendix 3

UK exports of manufactured cigarettes to principal destinations in Asia and Africa, 1906–48

Destination	1906		1907		1908		1909		1910		1911		1912		1913	
	000 lb.	(%)	000 lb.	(%)	000 lb.	(%)	000 lb.	(%)	000 lb.	(%)	000 lb.	(%)	000 lb.	(%)	000 lb.	(%)
China	1,259	26	1,889	29	2,639	35	3,608	39	5,764	52	6,481	54	7,697	54	11,421	60
Hong Kong	375	8	608	9	1,057	14	1,274	14	1,083	10	773	6	995	7	867	5
Kwantung Peninsular																
Straits Settlements	259	5	220	3	216	3	349	4	643	6	817	7	805	6	1,061	6
Federated Malay States															30	0
Java & Dutch possessions							6	0	9	0	17	0	33	0	107	1
Siam/Thailand															45	0
British India	1,477	30	2,044	32	1,855	24	1,952	21	1,149	10	1,230	10	1,211	9	1,514	8
Ceylon	112	2	145	2	165	2	181	2	237	2	204	2	308	2	331	2
Aden																
Asia subtotal	3,482	71	4,906	76	5,932	78	7,370	80	8,885	81	9,522	80	11,049	78	15,376	81
South Africa	201	4	95	1	65	1	114	1	123	1	132	1	168	1	174	1
British East Africa															111	1
British West Africa	59	1	71	1	98	1	138	1	239	2	275	2	417	3	457	2
Egypt															46	0
Africa subtotal	260	5	166	3	163	2	252	3	362	3	407	3	585	4	788	4
Total exports	4,907		6,453		7,612		9,261		11,002		11,967		14,192		19,000	

Appendix 3. (*cont.*)

Destination	1914		1915		1916		1917		1918		1919		1920		1921	
	000 lb.	(%)	000 lb.	(%)	000 lb.	(%)	000 lb.	(%)	000 lb.	(%)	000 lb.	(%)	000 lb.	(%)	000 lb.	(%)
China	9,901	54	9,722	53	8,252	41	1,623	12	747	7	387	3	1,806	11	2,074	22
Hong Kong	1,532	8	790	4	1,178	6	270	2	225	2	118	1	201	1	133	1
Kwantung Peninsular																
Straits Settlements	1,172	6	1,008	5	1,365	7	1,058	8	1,200	11	270	2	672	4	857	9
Federated Malay States											6	0	27	0	11	0
Java & Dutch possessions	124	1	158	1	176	1	152	1	150	1	174	1	439	3	455	5
Siam/Thailand	73	0	124	1	178	1	102	1	133	1	68	1	74	0	50	1
British India	1,230	7	1,605	9	2,175	11	3,574	27	2,933	27	2,142	17	3,285	20	1,714	18
Ceylon	325	2	229	1	344	2	385	3	325	3	150	1	461	3	248	3
Aden																
Asia subtotal	14,357	78	13,636	74	13,668	67	7,164	55	5,713	53	3,315	26	6,965	43	5,542	59
South Africa	158	1	98	1	86	0	75	1	36	0	56	0	75	0	42	0
British East Africa	165	1	259	1	486	2	638	5	598	6	222	2	301	2	216	2
British West Africa	334	2	343	2	499	2	409	3	486	5	777	6	1,120	7	177	2
Egypt			579	3	331	2	361	3	388	4	130	1	138	1	245	3
Africa subtotal	657	4	1,279	7	1,402	7	1,483	11	1,508	14	1,185	9	1,634	10	680	7
Total exports	18,448		18,335		20,339		13,144		10,680		12,638		16,262		9,448	

Appendix 3. (*cont.*)

Destination	1922		1923		1924		1925		1926		1927		1928		1929	
	000 lb.	(%)	000 lb.	(%)	000 lb.	(%)	000 lb.	(%)	000 lb.	(%)	000 lb.	(%)	000 lb.	(%)	000 lb.	(%)
China	1,075	9	1,492	10	1,538	10	1,144	7	1,442	7	991	5	2,322	9	3,171	10
Hong Kong	209	2	374	3	810	5	385	2	371	2	437	2	754	3	1,401	4
Kwantung Peninsular																
Straits Settlements	1,037	9	1,627	11	2,211	15	3,553	21	4,397	22	4,797	22	5,552	21	6,459	20
Federated Malay States	29	0	105	1	164	1	332	2	399	2	775	4	546	2	774	2
Java & Dutch possessions	451	4	364	2	264	2	208	1	344	2	480	2	678	3	748	2
Siam/Thailand	82	1	79	1	138	1	301	2	465	2	727	3	1,432	5	2,419	7
British India	3,655	31	3,378	23	2,702	18	3,161	19	4,033	20	5,546	25	5,070	19	5,114	16
Ceylon	353	3	308	2	450	3	439	3	577	3	518	2	651	2	502	2
Aden											65	0	167	1	169	1
Asia subtotal	6,891	58	7,727	53	8,277	56	9,523	57	12,028	60	14,336	65	17,172	64	20,757	63
South Africa	44	0	45	0	36	0	39	0	40	0	60	0	52	0	82	0
British East Africa	259	2	290	2	513	3	682	4	684	3	861	4	1,019	4	1,132	3
British West Africa	685	6	715	5	836	6	948	6	1,101	6	1,319	6	1,646	6	1,244	4
Egypt	163	1	304	2	321	2	280	2	372	2	433	2	513	2	554	2
Africa subtotal	1,151	10	1,354	9	1,706	12	1,949	12	2,197	11	2,673	12	3,230	12	3,012	9
Total exports	11,795		14,610		14,817		16,766		19,881		22,003		26,668		32,842	

Appendix 3. (*cont.*)

Destination	1930		1931		1932		1933		1934		1935		1936		1937	
	000 lb.	(%)	000 lb.	(%)	000 lb.	(%)	000 lb.	(%)	000 lb.	(%)	000 lb.	(%)	000 lb.	(%)	000 lb.	(%)
China	5,414	17	4,499	23	635	4	324	2	262	1	206	1	165	1	153	1
Hong Kong	1,178	4	839	4	1,180	8	514	3	396	2	337	2	332	1	468	2
Kwantung Peninsular							51	0	191	1	290	1	89	0	114	0
Straits Settlements	4,535	15	2,941	15	3,609	23	6,058	37	7,995	41	8,481	38	8,509	35	9,516	35
Federated Malay States	1,219	4	496	3	261	2	309	2	405	2	1,328	6	2,559	11	4,154	15
Java & Dutch possessions	763	2	371	2	441	3	261	2	239	1	190	1	241	1	424	2
Siam/Thailand	3,486	11	3,085	16	3,812	24	3,132	19	4,142	21	4,098	19	3,552	15	2,682	10
British India	3,408	11	1,847	9	697	4	581	4	613	3	824	4	1,002	4	1,138	4
Ceylon	286	1	136	1	111	1	130	1	84	0	88	0	58	0	49	0
Aden	161	1	152	1	154	1	218	1	286	1	362	2	595	2	450	2
Asia subtotal	20,450	66	14,366	73	10,900	70	11,578	70	14,613	74	16,204	73	17,102	71	19,148	70
South Africa	125	0	116	1	95	1	120	1	159	1	184	1	206	1	190	1
British East Africa	1,055	3	934	5	727	5	757	5	778	4	936	4	939	4	1,122	4
British West Africa	1,508	5	928	5	1,070	7	1,117	7	885	4	1,205	5	1,558	6	1,858	7
Egypt	248	1	121	1	163	1	176	1	177	1	225	1	347	1	217	1
Africa subtotal	2,936	9	2,099	11	2,055	13	2,170	13	1,999	10	2,550	12	3,050	13	3,387	12
Total exports	31,068		19,720		15,670		16,484		19,720		22,124		24,194		27,546	

Appendix 3. (*cont.*)

Destination	1938		1939		1940		1941		1942		1943		1944		1945	
	000 lb.	(%)	000 lb.	(%)	000 lb.	(%)	000 lb.	(%)	000 lb.	(%)	000 lb.	(%)	000 lb.	(%)	000 lb.	(%)
China	104	0	113	0	129	1	184	1								
Hong Kong	548	2	544	2	403	2	312	1	4	0					59	0
Kwantung Peninsular																
Straits Settlements	8,831	33	9,238	37	8,891	40	8,149	33	658	4					725	2
Federated Malay States	3,442	13	3,197	13	3,176	14	2,328	9	213	1						
Java & Dutch possessions	779	3	220	1	149	1	151	1	25	0						
Siam/Thailand	2,069	8	1,140	5	596	3	391	2	9	0						
British India	1,420	5	1,565	6	1,638	7	1,766	7	562	4	131	1	219	1	1,323	4
Ceylon	51	0	59	0	50	0	172	1	520	3	894	5	1,839	11	1,479	4
Aden	488	2	570	2	563	3	647	3	597	4	172	1	7	0	240	1
Asia subtotal	17,732	67	16,646	66	15,595	70	14,100	57	2,588	17	1,197	7	2,065	13	3,826	11
South Africa	205	1	215	1	189	1	481	2	307	2	147	1	143	1	137	0
British East Africa	1,274	5	1,154	5	909	4	1,752	7	853	6	1,024	6	889	5	639	2
British West Africa	1,545	6	1,450	6	991	4	1,994	8	1,866	12	1,658	10	1,268	8	1,414	4
Egypt	354	1	571	2	1,096	5	1,434	6	6,216	42	3,635	21	2,327	14	8,169	24
Africa subtotal	3,378	13	3,390	13	3,185	14	5,661	23	9,242	62	6,464	38	4,627	28	10,359	30
Total exports	26,456		25,123		22,194		24,567		14,950		16,984		16,315		34,003	

APPENDIX 3. (*cont.*)

Destination	1946		1947		1948	
	000 lb.	(%)	000 lb.	(%)	000 lb.	(%)
China	138	0	7	0	1	0
Hong Kong	1,538	3	3,485	7	3,255	8
Kwantung Peninsular						
Straits Settlements	13,900	28	16,491	34	16,102	38
Federated Malay States						
Java & Dutch possessions						
Siam/Thailand	53	0	319	1	239	1
British India	2,502	5	1,835	4	805	2
Ceylon	430	1	147	0	75	0
Aden	922	2	1,317	3	985	2
Asia subtotal	19,483	40	23,601	48	21,462	50
South Africa	484	1	471	1	312	1
British East Africa	660	1	474	1	216	1
British West Africa	2,260	5	3,193	7	1,988	5
Egypt	4,123	8	1,734	4	1,351	3
Africa subtotal	7,527	15	5,872	12	3,867	9
Total exports	49,035		48,770		42,584	

Notes
Asian and African subtotals include exports to all parts of the continent.
Figures for British India include Burma.
Exports to China exclude Manchuria (Kwantung Peninsular) after 1931.
Federated Malay States and Straits combined after 1945.
Source: Annual Statement of the Overseas Trade of the UK.

Appendix 4

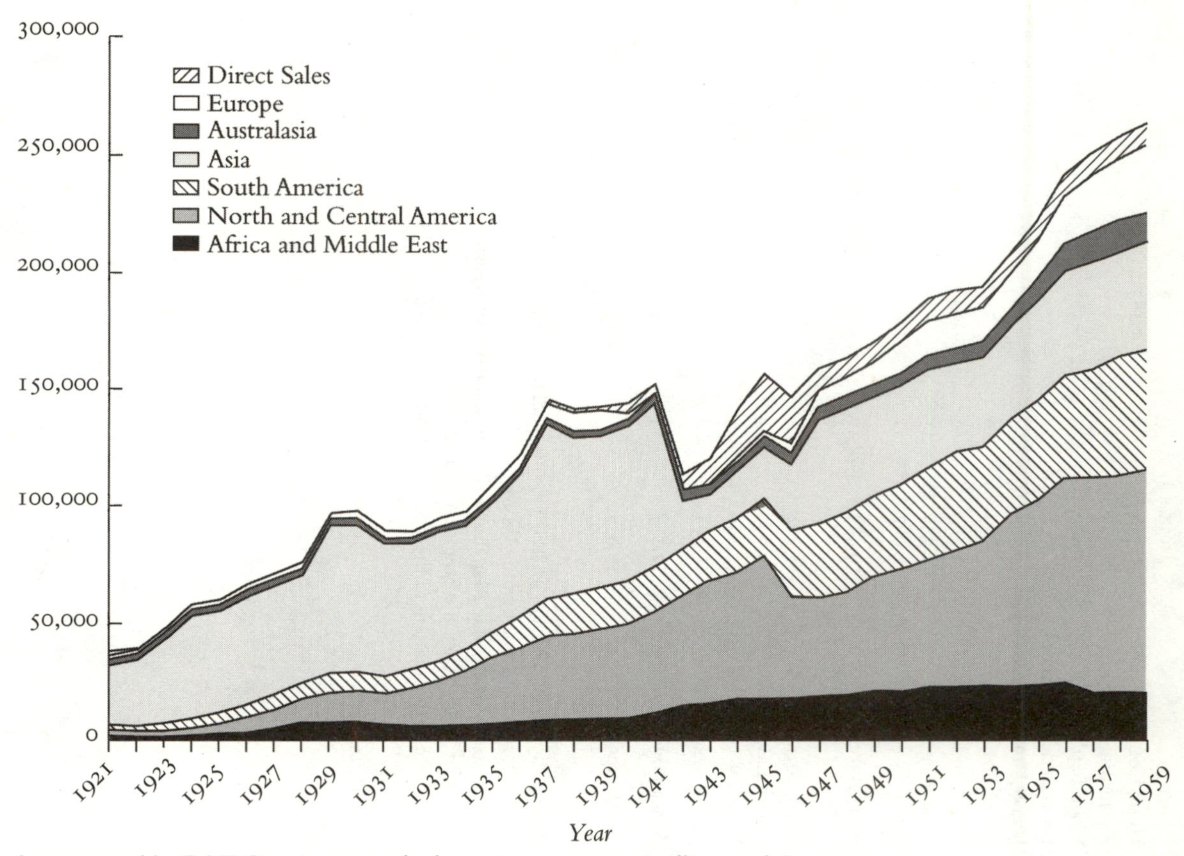

APPENDIX 4(a). BAT Co. cigarette sales by region, 1921–59 (million sticks).

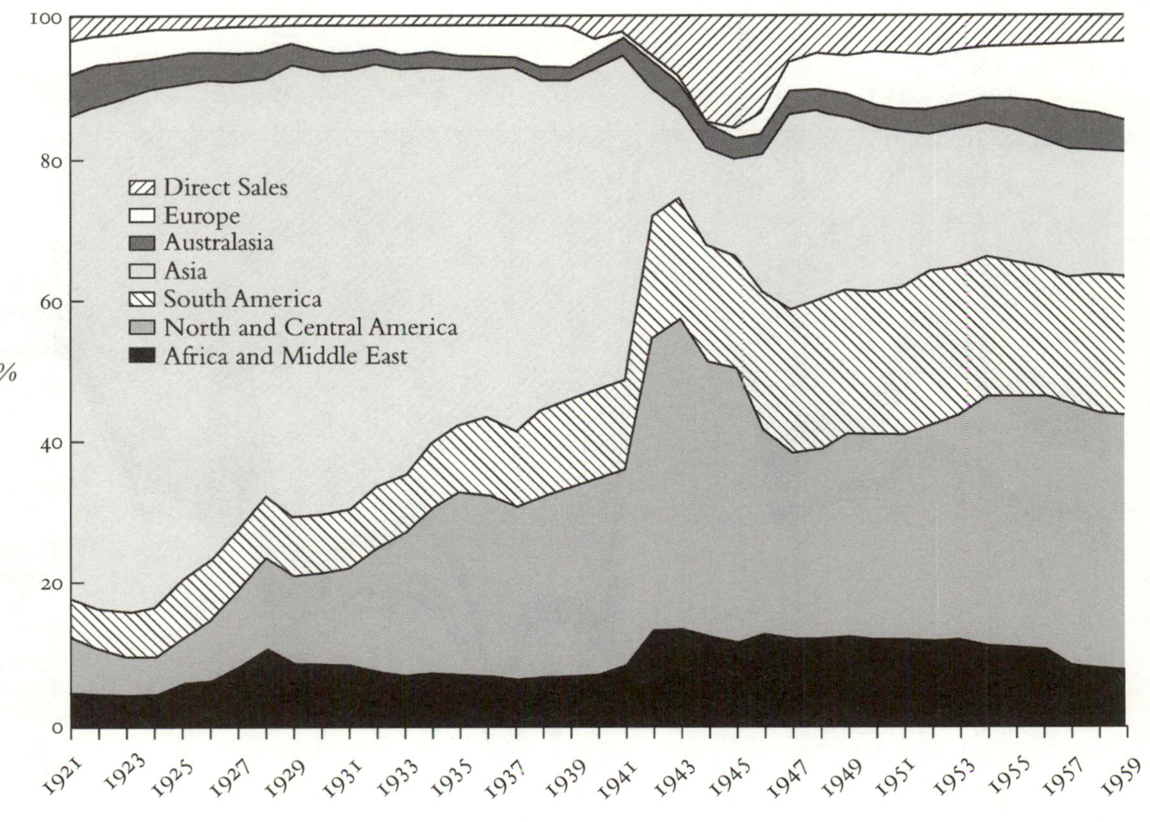

APPENDIX 4(b). BAT Co. cigarette sales by regional share, 1921–59.

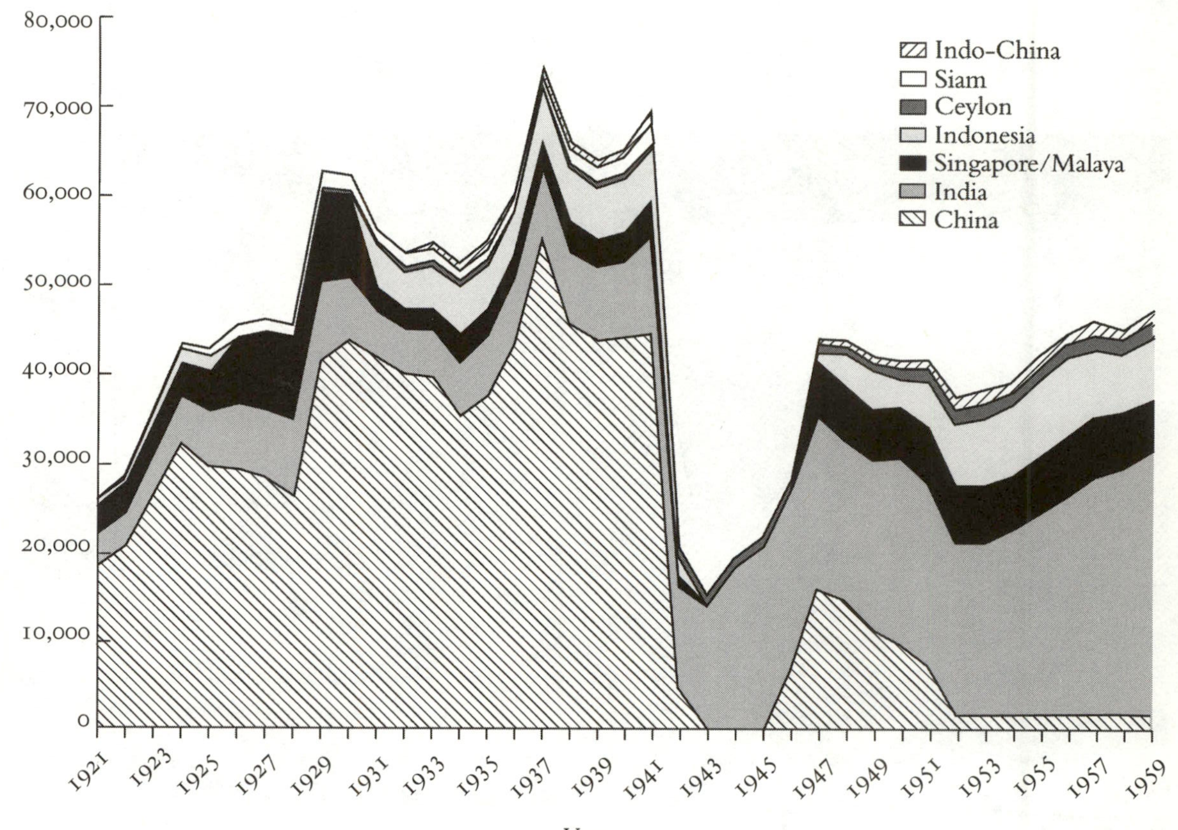

APPENDIX 4(c). BAT Co. cigarette sales: Asia 1921–59 (million sticks)

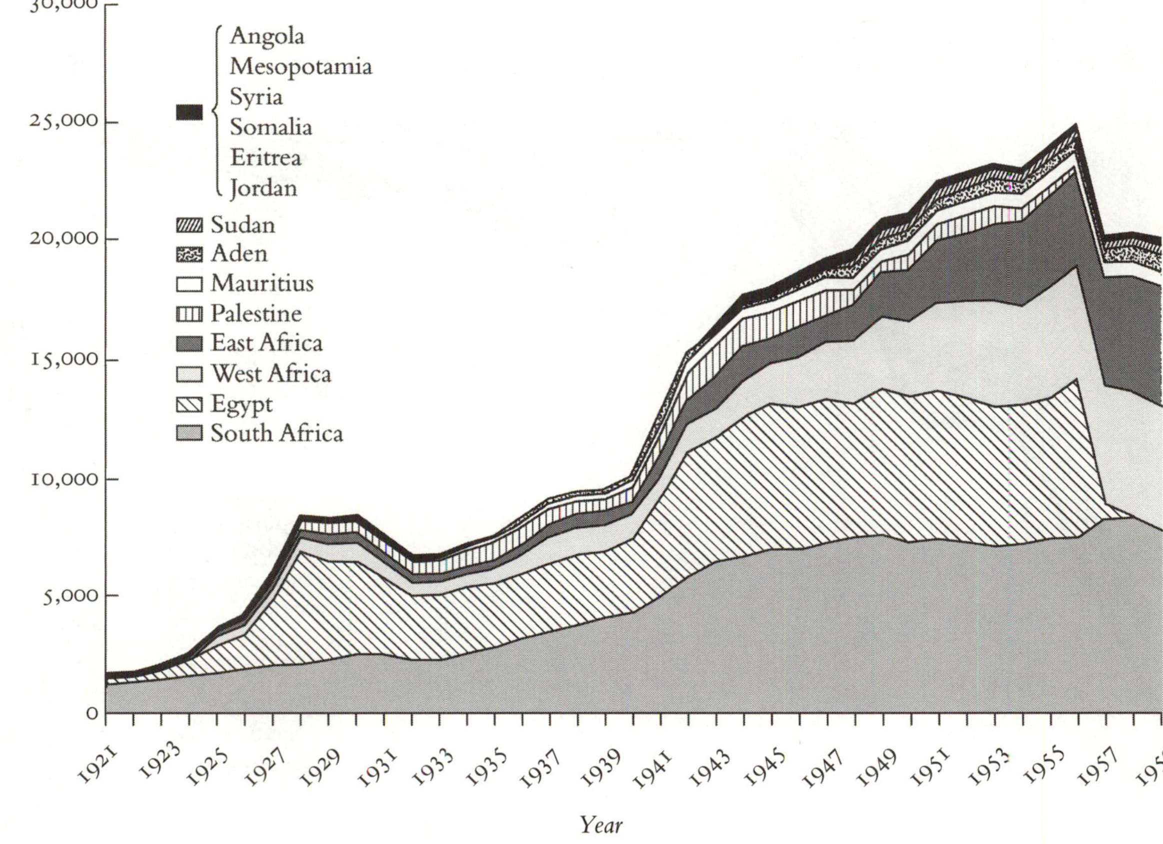

APPENDIX 4(d). BAT Co. cigarette sales: Africa and the Middle East, 1921–59 (million sticks)

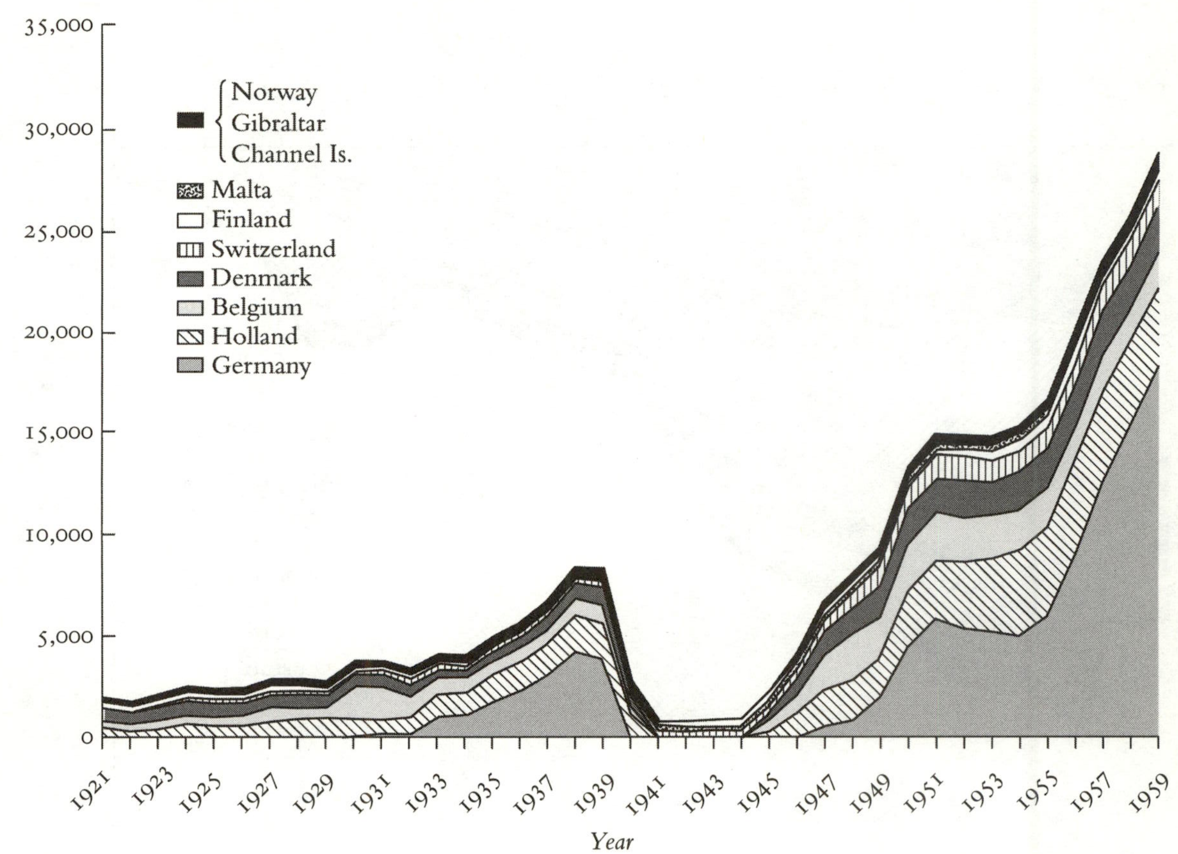

APPENDIX 4(e). BAT Co. cigarette sales: Europe, 1921–59 (million sticks)

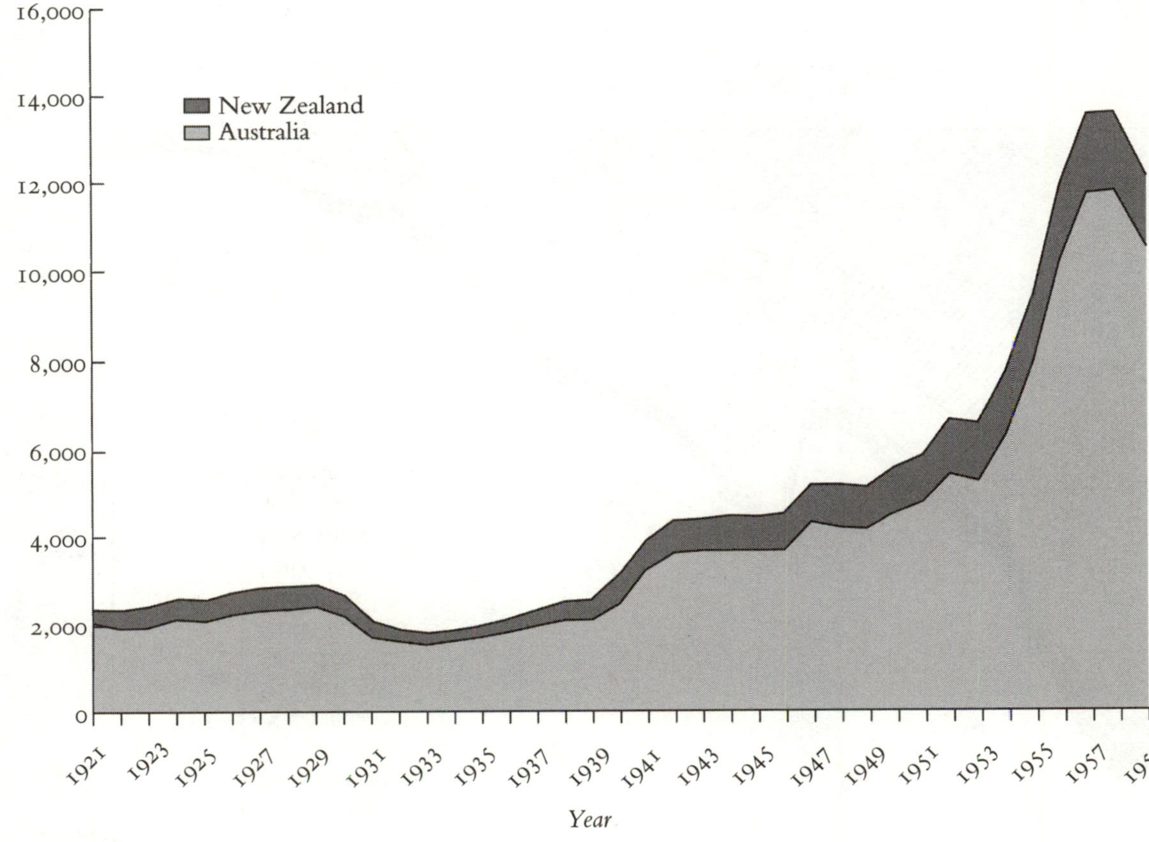

APPENDIX 4(f). BAT Co. cigarette sales: Australasia, 1921–59 (million sticks)

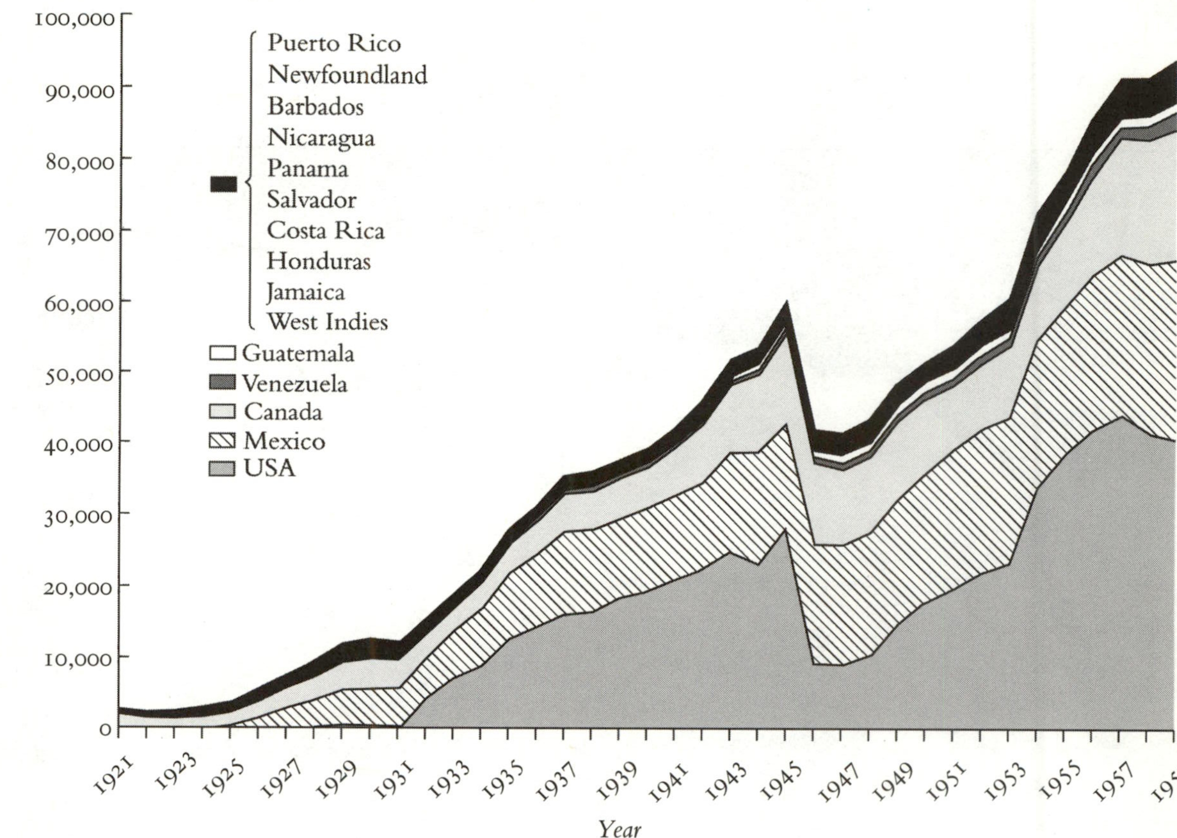

APPENDIX 4(g). BAT Co. cigarette sales: North and Central America, 1921–59 (million sticks)

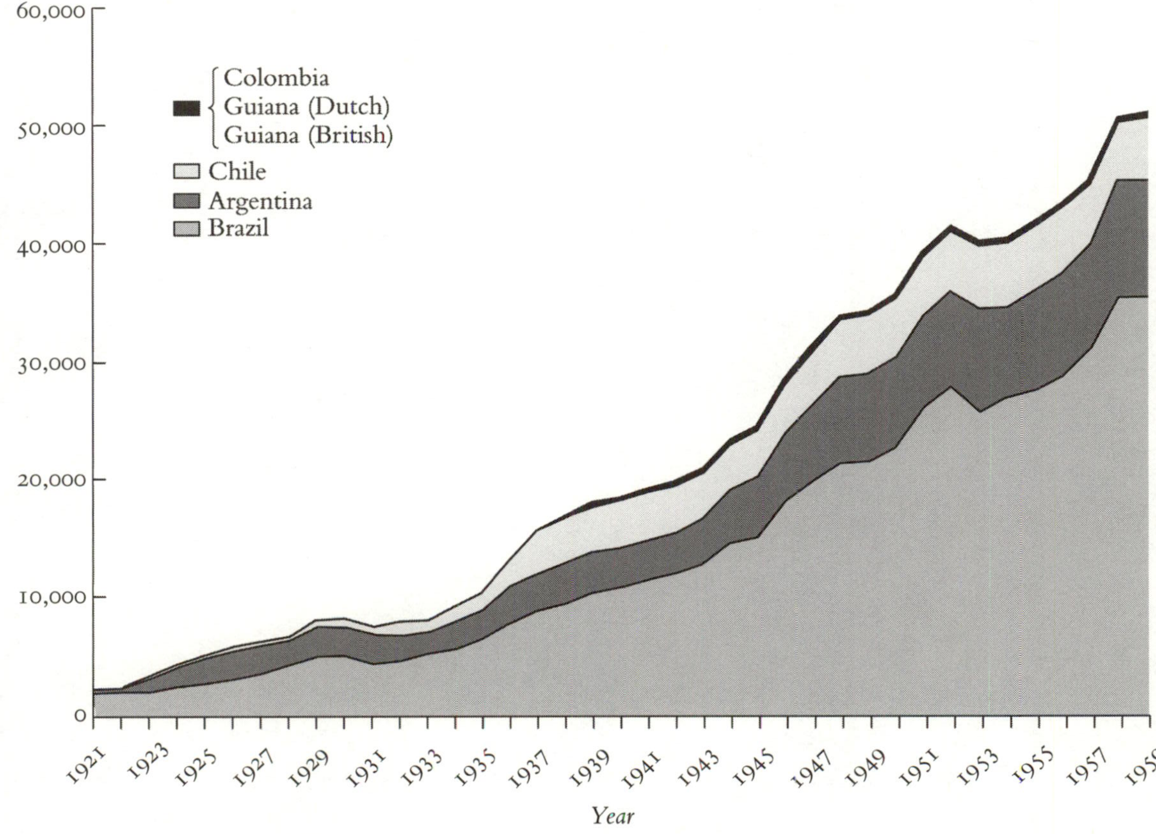

APPENDIX 4(h). BAT Co. cigarette sales: South America, 1921–59 (million sticks)

Index